Translated from the German
by Alex J. Kay and Anna Guettel-Bellert

Manfried Rauchensteiner

UNDER OBSERVATION

Austria since 1918

BÖHLAU VERLAG WIEN KÖLN WEIMAR

BUNDESKANZLERAMT ⁚ ÖSTERREICH   *ZukunftsFonds*
                                  der Republik Österreich

Veröffentlicht mit freundlicher Unterstützung durch das Bundeskanzleramt der Republik Österreich
und den Zukunftsfonds der Republik Österreich

First published in 2017 in the German language as "Unter Beobachtung. Österreich seit 1918"
by Böhlau Verlag Ges.m.b.H. & Co.KG., Wien – Köln – Weimar

Deutsche Nationalbibliothek Cataloging-in-publication data:
http://dnb.d-nb.de

Cover: Otto Dix, An die Schönheit, 1922 (detail) © Bildrecht, Wien 2018

Cover design: hawemannundmosch, Berlin
Endpapers: Stefan Lechner, Vienna
Typesetting: Michael Rauscher, Vienna
Printing and binding: Hubert & Co., Göttingen
Printed on acid-free and chlorine-free bleached paper
Printed in the EU

Vandenhoeck & Ruprecht Verlage | www.vandenhoeck-ruprecht-verlage.com

ISBN 978-3-205-20704-7

Table of Contents

Foreword

Otto Dix, one of the great painters and graphic artists of the twentieth century, lent me his eyes. His picture 'To Beauty', which provides the cover of this book with colour and expression, has been reduced to a detail. In the process, the painting is forced into a sort of straitjacket, which allows for a reinterpretation. It is the eyes that count, the stern look of a person whose attention, it appears, nothing can escape. It might be the case that the look also expresses something approaching disapproval. It is a self-portrait. The elegant couple in the background seem to be completely self-absorbed and evidently unaware that they are under observation. Only the present counts. That gives them a timeless quality. And it cannot be identified.

Like the painting, this book is also reduced to a detail. It deals with Austria, and it looks at events over a period of one hundred years. The deliberately stern gaze, seemingly external, is simultaneously a mirror image. The fact that narcissism also plays a role here corresponds to the subject. In the same year that Otto Dix pained 'To Beauty', 1922, Austria threatened to become ungovernable. It lurched between self-abandonment and visions of the future, and it was rescued with the help of the League of Nations. A conglomerate of historical entities, which first had to find a new commonality, was facing an uncertain future. It was no longer that which the Czech historian František Palacký had characterised it as in 1848, something indispensable, a European necessity, but instead a hard to define residue. Austria had gone from being indispensable to being in a quandary. But the country was under observation from day one. And the looks that Austria encountered were not always friendly. Concern, suspicion, pity, mistrust and greed were mixed with indifference, contentment and benevolence.

It was watched by the victorious powers of the First World War, the successor states to the Habsburg Monarchy and the League of Nations. But it was not only the others who watched. The internal gaze also reflected the full range of emotions that could be discerned among neighbours near and far. Austria was not a country in which great emphasis was placed on self-determination. And the will to assert itself emerged only at a late date. The awkwardness remained. Violence dominated. And in the eyes of many observers, contentment could be seen shining forth regarding the calm that descended

on Austria in 1938. 'Thank goodness, Austria is out of the way,' said one British politician. This was followed by the rueful realisation that the disappearance of one problem,
Austria, had been swapped for new problems. In 1945, it was as though the reset button
had been pressed. Much had changed. Austria was located between two blocs, liked
to think of itself as a bridge and played a role in which it experienced a new form of
oversight, more direct than anything that had gone before, and ultimately plunged into
a time in which general contentment took hold. The country was over the worst. The
awkwardness had suddenly become a stabilising factor. Admittedly, one thing did not
change: every time something happened in Austria, the land was under observation.
And even when nothing happened. Time and again, it was regarded as a problem zone,
then as a special case, as a model pupil, and on multiple occasions as a naughty boy, on
whom a sharp eye had to be kept.

An account of all that cannot be evenly spread out. Likewise, there can be no question of each event and every protagonist being described in all available details. Here
and there, we must pause for a moment to make use of the parallelism and the flow of
time for the narrative thread. We cannot always rush through the different time periods. One thing should be achieved, however: that the reader understands the history
of a country that sometimes does not take itself seriously as important for the overall
development of a continent and can admit that it is a stimulating history. It is no less
interesting when one attempts to survey a long time period. In the process, some things
will have to be brought to light that are already known and others that are unknown,
but where the view over a long period of time also offers possibilities for comparison
that invite us to stop and think: did not something similar once happen; are events or
non-events so unusual that it is impossible to find a precedent? And time and again the
question will arise: What would have happened if …? – If, for example, Ignaz Seipel
had acceded to the request of Bavarian authorities and again conferred Austrian citizenship on Adolf Hitler in 1924, if the Dollfuß assassin had missed, if the Allies had
agreed in Moscow in 1943 to divide Austria, if the Soviets had reoccupied Austria in
1956, as Marshal Zhukov wished, or if Jörg Haider had not been killed in an accident
in 2008? It is not a question of thinking the impossible but of thinking the possible. It
is also an invitation to see that which is transient.

When taking a walk through history, one passes many sites. They present themselves
with a never-ending willingness. One can take a break in the villa of Senator Giusti
near Padua or in Saint-Germain, Geneva, Berlin, Berchtesgaden, Sopron/Ödenburg,
Kragujevac, Stalingrad/Volgograd or Prague. Austrian history was written in London,
Moscow, Paris and Washington, and has also left its mark there and created sites of
remembrance. Ultimately, there is not a single place that would not hide a story, no
monument, no cemetery, not even a field or a meadow that could not be linked to an
event or a person.

It is frequently the case that stones and hallways divulge their stories only to those who live there and feel just as addressed by the 'moss on the stones' (Gerhard Fritsch), the glades and the furrows as those who allow themselves to reflect on monuments, statues or 'Stolpersteine' and like to make use of the narrative phrase 'Once upon a time …'.

No place exists of which it can be said that events took place there uniformly. And no cemetery exists in which those who one perceives to have been either the 'good guys' or the 'bad guys' do not lie side by side. Cemeteries, especially, are deeply democratic sites of remembrance, because to them applies most of all the interpretation offered by G. K. Chesterton of the tradition by which 'the most obscure of all classes' is given the vote – our ancestors (Chesterton, 'The Ethics of Elfland').

All of this is to be found in the history of a century. Towards the end, the narrative becomes slower, more tentative. Nothing will change regarding the awareness of being observed. No more than regarding the necessity to form an opinion ourselves. Nothing is yet concluded; it is in a state of flux. In the well-known stream of time.

1 The Experiment

1 The armistice signed in the villa of Senator Giusti del Giardino near Padua on 3 November 1918 ended Austria-Hungary's final war. More than 300,000 soldiers of the Imperial and Royal Army went into Italian captivity. Most of them were interned only for a short time. Some of the prisoners, however, remained in Italian camps until 1921. At that point, Austria (not including Burgenland) still counted around 20,000 prisoners of war and more than 22,000 missing persons. (Photo: Austrian State Archives / War Archives)

The queues in front of shops became ever longer. In 1918, the fifth year of the war, the people of Austria-Hungary were going hungry. At irregular intervals, posters were put up in the larger cities by means of which the people were called upon to collect stinging nettle leaves for textile production, coffee extract for oil extraction or cockchafers as chicken and pig feed. On the exceptional occasion that there was coal, this was also announced, likewise the release of potatoes, flour and milk. Donations were requested for those blinded in the war, war invalids, military widows, orphans and dozens of other groups of people in need. Farmers established watch posts in order to prevent potatoes and turnips being stolen from the fields. The confidence still in evidence in December 1917 to the effect that the war would soon be over, was replaced in January by widespread disappointment. In some large cities and industrial centres of the Habsburg Monarchy, the war was boycotted. Then the people returned to work, briefly renewed their hope and were disappointed once more.

The distress stemmed not only from hunger, however. Most people not only had nothing left to eat, but also scarcely any hope or prospects. They did not know whether Austria-Hungary would continue to exist or whether it was approaching dissolution. The people often did not even know what they should hope for. The speech of American President Woodrow Wilson in Congress in Washington on 8 January 1918 had only made everything more difficult. In announcing his Fourteen Points, Wilson had named as Point Ten: 'The people of Austria-Hungary, whose place among the nations we wish to see safeguarded and assured, should be assured the freest opportunity to autonomous development.' Self-determination thereby became a special topic that was seized upon by all belligerents. The eleven nationalities of the Habsburg Monarchy were no exception. The question was merely: did this apply to all peoples?

Between 13 and 15 June 1918, the Austro-Hungarian troops lined up from the Dolomites to the Adriatic for their final offensive. The Allies knew about the timing of the attack and had no difficulty in repelling the oncoming armies. From late June, Austria-Hungary was unimportant as an adversary. Now it was no longer necessary to bring American troop formations to Italy. Instead, they were sent to France. Discipline was as yet still being maintained among the combat troops of the Imperial and Royal Army, but it deteriorated by the day. Aversion and the long-simmering, mutual hatred among the peoples of the Habsburg Monarchy, which arose with increasing regularity, gained ever more ground. In view of the dismal situation at the front and in the rear, Emperor Karl attempted at the last moment to find a solution that might ensure the survival of his empire. The response of the Slovene Anton Korošec, 'Majesty, it is too late,' basically said it all.[1] The Emperor unilaterally took steps to bring about a peace. The Allies reacted merely with the observation that first Germany had to surrender; only then could Austria-Hungary's wishes be addressed. Another hope had been dashed.

The Dissolution Order

One month later, on 16 October 1918, Emperor Karl issued a so-called 'People's Manifesto', according to which Austria-Hungary should continue to exist as a league of free nations.[2] The Hungarian government, however, managed to prevent the manifesto from also applying to the Lands of the Crown of St. Stephen. But even Hungary could not escape the unavoidable fragmentation of the Empire. Reactions to the manifesto demonstrated, however, like the words of the Slovene Korošec, that it had come too late. It was regarded as carte blanche, as a type of dissolution order permitting all the peoples of the Habsburg Monarchy to go their own way. And the enemy powers did everything to encourage the decline. On 24 October, the Italian army commenced the final offensive together with British and French troops. It was the anniversary of the great victory of Austro-Hungarian and German troops over the Italians a year earlier. A counteroffensive was out of the question. The front began to disintegrate after two days.[3] One of the last regular holidaymakers to travel to the north was Territorial Infantry Lieutenant Engelbert Dollfuß. He overnighted in Trento (Trient) in the same hotel as the armistice commission, which had been sent to South Tyrol as a precaution and had been waiting since early October to make contact with the Italians. An almost fateful encounter of past and future. Emperor Karl finally made the long-delayed resolution to request an armistice or a special peace, irrespective of Germany. The Minister of Foreign Affairs, Count Gyula Andrassy, declared the alliance with Germany at an end. Austria-Hungary could not do anything else but act unilaterally. Now the time had come. The head of the Austro-Hungarian armistice commission in Trento, General Viktor von Weber, was instructed that he was empowered to conclude an armistice. He was allowed to accept all conditions, aside from those that the army's honour did not permit or that amounted to a complete disenfranchisement.

The Austrian commission was brought to the villa of Senator Giusti del Giardino near Padua, the guesthouse of the Italian Army Command. In the night of 1/2 November, the demands formulated by the Allied Supreme War Council in Paris were handed over. They amounted to an unconditional surrender and did not signal any willingness to compromise. The Habsburg Monarchy was to be crushed to the extent that it did not dissolve itself. There were admittedly some among the victorious powers who championed the retention of the Monarchy, but the Entente had done everything to accelerate the dissolution and signalised to the Northern and Southern Slavs that they would be recognised as belligerents on the side of the Entente. Italy itself had in any case been in the Allied camp since 1915. Thus, all considerations for retaining a reduced Habsburg Monarchy at least as a rump state were more or less obsolete. And after the real union between Austria and Hungary had been dissolved on 30 October, nothing remained of the Empire but memories.

Half an hour before midnight on 2 November, Emperor Karl empowered General von Weber to conclude the armistice. At the same time, the monarch surrendered supreme command over his troops to Field Marshal Hermann Kövess von Kövesshaza. The armistice demanded:

1. Immediate cessation of hostilities at sea, on land and in the air.
2. Complete demobilisation of Austria-Hungary and the withdrawal of all troops.
3. Withdrawal from all territories occupied since 1914.
4. Freedom of movement for Allied troops on the entire territory of the Habsburg Monarchy.
5. Withdrawal of all German troops from Italy and the Balkan front within 15 days.
6. Immediate repatriation of all prisoners of war and internees.[4]

There were also provisions for the fleet, but it had already been transferred by Emperor Karl at the suggestion of the last Commander of the Fleet, Rear Admiral Miklós von Horthy, to the National Council in Zagreb (Agram) on 31 October. The Allies, therefore, had to agree among themselves what would happen to the fleet. Italy then created a fait accompli by sinking the flagship of the Imperial and Royal Navy, the *Viribus Unitis*, in the bay of Pula (Pola) with limpet mines. The dreadnought could not be allowed to fall into Southern Slav hands. And then there was a special inaccuracy in the armistice agreement: it repeatedly mentioned Austria-Hungary and its territory, but only the Italian front featured in the detailed agreements, though not Romania or Serbia, let alone Russia or Ukraine. For the latter, the peace treaties of Brest-Litovsk and Bucharest, concluded in March 1918, were regarded as applicable. Therefore, future developments in the east and the southeast were addressed least of all in the Villa Giusti.

The Imperial and Royal Army High Command ordered the Austro-Hungarian troops early on the morning of 3 November 1918 to cease hostilities, even before the armistice agreement had been signed. Whether this was premature or negligent is contested to this day. Over 300,000 Austro-Hungarian soldiers ended up in Italian captivity. On 3 November 1918, at 3 p.m., the armistice document was signed. Twenty-four hours later, the ceasefire took effect. The war lagged days behind political developments.

The German Delegates

On 21 October, the German delegates of the Austrian Imperial Assembly (Reichsrat) had gathered in the Lower Austrian regional diet (Landtag) on Vienna's Herrengasse to discuss what would happen if the Habsburg Monarchy were really to disintegrate. By way of precaution, they had already been invited to this meeting on 17 October,[5] and they adhered to the provisions cited in the 'People's Manifesto'. 106 German nationalists from different parties, 65 Christian Socials and 38 Social Democrats, as well as one Free Socialist,[6] including delegates from Bohemia, Moravia and Silesia, drew the consequences from the hopeless situation of the Empire and sought a minimum consensus. Earlier that same month, they had already made attempts to explore what options might be available after the approaching end to the war and the probable disintegration of the Monarchy. Representatives of both parties of the masses, the Christian Socials and the Social Democrats, had sketched out two scenarios: in the event of a dissolution of the Monarchy, a loose association of state might emerge, or instead an annexation of the German territories of the Habsburg Monarchy by Germany. The latter could by all means be interpreted as a threat. If the others – the Poles, Czechs, Hungarians, Romanians, Italians, Southern Slavs – no longer wanted to maintain an alliance, then there would just have to be a Germany enlarged by the German territories of Austria-Hungary. The term 'German-Austria' (Deutschösterreich) was even already used.[7]

For the time being, the German delegates constituted on 21 October as the Provisional National Assembly. It was a step located somewhere between resignation, despair and hope. The chairman of the body, Viktor Waldner, began with the term of salutation 'Valued ethnic comrades' and described the purpose of the gathering. His speech and the contributions of the delegates were repeatedly interrupted by applause and calls of 'Heil', as the minutes of the session demonstrate. In fact, 'Heil' was the most common word of agreement. An executive committee was elected as the core of a future German-Austrian government. Other committees followed. The provisional state chancellor ought to have been the director of the library of the Imperial Assembly, Karl Renner, though it could not have been assumed that the Social Democrats would become the strongest political force. But they had a clear objective in view: the end of the Monarchy.[8] No one had a drift into isolation in mind, and the leader of the Austrian Social Democrats, delegate Viktor Adler, remarked: if the other states, the Romanian and the Slav, whom he congratulated on their independence, did not want to join Austria, then Austria would attach itself to the German Reich as a special federal state. This was proposed as a motion. The next session was scheduled for 30 October. In the nine days until then, Renner drafted a constitution, in which it still remained open what type of political system would be launched. It could be a monarchy or a republic, independent or part of a new whole.

The time had come on 30 October: the Provisional National Assembly adopted a resolution for the establishment of the state of German-Austria. The German delegates were the last ones to break with the Empire. They evidently feared that the peace would have its price and that most nationalities would blame the two dominant peoples of the Empire up to this time, the Germans of the Habsburg Monarchy and the Hungarians, for the war but also for the mistakes made under the governments of Emperor Franz Joseph I and Karl I. Attempts by Emperor Karl to share responsibility for the past and the future with representatives of the political parties had failed. Above all, the Social Democrat politicians strictly refused to assume government responsibility in an imperial cabinet. Karl Renner would admittedly have done this without further ado, but his party wanted to signalise a type of 'political innocence',[9] in order to make an attempt at a new start unburdened by the past. Thus, the pacifist and internationally-renowned expert on international law Heinrich Lammasch became the last Imperial Austrian prime minister. But he could only watch how an empire that had also been his was liquidated. The Council of State of German-Austria did everything to make it clear that it did not want to be associated with the past. Thus, its representatives consistently refused to contribute to the conclusion of an armistice. It had not been German-Austria's war, and therefore the 'factor' that had declared war should also be the one to end it. Emperor Karl could only respond by pointing out that he had also not been that factor, but he had to attempt to make the laying down of arms still appear like a sovereign act.

Germany wanted to recognise German-Austria. For the enemies of Austria-Hungary, this was an irrelevant procedure, because they were still at war with the Habsburg Monarchy and needed an adversary in order to be able to dictate a peace, and not a new creation.[10]

In order to avoid the necessity of having to elect a head of state – an 'anti-emperor', as it were – and because it was still impossible to predict whether and how Emperor Karl would seal the fate of the Monarchy, the Provisional National Assembly made do with a particularly cumbersome construction: three presidents were elected, or rather chosen, of which one would chair the National Assembly, another would be chairman of the Council of State and the third chairman of the Cabinet Council. The three had to alternate in their functions on a weekly basis. But it was only intended as a provisional measure, just as everything was provisional for the time being.

After the act to establish the state had been adopted, speeches were held in due form. Outside, on Herrengasse, the people were standing shoulder to shoulder. The majority cheered and shouted 'Heil'. Black-red-gold and red flags could be seen. There was some rioting. The Emperor was not mentioned.

A state of limbo existed. While a new statehood emerged and parallel institutions to the Imperial ministries appeared, the latter continued to work. At 7 Herrengasse in Vienna, the Imperial and Royal Prime Minister Heinrich Lammasch held office and, like the Imperial-Royal ministries of the Austrian half of the Empire, which were spread over the Imperial capital and seat of royal residence, attempted to administer something that no longer existed. Only a few doors down, the German-Austrian Council of State carried out its activities. The three joint ministries of Austria-Hungary continued to exist, which considered themselves responsible for foreign affairs, war and finances of the Habsburg Monarchy and whose heads met on Ballhausplatz in the Ministry of Foreign Affairs. Not to forget the Imperial Assembly, which was housed in the parliament building on Ringstraße and whose officials – although it had been adjourned – sat in the offices that had once been assigned to them and into which the staff of the Provisional National Assembly of German-Austria now forced themselves.

The new Austrian statehood started with a mistake. The end of the war had been expected in spring 1919, not in November 1918. But that is not what happened. Emperor Karl had hoped that Austria-Hungary would retain some type of commonality, preferably in the form of a league of states – he was mistaken. The German delegates of the Austrian Imperial Assembly feared total chaos as soon as the old political system collapsed and sought advice and assistance one after another from the Imperial and Royal Army Command, the victorious powers and, above all, the leadership of the German Reich. They all said it was not their responsibility. The next and most fundamental mistake was that the German Austrians of the Habsburg Monarchy were under the illusion that their state would not be so small. This had been casually stated on 21 October and could be found nine days later in the (first) state constitution. The territories to which a German Austria laid claim were then counted: German Bohemia, German southern Bohemia (Bohemian Forest Region), German southern Moravia, the German territory around Nová Bystřice (Neubistritz), the Sudetenland and the German linguistic enclaves of Brno (Brünn), Jihlava (Iglau) and Olomouc (Olmütz). This land mass, which was admittedly not contiguous but nonetheless considerable, would in any case possess sufficient resources to grow into an orderly state. And regarding the other peoples of the disintegrated Empire, after disengaging they would surely also search for some sort of commonality. This also proved to be incorrect.

Everyone automatically gave thought to the future and would have gladly undone past events. They could at least be suppressed somewhat. It was therefore least of all the case that they self-critically questioned whether it was above all Austria that bore a greater degree of responsibility for what had happened than others did. And it was then only a few who, like the editor-in-chief of the *Arbeiter-Zeitung*, Friedrich Austerlitz, made the rhetorically-sounding question of the 'Deserved Fate' the subject of an editorial on 5 November 1918. Not only the victorious powers wanted to saddle Austria and Hungary with a historic guilt, but also those who regarded themselves as 'oppressed nations'. They had ultimately also played their part in events, in the successes and the failures, right up to the collapse of the Habsburg Monarchy. But they exclusively blamed the German Austrians and the Hungarians. It was they, therefore, whom the 'deserved fate' should befall.

Who, however, were 'the' Austrians, and where was their place in post-war Europe? Should that which American President Woodrow Wilson had said about the right of all peoples to self-determination not also apply to them? There were good reasons to grant the same status to the entity emerging from the collapse of the Habsburg Monarchy – the 'residue' as French Prime Minister Georges Clemenceau was said to have briefly and accurately formulated it[11] – as to the non-German and non-Hungarian parts of the Empire, which were then simply successor states. An argument against this, however, was not least the sense of self-worth that was especially typical of the German Austrians. They did not regard themselves as a 'residue'. The Habsburg Empire had, after all, emerged from the German core or hereditary lands. Austria had always borne a greater responsibility as well as burden than others, had always been at the centre of things and had identified itself with the Empire to a far greater extent than the other parts of the Habsburg Monarchy. But what was Austria really?

There was broad agreement that German-Austria (South-East Germany, as it was also occasionally called, if one did not want to go so far as to use portmanteau words like 'Ostass', 'Danube-Germania', 'Treuland' or 'Teutheim')[12] should become a democratic republic. This was conditional on having a bourgeois order and a political system comparable to that of the Western democracies. And something else: the 'trench community' of Germans and Austrians, as Karl Renner had described it,[13] should become a Central European state. It was assumed that this would happen in unison with Germany. For several days in November 1918, it was admittedly unknown whether the forms of government could be reconciled, because whereas German-Austria had made a clear commitment to the democratic republic, Germany was still an empire. Only two days after 9 November, it could be established that the necessary agreement existed. The German Kaiser Wilhelm II fled to the Netherlands and cleared the way for a German republic. Philipp Scheidemann proclaimed the republic in Berlin. Now it was again Austria that had to follow and take the last, decisive step towards a republic.

Initially, it was a question of the person of Emperor Karl. He fought to retain his power, but he no longer had any instruments of power. To the last, he had still claimed that there would be a common future for him as well as for the Habsburg Empire: 'It will be possible,' he said in late October to the General Council of the Austro-Hungarian Bank, Michael Hainisch.[14]

The Emperor had even made a concession that was designed to make him acceptable even for the radicals: on 6 November, he amnestied Friedrich Adler, the son of the leader of the Social Democrats, who had been sentenced to death in 1916 after the murder of the Austrian Prime Minister Count Karl Stürgkh and whose sentence had then been commuted to life imprisonment. Should Karl have hoped to have earned some kind of reward for the release of Friedrich Adler, he was also mistaken. But no one yet wanted to simply ignore him. In spite of his inability to lead Austria out of the war in any other way than via unconditional surrender and as a shattered state, there was still a high degree of loyalty and respect towards the monarch. And the Allies perhaps preferred to negotiate with him than with representatives of the new creation of German-Austria. The monarch should admittedly be removed as a political factor, otherwise the reference to a democratic republic would not enjoy any validity. After lengthy hesitation and many objections, the Emperor consented on 11 November to renounce any claim to participation in the political affairs of German-Austria. The document, which was burned in July 1927, stated: 'I renounce any part in affairs of government.' The Emperor was thus not removed and banished from the country but was instead edited out of events in a very moderate way. He removed the last Imperial government from office, left the Schönbrunn Palace and relocated to the Marchfeld in order to await further developments in Eckartsau Castle. There, on 13 November, he signed a waiver for Hungary, similar to that which he had accepted for Austria two days earlier.

As the Emperor had no power henceforth and the last Imperial government and the Army High Command would only be permitted to liquidate the Empire and its armed power, the question remained as to who would empower the new state. The problem, namely, was that German-Austria only had a chance of making a fresh political start if it also possessed the power to implement the resolutions of the Provisional National Assembly and their legislative acts and earn respect. Therefore, on 30 October 1918, a start was already made on the establishment of a new military institution, the People's Militia (Volkswehr). Banally enough, it was a question of guaranteeing the new state a minimum level of security, because the city commander of Vienna, Major General Baronet Johann von Mossig, had only four companies at his disposal, that is, around 500 men, with which he was able to prevent neither plundering nor the rioting of re-patriated soldiers, not to mention a more far-reaching change, a Bolshevik revolution. Returning soldiers were compelled to exchange the Imperial colours on their caps for red cockades. Officers occasionally had their insignia torn off. For several days, the Council of State feared that the government could be overthrown. And Renner is sup-posed to have said: 'Whenever I now pass a lamppost, I always have a strange feeling.'[15] He openly stated that the coalition of citizens, peasants and workers was a very fragile construction and rejected by the working class.[16] But it was only a few radicals who wanted to use violence. And it was not least they who should be disciplined by means of the People's Militia. The vast majority of the tens of thousands of members of the People's Militia were in any case content to have a roof over their heads and free of the most pressing existential worries. They had no thought of revolution. Before long, the

People's Militia then became far more a social institution rather than actually being called on for military operations.[17] This very soon became clear.

In early November, Slovene troops from the new Southern Slav State of Slovenes, Croats and Serbs (SHS) began to occupy the southern territories of Carinthia and Styria, which were partially populated by Slovenes. They initially encountered only the resistance of local citizens' militias. An armed conflict was looming. The People's Militia did not play any part in it. Salzburg and Tyrol as far as the Brenner Pass were occupied by Bavarian troops from 6 to 11 November. On 9 November, Italian units began to advance northward, crossed the Brenner Pass and eventually occupied Innsbruck. As one of the victorious powers, Italy was entitled to do this. It remained completely unclear where the frontiers would be drawn in the north and the east. The People's Militia, in any case, was unable to exert any influence on this.

Violence gained ground. Instead of granting the state executive power and solving security problems, the People's Militia became part of the problem. The idealistic assumption that the new state would be able to manage without a military, as advocated, among others, by the last chief of staff of the Isonzo Army, Colonel Theodor von Körner, and reflected in the rhyme 'Ohne Waffen, ohne Pfaffen wird die Jugend sich die Zukunft schaffen' (Without weapons, without papists, the youth will create the future),[18] did not match the reality of the post-war period. Red guards and soldiers' councils were time and again willing to use violence. And they did not want to simply watch how a new state defined itself, in a very orderly and thoughtful fashion, always taking administrative procedures into account, preserving legal continuity and to a certain degree legitimate. A handful of radicals believed that now the time had come to set up councils, like in Russia, and trigger a Bolshevik revolution. In fact, it was still unknown what the state would look like; not even the name was beyond dispute. Both parts of the word German-Austria were unsatisfactory. And once doubts were raised as to whether the victorious powers might understand the term Austria as a cue to saddle this one remaining Austria with the entire war guilt – then no one was satisfied any longer with the official name. Nonetheless, the word continued to be used, not least in the provisional constitution and in the draft law for the political system, in which it was specified that German-Austria was to be a democratic republic. § 2 stated: 'German-Austria is part of the German Republic.' Thus, this was not an expression of intent but rather a pretence that everything was already certain. Only a single delegate hesitated. The Christian Social Wilhelm Miklas would have liked to see the decision regarding the system of government subjected to a popular referendum. But it was decided that the minimum consensus should be preserved; so Miklas relented.

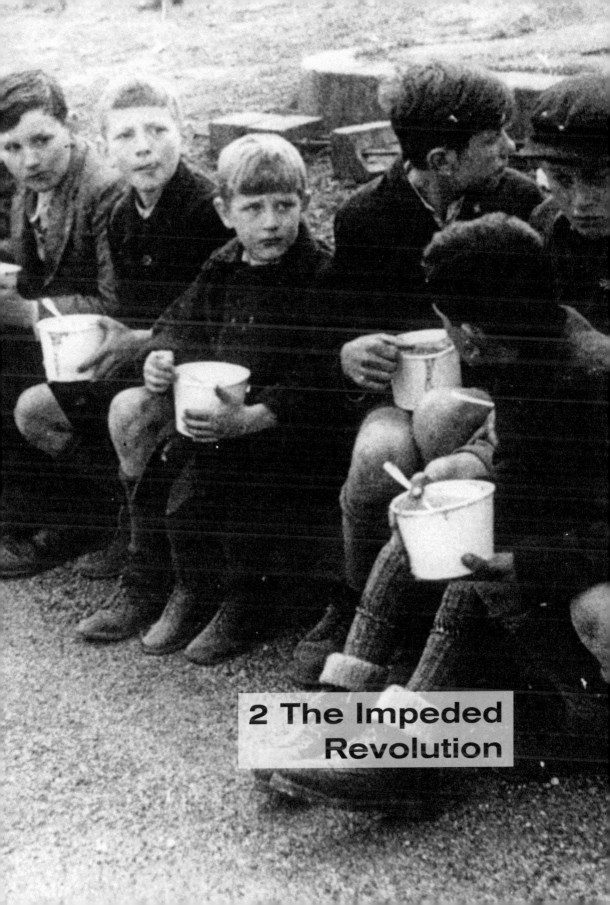

2 The Impeded Revolution

2   Free meals for children in Vienna, 1919. In the months after the end of the First World War, the urban population was able to survive only by virtue of foreign aid. At the start of the free meals campaign by the Anglo-American Society of Friends, it was ascertained that in Vienna and Lower Austria 72 per cent of schoolchildren between the ages of six and 14 were poorly or very poorly fed. In order to provide effective assistance, 300,000 free meals were distributed every day during the first years after the war. Half of them were accounted for by Vienna and the rest by the other federal states. In 1919, 40,000 children found foster parents, above all in Switzerland and the Netherlands, who took them for three to six months. Foreign committees, such as New York's Vienna Milk Relief, operated their own childcare institutions. (Photo: Vienna City Library)

It could be one of the more difficult questions in a quiz: on which day did the First Austrian Republic begin, 30 October or 12 November 1918? The answer would perhaps result in a debate. Legal historians could argue that the beginning was marked by the resolution of the Provisional National Assembly on the founding of the state of German-Austria on 30 October 1918.[19] Karl Renner instructed in 1947 for the 'proclamation of the Republic on Herrengasse on 30 October 1918' to be recorded in a painting by Max Frey, which was intended for the Museum of the First and Second Republic, initiated by Renner. A watercolour by Moritz Ledeli records the same scene from a different perspective. The argument that the founding of the state had been executed with the resolution on the basic institutions of state power could be countered by pointing out that the session in the Lower Austrian regional diet (Landtag) was merely a declaration of intent, because on 30 October Austria was still a monarchy. Only after Emperor Karl's renunciation was the path clear for the proclamation of the Republic. The history of the Republic thus began on 12 November 1918 with the resolution of the Provisional National Assembly on the Provisional Constitution and with the proclamation of the Republic before parliament. It's certainly the case that this day has taken hold in historical memory, that the memorial to the founding of the state not far from the parliament building bears this date, that the section of Vienna's Ringstraße between Bellaria and the town hall was called 'Ring of 12 November' from 1919 and 1934, that on 25 April 1919 the Constituent National Assembly declared 12 November to be a national holiday[20] and that on 1 May 1934 – the day on which the end of the Republic had come – it was heard that now 'the Austria of 12 November 1918' was being 'carried to its grave'. Accordingly, 12 November 1918 would be the correct answer. This day and the events before parliament were also recorded in a painting by Rudolf Konopa.[21] The paintings by Frey and Konopa unmistakeably carry the designation 'proclamation of the Republic'. Only the places and dates are different. What is correct? Let us abandon the debate.

A State Emerges

The 12 November 1918 did not end so peacefully as it had begun. On the afternoon, it was intended that the Provisional National Assembly adopt the state constitution and that the, as it were, official proclamation of the Republic take place. Everything was prepared, the individual marching columns, which were supposed to meet in front of parliament, had been given detailed instructions. The crowds were estimated to number 150,000 people. Light rain could not spoil the festive mood. Most people, men and women alike, were well dressed. Hats were worn. When the members of the Provisional State Government stepped on to the ramp of parliament after the adoption of the Provisional Constitution, in order to proclaim the founding of the Republic to a crowd waiting in the falling darkness and the red-white-red flag was raised, which replaced the old black-yellow of the imperial era, a few members of the Red Guards pulled the flag down again. They tore the white of the middle stripe and hoisted the red rags, tied together, as a symbol of the beginning of the revolution. Subsequently, speeches were held and the Workers' Choral Society sang a song. Then, however, a dozen Red Guards attempted to force their way into the parliament building and began a wild shootout. Calm could be restored only with difficulty. But the spectre of the revolution began to take shape. The fact that it did not thrive was only because the future of the country appeared relatively secure in spite of all loans. At the outset, there was no question of Austria's inability to survive. People continued to hope that German-Austria would have a sizeable state territory. In the Law on the Scope and Borders of State Territory from 22 November 1918, those regions and cities were finally named to which territorial sovereignty should extend, and these were primarily areas and linguistic enclaves in which German was spoken but which were also claimed by the Southern Slav SHS state and the new Czechoslovakia or were located in Poland, like Bielsko Biała (Deutsch-Bielitz), for instance. It was unrealistic. In such a way, an artificial construct would have emerged that would have been without any coherence. But the very one-sided declaration with which Vienna decreed what belonged to German-Austria and what should ultimately have a seat and a voice in the intended new parliament with 225 seats had in any case not been reconciled with the other successor states of the Habsburg Monarchy. And they had no intention whatsoever of complying with German-Austria's notions.

In German-Austria's leading economic circles, too, a sense of cautious optimism still prevailed in November 1918. This was based not least on the fact that a type of government of national unity had been formed and gave the impression that all political forces wanted to assist in the construction of a new state. The country was regarded as a state of national unity and not as the wreckage of a great empire. And then they added together everything that this new state would have – always provided that those things would fall to it that it had made a claim on from the start: productive industries, iron, timber, hydropower and above all capital. Vienna had been the banking centre of the Monarchy, and there was still plenty of money. After all, Austria-Hungary had not been bankrupt in November 1918. The company directors in Vienna also believed that the Bohemian industries obtained their loans primarily from German-Austrian institutes. The war profits would have to be invested and the factories adjusted to new products, and when all this was under way the viability even of a downsized country would not be an issue. As long as the state ensured internal order, the people would surely soon place their trust in it.

Unlike in Germany, there was no seeking of refuge in the myth of the stab-in-the-back to which Austria-Hungary had supposedly fallen victim. Admittedly, as during the war years themselves, the attitude of the Northern and Southern Slavs was regarded as causal for the collapse, but at the same time with a certain satisfaction that one was now free to make decisions. Now there was no need to take consideration of Hungarians, Czechs and other peoples of the Habsburg Empire readily perceived as the 'gravediggers' of the Monarchy; now German-Austria could go its own way, undeterred. Politicians, the public and, not least, the Catholic Church agreed on this, and it was especially the latter who successfully accomplished the transition from a pillar of the Habsburg dynasty to a pillar of the democratic republic comparatively harmlessly. It might be that it remained a 'bloody wound',[22] but it could be concealed. The clergy was called on to exhort the faithful from the pulpit to display 'unconditional loyalty towards the now lawfully existing state of German-Austria'.[23]

That which had changed and would happen admittedly had to be explained and the children were a good starting point. For this reason, reading material in primary schools stated:

> Some of the things the grown-ups are currently talking about, you ultimately cannot yet understand. They are presently saying: our fatherland is now Austria – no, they now call it German-Austria – German-Austria is now a republic and we are republicans. What might that mean? … We who speak the German language now want to join together and set up house as we please. No individual ought to be able to dictate anything to us; instead, we want to do that which the majority of us regards as good. … Yes, but we are ten million people in German-Austria. Should they always be asked what they want? Surely not, because that would be too cumbersome. Therefore, the ten million people elect from time to time people whom they trust. These people then get together and make laws, with which we all have to comply. That is how it is done in a republic. … When you grow up, our beloved German-Austria should be a happy, joyful country again and you should be proud of your fatherland.[24]

The transition from monarchy to republic appeared to be so natural that, though most people were aware of the caesura, they also experienced it as an experiment, of which they were a part. No one had any experience of democracy. In spite of all indications of a secure future in a democratic state, for the mass of the population existential worries came to the fore and the desire for stability in a world falling to pieces. Union with Germany appeared to be the solution to everything. The Greater German parties and the Austrian Social Democrats advocated this out of complete conviction; the Chris-

Map 1: Intended
Scope and
Borders of the
State Territory of
German-Austria,
November 1918

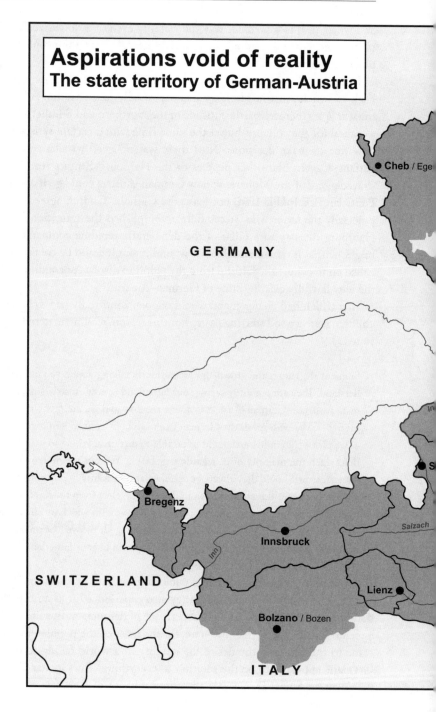

Aspirations void of reality
The state territory of German-Austria

GERMANY

● Cheb / Ege

SWITZERLAND

● Bregenz

Innsbruck ●

Salzach

Lienz ●

Bolzano / Bozen
●

ITALY

POLAND

Liberec /
Reichenberg

⊙ Prague

CZECH REPUBLIC

Bielsko /
Bielitz

Isen

Olomouc /
Olmütz

Jihlava /
Iglau

Brno /
Brünn

Český Krumlov /
Krumau

Znojmo / Znaim

SLOVAKIA

Danube

Danube

Morava

Linz

Vienna

Bratislava /
Pressburg

St. Pölten

Eisenstadt

Sopron / Ödenburg

Budapest ⊙

Enns

HUNGARY

Mur

Graz

Klagenfurt

Drau

Mur

Maribor /
Marburg

SLOVENIA

	Scope and borders of state territory according to the law of 22 November 1918

The map is based on today's state borders.

tian Socials with some hesitation. The Social Democrats expected a complete national unity to bring a swift establishment of a socialist social order. It was for this reason that they claimed – and here the contrast with capital becomes clear – that an independent Austria was not viable.[25] Union with Germany was admittedly not completely unquestioned among the Social Democrats, and State Chancellor Renner would have by far preferred a league of independent states with a common central administration. It remained unclear who would belong to the league.[26]

A little later, the aspiration to combine with Germany was qualified and it had to be acknowledged that Germany was only moderately taken with Austrian advances. Berlin feared above all that the addition of Austria – if at all possible – would be answered by the victorious powers with intensified peace terms. In such a way, Germany would have come out of the war stronger. Therefore, the Minister of Foreign Affairs, Wilhelm Solf, signalled his rejection. However, when it came to drawing up the Weimar constitution, representatives of German-Austria were nevertheless invited to assist in this work.[27] Germany was thus not so certain after all and preferred to keep an iron in the fire.

The union issue was something of a political card, however, which was played once and held another time up one's sleeve. Austria's union with Germany would most certainly prevent both a return to the monarchy as well as a Bolshevisation.[28] The victorious powers considered the latter to be a real danger, which they wanted to confront, but at the same time they had to admit that they hardly had any options. It was not yet a foregone conclusion that the experiment with the democratic republic would succeed and that radical groups would not capitalise on the expiration of the old Austria and provoke a revolution. The violence that had become so commonplace during the war did not look like abating. The call for the Allied military or at least law enforcement troops could be heard time and again. Admittedly, the British government was not keen on French and Italian plans to send troops to Austria. Eventually, the three powers agreed to install small diplomatic or military missions in Vienna. They wanted at least to be able to observe developments at close quarters. On 30 November 1918, the War Office in London commissioned Lieutenant Colonel Sir Thomas Montgomery-Cuninghame to go to Vienna as the British military plenipotentiary. Montgomery-Cuninghame had been military attaché in Vienna until 1914. Now – almost like old times – he was supposed not only to enforce the will of the Allies in German-Austria but also be responsible for Hungary and regularly report from Czechoslovakia. His first messages from Vienna already sounded alarming. German-Austria was threatened with a catastrophic famine.

As early as late October 1918, the last Imperial Minister of State for Food, Johann Löwenfeld-Russ, had pointed out that it would not be possible to feed Austria in the medium and long term. He would prove to be right. The Allies, namely, left the wartime blockade in place, and in view of the food catastrophe or at least scarcity in many European states there was also little prospect of imports.

The only hope held by Löwenfeld-Russ, who, as minister, had become – without a break – a member of the Provisional State Government of German-Austria, was that Austria might be able to overcome its existential problems with the help of Germany. But in November, Germany cancelled the deliveries it had already agreed to make. It was fighting for its own survival. And then it got worse: in view of the looming quarrel over the affiliation of southern Bohemia and Moravia as well as the German territories of Silesia, the Czechs were no longer prepared to deliver foodstuffs to German-Austria. They were also thoroughly alarmed that German-Austria had simply written into its constitution that it would be part of Germany, because if indeed all those territories claimed by Austria became part of (a Greater) Germany, Czechoslovakia would be positively encircled. This was unimaginable for the Prague government. It responded accordingly. If Austria did not want to starve to death, it would have to, at least temporarily, defer its territorial desires and talk to the Czechs. Löwenfeld-Russ then made unmistakeably clear in the session of the Council of State on 8 November: 'With all due respect to national feeling, the question must be asked: is it possible to force through our national and political desires if we have already starved to death?' The answer was self-evident. It would prove to be immensely difficult, however, to come together in conversation with the new Czechoslovakia. But there was still a flicker of hope: five days after the conclusion of the armistice in the Villa Giusti, the American government had announced that it would support the 'liberated peoples of Europe' with foodstuffs.[29] The German-Austrian Minister for Foreign Affairs, Otto Bauer, successor to the suddenly deceased Viktor Adler, therefore notified the Americans not only of the new Austrian creation but also reflected on the American offer. German-Austria was also one of the 'liberated peoples', he argued, and would therefore also be supplied with foodstuffs from the USA. President Wilson communicated in his answer that the USA would indeed enable the country to import foodstuffs, but only against payment. Admittedly, the USA did not want to adopt the British-French stance and continue the blockade measures beyond the end of the war. Therefore, Germany was not supplied until March 1919; in the case of Austria, however, an equalisation was silently made with the liberated nations, even if the start of aid deliveries was dramatically delayed. It even took until the end of the year before it was at all possible to speak with the director of the American Relief Administration, Herbert Hoover. Until then, all food it had been somehow possible to rustle up in German-Austria had been exhausted. The people survived from January 1919 with the help of foreign aid. As announced, however, this aid was not free of charge. Instead, payment agreements were concluded – it was a question of indemnities, without which no help could have been expected.

For the willingness of the USA to provide food credit to Austria and in this way ensure its survival, it was ultimately decisive that the looming spectre of Bolshevisation was taking on concrete form. It was not a question of generosity, and when the USA advanced German-Austria money, with which the food deliveries were to be paid, German-Austria had to pledge considerable state revenue to the USA in return and eventually agree in June 1919 to the temporary transfer of the Austrian gold and foreign exchange reserves to Italy.[30] The Americans and the French also ultimately persuaded Czechoslovakia to supply Austria with coal for the production of gas.[31]

The daily arrivals of flour and cereals grew significantly. In April, the flour contingent per person was doubled, likewise the fat contingent. Both, however, only reached the (exceedingly modest) quantities of December 1917 and January 1918.[32]

Elsewhere, the crisis continued to escalate. Austria's major banks had to sell off their holdings. They were unable to do anything else, because the loss of their solvency loomed. They sold their majority shares to the then Italian shipyards in Trieste (Triest) and Rijeka (Fiume). The Czechs invited French financial institutions to purchase hitherto Austrian shares in the Škoda company. Škoda was then acquired by Schneider-Creuzot. When the Italian Fiat company succeeded with the help of the notorious speculator Camillo Castiglioni in acquiring the share packages of the Austrian Alpine Montan Company (Österreichisch-Alpine Montangesellschaft), another major Austrian enterprise was transferred into foreign hands. It did not make matters any better that the Austrian Ministry of Finance under the short-lived minister Joseph Schumpeter had a finger in the pie. It was precisely such actions, which prevented an emergency nationalisation of large firms, that were grist for the mill of those who regarded economic questions from an ideological viewpoint. And for the Social Democrats, the sell-off amounted to a loss of jobs and could be interpreted in this way from the perspective of the class struggle as the 'West' being imperialist and capitalist, and it by all means allowed for the adoption of the slogans of the Russian October Revolution.

In spite of increasing verbal radicalism, the Social Democrat party leadership of German-Austria attempted repeatedly to provide reassurance. Permanent Secretary for the Army Julius Deutsch also played down the issue when there were several indications that the political leadership might lose control over the People's Militia. Vienna, above all, regarded it already as a veritable scourge, and its strength of more than 15,000 men gave cause for concern. Individual People's Militia squads began not only to search guest houses and shops for foodstuffs and other items they could make use of. Now private apartments were added. There was plundering. The police were powerless. Military intervention still appeared too risky for the Allied military missions. They had only 200 men at their disposal and were thus confronted by far superior numbers.[33]

In other respects, too, things did not look good. Slogans in favour of union with Germany were repeatedly sighted. Anti-Semitism, which had already been latent before the war, was increasingly directed against those Galician Jews who had remained in Austria, above all in Vienna, as well as the 'local' Jews. Everywhere, things were threatening to boil over. The government did what it could and attempted to fight off the threat of revolution with a whole raft of reforms. The coalition voted in the eight-hour day for factory workers and a general 48-hour working week, secured holiday entitlement and unemployment insurance, all things that had already been demanded during the wave of strikes in January 1918. Of course, some desires remained unfulfilled. However, good behaviour was the order of the day until the issues deriving from the peace treaty had been settled. Unrest should be avoided, if at all possible, because it might otherwise be claimed: Austria is becoming communist.

The first general election was announced for 16 February 1919, the first since June 1911, and the first in which women could also exercise their right to vote. The pre-election period naturally brought an additional polarisation and radicalisation. For a time, there were thoughts of simply naming delegates for those German territories of the former Monarchy separated from German-Austria, because they could not take part in the elections, but it was ultimately refrained from doing so. As it turned out, the result of the elections was clear-cut: with 72 parliamentary seats, the Social Democrats obtained a relative majority; the Christian Socials received 69 seats in parliament, which was designated the Constituent National Assembly; German nationalist groups got 26 and splinter parties a further three seats in parliament, which had 170 seats. In fact, only 159 delegates had been elected; eleven were co-opted.[34] Karl Renner became state chancellor. The government was established in the form of a grand coalition of Social Democrats and Christian Socials; with 141 delegates, it enjoyed a very comfortable majority. One of the first resolutions of the newly-elected Constituent National Assembly was to confirm the constitution of 12 November 1918. German-Austria was a democratic republic. And German-Austria was an 'integral part of the German Republic'.[35] At least on paper.

One Emperor Too Many

The building of the Imperial Assembly (Reichsrat) on Vienna's Ringstraße was vacated by those who no longer had anything to do there. It was also no longer called the building of the Imperial Assembly, but rather the parliament. Only the largest assembly hall retained its name: it was the Reichsrat Assembly Hall. But it was hardly needed. The Constituent National Assembly managed without it. It did, however, have an overflowing agenda. Again, as in November 1918, the main concern was initially the person of the Emperor. He had by no means become a non-person, even if he was accused of many things and verbal attacks were directed in equal measure against him, the aristocracy and, above all, the wartime military leadership. The fact that the Emperor was a type of nuisance factor, however, appeared evident. To the last, he had driven through Vienna in an open-top motor car and been acclaimed, then he had relocated to Eckartsau Castle and waited there for a signal from one of the successor states, welcoming him. It did not come. Like many, the former Emperor had the Spanish flu. His diet was a little monotonous, as there was game almost every day. And he waited.

It was noticed that the Emperor had not disbanded the armed forces of the Dual Monarchy, which had taken an oath to him, or released them from this oath – in contrast to the last Imperial Austrian government. Was it an omission that just happened or should the fiction of a still extant supreme command be nurtured in this way? No one knew. Karl remained in Eckartsau Castle and his intentions were unclear. A solution had to be found.

After the elections in February, the German-Austrian National Assembly prepared a law on the exile of the Habsburgs. There had already been considerations at the Council of State session on 20 December 1918 to 'outlaw' the Emperor. An obstacle to this was still the idea of involving Emperor Karl in the negotiations for a peace treaty. Renner travelled to Eckartsau, but evidently did not have an opportunity to speak to the former Emperor, because the latter avoided an encounter and Renner had to return home without having achieved anything.[36] Karl doubtless felt that he had gone too far with his declaration of renunciation from 11 November and had adopted the view of his wife, Zita, to the effect that a ruler cannot simply abdicate. He could be killed; then another would simply follow in his footsteps.[37] But to abdicate: never!

On 12 March, the British Prime Minister David Lloyd George addressed the question of war guilt of the Austrian Emperor to the Supreme Allied Council in Paris. The Council decided that Karl was not personally guilty and that they would be grateful if Switzerland were to take him in. In Vienna, however, Karl's refusal to abdicate led to a further escalation. Rumours circulated to the effect that the life of the Emperor was in danger, though they had admittedly been plucked out of thin air. He had become an embarrassment – nothing more. And, unlike Kaiser Wilhelm, he did not want to flee. State Chancellor Renner overtly threatened: if Karl did not abdicate or go into exile, he would be interned. Eventually, the former Emperor did resolve to emigrate after all and was brought to Switzerland by special train on 24 March 1919. Stefan Zweig travelled in the opposite direction. He who had regarded the start of the war in 1914 and the awakening of the masses as 'something magnificent, captivating and even seductive', but had then travelled to Switzerland because he was surplus to requirements, returned to Austria in March 1919, to an Austria 'that now only dozed as an uncertain, grey and lifeless shadow of the former Imperial Monarchy on the map of Europe'. In Feldkirch, Zweig claimed to have come to a standstill exactly next to Emperor Karl's saloon and watched as the latter's train departed:

> The officials gazed after him, respectfully. Then they returned to their places of work with the same certain awkwardness that can be observed at burials. ... I knew it was a different Austria, another world to which I was returning.[38]

Before crossing the frontier, the former Emperor withdrew his waiver of 11 November of the previous year with the explanation that no one, whoever it was, had the right to depose an emperor 'by the grace of God'. 'I continue to believe in the "divine right of kings". I am the legitimate ruler. All anti-kings, even if they are chosen by the grace of the people, are illegitimate and traitors. My Austrian and Hungarian proclamations were imposed on me and are, therefore, invalid.'[39] The Republic responded on 3 April 1919 with the unconditional exile of the 'former bearer of the crown' and the expulsion of all members of the House of Habsburg-Lorraine who did not expressly acknowledge the Austrian constitution.[40] Their civil rights were restricted. The Republic declared itself the owner of all Habsburg property situated on state territory, so far it was not verifiably private property. Oaths taken to the Emperor were to be regarded as 'non-binding'. Aristocratic titles and privileges were abolished.[41] In this way, a problem had been radically solved. Reactions like that of (Count) Adalbert Sternberg are to be regarded as episodic: he had business cards printed on which he annotated his name with 'Ennobled under Karl the Great / disennobled under Karl Renner'.[42]

Attempted Coups

The law of 3 April 1919 at least made it clear to some extent that German-Austria could also show its revolutionary side. The victory of the radicals in Hungary and the formation of a Communist council government there had doubtlessly contributed to its determination. On 21 March 1919, Béla Kun, who had been radicalised during the Russian Revolution, took over the reins of government in Budapest. Austria also understood this as a signal: the left hoped that the revolution would cross the border; the vast majority of the population, above all in the west of the country, was shocked. The nervousness was increased when the British Lieutenant Colonel Montgomery-Cuninghame returned to Vienna from Budapest in March in an alarmed state and spoke of an immediate danger. The Austrian Minister of Foreign Affairs, Otto Bauer, attempted to provide reassurance: there was also talk in German-Austria about a Communist government, but it was merely an academic discussion. Moreover, developments in Austria did not depend on Hungary but on Germany.[43] Precisely this was the problem, however, because on 5 April a council republic was also proclaimed in Munich. Was it the beginning of a Bolshevik revolution in Germany? Would it trigger an 'Austrian Revolution', which had so far failed to materialise and had at most been promulgated?[44]

On 27 March, strikes began on the Southern Railway and the Western Railway. Trains with foodstuffs were halted and redirected. It was once more the People's Militia that was a cause for concern. Minister of Finance Schumpeter strongly advised the Western powers to disarm the People's Militia and suggested to the representatives of the victorious powers that State Chancellor Karl Renner would also support such a step.[45] But the Allies were again unable to bring themselves to take any measure other than threats. In Vienna, the hour of the Social Democrats finally struck.

Although the Austrian left had a radical wing and took the class struggle seriously, it rejected the request of the Hungarian Communists for active support. In spite of much sympathy for a left-wing experiment, the Austrian Social Democrats – who sympathised with Béla Kun – did not consider the situation comparable. It was argued above all that a dominant left existed in Vienna but not in the rest of Austria, where the strongholds of the peasantry and the Christian Socials were located, who were vehemently opposed to the call for joint action with the Hungarian Communists.

The possibility of an affiliation of Austria and Hungary, however, set the alarm bells ringing among the victorious powers. They now discussed the option, after all, of transferring troops to eastern Austria. Even a regiment in Vienna would suffice, they argued. The idea suddenly attracted the interest not only of the French but also the Americans and the British. The French wanted to make a start with 500 men. But interventionism had already seen its best days. The militaries continued to make plans to intervene, but the political leaderships in Paris, London and Washington put them off time and again. A contributing factor was the only limited success of Allied intervention in Russia. To saddle themselves with an additional problem in the form of Austria and, potentially, Hungary was not in the interests of the West.

More nuanced was Italy's approach, which did not rule out a French intervention in the Danube region but wanted to safeguard its own interests there. Italy, therefore, advocated an intervention and, should the occasion arise, wanted to see an Austria occupied and controlled by Italy and a Hungary controlled by the French.[46] The Vatican also desired Allied intervention in Austria. As early as 27 March 1919, however, the victorious powers agreed during the Paris Peace Conference that there would be no intervention. Thus, the plans of Montgomery-Cuninghame and his colleagues in Vienna, the Italian General Roberto Segré and the French diplomat Henri Allizé were definitively rejected. A swift conclusion of peace and resumption of international trade would, in Paris' view, combat the danger far more effectively than a military intervention.[47]

On 8 April, a positively catastrophic mood emerged among the 'Big Four'. The Italian Prime Minister Orlando announced that he had received reliable reports that the proclamation of a Soviet republic in Vienna was planned for 14 April. The British had received similar information.[48] The day was incorrect, but there was substance to the rumour. The reaction of the Allies, however, was rather odd: the British Foreign Secretary, Lord Arthur James Balfour, said: if the country were to sink into chaos or even become communist, deliveries of foodstuffs would immediately be stopped. And Lieutenant Colonel Montgomery-Cuninghame caused a stir with the remark: 'Unrest … will be punished with death by starvation.'

In spite of the aid deliveries sent since January, the existential distress in Austria was still extensive, and because the Austrians were basically given next to nothing for free, it was only the fact that something was delivered at all that was worth pointing out. In March, the Allied blockade against Austria was demonstratively ended. However, Austria was not allowed to export any goods to Germany or Hungary. This, in turn, had a restrictive effect, and unemployment increased. The class struggle became more acute. It was not limited, however, to the radical left and their main ideological adversaries in the Christian Social camp but extended to the antithesis between a Vienna that was regarded as predominantly 'left' and the federal states, which were considered to be mainly Christian Social, or at least not left. But even within the left, the contrasts were tangible. Renner opposed the demand of the radicals for socialisation with the argument that 'one cannot socialise bankruptcy'. Eventually, the majority of Social Democrats distanced themselves from the council movement at a national conference of workers' councils in Linz in spring 1919.[49]

However, this by no means silenced radical expression. And it was not only expressions but time and again acts of violence that fanned the fear. Ever social group sought to shape the state according to their preferences. Bogeyman images were produced accordingly. Those who thought differently were 'class enemies'. In turn, words such as 'Bolsheviks' or 'Judaized' easily crossed the lips of the latter. Everyone believed they had a monopoly on the truth. The spectre of revolution loomed in Vienna. The federal states fought to save their territory. Understanding for the problems of the others could only be described as 'finite'. The escalation of violence could also be perceived, however, as a millionfold answer to the question of the meaning of life and, above all, the meaning of the mass mortality during the war. Was that it? Around half the male Austrians had gained military experience, been to war and survived. The repatriates were accustomed to violence. And violence in politics was commonplace after the war.

The radical left prepared an armed uprising for 17 April, which was also designed to install a council government in German-Austria. The Hungarian Communists placed all their hopes in this operation. Enthusiastic reports in the Hungarian press about the growing Communist movement in Austria increased day by day. Armed men from Hungary infiltrated their neighbour. The Communist regime in Budapest was also prepared to contribute to the cost of revolutionising Austria and sent money. Then came illegal emissaries, even including the People's Commissar for Education, Sándor Szabados, and Ernst Bettelheim as a representative of the Communist International. The first thing he did was to replace the leader of the Austrian Communists, who was too inactive for his taste.[50] Another brought pre-prepared proclamations, which were supposed to be put up after a successful Communist putsch. The placards bore the date of 16 April.[51] However, it was to be the day after.

Communist agitators exploited a gathering of repatriates and unemployed in Vienna to storm parliament. Sections of the People's Militia intervened on the side of the Communists. The mass of the People's Militia remained loyal to the regime, however, and followed the appeals and orders of Social Democrat politicians, above all those of Minister for the Army Julius Deutsch. A general uprising failed to materialise. The ringleaders were arrested, and it can be said with some justification that the revolutionising of Austria had foundered on the Social Democrats.

Things again became critical in June. There were two reasons for this: the Allies, above all the Italian plenipotentiary for supervising the armistice, General Segré, had issued an ultimatum regarding the reduction of the People's Militia, and the Hungarians – or, rather, the Communists – had put all their eggs into one basket. Money and agitators continued to arrive. The Hungarian envoy played a key role and attempted everything to take advantage of the commotion over the depletion of the People's Militia from more than 50,000 to 12,000 men. However, the chief of police in Vienna, Johann Schober, had 122 Communist functionaries arrested on the eve of the planned operation. The movement was leaderless and the storm on the prison on Rossauer Lände ended on 15 June in Vienna's Hörlgasse in a hail of police bullets. The Bolshevik dream of the rule of workers' and soldiers' councils was over. The radical left had suffered a debacle and henceforth played no further role. Now everyone could concentrate on something other than the Communist threat.

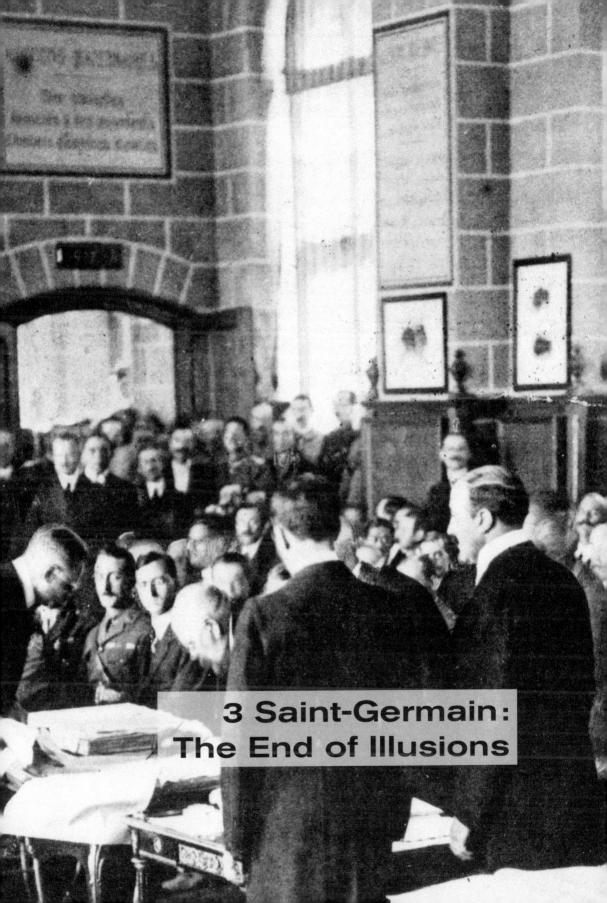

3 Saint-Germain: The End of Illusions

3   On 10 September 1919, State Chancellor Karl Renner signed the peace treaty between the Allies and Austria at the Château de Saint-Germain-en-Laye. 'It is a painful peace but it is a peace', said the Chancellor. The Romanian and Yugoslavian delegations did not take part in the signing ceremony, as they had objections to individual provisions. During the ratification debate in the USA, the House of Representatives refused to give its consent to the treaty. As a result, the USA remained officially at war with Austria until 8 November 1921. (Photo: Austrian National Library / Picture Archives)

Since December 1918, intensive thought had been given to what should be settled in the framework of a treaty between the victorious powers and German-Austria. As German-Austria regarded itself as a successor state and not the state that had waged war at the time, it was assumed that the Allies would conclude a state treaty with Austria, rather than a peace treaty. Again, one of the illusions or, rather, misapprehensions that accompanied the path of the Republic. Initially, it was also hoped that everything would be settled fairly quickly, because – as the state constitution declared – German-Austria was to become part of the German Republic. All that was important, therefore, was what the German peace treaty said. But developments wrought havoc with all plans, not to mention all hopes. There was, above all, the greatest uncertainty regarding the frontiers of the territory, which would either exist as an independent state or be incorporated into Germany. A central role was played here by the question of a union with Germany, both for advocates of independence and for those who put the case for incorporation: if German-Austria were to endure, literally every square kilometre had to be fought for; if it were to be consumed by Germany, it was not so important whether peripheral territories were included or not.

The Parts and the Whole

The question of what would happen resulted in territorial issues shifting from the level of the state to that of the provinces, because the federal states regarded themselves as historically evolved entities, and rightly so. They had existed earlier than the state; they were in some cases older than Habsburg rule in the Alpine region. The federal states, therefore, fought with stubborn determination to retain the historical entities and even occasionally questioned affiliation with German-Austria.

In the far west, in Vorarlberg, the right to self-determination was regarded as something that also allowed even small territorial entities the free choice of affiliation. As early as November 1918, a union of the province with Switzerland was touted. Several months later, on 12 March 1919, when the Constituent National Assembly voted on a union with Germany, a Vorarlberg delegate caused a stir when he voted against the motion, because Vorarlberg wanted to decide on its own affiliation, he said: 'Vienna does not know the people of Vorarlberg, and we do not want to know anything about the Vienna Jews,' he succinctly commented.[52] The President of the National Assembly, Karl

Seitz, remained calm and said that, for the provinces, it would 'prove very unpleasant if they want to segregate themselves from Vienna as one would from a leper', because 'without Vienna's steering power, the provinces would not survive'.[53] However, it was also suggested to unite Vorarlberg with Bavaria or Württemberg. In a popular referendum on 11 May 1919, around 80 per cent of the population voted for the union of Vorarlberg with Switzerland. Switzerland was conflicted, but ultimately decided only to accept a union with Vorarlberg in consultation with Vienna. Furthermore: the view prevailed in Bern that one should not start carving up Austria.[54] The Supreme Allied Council in Paris, which was preparing the judgement of the victors, could only agree.

Tyrol, which had belonged to Austria since 1363, hoped – against its better judgement – that South Tyrol, the territory south of the Brenner Pass as far as Salorno, would remain part of the historical entity. After all, Tyrol was older than the Habsburg Monarchy. It had now long been known that Italy had been awarded Tyrol as far as the Brenner Pass in the Treaty of London in 1915, but the state capital of Innsbruck did not regard that as definitive. Therefore, all possible options were explored for how Tyrol could preserve its integrity. The fact that the province had declared its accession to the state of German-Austria was one thing; the fact that the province might be torn apart was something else. The propaganda for a union was, therefore, very weak in Tyrol and was largely limited to Social Democrat and Greater German circles, whilst the Christian Social majority was split on the issue of the union. All forms of state autonomy were discussed, from a union of Tyrol – as a canton – with Switzerland via the creation of an independent Alpine republic to the neutralisation of Tyrol and its withdrawal from the German-Austrian association of states.[55]

Carinthia, which had become part of Austria in 1335, wanted to belong to the new state of German-Austria at all costs. As the Slovene national government in Ljubljana (Laibach) was anxious to take possession of as much territory as possible and wanted to incorporate Klagenfurt and most of Villach into the new Southern Slave state, Slovene troops began to occupy Carinthian territory north of the Karawanks. They were met with resistance. It was the beginning of the Austro-Slovene conflict in Carinthia. Citizens' militias, which were intended to halt the advance of the Slovenes, were formed from repatriates and volunteers. The Carinthian Provincial Assembly could not and did not want to wait until People's Militia forces enabled an orderly resistance. It decided to act independently: 'The Council of State in Vienna is to be informed immediately of this resolution.'[56] The defensive measures were in vain.

The Provisional Provincial Assembly in Carinthia eventually had to consent to a demarcation line on 23 November, which ran along the Gail and Drava rivers, that is, right through the middle of Carinthia. However, this did not bring an end to the armed conflicts. After an American academic commission had toured the province from January 1919 onwards, which spoke out against a partition of the Klagenfurt

Basin and wanted to draw the frontier along the main ridge of the Karawanks, the Slovenes sought to bring about a fait accompli. They began a large-scale offensive but were thrown back. This time, the People's Militia also played a role. One of the People's Militiamen deployed in Carinthia was Franz Jonas. Italy, which was already engaged at this point in time in a bitter struggle with the SHS state for Istria, Rijeka (Fiume) and the Dalmatian coast, was perfectly content with the Austrian victories. When Serbian troops intervened in the fighting, however, there was nothing left for the Austrian units to do but retreat. Against Entente troops, which also included the Serbians, no resistance could be offered on account of the armistice. Klagenfurt was occupied by SHS troops. The provincial government had to be evacuated to Spittal an der Drau. Until the time of a decision in the context of the peace treaty negotiations, the south of Carinthia remained disputed.[57]

From the outset, southern Styria, Austrian since 1282, with the predominantly German cities of Maribor (Marburg), Celje (Cilli) and Ptuj (Pettau), could not be held. Only for Maribor was a popular referendum considered, but it then did not come about. The SHS state had received massive support from France, and for Italy its own desires carried too much weight for it to risk becoming more than a verbal advocate for German-Austria. As in Carinthia, Slovene and SHS formations also advanced north into southern Styria and occupied Radkersburg, among other places. Despite repeated attempts to force back the SHS troops, the city could not be liberated.

Another territory remained disputed, and indeed for a longer period of time, namely the German-settled parts of western Hungary. Here, Hungarian, Austrian and, not least, Czech interests were at odds. Hungary wanted to retain the territory; Austrian wanted to obtain it; and Prague pursued the project of a Slav corridor, which would stretch from Slovakia via the three western Hungarian counties of Moson (Wieselburg), Vasvár (Eisenburg) and Sopron (Ödenburg) as far as Croatia. Until spring 1919, it seemed to be anything but a foregone conclusion that Austria would receive German West Hungary. But then the Béla Kun regime gave Austria the edge in the eyes of the Allies because they were inclined to honour the stance of Austria and ignore both Hungarian and Czech wishes.

Austria demonstrated compliance. Everything that might appreciably provoke the Allies or even its neighbours was eschewed. Although Austria received verbal praise for this, it was more than questionable whether the Allies would take this into account at the negotiations for a peace treaty scheduled near Paris. After all, they did not do it in the case of Germany, whose peace treaty was being discussed in Versailles. Meanwhile, the hope could be buried that there would not be any victor's justice in Paris, as had been the case in 1814/15 in Vienna. The pentarchy of the five European great powers from that time, the Concert of Europe and the old-style conference diplomacy were no longer in demand. Only the idea of a balance of power in Europe still had its advocates. Therefore, it was not only the Liverpool Professor of Modern History, Charles Webster, who took a detailed look at the Congress of Vienna of 1814/15; others did the same. Webster did it in a particularly impressive manner. Within eleven weeks, he wrote his remarkable book *The Congress of Vienna, 1814/15*,[58] in which he described the Congress as the only meeting that could act as a type of matrix for the forthcoming tasks of the statesmen in the palaces around Paris. However, the British scholar was unable to convince them. In Versailles and Saint-Germain-en-Laye, just as little as in Neuilly-sur-Seine, Trianon and Sèvres, the basic principles of the Congress of Vienna were not applied. The twentieth century had arrived.

In one point, however, Austria was wrong to be sceptical. It was feared that the victorious powers would know nothing about the countries with which they were supposed to conclude a peace. This may have applied to some politicians, but not to the experts who not only had to prepare the foundations for a solution to territorial questions but also discussed every detail of the generally comprehensive studies.[59] Until March 1919, for instance, the thinking within British institutions revolved time and again around a Danube confederation with Vienna at its centre. It was above all the finance and economics experts who had a type of Swiss model in mind. And they urged haste, because if the economic situation were to deteriorate still further, there would be a revolution in Austria, and in view of the Hungarian example this alarming observation did not seem to be plucked out of thin air. But the experts' problem was, as always, that they did not express a single position, contradicted one another and, in this way, accommodated political decisions to an exceptional degree. Thus, in such cases, it applied more or less across the board that the wishes of the victorious powers were to be considered where at all possible and those of the wartime opponents ignored.

Time of Uncertainty

Renner and the government of German-Austria waited for months for a formal invitation to Paris. Despite intensive preparations, however, they remained uncertain about very critical points. They did not know, above all, whether the union with Germany would be discussed. The Minister of Foreign Affairs, Otto Bauer, hoped that the United States and Britain would eventually agree to the union of German-Austria with Germany, after all.[60] He cherished his own personal illusions, because he must have been aware of the firm 'no' of the French. And it was hopeless from the start to attempt to play the Allies off against each other. The domestic political climate worsened. The Christian Socials were strictly opposed to Otto Bauer being the head of the Austrian delegation, just as Ulrich von Brockdorff-Rantzau – minister in the Foreign Office of the German government that had been based in Weimar since January 1919 – was. The argument was that Bauer, as an uncompromising advocate of the union and a sympathiser of the Hungarian council system on top of that, would provoke with his stance rather than signalling a willingness to compromise. Furthermore, his Francophobe attitude was a cause for concern. Whether the union with Germany could even still be attractive was questioned once more at this point in time. Thus, the leader of the Christian Social Party, Ignaz Seipel, remarked: 'We will only unite with Germany if it becomes a truly free state. In the Germany of today, in which terror by soldiers' councils and a socialist dictatorship exist … we have no place.'[61] Bauer, at least, was regarded as unsuitable to represent Austria in Saint-Germain. As no comparable leading representative could be found, State Chancellor Renner ultimately became head of the delegation. This was no doubt a good and sensible choice, because it was hoped that Renner would also find a sympathetic ear at the level of the heads of government and not only that of the ministers.

In mid-May 1919, the Austrian delegation went to Paris. It was interned in Saint-Germain. First of all, Renner was informed that the Austrians were only invited as respondents. They would under no circumstances be allowed to take part in the negotiations. Without beating about the bush, the status of Austria was made plain: Austria had been summoned, like Germany, as a belligerent and was therefore entirely responsible for the war and its consequences. The final illusions disappeared.

The question of legal continuity having passed from the Habsburg Monarchy to Austria had admittedly been discussed by the Allies, and President Wilson, like British Prime Minister David Lloyd George, was against viewing German-Austria as the legal successor. However, the interests of France, Italy and the new allies, above all the Czechs, ultimately counted for more. It was no coincidence that it was argued that the Germans in Austria had always been the bearers of the state idea. Therefore, they now had to accept liability for the war, too. And as far as territory was concerned, things were fairly straightforward: the Habsburg Monarchy had emerged in 1526 from a core of lands to which Austria was now to be reduced again.[62] Thus, territorial questions caused the Allies the least concern. And the French deleted the word 'German' from the name of the state. The state was simply designated Austria and would also call itself such in the future.

The affiliation of South Tyrol, which was claimed by Italy as far as the Brenner Pass, was not disputed by the victorious powers. It should go to Italy. There were strategic and economic reasons in favour of this. British Prime Minister Lloyd George had most of all been in favour of a departure from the Treaty of London. Ultimately, the British representative on the armistice commission in Vienna, Lieutenant Colonel Montgomery-Cuninghame, had also stated that the Allies would honour in the form of concessions the positive role played by Austria in containing the Bolshevik threat from Hungary. The last word had also not been spoken on the issue of South Tyrol. The

British then also contented themselves to fulfil those parts of the Treaty of London that concerned Austria. The Val Canale was also allocated to Italy without major discussion. This question was thus settled.

The Allies did not want any debates regarding the northern frontier, either. Since June 1918, France had supported the claims of exile Czechs to the so-called historical borders of Czechoslovakia. The other Allies had remained reserved. The Czechs, therefore, did not want to take any risks and, from December, had occupied all the territories claimed by them. It did not bother them here that the recurring historical borders of Bohemia and Moravia must inevitably raise the question of whether the borders of the crown lands that had been in place until the end of the war were not just as historical as the older frontiers of the Kingdom of Bohemia and the Margraviate of Moravia. Wherever a claim went beyond the historical borders, above all in the territory of Gmünd, Valtice (Feldsberg) and Břeclav (Lundenburg), reasons relating to traffic geography were cited.[63] At the new frontiers, the dawning of a new era was especially visible. If, until 1918, it had taken less than seven hours to reach Cracow from Vienna by train, the trains now stood for seven hours at Hohenau Station, waiting to be processed.

Prague was still not entirely satisfied. Eventually, President Tomáš Masaryk also addressed those wishes that constituted the real objective: Vienna and a major part of Lower Austria should become Czech. A land bridge would lead from Czechoslovakia to the State of Slovenes, Croats and Serbs and definitively separate Austria from Hungary. The justification for these demands, however, were merely a construction. Austria promptly protested and was informed by France that, until the peace treaty came into force, the historical borders of Bohemia and Moravia, as well as those of Silesia, would be valid. But when the occupation of the disputed territories by Czechoslovak troops and popular referendums were simultaneously rejected, it was clear that the drawing of borders would be an exclusively political act based on Western interests. It had long since been clear on which side France stood.

Renner, who constantly strove to maintain a good relationship between German-Austria and its northern neighbour, had attempted a very special idea. He proposed a federation to the Czechs. At the head of the league of states would be President Masaryk. The economy would be controlled by means of an instrument modelled on the Austro-Hungarian Compromise of 1867, namely an economic parliament based in Bratislava (Pozsony, Preßburg). It was also proposed to settle other matters with consideration of Czech interests. Prime Minister Karel Kramář and Foreign Minister Beneš were not interested. This was also a personal setback for Renner, because his family home in Dolni Dunajovice (Unter Tannowitz) would in the future be located in Czech Moravia.

The Carinthia question and the drawing of borders for Styria threatened to result in complete strife and war. After the occupation of parts of the Klagenfurt Basin by Southern Slav troops, a preliminary decision appeared to have been taken there, too.

But it also applied here that the borders would be drawn in Paris. On 30 May, President Wilson, with the complete agreement of Premier Clemenceau and Prime Minister Lloyd George, stated that a letter should be written to their 'Yugoslavian friends' making it clear that the results of the fighting would have no influence on the drawing of borders.[64]

As Yugoslavia did not want to accept the withdrawal of its troops to a demarcation line south of Klagenfurt and Lake Wörth, the Allies adopted a particularly threatening pose and declared that it had not yet been decided that Croatia and Slovenia were not enemy states, too, and action would be taken accordingly. The Italians even demonstrated this. But for them it was of course primarily a question of Istria and the opposite coast of the Adriatic Sea, and less of Carinthia. Austria had to note, however, that Italy was transforming from an archenemy into its only European partner.[65] Rome could also be generous, because it seemed that all its own wishes were being fulfilled.

The question of Burgenland proved to be no less problematic. The first draft of peace conditions made no mention, in any case, of Austria receiving western Hungarian territories. At least in this case, the Austrian delegation proved to be persuasive with its arguments, and the German territories of western Hungary were allocated to Austria.

The Moment of Truth

It was against this backdrop that the issues to be solved in the peace treaty were to unfold. Many parts of the treaty were already finished when the German-Austrian delegation arrived in Saint-Germain. Entire sections of the agreement had been adopted from the Covenant of the League of Nations; other sections, above all for the introduction, were already in the Treaty of Versailles for the peace with Germany. Austria – like Germany – was regarded as bearing complete liability for the war; this war guilt provided the basis for imposing obligations on the defeated Austria. Thus, Austria was subjected to some of the hatred that was directed primarily against Germany.

Article 177 of the treaty on Austria was then formulated accordingly, where it stated: 'The Allied and Associated Governments affirm and Austria accepts the responsibility of Austria and her Allies for causing the loss and damage to which the Allied and Associated Governments and their nationals have been subjected as a consequence of the war imposed upon them by the aggression of Austria-Hungary and her Allies.' It was made clear to Austria that it was liable for unleashing the war and for everything that followed, thus also for the wars then declared by others on the Habsburg Monarchy, like, for example, Italy and Romania.

It was almost unavoidable that the victorious powers would edit out their own role in the prehistory of the war and were merely anxious to assign guilt. This was also the most effective way to then derive demands from the war guilt assigned to one side. It was owing to the politics of the day and lacked a careful treatment of historical facts.

On 2 June 1919, the chairman of the peace conference, French Prime Minister Georges Clemenceau, gave Karl Renner the draft treaty. The shock could not have been greater. The state that would have liked to have seen itself as a new creation and had always made reference to discontinuity was literally cudgelled back into history by the Allies. Although they were actually already aware of most essential points and the prohibition of the union could already be read in the German Treaty of Versailles, the members of the peace delegation and, above all, the people back home had still cherished the hope that it would not turn out so badly. But it was as they had feared, and Renner stated outright that if the treaty were to come into force one-to-one, the Allies would 'load a corpse on to their triumphal chariot'.[66] The President of the Constituent National Assembly, Karl Seitz, stated in the Viennese parliament: 'We know that this sentence is a death sentence', and Foreign Minister Otto Bauer, who was still in office, availed himself of a phrase already common in Germany: it was a peace 'dictated by the victors'.[67]

As demanded, the delegation in Saint-Germain presented its objections in writing. Territorial issues were one thing. But Austria was also supposed to pay reparations. The amount had not yet been fixed. It was also a question of Austria-Hungary's foreign investments and debts. It was above all British economic experts who agreed that it would be preposterous to apply to Austria the terms developed for Germany. In the case of Germany, the aim would be to inhibit economic development, whereas in the Austrian case it would have to be promoted. Several memoranda by Sir Francis Oppenheimer regarding the catastrophic financial and economic situation in Austria eventually brought about a change, and the view prevailed that the reparations for foreign investments and likewise the clearance of financial debts could not simply be unloaded on to Austria, because this would promptly bankrupt the country. Instead, a ratio of distribution among nationalities should be agreed on, on the basis of which every successor state would assume a proportional share. The foreign ministers and the Supreme Allied Council agreed with their experts after some hesitation and ignored the wishes of the friendly successor states. Another part of the treaty had been completed.

At intervals of weeks or even months, each and every part of the treaty was handed over to Austria. There were still no negotiations. But there were interludes that suddenly showed some things in a different light.

Paris was concerned in June 1919 about the Hungarians' progress in their military undertaking in Slovakia. The Romanian and Czechoslovak offensive against Hungary progressed differently to what the Allies had expected and hoped for, and it did not lead to the rapid collapse of the Béla Kun regime. (1,200 volunteers from Austria had also contributed to the temporary victory of the Hungarians.) Hungary subsequently remained isolated, because there would be no negotiating with Bolsheviks, and the Allies began to pressurise Austria to adopt a more active role in the containment of communism. Soon, it was said that the incorporation of German West Hungary and Burgenland into Austria would be favourably reviewed in the framework of the peace negotiations if Austria were to alter its stance towards Hungary. The Allies would not settle for the Viennese government – in the case of the Social Democrats, with great reluctance – to refuse to support the Communist regime in Hungary. The Allies wanted more. Austria would have to agree to representatives of the victorious powers monitoring the demanded blockade measures at the Hungarian border. As so much was being monitored in any case, this would not ultimately make a difference. The result, admittedly, was the collapse of bilateral trade with Hungary. Yet it was still not enough. The Czechs wanted to receive additional contingents of weapons and ammunition from the dissolved assets of the Imperial and Royal Army. In the event of a refusal, they intended to stop coal deliveries. The Allies increased the pressure: if Austria did not fulfil Czech demands, they would discontinue food deliveries. The head of the Ministry of Foreign Affairs, Otto Bauer, assured the Hungarians of his sympathy and emphasised that Austria was acting under duress and therefore could not risk a revolution like in Hungary. In the other direction, namely to Czechoslovakia, 150,000 rifles and 200 machine guns as well as large amounts of ammunition were shifted, with the instruction that the public should learn nothing of it.

Austria continued to receive foodstuffs. At the same time, the next sections of the agreement were handed over in Paris. This time, the incorporation of the German territories of West Hungary were also included. This was something of a carrot and stick approach. An important point in the treaty had not yet been addressed by the summer, however, namely the question of a union of Austria with Germany. For the Allies, like for Austria, this was surely by no means a side issue.[68]

Initially, the prohibition of a union had only really been desired by France, in order to prevent a potential increase in German territory. The USA, Britain and Italy were inclined to be in favour of a union; at least it was less important for them. In March 1919, however, whilst the frontiers of Germany were being fixed in Versailles, a border was also drawn in the south-east that was designed to prevent Germany from being enlarged. With this stipulation, France complied with what a whole series of states had expected and positively demanded. Czechoslovakia was against the union. Yugoslavia was against it; even Switzerland protested against the 'hypothesis of unification'. Austria, intended for independence by means of a detour via Germany, and which became a sort of function of the treaty on Germany, was to be neutral, and in order that it remained this way, the League of Nations – in accordance with French notions – was to provide a guarantee. The idea was not entirely new. In March 1919, the semi-official French daily newspaper *Le Temps* had written about it. The final Imperial Prime

Minister of Austria, Heinrich Lammasch, formulated it in a very similar fashion when he wrote about a neutral 'Noric' or 'eastern Alpine' republic.[69] Soon thereafter, however, France no longer showed any interest in a neutral Austria, because the French General Staff had evidently argued that it would be far more practical if one could, if necessary, intervene in Hungary via Austrian territory. Furthermore, it was deemed imperative to weaken Germany, or at least not allow it to become stronger.

By early August 1919, the Hungarian Council Republic was history, and this changed the status of the question of union. And only now, with the third draft of the peace treaty, was the Austrian delegation officially informed of the prohibition of a union with Germany. But if anyone had pretended until now that he had been caught unawares by this and had known nothing about it, then he had failed to notice that the corresponding passages were in the Peace Treaty of Versailles as Article 80, which it had been possible to consult since June 1919. There, it was also clearly stated that Germany was obliged to preserve Austrian independence.

It was for this reason that the prohibition of a union with Germany also found its way, as Article 88, into the Peace Treaty of Saint-Germain. (In 1920, the imperative to preserve the independence of Austria was also written into the Hungarian Peace Treaty of Trianon.) 'The independence of Austria is inalienable otherwise than with the consent of the Council of the League of Nations.'

Otto Bauer used the occasion of the prohibition of union to resign from his post, because, he said: 'If the union does not happen, Austria will become a miserable peasant state in which it is no longer worth pursuing politics.' He rejected all responsibility for the peace treaty.[70]

After the whole raft of terms had been handed over in early September, Karl Renner demanded time to be able to study all 381 articles of the treaty and discuss them in the National Assembly; but he received only an additional 48 hours. On 10 September 1919, he signed the Peace Treaty of Saint-Germain standing up.

Not that the treaty was already valid with his signature. Only now did the tiresome process of national ratification and filings begin. Austria ratified the treaty on 25 October 1919. France delayed its signature by ten months and, in doing so, ensured, among other things, that the SHS troops did not withdraw from Radkersburg until July 1920. But it was advisable for Austria to adhere to the wording of the terms and to accept the conditions.

The balance sheet of the non-negotiations was mixed. By virtue of the embedding of the treaty in the Covenant of the League of Nations, the community of state would guarantee the existence of the country. At the same time, Austria was deprived of any right to self-determination.[71] The debts of the Monarchy had been divided up, so that Austria was prescribed a share of only around 8.5 per cent. The radical military stipulations to the effect that Austria's federal army should have only 30,000 professional soldiers, no general staff and no air force, and only a small number of heavy weapons, was regarded primarily as a social problem, because around 25,000 people, who had been part of the People's Militia, would now definitively have to be 'cut' and the army of unemployed multiplied at one stroke.

South Tyrol was transferred to Italy without any provision for autonomy and without protection of minorities. Nothing stood in the way of an Italianisation of the country. In North and East Tyrol, a nationwide day of mourning took place on 10 October 1919, and for every year until 1936.[72] The northern border had been drawn by the Czechs. It had to be accepted. On 24 September 1919, the Sudeten territories, which, in the Law on the Scope and Borders of State Territory, had once been declared a part of German-Austria, were solemnly removed.[73] For the disputed territory of Carinthia, a popular referendum had been appointed in Saint-Germain, which, with around 60 per cent voting 'yes' on 10 October 1920, resulted in a clear vote to remain in Austria. The Austro-Slovene conflict in Carinthia, economic interests and the traditional bonds of the Slovene population had evidently tipped the balance.

The issue of Burgenland remained a controversial one, although it should have been perceived as having already been settled in the peace treaty. In fact, after the end of the Communist regime in Hungary, the Allies had lost interest in a union of German West Hungary with Austria. The new eastern border was admittedly fixed in the treaty. But alterations were not ruled out and were to be arranged bilaterally. The new Hungarian state leadership under the former Vice Admiral Miklós Horthy, who was acting as regent, hoped that time would tell. Renner secured the support of the Czechs, for he had no particular sympathy for Hungary, and in January 1920 an Allied military mission went to Sopron (Ödenburg) at the request of Austria. In August 1920, the Allies issued Hungary with an ultimatum to hand over Sopron. It did not help. Hungary pinned its hopes on negotiations and applied a proven remedy: the supply of Austria with foodstuffs. But this time it did not prove to be so easy.

The government in Budapest then resorted to force. Guerrillas advanced into southern Styria. Austria sent gendarmerie and then Federal Army units. Fighting took place at Kirchschlag and Ágfalva (Agendorf) near Sopron. There were several dozen dead. Czechoslovakia and Italy now intervened and offered to mediate. Austria decided this time in favour of the Italians and ultimately accepted their proposed solution: contrary to the settlement in the peace treaty, a popular referendum would take place in Sopron and eight surrounding municipalities, which was held on 14 and 16 December 1921. In Sopron, a substantial majority voted to remain in Hungary, and it made no difference that Hungary had manipulated the voting lists. In the eight surrounding municipalities, there was a clear majority for Austria. However, the localities were left with Sopron, or rather Hungary. Until everything was finally settled and small villages had also been traded, it was 1924.[74]

The Balance Sheet

It was almost inevitable that the secession of territories or their union would now lead to friction, and subsequently perhaps nothing contributed so much to the destruction of the old bonds of the Habsburg Monarchy and the emergence of new state entities as the numerous conflicts over the drawing of borders. Over the union of the German territories of Bohemia and Moravia, Austria and Czechoslovakia got into a conflict that lasted decades. Despite all later protestations, Italy and Austria could not simply ignore the fact that German South Tyrol had been handed over to Italy. Tensions repeatedly flared between the majority population and the minority in Carinthia and several border areas of Styria. And in the case of the two brothers-in-law, Austria and Hungary, it was to be expected that the cession of Burgenland would arouse a hostile mood and much resentment. Perhaps it was not unwelcome for several victorious powers, above all France, that tension, conflict, threats to deploy the military, and indeed hostilities occurred, because the break-up of the Habsburg Monarchy aimed above all at destroying the old structures.

It could have been a source of hope that the Treaty of Saint-Germain was not supposed to remain valid in perpetuity and that the theoretical possibility at least existed that the League of Nations might repeal some conditions. As so often, it depended therefore on how the treaty was interpreted and how it was applied to a given situation. And this was not only done in accordance with objective criteria and by comparison with others, the Germans, the Hungarians, etc., but also the British, French or Italians, but instead primarily by direct comparison of workers, peasants, bourgeoisie, unemployed, proprietors, poor, war profiteers, locals, new arrivals, Jews, non-Jews, left-wingers, right-wingers and many other categories. The war and the 'deserved fate' did not have a levelling effect; instead, they merely created new categories and allowed differences to emerge. Envy, greed, lust for life and resentment became defining political categories. The fight for remembrance began. Ever more people, ever more combat veterans felt cheated, not only of the fruits of their struggle and suffering, but also their first post-war hopes. One thing had become evident, however: the victorious powers wanted to avoid at all costs the dissolution or self-dissolution of the new Austria. It had now indeed become a state and it exhibited all characteristics of one. Austria was a country of around 84,000 square kilometres. No one yet knew for sure, because the popular referendums on whether southern Carinthia and Sopron would remain were still outstanding. The country had around 6.5 million inhabitants. This remnant alone of the once 52-million-strong Habsburg Empire mourned for around 155,000 war dead and counted roughly as many war invalids.[75] As many as 50,000 people died from the Spanish influenza pandemic. The remark made by Magnus Hirschfeld, one of the pioneers of sexual research, regarding the war, also applied to Austria: it was the greatest sexual catastrophe 'that civilised humans had ever sustained'.[76] It was foreseeable that the social consequences of the war would still be tangible in years to come. Around 50,000 war widows and hundreds of thousands of orphans had to be fed. There was perhaps one thing that could be emphasised positively: there was as good as no war-related destruction, such as that suffered by the likes of Poland, Belgium, France and Serbia, for instance, but could also be seen in the former war territories now belonging to Italy or in Russia, Ukraine or the regions of the Middle East.

Many things remained unsettled. The question of reparations payments was still open and was ultimately neither solved nor properly updated by the victorious powers. Two years later, state bankruptcy loomed. The economy was in tatters. The partial sell-off had been to no avail. A cultural sell-off began. Private owners, churches and monasteries sold rare books in order to stay afloat. The key memory banks of Central Europe, the collections of the now State Archives in Vienna, threatened to be scattered to the four winds. For a time, anyone and everyone took whatever they could get their hands on.

Although Austria got off somewhat more lightly than Germany, the peace treaty was regarded as a catastrophe. The deletion of the article on union from the constitution on 21 October 1919 was accompanied by emotional scenes. The question of liability was answered by clearly establishing that Austria was a state that no one wanted and which had been deprived of all opportunities.[77] Special emphasis was once more placed on the prohibition of union. As it was not possible for the entire state to unite with Germany, in 1921 Tyrol, Salzburg and Styria carried out referendums one after another, the results of which were admittedly not valid but with approval ratings of 98 per cent for the union were hard to beat when it came to clarity.[78] The victorious powers then adopted a positively threatening stance. The spectre of the discontinuation of the delivery of essential goods was once more brandished. The French envoy in Austria, Pierre Antonin Lefèvre-Pontalis, threatened that Yugoslavia would occupy Carinthia with French approval and Paris would support Hungary's claim to Burgenland.[79] Even if the referendums in the federal states did not ultimately have a lasting effect, they led to the resignation of the federal government and contributed to a further emotionalization and to domestic conflicts.

The theory of an inability to survive increasingly became part of a 'rejection psychosis' and the myth of the enforced state. Austria did not just appear to have become but was in fact unmistakeably under foreign control and grossly dependent on it. And this would never change. It was this that made the transition from self-regulating major power to a small state appear so evidently and emotionally dreadful. And now even those who had originally painted a rosy picture began to doubt the continued existence of the new state.

The Fight for Remembrance

It was admittedly not easy to fight off the apocalyptic mood, evoke the start of a new era and demonstrate optimism. But this was exactly the job of politics. The original 'circle of gentlemen' in parliament had been loosened and jumbled in the meantime. Since the elections of March 1919, eight women also sat in the National Assembly. More crucial, however, was that those who returned home from the war, disappointed and often humiliated, forced their way into politics. They wanted to have their say, shape the future according to their ideas and, in some cases, take revenge. They had been doing this since 1918. New bogeyman images quickly emerged. The Austrian Social Democrats and Communists stirred up hatred not only against the old aristocracy, the war profiteers and the upper classes but also against the peasants, who still comprised approximately 40 per cent of the total population. For the left, class struggle was unavoidable. Terror as an instrument of class warfare and civil war as a form of revolutionary politics,[80] however, inevitably had an unsettling effect on many. The conservatives and German nationalist right-wingers, by contrast, regarded the left as the Evil Spirit, and could even pinpoint its whereabouts: it was at home in Vienna, where – as a result of the new conditions – a third of the population of Austria lived. There, too, were people who were perfectly suited to the role of bogeyman: the Jews. They were allegedly to blame for the outcome of the war, it was as simple as that. The one thing that all political and social groups had in common was the desire to settle accounts.

The law for the 'Investigation into Military Dereliction of Duty during the War' had existed since November 1918.[81] Intended first and foremost for high-ranking and senior officers, of whom a few were indeed put before a court, the law was also directed against academics. The most famous case was that in which the Viennese psychiatrist and later Nobel Prize winner (Baronet) Julius (von) Wagner-Jauregg was indicted. He was accused of having tortured mentally-ill soldiers and malingerers by means of electric shocks. Wagner-Jauregg was acquitted. Sigmund Freud had testified as a witness for the defence. And Julius Tandler, a no-less-famous Viennese physician and Social Democrat town councillor from Vienna, had done everything to exonerate Wagner-Jauregg. Tandler himself referred to malingerers and mentally-ill soldiers as 'deficit varieties of humanity' and held therewith a very widespread opinion.[82] The early anti-militarism and pacifism had rapidly yielded to new forms of militarism. Finally, the proclamation of the Republic had admittedly demonstrated altered forms of aggression, but this was actually more a continuation of the war by other means.

The repatriation of combatants, of whom the last returned home from Italian captivity in 1921 and quite a number from the new Soviet Union by detour via China, had made the soldiers omnipresent. It was they who started the fight for remembrance, who frequently blended the struggle for employment with the class struggle and who wanted to clean house wherever they found too much of the world of yesterday. The settling of accounts ultimately found its most powerful mouthpiece in the anything but 'left-wing' writer, Karl Kraus. In 1919, Kraus began with his periodical *Die Fackel* (The Torch) to publish the previously authored episodes of his anti-war drama 'The Last Days of Mankind'. The work was completed in 1922. It was both a settling of accounts and a satire, but it was certainly no pacifist work. In its ambivalence, it integrated itself perfectly into the beginnings of the Republic. It was above all the Social Democrats who wanted to teach peace among nations and combat the glorification of war, but who also, on the other hand, preached class struggle and the 'true peace', which would only then exist when socialism had prevailed. Pacifism, which had been a mass movement until 1914, was dead. Tellingly, when, on 6 January 1921, Heinrich Lammasch, a staunch pacifist, final Imperial-Royal prime minister and professor of international law in Salzburg, was buried, a mere six people followed his coffin.[83] One of those who then visited his grave was the Nobel Prize winner Alfred Hermann Fried. He had returned to Austria from Switzerland and had recommenced the publication of his periodical *Die Friedens-Warte* (The Peace Watch). But no one was actually interested in it.

The combatants continued to be omnipresent. The federal government nonetheless prevented a publication of files on the Great War in 1920, with was intended to start a process of academic reappraisal.[84] Perhaps they did not want to know too many details about certain things. The fight for remembrance soon became a cause, however, that not exclusively the new army had to serve but likewise the associations of former soldiers as well as the militant groups of political parties. Memories of the war continued to dominate thoughts and feelings for a long time to come. The dead returned in monuments and memorial services for war heroes. And after the decision had already been taken during the war to create municipal memorials as the most important sites of remembrance, the erection of war memorials commenced from 1920 on a large scale.[85] Virtually every locality received at least one, until as many as 4,000 existed in Austria. Contrary to some expectations, the message of the monuments was by no means revenge; instead, it was sorrow and a sense of meaning that dominated in the form of attributions: 'hero', 'heroic' and 'fulfilment of one's duty'. Literally next door, mutilated veterans of the Great War begged for a few crowns, which were fast becoming worthless. Anxiety about the future circulated. Emigration, in order to escape the hardship and the perceived distress, seemed a good possibility for leaving everything behind. Emigration was positively encouraged, and organisations were founded especially to help. The only question was: where? The most important country of emigration before the war, the USA, had shut down and made it difficult for potential immigrants to cross the Atlantic. The British, French and Italians promoted emigration to Tanganyika, Libya or the East Indies. But the idea to start a new life there as a smallholder was for many unattractive.[86] A majority of poor or impoverished farmers moved to the cities, above all Vienna, instead of letting themselves in for an African adventure.

The double-headed eagle was removed from many buildings and generally disposed of as a state symbol. It was again Renner who had suggested as early as 31 October 1918 to select the colours of the Babenberg coat of arms, red – white – red, as state colours and to exchange the double-headed eagle for a single-headed one, which should receive as attributes a black city tower as a symbol of civil society, red hammers for the workforce and golden ears of wheat for the peasants.[87] Black – red – gold: the colours of Germany. Thus, the symbols had been modified, but the coat of arms remained foreign. And in view of the general opinion of the state's inability to survive, the heraldic animal soon received the mocking name 'bankruptcy vulture'. Coat of arms and colours could be decreed. A national consciousness could not.

As an almost posthumous acknowledgement of the beginnings of the Republic, Karl Renner also supplied the text for a national anthem in 1920, which was set to the music of Wilhelm Kienzl: 'German-Austria, thou art wonderful, we love thee! / High from the Alps' dome-like glaciers, waters rush to the Danube / … We love thee, we protect thee.' The anthem, which – though almost impossible to sing – remained valid until 1929, disposed of a further symbol of the Monarchy, the Emperor's Hymn, *Gott erhalte* (God Preserve). Austria definitively relinquished the Haydn melody to Germany. But maybe this was only the surface appearance.

Parallel to the reappraisal and settling of accounts with the past, the search began for a new normality. A partially fatherless society had to struggle for its place in the new Austria. Women played an increasingly minor role here, for women had been quickly forced out of traditionally male occupations after the war ended. The repatriation of combatants had again made them superfluous. And they allowed themselves to be supplanted, while they, in turn, also supplanted others. Until 1918, marriage had been regarded as insoluble. Now, divorces occurred on a huge scale.[88] It was not only separation for years on end that had led to marriages being shattered and people no longer liking each other. In a large, though statistically not exactly verifiable, number of cases, bonds also broke as a result of men returning physically or mentally disabled and women being unable to bear a life together with a cripple or a nervous wreck, a 'shell-shock sufferer'.[89]

The loss of orientation gave rise to ever louder calls for direction. The awareness of living in something unfinished, leading an existence in limbo, led not only to resignation but also triggered creative processes. The hour of the educators and psychologists struck. Karl Popper worked on new narrative forms, Sigmund Freud wrote his *Beyond the Pleasure Principle* in 1921, though he did not only meet with approval. It was later regarded as a 'historical irony' that psychoanalysis, which practically all political forces in Austria rejected, took off in Vienna, of all places.[90] Karl and Charlotte

Bühler set up the Vienna School of Child and Adolescent Psychology. Coeducation was tested. Drugs were regarded as a vehicle for liberation and creativity. Free love was preached.

Others also became a talking point. Franz Werfel was at the heart of events in the revolution and was threatened with exile due to his involvement in the riots that followed the proclamation of the Republic of German-Austria. Rainer Maria Rilke and Stefan Zweig returned from Switzerland and picked up where they had left off, continued to write and completed works such as Rilke's *Duino Elegies*. Ludwig Wittgenstein had already completed his *Tractatus Logico Philosophicus* during the war. Arthur Schnitzler addressed *the* hot topic of the day with his *La Ronde*: sexuality. Ultimately, they all struggled for their very personal present and simultaneously fought the battle for remembrance, just as Franz Theodor Csokor did. The fight for remembrance was at its plainest among senior military officers and statesmen of the 'world of yesterday'. Much of what they wrote or said was naturally underpinned by the need to justify themselves.

Other things integrated themselves into the great narrative arc and frequently fitted into the overall structure of the political sphere, in which rejection continued to dominate. But it was also worth asking what had become of the social Darwinists, those seeking salvation and the radicals of 1914, who had longed for the war as the greatest event of the twentieth century. Were they all dead? By no means! Hermann Bahr and Hugo von Hofmannsthal were composing new written works. Josef Schumpeter had transferred to the political arena, whilst a whole host of diplomats, who had certainly contributed to unleashing the war, now served the Republic. Journalists who had played no small part in stoking the belligerent mood in 1914, continued to write, and the historians continued to teach. Many were reformed, had submitted themselves – like Friedrich Austerlitz – to the question of the 'deserved fate' and had to reorientate themselves. Others expressed their sorrow about the past, like Joseph Rath, and erected literary monuments to the world of yesterday, which clearly demonstrated that they were unable to find their bearings in the new age.

Ultimately, Austria was not prepared to regard the terms of the peace treaty as final, just as was the case with Germany, Hungary, Italy, Poland or Czechoslovakia; not to mention Bulgaria or Turkey. Feelings of humiliation, impotence, injustice and revenge overlaid the terms of the respective peace treaties and transformed their implementation into a series of coercive measures.

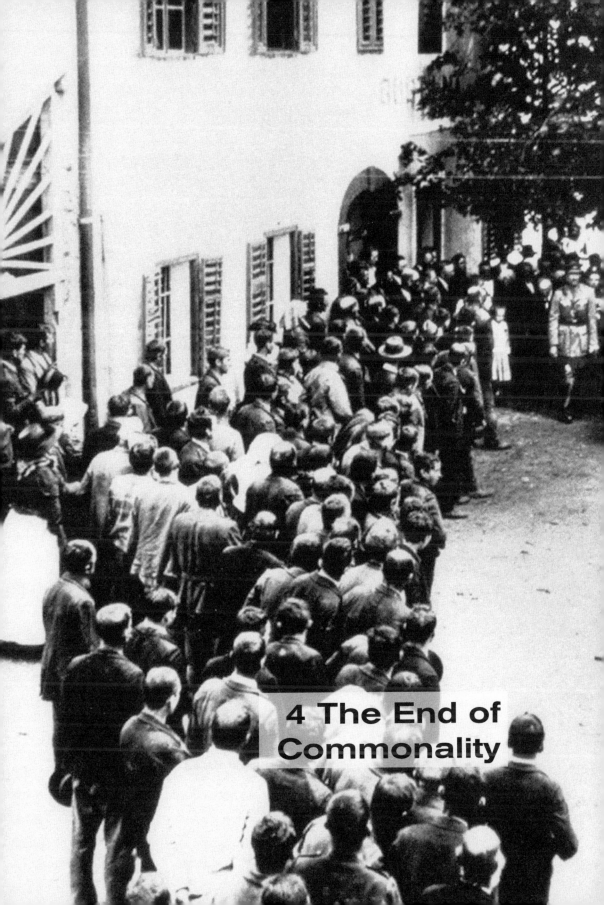

4 The End of Commonality

4 Plebiscite in Diex, north of Völkermarkt, on 10 October 1920. In the background, a British officer observes proceedings. The plebiscite in Carinthia decided on whether substantial parts of the former duchy would remain part of Austria. Diex was located at the edge of Electoral District A, in which 59.04 per cent of those entitled to vote decided in favour of Austria. The territory south of the Karawanks had already been assigned to the State of Slovenes, Croats and Serbs in the Peace Treaty of Saint-Germain. (Photo: Carinthian Regional Archives)

I t took a while before the excitement that had kept Austria on edge from June to September 1919 began to die down. Only gradually, something akin to normality began to return. However, in the government, fault lines were beginning to show. State Chancellor Renner knew that the parliamentary support for the government that he headed was extremely fragile. By now, cohesion was only temporarily maintained for practical reasons. One of these was the Treaty of Saint-Germain, which still had to be implemented through parliament, for which majority support would have to be secured. If this was not forthcoming, Austria threatened to sink into chaos. The other equally urgent measure was the adoption of a constitution. While a draft had already been produced by Hans Kelsen, professor for constitutional law in Vienna, it was not uniformly accepted.

One Constitution for Eight Federal States

Like Hugo Preuß in Germany and the experts in constitutional law in the successor states to the Habsburg Monarchy, Kelsen had combed through all official liberal constitutional models and sought to find more modern formulations wherever possible. As is so often the case, the devil was in the details. While for the most part the federal states had voluntarily declared their accession to the state of German-Austria, they had also submitted a significant number of objections in the interim. In particular, in places where the state as a whole was regarded as being an obstacle to their own development, such as in Tirol and Vorarlberg, possible solutions and at least special rights were discussed. The prohibition on a union with Germany only added further grist to the mill. The constitution drafted by Kelsen also contributed to the stream of protest, since it was based on very far-reaching centralism and granted the federal states only relatively low-level opportunities for participation. A rapprochement occurred only gradually. Renner chose to employ an instrument that had already proven effective many times in the past, and called conferences of the federal states in Vienna. These conferences were at the same time an outlet for the resentment and disappointment that had arisen above all in relation to the Treaty of Saint-Germain. As the governor of Vorarlberg, Otto Ender, so clearly put it, one felt 'temporarily forced by the peace treaty... to live in this state'.[91] Accordingly, the constitution was to express the fact that its authors were only acting under constraint. However, that was merely the declamatory part. At the heart of the

matter were the rights of the – at that time – eight federal states, which pushed forward
with their demand to be able to withdraw from the state at any time. Constitutional
laws were only to become effective when the federal state parliaments had given their
approval. For a time, the federal states asserted their independence outright and were
not even prepared to send representatives to the federal state conferences.[92] The discussion spiralled out of control after the coalition between the Social Democrats and the
Christian Social Party began to flounder. While this was not connected to the issue of
the constitution, representatives of both parties increasingly began to voice their dissent
in the National Assembly. This applied in particular to questions surrounding marriage
law, schools and therefore also the role of the (Catholic) church in the classroom or
within non-parliamentary institutions such as the workers' councils. The final rupture
occurred on 10 June 1920 during a debate on an apparently minor topic, the sphere
of activity of soldiers' councils. However, this was related to an issue of far-reaching
importance: should the People's Militia, which was controlled by the Social Democrats,
be laid to rest, or should there be a new, perhaps less politicised, army? A third option
was also available: would it be possible to do away with the army entirely by replenish-
ing the police and Gendarmerie as had been requested by several provincial governors?
This would however have meant that the provincial governors had executive powers over
their federal states – and that could not be in the interest of the state as a whole.

As yet, there was no dissolution of parliament, but merely governmental restructuring in the form of a proportional government, in which not even unanimity was
required. Renner stepped down as state chancellor and assumed the post of minister of
foreign affairs. The Cabinet was now led by Minister for Constitutional and Administrative Reform Michael Mayr, since the constitution continued to be the main point
of debate. However, the final drafts were not produced by the government, but by the
parties. Several items, such as the issue of fundamental rights, schools or financial compensation, were set to one side. Yet the delimitation of competencies between the federation and the states was agreed. A chamber of states was to have only a postponement
veto and could not entirely block a decision. There was to be a federal president, and
Lower Austria and Vienna were to be separate federal states. It would take at least one
more year before this could be turned into reality, but from 1 January 1922, Vienna became a separate and the newest federal state, and, following the addition of Burgenland,
Austria was accordingly divided into nine federal states. The 'colour doctrine' was clear
and continued to apply during the years that followed. Vienna was 'red', while all the
other federal states – except for Carinthia – were 'black'. However, the new constitution,
too, failed to resolve one imbalance: around a third of the population lived in Vienna,
which while being the capital city of the Republic of Austria was also a federal state. It
was known affectionately by its ugly nickname of 'Wasserkopf', or 'bloated head'. And

it was in a different situation, even though it was shrinking. By 1922, around 400,000 people had left the former imperial capital and seat of royal residence.[93]

With agreement reached on the constitution, the proportional government had now completed its task, and indeed, the Provisional State Government of 1918, the state government under Renner and its successor administration, which ruled for half a year, could look back on a notable achievement. Together with the federal states, they had created a country which ultimately also had all the characteristics of a state, namely a clearly defined state territory and a state people. They may have been acting in agreement with the victorious powers and the signatories to the Treaty of Saint-Germain, but through their actions, several gloomy predictions that had been made had failed to materialise. Despite the tendencies towards a union that were also promoted by political representatives, Austria remained a state unit and did not become a type of self-service store for its neighbours. The government had given the new state entity a constitution, and through negotiations with Austria's neighbours had not least also secured basic provisions for the population, which repeatedly threatened to be engulfed by famine, and which at any rate now had enough food to survive. However, it was all too easy to gain the impression that there was discord between the representatives of the parties and advocacy groups. This was confirmed by the large number of people killed as a result of disputes arising from trivialities. On repeated occasions, it appeared that everything had to start again from scratch. What was missing was a sense of commonality. Furthermore, it was disconcerting that other countries adopted a critical and unfriendly attitude towards this new country between Lake Constance and Lake Neusiedl.

Restorers at Work

In October 1920, elections were held for the second time in the history of the young Republic. The political balance of power shifted. The Christian Social Party achieved the strongest mandate. Theoretically, further shifts could also have occurred, since in Carinthia, votes had not yet been cast for the referendum on the continuance of voting zone A, as was also the case in Burgenland. There, the mandates were not due to be issued until June 1921 and June 1922, respectively. However, politics could not remain at a standstill for that length of time. The most obvious question was already difficult to answer, however: who would be willing to work together in a new government? The decision by the Social Democrats to go into opposition, which was in fact unexpected, left no option other than for the Christian Social Party to enter into a coalition with the third-largest party, the Greater German People's Party. Otto Bauer had presented the party executive of the Social Democrats with a paper that contained the following strictly confidential statement: as long as the Social Democrats are in government 'they cannot assign responsibility for the economic crisis to the parties of the middle classes'. And unequivocally: 'In the coalition, we no longer successfully push anything through.'[94] At that time, no one could have known that this would constitute the permanent departure of the Social Democrats from governmental responsibility. Yet here, the conflicting positions compared to those of the Christian Social Party, the frustration surrounding the cooperation with the three governments since 1918, and the ongoing desire for a left-wing experiment and a dictatorship of the proletariat were probably just as important a factor in their decision as their expectation that the other parties would fail to achieve their goals. The Christian Social Party also kept a low profile, agreeing only to nominate the already experienced Michael Mayr as interim chancellor. He formed a cabinet made up of public officials and several Christian Social Party members, which he then led as the head of government, or federal chancellor, according to the new name assigned to the post. Mayr made an honest effort, but neither from within the country nor from abroad was he granted the room for manoeuvre that he needed in order to overcome the crisis, which ultimately was more severe than others that had arisen before 1921.

Austria's economy found itself in a steep downward spiral. The main loser from the economic downturn was Vienna. Factories were no longer receiving orders. They also had excess capacity. Four of five locomotive factories in the Habsburg Monarchy were located in Austria – yet hardly anyone was ordering new locomotives. The west of Austria, which differed in so many ways from the large city, showed signs of wanting to leave. The food crisis was supplemented by an energy crisis. The banking centre of Vienna, in which so many hopes had been placed, since it was home to the largest credit institutions of the Monarchy, began to flounder. The successor states no longer met their monetary requirements in Vienna, but elsewhere. Trust within the financial world in the Austrian crown suffered as a result of the reparations payments that Austria was obliged to pay, even if the exact amount remained unknown. The victorious powers had rights of lien. To these were added so-called 'liberation debts', i.e. payments whose level was also unspecified, which the victorious powers were authorised to demand from the successor states to the Austro-Hungarian Monarchy for their liberation – although from whom they had been liberated remained unclear. At the end of 1921, the state food subsidies were terminated. This affected not only workers but to an equal degree also employees with low incomes and the unemployed. However, workers again saw themselves as bearing the brunt of the burden. In Vienna, there were unruly demonstrations and riots. The replacement of the broken glass on Mariahilfestraße alone cost two million gold crowns.[95] Some called for a proletarian revolution, while others wanted a union with Germany, regardless of the fact that this would lead to war and chaos. Michael Mayr could see no way out of the crisis and resigned as chancellor.

Once again, a new head of government was needed. He was found in the form of Johann Schober, the Viennese police commissioner who had successfully worked in security operations. He had already rejected the offer previously but was now willing to take on responsibility for the government. The problems remained the same, and Schober ultimately did not even have to look for other possible solutions. While he set about restoring funds for foreign credits, the Social Democrats in the opposition were in favour of domestic loans and capital levies, since they wanted to reduce dependency on foreign (capitalist) countries. In the view of Schober and his finance minister, Alfred Gürtler, both options were worthy of consideration. The Chancellor obtained a loan from Czechoslovakia for 500 million Czech crowns. One condition of the Treaty of Lány (Lana) was, however, that Austria should faithfully fulfil the requirements of the Treaty of Saint-Germain and remain neutral in the event of a war between Czechoslovakia and Hungary. It was the second time that the prohibition of a union was written into a treaty, as though there were uncertainty as to whether Austria would observe this requirement. The Greater German People's Party, on whose support Schober, like Mayr before him, relied, then threatened to withdraw its support from the government, since once again, the possibility of uniting with Germany, however fictitious this scenario may have been, had been relinquished. However, the final rupture came when the British controller for the observance of the peace treaty conditions, George Malcolm Young, praised Schober with the best intentions in a letter, attesting that Austria was creditworthy for the simple reason that the Federal Chancellor guaranteed stability and the continuation of independent statehood. And while the Chancellor, on an extension of his tour to gather support, negotiated with the victorious powers and potential creditors in Genoa and obtained assurances from most states that they would not make use of their general rights of lien, the Greater Germans toppled one of their own and, with him, the entire government.

Now, finally, someone appeared from behind the scenes of whom it had been long expected that he would not only take over the reins of the Christian Social Party but would also assume full responsibility himself: Prelate Ignaz Seipel. The 45-year-old was the embodiment of political and politicising Catholicism in Austria, had been minister for labour and social affairs in the last imperial government, and had been involved in the declaration of renunciation by Emperor Karl. Since then, he had remained in the background, and had only made an appearance in the role of an elected delegate. On 31 May 1922, he presented the National Council with his government. It was composed of members of the Christian Social Party and the Greater German People's Party, since the latter had clearly realised that the alternative would be a renewed version of a Christian Social – Social Democratic government. Simply tolerating the situation, as had been the case with Mayr and Schober, was no longer a viable option, and compromises had to be made. At a 'Reich party rally' in Graz, the delegates of the Greater

German People's Party approved the merger with the Christian Social Party. Seipel promised that the union policy would not be abandoned, and he was also not averse to including a passage in the coalition pact which stipulated: 'Effective protection of the local German population against the increasingly harmful influence of Jewry in all areas of public life.'[96] Thus, work could begin under the slogan 'The enemy is on the left and is Jewish'.

The problems had not abated. And the potential solutions were thin on the ground. In order to stabilise the currency, Seipel chose four options: increasing income and reducing expenditure, capital levies and foreign loans. However, none of these tried and tested means appeared to work. In June 1922, there was still hope that the impending crisis in the banking and currency sector could be fended off by founding a National Bank of Austria in the form of a stock company, which in a similar way to the former Austrian-Hungarian Bank would also function as a central bank, in other words, it would be authorised to issue bank notes. Suddenly, a period of wild speculation against the Austrian crown began. The Anglobank, which was majority British owned, and the French-dominated Länderbank, refused to invest share capital into the National Bank. The crown sank to one-14,400th of its gold value.[97] The money circulation, which in 1920 was still 12 billion crowns, increased to one trillion in August 1922. Consumer prices doubled within the space of a month.[98] The official price of one US dollar was 83,600 crowns. An egg cost 2,000 crowns, and 1 kilogram of butter 80,000 crowns. The economic destabilisation of the middle classes, public servants, pensioners and home owners proceeded apace, and the great sell-off began. Anyone with money stowed away abroad in sufficiently good time, who was in a position to purchase material assets, who lived on credit and who then paid it back with what was now worthless paper money, was able to amass a huge fortune. Sigmund Bosel and Camillo Castiglioni were well known examples of this.[99] Politicians also took their 'cut'. Tax income was unable to keep pace with inflation, and capital levies were no longer of any help. The fragile economic upturn was rendered ineffective by the fact that the state propped up the prices for basic foodstuffs, with 59 per cent of the budget having to be spent on support measures as early as 1921.[100] It was clear to everyone that things could not go on in this way. What was more, foreign countries were no longer willing to invest in the broken Austrian system. An application for a loan of 250 million dollars failed. In March 1921, the victorious powers had brought the problem of Austria to the League of Nations, which as a prerequisite for financial aid demanded that the Allies relinquish their general rights of lien in Austria.[101] Once again, hopes were dashed. Seipel began to spell out the consequences of an Austrian catastrophe: the state would dissolve. Austria would need help if all the effort were not to have been in vain. Since a solution was no longer possible in direct contact with the states that were potential creditors, Seipel decided to turn to the League of Nations. The League was simply representing the sum total of the individual interests of its members, but here, there was something akin to collective pressure and the necessity of making a public commitment.

The League of Nations Loan

Seipel prepared his journey to the headquarters of the League of Nations in Geneva carefully, travelled to Prague and expressed aloud that he was considering the possibility of Austria joining the 'Little Entente' of Czechoslovakia, Yugoslavia and Romania. In Germany, which at that time was still barred from joining the League of Nations, he was given assurance that no one in Berlin was in the slightest inclined to lend an ear to the demands of Austrian proponents of a union; and in Verona, he presented the prospect of a currency and customs union and a permanent orientation to Italy.[102] It was a balancing act, since in Rome, there was jealousy of Prague, while in Paris, there was jealousy of Rome, and so on. Seipel refused to be put off course by a motion of no confidence by the Social Democrats in parliament, but instead finally appealed at the League of Nations Assembly to the members of the committee headed by British Foreign Secretary Lord Balfour to help Austria. While a willingness to provide assistance was there, each of the potential creditors demanded a type of special treatment. For a short period, the British Prime Minister Lloyd George caused an upset when he said, in so many words, that he could not see the point in investing money in a state that was as broken as Austria. However, clearly, Seipel as well as the other attendees at the meeting succeeded in reassuring the Prime Minister. On 4 October 1922, the Protocol for the Reconstruction of Austria was signed. The British, Italians and Czechoslovaks were willing to lend Austria 650 million gold crowns for a period of 20 years.[103] Smaller states also wanted to lend money.

The loan amount was not huge, for it was far below the level of a single Austro-Hungarian war loan in former years. The interest was also high, at 10.2 per cent. Sweden and Britain were required to pay far lower interest rates during that time. However, it was money that was not forthcoming elsewhere, and it could be used to shore up the currency. Seipel is likely to have been aware that the League of Nations, which assumed liability for the amount to be provided, would attach conditions to its guarantee.

To secure the loan, Austria pledged its tobacco monopoly and customs revenue. However, it could now certainly be argued that the pressure to take decisive measures was not coming from the government, but from 'Geneva'. And the conditions were quite harsh: in the three Geneva protocols, Austria was again required to accept a prohibition on a union – for the third time. Within one month – in other words, by November 1922 – a package of reforms and reconstruction measures were to be presented that guaranteed that the state budget would be put to rights within two years. In order to make sure that the money would be used as intended and all agreements would be observed, Austria was required to agree that a general commissioner appointed by the League of Nations at the head of a four-member control committee of the creditor countries would monitor the proceedings. For the Social Democrats, this form of international monitoring was nothing short of 'foreign rule'.[104] Otto Bauer was also unequivocal in his criticism, saying pointedly that 'German-Austria [like Renner, he still used this term] has separated from Germany and thrown itself into the arms of the Entente.' It had become a 'colony of the Entente'.[105] Ultimately, the committee, which was led by Alfred Rudolph Zimmermann from the Netherlands as the general commissioner, one just one of many keeping watch over events in Austria. In addition, there was the armistice committee, the committee for the observance of the peace treaty conditions, the reparations committee, delegations for monitoring the use of the foreign loan funds received thus far, restitution committees, which monitored the removal of cultural assets, and delegations from several successor states, which combed through the files in the central administration and the archives, deciding on those that affected them (or not, as the case may have been) and removing them. Furthermore, there were the diplomatic representations, which felt it incumbent on themselves to monitor Austria and to issue threats to the country if necessary.

In Vienna, one could certainly gain the impression that Austria had been placed under guardianship. In the National Council, tensions flared again in relation to the Geneva loan. At the party conference of the Social Democrats, Otto Bauer proclaimed: 'I would say, therefore, that it is possible to fix the Austrian domestic economy without recourse to the five hundred [*sic*] million gold crowns, to the ill-gotten funds of the League of Nations.'[107] Here, there was opposition on a fundamental level. Since the government applied for special powers of attorney, which could only be obtained with a constitutional majority, in other words with the agreement of the Social Democrats, Seipel took a step to accommodate them and gave them the opportunity in an 'extraordinary cabinet council' to work together with government representatives to ensure that the powers of attorney were not abused. As a result, the Social Democrats both shared responsibility for the so-called 'Geneva reconstruction' and fought against it with all the means at their disposal. The fact that during the process, they chose to focus attention on the union prohibition, publishing articles in the *Arbeiter-Zeitung* on the 'Geneva treaty of enslavement'[108] may have been what many of their supporters expected, but it did not reflect reality. However, despite the domestic policy quarrels and several delays in the payment of the first tranche of the League of Nations loan, the path was cleared, and in December 1922, Mr Zimmermann could start his work in Vienna as the League of Nations commissioner.

The budget deficit was to be offset through radical cost-cutting measures. A nominal figure of 100,000 public service posts were to be dismantled, including many former soldiers and professional military personnel, or 'fee earners', who had hoped to make a living after the end of the war. The reduction in posts also affected many of the railway workers, who were also classed as public servants. In March 1923, an increased goods turnover tax was introduced, which immediately brought in nearly a tenth of the federal budget. Industrial production was to be boosted in order to halt the downward trend. Seipel also wanted to reduce the number of ministries. To accomplish this, he formally resigned from office on 16 April. For 24 hours, department head Walter Breisky led the federal government – the shortest time that a cabinet had been in office in the history of Austria. On the following day, Seipel presented his new, diminished government. Once again, events occurred in rapid succession. It was not always possible to quickly align wages and prices. As was to be expected, many people were unhappy. During the elections in October 1923, Seipel's efforts were acknowledged, but the Christian Social Party remained just below their anticipated absolute majority, with 82 seats, in a National Council that now had just 165 elected members.

Seipel continued with his efforts at reform. Finance Minister Viktor Kienböck prepared the introduction of a new currency, the schilling, on 1 January 1925. His aim was now to expand the cost-cutting measures to the federal states and local districts. In early January 1924, the National Bank, which was also the central bank, began operations. The flow of inflationary crowns was halted. However, resistance against Seipel grew. There was unrest within his own party, particularly since the federal states were not prepared to implement the federal cost-cutting measures in their own budgets and increasingly refused to do what Seipel wanted. The Greater German People's Party knew that Seipel's now clear refusal to countenance a union was a cause for resentment among its followers. At that point in time, somewhat episodic attempts, which were twice rejected by Seipel, were made to allow a certain Mr Adolf Hitler, who was incarcerated in Landsberg am Lech, to enter Austria, as the Bavarian Foreign Nationals Office had requested. According to Seipel, Hitler had become a German, and it should stay that way.[109] (What might have happened had Seipel decided otherwise and Hitler had again become an Austrian citizen?) Hitler remained stateless!

Ultimately, it was a strike by the railway workers that led to Seipel stepping down from office in November 1924. It is likely that on a human level he was deeply affected by the fact that he enjoyed so little support. In addition, he had been severely injured six months previously by an unemployed man who had made an attempt on his life, and he remained weak. Seipel suffered from diabetes and may also have taken on more than he could cope with. Finally, as with Bismarck, a fitting expression would have been that 'the pilot leaves the ship'. The event occurred without any drama, however, and it was a relief for many people. Admittedly, his departure would only be temporary.

5 Marching Season

5 March by members of the Republican Protection League in Eisenstadt, 1932. The Protection League and the (right-wing) Home Guard units were the largest paramilitary organisations in Austria. For varying lengths of time, they dominated the streetscape in many localities. During marches, weapons were also carried, which signalised their willingness to use violence. It was hoped that the union of 'German West Hungary', that is, Burgenland, with Austria, which did not take place until 1919, would stop this ninth federal state from being a stomping ground for paramilitary forces. The fact that things turned out differently, however, counts among the many breaches of taboo during the interwar period. (Photo: Austrian National Library / Picture Archives)

November 1923 might have been an occasion to celebrate Austria's fifth birthday. However, very few people were in the mood to do so. Only the Social Democrats made a cautiously positive assessment, of necessity ignoring the fact that they too had taken leave of so many of their ideas and demands of 1918. And they were no longer part of the government. The only place where the party enjoyed solid support was in Vienna. And that was not all: efforts had begun to build Vienna up as a type of Social Democratic model state. The city councillor for finance, Hugo Breitner, did not delay in tightening the tax screws and demanding that higher earning and the well-off citizens in particular should pay more. For those who still thought in terms of the old tax rates under the Monarchy, with a maximum levy of 6 per cent, this was an abomination. Breitner revealed a highly imaginative side to his nature, introducing a motor vehicle tax, a piano tax, a billiards tax, a light bulb tax and a luxury dog tax – and above all, a housebuilding tax, which made it possible to dramatically improve the precarious living accommodation situation within just a few years and in particular for the socially disadvantaged and people on low incomes to create affordable, small housing units.[110] Gradually, around 400 so-called 'social housing buildings' were constructed, and while they may not always have been revolutionary building complexes in architectural terms, they did ultimately characterise the urban landscape of Vienna beyond the Ringstraße. The building structures not only extended upwards, but also outwards. It was taken as a given that anyone wanting to live in the social housing would have to have a close relationship to the Social Democratic Workers' Party. Around a third of the population of Vienna were members of the party.[111] The money gained from the conscious redistribution was used to pay for popular education institutions, public baths, health centres, advice facilities for mothers, marriage guidance counselling, nursery schools, credit institutions and other facilities associated with the Social Democrats. Frequently, they bore the prefixes 'public' and 'workers'.

Paramilitarism

With the conscious permeation of an order that tended to be regarded as middle class, the process of the formation of rival camps intensified. The separation of the social groups was prevalent in an increasing number of areas. Later, a word borrowed from the Dutch, *Versäulung*, or 'pillarization', would be used to describe the situation. However, this phenomenon was by no means restricted to Vienna. Workers were expected to be 'left-wing' and Social Democratic, farmers were Christian Social; civil servants, who were collectively known as 'officials', were expected to be middle class and members of either the Christian Social Party or the Greater German People's Party. Each party made efforts to care for its clientele and had no scruples about further deepening the divisions and moving in closed social groups. Viennese citizens lived either in a workers' district or in a middle class one. They purchased goods in their separate shops, visited their separate guesthouses, theatres and places of entertainment, and only sought out those baths where they could be 'among themselves'. The 'middle classes' played tennis, went rowing, swam or pursued track and field sports; 'workers' played handball, took part in bicycle races and climbed mountains. Football was the only area of life where the two groups shared an interest, even if they played in separate clubs.[112] One group went to the Burgtheater, the other to the Deutsches Volkstheater; some read Anton Wildgans, Max Mell or Karl Heinrich Waggerl, while others preferred the working-class poets Alfred Petzold, Theodor Kramer or perhaps Josef Luitpold Stern. This cultural polarisation was a reflection of the deep fissure that ran through the population.

The compartmentalisation went hand in hand with a deep mistrust of the intentions of the other side, and almost as a matter of course resulted in a desire to protect oneself. However, this was not a procedure whereby it could be claimed that the actions or failure to act by the one side caused the other to take certain measures. Here, it was far more the case that the different factors were intertwined, although they did follow a basic pattern in that the contrasts between the political groups and, analogously, Vienna and the other federal states, became increasingly stark.

Perhaps initially, there had been disappointment over the fact that the state could not be formed as had been hoped. The feeling of vulnerability also played a role. The People's Militia, which had already been formed during the days when the Republic was created, and which during the winter and the spring of 1919 had grown to a considerable size, was still only highly limited in terms of its military deployment capacity. To a far greater extent, it was a social safety net rather than being of any use for foreign policy requirements. What really stuck in people's minds was that it was used to force farmers, who were frequently unwilling to hand over their produce, to make their deliveries. Disappointment over the People's Militia, which was often simply referred to in derogatory terms as 'that lot' became widespread. After all, they could not compare with the Imperial and Royal Army or the Imperial-Royal Landwehr (Austrian standing army).

The level of disappointment increased when it emerged that the state was not fulfilling the hopes of the provinces in providing protection from the outside in the form of pre-emptive defence. The People's Militia was not deployed where it might have succeeded in its mission, such as in the Austro-Slovene conflict in Carinthia, in order to cross the demarcation line on the Drava and Gail rivers and eject the Yugoslavian units from the country entirely. The fact that here, the People's Militia was obeying the orders of the Provisional State Government and had clear instructions from Renner was of little interest in Carinthia. The People's Militia was also not present at the battles in the Radkersburg region, which remained occupied by Southern Slav troops until 20 July 1920. The same applied initially in German West Hungary, and a certain presence might have been expected in Tyrol, too. Not least, disappointment spread because the People's Militia failed to act as a decisive force against the Czechs when there were disputes over South Bohemia and South Moravia. Then, too, it was of no interest to critics that the Provisional State Government had good reasons not to attempt a military campaign, and the People's Militia faithfully obeyed its orders.

The People's Militia was seen as being left-wing – and indeed it was. Two battalions were even communist. They were rendered ineffective through organisational measures and ultimately during the process of reducing the size of the People's Militia, although the People's Militia continued to be regarded as an institution that was by no means to be trusted. In accordance with the conditions of the peace treaty, it was converted into a far smaller federal army in 1920. Austria was granted 30,000 professional soldiers by the victorious powers. Initially, only half that number reported for service in the new armed forces. Ultimately, it offered almost no professional opportunities, although it attempted to create the impression of being an entirely normal army. However, by that time, the army was facing competition.

In the western and southern federal states, self-defence formations had been created, which – while they may initially have refrained from any political affiliations – soon did become politicised. In Carinthia, the first self-defence formations had already been established in November 1918, with others following in Tyrol in 1919, and so on. Some were directed against an external enemy; others wanted to defend themselves against the 'Bolshevisation' of the country. However, competition had also been established in the shadow of the People's Militia, where Social Democratic stewards' organisations had been formed, which were tasked with protecting what were seen as revolutionary achievements. For the self-defence formations and stewards' militias alike, there were waves of development that they not only failed to halt, but in fact allowed to flourish. And it was not at all difficult to find people willing to organise themselves, and who regarded the paramilitary groups as an attractive prospect and suited to satisfying their own needs. However, the state did not intervene, was too weak and failed to heed the first warnings – until it was too late. Paramilitarism may have been a common trend during that time, but it led to the crisis in state power more than almost any other contributing factor.

The only thing that the stewards' organisations, which were already established as an arm of the Social Democrats in 1918, and the workers' defence units and citizens' and farmers' militias, which were created at almost the same time, had in common was distrust. While some distrusted the organisations that were regarded as Marxist, and which were justifiably accused of being reactionary and at any rate ready to turn back the clock. To the citizens' and farmers' militias, which soon became summarily known as *Heimwehre*, or Home Guard units, the workers' defence groups were in turn regarded as being revolutionary guards who were ready at all times to use force of arms to help successfully assert Bolshevik ideas.[113] Every crisis of statehood and the permanent talk of the inability of Austria to survive appeared to bring the country one step closer to dissolution – and one needed to be armed just in case.

By 1920, when the People's Militia was disbanded, the Social Democrats were reliant not only on the state armed forces, but also the stewards' organisations and the workers' battalions that existed in the industrial regions and particularly in Vienna. (The name alone clearly exposed their paramilitary nature). After the end of the coalition governments and the assumption of the defence department by Carl Vaugoin, a Christian Social, a change in personnel began that was termed 'depoliticisation', which continued at a slow but steady pace and rapidly restricted the influence of the Social Democrats. The Social Democrat Minister for the Army, Julius Deutsch, lost his post. The highest-ranking officer, Brigadier Theodor Körner, was replaced as party spokesman for national defence issues for the Social Democrats in parliament. Those who managed to survive the reduction in personnel and who succeeded in joining the Federal Army either acted in an apolitical way or risked losing the extension on their contract, which was anyway limited to a maximum of six years. Minister Vaugoin by all means exercised the supreme command in person, even though in principle it was the remit of the National Council. As a result, the Federal Army soon no longer provided a backup for the Social Democrats. In response, at a meeting of the workers' councils and stewards' organisations held on 8 December 1920, they decided to form a central headquarters. At this point in time, around 47,000 men were deployed in the stewards' organisations. Two years later, Julius Deutsch suggested organising the formations as an association under the name 'Republican Protection League' (Republikanischer Schutzbund).[114] The membership figures increased steadily. The goal of building socialism and offering armed resistance to the 'exploiters' and 'reactionaries' was openly expressed. The members of the Protection League practised paramilitary sports and received military training. As early as 1923, Julius Deutsch is said to have proudly announced that the Protection League comprised over 220 infantry, twelve railway and eight assault battalions, as well as 80 machine-gun companies.[115] The only thing missing was artillery. Otherwise, there were substantial stockpiles of weapons available, however, which were openly flaunted on numerous occasions.

The 'right-wingers' also had nothing against paramilitarism and merely sought to outdo the 'leftists'. What began as a measure born of necessity continued to exist after the direct threat had disappeared. The state governments, particularly several state governors, were happy to accept the situation, since they then had a type of armed unit that was neither dependent on the People's Militia nor on the Federal Army, and which could be relied upon in a highly personal, or at least federal state-specific sense. The latter also did not conflict with a collaboration with the citizens' militias in the southern German region, particularly the organisations led by Georg Escherich and Rudolf Kanzler, which had participated in bringing down the Munich Council Republic and were endeavouring to expand their organisations to Tyrol, Vorarlberg, Carinthia and Salzburg. However, this was to be no more than a brief episode. Instead, on 23 February 1923, the self-defence formations of these federal states and Upper Austria decided to join together to form the Association of Alpine Self-Defence Formations. The Tyrolean Richard Steidle became its leader. The Styrian and Lower Austrian leadership wanted to go their own way, at least at first. And 'red' Vienna did not belong anyway, although in the City Guard, which was subordinate to the mayor and the state governor, it had a similar formation as the seven 'old' federal states. Only Burgenland lagged behind. In terms of size, the 'Alpine Self-Protection Formations', the Home Guard organisations, were just as powerful as the Republican Protection League. They proudly announced that they had 110,000 members. And even if neither the figures quoted by Julius Deutsch nor those given by the committee responsible for the Home Guard could be given much credence, one thing was clear: both the right and the left had a great deal of paramilitary capability to hand if needed. This would be of no consequence so long as the state did not suffer another crisis after Seipel's reconstruction measures and with the help of the recovery of the global economy that began in 1924. But if it did – what then?

Aside from the two major organisations, there was still a broad spectrum to the right of the centre that the 'Association of Combat Veterans' (Frontkämpfervereinigung) was keen to cover. It had emerged from the 'Economic Association of Non-Active Officers and Equivalent Ranks', and initially endeavoured to create job opportunities for former officers and high-ranking army officials and to assert their claims vis-à-vis the state, as well as to enable them to emigrate.[116] Gradually, the 'Combat Veterans' had become a particularly colourful 'bunch'. The paramilitary capability then expanded to include the farmers' militias, the Christian-German gymnasts, the 'Freedom League' and small, more or less private groups, who ostensibly aimed to foster a sense of fellowship, show solidarity, defend the groups close to them and their interests and at all costs be prepared for action if and when they might be needed. They all participated in the battle for remembrance and used every opportunity to attract attention. Naturally, all paramilitary organisations aside from the Protection League wanted to be present at the funeral of the Chief of the General Staff of the entire armed force of Austria-Hungary over many years, Franz Conrad (von) Hötzendorf. The field marshal had died in Bad Mergentheim in Germany. On 2 September 1925, he was buried in Vienna. From the officers' mess on Schwarzenbergplatz, the funeral cortege set off along Ringstraße.

Ministers, presidents and the highest-ranking officers from the 'old army' followed the gun carriage. Bodies of troops from three branches of the military marched and rode in the funeral procession, and an open flower carriage and a horse decked in funeral colours followed the gun carriage. Thousands lined the street. No comparable funeral procession had taken place since the burial of Field Marshal Radetzky. In the view of one folklorist: 'all the usual set pieces' had been brought out.[117] Certainly, it could not be argued that this was in keeping with the times; rather, it was a lament for a lost world and an objection raised against the present. While the funeral cortege was moving towards the Hietzing Cemetery, there was a bitter reckoning on the part of both Social Democrat parliamentary delegates and war veterans. As was so often the case, two versions of the truth came face to face with each other. And they opposed each other in an almost irreconcilable way.

The Latent Civil War

By 1926, it appeared that the most difficult storm had been weathered. As in most European states, there was an economic upturn. In Austria, it was even stronger than in Belgium, Germany or Italy. The economy grew by an average of 4.8 per cent per year.[118] Yet the country had remained a fragile entity. The expansion of the welfare state collided with the necessity for economic and financial reconstruction. The latter was one of the reasons for the return of Ignaz Seipel as head of government in October 1926. However, rather than that of a great, successful restructurer, his second term in office left a final image of a decisive, but increasingly authoritarian government leader.

Quite a lot had changed in Austria since his first period in office, and it had not changed for the better. In particular, the level of aggressiveness had increased. The fact that the chancellor's party was increasingly focussing on the Jews was in part due to its basic ideological principles, but also to the fact that in times of existential crisis, guilty parties are always sought (and found). The Christian Social delegate in the National Council, Leopold Kunschak, was just one of those who demanded anti-Semitism not only in words, but in deeds. The Social Democrats clearly did not want to get left behind, so they combined anti-Semitism with a criticism of capitalism and badmouthed 'money Jews'.[119] The murder of the Jewish writer and journalist Hugo Bettauer was an indication of the changing atmosphere. He had been killed by a member of what was then a still inconspicuous National Socialist movement. Yet the cheers from the Catholic-conservative camp in particular could not be overheard. It was claimed that only a 'popular judgement' had been passed on the 'pornographer' Bettauer. In 1926, the Christian Socials adopted the 'cultivation of German art' and the fight against the 'supremacy of the corrosive Jewish influence on intellectual and commercial life' into their agenda.[120] Around 100,000 people took part in a demonstration 'against the dictatorship of Jewry' and marched along Ringstraße in Vienna, chanting their slogans.[121]

Seipel had presumably warned Kunschak that he should allow the radical phase to run its course. However, in light of the radicalisation of politics, the Federal Chancellor also regarded the use of force as inevitable. Like others, he assumed that early elections would be called. He had already announced the possibility for doing so in his government declaration. Consequently, it was necessary to clarify positions. The Christian Socials did so, along with the Greater Germans, the smaller parties and above all the Social Democrats. Perhaps the pragmatists on the right wing of the party now realised that the refusal to enter into a government of national unity had been an error. Instead of lowering their sights, however, the Social Democrats set the bar higher. In Linz, they set themselves a new agenda.

From Linz to Schattendorf

With the Linz Agenda of November 1926, the Social Democrats unequivocally announced their desire to achieve power and set out their goals. It was a threat of unrestricted class war. According to the agenda, the bourgeoisie would not voluntarily give up their position of power. 'However, if ... a counterrevolution of the bourgeoisie were to succeed in destroying democracy, the working class could only conquer the state power through civil war.' And if the bourgeoisie were to try to prevent the social upheaval, 'the working class would be forced to break the resistance of the bourgeoisie by means of a dictatorship'.

Ultimately, it was these formulations that turned the Linz Agenda into a declaration of war, far more than the social-political goals, such as the right of asylum for political refugees, the removal of bureaucratic obstacles, greater protection for tenants, the construction of communal residential buildings, the creation of a tax-free minimum income, the expansion of a progressive tax system, involvement by workers in company decisions, equal opportunities for women, education about and provision of contraceptive methods by the health insurance companies, an extension of mandatory schooling, the determination of maximum pupil numbers in classrooms, or the complete separation of church and state. Some of these agenda items may have appeared utopian, and others unrealistic. Yet the real problem was that the Linz Agenda could not be viewed as a project for the whole of Austria, but instead showed a very strong orientation towards Vienna, the workers and the low-income social strata. Outside Vienna and the industrial areas, it had little to offer. It was only in the final passages of the Linz Agenda that the Social Democrats could count on the agreement of many, indeed the vast majority. The agenda expressed an objection 'to the interference of foreign states in the domestic affairs of the Republic'. And the second-to-last item in the section 'The Internationale' was also aimed at gaining broad support: 'Social Democracy regards the union of German-Austria with the German Reich as the necessary conclusion of the national revolutions of 1918. It aims to achieve union with the German Republic through peaceful means'.[122]

The Christian Socials quickly responded with their own agenda, which was intended to set out a clear counter-position. It was self-evident that the phrase 'dictatorship of the proletariat' was seized upon and perceived as a threat, that all collectivist tendencies were rejected and the protection of private property emphasised. The Christian Social counter-concept was particularly clear in its sections relating to cultural policy, setting out the relationship between church and state, as well as with regard to schools, marriage law and the prohibition of abortions. There was no mention of the union with Germany. However, the topic did play a central role in the third party agenda that was produced at the same time, that of the Greater Germans, and was intended to give them a clearer profile. All parties, including the smaller ones, had a verbal radicalism in common, which showed anti-democratic tendencies even in cases when they expressed their support for democracy.

The aim was still to test the impact of the agendas and the attractiveness of individuals and proposed ideas in the elections that were then brought forward. Seipel hoped that through the creation of a unity list with the Greater Germans he could achieve a convincing parliamentary majority on 24 April 1927 and marginalise the Social Democrats. In fact, the opposite occurred. The Christian Socials lost nine seats in the National Council, and it was only with the aid of the Rural League (Landbund) that a three-party coalition between the Christian Socials, the Greater Germans and the Rural League could be formed. However, instead of embarking on halfway normal parliamentary and governmental work, just a few weeks later, Austria veered towards its greatest crisis since the creation of the Republic. The 'civil war' of the Linz Agenda appeared to become reality in other contexts. Vienna – albeit via an indirect route – had become the flashpoint, with initial events unfolding in Burgenland.

On 30 January 1927, in the small municipality of Schattendorf, close to the border with Hungary, the comparatively insignificant Association of Combat Veterans wanted to prove its worth as a militia.[123] This was despite the fact that Burgenland was to be kept free of paramilitary formations, since it had only recently become a part of Austria in 1921. However, the Combat Veterans were not the only ones to see no reason to abide by this agreement. The Republican Protection League reacted with a counter-demonstration and succeeded in mobilising more members and in shorter time than the Combat Veterans. The mayor, who could have halted everything, was a member of the Protection League. Nobody intervened. Scuffles occurred as soon as the Combat Veterans arrived. The violence escalated. Some Combat Veterans fled into a tavern and began shooting at the members of the Protection League who were pursuing them. A war invalid and a young boy who got caught up in the events were killed. Three suspects were quickly identified and tried before a jury in a Vienna court. There, it could be quickly established who had fired the lethal shots, but not whether they had been fired with the intention to kill. The judgement was announced on 14 July 1927: not guilty. If this had been the culmination of a 'normal' criminal case, there would at most have been a listing in the events chronicles in the newspapers. However, the fact that the occurrence was the result of a skirmish between feuding paramilitary formations raised the matter to a very different, political level. This could already be seen in the run-up to the court proceedings. Ultimately, there was not just heavy criticism of the judge and jury, for example, or the sense and purpose of jury courts, but the judgement itself was evaluated as an example of class justice. The *Arbeiter-Zeitung Deutschöster-reichs* wrote of 'worker murderers', questioned the suitability of the eleven male and one female juror to make a judgement, and saw this not least as an achievement of a defence lawyer who as a 'swastika supporter' had made every effort to cast doubt over the robustness of the prosecution.[124]

Now, all that was needed was an editorial by the editor-in-chief of the *Arbeiter-Zeitung*, Friedrich Austerlitz, to cause an uproar among the Social Democratic workers. On 15 July, thousands of workers marched through the centre of Vienna. At first, it was not yet clear which institution or which building the demonstrators would turn against. They were forced to one side, and gathered in front of the Palace of Justice, which was viewed as a symbol of state jurisprudence. Gradually, a crowd of around 200,000 people was formed. Not all of them were 'activists'. Many had come out of curiosity. The first arrivals clearly expected violence to erupt, with many of the demonstrators arriving with missiles, although not with weapons. The masses gathered and finally attempted to penetrate the Palace of Justice. A fire was lit. It spread. The top floors, where the General Administrative Archives were housed, burned. The declaration of renunciation made by Emperor Karl went up in flames, as did the land registries and files of the central authorities of Old Austria. The mayor of Vienna, Karl Seitz, attempted in vain to calm the situation. The fire brigade was prevented from intervening. Fire extinguishing lines were cut. The Protection League, which – as stewards' troops – could have stepped in, failed to act or rather much too late. No one felt the need to request assistance from the Federal Army. The police were the ones who should take control of the situation. Police on horseback and armed police closed in, hoping to disperse the crowd, shooting at first above peoples' heads and then into the mass of bodies. 89 demonstrators, four policemen and one police detective were killed; well over five hundred people were injured.

The fire at the Palace of Justice, which could only be extinguished twelve hours later, was a shock. However, rather than leading to a careful search for the reasons behind the event, it resulted in an escalation of verbal violence. At the same time, the leaders of the Social Democrats called for a general strike. The spectre of the civil war, ever latently present, stalked everywhere. The general strike affected the postal service, telephone and public transport, and for two days, no newspapers were published except for a hastily put together *Mitteilungsblatt der Sozialdemokratie Deutschösterreichs* and a small communist militant publication; as a result, no reporting of the events in front of the Palace of Justice and their consequences was possible. All kinds of rumours circulated.[125] It was claimed that 1,000 people had been killed, and that Italian and Hungarian troops had intervened. Some people feared a return to war and started quickly hoarding stocks of food.

In the federal states, the population was mostly reliant on hearsay, and the newspapers in Upper Austria, Styria and Vorarlberg only reported the events in Vienna several days later. If they were Social Democratic publications, the talk was of the acquitted 'worker murderers' and 'class justice'. There were also claims that Federal Chancellor Seipel, who had not intervened directly, but had instead allowed events to take their course, had a huge amount of blood on his hands. He became the 'Blood Chancellor';[126] and when he defended the use of his executive power in parliament, the phrase 'prelate without charity' was born. Karl Kraus had a poster printed on which he demanded the resignation of Police Commissioner Johann Schober.

Although this only became clear in retrospect, the fire at the Palace of Justice was one, if not *the*, turning point in the history of the inter-war period. Until then, despite all the rivalries and acts of violence, there had been a type of commonality that at least kept the prospect alive of overcoming the existing contradictions. The lack of orientation, the hardships of the first post-war years, the departure from a bygone era, the phase of ceaseless monitoring by the victorious European powers and creditors, and finally a moderate economic upturn from which everyone benefited were what brought people together. The commonality even went so far that in light of the fear that Italy, now a fascist country, might wish to expand its territory over the Brenner to Tyrol, and that the Federal Army, Protection League and Home Guard militias announced their willingness to offer joint defence. However, on 16 July 1927, everything changed. The contradictions mutated into open hostility. What now began was a latent civil war, in which the fronts ran right through the country, the political parties, advocacy groups and individuals. However, the state, despite its theoretical monopoly on power, was unable to assert itself and increasingly left the public arena to the paramilitary formations. These groups claimed the right to the street for themselves and were the 'combatants' in the conflict. For a while, those in positions of responsibility in the government and the party leaders thought that they had found willing helpers to implement their respective agendas in the form of the militia groups. In reality, they became increasingly dependent on them, and might aptly have quoted Goethe's 'Sorcerer's Apprentice': 'Wrong I was in calling spirits, I avow, for I find them galling, cannot rule them now.'

6 Civil War Scenarios

6   The Federal Army on stand-by on 1 May 1933 in front of the Vienna Opera House. After the refusal of Federal Chancellor Engelbert Dollfuß to permit the National Council to continue its legislative activities, unrest was feared on the 'Day of Labour'. May Day demonstrations were prohibited. Chevaux-de-frise, barbed wire and machine guns were supposed to make it clear that the government was prepared to use armed force. Things remained calm in Vienna. Only in Altheim near Braunau did someone die as a result of clashes between Communists and National Socialists. (Photo: Austrian National Library / Picture Archives)

S eipel had probably hoped that the Home Guard (Heimwehr) units would provide backup support for his government. He therefore made conscious efforts to
promote them and saw in them a welcome phalanx against the Social Democrats and
the Republican Protection League. The Home Guard units saw their chance. They, too,
wanted to make a big impact with their demonstrations. However, with increasing frequency, their verbal resolve ended in violence. And there, too, Seipel willingly supported
them, occasionally even leading the way, and certainly appeared to acquire a taste for
authoritarian measures. More and more often, he showed himself willing to pursue the
path taken by an increasing number of European states and leave the laborious option
of agreeing on compromises behind. Here, too, the 15th of July played a decisive role.
The use of force appeared to be the only possible response to an unruly mob, and more
was required than following the standard approach of discussing the issues. The failure
of such a well-known individual as the Social Democratic mayor of Vienna, Seitz, was
regarded as an example of how ineffective control mechanisms such as common sense
and persuasion actually were.

The Day of Wiener Neustadt

The next stage on the road to violence was 7 October 1928. The Styrian Home Guard,
a particularly active group that was seen as a power base by the Styrian state governor,
Anton Rintelen, wanted to organise a demonstration in Wiener Neustadt, and make
their own contribution to the 'marching season'. Wiener Neustadt was a Social Democrat stronghold, and the march of the Home Guard could unequivocally be regarded
as a power demonstration and a challenge to a fight. Not surprisingly, the Protection
League responded by announcing a counter-demonstration. Both marches were approved and were to pass down the same street, at the same time. Prominent figures
were due to appear in the form of Karl Renner, Otto Bauer and the 'Protection League
general' Theodor Körner. To prevent a scenario that surpassed even Schattendorf, the
Wiener Neustadt garrison was mobilised. 1,000 soldiers from the Federal Army and an
additional 2,500 gendarmes and police turned the city into a fortress. Four emergency
hospitals and ten mobile walk-in medical facilities were provided to take care of the
injured. 380 journalists were waiting to see how events would unfold. They would be
disappointed.[127] The infantry battalions, squadrons and artillery batteries formed an

armed cordon along the marching route which was designed to prevent clashes between the demonstrators. The measure appeared to work. However, it might have been noticed that among the Federal Army units, an artillery division had also been put on alert and was moving out with its guns.

Despite the attempt to make a show of the state's monopoly on power, neither the federal government nor the parties and militia groups drew the necessary conclusions. Quite the opposite: on 24 February 1929, a type of standstill agreement was reached, and Home Guard formations were permitted to march along the Ringstraße in Vienna for the first time. Once again, members of the Defence League appeared to stage a counter-demonstration. The trial of strength continued.

The paramilitary forces of the left and the formations regarded as being at least supportive of the government if not loyal to it had already attracted a quarter of a million members each. The male divisions, battalions and squads, which were structured along military lines, were supplemented by women who were to be used for any medical services that might be required. And the number of formations continued to grow, with what must have been a noticeable increase in right-wing groups. Here, the combat organisations of the National Socialists, the Storm Troopers (Sturmabteilung; SA) and the Schutzstaffel (SS) were making their presence ever more strongly felt.

However, it was the Home Guard units that experienced the largest upturn in membership, and they quite clearly profited from the fear in non-Social Democrat circles that became a constant feature of political events after July 1927. The Home Guard units became increasingly radicalised, and also created a joint leadership when, in October 1927, the Tyrolean security director and Home Guard leader Richard Steidle was elected federal leader of the 'Federation of Austrian Citizens' Guards'. The deputy federal leader was the head of the Styrian Home Guard, Walter Pfrimer. The total membership of these organisations reached 300,000, of whom 52,000 were armed.[128] The accession of entire associations, such as the Lower Austrian Peasants' League, altered the Home Guard units to the extent that they were no longer regarded merely as paramilitary organisations, but as a political force that aimed to attain power in the state.

Among the Social Democrats, the opposite development could be observed. The 15th of July 1927 was – without them conceding that this was the case – a debacle. While the Protection League continued to create the impression of being determined and unified, it was in fact on the defensive. Many of its members had grown tired of being frequently on standby, and were critical of the leadership, which time and again prevented them from taking the offensive. While radical phrases continued to dominate, it was natural to question the condition of a party that quite evidently shrank from using force. Only one thing was clear: the Social Democrats continued to support democracy.

In 1928, the second period of office of the federal president came to an end. Michael Hainisch had remained unobtrusive, and had neither become largely involved in domestic politics, nor expressed a desire to represent Austria abroad. Seipel would have wanted a new federal president to have been chosen through direct presidential elections, instead of retaining the practice of appointing the head of state through the Federal Assembly. However, he would have needed the support of the Social Democrats to bring about a change to the constitution, and they unequivocally rejected the proposal of direct elections. As a result, the established practice was continued. The Christian Socials put forward the president of the National Council (Nationalrat), Wilhelm Miklas, as a candidate, while the Social Democrats proposed Karl Renner. The Greater Germans and the Rural League nominated Johann Schober. After two rounds of voting, there was still no majority. During the third round, the Social Democrats submitted blank voting cards. They knew that they would not be able to get Renner elected, and Schober, who as the police commissioner of Vienna was responsible for the use of executive authority on the 15th of July of the previous year, was out of the question for them as a candidate. The only person left was Miklas, the man who in 1918 had only reluctantly voted in favour of a union with Germany, but who was seen as the lesser of two evils. Seipel may have regarded the election of his candidate as a success. Nevertheless, he showed growing signs of resignation. The coalition with the Greater Germans had become increasingly frustrating. With regard to the matter of a new rent law, a very important issue for Vienna in particular, Seipel even found greater support among the Social Democrats than his coalition partners. However, this in itself should not have led to his resignation. And despite this setback, he should in fact have been highly satisfied when, in 1928, the monitoring by the League of Nations came to an end – a sign that the reconstruction measures introduced by Seipel in 1922 had clearly succeeded to the satisfaction of the financial monitors. Yet it was evident that he was disappointed, and he accepted the consequences. In April 1929, Seipel made the surprise announcement that he was resigning from office, leaving not only his own party, but also his political opponents at a loss.

For the second time, it could be said that the pilot abandoned ship. At best, one could only speculate as to why he gave up everything. One theory was that as a prelate, Seipel was exhausted by the many church appearances he had to make, and he related them to himself and his policies.[129] However, to an equal degree, he resigned in the face of the difficulties within the coalition. There was one more reason that led him to make his decision: the federal states increasingly insisted on independence, and they were not willing to accept compromises in this regard. However, this was precisely what Seipel aimed to achieve in his plans for a reform of the federal constitution. The conglomerate of federal states was to merge together to form a real whole. However, Seipel left without achieving the constitutional reform that had certainly already started to become evident.

His successor, the former professional officer Ernst Streeruwitz, was a stopgap solution. He had no 'power base' and could therefore only try to form a workable government. However, he lacked the most important source of support, namely that of the Home Guard units. There, the anti-parliamentary forces had increasingly gained the upper hand. Among the goals of the Home Guard, eliminating the Social Democrats ranked at the top. Confrontation was regularly sought. While the Home Guard units also wanted constitutional reform, they did not wish to see this within the parameters of a democratic political system. With increasing frequency, therefore, demands were made for the creation of a corporative state, modelled on Italian fascism and the authoritarian system in Hungary under István Bethlen. Since the Home Guard units had their centres in the federal states outside Vienna, the focus of events shifted away from the federal capital, and remote places became arenas for the latent civil war. The next confrontation after Wiener Neustadt occurred in the small Styrian town of St. Lorenzen in the Mürz Valley. And events took a more violent turn than the marches in Wiener Neustadt, the city known as the 'Eternally Faithful' *(Allzeit Getreue)*. When it was announced that the Styrian Protection League leader, Koloman Wallisch, who was known for being a radical, would speak in St. Lorenzen, members of the Home Guard occupied the site where the rally was due to take place. Although the activities of both sides had been made known, no one saw reason to take security precautions, to bring in Gendarmerie forces or even to request the assistance of the Federal Army. On Sunday, 18 August 1929, formerly the 'Emperor's birthday', the Styrian Home Guard and the Protection League waged nothing short of a battle, in which three Protection League members were killed. Thirty members of the Home Guard and two Protection League members were severely injured. A machine gun was even used from the church tower.[130] The incident was followed by mutual finger-pointing and judicial enquiries that delivered no results.

Calm Before the Storm

Federal Chancellor Streeruwitz was not willing to simply interpret events as an isolated outbreak of violence, and correctly surmised that the Styrian state governor, Anton Rintelen, was not only behind the Home Guard's actions, but was aiming to use the incident to bring about the demise of the government. The Home Guard units then also called for a 'march on Vienna' for 29 September. Streeruwitz felt unable to take effective countermeasures and resigned. This time, his successor was already waiting in the wings. Once again, it was Johann Schober – and he could count on a broad level of support. Since he was regarded as being a 'strong man', the Home Guard units felt sure that he would pursue their goals. Schober also enjoyed support from those citizens' and farmers' groups who hoped for an end to the violent clashes and for some form of disarmament. Not even the Social Democrats denied him their support. After all, it was Streeruwitz himself who had recommended Schober as his successor.[131] One might justifiably say that the decision had been made just in time. The 'march on Vienna' was cancelled.

Schober had already been pulling the strings for some time and had prepared for his second term as chancellor. He made promises and set out demands. He let it be known to the Home Guard units that he was in no hurry to revamp the constitution. However, he also demanded that he should be allowed to fill his cabinet with people who enjoyed his personal trust, rather than those who should be included in the government in line with some proportion quota. His request was granted. Among his ministers, the former federal president Hainisch, Theodor Innitzer, who would later become archbishop of Vienna, and the historian Heinrich Srbik stood out in particular. Christian Socials, Greater Germans and the Rural League were granted just one government seat each. The Home Guard was left completely empty-handed. This was a surprise to its leaders. Schober also disappointed Steidle & co by pushing through a reform of the federal constitution, contrary to his previous statements. Here, too, his actions were rooted in pragmatism, since he not only conducted the negotiations regarding the constitution, which had already been ongoing for a year, in person but also wanted to bring them to a conclusion in direct contact with the chief Social Democrat negotiator and president of the Vienna regional diet (Landtag), Robert Danneberg. This was also a necessity, since once again, a two-thirds majority was required in the National Council. In order to achieve this, the Social Democrats needed to be brought on side, and parliamentary democracy left undisputed. As soon as this was clear, changes could be made that had previously been unequivocally rejected by the Social Democrats. They waived the implementation of what had initially been a central demand, namely the abolition of the War Economy Enabling Act of 1917. It was allowed to remain in force. A further compromise was that the next federal president could be appointed by means of direct elections, and the authority of the federal president was to be considerably strengthened. Like the German Reich president, he was to have the right to appoint and dismiss the federal government and to dissolve parliament and, if urgently needed, to issue emergency decrees and exert (nominal) supreme command over the Federal Army. The right to hold a consultative referendum was introduced as a new plebiscitary means. Furthermore, the position of the federal states in relation to the federation was newly regulated, and the second chamber, the Federal Council (Bundesrat), was granted additional areas of authority. The compromise demanded that the government also renounce numerous demands. Danneberg insisted that the law of 3 April 1919 regarding the exile of the Habsburgs and the abolition of titles and privileges of the old Austrian nobility should remain in force, and that no changes should be made to the state coat of arms. This then also required agreement, and almost bordered on cosmetic specifications. In December

1929, parliament succeeded in passing the new version of the federal constitution of 1920. As had been hoped, a big step forward had been taken. Schober was also successful in other areas. He was able to improve relations with Italy, which since 1926 had been tense as a result of the Italianisation of South Tyrol. After Schober described the behaviour of the fascists in South Tyrol as a domestic matter for Italy, Mussolini ceased to maintain the blockade policy against Austria that he had applied until then. The result of this policy had been that Austria had not received a foreign loan that it urgently needed to expand its industry, and Italy had also been unwilling to waiver the general rights of lien stipulated in the Peace Treaty. Now, Mussolini assigned himself the role of attorney to Austria, and also abandoned his objections to a new loan.

Schober had another goal in mind, namely to regain the state's monopoly on power and the state executive authority. The paramilitary forces were to be pushed back. They had spread like wildfire. In December 1929, the Rural League had also decided to establish its own farmers' militia and no longer felt bound to the Home Guard. Schober therefore had to reckon with a large number of opponents, on the left and right, but for him, it was not the Protection League that presented a danger, but the Home Guard. The latter was namely not idle.

Escalation of Violence

In itself, the meeting that took place on 18 May 1930 in Korneuburg in Lower Austria appeared perfectly harmless. The federal leader Richard Steidle had called a conference of the Home Guard leaders and had a paper prepared in which the goals of the Home Guard were set out. Everyone gathered there was to swear an oath and pledge allegiance to the principles given in the paper. These included:

> We want to renew Austria from its foundations! / We want to seize power in the state and reorganise the state and the economy for the good of the entire people. / We must forget our own interests…, since we want to serve the community of the German people! / We reject Western democratic parliamentarianism and the party state! / In its place, we want to create self-administration of the corporate groups and a strong state leadership, which is formed not by party representatives, but is created from the leading individuals of the major corporate groups and from the most competent and experienced men of our popular movement. / We fight against the disintegration of our people by Marxist class struggle and liberal-capitalist management of the economy ….

Around 800 delegates swore the oath, which soon became known as the 'Korneuburg Oath'. The state leader of the Lower Austrian Home Guard, Julius Raab, was among them.[132] Yet not everyone was willing to swear. There was resistance among the Christian Socials, particularly in the form of Leopold Kunschak, and many Greater Germans also showed reluctance. The representative of the Rural League in the federal government, Vinzenz Schumy, refused to swear the oath and was excluded from the Home Guard, as a result of which the Rural League went entirely its own way, and like many Greater Germans turned to the National Socialists. The political spectrum became ever more colourful, and it was already downright confusing. The Republic had already 'used up' dozens of politicians. Idealistic approaches had run into the sand. Ideas had been replaced with ideologies. Those that were most likely to survive appeared to be the ones that were forcefully asserted. In so doing, they impressed not only their adherents, but also those who had grown tired of the inflation of ideas, and who were looking for salvation in the form of a strong leader. The crisis of ideas preceded even the next economic crisis. And there appeared to be no available cure.

Schober would not be deterred from pursuing his chosen course of action by the apparent determination of the Home Guard units, just as he was not prepared to follow an anti-democratic course. However, Schober's government had an expiry date. As soon as he acted openly against the Home Guard units and arranged for one of the most colourful personalities from their ranks, who was responsible for the murders of Rosa Luxemburg and Karl Liebknecht and for several putsch attempts in Germany, chief of staff of the Home Guard, Waldemar Pabst, to be arrested and extradited to Germany, he became the object of hatred among numerous members of the Home Guard who were ready to attempt a putsch. Ultimately, however, it was once again a trifling matter that led to Schober's fall from power. He refused to re-politicise the Social Democrat-dominated Federal Railways in a similar way to the measures taken with the Federal Army by Minister of Defence Carl Vaugoin. The governor of Styria, Anton Rintelen, recommended to Schober the director general of the Graz tram company, Georg Strafella, as the new director general of the Federal Railways. He had attracted attention for his illegal speculative trading. Schober refused to appoint him, leading to the resignation of Minister of Defence Vaugoin and Minister of Agriculture Florian Födermayr. Schober broke off his government. He resigned. However, this was not just a simple government crisis; there was much more at stake. The Home Guard penetrated through to the political arena. This was the precursor to the credo that would then apply in Germany: 'get into parliament in order to destroy it'. The Christian Socials, who like the Home Guard units found Schober increasingly problematic, wanted to install a chancellor from their party as the head of government. The Greater Germans and the Rural League were no longer content to play the role of providers of a majority. And while the Social Democrats had no chance of participating in government, they could certainly hope to gain lost territory in the elections. Federal President Miklas finally entrusted the man who had toppled Schober, Carl Vaugoin, with the task of forming a government.

There had rarely been such a dark period in domestic politics as the one at the end of 1930. Schober's fall had robbed the Republic of one more source of hope. Exasperation made itself felt – if it was not present already. The time of economic recovery, the brief period of prosperity, which had prevailed between 1925 and 1929, was brought to an end by the 'Black Friday' (which was in fact a Thursday) on the New York Stock Exchange on 24 October 1929. The markets shrank. Banks declared loans due for payment. American companies withdrew their money from Europe, and unemployment figures began to rise rapidly. Certainly, some counteractive measures could be taken through national efforts, but of course Austria, too, was not spared the crisis. There was not enough money for investments and the funding of employment creation programmes. While there were several 'doctrines of salvation' to hand, they contradicted each other, and even the most wonderful theories, such as had been developed by the Austrian national economist Josef Schumpeter, for example, or as set down by John Maynard Keynes in *Treatise on Money*, were unable to stop the disintegration of the global economy. Schumpeter, who now lived in the USA and taught at Harvard University, was quoted as saying: 'A dog is more likely to set aside a stockpile of sausages than a democratic government a budget reserve'[133] – the so-called Schumpeter theorem. The Harvard professor may well have been right, and Austria was a prime example of this. By 1930, it was too late. Mindful of the massive inflation at the start of the 1920s, however, this time nothing was to be done that might risk the stability of the currency. So it was that an increase in unemployment was accepted. Even the view to Germany, which over many years had been filled with longing, offered no solace, since Germany was even more severely affected by the crisis than Austria. And when it came to contrasting views and the radicalism with which ideas and utopias were presented, there was no doubt that Germany was one step ahead.

On 30 September 1930, Carl Vaugoin took over the reins of government. If he had not been so power-obsessed, he should in fact already have resigned in advance. The Greater Germans and the Rural League refused to enter into his government. The avowed anti-Marxist Vaugoin did not even consider the possibility of forming a coalition with the Social Democrats. A part of his own party, which still felt loyal to Schober, distanced itself from him. Vaugoin therefore had no choice but to cooperate with the Home Guard, who at the start of September 1930 had surprisingly toppled Steidle and made Ernst Rüdiger Starhemberg their new leading representative, now known as the 'Reichsführer' ('Reich leader'). Starhemberg became Minister of the Interior. However, Vaugoin was unable to form a parliamentary majority, and Wilhelm Miklas put a stop to the to-ing and fro-ing by dissolving parliament and announcing new elections. Vaugoin, however, used the period of his transition government to now make Georg Strafella the director general of the Austrian Federal Railways, and in deference to the Home Guard, as it were, he lifted the enforced exile of the German Waldemar Pabst. It is no wonder that among those observing these machinations from a distance, the sense of exasperation with the state and politics only increased further.

The turmoil continued. Starhemberg, who represented a clearly (German) nationalist agenda, sought an alliance with Adolf Hitler's National Socialists, who were campaigning in an election in Austria for the first time. However, understandably, Hitler, who was still stateless, wanted to head the list of candidates. The talks came to an end before they had even started. Within the Home Guard units, disputes broke out between the fractions, since the leader of the Vienna Home Guard, Emil Fey, disagreed with the goals set out by Starhemberg. Starhemberg rejected the proposal of a merger between the Home Guard units and the Christian Socials. So it was that the Home Guard units campaigned as a separate political party called the 'Homeland Bloc' (Heimatblock). As if this wasn't enough, representatives of the middle classes gathered around Johann Schober and finally contested the election to the National Council under the name 'National Economic Bloc' (Nationaler Wirtschaftsblock). However, the Social Democrats waited for their time to come, and nurtured the well-founded hope of returning from political isolation after the elections. They also refrained from acts of violence in the wake of targeted weapons searches decreed by Minister of the Interior Starhemberg. On 10 November 1930, the Christian Socials and the Homeland Bloc suffered a heavy defeat. However, the Social Democrats also came out worse than expected, even if they did become the party with the strongest mandate, putting them in a position to appoint Karl Renner as president of the National Council. However, they received no mandate to form a government. This would probably have been a futile undertaking anyway. The Schober block won 19 seats, and the Home Guard entered parliament. However, there was one more loser who did not attract enough attention. The National Socialists under Adolf Hitler were elected by around 110,000 Austrians. While they failed to achieve an initial mandate, and therefore did not win any seats, they were still a presence.

The process of governing in Austria had not become any easier. Now, parties had to work together who were divided by more than just the occasional area of hostility. One thing was clear: Vaugoin would no longer be able to obtain a majority in parliament. The Federal President finally entrusted the governor of Vorarlberg, Otto Ender, with the task of forming a government. Vaugoin's followers acquiesced. However, Seipel refused to enter the government. He was thinking increasingly along authoritarian lines, and Ender appeared to him to be too 'soft'. Schober was willing to cooperate. The Homeland Bloc was excluded. The opposition to the government, splintered as it was, was still more powerful from the outset. Ender therefore had no option but to follow the path of least resistance and offer compromises. This he also succeeded in doing when it came to dividing the tax revenue between the federation, the federal states and the municipalities. A project that was no less ambitious, namely the creation of a free trade zone between Germany and Austria, would end in fiasco, however.

Customs Union

Once again, Austria had arrived at a place where an agreement with Germany was sought in order to stabilise the economy. The brief period of growth was a thing of the past. Exports were declining, and foreign trade was halved. In Vienna alone, unemployment had risen by 24 per cent from 1929 to 1930. The suicide rate rose rapidly. In 1931, the share of unemployed in Austria climbed to around 20 per cent, and in some sectors even exceeded 50 per cent.[134] Young people and students became radicalised. A generation appeared to be growing up from whom all opportunities had been taken, and who no longer had any prospects for the future. The plans for countering this situation were not new, but the global economic crisis created a different, new sense of urgency. Once again, it was hoped that the successor states of the Habsburg Monarchy, primarily Hungary, would be a source of support. This promptly awakened the suspicions of the Little Entente and was met with bitter resistance from the Austrian Social Democrats. The spectre of a restoration of the Habsburgs stalked the room, although it should have been clear a long time ago that the Hungarian imperial regent, Miklós Horthy, would be at least as bitter an opponent of a Habsburg restoration as the Czechoslovak President Tomáš Masaryk, for example. However, the matter was not further pursued anyway, since in the interim, new possibilities had emerged.

For the first time since 1919, in fact, the desire for closer economic cooperation between Germany and Austria had been expressed in the German Reichstag on 14 March 1929 and had been met with unanimous agreement. For Ender, the minister of foreign affairs of the government, and the former federal chancellor Johann Schober, this provided a welcome reason to seriously pursue the project of forming a customs union with Germany. The goal was to remove the customs barriers between the two countries, dismantle obstacles to trade and to introduce a uniform customs system in relation to other countries. Since Austria's trade volume with the successor states was double that of Germany, the purpose of this system was also to introduce a new structure and prepare for a type of silent union. In principle, this approach followed through on ideas that had already been expressed in 1915, and particularly in 1918, when under the auspices of the Central European movement and finally of the 'Arms League' (Waffenbund) an economic interrelationship between Germany and Austria-Hungary had been considered. It is likely that the German Reich President Paul von Hindenburg had also been thinking of the time during the First World War, and he was then quoted by Reich Chancellor Heinrich Brüning: 'his [Hindenburg's] memories were such that one should never forge a common policy with Austria, since the Austrians never stuck it out and at a suitable moment would sell such agreements to others for a high price.'[135]

Now the field had been recently prepared, however. The Germans, particularly German industrialists, became insistent, and they could be sure of finding support in Austria, although precisely in business circles there was a fear of being overrun by the Germans. Yet most members of the government and the broad general public were in favour. And even if it looked a little like a boilerplate, the formulation of the president of the National Council, Karl Renner, on 29 April 1931 regarding the matter left no room for doubt: 'May it ... be accorded to us ... to unite economically with our mother country. In my own name and in all likelihood in that of all of you, I greet our great German mother people in this hour!'[136] There it was again, that emotively dressed-up desire for union.

Schober reached an understanding with the German Reich Foreign Minister Julius Curtius regarding the framework conditions. At the beginning of December 1930, Federal Chancellor Ender incorporated the formulation of the 'necessity of a gradual establishment of the European union',[137] while at the same time seeking to counter the first objections.

Immediately, there was resistance from France. However, instead of referring to the Treaty of Saint-Germain, France invoked the Geneva Protocol of 1922. Naturally, the French were primarily concerned with Germany but in Paris there was also the simpler strategy available of pursuing the indirect route and addressing the objections towards Vienna. However, there was also resistance from Rome, which was working on developing its axis with Hungary, and which would have like to incorporate Austria into its own sphere of power and interest, as well as from Prague, which was reminded of the Central Europe plans of German and Austrian politicians and intellectuals during the First World War, and which therefore indicated its rejection of the idea on principle. The Geneva Protocols offered a good lever for the purpose, even if they were used as a convenient cover, with their formal legal formulations. Finally, on the initiative of the British, the matter was taken to the Permanent International Court of Justice in The Hague, which on 5 September 1931 decided with a majority of 8 votes to 7 that a customs union would be an infringement of the Geneva Protocols. 'Austria is an essential element of the political order in Europe',[138] the statement read, and in Geneva, Austria had been obligated in 1922 to preserve its economic and thus also political independence. There was no mention of what might have happened if Austria had desired a customs union with Czechoslovakia. Yet that was not the issue. The German project had at any rate failed. In fact, the idea had already been stillborn long before September, and indeed as early as May and June of that year.

'South-Eastern Europe is in Flames'

During a meeting of the German and British heads of government in May 1931, the governor of the Bank of England is said to have burst into the office of British Prime

Minister Ramsay MacDonald at his country seat in Chequers and exclaimed in a state
of unfettered excitement: 'Sir, South-Eastern Europe is in flames. The Creditanstalt in
Vienna has closed its counters!'

It was not the first time a bank had collapsed in Austria since the war. Quite the opposite: banks had repeatedly become bankrupt, had to be propped up and cushioned by
other institutes. Thus, the Creditanstalt had taken over the Bodencreditanstalt following an intervention by Federal Chancellor Schober in October 1929 in order to prevent
a collapse of that traditional bank.[139] (The dubious business practices of the governor
of the 'Boden', Rudolph Sieghart, remained just as suppressed as the circumstance that
he had been one of the main funders of the Home Guard, but had recently conducted
business with the municipality of Vienna, in other words, the Social Democrats.) The
Creditanstalt was considered to be a 'Rothschild bank', solid to the core, and as one of
the few major banks had maintained its connections to the former crown lands of the
Habsburg Monarchy. If this bank collapsed, then there could be no faith in any other.
Yet this is precisely what happened. At first, it resulted in a series of bank collapses, the
most spectacular of which was the fall of Dresdner Bank.[140] In May 1931, the Creditanstalt needed to be kept afloat with 100 million schillings. The government issued
treasury notes. A storm on the bank began. Deposits were withdrawn, and savings were
taken out. Foreign creditors demanded that the federation assume liability. This was
granted, with an amount of 500 million schillings. The Austrian currency came under
pressure. The National Bank reacted with alarm. There were no longer any other major
banks in Austria. Salvation could only come from abroad. The foreign creditors of the
Creditanstalt enforced the appointment of a Dutch director general. The Bank of England granted the National Bank a loan of 150 million schillings. France also agreed to
help, but the offer came with two demands: renewed foreign monitoring of the financial management of the Republic of Austria – and the abandonment of the proposed
customs union with Germany.[141] Both had to be agreed to. Once again, Austria was
under observation.

The economic crisis and the bank crash were joined by a government crisis. Three
ministers resigned. Ender was left with no choice but to step down, too. Once again, a
successor had to be found. At first, it appeared as though Ender would succeed himself.
However, his own party, the Christian Socials, left him in the lurch. Again, Seipel offered to take up the post, with the idea of forming a government of national unity. The
Federal President urged his colleagues to embark directly on negotiations to this end.
And for a brief period of time, it really did look as though the feat might be pulled off.
Seipel wanted the chancellorship and was ready to give the Social Democrats control
over more ministries than the Christian Socials, and indeed, there were powerful voices
among the Social Democrats, such as that of Karl Renner, who spoke out in favour
of joining a cabinet under Seipel. However, the most important Social Democrat fig-

ure, Otto Bauer, decisively rejected the idea of participating in a government. In his view, the bourgeoisie would soon tear themselves to pieces, and as a result, the Social Democrats would be able to dictate the conditions under which they would be willing to cooperate. In retrospect, the question once again had to be asked as to whether a major opportunity had not been passed up here. What would have happened if a government of national unity had been formed which incorporated Christian Socials, Social Democrats, Greater Germans and the Rural League? Would everything have turned out differently? The decision lay with one man. And it appears that he made the wrong choice. The Social Democrats were willing to bear part of the burden of taking the necessary measures to refurbish the state finances, but they were not prepared to co-govern under the conditions set by Seipel. Here, the Social Democrats, like other parties, laboured under their unwillingness to compromise, and they were also not in a position to break out of their de facto isolation and gain a stronger foothold in the west and south of Austria.

Seipel continued his efforts and sought to form a government of the 'right'. However, the Home Guard units that had joined to form the Homeland Bloc remained at a distance, and the Greater Germans also refused to cooperate, since Seipel wanted to assign the post of finance minister to Viktor Kienböck, the man with whom he had implemented the Geneva reconstruction measures, and who was regarded as an uncompromising fixer of finances. Seipel was forced to set his request to form a government to one side. The Federal President put forward the idea of a cabinet of civil servants. This was also rejected by all sides. Finally, the Christian Socials, Greater Germans and the Rural League declared themselves willing to form a government under the chancellorship of Karl Buresch.

Buresch, who had been governor of Lower Austria since 1922, was to a large extent an unknown quantity in federal politics. There were rumours of corruption and susceptibility to bribery in connection with the collapse of the Lower Austrian Peasants' Bank, as well as the collapse of the Central Bank of German Savings Banks, yet Buresch did at least have some halfway functioning contacts to all parties, including the Social Democrats. He needed the latter in particular to push through a budget clean-up act in parliament, which was a precondition for requesting a loan – once again – from the League of Nations. However, the economic problems persisted, with Austria running short of money and unemployment figures rising relentlessly. In 1928, the official statistics showed 179,000 people claiming unemployment benefit. Around 80,000 others, known as 'eliminated' *(Ausgesteuerte)*, were no longer entitled to receive benefits and were dependent on charity. In the following year, the total number of unemployed counted 280,000, rising to 350,000 in 1930 and 400,000 in 1931. One in six people were without work.[142]

All Against All

The federal states appeared to be less severely affected by the plight of the state than the 'federation', and it was almost inevitable that one of those who believed that a violent solution would cure the country and its people from all its ills would start to make plans for an overthrow. This occurred in Styria, where the federal leader of the Home Guard, Walter Pfrimer, who had recently taken over the post from Ernst Rüdiger Starhemberg, called for a putsch, albeit a poorly prepared one, on 13 September 1931.[143] According to the rumours, it was the almost legendary defender of the Sette Communi plateau during the First World War, Brigadier Otto Ellison, who had made the necessary military preparations. However, this did not make the matter any better. While several federal state leaders declared their willingness to cooperate, the initiative remained largely limited to Styria. A planned 'march on Vienna', which was to start from Klosterneuburg, was abandoned. The Home Guard members involved were arrested. From Linz, a colony of lorries set out that was, strangely enough, only prevented from continuing its journey and not requested to surrender its 26 machine guns. In Styria alone, a curious image emerged, since the Styrian governor, Rintelen, together with Minister of Defence Vaugoin, prevented an effective implementation of executive forces for several hours, and only permitted the 4,000 Federal Army soldiers and the Gendarmerie and police to proceed during the afternoon. The only shots that were fired were in Kapfenberg, where members of the Home Guard killed two people and injured several more. It became clear by the evening that the attempted uprising had failed. The federal government promised to 'immediately hold accountable' those responsible 'and with the full force of the law'.[144] Starhemberg and other Home Guard leaders were arrested. Pfrimer, who had initially fled Austria and then returned, was put on trial and acquitted. This marked the end of the legal proceedings against around 4,000 Home Guard members. However, the entire undertaking was neither harmless, nor did it deserve to be simply referred to as an operetta. It was without doubt a serious attempt to attain power in the state. It had simply been engendered by the wrong person. And it was most certainly misleading to speak of a triumph or a victory for democracy.

Even if the Home Guard putsch organised by Walter Pfrimer was condemned, there were many people who were by no means outraged by his actions. The government was weak and quite clearly reluctant to act against the Home Guard. Even the occasional merger between the Home Guard and the National Socialists was not met with concern.[145] The Greater Germans continued to fly the banner for the idea of union with Germany, and they wanted Minister of Foreign Affairs Schober to continue to pursue a German course – otherwise, they would resign from the government. They were in an unfortunate situation themselves, since in the interim, far more radical proponents of a union with Germany had appeared on the scene in the form of the National Socialists.

However, Buresch knew very well that he needed the assistance of France in order to successfully request a loan from the League of Nations. For this reason, he could not allow himself to be blackmailed by those who sought a union with Germany. He resigned, and immediately afterwards formed a new cabinet, in which Schober and the Greater Germans, as well as the Home Guard, were no longer represented. The cabinet had no parliamentary majority behind it and was reliant on the support of the Social Democrat opposition. The government literally went through all possible options, and was given any amount of good advice, including from the French Prime Minister André Tardieu. He proposed a very different kind of customs union, suggesting that Austria, Hungary, Czechoslovakia, Yugoslavia and Romania should standardise their economic spaces. France wanted to play the role of financier. This in turn conflicted with the interests of the Italians, Germans and ultimately also the British. The Tardieu plan was quickly shelved.[146]

In a situation in which soon, everyone had turned against everyone else, Seipel against Buresch, Starhemberg against Steidle, Buresch against Schober, Renner against Bauer, and so on, there was only one party that recorded a continuous growth in support: the National Socialist German Workers' Party, the NSDAP. For them, it was of no interest whether France was prepared to lend money, and they unreservedly propagated a union with Germany, were openly anti-Marxist, while also being a workers' party, anti-democratic, like so many others in Austria, anti-Semitic, again, like so many others in Austria, and anti-clerical, something they had in common with, not least, many Social Democrats, who rejected political Catholicism if not religious convictions per se. They attacked democratic politics as 'bourgeois'[147] and accused them and their representatives of being lethargic, materialistic and unimaginative, with no visions for the future that spoke to the masses.

When, on 24 April 1932, there were elections to the regional diets in Lower Austria, Salzburg and Vienna and municipal council elections in Styria and Carinthia, there was a lurch to the right. All the established parties lost votes; the Greater Germans and the Rural League were marginalised and their supporters were thoroughly soaked up by the NSDAP. The National Socialists seemed to have future-oriented solutions readily available and were also far more suited for supporting the many activities with which the Greater Germans had until then sought to secure the loyalty of their supporters and sympathisers. The 'German School Association of the Southern March' (Deutscher Schulverein Südmark), the 'German-Austrian Alpine Association' (Deutschösterreichischer Alpenverein), the 'German Gymnasts' League' (Deutscher Turnerbund), student fraternities, territorial associations, singing groups and youth movements such as the 'Wandervögel' hiking organisation, developed all kinds of activities. They took responsibility for the German-speaking old Austrians in the Sudetenland and Carpathian regions, Galicia, Volhynia, Bukovina, Transylvania and the Danube Swabians, the Germans in Cilli (Celje), Marburg (Maribor), Pettau (Ptuj) and Gottschee

(Kočevsko), formed folk dance groups, and collected and transported books to South Tyrol in order to enable German to be taught, which was forbidden in Fascist Italy. The days of the Greater Germans were numbered. The National Socialists asserted a monopoly over union with Germany.[148]

The Homeland Bloc lost votes; losses for the Christian Socials in Vienna were particularly heavy. In the elections to the regional diets, one in ten Social Democrat voters had migrated to the NSDAP. As a result, the National Socialists were the clear victors. Now, with the aid of the politicians, a particularly common type of reinterpretation was possible: nine out of ten voters had still remained loyal to 'their' party and had not become National Socialists. However, it must in reality have been clear that this situation could not be allowed to continue. But which option was the most viable? In Austria, the decision was made to exclude the NSDAP, even taking into account the risk that they would present themselves as victims of the established parties and resort to terrorist methods.

Once again, Karl Buresch would attempt to form a government. Yet he was unable to secure a parliamentary majority and without further ado became one more statistic with regard to the average length of time in office of any cabinet of the First Republic: just eight months. Now, in May 1932, Miklas charged the minister of agriculture in the cabinet, Engelbert Dollfuss, with the task of forming a government.

84,000 Rifles and 980 Machine Guns

Dollfuss had been a member of the governments of Ender and Buresch since March 1931. Prior to that, he had been director of the Lower Austrian Chamber of Agriculture and most recently also president of the Austrian Federal Railways, in which function he was partly responsible for the nomination of Georg Strafella. It is likely that he regarded this as a necessary concession. However, Dollfuss had also been a different person in the past: a student of theology, a lawyer, an officer serving in the war with the Tyrolean Imperial Rifles, a member of the not very secret 'German Community' (Deustche Gemeinschaft) secret society, and an elder of a student association within the Catholic umbrella organisation 'Cartel Union' (Cartellverband). He was anti-Marxist and a strict Catholic. As a functionary of the Chamber of Agriculture and as minister of agriculture, he had certainly won the support of the Social Democrats, and he rarely met with open rejection in other circles, either. Now, he was to be the one who would succeed where so many before him had failed: in leading Austria out of the crisis. Dollfuss formed a government consisting of Christian Socials, the Homeland Bloc and the Rural League. It was a tried and tested combination – perhaps all too thoroughly so. And since the government had a parliamentary majority of just one vote, very few people thought that it would survive for long.

The economic and social problems piled up. The misery could not be stopped using the methods practised hitherto. Some of the Christian Socials and in particular the Homeland Bloc, the parliamentary representatives of the Home Guard units, already displayed very clear anti-democratic and authoritarian tendencies. The dispute with the Social Democrats had turned increasingly violent since 1927. Dollfuss therefore willingly followed those who were convinced that the 'true state' could not be built on the useless instruments of the parliament and the parties. They saw themselves as being students of the philosopher Othmar Spann, who was teaching in Vienna at the time, and were keen to pursue a new experiment after the one with parliamentary democracy was over: the authoritarian-led state. The fact that this might evolve into a type of 'rival fascism' was the least of their concerns.[149] And since multiple signals were coming from the economic sector that a 'regime on the basis of extended authorities' was seen to be urgently required and certainly worthy of support, the path already seemed to be cleared.

However, even with the first more significant measure, the government threatened to collapse. After more than a year's preparation, the League of Nations was ready to offer a new loan, this time of 300 million schillings. Once again, this was not a huge sum, and was far less than that lent in 1922. Furthermore, half of the loan would serve to settle old debts. It was therefore clear from the start that the money would not be enough. The British and French regarded the loan as a form of political credit that should be used both to bolster efforts to stop a union with Germany and against Italian ambitions. Again, one of the conditions was that no union with Germany would be permitted for a further ten years. Only then, in 1942 – at least in theory – would the League of Nations have been able to lift the prohibition on union with Germany set out in the Treaty of Saint-Germain. As if this were not enough, Austria was once again placed under observation. Meinoud Rost van Tonningen from the Netherlands, who had already worked on the staff of League of Nations Commissioner Zimmermann, subsequently monitored the use of the funds and the observance of the requirements related to the loan until August 1936.[150]

The National Council agreed to the Lausanne loan with a majority of 81 votes to 80. The prohibition on union with Germany and the renewed monitoring led to ferocious verbal battles. The government initially lacked the vote of Seipel, who was terminally ill. However, a replacement was found to fill the ranks of the government camp in good time.[151] In summary, there was a possibility that events would be repeated. This was clear not least to Dollfuss, who worked to broaden the government's base. He courted the Greater Germans but was unable to win them over. The Chancellor then tried the same thing with the Home Guard. At a meeting in Pörtschach, conditions and modalities were discussed. The leader of the Vienna Home Guard, Emil Fey, entered the government as permanent secretary for security and took over the command of the police and Gendarmerie. The hope was that through these measures, the wind would be taken out of the Home Guard's sails. This did nothing to change the majority ratios in parliament. They remained as follows: Social Democrats 72, Christian Socials 66, Schober block 19, Homeland Bloc 8. Nobody could have foreseen that from one day to the next, parliamentary democracy would not only be plunged into crisis, but that it would be dealt a fatal blow.

At first, as so often before, the subject of the article printed in the *Arbeiter-Zeitung* on 8 January 1933 may have been regarded as a minor matter: on the premises of the cartridge factory in Hirtenberg, Lower Austria, 40 wagons had arrived. They had been sent from Italy and were repaired and modernised before being finally transported onward to Hungary. 84,000 rifles and 980 machine guns became a problem and ultimately a scandal. They were booty from the First World War, which Mussolini wanted to move to Hungary. As an aside, a contingent was to be given to the Home Guard. Now it was announced that the transfer was in violation of the conditions of the Treaties of Saint-Germain and Trianon. The Austrian government disagreed. The French were furious – or at least, pretended to be so. The reaction reflected the conflicts between Italy and France, as well as the protective-power position that France exerted over the Little Entente. As a result, Hungary was to be refused permission to receive any more weapons. The government in Vienna could object as much as it liked, arguing that weapons had also been transported from Czechoslovakia to Yugoslavia via Austria. The matter might have been put to rest, since Italy offered to take the weapons back. However, the director general of the Federal Railways, Egon Seefehlner, attempted to bribe the railway workers' trade union with a significant sum of money in order to continue with the transport to Hungary. The incident came to light and Mr Seefehlner was dismissed. However, the government was forced to defend its stance both to France and Britain and to the Social Democrats, and it was left still waiting for the transfer of the millions of schillings from the Lausanne loan. Finally, the weapons were indeed returned. On 4 March 1933, the whole affair, which had been further exacerbated by a strike among the railway workers, was the subject of debate in the National Council. The Social Democrats submitted a motion of no confidence against the government. The whole matter rested on just one vote. Not entirely surprisingly, the first president of the National Council, Karl Renner, handed over the chair and wanted to vote with his fraction. After a discussion of the order of business, the second president, the Christian Social Rudolf Ramek, left the committee. Finally, the third president, the Greater German Josef (Sepp) Straffner also resigned from office. The meeting was not closed; the delegates left the room. Almost no one outside of parliament took any notice of what had happened. The newspapers reported the event in brief and in a neutral tone. It had simply been an unfortunate incident. In fact, however, a turning point had been reached.

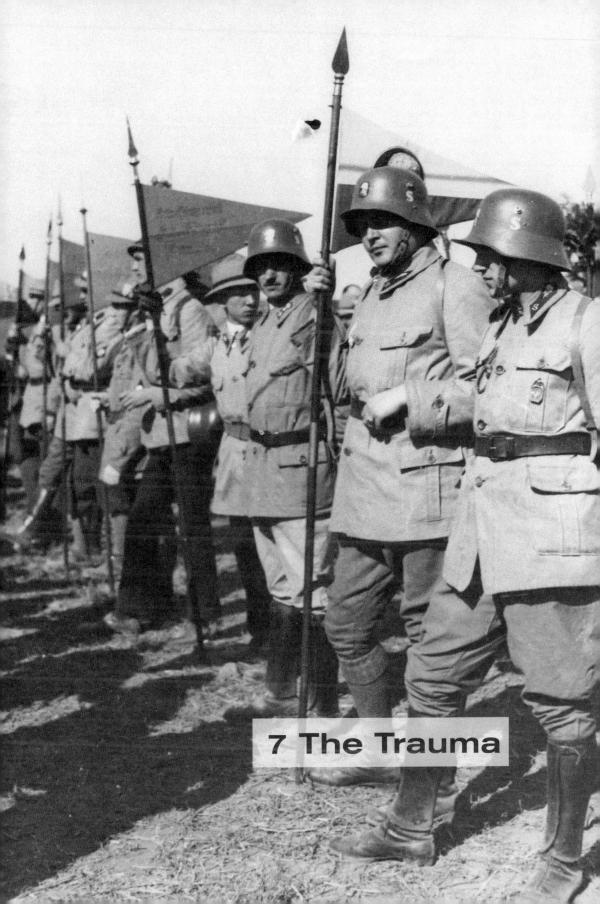

7 The Trauma

7 Regiment of the Home Guard. The Home Guard units, which had emerged in the federal states as local citizens' militias, became the most powerful paramilitary organisations in Austria in the mid-1920s. They demonstrated their claim to power by marching, frequently in competition with the Republican Protection League. They were regarded as pro-government but called into question practically all governments from 1927 onwards. Not until October 1936 did Kurt Schuschnigg succeed in dissolving the Home Guard units. However, they survived in countless so-called Veterans' Associations and continued to exert an influence on politics. (Photo: ORF Archives)

At first, the word was given to the constitutional lawyers. The situation could be regarded in such a way that the meeting of the National Council (Nationalrat) on 4 March – since it had not been closed – had only been interrupted and could be resumed on another day. Or, alternatively, that the federal president dissolved parliament and announced new elections. This appeared to be too risky to the Christian Social Wilhelm Miklas, since this might mean that the Social Democrats could emerge as winners from the elections and that the National Socialists might by all means enter parliament. It could already be seen from the example of Germany that this would not do anything to calm the political situation within the country. There, Reich President Hindenburg had appointed Adolf Hitler Reich chancellor on 30 January 1933. Five days before the confusion of the elections in Vienna, the Reichstag in Berlin had been in flames. And already the day afterwards, Hindenburg had issued a decree 'for the protection of people and state' (the 'Reichstag Fire Regulation'). This effectively nullified the basic rights contained in the Weimar Constitution in Germany and paved the way for the persecution of political opponents of the NSDAP by the police and the SA. However, the National Socialists wanted special rights that went much further than this. Was this to be the path taken by Austria?

By applying the War Economy Enabling Act 'for the prevention of overt, irreparable damage to the common good' at a time when the National Council was not in session and could not be convened quickly enough, Miklas could have taken measures himself by decree at the request of the federal government.[152] However, this required that the federal government submit such a request. And it was precisely this option that was thwarted by Dollfuß. After leaving himself a few days to consider his options, he was urged by his supporters throughout Austria to continue to govern without parliament.[153] He resigned, and – as had previously been arranged with Miklas – was reappointed. And this was one of three major wrong decisions that Miklas would make during the course of five years. A first step towards authoritarian rule had been taken.

The End of Parliamentary Democracy

The reappointed government had only been in office for a week when the third president of the National Council, Straffner, summoned the delegates to continue the meeting that had been interrupted on 4 March. Now, Dollfuß went into action. It had already been clear in advance that the parties from the government camp, with the exception of the Rural League, disputed Straffner's right to reconvene the delegates. Once again, a legal problem arose. The two ministers of the Rural League, Winkler and Bachinger, tendered their resignation. The Federal President refused to accept it. However, Dollfuß issued instructions that the National Council delegates should be prevented from entering parliament. The police took up their positions. Some of the Social Democrat and Greater German delegates were already inside the building. Dollfuß arranged for the building on the Ringstrasse to be cleared. When the Vienna Home Guard (Heimwehr) attempted to use this to strike out and turn violent what had until that point been an entirely peaceful overthrow, Dollfuß had them disarmed. He quite clearly wanted to avoid any pretext that would cause the situation to escalate further. Two days later, the Federal Council (Bundesrat) delegates were even able to enter parliament unhindered, and with a large majority passed a resolution in which the Federal President was requested to restore the constitutional conditions and not allow the legislation to be obstructed by the government.[154] This did not distract Dollfuß in the slightest. The National Council remained locked out. The Chancellor must have calculated that the Social Democrats would not simply take what had happened lying down. However, this is precisely what happened. No general strike or local walkouts were called. Nobody got upset about verbal radicalism any longer. On 19 March, the *Arbeiter-Zeitung* was seized after publishing the text of an interpellation in the Vienna regional diet (Landtag). Nothing happened. The 15th of March 1933 appeared to be a normal day like any other.

On 31 March, the Republican Protection League was banned. Stewards' groups were permitted to remain, however, as was the Vienna City Guard. May marches by the Social Democrats were prohibited. However, Dollfuß did not want to challenge the Social Democrats even further, no more so than the National Socialists. He, therefore, indicated that he was willing to talk. It must have been noticeable, however, that the permanent secretary in the Ministry of the Interior and the Vienna Home Guard leader, Emil Fey, struck a radical tone by elevating the Home Guard to the rank of auxiliary police, while the Tyrolean Protection League leader, Gustav Kuprian, was arrested after being accused of high treason.[155] When the Federal Council, which was still meeting, challenged several emergency decrees before the Constitutional Court and had good chances of winning their case, Dollfuß abruptly dissolved the Constitutional Court. Once again, the Social Democrats offered nothing but verbal resistance. For a brief period, the rumour circulated that the Christian Socials and Social Democrats would form a grand coalition, at which point the Home Guard threatened violence. Then it was claimed that the last commander of the Imperial and Royal Army, who had been stripped of his noble title, Count Aloys Schönburg-Hartenstein, could become a type of regent, but this was at best a rumour, and was vehemently rejected by all those who warned against a restoration of whatever personage. Clearly, there were no alternatives. However, there certainly were consequences.

On 18 May, the Rural League disbanded. Some of its members joined the NSDAP. Two days later, Dollfuß took the next step towards securing his position, merging the Christian Social Party with the Home Guard to form the Fatherland Front (Vaterländische Front, or VF). The Chancellor took over the reins of the new organisation as the 'front leader' *(Frontführer)*. Six days later, the Communist Party of Austria was dissolved. Its members were the first to be forced into illegality. Austria had caught up with Germany. There was no resistance.

However, in contrast to the Social Democrats, the National Socialists did not feel inhibited in their fight for power by the need to take democracy and legality into account. After entering three Austrian regional diets, in a development that was surprising for many, they were on their way to joining the National Council. Dollfuß had put a stop to this plan. Since the Berlin functionaries, and also Hitler, did not get directly involved, the party headquarters of the NSDAP in Munich went into action and persuaded Hitler to send Theo(dor) Habicht, who originally came from Wiesbaden in Germany, to Austria as regional inspector. Habicht had already held influence over the Austrian National Socialists since 1931. Now, he was to take them down a more radical path. Hitler agreed. In order to make the whole idea more palatable, the possibility was mooted of installing him in the German embassy in Vienna.[156] Austria refused to give him accreditation. Habicht, who had already arrived in Austria, was expelled on 17 August 1933. As a retorsion measure, the Austrian press attaché at the embassy in Berlin was declared persona non grata. Theo Habicht continued his activities from Munich. Immediately afterwards, the next escalation occurred. The National Socialists suggested to the Christian Socials that they form a coalition. The Rural League was to be ousted.[157] For Dollfuß, this was not an option. He decided to risk a confrontation – which then immediately followed.

While the party work of the NSDAP intensified, the Bavarian Minister of Justice Hans Frank was invited to Austria. During the parliamentary crisis of 8 March 1933, Frank had attracted attention after sending a greeting from Bavaria in a radio message 'to its suppressed ethnic comrades in Austria'. Minister Frank then had no qualms about disparaging Austria and the government. His appearances occurred simultaneously, of all things, with a major event organised by the Home Guard to celebrate the 250th anniversary of the Second Ottoman Siege of Vienna in 1683. When the Home Guard members marched away from Schönbrunn, they were heckled by Social Democrats and National Socialists. Frank was then urged to leave Austria as quickly as possible. He did so two days later, although not without first receiving declarations of sympathy by his supporters in a Salzburg café.

The factors that made this situation different in reality from the operetta-like Pfrimer putsch now had serious consequences. Almost immediately, the National Socialist terror began. While previously, this could be described as 'swastika daubing', now, the events that followed between March and May 1933 were an unequivocal expression of a profound disunion – and the reversal of how the situation had been perceived until then: since 1918, Austria had namely been the driving force behind a union with Germany. Now it was Germany. And these efforts were motivated not by any yearning, but by the unmistakeable, bare-knuckled thirst for power. During the course of the year, the National Socialist terror would be the cause of 20 deaths and dozens of injuries of varying degrees of severity.[158] The victims included innocent people and individuals who were not involved in any way, when an explosive device was set off in a train, a Jewish jeweller and a passer-by were killed in Vienna, or telephone booths exploded, creating the impression that the state was no longer able to protect its citizens, despite the presence of the police, the Gendarmerie, the Federal Army and the Home Guard auxiliary policemen. For the Federal Army, the consequences were particularly severe, since members of the army had already served around 150,000 hours as a political assistance force in 1932. In 1933, that figure doubled to 300,000 hours. The army was therefore no longer a power factor of foreign policy, but more than anything else an emergency response force at home.

The situation became even more confusing when the Nazi terror found no small number of sympathisers – and not only among those who hoped that National Socialism would offer a solution to their problems, but also among the Greater Germans and the Styrian Home Guard. The latter had already been using the swastika as its symbol for years.[159] Violence in politics was nothing new. But the spiral of violence continued to coil at a rapid pace. On 19 June 1933, the NSDAP was banned in Austria. Forcing the National Socialists into an illegal existence, however, did not lead to a sense of resignation among young people, in particular, or the unemployed. They had little to lose. In 1933, the number of unemployed reached 557,000.[160] The attacks continued. The prohibition of the party in Germany was seen as an affront, even as a kind of declaration of war. The government of the Reich responded by imposing the '1,000-mark barrier'. For journeys to Austria, regardless of their nature, German citizens were required to pay an exorbitant visa fee of 1,000 Reichsmarks – a severe blow to the Austrian tourism industry. And it had been tourism in particular that had mitigated the economic problems in the country, and which was viewed as a real source of hope. The 1,000-mark barrier was therefore a premeditated measure intended to damage the economic and political fabric. The number of German tourists declined from 749,000 in 1932 to less than a tenth of that figure.

The dispute now went far beyond a war of words. And the impact was certainly felt beyond the tourism industry, in commercial relations. 60 per cent of Austria's import and export transactions were now with Germany. Yet the blame for the debacle was sought not in Germany, but in Austria. The government was accused of failing, since it had not known how to prevent the measure.[161] Austrian National Socialists reported in Bavaria and were formed into an 'Austrian Legion'. The fact that as a result, they lost their Austrian citizenship and were expatriated was of little consequence to them. In the summer of 1933, the legion's camps already contained over 2,000 young people.

Dollfuß continued in his attempts to calm the situation. His tone remained authoritative. Demands for a boycott of German goods were made, with the threat of punishment for those who disobeyed.[162] In the international arena, before the League of Nations, confrontation was avoided. Austria was to continue to be regarded as a reliable partner. It's problem, however, was that it was weak and small, and was paid attention not for its own sake, but because of its geopolitical location. France and Germany intervened in Berlin and were promptly informed by the government of the Reich that this was a matter of concern for the governments in Berlin and Vienna alone.[163] Here, in July 1933, the Western powers were only able to summon the will to express formulations of a very vague nature, with reminders of the valid agreements. However, they began to look to Austria with increasing concern.

In the words of the British Ambassador in Vienna, Dollfuß was standing 'with his back against the wall'. He may wish to enter into a coalition with the Social Democrats, but that would lead to an uprising in the Home Guard. If he sought a path back to democracy, the unavoidable consequence would be that National Socialists would enter the National Council. Alfred Eduard Frauenfeld, the illegal regional leader of the illegal National Socialists, anticipated that his party would win 35 per cent of the vote in National Council elections. And at the drop of a hat, that share could be increased to over 50 per cent. This would make a legal takeover of power possible. If, however, Dollfuß were to postpone the elections for good reason, or even avoid them altogether, he risked a putsch.[164] The outlook was therefore gloomy.

Even more than his predecessor, Dollfuß therefore sought support from Italy. South Tyrol was to be no obstacle, and a relaxation on school lessons in the German language was welcomed by Austria as a real compromise. However, what counted was that Italy, in the pursuit of its power political goals, took Austria under its wing as a connecting link to Hungary. On several occasions, Dollfuß sought out Mussolini and was not in the least perturbed when in Riccione he found himself trudging across the sand next to a Duce in bathing trunks, dressed himself in shirt and tie, with his coat slung over his arm. One could certainly interpret this as 'small size charisma':[165] the Austrian Chancellor, governing in an authoritarian way while at the same time seeking help, and the 'great dictator'. What counted was the political and, if need be, military support to which Mussolini agreed. Mussolini also succeeded in stopping Germany from making propaganda flights over Austria and limiting itself to radio propaganda.[166] Mussolini was also unimpressed when Berlin described the Brenner border as unalterable. What weight did that have? Austria was still a sovereign state, the borders of which had been drawn by the victorious powers in 1919. No German assurances were required in order for the Brenner border to be observed. However, the fact that Italy also did not entirely understand Germany's objectives was reflected in the unequivocal manner in which Mussolini pointed out to Dollfuß that the Austrian Federal Army had 8,000 fewer soldiers than the 30,000 agreed in the peace accord. Military efforts would therefore certainly be appropriate. The Chancellor understood.

Nation versus Fatherland

Since Dollfuß had begun to steer an authoritarian course, he was coming closer not only to a type of European normality but was also increasingly conforming to the requirements of Fascist Italy. A key difference was that Dollfuß wished to reconstruct the state on Catholic foundations, more specifically, on the 'Rerum Novarum' papal encyclical of Pope Leo XIII. (1891) and the bull based on it by Pius XI's 'Quadragesimo anno' (1931). As well as Catholic social doctrine, he also incorporated a further element into his political work, namely Austrian history. This was already evident in March 1933. It was expressed in the commemoration of the Turkish siege in May and reached its present high point in a speech by Dollfuß on the Trabrennplatz in Vienna on 11 September 1933. Once again, the Turkish year of 1683 formed the historic backdrop for the Chancellor to announce his goals. The state was to be constructed on a professional basis, in other words, divided according to professional groups, without political parties and without a parliament being formed through democratic elections. The idea was not entirely new. It had already been proposed by Karl von Vogelsang at the end of the nineteenth century as a countermovement to capitalism and the workers' movement in order to protect several professional groups that were losing importance, particularly farmers and skilled craftsmen. During the 1920s, it had been propagated by the national economist and philosopher Othmar Spann, who taught at Vienna University, as a third path between democracy and Marxism. Spann used it as the ideological basis for the Styrian Home Guard in particular, and he set it down in his book *Der wahre Staat* (The True State). His ideas were transported and interpreted. Most frequently, the rejection of democratic parliamentarianism and the party state were selected for particular attention. What was left was 'the creation of true democracy through liberation from the party dictatorship', which was a contradiction in itself.[167] But there was so much that was contradictory.

Dollfuß considered reforming the constitution and invited philosophers and social reformers in particular to produce drafts for a new constitution. Johannes Messner,

August Maria Knoll, Friedrich Funder, Eugen Kogon and also Kurt Schuschnigg provided contributions. As a basic principle, it emerged that parity between employees and
employers, subsidiarity and self-administration of the 'corporate groups' should be anchored in the new constitution. Social Democrats also did not immediately close their
mind to a setup based on professional groups, and Otto Bauer wrote in the *Arbeiter-
Zeitung* that the Social Democrats could come to accept the idea of professional
self-administration, if it were built up from below.[168] For Dollfuß, this was clearly not
enough.[169] The term 'Austrofascism' began to do the rounds, although it was in reality
a combative word directed against the notion of the corporative state, and it was not
satisfactory. The president of the corporative state Federal Parliament, Rudolf Hoyos,
later claimed that 'the correct, compelling word for the specific type of Austrian fascism'
still had to be found.[170] Ernst Rüdiger Starhemberg put it more directly: 'Our agenda is
called Austrofascism'.[171] Quite evidently, the term was not seen as derogatory. The only
question was whether the word really hit the mark. (Would terms such as 'clericofas-
cism', 'government dictatorship', 'semi-fascism', 'imitation fascism', 'crisis dictatorship' or
combinations with 'repressive', 'totalitarian' or 'anti-modern' have been more fitting?)[172]

Dollfuß, however, also set an additional accent by replacing the widely used 'German'
with 'fatherland'. And 'Österreich' – Austria – began to be pronounced, as the Viennese
historian Alphons Lhotsky so succinctly put it, 'with three "Ös" at the beginning'. The
uniforms of the Federal Army, which in 1920 had been adjusted to the uniform of the
German Reichswehr, were now, in 1933, 're-Austrified', while the state coat-of-arms
was made to look like the double-headed eagle of the Monarchy, with some slight
alterations. Since the Renner national anthem, so denigrated by the Social Democrats,
had been discarded in 1929, a text composed by Ottokar Kernstock had been sung to
the old Haydn melody *Gott erhalte* (God Preserve). Systematic thought was given to
creating a national state consciousness with which the regional consciousness of the
individual provinces could be overlaid. All this testified to the 'yearning for a type
of "Reich"'.[173] However, before the state could be restructured, what remained of the
old, yet still existent, state system had to be removed. Austria was still a republic. The
constitution of 1920 was still valid in its amended form of 1929. There were still some
of the traditional parties, even if they had been forced into the background. Now one
event followed another. First, Dollfuß toppled the longstanding minister of defence,
who had briefly also been federal chancellor, Vaugoin, and pushed the Christian Socials
out of the government. The same occurred with the Rural League and its national party
chairman Franz Winkler. In addition to his actual tasks, the Federal Chancellor also
assumed responsibility for the interior, defence, security and agricultural ministries. A
further step towards a chancellor's dictatorship had been taken. Only the Home Guard
would not be brought into line so easily. It was not used to subordinating itself, and
continued to nurture its contacts, with Rome as well as with Munich and Berlin. This

was where the real test of power lay for Dollfuß – and it was a test he had no chance of passing. At the same time, however, he succeeded in giving Austria, which to some had seemed so ready to unite with Germany, clearer contours. Now, the goal was to set boundaries.

Dollfuß would have been happy to convince Hitler of his ideas. He made attempts to arrange discussions with Hitler and his regional inspector, Habicht, through various different channels, yet when Habicht was due to meet with Dollfuß, the plan was successfully torpedoed by Fey and Starhemberg. Habicht, who was already in the aeroplane from Munich and waiting to land at Vienna-Aspern, was forced to turn around, since Dollfuß had been obliged to 'disinvite' him, giving a new wave of explosions organised by Austrian National Socialists as the reason.[174] In this way, Dollfuß saw with his own eyes that he was far from having his own house in order. In January 1934, the Chancellor became aware of the fact that many contacts were being made without his knowledge, and that there were at least a dozen people who thought that their – and only their – connections to Berlin and Munich, to the government or party offices of the NSDAP, would be sufficient to solve all the forthcoming problems. The issues at stake were more or less the union with Germany, an end to the 1,000-mark barrier, an end to terrorist activities, which from the National Socialist side were simplistically and banally known as 'crashing Austria', and, not least, personal influence and personal conceitedness.

Dollfuß continued to seek a compromise – internally and externally. Yet success eluded him. The Chancellor was just as unable to break his ties to the Greater Germans, the Rural League and the National Socialists as he maintained loose connections to the Social Democrats. The latter certainly did not arise out of a heartfelt desire, and perhaps he drew the wrong conclusions from the behaviour of the Social Democrat leadership. Politically, the Social Democrats had become almost redundant outside of Vienna. With half a million unemployed, workers were only too aware of their precarious situation. To strike now meant risking your livelihood. A third of the party membership in Vienna left the Social Democrats. Now, the Protection League, which had once been so powerful and had ruled the streets, only made rare appearances. Yet it did still exist, and it still had weapons.

The Rebellion of the Oppressed

Since the closure of parliament and the prohibition of the Protection League had not triggered any direct violent reactions from the Social Democrats, a dual effect came into force. In the right-wing camp, the stream of newcomers to the Home Guard units increased, although it was evident that dubious types were accepted indiscriminately simply to make up the numbers.[175] On the left wing, however, a sense of helplessness became widespread. The failure to deploy the Protection League to save parliamentary democracy was regarded not as a humane and responsible act, but as a sign of weakness. It was seen as an admission that at the end of the day, the will was not there to do anything to preserve parliamentary democracy from being destroyed, as set out in the 'Linz Agenda', using force or an act of revolution if necessary. At first, attempts were made to explain the ensuing departure of Protection League members by claiming that the quicksand had moved on. In some cases, even targeted action could have been behind this development, as was reported from Bruck an der Mur, for example, where it was claimed that the Communists had joined the Home Guard en bloc in order to infiltrate it.[176] However, on the part of the Social Democrats, doubts were already openly expressed as to the political clout of the party leadership and its statements, since the discrepancy between words and action was all too evident. At the party conference of the Social Democrats in October 1933, attempts were therefore made to draw a recognisable 'red' line: if a new constitution were to be octroyed, if a new government commissioner were to be appointed in Vienna, if the Social Democratic Party were to be dissolved or if the free trade unions were to be brought into line, violent action would be taken.[177] A further decision of the extraordinary party conference deserved particular attention, however: the Social Democrats deleted the paragraphs in their agenda relating to a union with Germany. A union with National Socialist Germany, 'Hitler's house of correction', was out of the question.[178]

1934 began with a series of attacks by the National Socialists involving small cannon and explosive devices, drawing attention to this political group, which was pushing to gain power through increasingly violent methods. Quite clearly, the intensification of criminal law and the introduction of summary court martial proceedings in November 1933 had not had a sufficiently deterrent effect. However, it was not only domestic policy that began the year in sensational fashion; foreign policy, too, contributed to a sharp escalation of the crisis. On 18 January, the deputy secretary in the Italian Ministry of Finance and native of born Trieste, Fulvio Suvich, came to Vienna to remind Dollfuß that during the previous year, he had made promises to Mussolini in Riccione with regard to the alignment of Austrian politics with those of Italy. The political parties were to be abolished and constitutional reform implemented.[179] This by all means correlated with the aims of the Home Guard.

On 30 January, the Home Guard marched in Tyrol and forced the establishment of an advisory committee consisting of members of the pro-government defence units as an addition to the federal state government. This was designed to serve as a model for Austria, and to pave the way for replacing state governors with government commissioners.[180] However, as yet, there was no indication that an explosion was forthcoming. Then, the police began to search for weapons with increasing frequency.[181] The government and the Home Guard pulled no punches. The Linz Protection League leader, Richard Bernaschek, reacted by informing the Vienna party headquarters that if weapons searches were to be conducted in Linz, he would give the order to shoot.[182]

From 1929, the Protection League leadership had specific plans for armed conflict in Vienna. A key role in creating such a concept was played by the retired general Theodor Körner and the later chief of staff of the Protection League, Alexander Eifler.[183] Soon afterwards, Körner withdrew from the Protection League. He was no supporter of the use of paramilitary formations against the regular military. As a former chief of staff of the Isonzo Army, he knew what he was talking about. However, Eifler was of a different opinion. He was in favour of a concept that had been published under the pen name A. Neuberg, *Der bewaffnete Aufstand* (The Armed Uprising), in which the German Hans Kippenberger, the Soviet general Mikhail N. Tukhachevsky and the Vietnamese revolutionary Hồ Chi Minh had recorded their ideas. According to the book: 'Armed uprising is the highest form of the political battle of the proletariat.'[184] And Eifler drafted a plan for an uprising in Vienna, according to which after a general strike had been called, police officials, judges and high state functionaries were to be seized and kept as hostages. Then, the Protection League forces were to be consolidated. According to the plan, during the final phase, the Republican Protection League was to advance from the Wiedner Gürtel section of the Vienna Beltway towards the inner city. However, should the initial phases of this plan fail, Eifler decided that the Protection League should withdraw from the inner areas of Vienna towards the Laaer Hill and the Simmering district, from where a decisive attack was to be made against the city area. Körner took the following view in 1931: the plan of action for Vienna 'must contain some dreadful elements, if there is a plan for Vienna at all, and the hair-raising nonsense of clearing the inner districts, occupying and consolidating a cordon does not still apply'.[185]

On the morning of 12 February, the news from Linz came as a surprise. In the camp of the Social Democratic Party in the 'Schiff' hotel, a search for weapons was conducted, and Richard Bernaschek had put his threat of ordering to shoot into practice. He did what was to be expected: he hit out and in so doing, delivered a perfect reason for resolving the issue of who held power in the state once and for all. In Vienna, Otto Bauer and Julius Deutsch chose to attack as the best means of survival and attempted to take control of events by doing something that they had originally not at all intended, namely by forming a central battle command.[186] The most highly qualified leader, Alexander Eifler, had been arrested on 3 February. Towards midday of 12 February, large parts of Vienna were without power. This was designed to signal the fact that a general strike had been called. However, since power failures were not an uncommon event, the response was one of uncertainty. The Protection League and the executive made preparations to use force.

Initially, martial law was imposed. At the meeting of the Council of Ministers held that afternoon, the decision was made to dissolve the Social Democratic Party, to appoint a government commissioner for Vienna, to dissolve the trade union and to seize Social Democrat assets. Three of the four scenarios had therefore become reality, each individual one of which – according to the October resolutions of 1933 – was to be evaluated as a signal to take action. Now, however, they did not even lead to an escalation of the situation. During the early afternoon, the police began a systematic search of the Social Democrat districts. If they were met with resistance, or if there was shooting, they sent a request for assistance, which was usually met by the Federal Army with reserve units. Then, after resistance had been broken, the task of securing and searching the area again became the responsibility of the executive, or the defence units of the right-wing camp.

The armed uprising of the Protection League did not begin in an abrupt fashion. It flickered up here and there and then died down before flickering up again. If the resistance grew tougher and there were casualties on the side of the executive, artillery was brought in. The shooting was not always preceded by a warning, although warnings were given in most cases. It also occurred that a battalion commander asked the governor of a city district whether artillery should be used, and the governor expressly forbade it.[187] However, when artillery was used, the effect was precisely what the state authority had hoped it would be. However, in most cases it was not only the destruction and the casualties that resulted from the shooting that led to an immediate cessation in the gunfire, but also and above all its moral implications, which can still be felt today, and which are summarised by the words: the Federal Army used cannons to shoot at workers, women and children. And this moral impact that manifested itself in the fighting as a very direct sense of powerlessness, since the Protection League fighters saw that the rules of fair play had somehow been violated, explains a part of the bitterness towards the Federal Army that was clearly felt among the Social Democrats for a long period of time, and which occasionally also coloured their attitude in the Second Republic. In many cases, the municipal buildings had already taken on the characteristics of fortresses during the 1920s. We now know that there was a whole series of reasons for doing so when designing these buildings, among which a potential military function was likely to have been the least important.[188] One thing had certainly not been the intention: that a member of the Protection League might shoot out of the toilet window of his own apartment! During the fighting, however, it was no doubt the case that people used their own homes as a final place of refuge.

The individuals who conducted this fight for self-assertion fluctuated, fighting here, disappearing overnight or through the sewers, only to emerge later in other districts to continue the fight there. Here, resistance was very often not supported by the residents, since they would hardly have expected their apartments to be turned into fortresses. The deceptive protection offered by the large municipal residential complexes induced people to see them as something other than what they were: a place where many people lived, and in the case of the Karl-Marx-Hof complex, home to hundreds of families. Attempts to mobilise all members of the Protection League were far from successful. In Brigittenau, they simply refused outright.[189]

On 12 and 13 February, fighting took place on an even larger scale. It was during the fight for the Goethe-Hof residential complex in the Kagran district of Vienna that the only aerial attack occurred during the February Uprising. It was conducted by the air squadron of the Home Guard under the former field pilot of the Imperial and Royal Army and 'flying ace' Godwin Brumowski. On 15 and 16 February, the only thing left in effect for the Federal Army and the executive to do was to comb through the Karl-Marx-Hof and the Floridsdorf, Kagran and Stadlau districts, make arrests and seize weapons. The Karl-Marx-Hof was renamed 'Biedermann Hof' in honour of the commander of the Home Guard company that took part in the storming of the building. On the evening of the 16th, all Federal Army units had returned to their barracks. The armed uprising was at an end. Of course, the fight had been an unequal one.

The armed uprising had spread in several federal states, too, particularly in Styria and Upper Austria. In the industrial regions of what was known as the 'Mur-Mürzfurche', the valley formed by the Mur and Mürz rivers, fighting occurred in Bruck an der Mur, Leoben, Fohnsdorf and Knittelfeld, as well as in Graz, Weiz and Voitsberg. Linz, Steyr, Attnang, Wolfsegg and Ebensee were also impacted by the uprising. The fighting in Bruck an der Mur, which was well and truly conquered by Koloman Wallisch before the Federal Army overcame the resistance, was particularly severe. There was fighting in the Lower Austrian industrial areas, and also shooting in Hallein in the Salzburg region and in Wörgl in Tyrol. However, while small fires flared, there was no large-scale conflagration. The fighting always ended in the same way, with people dead and wounded, arrests and the imposition of martial law.

According to the official figures, the number of dead on the side of the executive and the Federal Army amounted to 118, with 196 on the 'other side'. However, it is likely that the latter suffered far heavier losses. There were mass arrests. 140 members of the Protection League were placed before a summary court martial; 20 death sentences were pronounced, of which nine were carried out.[190] Many hundreds of people fled. It was therefore not the fighting in itself – that had been a risk – but also the persecution measures conducted by the government that left indelible traces. The consequences of the uprising were therefore just as numerous and divergent as its roots. They made themselves felt in the domestic arena, and ranged from executions, prison sentences and periods in detention camps to the creation of new, now illegal party organisations and a not inconsiderable shift in political conditions.

Perhaps of more far-reaching impact were the reactions from outside Austria, however. In Italy, the aforementioned Deputy Secretary Fulvio Suvich announced that he had no doubt that the fighting in Vienna had been sparked by the Communists.[191] Dollfuß had been confronted by what he termed a 'Red Army'. Romania followed with concern the events in Austria and 'the fermentation in the Danube region that seeks to find a form'.[192] Yugoslavia kept Italy in its sights, which had recently been informed that if Italian troops marched into Austria, an invasion of Yugoslavian troops would also immediately follow.[193] Hungarian army and government circles praised the success of the Dollfuß government in bringing down the 'Marxist agitators'.

Czech newspapers reported that a German division had been standing ready near Passau, and that Hungary was concentrating its military on the border to Burgenland. Finally, on 15 February, the British consul general in Munich, Donald St. Clair Gainer, reported to the British ambassador in Berlin, Sir Eric Phipps, that he had received information in Munich that if the Social Democrat putsch had succeeded, the National Socialists planned to cross the Austrian border to help the Dollfuß government, in order to then obtain government positions in return.[195] In Berlin, Hitler told the French ambassador that Dollfuß had made a stupid criminal error by shooting at socialist workers, women and children. Now, he said, he had blood on his hands; he would soon fall and be replaced by a Nazi government. Evidently, everyone had something to say about it.

At the same time, Dollfuß was able to notch up a foreign policy success on 17 February, since Italy, England and France issued a declaration of guarantee of Austrian independence and integrity 'according to the valid agreements'.[196] However, this did not provide for freedom of action with regard to foreign policy. And the domestic policy barometer continued to point to a storm.

8 Corporative State without Corporations

8 Two boys of the Austrian Youth being sworn in. In August 1936, the youth organisations of the Austrian Home Guard and the Eastern March Stormtroopers, which were loyal to the regime, were consolidated in the Austrian Youth. All boys and male adolescents aged six to 18 were supposed to become members. In this way, an organisation emerged similar to the Hitler Youth in National Socialist Germany. The Law on the Patriotic Education of Youth from 29 August 1936 did the rest in compelling all youth organisations to join. In 1937, the Catholic youth organisations were also incorporated. The following year, the Austrian Youth counted 350,000 members. (Photo: Hanisch, *Männlichkeiten*)

T he Austrian Social Democrats had been defeated, the party dissolved and their assets confiscated. Prominent members had fled abroad, others had been taken to prison or detention camps and those who had been identified as ringleaders had been sentenced to death. A government commissioner had been appointed in Vienna. The free trade unions, which had been dominated hitherto by the Social Democrats, were on the verge of dissolution. It appeared to be the end of this party of the masses. Dollfuß regarded himself as the victor. As in March 1933, he had exploited the situation to eliminate an opponent. He had acted in the way he had promised Mussolini he would in Riccione in 1933. Now, however, no more small steps were required. If he wanted to ensure the continued support of Italy, he would have to eradicate the remains of democracy, dissolve all political parties and implement constitutional reform. Austria should become an authoritarian state. Fulvio Suvich had demanded it. And, naturally, he had praised the Italian model of an authoritarian state, in which society should be represented by associations rather than classes.[197] From mid-February, Austria also appeared to be well on the way to becoming this. Rome did not conceal its approval during the removal of the Social Democrats, and only a month later the Rome Protocols were signed, which envisaged Italy's close cooperation with Hungary and Austria, especially in economic matters. In Berlin, news of the agreement came 'like a bombshell'.[198]

For Dollfuß, it was time to take the next step. It was a question of a new constitution. Social Democrats and National Socialists were not to be considered, but by all means the various Home Guard (Heimwehr) organisations and other still extant, pro-government defensive formations. It was intended that they be incorporated into the 'Fatherland Front' (Vaterländische Front), which was brought into being on 20 May 1933, and they engaged in fierce battles for position.[199] Likewise, the Christian Social Party need not be considered any more. Since autumn 1933, it had been clear that its days were numbered. On 6 December 1933, its strongest pillar of support fell away, when the Catholic Bishops' Conference announced the withdrawal of all priests from their political functions.[200] Previously, Catholic priests had held three seats in the National Assembly, three in the Federal Council (Bundesrat), as well as a series of positions in regional politics.[201] Meanwhile, the primary objective of the Catholic Church, the Concordat, had been achieved. The Christian Socials were no longer needed.

The 'May Constitution'

The completion of the constitution was repeatedly delayed. The 1st of May was finally fixed as the day on which the corporative constitution was to come into effect with the help of a regulation issued by the federal government. For Dollfuß, it was a sort of personal triumph. He had previously regarded the signing of the Concordat with the Holy See as the highpoint of his political career. The new constitution now built on this state treaty and on the papal encyclicals, which had already constituted the foundation of his political actions since March 1933, and the introduction therefore stated: 'In the name of God, the Almighty, from Whom all law emanates, the Austrian people receive this constitution for their Christian, German, federal state … .' From the outset, there were discussions regarding the legality of the realisation of the new constitution, for it could only be adopted with the aid of the Wartime Economic Enabling Act, whose application fifteen years after the war must be regarded as a legal trick and master stroke on the part of Dr Robert Hecht, one of Austria's leading lawyers. Having said that, the Social Democrats had already expressly confirmed the validity of the Enabling Act in 1929. Shortly after midnight on 1 May, the Federal President signed the Concordat, which had already waited a year for his signature.[202] At lunchtime, the Austrian National Council – or rather that which still existed as a rump parliament – convened once more and adopted the Law on the Field of Application of the Wartime Economic Enabling Act. Out of 76 delegates, 74 voted in favour of a new 'federal constitution law on exceptional measures in the area of the constitution'. In the afternoon, the Federal Council – which now also met without Social Democrats – likewise approved the law. Noting that from this day another constitution was in any case valid, and that legal continuity had been maintained in every respect, the Federal Council then ended its activities, and its chairman, Franz Hemala, who had administered his office for a single day, concluded with words that were to be frequently used in similar expressions on 1 May:

> 'Today, we carry the Austria of 12 November 1918 to its grave. Long live the new Austria, the free, Christian and socially equitable, German Austria of the future.' This was followed by 'lively applause and calls of *Heil*'.

Even apologists of the Corporative State (Ständestaat), who fundamentally advocated a bond between German nationalism and Catholicism, were ultimately unable to decide 'whether the teachings of the Corporative State were a universal profession of faith or intended exclusively for Catholic Germans'.[203] Federal President Miklas had signed the constitution, and because he held office by virtue of a democratic election in the Austrian Federal Assembly, one ultimately had to assume in his case that he was acting legitimately. And it certainly did not fit the facts to claim that what followed was a 'pseudo mediaeval construction'.[204] Neo-romanticism was more fitting here. The key point of the May Constitution was an authoritarian government. Power was shifted from parliament to government.

The federal president, whose term in office was extended to seven years, and above all the federal chancellor received considerably expanded authority. Four bodies were to consult in advance on legislation and constituted a type of mock parliament: the Council of State, the Federal Council for Culture, the Federal Council for Economics and the Council for the Provinces. They sent representatives to the Federal Parliament, which was organised on the basis of professions – or, rather: they *should* have sent representatives to the Federal Parliament. The establishment of the professional bodies remained, namely, in its infancy. Nonetheless, the May Constitution was valid from the first day onwards. In many places, patriotic demonstrations were held, with the largest march of the corporations taking place in front of Vienna's town hall. The painter Ludwig Koch recorded the scene in a painting. As it had been commissioned, he painted at the centre of a group of people, who comprised representatives of the seven estates, the leader of Vienna's Heinwehr, Emil Frey, on horseback and dominating events. In actual fact, Fey was in Graz at the time. And, furthermore, he was replaced as chancellor on the very same day by his rival Ernst Rüdiger Starhemberg. The new constitution had evidently not brought an end to quarrelling within the government camp.

The Murder of the Chancellor

Many things still awaited more clarification and moulding. But some things could no longer be ignored. The Federal State of Austria, as it was officially known from May 1934, had transformed into an authoritarian state. If Dollfuß had gone as far in his claim to power as Hitler had done in Germany, the term 'dictatorship of the chancellor' would have been applicable. But Dollfuß was a long way from securing the type of position that would have brought him dictatorial powers. The organised left had admittedly been destroyed; the conflicts over ideology and future developments took place among the right-wingers. Dollfuß also had to keep in mind that, in Miklas, he had a head of state at his side – indeed, in the same building on Ballhausplatz – who was committed to the old regime. This was a federal president who may have been compliant enough in 1933 to facilitate the suppression of parliament, but whose repeated objections caused the Chancellor discomfort. There had been deliberations on whether or not to end Miklas' term of office prematurely, but then the view had prevailed that he should be allowed to serve out his time until 1936. Only then would the mayors be called upon to elect a new head of state. This did not happen. Miklas had not been willing to demonstrate solidarity with the Heinwehr, and it had also not been forgotten that it was Wilhelm Miklas who had objected to the wording 'German-Austria is part of the German-Republic' during the vote on the Republic's first constitution. Dollfuß, too, was surely aware of this and it led him to fashion a tighter alliance.

He did not need to expect any resistance on the part of the Federal President, though he had to admit to himself that he could not rely on the armed formations swallowed up by the Fatherland Front, in spite of all his efforts. Starhemberg and Fey continued to play a role here. Dollfuß was admittedly the federal leader of the Fatherland Front, but Starhemberg was his deputy. And Emil Fey was still powerful, even if he was no longer vice chancellor. The Chancellor also lacked any means of enforcing his claim to power vis-à-vis the National Socialists and had to stand by pretty much helplessly and watch how the National Socialist terror increased again from February 1934. This underlined the difference between the 'Führer' Adolf Hitler and the 'Federal Leader' Engelbert Dollfuß. Dollfuß was and remained dependent, and Austria had to endure the terror and simultaneously exude affability.

The authoritarian regime proceeded with small steps to alter the political structures and establish the Corporative State. In the process, anti-capitalist tendencies also came into play. The most enduring changes were of a socio-political nature. As early as January 1934, a decree issued by the Federal Ministry of Education demanded that all teachers join the Fatherland Front. Other professions followed. Once the Concordat and the May Constitution came into effect, marriage laws were refashioned. From here on in, church marriage was the only legal form. The detention camp of Wöllersdorf near Wiener Neustadt, which was created in September 1933, was filled many times over.[205] After February 1934, the detainees had been primarily Social Democrats; now the National Socialists again predominated. Kaisersteinbruch Camp, which in early April 1934 already held 629 prisoners – predominantly illegal National Socialists, such as the Viennese lawyer Ernst Kaltenbrunner – was also added to Wöllersdorf. The prisoners were transferred to Wöllersdorf at the end of April.

The NSDAP grew and grew. Since Hitler's assumption of power, the number of party members in Austria had doubled and counted around 90,000 in July 1934.[206] Terror was openly called for, and suicide attacks were also recommended with unspeakable frivolity. If someone wanted to kill another person, he could 'die a hero's death and always take with him a few of those guilty for their misery'.[207] If necessary, the frequently invoked Germanness was no longer valid. Maribor (Marburg) and Ljubljana (Laibach) became strongholds of the Austrian National Socialists, from where they unfolded their anti-Austrian activities. Slovenia was unashamedly offered to cede to Yugoslavia the formerly disputed territory in southern Carinthia in the event of a union with Germany.[208] Most of those who were arrested on suspicion of having carried out attacks were released against a pledge – but they failed to keep their promises. The government increased the economic pressure and strove to bring non-conformists to their knees by rounding up hostages, where necessary. Finally, the executioners also took action and carried out death sentences. This had been threatened following an attempt to shoot Dollfuß on 11 November 1933, in the event that martial law was imposed. The death penalty was handed down for murder, arson and malicious criminal damage. It was applied from February 1934. On 1 July 1934, the death penalty was also enforced in ordinary proceedings for the aforementioned crimes as well as manslaughter and offences involving explosives. The Chancellor was reacting here to the increasing number of explosives attacks. Possession of explosives was also a capital offence. On 24 July, Josef Julius Gerl was executed in Vienna's regional court; he was not a National Socialist but rather a Social Democrat who had carried out an explosives attack on Vienna's Danube Riverbank Railway.[209] The next day, on 25 July, the terror reached a new and final peak. Around midday, 154 members of the SS dressed in Federal Army uniforms left Vienna's Monastery Barracks in Federal Army trucks and arrived at Ballhausplatz in time for the change of the guard of honour in front of the Federal Chancellery.[210]

The operation had been considered for months and planned for weeks. Hitler had been informed and had agreed, though he initially only pursued the aim of appointing a chancellor in Austria who was friendly towards the German regime and of involving the National Socialists in government. This approach corresponded to what Hitler and Mussolini had discussed at a meeting on 14 June 1934 in Villa Pisani in Stra. Hitler had at least understood that Italy would not stand in the way of a change of chancellor and regime in Austria.[211] The prehistory of the events of 25 July was not only accompanied by high politics, however, but also by a whole host of personal vanities, intrigues, whistleblowing, spies, informants, treason and – time and again – coincidences. The putsch had been planned for the 24th, as the final session of the Council of Ministers before the summer break was due to take place. The day before, the leaders of the conspiracy, the Bavarian Rudolf Weydenhammer, the Viennese lawyer Otto Gustav Wächter, who now led the illegal NSDAP in Austria, and the former sergeant in the Federal Army Fridolin Glass, who was supposed to carry out the operation, met. Aside from these three, a whole host of others were more or less well informed. The German envoy, Kurt Rieth, was also aware of what was planned.[212] The same applied, naturally, to Anton Rintelen, former governor of Styria and twice federal minister, now Austrian envoy to the Vatican, who was slated to replaced Dollfuß. He had volunteered his services.

As is so often the case, however, chance reached historic proportions. Clausewitz called it friction, when the most sophisticated plans are undone by something unforeseen. When the operation was supposed to start with troops detaining Federal President Miklas in Velden am Wörthersee, while the rebels went into action in Vienna, Rintelen learned that the scheduled session of the Council of Ministers had been postponed until the following day. The rebels, for the most part members of the illegal SS Regiment 89, did not leave the Monastery Barracks until midday on 25 July. They were seen. Reports abounded in Vienna that something was in the pipeline and plans were being made to storm the Chancellery. In some cases, the calls reached the wrong people, arrived too late or were not given sufficient attention. Instead of the gates of the Chancellery being closed, they remained open, and it did not seem to bother anyone that eight (or more) trucks with soldiers, police officers and civilians attempted to drive up to the Chancellery. The rebels stormed the building, searched it and discovered that they had come too late. Dollfuß, who had feared an attack on the basis of the rumours that had also reached him, had aborted the session of the Council of Ministers after quarter of an hour; most of the ministers had already left the Chancellery. The Federal Chancellor, Emil Fey, who had been degraded to 'General Commissioner for Emergency Security Measures for Combating Subversive Endeavours in Private Industry', Permanent Secretary for Security Carl Karwinsky and several attendants had remained in the building. Shots and cries alarmed the Chancellor. He attempted to escape via an emergency exit to the State Archives, which were connected to the Chancellery. A porter attempted to unlock the door but he was not quick enough. Ten men armed with pistols attacked the Chancellor. Two shots were fired, the first from close range. And it was fatal.

The killing of the Federal Chancellor might not have been the intention of the rebels; they wanted to arrest him. But they did not shy away from wounding or even killing him. Over the radio, the rebels announced the toppling of the government and the appointment of Anton Rintelen as federal chancellor. It was premature. A second squad of troops had driven to the broadcasting building on Johannesgasse in Vienna's 1st District and ensured that the report of the assumption of the chancellor's office by Rintelen was swiftly circulated. The report was read out twice in quick successions. Then a shot by a policeman destroyed the transmitting tube.

In the meantime, the Chancellor succumbed to a slow death. He was refused medical help. His request for a priest was ignored. Dollfuß died. Negotiations regarding the withdrawal of the rebels were conducted but ended with their arrest. And because there had been a death in the Chancellery, all promises for an unhindered withdrawal became null and void. In martial law proceedings, thirteen men who were identified as leaders or who admitted, like Otto Planetta, to having fired the shots at the Chancellor, were sentenced to death and executed.[213]

Outside the capital, the SA wanted to contribute to the political coup, so that the SS did not get all the 'glory'. The brief radio announcement had sufficed to sound the alarm. It was clear what had to be done. Swastika flags were hoisted. On posters, not only was the assumption of power announced but also an example for self-deception or sheer disinformation was provided, for the talk was of an Austria that should be independent on all sides. To this end, a popular referendum was to take place. There was no talk of a union with Germany.[214]

In the days that followed the putsch attempt in Vienna, fighting took place in several federal states, the reasons for which are still unclear. Did the SA still want to steer the ship around? In June, the leader of the Austrian SA, Hermann Reschny, had arranged the preparation of plans for the murder of Dollfuß and now saw himself forced into the background by the SS.[215] Was the intention of the armed uprising to demonstrate to the SS that the SA could successful carry out a coup? Were regional SA leaders making themselves independent? In Lamprechtshausen in the province of Salzburg, during the night of 27/28 July, after martial law had once more been imposed, a wild shoot-up took place with eight dead.[216] Fighting flared up in the Pyrenees, in the Enns Valley and likewise, for a short time, in Carinthia, where an attempt to arrest Federal President Miklas had failed. Some National Socialist squads were able to make it to Yugoslavia and were ultimately redirected to Bavaria, where they strengthened the Austrian Legion (Österreichische Legion). The latter had prepared itself to march into Austria. Some legionnaires did indeed cross the border to the Mühlviertel and, after a few attacks and one shoot-up near Kollerschlag, were swiftly ordered to return. An international incident could not be risked and a war of sorts unleashed.

The rebels must have reckoned least with the Federal Army giving no indication of potentially wanting to join the rebels. The fact that a considerable number of army members were illegal National Socialists did nothing to change this. Wherever executive forces were deployed, they proceeded ruthlessly against National Socialist troops. The fact that not everything had gone smoothly and that the police was also teeming with Nazi sympathisers could only be discerned when around 200 police officials were later investigated, the head of the criminal investigation department in the Viennese Federal Police Headquarters, Otto Steinhäusl,[217] once highly decorated for his role in solving the spy case involving Colonel Redl, was discharged and other senior police officials were arrested. Emergency detention areas were set up in schools and dance halls, to which a steady flow of thousands were brought in who had taken part in the uprising of the National Socialists or were under suspicion of having done so. In mid-August, around 2,000 prisoners were counted in Klagenfurt, 1,300 in Upper Austria and 1,200 in Styria. By means of special judicial measures, six military tribunals were set up. For a period of time, the federal government – which met briefly under the direction of Starhemberg and then under that of Minister of Justice Kurt Schuschnigg – considered exercising leniency. But then the view prevailed that severity had to be exercised. Assets were confiscated and forced labour was imposed. The detention camps counted 13,388 political prisoners as of 23 September; approximately one third of them had been involved in the attempted uprising.[218]

Depending on political views and sentiments, the murder of the Chancellor was a cause for sorrow, celebration or indifference. Reference was soon being made to the 'heroic chancellor'. It was not difficult to assign him the role of martyr. He had 'died for

Austria'. Crowds flocked to the funeral rally on Vienna's Rathausplatz. The farewell to the Chancellor and the funeral cortege through the city brought hundreds of thousands on to the streets. Outside of the elites of politics and diplomacy, it was perhaps surprising that it was Karl Kraus, of all people, who made reference in the *Fackel* to those who dared 'to vilify him [Dollfuß] even in death'.[219]

And Hitler? He had been informed about events in Vienna during a performance of Wagner's *The Rhine Gold* in Bayreuth. In view of the failed uprising, it was merely a question of damage limitation. This was all the more the case because Mussolini reacted very differently to how Hitler had expected. The 'Duce', who had the task on the evening of 25 July of informing Alwine Dollfuß, who was holidaying in Riccione at his invitation, of the death of her husband, redirected two Italian divisions that were participating in manoeuvres in South Tyrol to the border with Carinthia and Tyrol. He moreover made no secret of his disgust about what had happened. Hitler could not rule out the possibility that France and Italy might agree to undertake a joint operation, should the Austrian Legion march into Austria and provoke a military escalation. He was deeply indignant about Mussolini's attitude. Propaganda Minister Goebbels noted that Hitler had inwardly broken with Italy: 'It's over with Italy. The old infidelity.'[220] But Hitler acted quickly. The German envoy to Vienna, Kurt Rieth, was recalled in the night of 25/26 July. German involvement in events was, of course, denied. The Austrian Legion had to surrender its weapons to the Reichswehr. All documents that were in any way incriminating had to be destroyed on Hitler's orders. Indeed, only statements, trial records and memoirs survived. A dead chancellor remained; his murder did not provoke any domestic crisis but instead triggered the next political shift and a change in protagonists.

A Better Germany?

As is so often the case after such an event, questions began to be asked about what had happened and its background: who had known about the plans for a putsch? Was Planetta the only one to have shot at the Chancellor? What part had been played by Anton Rintelen, who sat in a Vienna café and waited to move into Kaunitz Palace on Ballhausplatz as the new chancellor? Why did the uprising in Lamprechtshausen not begin until the evening of 27 July, when everything was actually already over? And, repeatedly: who within the Nazi leadership had known about the preparations and what consequences should this all have had? As the uprising had been suppressed, or rather done the job itself, and Germany showed no signs of supporting the revolt, the consequences of 25 July 1934 for foreign policy had been negligible. After he had received the news of the death of the Federal Chancellor, the Federal President had entrusted Kurt Schuschnigg with the conduct of official duties. Schuschnigg, who had been a member of the Cabinet as minister of justice since 1932 and had additionally been appointed minister of education in 1933, could demonstrate continuity. More importantly, however: he was 'Reich leader' of the Eastern March Stormtroopers (Ostmärkische Sturmscharen), i.e. not a functionary of the Home Guard (Heimwehr), and therefore neither in Starhemberg's 'camp' nor in Fey's. It complicated matters, however, that Starhemberg remained vice chancellor and also became federal leader of the Fatherland Front; Schuschnigg was appointed his deputy. Thus, the two were alternately subordinated to each other. But the picture of two consuls who mutually imposed on one another was deceptive. It was Schuschnigg who determined policy.

In the west, among the British and French, the hope predominated that he would continue the course set by Dollfuß, for which sympathy had increased bit by bit because it had proved to be a buffer against National Socialist Germany. Schuschnigg could count on support from Italy, because he promised to retain the course towards Italy set by his predecessors, above all Dollfuß. For the major as well as the minor European powers alike, however, Austria was in any case a matter for Germany, indeed – as Hitler saw it – an 'internal matter'. Thus, Hitler doubtless counted more than Dollfuß and, especially, Schuschnigg. The latter had to fight with a whole host of handicaps: he lacked the winning way of the murdered chancellor, who had been willing to overlook some things. Schuschnigg was stiff, and this led increasingly to his isolation. In his encounters with foreign statesmen, he placed an emphasis on being polite and proper, but lacked all warmth. Schuschnigg was a legitimist and enforced his rule only out of political necessity, not out of any conviction for the Habsburg laws of 1919. This ensured him the deep mistrust of the successor states. In domestic politics, he was also unable to count on any particular sympathy. The Social Democrats had not forgotten that he had reintroduced the death penalty in December 1933. And he confirmed the verdicts. Minister of Justice Schuschnigg had enforced nine of 20 death sentences in February 1934, including the judgement against the seriously wounded Karl Münichreiter. For the Social Democrats, therefore, he was no less stigmatised than Engelbert Dollfuß. The Austrian National Socialists regarded him as an enemy, because he also did not hesitate in their case to punish with death those who had committed serious crimes, above all murder. After the murder of the Chancellor and the fighting during the aftermath of the July putsch, Schuschnigg had seen no reason to exercise leniency.

From the outset, therefore, the new chancellor was not a popular figure. Schuschnigg gradually became aware of Austria's foreign policy situation. In August 1934, during his first official visit to Rome, he had to acknowledge that Dollfuß had not only concluded economic agreements with Mussolini and agreed to a close collaboration of Austria with Italy and Hungary by signing the Rome Protocols, but also made considerable military promises to Italy that were more than problematic, for example the right of passage through Austria for Italian troops in the event of a war with Yugoslavia. Italy was also permitted, however, to transfer troops to the north via Austria in case Italy had to provide military support to Austria against Germany. In this context, the further construction of the half-finished Grossglockner High Alpine Road gained additional importance, because it created not only jobs but also a strategic route.[221] The regime pumped fourteen per cent of its entire road construction budget into the Glockner Road. More than 3,000 labourers participated in its construction. Thus, everything seemed to be clear with Italy. In January 1935, the British and French issued a strong statement on the maintenance of Austrian independence and agreed a few weeks later to consult each other in the event of a threat to Austrian integrity.[222] In April 1935, the British and French once more announced in the concluding resolution of a conference in Stresa that they were determined to guarantee the preservation of Austrian independence.[223] National Socialist Germany appeared unimpressed. Schuschnigg solicited the League of Nations in Geneva for guarantees of Austrian independence. He did not get them. The term that now did the rounds and also flowed into a Franco-Italian agreement was 'non-intervention pact'.[224] However, Yugoslavia and Czechoslovakia but also Hungary and Germany were against contractually conceded non-intervention. It could be concluded from this that they either wanted to intervene or at least left this option open. Thus, there was a lot of talking about this but nothing was agreed in writing. The union between Austria and Germany was still prohibited, but it was not in the interest of the European states to safeguard Austria's independence by, if necessary, military guarantees. Austria itself should make sure that it remained separated from Germany. Mussolini urged Austria to accelerate its arms build-up. This would provide the country not only with more security but also the opportunity to work together with Germany and be involved in the German attack on Czechoslovakia expected by Mussolini.[225] Mussolini also informed Schuschnigg that, internationally speaking, the military potential of a state was not measured in brigades but in divisions. Austria should, therefore, make the transition from eight small brigades to the larger divisions. Schuschnigg did as Mussolini advised. And Italy once more promoted an Austrian arms build-up by delivering armaments but above all by assuming around two-thirds of the costs.

Having an adequate army with reasonably modern weaponry admittedly required the abolition of numerous military terms in the Treaty of Saint-Germain. This faced resistance from the Little Entente, whose partners feared that Hungary would then also want to draw level. The trigger ultimately came from the outside: Hitler declared that he no longer intended to adhere to the armaments restrictions imposed by the Treaty of Versailles. The previously secret arms build-up was now pursued openly. In March 1936, Hitler arranged for the German Wehrmacht to occupy the demilitarised Rhineland. France tolerated it. On 1 April 1936, Schuschnigg announced the nationwide introduction of compulsory military service. Male Austrian citizens aged between

18 and 42 were now to be called up for military or non-military service. According to the legislation, it was the natural duty of federal citizens to perform one year of public service in return for what the state delivered 'if the general public has need of these services'.[226] Once again, several states of the Little Entente objected to this measure and protested 'energetically' in Vienna. The major powers, however, tolerated this step, which was regarded as unavoidable and completely in accordance with the concept of non-intervention. It evidently depended on how one looked at it. Adolf Hitler ignored the Treaty of Versailles and exuded confidence, whereas Austria was time and again admonished to adhere to the provisions of Saint-Germain.

Despite or precisely because of the rivalries, Germany became a role model for Austria. Germany had evidently found a remedy for unemployment; the country prospered. Austria, by contrast, only gradually retreated from the maximum number of 560,000 unemployed. By all accounts, law and order prevailed in Germany, there were clear political and social structures, whereas the Corporative State continued to be torn apart by separatist interests and disparate groups. Admittedly, it was the NSDAP that was responsible first and foremost for this, but this did not prevent Hitler and his party from acquiring ever more supporters. And Austria was on the verge of squandering sympathy abroad.

Schuschnigg was able to score points in only one respect: he extolled Austria as 'the better Germany' and offered refuge to those who fled National Socialist Germany for political and, above all, racial reasons. It was the shortest route to entering a country in which the Jewish intelligentsia demonstratively identified with the state and rejected National Socialism. Karl Kraus, Felix Salten, Franz Werfel, as well as Ernst Gombrich, Karl Popper and Sigmund Freud, originally party members or at least sympathisers of the Social Democrats, pledged themselves to the Corporative State and could themselves be regarded as symbols of a better Germany.[227] Austria, according to the slogan, 'embodies true Germanness'. It should lead the struggle against National Socialism 'without violating pan-German interests in the process'.[228] This might have reflected well on the heralds of this balancing act, but it could not solve Austrian problems in the long term. And on closer inspection, doubts emerged regarding the 'better Germany'.

Austria had quite positively committed itself to a patriotic course. Pride in its history, the historic role of the country and especially the military successes and civilising achievements had replaced the always inaccurate picture of a state that no one wanted. Now it was a question of exploiting the past. Austrianness was already being taught in primary schools.

According to the school chronicle of the small Weinviertel municipality of Rabensburg, 'In the school year 1935/36', there was a change 'in history lessons, language instruction and physical education. ... Particular emphasis was now placed on religious ideas regarding the

fatherland. Wherever possible, education regarding the fatherland was deepened in the individual subjects. … In singing, old soldiers' songs were practised more. … The teachers' library
was equipped with suitable material. (Military geography of Austria, pre-military youth education, soldiers' bulletin). … Physical education was given a special touch in the form of
pre-military youth training.'[229]

Thousands of others contained very similar formulations. Admittedly, the concomitant
effects were by all means suited to fostering scepticism.

In Germany, the swastika had been an omnipresent symbol. The Corporative State
countered with the cross potent. The greeting of the Fatherland Front was 'Front Heil'.
Uniforms became pervasive. Civil servants wore uniforms; members of the Home
Guard, the mutated remnants of former armed formations and countless other organisations wore clothing reminiscent of uniforms. Without them, one felt the absence of
an identifying mark and was positively 'naked'. Grammar school pupils felt the same
when they did not wear the 'Unite!' *(Seid einig)* school badge of the Fatherland Front.[230]
On 30 January of all days, the day of Hitler's assumption of power in Germany, the 'Day
of the New Austria' was celebrated in 1935 with torchlight processions and marching music.[231] The Mothers' Protection Agency (Mutterschutzwerk) and the Agency for
Children's Holidays (Kinderferienwerk) were very similar to National Socialist institutions. The Austrian Youth (Österreichisches Jungvolk), to which 350,000 children
and adolescents between six and eighteen years belonged, was comparable to the Hitler
Youth. Germany accelerated the expansion of infrastructure and built roads. Austria attempted to pull level but had less money at their disposal and remained in debt. Nonetheless, large-scale projects such as the Reich Bridge and the Mountain Road, both in
Vienna, and roads over the Pack Saddle, the Plöcken Pass, the Gerlos Pass, the Iselsberg
Pass and the Hochtann Mountain Pass were started, for which as few machines as
possible and all the more people were to be employed. These were perhaps initially 'un-
productive investments',[232] but they at least created some relief, as they were designed to
help fight unemployment among youths and undermine German propaganda.

With its brutal persecution of Communists and ideological opponents, Germany
had triggered a state of shock, and with the creation of concentration camps it had
mapped out a course that Austria willingly followed, if not with quite the same degree
of brutality. The Austrian version, the detention camps of Wöllersdorf and Kaierstein-
bruch, could at the very least be regarded as an enduring threat. And the measures of
the government became increasingly authoritarian. The end of paramilitarism did not
mean the end of the armed formations. Only a few had been prohibited. Representatives of others sat in the government, at least temporarily. Despite its withdrawal from
political bodies, the Catholic Church had attained such a dominant position, or rather
been assigned one, that membership in it was in many cases decisive for getting a job,

and where this was not the case, the membership card of the Fatherland Front should at least furnish proof of an avowed Austrianness. In Germany, one strove to be accepted into the NSDAP. In Austria, it was the Fatherland Front.

Beyond politics, one did not grow tired of pointing out the similarities and overlaps between Austrian and German academic trends. The Reich Archives in Berlin and the War Archives in Vienna worked closely together in compiling major works about the First World War. At Austrian universities, central importance was given to reappraising the history of the Empire. Heinrich Srbik's four-volume work *Deutsche Einheit* (German Unity) was an eloquent expression of this.

Economists and natural scientists took similar views and engaged in normal academic dialogues. Particularly striking were the identical opinions of the eugenicists. Especially when it came to racial doctrine, they considered themselves furthermore to be in a type of global network. Racial hygiene was regarded as something that was supposed to help create a better human being. There appeared to be no ideological limits here, because racial doctrine brought together Social Democrats, liberal reformers, conservatives and right-wing advocates of an authoritarian state. The goal was the same for them all; the path taken to achieve it differed. Social Democrats focussed on the living conditions of the predominantly urban workers and the future of the city. Conservatives equated health with land, soil and physical labour. The former Social Democratic city councillor of Vienna, Julius Tandler, the psychiatrist Julius Wagner-Juaregg and the behavioural scientist Konrad Lorenz evolved into leading eugenicists. They considered themselves of one mind with Alfred Ploetz, Theodore Roosevelt, George Bernard Shaw or even Winston Churchill. Imbeciles and lunatics were regarded as a threat to a society's affluence, vitality and strength. Thus, it was not 'crackpots' who – like the National Socialists – considered eugenics to be a tool for (un)natural selection. Lorenz was convinced that the domestication of humans as a result of modern life led to 'racial decline' and was 'contrary to true evolution'.[233] The construction of social housing, allotment gardens and the relocation of construction activities from the centres appeared to be effective means for counteracting the decline. American and British settlement forms sometimes had a role-model function here. Preventing a rural exodus was a major goal. New open-air swimming pools and sports stadiums were to be built. It almost appeared as though the Corporative State was taking a leaf out of the Social Democrats' book. The course to creating new human beings was mapped out. It could be made passable by means of the carrot or the stick.

In spite of a whole host of echoes, there was no doubt much that separated Austria from Germany and forbade an equation of National Socialism with the Christian Corporative State. One thing was decisively different though: Germany aroused fear; Austria aroused, at best, pity. It was independent and under constant observation. This could be seen time and again. And it threatened to drift ever further into isolation.

When Italy not entirely unexpectedly unleashed a war in Abyssinia in October 1935, which was designed to establish Italian domination of the country, Austria's only protector was admonished by the League of Nations Assembly and subjected to sanctions. Only Hungary, Albania – which was completely dependent on Italy – and, above all, Austria voted against the imposition of sanctions. The Austrian envoy to the League of Nations, Emmerich Pflügl, justified this with a certain helplessness, by pointing to Italy's role in the aftermath to Dollfuß's murder: Austria could not forget that Italy, 'at a critical moment by virtue of its intervention', had 'effectively contributed to maintaining Austria's integrity and independence'.

Austria's stance was regarded, not least by the major colonial powers of Britain and France, as unbecoming, and it would have consequences. Italy had violated not only the Covenant of the League of Nations but also the Geneva Protocol for the Prohibition of Poisonous Gases. It had conducted a brutal, genocidal war. As the Western powers did not want to deal too harshly with Italy, however, it was much easier to create difficulties for Italy's vassal, Austria. It was at precisely this time that Austria was seeking a deferral of credit repayments from the British, which had been granted following the debacle with Creditanstalt. Britain, however, demanded punctual settlement. France blocked the disbursal of the Lausanne loan. The result was a tightening of austerity measures. Schuschnigg had to furthermore acknowledge that Mussolini did not honour the Austrian government's course vis-à-vis Italy but instead sought to counter the sanctions against his country by making an approach to Germany. Austria had no part to play in this manoeuvre. It was once again caught between two proverbial stools. Not even the approach to the Little Entente succeeded, although Czechoslovakia reacted positively to Schuschnigg's efforts. Yugoslavia, however, put no value on friendly relations and focussed not on the 'dying' but on the presumptive heir.

Going for Broke

Schuschnigg endeavoured to at least bring calm to domestic politics, for that which appeared from outside to be united and consolidated was in reality a web dominated by power struggles, vanity and corruption. The factions of the Fatherland Front continued to compete with one another. They courted influence and were melting pots for all and sundry. The most important thing, of course, was to be organised. The Freedom League (Freiheitsbund), founded in 1927 and still extant, gradually became a reservoir for prohibited 'leftists' and, even more so, National Socialists. It was sharply at odds with the Home Guard and repeatedly made it clear that it was only of necessity that it adhered to the authoritarian course. The Eastern March Stormtroopers, founded in 1930 and the Chancellor's very own organisation, referred to themselves as a 'Catholic movement for cultural-political renewal and protection' and likewise claimed to have nothing in common with the Home Guard and, above all, its special paths in foreign policy, which sometimes pointed towards Italy and sometimes to Germany. Starhemberg resolutely wanted to take the Italian route, though he was not averse to a legitimist experiment; Emil Fey, though in fact neutralised, maintained permanent contacts with National Socialist circles and had sided with the government on 25 July 1934 only at the last moment. He was still waiting for his hour to strike. The Christian-German Gymnast Militias (Wehrturner), the Burgenland Territorial Infantry (Burgenländische Landesschützen), the Green Militia (Grüne Wehr) and other small armed formations no longer played any part. Several of them, such as the Association of Combat Veterans (Frontkämpfervereinigung), had been dissolved or merged into other organisations. Most of them were 'right-wing', and those that were not were pulled into the right-wing camp by means of infiltration.

In June 1935, all large armed formations were declared to be protective corps units. This, however, was not only a step towards uniformity but also one that aimed at the dissolution of the armed formations. The objective was for the state to finally regain the monopoly on power that it had lost to the armed formations over the course of years. But it appeared to be anything but straightforward. It was eventually pure chance that came to Schuschnigg's aid. Starhemberg let himself get carried away and sent Mussolini a telegram congratulating him on the conquest of the Abyssinian/Ethiopian capital Addis Ababa in early May 1936 and attacking the Western powers – for Starhemberg, who had received the considerable sum of 3.5 million lira over the course of four years for himself and his Home Guard[234] and who was personally close to Mussolini, this was evidently a natural thing to do. Not without vanity, he characterised himself in his cable as the 'leader of Austrian fascism'.[235] The telegram was published. The envoys of Britain, France and Czechoslovakia protested to the Chancellor. Schuschnigg reacted promptly and removed Starhemberg as vice chancellor and head of the Fatherland Front, whose leadership he himself now assumed. Federal chancellor, federal head of the Fatherland Front, minister of defence, foreign minister – all functions that Schuschnigg henceforth united in his person, could have signified a sufficient plenitude of power for him to steer an authoritarian course without having to take particular considerations. Schuschnigg went one step further: in May 1936, he ordered the establishment of a uniformed formation within the Fatherland Front based on military principles, the so-called Front Militia (Frontmiliz). The Chancellor appeared once more to have taken a decisive step in the expansion of his power. Ultimately, however, he was still dependent on considerations, and it was not least second-tier men who did not want to accept the dissolution of the political parties and the armed formations and who had not surrendered their Christian Social or even Greater German (though not National Socialist) ideology along with their party membership books. It was above all the illegal and nonetheless omnipresent National Socialists, however, who troubled the Chancellor. Schuschnigg wanted to reach out to them. From here on in, he orientated himself towards Germany rather than Italy. Italy's rapprochement with Germany as a consequence of the Abyssinian War had resulted in the evaporation of its backing for Austria. A reaction had to come.

The successor to Envoy Rieth, the former German Reich Chancellor Franz von Papen, could react to Schuschnigg's advances all the easier for being directly subordinated to Hitler as his 'special plenipotentiary' and having the task of bringing about an accommodation with the Corporative State. Von Papen had advised Hitler to let the question of a union cool down.

> Austria must become uninterested. If no one speaks about Austria any more, because the issue has begun to get boring, then the Austrians will have time to address their own domestic affairs … and realise with astonishment that they have a dictatorial government that puts everything in the shade that is happening in this respect in the so-called fascist countries.[236]

Hitler demanded another two years of von Papen before addressing the Austrian question. The immediate result was the discontinuation of acts of terror. Joseph Goebbels instructed the German press to 'largely hush up' the subject of Austria.[237] However, the propaganda continued.

Schuschnigg and von Papen negotiated for a year over an agreement. There were numerous spanners in the works. Starhemberg was opposed; the German Reich stalled.[238] Negotiations continued. Ultimately, von Papen and Schuschnigg agreed to a 'treaty on normalisation and friendship', which was signed on 11 July 1936 and was supposed to bring solutions to a whole host of questions. The normalisation of relations had top priority. The government of the German Reich recognised the full sovereignty of Austria. Political affairs were to be regarded as an internal matter, on which no influence should be exerted from abroad. Austria would shape its foreign policy in the awareness of being a German state, though the treaties with Italy and Hungary would retain their full validity. The agreement was otherwise full of rhetorical catchwords. But that was just the published text. Other parts of the 'July accord' were to remain secret and were characterised as a gentlemen's agreement. It was subsequently possible to deduce its contents from a series of individual measures: the fact that Schuschnigg appointed two new Cabinet members during the course of a reshuffle, who were supposed to guarantee a course acceptable to Germany, namely Director of the War Archives Edmund Glause-Horstenau, who joined the government as minister without portfolio, and the deputy chief of staff to the Federal President, Guido Schmidt, who became permanent secretary in the Foreign Ministry. It soon became clear, however, that the National Socialists were given a certain degree of political freedom, that there was to be a sort of press freedom and that the restrictions on tourism – the 1,000-mark barrier – would be gradually abolished. The secret agreement also stipulated that convicted National Socialists who were serving time in prisons or detention camps for something other than serious crimes such as murder should be amnestied. This applied above all to the approximately 500 of what had once been 5,000 National Socialists in the Wöllersdorf detention camp. In addition, there was to be a great deal of economic relief for Germany even without a customs and currency union. It was especially in this regard that the impression inevitably arose that Schuschnigg had veritably bought the July accord.

The press, which had been subjected to widespread enforced coordination, applauded the agreement. It did indeed seem to bring about a relaxation of relations. The government's course had received confirmation. Austrian independence appeared secure, and it was regarded as positive that a German-Austrian committee should oversee the fulfilment of the agreement's terms.[239] The threat of terror appeared to have been removed. But the satisfaction was deceptive. In both Austria and Germany, there were opponents of the agreement, such as Vienna's mayor Richard Schmitz, Joseph Goebbels, Reichsführer SS Heinrich Himmler and Hitler's deputy Rudolf Heß.[240] On flyers, Hitler was accused of 'treason' by Austrian National Socialists. But everyone had to accept things as they were. The German press extolled Hitler's will to peace. In Italy, 'the statesmanship of the Duce'[241] was commended, though, in truth, he had contributed little to the treaty. For many Austrian National Socialists, however, the agreement did not go far enough. They could say that, for them, the time of illegality was at an end and that, above all, Germany's influence on Austria had not become less but considerably more. And, sooner or later, this would lead to the union. It appeared to be a straight road.

Schuschnigg also used the agreement to sideline his domestic opponents, first and foremost the 'prince of the Home Guard' Ernst Rüdiger Starhemberg. The latter regarded himself as the victim and refused to accept Schuschnigg's offer to assume a different task. The Chancellor then made short shrift of things and dissolved the Home Guard on 9 October 1936. The 'Federal Law for the Dissolution of the Voluntary Armed Formations' liquidated all armed formations. The men of the protective corps could apply voluntarily for incorporation into the Front Militia of the Fatherland Front. If required, it should serve to support the Federal Army and the executive. This indeed appeared to spell the end of the party armies. The Federal Army would be consolidated with 110,000 men from the Voluntary Protective Corps.

The country's ability to defend itself had grown, at least on paper. Italy was still calculated to be the protective power; relations with Czechoslovakia could be regarded as good; those with Hungary were very good and even led to joint operative arrangements being made in the event of one of the two countries being involved in a military conflict. Brief irritations, when Hungarian Prime Minister Gyula Gömbös characterised Burgenland as one of Hungary's 'unsolved questions',[242] were forgotten. It was hoped that an improvement of relations with Germany would ensure peaceful developments for the second German state, Austria. Admittedly, this did not prevent the Austrian chief of the General Staff, Alfred Jansa, from instructing his operations department to plan for all possible operational scenarios. These included the war scenario C + Yu (Czechoslovakia and Yugoslavia), which was based on an attack against Austria, but also a joint attack with I + H (Italy and Hungary) against C + Yu. Most consideration, however, was given to war scenario GR (German Reich), which was tellingly termed 'War Scenario I'. This could be regarded as a 'sin against the spirit', but there had been similar blueprints before the First World War and it was considered to be normal General Staff work. It was ultimately seen as a contingency plan.[243] This time, there were no allies. Austria had more or less written off Britain. France gave thought to arms deliveries, but that did not increase Austria's security in the slightest. Yugoslavia was not sympathetic and interested primarily in good relations with Germany. It was inevitable, therefore, that the question about Austria's capacity to survive was posed again and with a new sense of urgency.

Schuschnigg was soon subjected to Hitler's accusation of not fulfilling the July agreement either literally or in spirit. Austrian foreign policy differed markedly from Germany's above all in one respect: Austria made no move to leave the League of Nations, as Germany had done. At least to a certain extent, the community of nations gave it a feeling of something like collective security. It was not forgotten, furthermore, that the League of Nations had guaranteed both the Geneva and the Lausanne loans. Schuschnigg was accused by Hitler of including in government, in the shape of Guido Schmidt, one of his own confidants rather than a politician who was genuinely sympathetic to National Socialism. Where was the second minister whom Hitler had been granted in the gentlemen's agreement? Mussolini also insisted on the inclusion of more National Socialists in government. Schuschnigg wanted to grant this but was forced to read in the newspaper of his readiness to do so even before he had taken the corresponding steps. He was furious and dropped the matter. In February 1937, he believed he could demonstrate his good intentions by incorporating an 'Ethnic Policy Department' into the Fatherland Front, in agreement with the German foreign minister, Konstantin von Neurath, and placing it under the control of the Viennese lawyer Arthur Seyß-Inquart. He was a moderate National Socialist and not uncontroversial among kindred spirits, because he was not radical enough. The radicals supported the leader of the Vienna NSDAP, Josef Leopold. Ultimately, one year after the conclusion of the July agreement, everyone was back where they had started: helplessness prevailed. One particular change of course was considered but then discounted as impracticable: the return of the Habsburgs. Otto von Habsburg indeed became increasingly insistent in his contact with Schuschnigg and claimed that he was the only one capable of standing up to Hitler.

The monarchist movement, which was convinced of the legitimacy of Otto von Habsburg's claim to power in Austria even in its reduced form, was prominently represented in the Home Guard and then the Fatherland Front, and Otto could also rely on a certain sympathy on the part of the Chancellor. Otto had met with Schuschnigg on 14 August 1936 in Geneva and on 7 January 1937 in Einsiedeln in Switzerland. Schuschnigg could pride himself on having altered the Habsburg Law of 3 April 1919, rescinded the expulsion from the country and returned assets in 1935. Moreover, he time and again emphasised the correlation of legitimistic and corporative aims. Like Dollfuß, Schuschnigg also wanted to remove 'the revolutionary rubble of 1918' and build 'on the loveliest times in Austrian history'.[244] He openly played with the legitimistic option and told Czechoslovak Prime Minister Milan Hodža: before losing its independence and being incorporated into the German Reich as its eighth Gau, Austria would 'rather take the path to restoration'. In this case, Schuschnigg had a 'territorial principality' of the Habsburgs in mind.[245] But he shied away. The German foreign minister, Konstantin von Neurath, had told him outright in February 1937 that the German Reich would intervene militarily in the event of a Habsburg restoration in Austria. And it was well known that the Little Entente considered the prevention of a Habsburg restoration as a basis for existence. Italy eventually also came into line with the Germans, Czechs, Romanians and Yugoslavs.[246] It would thus have constituted a complete denial of reality had Schuschnigg not recognised the signs of the time. This did not apply to Otto von Habsburg. He counted on the help of the Western powers, but they completely rejected the idea of supporting Otto.

In the deliberations on a solution to the Austrian question, everything surfaced that had at some point played a role, including the absurd idea – brought into play by Romania – that Austria could make an approach to the Soviet Union and receive a Soviet guarantee for its continued statehood.[247] Foreign countries were ruled out but they became increasingly dismissive and mistrustful.

In terms of domestic politics, there was likewise scarcely a glimmer of hope. The Social Democrats understandably demanded services in return for agreeing to back Schuschnigg. Those around Josef Leopold began to work towards a new putsch. In order not to be disturbed in their preparations, the followers of national leader Leopold were forbidden any contact with von Papen and Seyß-Inquart. Leopold did not want to wait any more. This time – as Leopold's deputy, Leo Tavs, wrote in a secret paper – an attack on German diplomats was to take place, in order for German military intervention to then be requested. The paper fell into the hands of the police during a search of the offices of the leadership of the Vienna NSDAP. Hitler had evidently not been informed about the fanciful plans, but he had long since decided in favour of a solution by means of force.

The Reich Ministry of War had already commissioned the chief of the General Staff, Lieutenant General Ludwig Beck, on 24 June 1937 with the preparation of an

operational study codenamed 'Special Scenario Otto'. This was designed to signalise
the readiness of the German Army to response militarily to any attempt to restore the
Habsburgs in Austria. Beck had admittedly stated that he was not in favour of such a
draft, and he cited political – though also relative force strength – considerations for
this, but he was ultimately left with no other option than to at least give the scenario
some thought. Hitler became more definite on 5 November 1937 when, at a secret
meeting with the Reich foreign and war ministers as well as the commanders-in-chief
of the three branches of the Wehrmacht – army, navy and Luftwaffe – he reflected
on the steps necessary in order to ensure the 'security and preservation of the German
masses'. Germany was faced with the question of 'where the greatest gains' could be
made 'for the least effort'.[248] The deliberations did not suggest anything that might
have indicated deference to any considerations. It was merely stated that Austria, like
Czechoslovakia, would have to be neutralised before a war with France and incorporated into the Third Reich. This would improve the food situation in the Reich and
yield troops. One of the prerequisites for this, they continued, was the resettlement
of a million people from Austria (and two million from Czechoslovakia). It was still
unclear, they said, how Italy would respond to the occupation of Austria, but as long
as the Duce was alive, no particular problems were to be expected. From 5 November
1937, therefore, it was only a question of when and how, but he was fundamentally
willing to use force.

Berchtesgaden

Soon, speculation abounded regarding the imminence of a German invasion or the
likelihood of an uprising. Since later autumn and winter 1937, Hitler's deputy, Rudolf Heß, the commander-in-chief of the Luftwaffe, Hermann Göring, Reich Foreign
Minister Konstantin von Neurath and others freely and independently of one another
stated that the 'Anschluss' of Austria would happen sooner or later. Hitler himself, it
is well known, was quoted as saying that Austria was an 'internal matter for Germany'.
Regarding the question of a potential reaction by the neighbouring countries, it was
stated that Italy would not lift a finger.[249] French newspapers reported that the German ambassador in Vienna, von Papen, would be removed in order to allow for a more
radical course of action. This rumour was related to the fact that Hitler, like a bolt out
of the blue, had made himself supreme commander in early February 1938 and also
wanted to initiate a new direction in foreign policy. Joachim von Ribbentrop switched
from the embassy in London to Berlin as Reich foreign minister, and Franz von Papen
would indeed leave Vienna. For more than two years, he had endeavoured to breathe
life into the July agreement. He had not succeeded. His removal could by all means be

interpreted, therefore, as Hitler having abandoned his evolutionary course and desiring the annexation of Austria by force, if necessary.

Berlin made repeated complaints to the effect that Austria was not fulfilling the agreement. Assurances that this was not the case failed to have any effect. Vienna's Foreign Ministry nonetheless attempted to address the contentious points in the favoured dilatory way, that is, to procrastinate. This did not contribute to solving the problems. On the occasion of his imminent transfer, von Papen informed the Führer and Reich Chancellor of the desire of the Austrian Federal Chancellor to meet with Hitler. The latter agreed. It was later disputed from whom the initiative had come. During the course of the 1947 trial for high treason of the permanent secretary in the Foreign Ministry, Guido Schmidt, it was claimed that von Papen had told Schmidt on 7 January that it was also Hitler's opinion that the exchange of memoranda would not lead to the removal of differences. Schuschnigg apparently shared this view and was in principle willing to meet.[250] On 8 February, he received the invitation. The meeting at the Berghof near Berchtesgaden was scheduled for 12 February 1938.

Schuschnigg knew that he was risking a great deal, so he kept the matter secret, although he would have liked to have obtained backing for his plan. He pinned his hopes on England and explained the situation and his concerns to the Austrian ambassador in London, Sir George Franckenstein. The British Ambassador in Austria received a copy.[251] It was a type of cry for help. London remained silent. One week later, Schuschnigg tentatively enquired in London whether he might quickly come to England for an oral presentation. The British foreign secretary, Sir Anthony Eden, turned him down. A visit in London might be misunderstood, even if it was ostensibly only a question of a presentation.[252] England did not want to go out on a limb. But the British naturally swiftly enquired in Vienna whether the meeting did not carry a big risk. Guido Schmidt reassured them.

Schuschnigg, who was purportedly on his way to Innsbruck, travelled – accompanied by Schmidt – to Berchtesgaden. As a precaution, the Salzburg garrison was placed on a state of alert the entire day.[253] The Federal Chancellor intended to submit to Hitler a list of proposals for a further expansion of relations and for a type of 'extended July agreement'. Guido Schmidt and Seyß-Inquart had prepared the draft. Like almost everything that was said or written in the Austrian ministries or offices of the Federal Army, Berlin knew about it long before Schuschnigg arrived in Berchtesgaden. Hitler welcomed him in the presence of the chief of the High Command of the Wehrmacht, Wilhelm Keitel, the commander of Luftwaffe Group Command III (Munich), Hugo Sperrle, as well as the commander of Army Group Commando IV (Leipzig), Walther von Reichenau. Schuschnigg had been informed that several generals would be residing 'by chance' at the Berghof, but the demonstration was not lost on him. Hitler did not waste any time on the polite submissions of his Austrian guest. Normal diplomatic form did not apply here. He

also exploited an aspect of weakness on the part of Schuschnigg, who was a chain smoker
and whom Hitler did not allow to smoke. The Federal Chancellor became increasingly
nervous. The presence of the soldiers played its part in pressurising Schuschnigg.[254] Hitler held a monologue and claimed to have then proposed that a popular referendum be
held in Austria, which Schuschnigg dismissed with a reference to the May Constitution
of 1934. Afterwards, there was a 12-minute lunch break, during which Hitler contented
himself with spinach.[255] They resumed their discussion in the afternoon. Schuschnigg
made concessions, but simultaneously pointed out that he still had to obtain the approval
of the Federal President – which was an excuse. Finally, Schuschnigg and Hitler initialled
the agreement. In doing so, the Austrian Chancellor did far more than just engage in an
undertaking, on which first Miklas and perhaps also the Federal Assembly had to decide.
A non-intervention in internal matters was once again pledged – as though it could ever
have been possible for Austria to intervene in German affairs. Austria furthermore had to
commit itself to pursuing foreign policy only in unison with the German Reich, to transfer the ministries of the interior and of security to Seyß-Inquart, to allow members of
the NSDAP complete freedom of action and to pardon those members of the party who
had not yet been amnestied. Dismissed officials and officers, the latter due to their membership in the National Socialist Circle of Soldiers (Nationalsozialistischer Soldatenring),
were to be reappointed. The chief of the General Staff, Alfred Jansa, who had planned
the deployment of the Federal Army and the Front Militia in the event of an invasion by
German troops, was to be discharged. He was to be replaced as chief of the General Staff
by a sympathiser of the Nazis, Lieutenant General Franz Böhme. Economic cooperation
was to be consolidated even further.

Hitler's adviser in economic matters, Wilhelm Keppler, who had endeavoured since
1937 to accelerate the evolutionary path to the 'Anschluss', had presented a paper to
Permanent Secretary Schmidt while Schuschnigg was talking to Hitler, which held
out the prospect of an unrestrained economic penetration of Austria. This involved
an incorporation of Austria into the German Four-Year Plan, a customs and currency
union and trade benefits. The doors were to be opened wide for German firms. Guido
Schmidt did not want to comment on it. Only a few days later, the German envoy, Carl
Clodius, travelled to Vienna and claimed that the matter had been decided in line with
German thinking. He departed dissatisfied.

Economic circles were alarmed. The president of the Austrian National Bank, Viktor
Kienböck, noted that speculation against the schilling had begun. Foreign currency
became more expensive on an almost daily basis. Kienböck anticipated capital flight.
He concluded, full of gloom: 'If there's no intervention from abroad, Austria's position
is untenable.'[256]

No one doubted that Schuschnigg would completely fulfil the Berchtesgaden agreement. Immediately after his return, he began to implement it. Seyß-Inquart became

minister of the interior and of security. Freedom of action for National Socialists as well as their amnesty were immediately decreed, and this drove tens of thousands into the streets to engage in manifestations of joy. Countless people moved through the streets crying 'Heil Hitler', 'Sieg Heil' and 'Schuschnigg, perish!'[257]

As a sort of compensatory measure for his concessions towards the National Socialists, Schuschnigg had also determined on amnestying the imprisoned Social Democrats and Communists, too. But he saw ever more clearly that he was on the verge of gambling away Austria and that his hope of at least having gained some time would prove to be illusory. He consoled himself with the fact that Seyß-Inquart was a practising Catholic and that limits would be placed on him by virtue of the appointment of a permanent secretary, Michael Skubl. Others were not so optimistic and gave Schuschnigg half a year at most before he would be forced to transfer the chancellorship to Seyß-Inquart.[258]

But Schuschnigg did not intend on giving up just yet. He appeared on 24 February before the Federal Assembly in the old Reichsrat Assembly Hall of Vienna's parliament building. The speech had been billed as historic. Events were cancelled nationwide and the universities closed at 6 p.m. in order to give as many people as possible the opportunity to hear the Chancellor's words. Schuschnigg appeared before the assembly as leader of the Fatherland Front and spoke for two hours: 'In this decisive and grave hour…'. In general terms, he reported on Berchtesgaden and defended its outcome. The meeting, at the invitation of the Führer and Reich Chancellor, had rightly been assessed as a political sensation, he claimed. A five-year war between brothers was at an end. 'And now there shall be peace.' Schuschnigg spoke not only of the meeting with Hitler, however. He described at length how Austria had developed positively during the preceding years, how the numbers of unemployed had dropped by about a third, what a success the reduced return tickets on the federal railways had been, and how road traffic would soon adjust to the obligation to drive on the right. Addressing his domestic opponents, the Chancellor stated that there should finally be an end to the incessant demands, resolutions and group demonstrations. It was necessary to show unity, a type of German unity, for the word 'German' was mentioned in the most varied combinations around one hundred times in his speech. Towards its end, Schuschnigg called Dollfuß and 'all martyrs of this nation' to the witness box. 'And because we are determined, victory is beyond doubt. Until death, Red-White-Red! Austria!' The *Wiener Zeitung* reported that his speech had been followed by cries of 'Heil', the waving off flags and the tossing of hats.[259] The members of the Federal Assembly stood and intoned the national anthem and the 'Dollfuß Song'. It was claimed that everyone joined in the singing: 'You young ones, tightly close your ranks / A dead leader marches ahead / He gave for Austria his blood / A true German man …'.

Hitler and the Nazi leadership did not allow themselves to be impressed by this. On the contrary, they regarded Schuschnigg's speech as a departure from the Berchtes-

gaden agreement and responded with new demands. It was Hermann Göring, the plenipotentiary for the German Four-Year Plan and Prussian state governor, who issued
the demand for a strict foreign exchange control in Austria, in order to combat capital
flight. It was claimed that Jews and political dissidents would attempt to transfer their
assets abroad.[260] A check would have to be placed on them. In fact, Göring wanted to
prevent anything reducing the rich booty that already seemed certain.[261] On 5 March,
Seyß-Inquart demanded more influence for National Socialist functionaries in the federal states and the governor's office in Styria, as well as several deputy governor positions. Whoever had believed that the pressure on Austria would lessen, saw themselves
deceived. One gathering followed another. Whenever there was any mention of Hitler,
it was followed by cries of 'Sieg Heil'; whenever Schuschnigg was mentioned, there was
an icy silence or the Horst Wessel Song was sung. After a visit by Seyß-Inquart to Graz
in early March, even the 'Song of Germany' – 'Germany, Germany, above all ...' – was
allowed to be sung, provided that a verse of the Austrian national anthem with lyrics by
Ottokar Kernstock was sung beforehand:[262] 'Be blessed without end, wonderful native
land ...'. The melodies were, by this time, identical. And Schuschnigg's options were
zero.

9 The Failure

9 8 August 1934: funeral rally of the Fatherland Front for Federal Chancellor Engelbert Dollfuß, who had been murdered on 25 July 1934. The event was announced as a 'Host of grief and loyalty'. It was intended to demonstrate 'the unity of the people and the state in Austria' *(Wiener Zeitung)*. It was probably the largest mass rally ever held on Vienna's Heldenplatz. (Photo: Association for the History of the Labour Movement, Vienna)

In terms of foreign policy, Austria was isolated. Mussolini had come into line with Hitler, and he believed that he could realise his dreams of great power status with German help. Hitler, for his part, made it clear that he did not want to question South Tyrol's belonging to Italy. Mussolini believed him. France, whose left-wing politicians fundamentally rejected the Corporative State, did not react. Telegrams sent by the French envoy in Vienna, Gabriel Puaux, who was replaced as of March 1938, went unanswered. The same applied to his final telegram of 7 March. France wanted to proceed only in unison with Britain. London, however, saw no reason to confront Germany for Austria's benefit. The neighbours in the north, east and south did not want to go out on a limb and risk their own future. It was too late for a liberating strike in domestic politics, and Schuschnigg sent, at best, half-hearted signals to the – still prohibited – Social Democrats. The illegal trade unions thereafter issued a resolution stating their 'passionate will ... to champion the freedom, dignity and independence of Austria'.[263] But there had been enough declarations. Eventually, Schuschnigg brought an idea into play that had essentially been recurring since 1933, namely the holding of a consultative referendum. It would not be a popular vote, however, because that would have been binding. In the event of a negative result for the government, a consultative referendum still allowed some room for manoeuvre and at least possibilities for interpretation.

Schuschnigg claimed to have had the idea for a consultative referendum on Sunday, 6 March. The next day he discussed the matter with several confidantes. One of them was the general secretary of the Fatherland Front and minister without portfolio, Guido Zernatto. Zernatto's secretary, one of hundreds, if not thousands, of National Socialist informants, promptly reported to Berlin that Schuschnigg intended to hold a consultative referendum on the independence of Austria as early as the following Sunday, 13 March.

The Consultative Referendum

Mussolini strongly advised Schuschnigg against taking this step. The Chancellor had informed him in the hope that the 'Duce' would agree to act once more as Austria's protector. He was disappointed, but he did not want to turn back now. Schuschnigg did not allow himself to be put off by the chaotic start to preparations for the consultative referendum. Seyß-Inquart, who had officially been informed only after Mussolini, the

Italian ambassador in Vienna, Pellegrino Chigi, and others, protested and regarded the Chancellor's actions as illegal. Only the federal president, he claimed, had the right to schedule a consultative referendum. Schuschnigg, however, based his actions on Article 93 of the May Constitution of 1934, according to which the federal chancellor determined policy guidelines, and announced on Wednesday, 9 March, his intention and the question to be posed. At a gathering of functionaries of the Fatherland Front in Innsbruck he proclaimed what should be achieved in four days' time. He again took a sweeping approach, spoke about the youth, social progress and the question of public holidays, before then – with repeated reference to the 'heroic chancellor' – listing the relevant points:

> What we want:
> We want a free and German Austria.
> We want a Christian and united Austria.
> We want bread and peace in the country, and we want equal rights for everyone who is committed to our people and our homeland.[264]

These three points could ultimately be found on the slips of paper that were hurriedly drawn up for the first ever consultative referendum in the history of Austria. Nothing had been properly prepared. There were no lists of voters; indeed, it was initially unclear who could even take part in the referendum. There was also terminological confusion, for the public proclamations also spoke of 'vote', 'electoral committee', 'those entitled to vote', etc., which did not really fit with the idea of a referendum. All Austrians, male and female, who were already 24 years of age as of 13 March were called upon. Members of the Fatherland Front collected money to finance canvassing measures. Four-and-a-half million schillings were collected. It was above all Jews who readily donated and entered themselves into lists that then fell into the hands of the National Socialists.[265] Like many intellectuals and artists, Anna Mahler championed Schuschnigg's course. Others, who perhaps had a corresponding sense or, like Alwine Dollfuß, the widow of the murdered federal chancellor, were sceptical, left Austria. Mussolini had warned her and, a week before the consultative referendum, suggested that she leave the country.[266]

Former vice chancellor Emil Fey, already in a position of political seclusion, spoke up with an exhortation to members of the erstwhile Home Guard (Heimwehr). His appeal for them to vote 'yes' in the consultative referendum culminated in the sentence: 'Only my word is valid for you!' Perhaps he again wanted to slip into the role of saviour of the fatherland, just as he had done on 25 July 1934.

From all federal states with the exception of Styria, Schuschnigg received comforting assurances regarding the outcome of the referendum. They believed that the text sufficiently accommodated the National Socialists for them to drop a slip of paper with 'yes' in the hurriedly prepared receptacles, instead of resorting to using the 'no' slip or a blank one. Schuschnigg also expected the votes of the 'left', although he had refused to the last to rescue them from illegality and fulfil their demands to be allowed back into the political fold. But the signals he received from the Revolutionary Socialists (Revolutionäre Sozialisten) gave him reason to be confident. But they were between a rock and a hard place.

Seyß-Inquart pressurised Schuschnigg to cancel the consultative referendum. The Chancellor did not budge. He was confident of attaining a comfortable majority. According to one naive assessment of the situation, a third of the population supported the government, a third was against it and would vote 'no', and a third was still undecided, but would for the most part side with the advocates of independence. While Schuschnigg made a show of strength, Seyß-Inquart hesitated. The national leadership of the NSDAP proclaimed the referendum slogan 'abstention'.[267] It turned out on 10 March that numerous members of the national leadership and also several of the (illegal) Gauleiter did not want to adhere to this. They put the illegal armed formations – SA and SS – on standby. It was clear by 11 March that the National Socialists wanted to prevent the referendum from taking place. Their guiding principle, with which they defied Seyß-Inquart, was as follows: we organise the grass roots against the leadership. During the course of the day, one federal state after another fell to them. Here and there, violence threatened to break out, but eventually things passed off everywhere without bloodshed. The mood assumed a tone of mass hysteria. Demonstrations and canvassing took place. The federal government still called on the people to vote 'yes' on 13 March. In the meantime, the National Socialists had in any case created a fait accompli.

Schuschnigg had initially believed he had everything under control to such an extent that he did not entertain the idea of mobilising the Federal Army. He considered such a step to be too threatening. The Chancellor had furthermore needed parts of the army for the past few days to contain National Socialist unrest and for the orderly implementation of the consultative referendum. Only on the afternoon of 11 March was 'consignment' decreed, and the troops were no longer permitted to leave their barracks. The Operations Division of the Defence Ministry issued the order to make carriages available the next day for transporting units of the Federal Army.[268]

If Schuschnigg had acted differently, perhaps Hitler would have immediately uttered threats. But the Führer and Reich Chancellor ordered silence. From one day to the next, he had been provided with a pretext to think through to the end his thoughts from 5 November of the previous year for 'Scenario Austria'. Several things had changed for him in the meantime. Not, though, as a result of the encounter at Berchtesgaden but because he had neutralised the resistance of some German generals, which he was of course aware of and had also encountered in the case of preparations against Austria.

The Invasion

At midday on 10 March, the chief of the Operations Staff of the Wehrmacht was ordered to prepare plans for an invasion of Austria on 12 March. Codename: 'Scenario Otto'. Hitler hesitated, however, with the mobilisation order and only issued it at the urging of Göring. On the evening of 10 March, German military preparations commenced in earnest. Commanders-in-chief and other generals were hurriedly ordered to Berlin; the chief of the Abwehr (counterintelligence service), Vice Admiral Canaris, was to report on whether any European power was making military preparations. The main focus here was on France. Canaris was able to reassure Hitler. France was absorbed with itself.

The Army Group Command in Dresden set up a field army command, which was given the number eight. The two south-western Military Districts VII and XIII were subordinated to the new High Command of the Eighth Army and were obliged to mobilise their troops. SS Dispositional Troops (SS-Verfügungstruppen), Order Police and Luftwaffe formations were placed on alert. Everything happened under the pretext of a parade in Munich, mobilisation exercises and the like. In Austria, however, events came thick and fast.

While the German Eighth Army prepared itself to invade, Vienna continued to hesitate to take military action. Theoretically, a mobilisation would also have been feasible, but the Chancellor had decided otherwise.

All in all, the Federal Army had less than 60,000 men at its disposal, which could be increased to 125,000 men after mobilisation in the event of war. The length of time required to do this, however, was one week.[269] Since the introduction of general conscription on 1 April 1936, the forces of the Federal Army had included those of the Front Militia. On paper, this meant another 100,000 men. Some of these people, who were inadequately armed and possessed only ten bullets for their weapons, had experienced war and – as was so often the case in Austria – were supposed to offset the lack of weapons with bravery. Federal Army and Front Militia were not attuned to one another, and the army did not regard the militia as a supplement of full value. Schuschnigg ordered the mustering of the reserves born in 1915, in itself a completely senseless measure, because it meant only that here and there a few soldiers could be enlisted to fill up the units. Of those to be mobilised, approximately 10,000 men responded to the call-up order and enlisted at the barracks. Some of them wore swastika armbands. The display was all too clear.

At midday on 11 March, two battalions, that is, a little over 1,000 men, departed to strengthen the garrisons in Upper Austria. It was intended that they should monitor the border. This was nothing more than a show of strength, however, as no attempt was made to implement the Jansa plan or any other pre-prepared plan. The general inspector of troops, Lieutenant General Sigismund Schilhawsky, informed the Federal Chancellor at the same time that 'resistance ... under these circumstances, if we cannot depend on immediate support from abroad, ... is futile and not to be advised'.

Schuschnigg had understood. He now declared his willingness to cancel the consultative referendum and also held out the prospect of his resignation. At the same time, those who still hoped that the referendum would be held in defiance of all pressures, still clutched at every last straw of hope. The front pages of the evening editions of the Jewish newspapers were unchanged; they still announced: 'We affirm Austria! Everyone to the election urns.'[270] In the afternoon, Germany increased the pressure. Göring demanded Schuschnigg's resignation within the hour and the entrustment of the chancellorship to Seyß-Inquart. But Federal President Miklas refused to entrust the Minister of the Interior with the task of forming a government. At 8 p.m., Schuschnigg announced his resignation over the radio. He ended his speech with the words: 'God preserve Austria!' Units of the Federal Army were ordered not to offer resistance and to withdraw to the east. A little later, the formations of the German Eighth Army received the order to march into Austria. The situation changed practically within the space of minutes.

After Schuschnigg's resignation, the Federal President searched for candidates for the Chancellery. Finally, he had no choice but to surrender to the pressure from Berlin and entrust the Minister of the Interior and of Security with the task of forming a federal government. Seyß-Inquart, who had known of preparations for the invasion of German troops, would have liked to have prevented it. Hitler, likewise, did not seem absolutely determined. But Seyß-Inquart's hesitation to solicit military intervention, as demanded of him, was eventually subverted by Göring, who – without informing Hitler – sent a telegram in the name of Seyß-Inquart, in which the entry of German troops was requested. The Eighth Army began to move. There was no resistance. The new federal chancellor, Seyß Inquart, did not even consider it necessary to prohibit the Federal Army from engaging in any resistance. His predecessor had already done that.

Notwithstanding the confusion surrounding a military invasion, Seyß-Inquart compiled his government list, wanted to form a federal government and received the approval of Wilhelm Miklas, who signed the list of ministers and permanent secretaries. He did this a second time when Seyß-Inquart reshuffled the government, which did not even really exist yet, and replaced two permanent secretaries. Miklas signed again. Only when Seyß-Inquart submitted the 'Federal Constitutional Law on the Reunification of Austria with the German Reich' to him on 13 March for his countersignature did Miklas declare that he was being hindered in the performance of his duties and resign from office. The authority of the federal president was thereupon transferred to the federal chancellor, who signed the Anschluss law.

When the German formations advanced on 12 March, they were not only met with no resistance; they gained the impression that they were entering a jubilant country.

Along the streets and, when Adolf Hitler then arrived in Austria on the 13th, from everywhere it resounded with calls of 'One people, one Reich, one Führer!'. The image of the unimpeded, advancing troops conceals a great deal, not least the seizure, like lightning, of Vienna, which was occupied around ten hours before the arrival of German ground troops via an airborne operation and the securing of all sensitive points and buildings. By the early morning of 12 March, the city was already firmly in German hands. The corresponding newspapers report stated dryly: 'Reichsführer SS Himmler, travelling by plane from Munich, arrived in Vienna at around 5 a.m. He is accompanied by the chief of the Urban Police, SS Major General Heydrich, the chief of the Order Police, Lieutenant General Daluege, SS Senior Colonel Jest, SS Colonel Müller and Lieutenant Colonel of the Urban Police Meißner.' Himmler and the SS were followed by the army formations, which were in turn followed by Hitler.

As none of Austria's neighbours made a single gesture that might indicate military preparations or even hostile intentions, the German troops, by contrast, scrupulously maintained their distance from the frontiers, especially the border with Czechoslovakia, and Italy did nothing to help Austria, which Hitler assured Mussolini he would 'never forget', the occupation of Austria on 12 March was no longer a military problem.

'Vienna, 13 March. It is officially confirmed: Yesterday, at 8 in the morning, German motorised troops crossed the Austrian border for a friendship visit.' The announcement, intended not least for the international press, described in a few words – and falsely – what had happened. Hungary closed its borders for refugees from Austria. Czechoslovakia reacted similarly. Passengers with Austrian passports were removed from the last train to Břeclav (Lundenburg) and had to return to Vienna, 'where they were arrested by a mob of triumphant SA men'.[271] The states of the Little Entente could tell themselves that there had been no occasion to intervene, for their alliance was based on a Habsburg restoration. The fact that Austria no longer existed was a fact for them. They had waited for this. Like the rest of the world.

Obituary for a State

No question: it was a fragile entity that had emerged in 1918 from the ruins of a great empire. Within the space of around two weeks, a conglomerate of historical crown lands, duchies and counties was supposed to define itself as a federal state and the previous imperial capital and seat of royal residence assume the function of a federal capital city. The remains of an empire were supposed to become a democratic republic, and all this, as it were, from a standing position, for it had not emerged underground, in exile or on the drawing board. It had been an experiment. Everything was uncertain: the borders of the state, the people of the state, the political structures. The vast majority of people regarded themselves as victims and not as responsible for what had happened. There was little cause for hope, at most the circumstance that there was to be something akin to self-determination. This proved to be an illusion, just as so many things were based on illusions.

The future was shaped by treaties – just as most things in the coexistence of human beings are based on treaties. The Treaty of Saint-Germain was the most important instrument, and every time something seemed to be going off course, insistent references were made to Saint-Germain and the observance of treaty stipulations. From the outset, violence was a means of policymaking. Violence was used by those who wanted to achieve an objective, and likewise by those who wanted to prevent something from happening. State power became a more than dubious concept. The state initially appeared to have scarcely any power to apply internally or, still less, externally. It was enough to be able to prevent another coup. It was not the case that Austria was all that different from its European neighbours. There was tension everywhere, violent conflicts, coups and murder. But Austria was almost exclusively absorbed with itself. Governments came and went. The heralds of 'doctrines of salvation' multiplied and were met with both acclaim and rejection. Commonality was played down and projected on to independent projects. The years in which there was a comparatively peaceful development could be counted on one hand. At the same time, readiness to use violence increased continually, resulting in armed uprisings and the murder of a chancellor. And when it came to adding up the figures for the years 1918 to 1938, it could be noted that there had been 338 attacks and that 836 people had been killed and around 2,000 injured in the various acts of violence.[272]

An economic upsurge could not be achieved, either, though it was admittedly a combination of the legacy of the Monarchy, mismanagement and corruption that led to the collapse of large credit institutions and economic enterprises. Mistrust of most politicians but also the attacks from abroad, ideological entrenchment and, finally, the policies of National Socialist Germany, which were directed systematically against the survival of an independent Austria, took on an increasingly threatening character. It was permitted to happen, although those states who had allowed this Austria to come into being, above all Britain and France but also Italy, were thoroughly aware that Austria could not be helped with encouraging assurances but needed effective help. The question, of course, was what this help should look like.

The British ambassador in Vienna, Sir Walford Selby, posed the direct question as early as 1933 in a private letter to the permanent secretary in the cabinet of Ramsey MacDonald, Anthony Eden: 'What has England done to help Austria economically?'[273] Nothing! It could have intensified bilateral trade or relieved Austria somewhat of its burden of debts. But nothing happened. And the last British chargé d'affaires at the embassy in Vienna, William Henry Bradshaw Mack, observed a further failure: England could have used the talks started with Italy in January 1938 to re-establish the axis of the First World War and remind Italy of the Treaty of London from 1915, for which it had its great power status to thank.[274] But it had not been done. To alter the disastrous conditions of domestic policy evidently exceeded the possibilities of one that considered itself the midwife of an Austria created in 1918. Italy provided some support until 1936, but – though this cannot be held against it – had its own interests in mind. But then it quickly came to an end. Dollfuß had enjoyed notable sympathies, even if his regime did not meet with the approval of Western Europe. Schuschnigg could not take advantage of this sympathy bonus, lost the support of Italy, attempted to play the German card and had to acknowledge his own impotence. The others looked on and knew very well that this was not an isolated case but a wider Central European problem.

Austria had failed as a state by 1938. Twenty years earlier, it had already been part of a failed state. Both events left their mark and damaged self-confidence. Why had this had to happen? Was it down to the geographical or the power political prerequisites, which could not be altered? Fatalists would have liked to think so. Was it due to the people, their mentality, one or more political castes? Had decisive changes of course been wrong? Was there a single moment in the historical course of events where one could say: this was the turning point?

Obituaries must always attempt to put into words something final and irreversible. Where the obituary to a state is concerned, however, the words 'de mortuis nil nisi bene' do not apply. Criticism is required. Those who voiced it at the time must have also understood it as self-criticism. Nothing of the sort flowed into the obituaries that could later be heard. It was, at most, regret that was expressed. The criticism, however, was directed against those who had allowed things to get this far. British Prime Minister Sir Neville Chamberlain found suitable words in the House of Commons and cautioned at the same time against overhasty conclusions. Leopold Stennett Amery was more forthright; he had already warned in 1918 that the collapse of Austria-Hungary could have unforeseen consequences. Winston Churchill used his obituary in the British parliament on 14 March to indirectly criticise Chamberlain and point to the consequences of the Austrian Anschluss for the whole Danube region. He spoke of a looming suppression of the Catholic population and the working classes by the National Socialists. One could not simply skate over the issue by concluding 'what's done is done'.[275]

This was surely very honourable. Far more sensitive, however, was the parting dispatch of the British chargé d'affaires in Vienna, Henry Mack, which told above all of wistfulness:

'So ended Austria – the Austria of the Treaty of St. Germain, whose independence was declared by that Treaty to be inalienable otherwise than with the consent of the Council of the League of Nations. What the future will bring, it is difficult to foresee. Austrians of the old school felt that their country had really ended with the cessation of hostilities in 1918. For this class, most of them Legitimists, the future holds out little hope. The workers in the towns and the peasants on the land will no doubt have greater opportunity for work, and unemployment will, as in Germany, to a large extent, cease. The German authorities lost no time in evincing the greatest interest in the welfare of the workers and it seems that it will be one of their main objects to ensure their willing support. ... The Jews will be oppressed as they have been in Germany and will be given no opportunity of taking any part in public life and very little of achieving anything in commercial life. The leaders of the Church have accepted the inevitable and have willingly, or unwillingly, exhorted their flocks to the effect that their duty in the plebiscite is to cast their votes in the affirmative. There is little doubt about the enthusiasm of the youth of the country for the Nazi regime and many Austrians consider that the future holds out much greater hope for the lower-middle classes, owing to the larger opportunities for work and activity which exist in the great unit of which Austria is now a part. Vienna is already, in appearance at least, a German town.' The enthusiasm with which Hitler was welcomed may have soon faded away. 'For the moment, however, it must be said that the spire of St. Stephen's towers over a city which has become Germanised almost in a night and that the city which served as the bulwark of civilisation against the Turks in 1683 has been converted into the eastern bulwark of a country dominated by a race whose culture and philosophical outlook is the negation of many of the principles for which civilisation stands.'[276] (Seven years later, in 1945, W. H. B. Mack would see Vienna again as a British member of the military government for Austria.)

The law of 13 March described the events of the Anschluss as 'reunification'. This was, of course, nonsense, for the Austria of 1938 had never been united with the German Reich. Seven years later, the incorporation of Austria by the German Reich would be characterised as an occupation. From that point on, the advocates of both the annexation and the occupation theory cited countless arguments to apply a term to events that was appropriate from the view of international law. All sorts of terms were used: desire for the Anschluss, disunity, evolution, reactionism, radicalism, the more or less nonviolent assumption of power by the National Socialists even before German troops marched in, the absence of military resistance and the jubilation on the one hand, the threats, coercion and the deployment of an entire German army on the other hand. Ultimately, all these aspects have something to offer. The emigrated Social Democrats attempted it with a special artifice: as the word 'Anschluss' was already established in the existing vocabulary, which they did not want to surrender to the National Socialists, the process of incorporating Austria was termed 'annexation'.

Even among those who rejected National Socialism, there were advocates of the Anschluss. However, while the fate of those who had felt bereaved from the very outset was admittedly taken note of, a mental attempt was made for the most part to ignore it. It did not fit the overall picture.

10 The Nazi Revolution

10 During the night of 11/12 March 1938, red–white–red flags disappeared from public spaces. Swastika flags also flew in front of the parliament building in Vienna. The building was subsequently used by the 'Reich Commissioner for the Reunification of Austria with the German Reich', Josef Bürckel, and then became the 'Gau House' of the Greater Vienna Reich Gau as the headquarters of the Gau leadership. On 10 September, the parliament building was badly damaged during an American bombing raid. (Photo: Association for the History of the Labour Movement, Vienna)

After Hitler had received the reassuring message on 10 and 11 March that no notable objections would be raised abroad to the swift and forced annexation of Austria, any potential later reactions could no longer irritate him. In fact, the British and French governments only criticised in a thoroughly reserved fashion the way in which the Anschluss had taken place, though not the fact itself. In Moscow, the people's commissar for foreign affairs, Maksim Litvinov, expressed the disapproval of the Soviet government with the drastic formulation 'international crime'. Not surprisingly, there was no reaction to his tentative call for a joint response against Germany's 'illegal aggression'. Only in Geneva, at the headquarters of the League of Nations, to which Germany had no longer belonged since October 1933, was there a formal protest. This was not issued, however, by the Austrian envoy Pflügl. He had sent a succinct telegram to the Foreign Office in Vienna on 12 March: 'Request that you take note of my resignation from my employment relationship hitherto with the Federal Government.' The Mexican envoy, however, delivered a note in the name of his government to the secretary general of the League of Nations, Joseph A. Avenol, on 19 March, in which the 'political death' of Austria was characterised as a serious violation of the Covenant of the League of Nations and the 'sacred principles of international law'. The Mexican government had reacted similarly to the crises in Abyssinia, China and Spain. A joint response had not occurred.[277] It was the same story in the case of Austria. The Mexican note was also contradicted by the fact that Mexico was simultaneously – and successfully – negotiating with Germany over deliveries of mineral oil and did not want to disturb the discussions by all too harsh criticism within the League of Nations.[278] Mr Avenol had in any case already deleted Austria from the list of members.[279] It was back to business as usual.

The Plebiscite

For a period of 24 hours, one might have believed that Hitler would grant Austria a special status within the German Reich and that he would prefer a gradual transition, comparable with that of Bavaria in 1871. He himself had spoken of giving Austria fifty or even eighty years. A personal union had also been discussed: Hitler as Reich chancellor in Germany and federal chancellor in Austria. But these deliberations had become irrelevant on 13 March. Hitler determined on another route. Austria would be incorporated immediately and completely. In this way, those, too, who had dreamed of a National Socialist Austria would have to abandon their illusions. Their disappointment was of no interest to Hitler. Now the radical assimilators were in power and quickly made it clear that it was no longer just a question of the Anschluss but also of revenge. The centres were occupied and potential opponents of the regime were arrested within the first hours. Whoever was able, attempted to flee abroad. Exponents of the Home Guard and the Corporative State sought death. The permanent secretary for national defence, Lieutenant General Wilhelm Zehner, was murdered in unexplained circumstances; Odo Neustädter-Stürmer, multiple minister and prominent leader of the Home Guard, who feared the vengeance of the National Socialists due to his role in the July putsch of 1934, committed suicide; the former vice chancellor and Home Guard leader Emil Fey threw himself out of a window. The cultural philosopher Egon Friedell, who was to be picked up in order to scrub streets, followed suit.[280] These were just a few of the 220 suicides. Schuschnigg was placed under house arrest, was then taken to prison and was eventually subjected to a curious special treatment as a concentration camp inmate, with visiting rights for his wife. Federal President Miklas, however, was not prosecuted, evidently in recognition of his acquiescence. He was permitted to remain in his villa and retained his official motor car. There were more than a few who could not understand this.[281]

A particular concern of the assimilators was the takeover of the executive and its swearing an oath to Hitler and the Nazi state. Anyone who might have been concerned about potential resistance to this could rest easy. The integration of police, gendarmes and Federal Army went without a hitch. After Schuschnigg had ordered the troops to enlist and as the Federal President as nominal supreme commander of the Federal Army evidently did not desire any deployment of the military, the soldiers drove and marched back to their barracks. The state leadership had made the conscious decision not to make use of their only more or less functioning instrument of power. Some of the soldiers and, above all, the officers had been disorientated, but there was no doubt about their loyalty. Germany, however, did not allow any time to elapse before securing this tool of power.

On the occasion of the Federal Army's swearing an oath to Adolf Hitler, only a small group of senior officers did not fall in. Four of around 2,000 officers, as well as 123 NCOs and enlisted men from 55,000 soldiers expressly refused to swear the oath.[282] The overwhelming majority took part in the collective swearing-in. Should any of them have not wanted to take the oath and instead only moved their lips, it went unnoticed in the crowd – and changed nothing. The haste with which this was all done became clear shortly thereafter, when it was noticed that Jewish officers and enlisted men as well as opponents of National Socialism had been automatically sworn in, too. Perhaps they had hoped that they would be allowed to continue serving in a German uniform.

It did not take long before they were dismissed on the basis of an examination of each and every individual. 440 officers of the Federal Army were discharged. Quite a number were later persecuted, sent to concentration camps and killed. To some extent as a quid pro quo, 50 officers who had been disciplined during the time of the Corporative State were reappointed. There was no doubt, however, about the overall picture: the Federal Army had become part of the Wehrmacht and paraded on 15 March before its new supreme commander. Everything seemed to be a matter of course. It was a similar story with the police and Gendarmerie. In terms of power politics, Austria was a part of the German Reich from the first day on. Adolf Hitler arrived in a country that dropped into his lap like a ripe fruit.

When the Führer and Reich Chancellor then proclaimed from the terrace of the New Hofburg the 'accession' of his 'homeland Austria into the German Reich' and announced to the 'oldest eastern march of the German people' its mission as the 'youngest bulwark of the German nation', the jubilation – controlled or otherwise – took on mass hysterical tendencies.[283] Echoing the sentence spoken by Joseph Roth in 1925 on Moscow's Red Square, one could also say: and behind the Heldenplatz, 'on the streets, there stands world history with a veiled face'.[284]

The fact that more people were present on Heldenplatz for the memorial ceremony of the Fatherland Front for Engelbert Dollfuß on 8 August 1934 than there were on 15 March 1938 and that the photos of the latter were edited is now evident. There is no doubt, however, that masses poured into Vienna's city centre to watch the spectacle. The jubilation was mixed with relief, for war had been averted. A day later, preparations already began for a plebiscite on Austria's annexation by Germany. Schuschnigg had not dared to hold one, for the result would have been binding and the time available would surely not have sufficed for the preparations. Hitler did not hesitate and applied the plebiscite to the whole of Germany. The NSDAP apparatus began to secure the results. Nothing should be left to chance. An approval rating as close as possible to one hundred per cent was the aim.

It was not even the incumbent Federal Chancellor Seyß-Inquart who would make the preparations but a man who had gathered relevant experiences in Saarland, the Gauleiter there, Josef Bürckel. On 13 March, he was tasked with reorganising the NSDAP in Austria and preparing the plebiscite. And he made a good job of it.

A propaganda operation was carried out on a scale unknown in Austria. The aim was to emphasise Anschluss aspirations, ensure that the times of rejection on the part of Germany were forgotten, and suppress a certain malicious glee that could often be heard from the Germans towards the backward Austrians, 'Comrade Lace-Up' from the First World War, just as, by the same token, there ought no longer to be any talk of the Slavic Old Prussians who still lived in swamps at the same time as the 'Song of the Nibelungs' had already emerged in Austria.[285] Political celebrities of Germany – now referred to as the 'Old Reich' *(Altreich)* – were engaged for large-scale rallies. Hitler, too, did not flinch from making a tour, which was accompanied by both spontaneous and organised rejoicing. Wherever he went or even wherever his train stopped, flowers were handed over, poems recited and cheeks fondled. Schoolchildren were given the essay topic 'My loveliest moment' and generally wrote using the 'German' running hand about the 'friendly, benevolent face' of the Führer: 'He stroked my cheek with his soft, manicured hand. … I will never be able to forget this moment as long as I live,' wrote a ten-year-old girl from Schwarzach im Pongau.[286] Tens of thousands followed suit. Wherever Hitler did not visit, the authors of local and school chronicles nonetheless let themselves get carried away with eulogistic formulations. The 'greatest son ever born by Austrian soil' had just returned home. He seemed to be emperor and messiah rolled into one.

In Berlin, Reich Foreign Minister Joachim von Ribbentrop assured the British Ambassador that Germany would be generous in the hour of its triumph. At the same time, he badmouthed Schuschnigg und accused him of having engaged in intrigues.[287] Ambassador Nevile Henderson feared that Schuschnigg would be put on trial. In view of the course of action against institutions of the Corporative State and members of Schuschnigg's government and the dissolution of unpopular organisations, the British Ambassador to the German Reich had every reason to be suspicious. But the rumours to the effect that Schuschnigg would be put in front a special tribunal proved to be untrue. The Fatherland Front was dissolved. Thirty legitimist organisations and associations were banned and membership in them was made punishable as a criminal offence. Priests were forced to leave their parishes. So-called celebrity transports were assembled and sent to Dachau concentration camp. The first transport, with 151 people – politicians, opponents of the National Socialist regime, Christian Socials, monarchists, Social Democrats and Communists – departed on 1 April 1938. More than a third of them were Jews. Whoever did not want to risk being arrested and was able to, fled. It was above all two countries that lent themselves to this: Czechoslovakia and Switzerland. Shortly thereafter, the latter initiated – as it called it – a 'fight against foreign alienation'. After Switzerland had accepted 3,000 people, a visa requirement was introduced on 28 March. Thereafter, the succinct formulation of the police commissioner in the Swiss Federal Justice Department applied: 'Let's not get bogged down in sentimentalities.'[288]

In Austria, repressive measures against the Jews were introduced overnight. They constituted approximately four per cent of the population. Not unlike what had happened in the Corporative State, only with inversed omens, so-called scrubbing troops had to remove the slogans for Schuschnigg's consultative referendum and the symbols of the Corporative State.[289] The comparison with the 'cleaning droves' of earlier years was admittedly inappropriate. The images were shocking, the large number of smeared windows and street fronts, and calls of 'Judah perish' and plundering lasting for days illustrated the difference all too clearly. Simultaneously, the exodus began and was accompanied by particularly sickening excesses. The aim was to humiliate the Jews.[290]

A positive race began to obtain the vote of prominent Austrians. Karl Renner was one of these and he was fully in agreement that his 'yes' to the Anschluss be used for propaganda purposes. However, the Nazi rulers did not want him to make any appeal whatsoever of his own accord, regardless of whom it was directed at. Nonetheless, an interview would be conducted with him and published.[291] Renner agreed. In spite of the radically German nationalist stance of the Nazi leadership, the Slovene organisations in Carinthia also advocated coming out in force on 10 April and voting 'yes'. They did not want to provide any excuse for persecutory measures.[292] It was somewhat more difficult to obtain a positive vote from the Catholic Church, until the Cardinal-Archbishop of Vienna, Theodor Innitzer, announced his 'yes' to the Anschluss in a letter to Josef Bürckel and received the support of the Catholic Bishops' Conference to publish this 'yes' and for the Church chancelleries to proclaim: 'On the day of the plebiscite, we, as Germans, will announce our allegiance to the Reich, and we also expect from all practising Christians that they know what they owe their people.'

It was clear that one of the pillars of the Corporative State – if not *the* pillar – had come into line with the advocates of the Anschluss, regardless of its reservations and knowing that it had squandered its role as supporter of the state. Innitzer had to justify his 'yes' in Rome. His letter to Bürckel had not in fact been published in full, as it contained a concluding passage referring to Church laws and Catholic doctrine.[293] Radio Vatican formally distanced itself from the letter of the Austrian bishops and emphasised on 2 April that the 'Solemn Declaration' of the Austrian bishops had been composed and sent without the knowledge of the Holy See. On 5 April, Innitzer travelled to Rome and had to endeavour to find a means of ensuring that neither the Vatican nor himself lost face vis-à-vis the leadership of the German Reich.[294] While he was still on his way back to Vienna, a second declaration concerning the first declaration was published in *Osservatore Romano*; it had been formulated primarily by Cardinal Secretary of State Eugenio Pacelli and approved by Innitzer.[295]

The Protestant Church in Austria also did not hesitate to announce its 'yes' to the Anschluss. The member of the Protestant High Consistory Robert Kauer greeted Hitler in the name of 330,000 Protestant Germans and enthusiastically wrote to him: 'After years of oppression that were reminiscent of the most terrible times of the Counter-Reformation, you came as our saviour.'[296]

The elimination of the political leadership and its replacement with people who were committed to the Nazi regime, the overnight reorientation of the executive to German command authorities and the suppressive measures, of which there were already noticeable indications, had already initiated a process in Austria, weeks before the scheduled plebiscite, that was characterised as 'enforced coordination' (Gleichschaltung) but also brought about something that had not existed in Austria in 1918, namely a revolutionary change. It was not only a question of substituting one political system for another and removing a few people from the leadership and the administration. It was also a question of replacing the elites and bringing about a social sea change. The unmistakeable threat that emanated from the invading Eighth Army, the arrests, as well as the violence and sanctioned arbitrary measures of Nazi formations like the SA and the SS were a part of this and rounded off the picture of a brutal revolutionary transformation.

At the same time, a disintegration took hold designed to destroy the old existing bonds.[297] The catchword with which the reconstruction of society was proclaimed was 'ethnic community' (Volksgemeinschaft). The culture of memory was also placed at the disposal of the revolutionary upheaval, and it was a widely visible symbol that the Rathausplatz in Vienna was renamed 'Adolf-Hitler-Platz' on 12 March. Thousands of other street and square names were also changed. There, where the attempted putsch of 25 July 1934 had begun, the Siebensterngasse in Vienna was renamed 'Street of the July Fighters' (Straße der Julikämpfer). It was only a matter of days before the crypt in the Seipel-Dollfuß Memorial Church in Vienna's 15th District was blocked off. There was no place in the collective memory of the Nazi state for either of them, least of all Dollfuß.[298] It was telling that the transfer of the coffins did not take place during the day but instead during the night of 23 to 24 January 1939.[299] The formal sealing of the revolutionary process took place on 10 April, when 99.75 per cent of those entitled to vote in Austria agreed to the Anschluss. In the 'Old Reich', the number was somewhat lower, but this was insignificant. The Federal Constitutional Law of 13 March had been likewise impressively confirmed. Incidentally, this was the third time since the end of the First World War that a constitutional law had stated that Austria was part of the German Reich. This time, it was considered irreversible.

The Country of Austria

During preparations for the plebiscite, German economic experts moved into the Austrian ministries and company management committees. They were tasked with preparing a balance sheet. The president of the Reichsbank, Hjalmar Schacht, did not paint a very rosy picture of the 'hostile takeover' of Austria. He claimed that the costs in the financial sector were higher than the profit, for the German Reich now inherited Austria's foreign debts and – as a result of the loans from the League of Nations – they were considerable. Eventually, the Reichsbank committed itself to making interest payments and to paying off the debts. However, the Reichsbank also liquidated the foreign assets of the Austrian National Bank with the Bank of England, which brought Chancellor of the Exchequer Sir John Simon several critical questions in the British House of Commons.[300] London's financial experts were doubtlessly satisfied, though, that Germany promised to be just as exemplary in its role of debtor as Austria had been. In his comments, however, which only touched on the monetary side of things, Schacht intentionally brushed certain matters under the table. For example, the fact that the Austrian National Bank had to pay 230 million Reichsmarks, plus settlement loans of 75 million, gold worth 148 million and access options on privately stockpiled holdings of gold and foreign currency in the amount of 875 million Reichsmarks. All in all, this was far more than the total reserves of the German Reichsbank.[301] The Austrian gold and foreign currency reserves were already brought to Berlin on 17 March.

There were also other things that triggered a gold-rush mood in Germany. It was namely not only the state but also private individuals who could undertake veritable raids and snap up companies. Before the Anschluss, German shares in industrial enterprises in Austria totalled between ten and twelve per cent and in credit institutions eight per cent. These shares later grew by virtue of buying but also considerable investments to a total of 57 per cent and became known as 'German Assets' (Deutsches Eigentum).[302] The proportion of the economy of the 'Old Reich' that Austrian firms could purchase was far more modest, but even if Austrian businesses, with a few exceptions, were much smaller than German companies, there were many opportunities for them in light of the tenfold market increase. It was also beyond doubt that the parameters would change. Many Austrian business owners and chief executives had no problem with the new era. Leading industrial enterprises, including the largest Austrian conglomerate, the Austrian Alpine Montan Company, which was owned by the United Steel Works in Düsseldorf, had started to support the NSDAP years earlier. Some of the firms had been run by illegal National Socialists and had preferred to employ National Socialists.[303] This could now be regarded as an investment in the future.

The Anschluss of Austria occurred half way through the concept adopted in 1936 by the Prussian governor, commander-in-chief of the Luftwaffe and plenipotentiary for the Four-Year Plan, Hermann Göring, to enable the German economy within four years to become autarchic in terms of food and to accelerate the arms build-up to such a degree that Germany would be capable of waging a war of aggression. This was based on Hitler's conviction that a war against the Soviet Union was unavoidable.[304]

Göring's insistence on a swift Anschluss therefore aimed from the outset to exploit Austrian potential as quickly as possible, in order to fulfil the targets of the Four-Year Plan. And Austria had a lot to offer: ores, above all iron and magnesite, as well as mineral oil. In addition, there was an abundance of timber and water and extensive possibilities for establishing new industries, as well as the potential offered by around 400,000 unemployed and those no longer receiving any social security benefits for remedying the labour shortages in Germany.[305] One hundred thousand found work in the 'Old

Reich'. In Austria itself, 300,000 found employment. They began building the Salzburg section of the Reich motorway from Munich to Vienna. They were supposed, furthermore, to start work on the storage power plant at Kaprun and were, not least, procured by the arms industry. It generally appeared that the hopes of the workers, but also the technicians, salaried employees, small businessmen and all manner of professions, that the Anschluss would have a positive effect would now be fulfilled.

In agriculture, things seemed to develop equally positively at first. The debt burden of the farmers had already grown in the 1920s. The number of foreclosures had increased from year to year. Between 1933 and 1937, 16.7 per cent of Austrian agricultural enterprises had to be sold.[306] In Styria alone, more than 1,000 farms went under the hammer every year during the 1930s.[307] The difficult situation of the farmers made it easy for the Nazi regime to proclaim an immediate turnaround in the economy. As early as 5 May 1938, the Austrian Debt Relief Regulation was enacted. The German Reich assumed part of the farmers' debt, extended the annuity rates to up to 60 years and published development studies that aimed to retain and consolidate farming enterprises, because they were desperately needed in order to achieve the intended autarchy and fulfil the Four-Year Plan.[308] Two weeks later, the Reich Food Estate Law (Reichsnährstandsgesetz) came into effect. It was designed to bring about a reorganisation of agriculture and the implementation of the agricultural policy measures of the Nazi state. It was admittedly not as successful as had been hoped, for the rural exodus increased. Industries had an enormous demand for workers and tempted them with jobs.

Soon, a different problem emerged: the amount of work exceeded the number of available workers. The success of the bundle of measures could not only be seen in the disappearance of unemployment and the debt relief operations for the farmers, however. The success also entailed the fact that the National Socialists had won over not only the Social Democrat workers but also the Christian Social farmers in a minimum of time. Evidently, their measures had far more success than those of the political organisations of 'old' Austria.

Something else also contributed to the dwindling human potential: the German Wehrmacht, Party formations and the construction of the surveillance state caused a veritable extraction of the people, above all the men. From 1935, attempts had also started in the Corporative State to fully exploit the country's military strength. The restrictive terms of the Peace Treaty of Saint-Germain were gradually rescinded until, in 1936, general conscription had been introduced and an open arms build-up begun. The victorious powers of the First World War, who had repeatedly issued threats to Austria, pretended to ignore the armament measures. Compared with the German Wehrmacht, however, the Federal Army was a pocket-size military instrument. This changed in summer 1938. With the adoption of German mustering norms and by means of a far more consistent call-up procedure, so many men became liable for military service or chose the path of professional soldiers that the Austrian proportion of the German Wehrmacht soon counted eight to ten per cent.[309] Officers, insofar as they were retained, NCOs and a small number of enlisted men were initially distributed among all military branches and military districts for the purpose of retraining and then in order to integrate them as swiftly as possible. The subsequent claim that the Austrians had been vigorously divided up and mixed with formations from the 'Old Reich' because those from the 'Eastern March' (Ostmark) were generally mistrusted was never the case and is purely a construction.[310]

It is also not true that no 'Austrian' troop units existed, for the 2nd and 3rd Mountain Divisions, as well as individual army divisions recruited primarily from those territories referred to nationwide as the 'Eastern March' – the 44th, 45th, 297th Infantry Divisions, the 2nd and 4th Panzer Divisions and the 4th Light Division – contained a disproportionately high number of soldiers from Austria.[311] Others were later added. The formations of the Wehrmacht were not dissimilar to the regiments of the Imperial and Royal Army, which had likewise not contained any purely German, purely Hungarian or purely Czech units, but instead only such where a single nationality predominated. Among the SS Dispositional Troops, referred to from 1939 as the Waffen SS, it was above all the 2nd SS Panzer Division 'Das Reich' that possessed a high proportion of Austrians.

Great value was attached to service in the Wehrmacht and the SS not only for purely military reasons but also because it was a leveller like nothing else. Those in the Wehrmacht who were academics or had a school-leaving certificate of course differed from those among the drafted enlisted men with a low level of school education, but there was no difference in the treatment of workers, farmers, craftsmen, tradesmen and retailers, but also between former Social Democrats and former Christian Socials.[312] In the SS Dispositional Troops, officer rank was not even tied to the successful completion of junior school. One difference soon emerged, however: members of the Wehrmacht were subjected to National Socialist indoctrination far less than the civilian population, and ultimately for Party members and Party aspirants the principle applied: for the period of service in the Wehrmacht, Party membership was suspended. This initially pertained to the two-year period of military service and was then extended for the war years. There was no shielding from propaganda. On the contrary: the Wehrmacht became a fundamental component part of the propaganda. It was not a question of blind obedience and merciless drill, while the exertions were regarded more as a challenge and a demonstration of masculinity, or at least this was how they were portrayed.[313]

For many more, what counted were new weapons, modern technology, the opportunities of flying with modern machines, or even service in military branches such as the navy, which had been non-existent in Austria. These things had the potential to seduce the men.

There were reports as good as every day proclaiming an end to shortages and every-day worries and propagating an upswing: 'Systematic placement of the unemployed', 'Lower Austria becomes a tourist destination', 'A major offensive against economic scarcity begins', 'Easter joy for 15,000 no longer receiving any social security benefits' announced *Das Kleine Volksblatt* at daily intervals; '75,000 receive benefits again' was one headline in the *Kronen-Zeitung*. On the occasion of Hitler's birthday, it was stated quite simply: 'The architect of Greater Germany'.[314]

Josef Bürckel, who had administered the plebiscite, became Reich commissioner for the reunification and was supposed to implement a complete administrative and le-gal alignment within the space of a year. He made no attempt to take consideration of anyone else, but he was bothered by the opposition of those who did not want to simply accept the disappearance of Austria. Most of them had already been arrested by 10 April 1938, had fled or at least been muzzled. But he did attempt to scotch the cases of wild Aryanisation and criminal fundraising operations, making himself unpopular with numerous Party big shots in the process. Otherwise, he tackled in ex-emplary fashion those who attempted to force themselves to the forefront of the Party and vied for power and influence. And it was no small number who attempted this, including Bürckel himself. In Vienna alone, 100,000 people were soon in the pay of the NSDAP.[315] Although Party membership was tied to a whole host of conditions, the number of those who at least aspired to become Party members continually rose. They strove to demonstrate their solidarity and affiliation. Opportunism played its part, though this was certainly not an exclusively Austrian characteristic. Even without ac-tual Party membership, someone could still belong to one of its many retinues. Often, it was unclear how someone was incorporated so quickly and without their personal con-tribution. This also applied to women, of whom in December 1938 more than 100,000 already counted among the members of Nazi women's organisations. Added to these were the female adolescents who were claimed by the League of German Girls (Bund Deutscher Mädel, or BDM) – the counterpart to the male Hitler Youth (Hitlerjugend). The tendency was rising.[316] The density of organisations exceeded that of the 'Old Reich' by far. The benefits of membership were obvious. If someone belonged to 'the Party' or one of the National Socialist organisations or was at least a recognised part of the eth-nic community, then he/she had work and benefitted from a whole host of privileges. One of the prerequisites for membership in the ethnic community was admittedly the production of an 'Aryan attestation' (Ariernachweis). Registry offices and churches were overwhelmed, because everything of course had to be dealt with swiftly. A large number of people were to be disappointed who had expected preferential treatment on the basis of their earlier illegal status. These included the 3,000 members of the Austrian Legion. Two weeks passed after the German invasion before they were even permitted to enter the country of Austria.[317]

The Nazi state promoted the construction of social housing, undertook widespread child education, guaranteed holidays and medical care and consciously (or, perhaps, unconsciously) built on the state welfare policies of the Austrian Social Democrats. If someone did not fulfil the criteria demanded, then he/she became an outsider and was made to notice it. There were sanctions due to 'work disloyalty', breach of employment contract, slacking or refusal to work. The 'Gau administrators' of the German Labour Front ensured that every single person contributed to building the Greater German Reich.

The surveillance state became omnipresent. The regime controlled marriages and reproduction, and it relentlessly took action against those who did not meet racial-ideological expectations.[318] It engaged in systematic exclusion to the point of forced sterilisation and killing. The idea was to make people 'available without limits'.[319] The state ultimately made a claim on the life of the members of the ethnic community.

The Other Side of the Coin

Some 'breathing space' was required in order to even remotely grasp how much the measures of the new state leadership intertwined. First of all, the exchange of elites resulted in the pillars of the Corporative State not only losing their function but also their freedom; they were eliminated and were only gradually released. The majority of those arrested in March and April were admittedly freed before the plebiscite but they lost their jobs and in many cases were later arrested again.

As of 1 June 1938, the 'country of Austria' was initially divided up into eight (Party) Gaue, which only partially corresponded to the old federal states. On 15 October, Burgenland was summarily divided up between Styria and Lower Austria. Ninety-seven surrounding communities were added to Vienna, so that it mutated to become the Gau of 'Greater Vienna'. However, it lost its function as capital city, to the annoyance of many, and was reduced to the status of a large provincial city. The parliament, the old Imperial Assembly building, became a 'Gau house' as the headquarters of the Gau administration. The Ausseerland region was transferred to Upper Austria. Vorarlberg – as a special type of administrative district – was combined with Tyrol, thus disregarding the common phrase in both Tyrol and Vorarlberg that one should not combine 'what God has separated'. Ultimately, there were only seven Reich Gaue. At the head of each of these, Gauleiter assumed the most important function. The objective was the unity of Party and state. As the name of Austria ought to disappear, the largest Party Gaue were promptly renamed Lower Danube and Upper Danube. Every hint of Austrian consciousness was to be removed and left to the historians.

On 14 April 1939, the name 'Austria' disappeared altogether. This, at least, was envisaged by the Eastern March Law, which was published on this day in the *Reichsgesetz-*

blatt and came into effect on 1 May.[320] In this way, the administrative structure of the country was aligned with the political structure of the Party. The Gauleiter also became Reich governors (Reichsstatthalter), which clearly demonstrated the tendency towards a preponderance of the Party.[321] That which was demonstrated in the Eastern March was supposed to be a model for the 'Old Reich'. The word for 'district' was renamed from *Bezirk* to *Kreis*, headed either by regional councillors or head mayors. A new Gau capital city was also stipulated: Krems would become the new Gau capital of Lower Danube, even if Vienna was the headquarters of the Gau leadership. Soon, the organisation of authorities in the Gaue of the Eastern March did not differ in the slightest from their equivalent in the 'Old Reich'. There was, however, one difference: The Reich Gaue of the Eastern March were in some cases considerably smaller than those of the 'Old Reich'. In this way, at least the historical units were preserved. The ultimate objective, however, was to merge the Reich Gaue of the Eastern March in order to create larger units. This never happened. Even so, enlargement was the order of the day.

While the reordering measures were still being implemented, there was a series of further far-reaching events that stemmed from the continuation of Hitler's expansive politics. After months of threats and negotiations, Britain and France approved via the Munich Agreement the separation of the so-called Sudetenland from Czechoslovakia and its attachment to Greater Germany. Czechoslovakia saw no possibility, either political or military, to oppose this step. When, from 1 October, German troops then marched into those territories of Czechoslovakia that were settled by a majority of Germans and also occupied the territories of southern Bohemia and southern Moravia by 10 October, Hitler and the National Socialists could once more be certain of the enthusiastic approval of a majority of the Austrian population. They had not forgotten the role of many Czechs during the course of the First World War, and likewise the futile struggle for the annexation of southern Bohemia and southern Moravia to German-Austria in 1918 and 1919. The newspapers fell over themselves: 'Our troops advance into southern Moravia', 'Celebration of freedom in German Znaim', 'Nikolsburg and Lundenburg brought home to the Reich', 'The advance of Bernhardsthal', 'German troops reach the finish line everywhere'.[322] It was intended that Petržalka (Engerau), the part of Bratislava (Preßburg) south of the Danube, be transferred to Lower Danube. Around 320,000 people lived in the annexed territories, with only 21,000 Czechs among them.[323] It appeared that the Peace Treaty of Saint-Germain had once again been suspended. For the soldiers from Austria, deployment during the occupation of southern Bohemia and southern Moravia was no acid test. They did feel the intoxicating effect of the jubilation, however, and they succumbed to it. Like the politicians of the Western powers, they believed Hitler's assurances in his speech in Berlin's Sportpalast on 26 September, to the effect that this would be the final territorial revisionist demand.

Amidst the rejoicing over the solution of the Sudeten question and the enlargement of the Gaue of Upper Danube and Lower Danube, one event was overlooked that revealed the pitiless side of the regime and made clear once again that the Nazi leadership would not hesitate for one moment to demonstrate particular severity when any resistance stirred. On 7 October, thousands of adolescents (there was talk of 15,000) made their way to St. Stephen's Cathedral on the occasion of the Feast of Christ the King. At the end of mass, Cardinal Innitzer expressed it in a considered or ill-considered way, as the case may be: 'You have one leader, your leader is Christ. If you stay true to him, you will never be lost.'[324] This had to be understood as a response to the slogan of Reich Propaganda Minister Joseph Goebbels from 26 September: 'Führer ordered, we followed!' The Catholic Youth of Vienna acclaimed the Cardinal at the top of their voices. A day later, members of the Hitler Youth stormed the Archbishop's palace and laid it to waste. The words of the Cardinal were remarkable not only because they were uttered less than seven months after the Anschluss. They were also directed against the claim to power of a regime that prided itself on its youthfulness and its particular advocacy of youth.

The Cardinal was of course riled by the anti-church policies of the regime, which found their expression in the repeal of the Concordat of 1933, the arrest of hundreds of priests, the closure of around 1,400 Catholic private schools and seminaries and an increasing number of secessions from the Church. Innitzer could not do any differently than to challenge the regime. The reaction was not long in coming. During a mass gathering of 200,000 people on 13 October, Bürckel went one step further and denounced the Church as the 'bearer of political Catholicism' and accused it of treason.[325]

No press coverage appeared, however, of the uprising of the Catholic youth, the brief arrest of the Graz Prince-Bishop Ferdinand Pawlikowski and the mounting alienation of the Catholic Church. It was reported, however, that unemployment had decreased by 500,000 people, and that there was a labour shortage outside of Vienna. In order to combat this, Czech, Slovak, Italian and Yugoslavian workers, male and female, were voluntarily recruited. It was only the beginning, but it was doubtlessly a signal. And the press reported on it.

The Nazi regime made perfect use of the human propensity for selective perception. The strategies had long become obscure. The media controlled by the press chief of the Reich government, Otto Dietrich, were officially committed to portraying developments in all areas of life as desired and sustainable. A similar form of portrayal had also been attempted by the Corporative State but it had never succeeded in silencing the opponents of an Austrian path. The National Socialists did not have a problem with constructing unanimity. They simply did not report on setbacks and problems, and reports from abroad were in any case not believed in the ideologically heated atmosphere and, furthermore, interpreted and relayed in a way that was agreeable to the regime.

The propensity for selective perception also resulted in practically everything being ignored that did not affect – and thus disturb – one's own sphere of life. People began to excuse to themselves the persecutory measures of the Nazi regime, which were very visible and open to scrutiny. They took the view that one cannot make an omelette without breaking eggs, if a backward country is to be aligned with the modernity of Germany. Freeloaders had no place in the ethnic community. The state was everything, its Führer knew everything; the individual was nothing – and knew nothing.

Perceptions became ever more subjective. The willingness to subordinate oneself made things much easier for those in power. And they had it within their control simply not to allow anything negative to find its way through to the citizens of the Reich. What would the residents of Vienna have said, for example, if Heinrich Himmler's plan to move the confiscated art objects abroad and concentrate them in Munich and Berlin, including the huge art collection of Alphonse de Rothschild, had become known? Hitler prohibited their removal, although – or perhaps because – he had become aware that Vienna was not quite so completely in favour of the Anschluss as the federal states were.[326] The injustice that was being done here, however, affected only a very few. The museums scrambled to obtain the gems of the collection. The Jew Rothschild, that was one thing; his collection was something entirely different. The Reich commissioner for the reunification, Bürckel, shared Himmler's view, however, because for him it was a question of making historic Austria and its cultural heritage disappear as far as possible.

One had to keep repeating to oneself that the Anschluss with Germany had been desired. In one way or another. This 'in one way or another' had also applied initially for many Jews. They had learned to fear National Socialism before 1938. But they also cherished hopes. In the first days after the Anschluss, they had often been the victims of private raids, which even Bürckel and Vienna's SA leadership then opposed, speaking of 'irresponsible elements' who were exploiting the period of 'upheaval' to 'misappropriate the property of others'.[327] It must have been positively alarming that – regardless of the fact that the 'Nuremberg race laws' did not yet apply to Austria, 210,000 Jews were not permitted to take part in the plebiscite. They were excluded and had to return the polling cards they had already received, as did 150,000 Austrians who were classified as opponents of the regime.[328] Jews lost their status in society, were cast out and – in the event that they had not attempted to flee – forced to emigrate. Hand in hand with this, they were deprived of their possessions. The approach towards the Jews fatally combined local, long-held prejudices with ideological factors. Jews made up 9.4 per cent of the Viennese population. In some areas, Jews had obtained a dominant position. In Vienna, the most important publishing centre for German-language literature after Leipzig, there were around 200 publishing houses headed by Jews. Jews dominated banking, trade, journalism, film, press, medicine and the practice of law. This already aroused envy in the 1920s, and it did not take much for the envy to turn into hatred.

Intellectual professions were not something that appealed to the lower social strata. It was not a question of envying a doctor for his profession, but he was envied for his affluence, and it seemed so easy to usurp Jewish property with the help of 'the Party' and to acquire the housing for 100,000 people promised by the National Socialists. Members of the 'old guard' wanted to be rewarded for their years in illegality.

Sixty-three Jews were sent with the first transport to Dachau. In the Jewish Religious Communities, donation receipts could be found for more than 800,000 schillings, which had been handed out for the promotion of Schuschnigg's consultative referendum. The specialist for Jewish affairs (Judenreferent) of the Secret State Police (Gestapo) sent to Vienna, Adolf Eichmann, demanded the same amount for the plebiscite. In May, around 2,000 Jews were arrested. This could only be understood as a downright threat. It was followed by harassment, and occupational bans for journalists, actors, musicians and lawyers. Schoolchildren had to leave their classes; students were unregistered. More than half the lecturers at the University of Vienna were dismissed.[329] Around 25,000 businesses and firms owned by Jews were placed in the hands of provisional administrators. Arthur Seyß-Inquart, who had mutated from federal chancellor to Reich governor, played an important role here and increasingly became the accessory of the Nazi state.[330]

The unregulated Aryanisation was followed by the 'regulated Aryanisation'. In late May 1938, the Nuremberg race laws of September 1935 were extended to Austria. In this way, the arbitrariness would be controlled and the 'legal' disenfranchisement of the Jews would begin. The economy was to be 'de-Jewified' (entjudet); troublesome competition eliminated, Jews removed from the markets and excluded from trade in grain and cattle.[331] It appeared most effective to increase the pressure to such an extent that the Jews were left with no alternative but to abandon everything and leave the Greater German Reich. An initiative of the American President Franklin D. Roosevelt led to the holding of a conference from 6 to 15 July 1938 in the French resort of Évian, whose aim was to enable the Jews to emigrate from Germany and, above all, explore the willingness of 32 participating states to take them in. The fate of 480,000 people hung in the balance. There were no official delegations from the 'Old Reich' and the Eastern March, though Seyß-Inquart did allow a representation of the Israelite Religious Community of Vienna to travel to Évian. It was not only a question of the legal departure of the Jews but also the material parameters. The Nazi leadership was interested in their departure but not in the Jews taking their assets and their possessions with them. Given, however, that the Dominican Republic was the only participating state that was willing to commit itself to taking in Jews, the Évian Conference ended in a fiasco. In the *Völkischer Beobachter*, the 'Militant paper of the National Socialist movement of Greater Germany' (Kampfblatt der nationalsozialistischen Bewegung Großdeutschlands), one could read that Germany had offered the world its Jews but no one wanted them.[332]

Ultimately, everything was done to enforce the emigration of the Austrian Jews. The Reich Flight Tax (Reichsfluchtsteuer), the Jewish Property Levy (Judenvermögensabgabe) and a passport charge were assessed in such a way, however, that the emigrants were left with nothing. Their bank accounts were blocked and, in this way, their cash on hand effectively confiscated. All this was observed but it nonetheless belonged in the realm of selective perception.

A multitude of laws and decrees exacerbated the measures already enacted. As of early 1939, Jews had to bear the additional first name of Sara or Israel. From 15 November 1938, Jewish children were excluded from attending schools. Jewish doctors were deprived of their licence to practise medicine and were permitted only to treat Jewish patients. Park benches displayed the inscription 'Only for Aryans'.

If one could speak of indirect violence until November 1938, this changed on the late evening of 9 November with the so-called Night of Broken Glass (Reichskristallnacht). During the course of the excesses, which were purportedly a spontaneous protest over the murder of a German diplomat in Paris, synagogues and Jewish prayer houses were destroyed, businesses plundered, apartments confiscated, people beaten and a large number killed. The Jews of German nationality were ordered to pay a billion Reichsmarks. A substantial part of this sum had to be raised in Austria. This made it entirely clear that the anti-Semitism also had a marked economic component alongside the racial-ideological aspect.[333] Everything continued to be done to force the Jews of the Greater German Reich to emigrate. In Vienna, 70,000 apartments inhabited by Jews were gradually 'aryanised', which satisfied the housing demand.[334] During the course of their Aryanisation policies in Vienna between 1938 and 1941, the National Socialists took possession of more apartments than had been built in 'red Vienna'.[335] By 14 May 1939, around 100,000 Austrian Jews had emigrated, most of them from Vienna.[336] Nonetheless, some small localities, such as Deutsch Wagram in the Marchfeld, prided themselves on having become 'free of Jews' (judenfrei). The Gauleiter of Salzburg reported on 12 November 1938 that his Gau was 'completely free of Jews'. The Semmering resort was 'free of Jews'. For a time, the intention was to resettle the Jews in Madagascar. This proved to be impossible. But then Poland and the 'Reich Commissariat Ostland' in the Baltic and Belarus lent themselves as territories for forced resettlements. A new chapter was opened, which was then euphemistically called the 'Final Solution to the Jewish Question' (Endlösung der Judenfrage) and which in reality meant mass murder.

Ethnic Community

That which had so euphorically been termed the Anschluss, had in the meantime become the everyday life of the ethnic community. People searched for normality and found it. At irregular intervals, they were summoned to roll calls, presentations, rallies, troths, schooling and courses. Male and female ethnic comrades were addressed in equal measure and obliged to take part. What had once been regarded as rivals to the institutions of the Corporative State, such as the 'Ethnic-Nationalist Emergency Relief' (Völkische Nothilfe), the 'Voluntary Labour Service' (Freiwilliger Arbeitsdienst) or the 'German School Association' (Deutscher Schulverein), now became the sole determinants. Working life was just as organised as family life. Block and cell leaders controlled everyday life and were regarded as public authorities: 'The public authority must take care of everything. He must be aware of everything. He must be involved in everything', as a directive of the Main Schooling Office of the NSDAP stated.[337] There were female local administrators and leaders of the Gau Women's League, in order to ensure that the women were just as organised as the men.[338] The endowment of the Cross of Honour of the German Mother was also directed at women. It was conferred from December 1938 in bronze for four or five children, in silver for six or seven and in gold for eight or more children, though it was clear that only mothers of 'German blood and sound genes' were to be honoured in this way.

Life appeared to consist of abbreviations: NSDAP, Pg (Party member), SA, SS, RSHA (Reich Security Main Office), HJ (Hitler Youth), BDM (League of German Girls), NSDStB (National Socialist German Association of Students), DAF (German Labour Front), WHW (Winter Relief Agency), NSF (National Socialist Women's League), DFW (German Women's Agency), KdF (Strength through Joy) and many more. The new vocabulary was regarded and used as self-evident, and, if this was even possible, language became ever more violent or just more cryptic. New public holidays were instituted. Schools observed 'German Savings Day' on 30 October, the 'Memorial Day for those Killed in the Name of the Movement' on 9 November, the 'Day of German Salon Music' on 19 November, 'Winter Solstice and German Christmas' on 21 December, the 'Day of the Seizure of Power' on 30 January, the 'Memorial Day for the Eastern March' on 13 March, 'Heroes' Memorial Day' on 16 March, etc., etc.[339] In nursery schools, the infants fervently recited verses such as 'Hold hands, lower your head and think of Adolf Hitler'. Dear God had to make way for the Führer, and National Socialism became a substitute religion. The foundations had long since been laid, for nationalism, racism and the desire for a single-minded, determined state leadership were not new. Only the methods had changed. Like so many things: not new, just different. The Corporative State had also had its own personality cult. Now Hitler and the swastika were omnipresent, and one could escape neither the image of the Führer nor the sign of joy and blessing, which the swastika was regarded as.

From newborns to the dying, everyone found themselves in one or another drawer of the Nazi state. Everything seemed to be uncommonly efficient and, what was more, legitimated by the rule of law. People worked not only for their own wellbeing but also for the state and the ethnic community. Freeloading, it seemed, no longer existed. Profiteers continued to exist but they were political persecutees of the 'time of the system' (Systemzeit), who had a right to indemnification. And if one person did not like another, all he had to do was suspect him of something and report him to the police. Doubts about Germany's sustainability were out of place. It was beyond doubt that the accomplishments of the ethnic community had to be safeguarded. Finally, the life of every individual was to be orientated towards the demands of a war. A home front was already created during peacetime.

Fascination with the economic development of the Eastern March had not yet disappeared, however. The country experienced a modernisation surge. Not only the east of the country, Greater Vienna, would profit but the west would also catch up in industrial terms. Of the approximately 100,000 Austrians who had been conscripted for work in the 'Old Reich', most returned home. Only 15,000 remained.[340] There was now enough work in Austria, too. On 13 May 1938, Hermann Göring had made the first cut of the spade for the Linz foundry of the 'Reich Works for Ore Mining and Ironworks Hermann Göring'. It would become the largest conglomerate in the Eastern March. Another six industrial groups belonged to it, from Steyr-Daimler-Puch to the Danube Steamship Company DDSG. The construction of a Luftwaffe plant was commenced in Steyr; the Nibelungs Works emerged in St. Valentin as a pure armaments factory. In Upper Danube, which recorded the largest number of new enterprises, the Eastern March Nitrogen Works were founded, while in Ranshofen work was started on the construction of an aluminium plant. In Wiener Neustadt, an armaments complex for the production of fighter planes was set up. Existing industrial enterprises such as the Böhler Works in Kapfenberg, the ammunition factory in Hirtenberg and, above all, the factories and manufacturing plants in Vienna were massively expanded. In a minimum of time, many of the most important production sites became suppliers of the armaments industry. In Styria and the industrially underdeveloped Carinthia alone, 126 companies were declared to be arms factories. Hundreds of thousands of men and women worked on behalf of the High Command of the Wehrmacht.[341]

Power stations were built, electrification was promoted and modernisation was in evidence on all sides. It again seemed as though things were picking up everywhere. One of the downsides was that almost all banks and credit institutions, as well as a substantial number of large firms were transferred to German ownership or at least placed under German management. Something similar had been planned by the Supreme War Command set up by Germany in 1918, just as the question repeatedly posed itself regarding the extent to which National Socialism was building on things already begun in the 1920s. Back in May 1918, enforced coordination had already been contemplated, and no consideration had been taken any more of circumstances and the needs of Austria-Hungary. It had exclusively been a question of increasing efficiency and achieving a victorious peace. That which had been contemplated back then was now being realised. Workers and salaried employees were content. The workforce did not have to worry about employment, and even if individuals rejected the regime for whatever reason, they fell in line. As one female worker in the Hallein Cigar Factory in Salzburg put it: 'The main thing is that we had work, that's what we thought. There was in any case nothing you could do in the face of the major changes imposed by the state.'[342]

Admittedly, many were not content to just have work and witness the changes. They wanted to play their part, actively participate, achieve something within the Party and its structures that they would have otherwise been denied. Around ten per cent of adults strove to join the NSDAP. One did not have to be a Party member or belong to the SA or the SS, however, in order to show appreciation for the Nazi state. The incorporation of southern Bohemian, southern Moravian and Slovak territories was perceived as righting a wrong. It remained to be seen whether the final word had been spoken in this respect. It had long since become evident that the peace treaties after the First World War no longer had any relevance. This could be seen time and again, and Vienna – reduced to the status of a Gau capital – seemed to be recovering some of the glamour of the former imperial city. It was at least the venue for transregional political decisions on more than one occasion.

Less than one month after the occupation of the Czech territories, one could again go and see Nazi celebrities in Vienna. The 'First Vienna Award' of 2 November 1938 assigned extensive territories in southern Slovakia to Hungary, which in this way came a great deal closer to achieving its aim of revising the territorial stipulations of the Treaty of Trianon. Czechoslovakia and Hungary had agreed to transfer to Germany and Italy the settlement of the question of territorial cessions. The German Reich Foreign Minister Joachim von Ribbentrop and the Italian Foreign Minister Count Galeazzo Ciano drew a new border. The Vienna Award was signed in Belvedere Palace. The objective pursued by Hungary and Germany, namely to completely smash Czechoslovakia, was palpable. It then only took until 14 March 1939 before Slovakia – with German backing – declared its independence and German troops invaded the so-called rump Czech state the next day, which was then incorporated into Greater Germany as the Protectorate of Bohemia and Moravia. London and Paris had reckoned with this and once again showed no reaction.

As with the invasion of southern Bohemia and southern Moravia, units of the army divisions stationed in Austria once more took part in the invasion. Not only that: for this 'Scenario Green', those plans that had been composed by the Operations Division of the Federal Army in 1937 were to have been communicated to Berlin, in order to occupy Czechoslovakia in a joint operation with the Wehrmacht and Hungarian troops and, with this sign of cooperativeness, preserve the independence of Austria. By 1939, this was, at best, only a memory.

After a year of Austria belonging to the German Reich, it could be established that the National Socialist revolution had completely changed the country. A widespread exchange of elites had taken place. Attempts had been made to loosen the traditional bonds with family, church and a Habsburg-Austrian history as quickly as possible. The introduction of the obligatory civil marriage instead of the exclusively church wedding contributed significantly to this. The Hitler Youth replaced the Catholic youth organisations. Male adolescents competed in small calibre-shooting, organised field games, marched, engaged in drill exercises and volunteered as soon as possible for service in the German Wehrmacht or – for the very spirited – the SS. They did not care that this served preparations for war. The life of every individual was organised through and through. Around 221,000 kinsmen of the Eastern March had obtained Party membership by March 1939, at which point a ban on new intakes was imposed.[343] Though not for long.

From October 1938, young men between 17/18 and 25 years of age were obliged to perform six months of labour service. The Reich Labour Service was also intended to force those who were not accustomed to physical work to serve the ethnic community. The slogan was 'service with the spade' in 'German soil'. Analogous to this, there existed for young women – who were now called labour maidens – the Reich Labour Service for Female Adolescents (Reichsarbeitsdienst für die weibliche Jugend). For the young men, it was the prelude to military service; for the young women, it was the prelude to motherhood. For those who were single and did not have children, the labour service was extended by six months in 1941 and had to be performed as wartime auxiliary service.[344]

Pressure was exerted on most members of the important professional groups, above all those that sent a powerful signal – teachers, lawyers, physicians, technicians and journalists – to join a Party organisation. One could attempt to thwart these efforts, like the later Austrian Federal President Adolf Schärf, by submitting a declaration of accession to the National Socialist Association of Legal Professionals but 'forgetting' to place it in the envelope. Whether one would succeed in this way until the end of the regime, however, was highly doubtful. The vast majority of people believed that they were safe and were not unsettled when they realised that the Nazi state demanded more than just staying put. In this way, those who had at least hesitated now found themselves willing, when in Rome, to do as the Romans do. Whoever wanted to continue to work or be creatively active had to make a decision. The painters Max Weiler and Herbert Boeckl, as well as the sculptor Gustinus Ambrosi were excellent examples of this.[345] Their art was only in demand again once they had joined 'the Party'. Hans Fronius became a war painter and went to the front. Heinrich Jungnickel now only drew and painted animals and tried not to have anything to do with the Nazi regime. Franz Lehár and Hans Moser came to terms with the regime in order to protect their

Jewish wives, just as Richard Strauß had done in Germany for the benefit of his family, which was 'Jewish by miscegenation' (jüdisch versippt). Edmund Eysler initially remained unmolested, despite being a Jew. His operetta, *The Golden Mistress*, was one of Hitler's favourites. This saved Eysler's life, or it at least preserved him from having to flee Austria. One thing could not be overlooked, however, and should have been shocking: the universities were subjected to a veritable deforestation. At the country's largest university, Vienna, 252 lecturers lost their positions within the space of a few days. They would be followed by a further 518.[346] The youth psychologist Charlotte Bühler, like her husband, the philosopher Karl Bühler, the Romance philologist Elise Richter, the physicist Hans Thirring, the chemist Hans Mark and the physician Karl Fellinger were just a few of them. The list could be continued at will. The exodus of artists and cultural workers, above all the flight and expulsion of poets and writers, was not less dramatic and Austria was all the poorer for it; indeed, it impoverished Austria.

Where were they, the representatives of what was termed 'degenerate' music, whose Jewish background or modernity had sealed their fate: Erich Wolfgang Korngold, Arnold Schönberg, Viktor Ullmann, Egon Wellesz and others? Georg Trapp, who had refused to serve the Nazi regime with his family as a figurehead, immigrated to the USA. Where, too, were painters like Oskar Kokoschka, Albert Paris Gütersloh and Wilhelm Thöny, or architects such as Clemens Holzmeister, a dozen important filmmakers, popular actors and singers? Whoever fled risked ending up in poverty. Whoever remained and could not produce an 'Aryan attestation' risked their life. Ultimately, everyone was forced to decide on his or her own subsequent fate.

The three Nobel Prize winners still living and teaching in Austria at the time of the Anschluss, the atomic physicist Erwin Schrödinger, the physicist Viktor Franz Hess and the pharmacologist Otto Loewi, were prohibited from teaching, were persecuted and then emigrated. Sigmund Freund was permitted to emigrate and died in September 1939 in London. The philosopher Ludwig Wittgenstein also turned his back on Austria and applied for British citizenship in 1938. Othmar Spann, the ideologist of the Corporative State, was also prohibited from teaching and sent to a concentration camp. In the musical theatres and concert halls, Emmerich Kálmán, Ralph Benatzky, Oskar Straus, Hermann Leopoldi and many others were suddenly absent. Whoever had enjoyed political cabaret and witty jokes had to increasingly content themselves with caricatures and (bad) cartoons. Among literary figures, the loss of exceptional people was particularly noticeable. New leading figures such as Erich Guido Kolbenheyer, Maria Grengg, Egmont Colerus, Fanny Wibmer-Pedit, Gertrud Fussenegger or Bruno Brehm, who advanced to become established stars of the Nazi regime, had already been well-known writers and became, like Josef Weinheber, celebrated (homeland) poets, whereas Stefan Zweig, whose books assumed a prominent place in the 'list of banned authors', definitively left Austria and ultimately immigrated to Brazil via

London. Franz Theodor Csokor believed he was safe in Poland and then fled to Romania, Yugoslavia and, finally, Italy. Carl Zuckmayer, who had already been forced to leave Germany before 1938, moved on. Adrienne Thomas fled via France to Spain and, eventually, the USA. Friedrich Torberg took a similar path. Franz Werfel found refuge first in France and then in Spain. All at once, the so-called coffee house and asphalt literature of Felix Salten, Peter Altenberg, Anton Kuh and Hans Weigel was taboo, as was an old Austrianness, as exemplified by Joseph Roth. To conclude from this that only the 'poetic mediocrity triumphed, the hour of the market criers and the rapturous Nazi bards had come'[347] no doubt falls short and ignored the literary creativity of Alexander Lernet-Holenia, Heimito von Doderer or Friedrich Heer. Most of the 'rapturous Nazi bards', however, had to content themselves after the war with modest positions in the literature scene, were shunned for a time, or at least no longer in demand as they had been before, since they were not required any more to inspire the people and, especially, the youth for the Nazi state.

From April 1939, all male and female adolescents were obligated to serve in the Hitler Youth or the League of German Girls. They received their own cultural programme, which was not intended for Jews, Communists, Freemasons, members of non-Christian religious communities, pacifists and nonconformists. They were components of an image of the enemy that served preparations for the next expansive steps of the Greater German Reich. And they were not long in coming. On 1 September 1939, the invasion of Poland by the German Wehrmacht took place, which marked the beginning of the Second World War and once again brought about many changes.

Conscripted Soldiers

In military terms, Austria was thoroughly organised from March 1938. The eastern part of the country, with Vienna, Lower Danube and Upper Danube, constituted Military District XVII; the rest was Military District XVIII. The Luftwaffe covered the greater part of the country with Air Gau XVII. Only the Gaue Tyrol-Vorarlberg and Salzburg belonged to the (Munich) Air Gau VII. The Navy and the SS also contributed to Austrian military strength. The replacement authorities of the Wehrmacht established the eligibility of the young men for all branches of the Wehrmacht and the SS Dispositional Troops. Around half the senior officers had by this time been dismissed. Younger and lower-ranked officers had replaced them; they were regarded as 'cultivable', and they advanced quickly.[348] The training of the soldiers took place in close proximity to the war. Ultimately, one should sometimes learn to fear the trainers more than the 'enemy'. New barracks were emerging, above all those for the SS Dispositional Troops in Vienna, Graz and Klagenfurt. The thought that there would be war did not, as a rule, have a discouraging effect. The men were armed, materially and mentally. The depiction of hostilities in the First World War, literature that ranged from the Peasants' Wars via the Turks and the French to the most recent major war, the experiences of the Hitler Youth and naive wishes were mixed with patriotic feelings and the negation of personal peril. In spite of the experiences of the First World War, war still seemed to be one big adventure. Only weaklings stayed at home when the Führer called. In any case, the men had little choice in the matter, unless they dodged service in the Wehrmacht and, in so doing, risked their lives.

When, on 28 August 1939, ration coupons were introduced and the control of essential goods began, those who had experienced the First World War must have said: the time has come again. Four days later, these suspicions came true. War had come. On 1 September, all army divisions stationed in the Eastern March found themselves part of the Fourteenth Army and participated in the campaign against Poland. The command of Air Fleet 4, set up in Austria under Air Marshal Alexander Löhr, ordered the Luftwaffe formations to support Army Group South. They carried out the first heavy air raid on Warsaw. The radio stations in the Reich and the daily newspapers fell over themselves to report the successes. It was not the death and destruction that counted but reports of the victories leading to the defeat of the Polish armed forces.

If anyone had expected the Austrians to behave differently to soldiers from other parts of the Reich, to go to war less willingly, to fight less bravely, to desert at the first available opportunity, they were wrong. The Austrians did everything they could to fall in line, not to attract attention and, if possible, to dispel potential prejudices by demonstrating particular zeal and courage. Those who had already been soldiers in the First World War, the 'veterans of the Great War', had been tentatively informed that they would no longer be called up for a new war, but even these older cohorts– provided they were still fit for military service – were included in the mobilisation. They were supposed to balance out the initially minor exhaustion of military strength and offered something that most of the 230,000 Austrians called up in 1939 lacked:[349] experience of war. The German victories in the Poland campaign meant that both the older and the younger generations, who had not yet served, were confident of continued success in this war and could suppress the feeling of defeat that had remained from the First World War.

Two days after the start of the Poland campaign, Britain and France declared war on the Greater German Reich. Events expanded in this way to became a major European conflict and approached the picture of the First World War. But it was difficult to argue that these new events paralleled the earlier ones. One would have had to be very gullible, however, to accept the propagandistic story of a defensive war forced on Germany. The war did suffice, however, to present the austerities and oppressive measures as wartime necessities. Emphases shifted. Until 1939, the enforced coordination and the forcing through of the NSDAP's claim to power had been used as arguments for the coercive measures; from September 1939, it was the war. And it claimed many lives. It was not taking place somewhere 'out there' but also inside the Reich, as a result of which the term 'home front' definitively established itself. The words 'fight' and 'struggle' found their equivalents in the civilian sector. And it could already be observed in 1939 that the Second War picked up where the First had left off.

As of 1939, a third of all married women and more than half of all single women between the ages of 15 and 60 years were gainfully employed.[350] As in the First World War, only to a much greater extent, they were deployed in the armaments industry. They had not only become part of the world of work, however, but also the race policies of the Nazi system. They were supposed to 'bestow' one child after another on the Führer in order to underpin those racial-ideological demands and fantasies that were heralded by a new master race and which it also wanted to achieve by means of the killing of so-called worthless life (unwertes Leben). The National Socialists implemented what the eugenicists had discussed for years. From summer 1939, idiotic children and those with physical deformities were killed. The Am Spiegelgrund clinic in Vienna gained sad notoriety for this.[351] But this was only the beginning of the killing operations.

Based on the model of the 'euthanasia' centres in Grafeneck and Brandenburg an der Havel, Hartheim Castle east of Eferding was converted into one of eventually six killing centres of the so-called T4 programme. It was one of many forms of organised murder. In May 1940, the first transport arrived at the institution and was the prelude to the killing of more than 25,000 people with physical or mental disabilities.[352] They came from psychiatric institutions and facilities for the disabled but also from Mauthausen, Gusen and Dachau concentration camps. It was then primarily Catholic offices that put a stop to the large-scale killings, which could scarcely be concealed, although they admittedly did not really end. But it was unmistakeable what the St. Pölten Bishop Michael Memelauer preached on New Year's Eve in 1941: 'There is no unworthy life in the eyes of our Lord …. The unfortunate, whose senses are confused, the child, who enters this world as a cripple … has a right to live.'[353]

Unlike the 'euthanasia' programme, which the Christian churches opposed, there was no official protest against the persecution of the Jews. Most people appeared to accept that the Jews were not part of the ethnic community.

The Camp Complex

The term 'camp' (Lager) was everywhere. People still knew the names of those camps that had been established during the First World War for the intake of refugees, internees and prisoners of war. They had ceased to exist in 1918/19 and survived primarily in local records. The Corporative State had established camps in 1933 in order to intern political opponents. The idea was evidently in the air and also not foreign to the Austrian Social Democrats when it came to planning a civil war. But there was a difference between thoughts and reality, just as there was a significant difference between those concentration camps established in Germany from 1933 onwards by the National Socialist rulers and the detention camps of the Corporative State at Wöllersdorf and Kaisersteinbruch. The fact that this was something different in Austria from 1938 became clear overnight. First Dachau and then Mauthausen forced people to change their way of thinking.

Mauthausen has long since been a synonym for the Nazi regime's reign of terror in Austria. But it is scarcely imaginable now that the erection of the camp in 1938 outside the idyllic Upper Austrian town north of the Danube near Grein was held up as an accolade. The governor and Gauleiter of Upper Austria, August Eigruber, proudly proclaimed as early as March 1938 that it was a great honour that the concentration camp 'for the traitors from all Austria' was coming to Upper Austria.[354] Mauthausen was chosen because the granite quarries there were supposed to provide the material for showpiece architecture. A second, similar camp was planned for nearby Gusen.

Work in the stone quarries was to be carried out by prisoners. First of all, they had to build barracks. The camp complex grew. In November 1938, the first train with prisoners arrived in Mauthausen from Dachau concentration camp. They did not know that their categorisation would drastically reduce their chances of survival. They arrived at a camp that was intended, according to a decree from the chief of the Security Police and the Security Service, Reinhard Heydrich, 'for grievous, irredeemable and at the same time previously convicted and antisocial, in other words, scarcely educable prisoners in protective custody'.[355]

For the latter, there also existed work education camps. The political prisoners of the first months were joined by criminals, homosexuals, Bible students, 'antisocial elements' and, finally, Czechs. The number of Austrians remained low,[356] because they were brought primarily to Dachau, Theresienstadt, then Buchenwald, Oranienbaum and, finally, to the concentration camps and killing centres in Poland and Belarus.

At least initially, relatively few Jews were sent to Mauthausen. Sinti and Roma were likewise sent there in only small numbers, as a camp was set up in Lackenbach in 1940 especially for the 11,000 members of this ethnic group, who lived mainly in Burgenland. There and in other camps, from 1942 in the Chełmno nad Nerem (Kulmhof) extermination camp in Poland, perhaps two-thirds of them were killed or died.[357]

Mauthausen concentration camp was filled with other inmates. Prisoners of war arrived, although it was not a POW camp. As soon as they arrived, they were deployed to expand the camp and its facilities and for building sub-camps, where they were then utilised in the related industrial enterprises for the construction of aircraft, engines and weapons systems of all kinds but also for the erection of transportation structures such as the Loibl Tunnel – to the point of total exhaustion. The fact that they were not simply killed was the result of a very basic observation: as of 1942, the Greater German Reich was running out of people able to work. Thus, ever larger contingents of prisoners were to be assigned to the concentration camps in order to balance out the call-ups to the Wehrmacht and to deploy the concentration camp inmates, provided they were fit for work, as slaves. For them, the statement made by the chief of the SS Economic Administration Main Office, Oswald Pohl, on 30 April 1942 in a circular letter to the camp commandants applied: 'The camp commandant is alone responsible for the deployment of the workforce. This deployment must be exhaustive in the full sense of the word.'[358] Bit by bit, sub-camps emerged, the largest of them in Gusen, Ebensee and Melk. Eventually, there would be 48 of them.[359] A warrant for protective custody from the Gestapo sufficed for someone to be sent to a concentration camp without trial. Mauthausen became a hub of death. In 1940, Poles and Spaniards arrived, primarily children of Social Democrats and Communists who had fought in the Spanish Civil War. They were followed, in 1941, by Dutch Jews, Yugoslavs and Soviet prisoners of war, of whom it was said that they were to be sent to 'their deaths through work in the quarry'.[360] In May 1942, 3,844 prisoners worked in the stone quarries. A year later, the number had risen by 1,000. In 1942, the Mauthausen complex continued to fill up with Belgians and French, both European and African, more Dutch Jews, Serbs, new Soviet POWs and people who were taken into 'preventive detention'. And so it went on. Prisoners from other concentration camps were repeatedly absorbed; each one received a number, until in Mauthausen the last prisoner number of 139,317 had been issued.[361] The number who ended up in Mauthausen was much higher, however, for Soviet prisoners of war did not receive new numbers but were recorded under the number of their POW main camp. It also applied to the Soviet prisoners of war that if they were sick upon their arrival in Mauthausen, they would be killed before their registration. They were gassed. Only those were recorded who were regarded as 'fit for work in the quarry'.

The statistic, according to which around 69,000 of the 194,200 prisoners in Mauthausen and its sub-camps died or were killed, says it all. However, it is deceptive to the extent that those who were admitted towards the end of the war had a better chance of survival than those who had arrived earlier. Prisoners of war had little chance of surviving. Most of them were Russian.[362]

Even more difficult than the attempt to establish precise figures for the concentration camp complex of the Nazi period in Austria is the ascertainment of even remotely concrete numbers for the prisoners of war. Preparations for accommodating POWs had been made in Germany from 1937. In August 1939, Kaisersteinbruch was then the first transit camp to be established on Austrian soil, which was followed from September by main camps for enlisted men and officers.[363] They were hardly used, however, although around 400,000 Polish soldiers fell into German captivity during the course of the Poland campaign. They were not treated in accordance with the provisions of the Hague Convention on the Laws and Customs of War on Land or the Geneva Convention relative to the Treatment of Prisoners of War, however, but instead robbed of their status by means of an arbitrary legal act. According to Berlin's interpretation, Poland had ceased to exist as a state following the German victory and the subsequent occupation of the country by German and Soviet troops. Thus, the prisoners of war were no longer protected by international law. Approximately half of the Poles were released from captivity but 200,000 were taken to Germany for forced labour. The same thing happened to a further 200,000 Poles who were classified as potentially hostile to Germany. In this way, 400,000 forced labourers were taken to the territory of the Greater German Reich and constituted a first contingent of slave labourers. The number of Poles converted from POWs to civilian workers in Austria increased bit by bit to 87,000. They were deployed predominantly in industry, construction projects and agriculture.[364]

The expansion of the war again washed masses into the POW camps. French, British, Belgians and Dutch arrived. They could not be treated in the same way as the Poles. Therefore, in Kaisersteinbruch, Krems-Gneixendorf, Döllersheim, St. Johann im Pongau and a dozen other places in Austria, large main camps for soldiers and NCOs as well as officers' camps and transit camps were created or for the time being just outlined. Again, one could recall the First World War, when – like back then – camps emerged in Wagna near Leibnitz or in Wolfsberg, which accommodated far more people than the number of residents in the localities themselves. Unlike during the First World War, however, the civilian population was forbidden to have any contact with the prisoners of war on pain of punishment. POWs were supposed – like previously – to replace the loss of people who were now needed for the war. That was legitimate. But the fact that dozens died of hunger and epidemics every day in a camp like St. Johann in Pogau, where around 30,000 prisoners were accommodated, made any comparison with the First World War inadmissible.[365] And it was only the beginning.

The Loss of All Restraint

The invasion of Norway and Denmark by the German Wehrmacht on 9 April 1940 and the start of the offensive against France on 10 May demonstrated once more that the Austrians in the Wehrmacht differed in no way to their comrades. The lightning victories, the expulsion of the remainder of the French army and the British Expeditionary Corps from the mainland, and the subsequent surrender of France far exceeded the euphoria of the victory over Poland. Nothing seemed to be able to withstand the Wehrmacht, and what Sebastian Haffner hypothetically suggested would have found its analogy in Austria: if Adolf Hitler had died or been assassinated after his apparent political and first major military successes, he would without doubt have gone down as one of the greatest, if not *the* greatest German.[366]

In the Eastern March, too, people were fond of saying: 'Today, Germany is ours and tomorrow the whole world.' Both the 'soldier in the Danube Gau' and the 'soldier in the Alpine country' could feel like a victor. Taken together, the first two years of the war saw around 550,000 Austrians serve in the Wehrmacht. Nothing whatsoever suggested that those from the Eastern March would not fight in just the same way as others for 'Greater Germany's struggle for survival'. Austrian officers had advanced to fill senior command positions. It might have been noticed eventually that they played an exceedingly minor role in the High Command of the Wehrmacht, as well as the High Commands of the Army, Navy and Luftwaffe. Hitler preferred to rely there on others. But the integration of Austrians into the Wehrmacht was at such an advanced stage that only common enemies now existed, the badmouthing of slackers and life in the rear areas took place collectively and local differences played next to no role at all. The Austrians had become willing soldiers, no more and no less. They were far more willing, in any case, than the 'ethnic Germans' (Volksdeutsche) or the soldiers recruited in Alsace-Lorraine and Luxembourg, who were run down and condescendingly dismissed for their often-limited fighting value and their tendency to desert.[367] Like in 1939, after a few weeks where hopes had been nurtured that the war might be over, the assembly of new divisions began in 1940.

In order to train them, the largest military training area in the German Reich had been set up around Allentsteig and Döllersheim in the Waldviertel. As early as 1938, the inhabitants of 45 municipalities and seven manor estates had been summoned to leave their homes and then resettled. The villages and farms were then destroyed during the course of military exercises. The mountain troops also needed training areas, likewise the anti-aircraft artillery, who received a firing range near Oggau on Lake Neusiedl, now in Lower Danube. Those born in 1923 were called up. Practically everyone obeyed the enlistment order and ultimately swore the oath to the Führer demanded of them:

> I swear to God this sacred oath that I shall render unconditional obedience to the Führer of the German Reich and people, Adolf Hitler, the supreme commander of the Wehrmacht, and that as a brave soldier I shall be prepared at all times to give my life for this oath.

It was not an oath to the fatherland but instead a personal oath to the Führer aimed at unquestioned loyalty. It must have occurred to very few that the Führer did not know how to direct the Reich and, above all, the war. And, like in the First World War, there were plenty of adolescents, Hitler youths, who feared that they would arrive too late to play their part in the victories of the Wehrmacht. They were to be thoroughly mistaken.

11 The War of Attrition

11 For his 52nd birthday, during the Balkan campaign of 1941, Adolf Hitler was given a peculiar present: in the saloon of the so-called America Train near Mönichkirchen, in which the Führer's Headquarters had been temporarily established, he received a memorial plaque dismantled in Sarajevo commemorating the murder of the Austro-Hungarian heir to the throne, Archduke Franz Ferdinand, by Gavrilo Princip on 28 June 1914. The plaque was eventually taken to the Armoury in Berlin, where it was destroyed during an air raid. (Photo: Author's archive)

On 30 August 1940, the Viennese once again had the opportunity to have a closer look at well-known figures and to witness the ascent of a motorcade to the Upper Belvedere Palace. As in 1939, the matter in hand was the resettlement of territorial affairs in East-Central Europe. This time, Romania's borders were to be shifted. The Soviet Union had initially demanded Bessarabia and Northern Bukovina from Romania. Stalin had gone about enlarging the Soviet Union to some extent in the slipstream of Germany. It was no coincidence that he was called 'Vozhd' – leader. In view of the Hitler-Stalin Pact on the eve of the war against Poland, Romania could not expect any support from Germany. Britain and France had no way of intervening. What was more, Bulgaria demanded Southern Dobruja. And then came Hungary. It had not forgotten the cession of Transylvania to Romania or the advance of Romanian troops as far as Budapest in 1919. Hitler was once more prepared to support Hungarian demands. Thus, as before, the new borders were drawn in Vienna. On 30 August 1940, Foreign Minister Ribbentrop and his Italian colleague, Count Ciano, confronted the Romanian delegation with the results of their deliberations. Romania had to agree to the decision and lost a third of Transylvania and neighbouring territories, though it did receive a promise of protection from Germany in return.

And Vienna was to be the setting for events yet again. On 25 March 1941, the Kingdom of Yugoslavia joined the Tripartite Pact of Germany, Italy and Japan in Vienna. Two days later, the Belgrade government was overthrown. Although the new government immediately declared its readiness to fulfil the terms of the Tripartite Pact, Hitler determined on a swift military strike. He did this not least to save Italy from failure in a war it had started with Greece. Hitler did not want to risk the situation in the Balkans and Greece getting out of hand during his already planned campaign against the Soviet Union.

Hungary and Bulgaria wanted to participate in the war. Aspects of this approach appeared logical, to the extent that this word could even be used to describe the war. But it meant another expansion of the European war and the acceptance of unforeseen consequences.

The Princip Plaque

In late March and the first days of April 1941, large German formations – designated the Second Army – were deployed in the Carinthia-Styria border areas and in western

Hungary. The German Twelfth Army was to attack from Bulgaria. Since summer 1940, a large supply basis had been set up in the vicinity of Vienna, which now allowed for a swift concentration of troops.[368] The High Command of the Wehrmacht moved into the Officer Cadet School in Wiener Neustadt, the former military academy. The high command of the Second Army arrived in St. Radegund near Graz. From the 'Führer's train' near Mönichkirchen, Hitler followed the course of the campaign, which began on 6 April with the heavy bombardment of Belgrade by Air Fleet 4.

As had been the case in Czechoslovakia, Yugoslavia crumbled after a few days. The remainder of the Serbian army surrendered on 17 April. Two days earlier, Croatia had declared its independence and, as a sort of reward, received Slavonia, Srem (Syrmien), almost the whole of Dalmatia, Bosnia and Herzegovina. Hungary took Prekmurje (Übermurgebiet), southern Baranja and Bačka, while Bulgaria secured the majority of Macedonia. Italy occupied Montenegro. The Italians and the Germans shared a downsized Slovenia as an occupation zone. Hitler wanted to restore the borders of the former crown lands. The Meža Valley (Mießtal), Upper Carniola (Oberkrain) and Lower Styria, which had been enlarged by a border strip, were therefore allocated to the Reich Gaue of Carinthia and Styria as 'occupied territories'.[369] Serbia, however, which now only existed as a rump state, was placed under German military administration.

On the occasion of 20 April 1940, Hitler's 53rd birthday, he was presented with a special gift: following the occupation of the Bosnian capital Sarajevo, Wehrmacht soldiers had dismantled a memorial plaque near the Latin Bridge over the Miljacka, which was affixed to a corner house, in front of which Gavrilo Princip had murdered the heir to the Austro-Hungarian throne, Archduke Franz Ferdinand, and his wife on 28 June 1914. The plaque was brought to Mönichkirchen and presented to Hitler in the 'Führer's train'.[370] This was again heavily charged with symbolism: the native Austrian Adolf Hitler had, by all accounts, taken his revenge for Sarajevo. The double murder, which was regarded as the cause of the First World War, had been avenged.

On 18 May 1941, Germany proclaimed the legal end of the Kingdom of Yugoslavia. Once again, though with considerable deviations, contours of the old Austria appeared to have been re-established. The campaign and, above all, its results were celebrated accordingly. This was all the easier because comparatively few troops from the Eastern March had been required to participate in the campaign and there had, therefore, been only few casualty reports.

The 344,000 Yugoslavian prisoners of war were treated in accordance with their respective ethnic affiliation. The Slovene, Bosnian-Muslim, Croatian, Hungarian and Yugoslavian-German soldiers were released. Around 180,000 Serbs and Montenegrins were sent to Germany for labour deployment. Approximately one tenth made their way to the Eastern March.

The next stop after Serbia and Macedonia was Greece. Again, nothing seemed to be able to hold back the Wehrmacht. Now, soldiers from Austria were brought in, above all mountain troops, and it was anticipated that only onerous occupation tasks would be fulfilled. During the Balkan campaign, the assembly of two new divisions in both Eastern March military districts had commenced, which were to subsequently assume occupation duties in Serbia and Greece. In this way, the field divisions could be swiftly separated off after the end of the campaigns and made available for the war against the Soviet Union. In Serbia and Greece, however, those were deployed which, it was assumed, would be sufficient to hold down the occupied territories and furthermore exploit them for the German war economy. A fatal error, as it would soon turn out. Austria-Hungary's experiences in the First World War should actually have forewarned the High Command of the Wehrmacht.

Resistance soon emerged and attacks on occupation troops began to occur, which made it clear that the Balkans had their own rules for waging war. The reaction of the Wehrmacht leadership consisted of repressive measures aimed at nipping a partisan war in the bud. They would not succeed. As early as summer 1941, resistance formed, whereby partisans loyal to the king and communist underground fighters struggled for supremacy in the fight against the German occupiers and opened up a sort of ancillary front. This seemed to be a comfortable situation for the occupying power, for it believed it could proceed in accordance with the old principle of 'divide and rule'. This was another misapprehension, as it would soon become clear. The two divisions introduced from the military districts of the Eastern March, the 717th and the 718th Infantry Divisions were involved in massacres and sanctions in no time at all. It would become the worst form of partisan war to take place anywhere, including the Soviet Union, France and, later, Italy. Instances of slaughter – where 50 civilians from the occupied territories were killed for every wounded German soldier, and 100 were to be killed for one dead German soldier – were often just used as a pretext to punish partisan atrocities with mass murder.[371] An attempt was made to gloss over the deployment of soldiers from Austria and a whole series of high-ranking officers and administrative officials, who were then involved in crimes of the Wehrmacht, with the explanation that the Austrians traditionally knew how to handle members of the Slav peoples and boasted a special affinity with them. For many of the soldiers involved, who could be accused a priori neither of inhumanity nor of an inclination towards hostage shootings, this form of warfare degenerated in such a way that they incurred a type of collective guilt. They were involved in a war of aggression, were misused and let themselves be misused. And the longer the war lasted, the more numerous became the possibilities to commit injustices and to act with brutality. Many who became guilty of this were held accountable after the war or at least mentioned by name in relation to the repressive measures. They attempted to justify themselves by claiming that the acts of repression

Map 2: The Reich
Gaue of the
'Eastern March'
from late April
1941

The Alpine and Danubian Reich Ga
of the Greater German Reich
End of April 1941

GERMANY

Jungholz

Bregenz

Kl. Walsertal

Innsbruck

Inn

SWITZERLAND

Lie

ITALY

	Reich Gau Tyrol-Vorarlberg
	Reich Gau Salzburg
	Reich Gau Carinthia
	Reich Gau Upper Danube
	Reich Gau Styria
	Reich Gau Lower Danube
	Reich Gau Greater Vienna
◉	Reich capital cities
✕✕✕✕	Territorial expansion in October 1938
⧄⧄⧄	Territorial expansion in April 1941

The map is based on today's state borders.

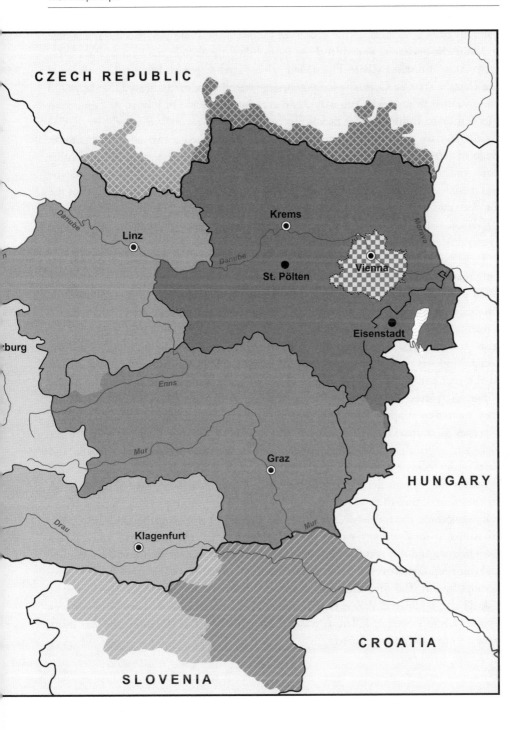

had only been a response to the actions of the partisans. Naturally, this did not suffice to justify the massacres and shift the responsibility. The former minister in the Corporative State, Edmund Glaise-Horstenau, who shared responsibility for the policies of the 'Ustashe' state as 'German plenipotentiary general for Croatia', feared that he would be extradited to post-war Yugoslavia and committed suicide in July 1946. Lieutenant General Franz Böhme, whose task it was to suppress the revolt of the Serbs in 1941 as plenipotentiary commanding general in Serbia, established a two-and-a-half-month reign of terror and was responsible for massacres in Kraljevo, Kragujevac and other cities and regions, during which the killing ratio of 1:50 or 1:100, as the case may be, was mercilessly applied, killed himself in May 1947.[372] The commander-in-chief of the air fleet that had bombarded Belgrade and who commanded German troops in the Balkans towards the end of the war as commander-in-chief of south-eastern Europe, General Alexander Löhr, was sentenced to death in Serbia and shot in February 1947.

However, the aforementioned immediate consequences for the Eastern March not only manifested themselves in the deployment of Austrians during and in the aftermath to the Yugoslavian campaign, as well as in the partisan war in the occupied territories, which started without warning, but also in Carinthia and Styria. There began a manifold and often confusing interplay in this war without fronts, whereby the German (and Italian) occupation of Slovenia, the rejection of the German regime and the compulsion – even as a Slovene – to enlist in the German Wehrmacht, were the cause of the partisan war. For a growing number of Slovenes, the war against the Soviet Union also played a role, for the Russians were regarded as a Slav sister people, whom they wanted to support. However, probably nothing stimulated the resistance of the Slovenes more than Hitler's directive: 'This land is to be made German again.'[373] Racially and politically undesirable people were to be resettled in Serbia and Croatia, and parts of the Slovene population of Carinthia were to be brought to camps in Germany. Whoever was able to flee, did so. Some of the young men, who wanted above all to escape conscription in the Wehrmacht, disappeared in the inaccessible regions of the Karawanks or in the Italian occupation zone. The will to work together and the particular sympathy for Germany, which had still existed before the war, transformed into a deep hatred. And this was the ideal breeding ground for the partisan war. Communists and some representatives of bourgeois parties established the 'Liberation Front' (Osvobodilna fronta). The first attacks took place. Whoever cooperated with the Germans risked being liquidated. Whoever was suspected of sympathising with the partisans was deported, imprisoned or killed. It was a thoroughly hopeless situation. The war in its ugliest form had reached Austria.

Operation 'Barbarossa'

The 22nd of June 1941 came as a shock. In the early hours of the 'longest day', three million soldiers of the German Wehrmacht attacked the Soviet Union. The newspaper headlines on the following day did not reveal the truth: 'Appeal by the Führer to the German people: Reckoning with the malicious traitors in the east – continued blackmail – rabble-rousing agitation and massing of troops. The Pact despicably violated. Opening hostilities on the Soviet border …'. In this way, the newspapers circulated the information – in fact, disinformation – approved by the Propaganda Ministry in Berlin regarding the start of the campaign against the Soviet Union.[374] For most people, this news was like a bolt from the blue. The Battle of Britain had dominated reports in the preceding days and weeks. One victory after another had been reported. And now, suddenly, the Soviet Union was the target. People asked after the reason for the attack: 'In Poland, the persecution of the Germans was cited as the reason for the war; with France we were already at war (which had been declared by France and Britain). Yugoslavia had been guilty of violating a treaty. But we had supposedly lived in the deepest peace with Russia until this hour,' as Second Lieutenant Christoph Allmayer-Beck summarised.[375] And while the contractually guaranteed deliveries from the Soviet Union were still rolling across the border with the Reich in the west, the Wehrmacht attacked, though six weeks later than Hitler had planned. Furthermore, 22 June might have been regarded as a bad omen, because Napoleon had also begun his Russian campaign on this day in 1812. But the initial successes seemed to belie such historical comparisons.

Most of the field divisions, Luftwaffe formations and SS Dispositional Troops set up in the Reich Gaue of the Eastern March were part of the armed force that was divided into three army groups, and which was joined by Italians, Hungarians, Romanians, Slovaks and European volunteers. Once again, one victory after another was reported. A new lightning campaign appeared to end with the defeat of the Red Army and the occupation of huge swathes of Soviet territory. In fact, as early as 1941, the campaign turned into that which Nazi propaganda had presented it to be – as a justification – from the very outset: a struggle for survival. In substantiating it, it was not Hitler's statements in *Mein Kampf* that were cited, to the effect that a war against Soviet Russia was unavoidable. Instead, it was claimed that Germany had only forestalled an attack by the Russians – an explanation that still has its advocates to this day. If the impression might still have been gained at the outset that the campaign would end in 1941 with the defeat of Russia, doubts began to emerge from autumn 1941. The entry of the United States into the war and the German declaration of war on the USA on 11 December 1941 strengthened these doubts considerably. The numbers of prisoners captured in the major battles of encirclement in Russia, however, seemed to prove the doubters wrong. No words were lost on the campaign having been begun without a declaration of war, or that – as already in the case of Poland – no convention on the treatment of POWs was in place. Time and again, Franz Liszt's *Les Préludes* could be heard over the Reich's radio station in Vienna as the prelude to a special report from the High Command of the Wehrmacht: 'Whenever victories were reported …, I still remember how Mrs Z. always opened the window and turned the radio up. … Yes, people were positively excited,' as a woman from Upper Austria stated more than sixty years after the war.[376] The fact that ever more people appeared on the streets dressed in black was regarded as a concomitant of the struggle for survival. People died, just as they did in every war; this time it happened to be for 'Führer, people and fatherland' and for the victory of the German Wehrmacht, as those laconically claimed who were not directed affected by it.

'Like on the entire German army, the east also exerted its unnatural pull on the Eastern March divisions,' wrote Allmayer-Beck.[377] The censored field post corresponded with the reports of the Reich's radio stations and the newspapers that circulated daily messages of jubilation. A campaign was being waged against 'Bolshevik subhumans', the 'mortal enemy'; derogatory statements were made with glee, though they corresponded less and less to reality. The aim was supposedly still the conquest of living space (Lebensraum); reference was made to the AA-line, which ran from Archangelsk to Astrakhan and westwards of which the Greater German Reich would unfurl. Even non-farmers began to dream of goods, for whose exploitation the conquered would be enlisted. Resettlers or even the South Tyrolean optants who had struck out to find a new home and land outside Italy, were veritably enticed with references to the conquered eastern territories. Highly-regarded recipients of the Knight's Cross were presented the prospect of receiving manor estates. Propaganda and wishful thinking formed an unspeakable symbiosis.

Even in 1942, the war in the east still appeared winnable, likewise the war in North Africa, which was increasingly turning from an Italian to a German theatre of war. The Battle of Britain, however, had been broken off. The navy, in which those crew members from the Eastern March had a large share only in the Danube Fleet and a handful of submarines, hesitated – as in the First World War – to deploy its larger units and increasingly shifted its focus to the submarine war. But wherever they went, the Austrians were 'soldiers like any other', equal among equals. They appeared largely immune to Soviet propaganda, which called on them to desert. Promises of good treatment were not believed.

Though we cannot go into much detail here, it can be assumed that the Austrians in the Wehrmacht had an eight-per cent share in abuses, plundering and that which later – long after the Second World War – caused indignation and pause for thought as 'crimes of the Wehrmacht'. During the Polish and the Western campaigns, rigorous penalties had applied in the event of plunder and pillage. In the case of the campaign against the Soviet Union, Hitler himself had given the signal to disregard the international laws of war and humanity. Furthermore, this not only applied to political commissars, whose status as combatants was denied. Executions and murder were daily occurrences, and when houses, villages and entire neighbourhoods went up in flames, the attempt was made to explain it by claiming that Stalin had been the first to issue the order for 'scorched earth'. In partisan war zones and in the event of military setbacks, any consideration disappeared entirely.[378] And the Austrians were soldiers like any other.

Not even catastrophes such as the encirclement of the German Sixth Army in late 1942, in which, by a series of coincidences, the share of Austrians was higher than in other sectors of the front, could bring about a lasting reversal of opinion and strengthen even the beginnings of a feeling that the war could not be won. The inspector of the military replacement district of Vienna reported as late as June 1943, at any rate, that enthusiasm for the war among the recruits born in 1926 was high, 'or even very high'. There were no malingerers, and some of those drafted had even attempted to conceal their illnesses.[379] In 1941 and 1942, another 100,000 men had been called up, and around 40.5 per cent of the male population of pre-war Austria had now become eligible for military service.[380] There were admittedly cases of desertion and undermining of military morale from time to time. They had increased since the start of the campaign against the Soviet Union but they did not differ in terms of percentage from comparable cases, in which soldiers from other Reich Gaue of the Greater German Reich became noticeable. Desertion, one of the biggest problems of the Austro-Hungarian army during the First World War, was punishable by death. It would be applied mercilessly. Up to 1943, however, only several dozen soldiers from the Eastern March were arraigned for desertion and, for the most part, executed.[381] Considerably more had deserted or surrendered without a fight. Nonetheless, they, too, were at most small statistical values. The belief in an early end to the war, if not the 'final victory', remained. Stalingrad, however, had a lasting impact on the morale of the civilian population. And the latter was to be subjected to further burdens, and indeed became the actual target of the Allied war effort. Back home, as at the various fronts, the people experienced the horrors of total war.

The 'Home Theatre of War'

The first signs that Austria could be reached by Allied aircraft were the incursions of British bombers, which reached Vienna at high altitude and already dropped flyers in winter 1939/40. This could be viewed in the same way as the raid on Vienna by the Italian Gabriele D'Annunzio, who dropped 50,000 leaflets from seven biplanes on 9 August 1918 and sought, in this way, to demonstrate that the imperial capital and seat of royal residence could no longer be defended. The incursions of the British increased from 1940 onwards. In August 1940, a bomber crashed in Vorarlberg. Of course, this was not yet the strategic air war that the Allies, like the German Luftwaffe, wanted to conduct. Nonetheless, the home theatre of war (Heimatkriegsgebiet), as it was so unequivocally called from August 1940, was made ready.

If the expansion of airfields had initially – in 1938/39 – been given priority among military construction projects, building activity shifted very quickly from the beginning of the war to passive and active air-raid protection. Air-raid protection measures were compulsory for the entire population.[382] Localities were classified as first-, second- or third-order air-raid protection sites depending on their probable exposure to danger. From the beginning of the war, blackout regulations applied. The fact that three Yugoslavian planes penetrated the air space over Styria and dropped a few bombs, which caused no appreciable damage, was at most a local sensation. The incursion of the British, however, led to the acceleration of the construction of air-raid shelters and bunkers and, above all, the intensification of anti-aircraft defence. Instead of captured Russian artillery, the German standard guns for anti-aircraft defence, 8.8-cm cannons, arrived everywhere where a threat was assumed. Meanwhile, it could be traced how the air war against the cities of the 'Old Reich' developed and how British bomber formations carried out their first night-time attack with around 1,000 bombers in late May 1942. Shortly thereafter, the transfer of American bomber formations to Britain and North Africa commenced.

Until August 1943, the Austrians could entertain the illusion that the Allied air fleets would spare Austria. But the Western powers had no intention of doing this. On 13 August 1943, a formation of the American Ninth Air Force coming from Libya reached Wiener Neustadt, bombarded the greatly expanded aircraft factory there and left a trail of destruction for the first time.[383] And it perhaps had a more lasting impact that the people felt exposed. The war that was being waged in Russia, North Africa or somewhere else far away had suddenly become very close. In this way, even the empty propaganda phrases acquired a different significance. The 'crimes' of the others were emphasised, there was talk of 'air gangsters' and 'terror', while simultaneously air raids on English cities and 'obliteration', 'extermination' and 'retaliation' were reported.[384] Occasionally, there was a noticeable loss of authority on the part of the National Socialist regime. It was increasingly just endured and lost its appearance of infallibility.

After the first attack from North Africa, four further American raids on targets in Austria followed, which were launched from bases in Libya. On 1 October, Feldkirch became a target of opportunity and was bombarded after an American attack on Augsburg. There was no heavy anti-aircraft artillery anywhere in Vorarlberg.[385] In the meantime, the Americans and British had advanced so far into Apulia that they were able to commence the construction of huge airfields in the vicinity of Foggia. It was intended

that the flight times to regions located further north would be considerably shortened
in this way. The American air force began to develop a new air fleet, the Fifteenth Air
Force. It was strengthened by the No. 205 (Heavy Bomber) Group of the British Royal
Air Force. The by now roughly 1,300 four-engine bomber aircraft were then augmented
by the American Twelfth Air Force, whose main task it was to support the fighting of
ground forces, as well as fighter units, which were transferred ever further northwards,
in order escort to the bombers as far as possible. The bomber formations flew in various sizes and combinations over the Adriatic and then overland northwards, generally
distributed themselves among different target areas, banked and began to drop bombs
on their primary targets. If these could not be hit as desired, they headed for alternative
targets and eventually dropped bombs on targets of opportunity before they returned.
The main load of the American bomber formations comprised explosive bombs and –
unlike with the British, who attacked targets in Western Europe and the northern
Reich territory – comparatively few incendiary bombs. In January 1944, the American
Fifteenth Air Force received the basic mission, quite simply, of destroying German
industrial bases and breaking the morale of the people.[386] The latter was teetering on
the brink. And only those who looked away or were particularly naive could not see the
writing on the wall.

It had already started in 1939. The situation reports of the Security Service of the SS
(Sicherheitsdienst der SS, or SD) contained references to a deterioration in relations
between Germans from the 'Old Reich' and locals.[387] The first doubts about the German path were voiced. This could be dismissed as grumbling and typical for those from
the Eastern March. However, the following incident in the German People's Theatre in
Vienna, described by Ernst Bruckmüller, left nothing to be desired in terms of clarity:
in the monologue of Ottokar von Horneck during a performance in 1940 of *König
Ottokars Glück und Ende* (King Ottocar: His Rise and Fall), 'the Austrian then steps in
front of him / thinks his thoughts and lets the others talk', at which point spontaneous
applause burst forth.[388] The authorities were alerted, and with good reason. Exhorta-
tions to hold out replaced the certainty in victory.

Partisans

The war had also come closer in another respect, which gave the phrase 'home theatre
of war' its special significance. What had initially looked like a withdrawal and was then
perceived as a particularly brutal way of waging war in the occupied territories of the
former Kingdom of Yugoslavia had now become a war on Austrian soil: the partisan
war. The Osvobodilna Fronta had already succeeded in 1941 in stirring up the readiness
to revolt in Slovenia and expanding the partisans' reach. Neither the taking of hostages

and shootings, nor the burning down of scattered farmsteads and entire villages or the expulsion of the Slovene population could prevent this.

On the morning of 14 April 1942, the deportation of around 1,000 Carinthian Slovenes had begun ambush-style. Most of them were sent to camps in the 'Old Reich'. Criticism of this measure voiced by well-known Carinthian figures, for instance the poet Josef Friedrich Perkonig and the chapter vicar of the Diocese of Gurk, Andreas Rohrracher, delayed the operation but did not stop it. Even officers of the replacement authorities regarded it as particularly counterproductive that Slovene families were expelled whose relatives served with the German Wehrmacht. But their protests were ultimately in vain.[389]

The resettlement operation pursued two objectives: on the one hand, to expel the Slovenes from Carinthia and render it impossible for them to ally with the ethnic group living south of the Karawanks. On the other hand, however, inhabitants of the Val Canale – who, like 75,000 South Tyroleans, had opted for Germany and were supposed to leave Italy – were to be settled in the farms to be vacated by the Slovene farmers.

As a result of partisan activities, which were also increasing in Carinthia, dozens, then hundreds of people were accused of having harboured and actively supported 'terroristic, communistically-inclined, armed gangs'. On 29 April 1943, the first twelve people were executed on the basis of this charge.[390] But even the terror could not prevent the development of partisan activities. Carinthia had become a war zone. Deserters from the German Wehrmacht and above all escaped Soviet prisoners of war, who had fled forced labour deployment, joined the partisans from Upper Carniola, the Meža Valley, Lower Styria and Carinthia. When they encountered German security forces, they fought for their lives, and for good reason. They operated in the inaccessible terrain of the Karawanks as far as the Drava and on the Sau Alps. Their main aim was to conduct ambushes and acts of sabotage. Units of police and territorial infantry accomplished little. Partisan operations increased until, in spring 1944, SS Police Regiment 13 was transferred to Carinthia and brought with it experiences of the partisan war in Belarus. The SS unit, which comprised men from Hannover, Braunschweig and Magdeburg mixed with Croats, Poles, Hungarians and Ukrainians, succeeded with its systematic approach in permanently weakening the partisans. Nonetheless, the guerrilla war continued, the main victims of which were the people in the still multilingual territories. Murder was the order of the day. For a time, the partisans were able to extend their operations to the region of Wolfsberg in the east and Arnoldstein in the west. Then the leader of the communist partisan movement in Yugoslavia, Josip Broz Tito, decided to withdraw and partially dissolve the partisans in the so-called 4th Operations Zone. At the same time, the Wehrmacht accorded the partisans combatant status. In the event of their capture, they were to be treated like prisoners of war.[391] The fighting abated. Individual operations continued to take place. Rejection and mistrust remained, as did the question of whether the partisans were fighting first and foremost for Slovenia or for Austria. It was beyond dispute that they strove to shake off German rule and that they claimed their place in a listing of Austrians among the armed forces of the Allies.

The Shadow Army

Initially, they had been nothing more than foreigners, those refugees, namely, who reached France, England, the Americas, Canada, China or another country willing to take them in and who believed themselves to be safe. Totalling more than 100,000 refugees and expellees, the Austrian Jews comprised by far the largest contingent of the homeless. On 3 September 1939, the day on which the Western Allies had declared war on the Greater German Reich, France and Britain's receptivity fundamentally changed. Refugees were also regarded as enemy foreigners, and regardless of whether they had fled for political reasons, were Jews or non-Jews. They had been called upon to gather at collection points and were then distributed among internment camps. In France, around 5,000 Austrians were affected by this measure; in Britain the number far exceeded 30,000.[392] In both cases, it was Jews who comprised the majority. The fact that they, of all people, were interned, however, was quite beyond their understanding. Jews and non-Jews alike were then given the opportunity to report for military service. In France, 1,500 are said to have volunteered at this point for the Foreign Legion; there was no alternative. They were sent to North Africa.

The British attempted to establish pioneer units composed of refugees, first in France, then in England. Five of them also contained several hundred Austrians. The next initiative was taken in 1941. It was again a few hundred Austrians who sought to evade the internment camps by reporting to the Allied armed forces, and to furthermore make an active contribution to the fight against 'Fortress Europe' held by the Wehrmacht. Only in early 1943 could Britain bring itself to allow refugees from the enemy states into all military branches.[393] At the same time, the British attitude towards the refugees changed fundamentally. The latter were released from the internment camps. Austrian exile organisations, above all the Free Austrian Movement, which had set itself the target of uniting all exile organisations regardless of their political orientation, encouraged them to join the British military. The Royal Air Force also accepted Austrians. The latter wanted to join only on the condition that they were not deployed against targets in Austria. This was easy to agree to, as the vast majority of British night-time bombing raids were against German cities. Austrians also volunteered for intelligence activities and were flown to partisan regions in the Balkans but also to Austria for deployment. Ideological questions were secondary: whoever volunteered and was considered suitable would be deployed, regardless of whether he was a legitimist, a Christian Social, a

Socialist or a Communist. The total number of volunteers is likely to have been around 3,000. Women were also permitted to report to serve in the British army and were assigned to the Auxiliary Territorial Service and other parts of the army.

The Soviet Union, to be sure, was mindful of whether someone had an appropriate ideological mindset. Ideological diversity was not in demand. In order to be deployed, one had to be a Communist. And the number of those who were regarded as eligible to fight for the Soviet Union remained manageable. However, Austrian emigration to the Soviet Union had a certain tradition. The emigrants came from a varied assortment of groups, were decimated by Stalin, replenished from February 1934 and then decimated again. Whoever was able and wanted to, reported for service in the Red Army from June 1941. Others were interned and deported. The Austrian Red Army soldiers served in normal army formations, in the intelligence service, as scouts and as partisans.[394] There was one thing that even they were not allowed to do: form an Austrian unit. Proletarian internationalism replaced nationalist sentiments. The Soviets eventually availed themselves of a small group of Communists in order to support the partisan war in Yugoslavia and the struggle of the People's Liberation Army there. The Communist emissaries around Franz Honner and Siegfried (Friedl) Fürnberg gradually succeeded in establishing five so-called Austrian battalions, which were to be led from Slovenia to Austrian territory. In fact, only one of these squads was deployed – to costly effect – in February 1945.[395] Most members of these formations would only play a part after the war.

Their experience was thus similar to those Austrian prisoners of war who reported to the French for duty in one of the Austrian battalions after the surrender of the German Army Group Africa. Initially, the French were not very interested in these people and merely offered them the chance of serving in the Foreign Legion. In late 1944, however, an Austrian battalion was set up after all. 280 Austrians signed a declaration, in which they committed themselves to fight for the liberation of their homeland Austrian 'with weapon in hand'. It was too late for a combat mission, however. The Austrian battalion established within the framework of the French army was sent to Vorarlberg only after the war.[396] The situation in the USA was initially similar to that in Britain and France. Austrian emigrants, both Jews and non-Jews, were interned in late 1941 as enemy foreigners. Most of them were then released months later following thorough examination. Between 3,000 and 4,500 Austrians volunteered for service in the US army.[397] Several hundred worked for the intelligence service (Office of Strategic Services) and the propaganda department OWI (Office of War Information). As a rule, after three months of service, the Austrian refugees received American citizenship – for some, this was perhaps a reason for volunteering.[398]

Otto von Habsburg's attempt to set up an Austrian battalion in the USA in 1942 ended in a quarrel among the exile organisations, in which the Czech exiles energetically interfered. The matter was complicated even further when the minister without portfolio in Schuschnigg's government, Willibald Plöchl, who had fled from Austria, regarded himself as authorised to bring into being the Free Austrian National Council and to characterise it as the legal successor to the last Austrian government. The founder of the Pan-Europa Movement, Richard Coudenhove-Kalergi, also attempted unsuccessfully to found an Austrian government-in-exile. The various initiatives received only very lacklustre support from the Americans, and the American Secretary of War Henry L. Stimson distanced himself in 1942 from the idea of establishing Austrian battalions and renounced any form of recruitment aid. The battalion that was already in the process of being set up was dissolved again in May 1943. Another initiative had failed. And perhaps this was not a bad thing. It was namely unmistakeable that the representations of the political emigrants were attempting not only to gain recognition but also to make some sort of claim to sole representation and wanted to deploy the military units as liberation troops, if not as an 'Austrian army'. That, in turn, would have led to similar attempts being made elsewhere. And that would perhaps have torn Austria apart even before it had been reconstructed. Around 10,000 Austrians who served within the framework of the Allied armed forces during the course of the war made it clear, however, that the Second World War was not just associated with the service of Austrians in the German Wehrmacht. Admittedly, it would prove almost impossible to earn unreserved recognition for those Austrians who had served in Allied formations or with the Yugoslavian partisans. They remained, as one would say in military jargon, a 'shadow army'.

War of Annihilation

It was 2004 when, during a lecture event, the aged and almost blind physician and psychiatrist Viktor Frankl was suddenly asked by a female member of the audience: 'Why did you survive?' The question related to the concentration camps in which Frankl had been – Theresienstadt, Buchenwald, Auschwitz and Dachau – and which he had survived. He did not have an answer, although he had thought about it for decades. He knew only one thing: he was still alive, whereas a large number of his fellow sufferers had been killed. And he also knew that there was no rational explanation for this. In view of the mass mortality that he had witnessed, it was not surprising that his motto became 'Yes to life'.

At a time when the war had long since passed its military culmination point, those towards whom the pathological hatred of the Nazi regime was directed met their fate. From August 1941, Jews capable of work were prohibited from emigrating from the 'Third Reich'.[399] One month later, the regulation was issued on the marking of Jews with the so-called Jewish star. At the same time, they were forbidden to leave their residential areas. The next step was the completion of ghettoization. Finally, those Jews earmarked for deportation were interned in four assembly camps in Vienna's 2nd District, on Kleine Sperlgasse, Castellezgasse and Malzgasse. In October, their transportation to those eastern territories began, where the majority of them would meet their fate. From Vienna, they were initially sent to Theresienstadt, north of Prague, and primarily to camps in Poland and Belarus.

From February 1942, the measures that had been decided at the Wannsee Conference of 20 January 1942, and which aimed at the systematic annihilation of the Jews, were implemented. People were no longer to be killed in individual operations but instead murdered systematically and en masse. Bureaucrats of death initiated the deportation to the extermination camps and availed themselves of a subtly sadistic method, for it was left to the Jewish Councils to draw up the lists of those to be transported to the death camps. Millions upon millions were sentenced to death, around 66,000 Austrians among them, and became part of the systematic killing of the Shoa.[400] Their names are for the most part known; the railway stations from where they were dispatched, Vienna's Aspang Station or Strasshof Station on Nordbahn, are special types of memorial site.[401] The names of those responsible, the camp commandants and their helpers, are also known. The question of historical guilt is not answered in this way, though, and it perhaps never can be.

An accusation made for decades is that Austrians, measured against their share of the total population of the Greater German Reich, had a disproportionately high share in the Holocaust. For a long time now, perpetrator research has therefore been the order of the day. Simon Wiesenthal suggested that 40 per cent of crimes under Nazi rule had been committed by Austrians.[402] Other figures have also been cited: 20 per cent, or even just 4.65 per cent.[403] Depending on which concentration camp, which measure of annihilation or, above all, which group of people was examined, the most varied numbers have been floated. For all concentration camps, it was very recently ascertained that of the SS guards in the years 1940 to 1945 between 1.8 and 4.5 per cent were Austrians. Most of them were deployed in Mauthausen and Sachsenhausen. In Auschwitz I-III, the figure was 1.8 – 7.6 per cent.[404] It is striking that many commandants of concentration camps were Austrians. This considerably increased the share of this group of people above the statistical share of Austrians – 8.8 per cent – among the population of Germany. There is no doubt, however, that most figures are vague in many respects. This vagueness was increased by the fact that the term 'Austrian' was often used in an undifferentiated way. Sometimes it was old Austrians, that is, people who were born on the territory of the Habsburg Monarchy; at other times people who were actually born on the territory of the Republic of Austria. On occasion, southern Carinthia and southern Styria were included, as were southern Bohemia and southern Moravia; on other occasions, they were ignored. One of the worst criminals, Odilo Globocnik, was born in Trieste. His mother came from Upper Carniola (Tržič/Neumarkt), his father from Vršac (Werschetz) in Vojvodina. Odilo Globocnik went to Klagenfurt at the age of 15 and was regarded from this point as Carinthian.

Attempts will continue to be made to explain many things and, perhaps, also white-wash them. But there is no ignoring the principle facts. And it was not just a question of the concentration camp guards. There is no doubt about the fate of those who were imprisoned in Mauthausen and its sub-camps. The camps were part of the machinery of annihilation and settings in the war of annihilation. In the 48 sub-camps that were des-ignated 'labour camps of the SS' and which existed for different lengths of time, those goods were produced that were designed to enable the Nazi regime to at least survive a while longer. The first big sub-camps of Mauthausen emerged in Wiener Neustadt near the aircraft factories there and in Wiener Neudorf near the 'Ostmark' aircraft engine works. They were followed by Schwechat-Heidfeld, Redl-Zipf and Ebensee. Camps in Melk, the Floridsdorf district of Vienna, St. Valentin and in Hinterbrühl near Mödling were later added – to name only the most important.

In Melk, Ebensee, Gusen II, Peggau, Hinterbrühl, Schwechat and Leibnitz-Graz, work was carried out in tunnel facilities on so-called miracle weapons and particularly sensitive products were manufactured. The rapid expansion of the concentration camp complex naturally required ever more guard personnel. The SS guards were not suffi-cient, so members of the Wehrmacht were requested. The army also had too few men, so the Luftwaffe helped out. By early 1945, around 20,000 Luftwaffe servicemen had been transferred to the SS and deployed as concentration camp guards.

The vast majority of the sub-camps were created for men. But women were also sent to concentration camps. Some were sent to Mauthausen. In addition, female camps were set up in Amstetten, Hirtenberg, St. Lambrecht and Lenzing. In late 1944, around 60,000 people were accommodated in the sub-camps of Mauthausen, who had to per-form forced labour: six times as many as the number that remained in the main camp of Mauthausen.[405] Whoever was not forced to work but instead left to vegetate in the main camp was frequently subjected to the most varied series of experiments: hormone experiments, lice experiments, dietary experiments, tolerance experiments, vaccination experiments ... The prisoners were also supposed to test completely inedible synthetic foodstuffs like mycelium-protein sausage from the refuse of the filament factory in Lenzing. 25,000 people are believed to have lost their lives during the medical experi-ments carried out at different locations.[406]

The existence of concentration camps was, of course, known, not only in the imme-diate vicinity but also further away. The camps were supplied by ordinary business es-tablishments. Prisoners marched out for work deployment. The thousands that begged for food and water at railway stations, were herded through streets and localities, then accommodated in the camps and hired out to industrial enterprises to slave away, could not be concealed. The simple explanation offered was that criminals, antisocial elements, enemies of the regime, Jews and prisoners of war were being forced to work here in the service of the German people. Reference was made to necessary selections and the treatment of the POWs was justified with the defensive war supposedly forced on Germany.[407] Once again, the instrument of selective perception was applied in order to block out anything unpleasant or distressing. There was already so much suffering in this war, so many worries. Why bother oneself with such things on top of all that? The possibility that one of the prisoners might talk about his or her experiences was excluded from 7 May 1944 at the latest, after Reichsführer-SS Heinrich Himmler had issued the order: 'For the duration of the war, I forbid any release of prisoners from Mauthausen concentration camp for reasons of secrecy.'[408]

But more and more people refused to content themselves with simple answers. They looked for confirmation of their suspicions and, in the process, risked falling under suspicion themselves. The millions of dead and wounded Wehrmacht soldiers unsettled them and likewise the disappearance of people whom they were close to or had at least known. There were no plausible explanations for these things. The number of arrests increased. It was, after all, so easy to fall under suspicion or be prosecuted for one of those forms of resistance that practically anyone could be guilty of, such as expressing doubts about the verisimilitude of reports, criticising local or major Nazi figures, or making reference to information from 'enemy radio stations'. Rumours replaced facts but it was sufficient in order to be charged on the basis of one of the countless denunciations. Dissidents and sceptics were labelled enemies of the people. Complaints of 'undermining military morale', 'treasonous propaganda' or 'conduct damaging to society' led to court proceedings, prison and concentration camp. Violations of one of the regulations that restricted the life of every single person were severely penalised and frequently punished with the death penalty. Franz Jägerstätter from Upper Austria was executed due to his refusal to serve in the Wehrmacht. This was evidently also intended as a warning to others that the same could happen to anyone who refused to serve on the basis of his Catholic beliefs. Not very different was the fate of religious communities such as the Jehovah's Witnesses and the Adventists, who refused to perform military service for reasons of conscience and were sent to a concentration camp or the ranks of a penal battalion, where their chances of survival were low.

But that which was so positively termed 'ethnic community' (Volksgemeinschaft) continued to survive. And it survived even though most people were already feeling the direct effects of the war and a threat that increased day by day. The days on which the air-raid warning was given and the sirens howled became more and more frequent. The destruction of the Luftwaffe industry and other parts of the arms industry was followed by so-called oil targets and transportation targets, railways stations, trains, bridges and roads. The Allies were also waging a total war. Gradually, however, the time had come for them to agree on their post-war aims. Victory over Germany was one thing. What followed was something else. And around five-and-a-half years after the Anschluss, the Allies sent a clear signal to Austria that it could expect what Friedrich Heer – by analogy with the upheavals of the year 1938 – would then term a 'regressive breach' (*Rückbruch*).

12 Back to the Future

12 Members of the Reich Labour Service (RAD) and the Hitler Youth operating an 8.8-cm Flak 37 anti-aircraft gun to the south of Vienna. With multiple batteries of up to 94 guns of different calibres, they attempted in Air Gau XVII to hit the bombers of the American Fifteenth Air Force flying at a height of 6,000 to over 8,000 metres during their attacks on Gau capital Vienna. To this end, the 24th Anti-Aircraft Division deployed 16,000 people until the end of 1944, including 4,000 adolescent Luftwaffe auxiliaries and 3,500 female anti-aircraft auxiliaries and RAD girls. In view of the size of the formations – more than 700 four-engine bombers – the effectiveness of the anti-aircraft artillery was modest. (Photo: Rauchensteiner, *1945. Entscheidung für Österreich*)

The language of Nazi propaganda had become monotonous. Reports on the enormous amounts of sunken tonnage of Allied shipping alternated with reports about battles, in which huge losses had been inflicted on the enemy. There was no mention of National Socialist Germany having started the war by attacking Poland, that it had attacked Belgium, the Netherlands, Denmark, Norway, Yugoslavia and Greece and, finally, that with the invasion of the Soviet Union the decisive step had been taken in unleashing a total war. Now it was a question of repeatedly hammering home to the 'ethnic comrades' (Volksgenossen) the necessity of a defensive war. 'Fight until the salvation of Europe from Bolshevism', as could be read in *Das Kleine Volksblatt* in 1943. 'In January, 522,000 gross register tons in submarines and aircraft sunk'; 'They died so that Germany can live'; 'People, arise, and storm, break loose!'; 'The Führer honours Vienna and her sons: "Reich Grenadier Division Grand and German Master". Title conferred on the 44th Infantry Division'.

Only a small column with eight lines was devoted to the first air raid on Wiener Neustadt: 'Enemy incursion in the south-eastern part of the Alps and the Danube Gaue'. There was nothing more to be read about it in the national newspapers. It was a different matter regarding the 'Culmination of the defensive battle in the east'; 'The Führer calls on German youth'; 'German Wehrmacht, the final defence of freedom'.[409]

The people were jaded. Stalingrad had brought about a change of thinking, especially in the Alpine and Danubian Reich Gaue. One simply had to bring to mind the annihilation of the German Sixth Army, the end of Army Group North Africa, the failure of the German summer offensive in 1943 (Operation 'Citadel') and the first strategic aerial warfare against an Austrian target in order to be clear about the situation. How, one asked, would it all end? The Allies gave first indications in autumn 1943. And for those who were prepared to break away from the idea of an eternal Anschluss, there was even a concrete hint.

The Moscow Declaration

In mid-October 1943, the foreign ministers of Britain, the Soviet Union and the USA met in Moscow. The conference had been prepared for months. Notes had been exchanged, attempts made to ascertain intentions and many things revived that had remained dormant for months or even years. As early as 16 December 1941, Stalin had delivered a memorandum to British Foreign Secretary Anthony Eden in Moscow, in which the demand for an independent Austrian state in its pre-war borders was mentioned.[410] In 1943, an Austrian section of the 'anti-fascist school for prisoners of war in the Soviet Union' had also been founded. British politicians, above all Winston Churchill, had listed Austria among those countries that were to be liberated. Finally, a paper with the title 'Declaration on Austria' arrived in October at the guest house of the People's Commissariat for Foreign Affairs in Moscow, which contained the history of the process of Allied self-discovery. The route taken by the British, in particular, had covered a lot of ground. In March 1938, the British Permanent Under Secretary of State Sir Alexander Cadogan had still stated: 'Thank goodness, Austria is out of the way.' One problem less, as far as he was concerned. But this had proved to be a misapprehension and it was not least the British who wanted to correct their own error. Thus, in October 1940, the government advisor and diplomat Robert Vansittart, stated that Britain had every reason to restore Austria. He had been contradicted and his comments dismissed as an expression of his fanatical hatred of Germany. The times were gone when one created small, independent states that were not economically viable or capable of surviving. Furthermore, the matter was in any case outdated, because Austria was firmly in Nazi hands. Seventy per cent of the people were Nazis, it was claimed. Ten months later, in August 1941, the question of Austria's future invited new intellectual debate. Mr H. R. P. Laffan from the Foreign Research and Press Service, one of the think tanks of the British War Cabinet, listed what might happen with Austria after the war: it could be left in a union with Germany, its independence could be restored or it could be allowed to merge with a new Danube federation. A fourth option was also discussed, namely its partition, whereby the western part could go to Germany or Switzerland and the eastern part could be assigned to a Danube confederation. In view of the war situation, this was an equation with many unknowns. British Prime Minister Sir Winston Churchill struck a propagandistic tone when he stated in London on 18 February 1942: 'We can never forget here in this island that Austria was the first victim of Nazi aggression … and in the victory of the Allies, Free Austria shall find her honoured place.'[411] Regardless of how this was meant, Austria had now become an issue! And the British assumed the leading role.

The participants continued to write about and discuss the matter. The longer the war went on and due to sympathy with at least some Austrian émigrés, the view had consolidated itself that Austria should be restored. Now, another Briton, Geoffrey Harrison, came into play and began in February 1942 to repeatedly debate the Austrian question in position papers. He was eventually able to convince with his argument that one ought to view the Austrian question from a positive, viable perspective and not just tinker with various formulations that might be understood as a call for resistance and contained hidden threats. Harrison summarised the initially disparate thoughts, and that which had been formulated in the Foreign Office read very well: Austria had been the first country to fall victim to a typical act of aggression by Nazi Germany. In order to make it still clearer, 'Nazi' was then replaced by 'Hitler's'. The Anschluss of 15 March 1938 was declared null and void. In this way, British politics, not least, were to be subjected to a review. The citing of the wrong date – 15 rather than 13 March – was a lapse. There was, indeed, an inflationary accumulation of dates. In any case, Austria was to re-emerge as an independent state. In order to ensure that the country remained stable in the long term, it should be given the option to merge with (unnamed) neighbouring states that would have similar problems to Austria. Things did not entirely pass off without threats, however: for their participation in the war on the side (*sic*) of Hitler's Germany, the Austrian people, according to the British, would bear a responsibility that they could not escape. And they would also take into account what Austria itself had contributed to its liberation.

Foreign Secretary Eden arranged for the paper to be subjected to a widespread evaluation. The reaction of the Soviet government, which received the draft of a declaration on Austria on 24 August, was cautious. The British Ambassador in Moscow soon let it be known, however, that the Soviets took exception to the idea that Austria might merge with its neighbouring states. In any case, that would still have to be discussed. Americans, British and Soviets agreed to a meeting at senior level.

During the course of preparations, the Soviets also set about formulating their objectives. To this end, the Soviet ambassador in the USA and former foreign minister Maksim Litvinov was summoned to Moscow and appointed chairman of a commission that should not only work out an agenda but also establish the lines along which negotiations would then take place. Once the time came and, on 18 October, an American delegation – headed by Secretary of State Cordell Hull – met with a British delegation under Anthony Eden and the Soviet negotiators, the claims were to some extent defined. Austria was one topic. In the framework of the Litvinov commission, the Soviets had committed themselves to several principles, which constituted an opposite standpoint to the British proposals to the extent that the crucial point was not the restoration of the country but the question of a union of states. This touched, namely, upon an issue that was fundamental for the Soviets: after the expected victory over Germany, they wanted to lay out a belt of countries in which Moscow called the shots. Austria was not one of them. Thus, it was not to be combined with a new Czechoslovakia, Hungary or any Balkan countries. Litvinov also cited the Czechoslovakian president-in-exile, Edvard Beneš, as a witness in favour of Austrian independence. And he noted that Austria should not simply be left to the 'West'. It should fall between East and West. A power-political neuter, as it were; an admittedly 'viable but small state'.[412] The Soviets had no objection to the small amount of menace at the end of the declaration. The British had no doubt formulated it very well. Thus, in the context of the Moscow Conference, the foreign ministers no longer had to attend a great deal to the Declaration on Austria. The few differing viewpoints were to be cleared up within a committee. And this is indeed what happened. However, the Soviets demanded that it should not stipulate that the Austrian people were to be made to discharge their duties – as the British had formulated it – but rather the state of Austria, which first had to be re-established. This might perhaps sound senseless, but it was a question of anticipating interstate and not interpersonal communication. The Americans and British were not particularly happy about this but they did not want to question the entire document due to such trifles. Annex VI of the minutes of the Moscow Conference of Foreign Ministers had been born.[413] It was the 30th of October 1943. The next day, the guests of Soviet Foreign Minister Molotov took their leave, though not without first agreeing on which results of the gathering were to be published and what had to remain strictly secret. The Declaration on Austria was intended for the general public. It was not a secret paper and was thoroughly acknowledged as early as 3 November in the Vienna edition of the Nazi central organ *Völkischer Beobachter* – in line with Party principles, of course! There was talk of 'cutthroats' in Moscow who wanted to restore the non-viable state that National Socialist Germany had saved from catastrophe. It had not crossed the 'rogues'' mind that they might be acting in this way against the will of the people of the Eastern March. But they would certainly give the 'riffraff' the right answer and make their contribution to final victory.

The Moscow Declaration thus very quickly became public. And whoever did not read the *Völkischer Beobachter* or any other 'coordinated' newspaper, no doubt heard in conversation that Austria had been Hitler's first victim – in the view of the Allies – but that it was to re-emerge as a new/old state and was heading for a future in peace and prosperity, guaranteed by the Allies. Some thought had to be given, of course, to the question of Austria's contribution to its own liberation. But nothing was written about this and a longer period would be required before Allied propaganda would also publicise this key element of the declaration. This also did the rounds. As early as November 1943, the declaration was instrumentalised and in December 1943, when the removal of the Vienna Gauleiter and Reich Governor Baldur von Schirach – who had attempted since August 1940, with little success, to build on the tradition of the imperial capital and seat of royal residence – appeared to be imminent, one of the arguments for his retention was that, in the event of his dismissal, it could be expected that in the Allies' signalised war of nerves the Moscow Declaration would boost 'elements in Vienna hostile to the Old Reich for sure'.[414] This was not merely pure invention because the idea of an independent Austria had not so completely disappeared as might have been assumed in 1938. One thing could be established after a short time: the Moscow Declaration had practically no impact on the conduct of the Eastern March soldiers, among whom an increased tendency to desert might have been expected. And this was in spite of the fact that the Wehrmacht was retreating on all fronts and that the time was long since over when the inhabitants of the Greater German Reich noted with fascination the vast numbers of POWs. In the meantime, hundreds of thousands of soldiers of the German Wehrmacht had also been captured; their relatives were concerned about them and rightly worried that they might suffer the same fate as the Allied prisoners of war in German camps.

The Human Factor

The people living in the Alpine and Danubian Gaue of the German Reich had also long since had to get used to receiving a postcard with the notification that such and such a relative had been reported missing after the fighting in such and such a place and had probably been captured. This might have initially confirmed that those whom the people were anxious about were still alive. Nothing more was known, and one could only hope for the best. After Stalingrad, the military registration offices had sent a particularly high number of such notifications. Frequently, this optimism then proved to be premature. In the pocket and the adjacent sections of the front, more than 300,000 Germans, as well as Italians, Romanians and volunteers from a dozen European countries, had been encircled. Around 40,000 soldiers were from the Military Districts XVII and XVIII. Thousands had been killed by February 1943 or successfully flown out at the last moment, injured. 15,000 were taken prisoner. The soldiers of the 44th and the 297th Infantry Divisions, as well as the 100th Light Infantry Division, were among them.

Added to those who had fought in the central sector of the front, were killed in action, taken captive or reported as missing, were those, primarily mountain troops, who had been deployed in Finland, northern Russia or the southern sector; those who had fought in North Africa against British, Canadian, American and French troops, and those who found a use combatting partisans as occupation troops in France, Belgium, the Netherlands, Greece, Serbia, from summer 1943 in Italy and, above all, in the hinterland of the eastern front; furthermore, members of the aerial formations, the Luftwaffe ground crews, the navy, the anti-aircraft troops, who were constantly being built up, and the Waffen SS. Gradually, only statistics appeared to be a reliable source of information; at least they gave some indication of the course of the war and the suffering. Beyond all statistics were those who cracked under the pressure of the war and could not endure the shock of the fighting, the dying and the infliction of suffering on others. They were probably far fewer in number than the shell-shock sufferers from the First World War. The methods of treatment were similar, however. Attempts were made during and after the war, not least in Austria, to treat the mentally ill with electricity and insulin shocks. For the most part, they remained human wrecks for the rest of their lives.[415]

From October 1942 to October 1943 alone, an estimated 13,000 men from the Eastern March had been killed in action or succumbed to their wounds or illness.[416] During the same period of time, around 36,000 were reported as missing. The majority of them had been left in Russia or North Africa. And it was no consolation that the losses of the wartime opponents steadily rose. The POW camps overflowed.

It was not left at the first camps; new ones had long since been added. In December 1941, around 100,000 French prisoners of war, 28,000 Serbs and others could be counted in the Kaisersteinbruch, Krems-Gneixendorf, Pupping, Wolfsberg, Spittal/Drau, Markt Pongau, Maribor (Marburg), Lienz and Wagna camps.[417] The camp inmates were separated. Western and Soviet prisoners of war were not to have contact with one another. There were namely differences not only in the camps themselves but also where labour deployment was concerned. Soviet POWs were deployed for heavy-duty work with even lower daily rations than the Western prisoners and without any kind of subsidies such as those received by the 'Westerners' from their home countries or the Red Cross. An order issued by Military District Command XVIII on 5 September 1941 stated: 'Any kind of sympathy towards the Soviet POWs would demonstrate abject weakness. At the first sign of active and passive resistance, action is to be taken with the utmost rigour and use made of the weapon.'[418]

The masses of captured Red Army soldiers following the large encirclement battles in autumn 1941 no doubt confronted the Wehrmacht with problems of a special nature. But the way in which the Soviets were dealt with exceeded all expectations. As of 20 December 1941, the High Command of the Wehrmacht counted 3,350,639 Soviet prisoners of war. Several millions were added in 1942 and 1943. As many as two million Red Army soldiers did not survive the first months of captivity. In this case, too, it very quickly became clear that human life was worth nothing. On the basis of the 'Commissar Order', the members of the Soviet political administration – the 'political commissars' – were shot, the prisoners starved to death, transported in open carriages even in winter and decimated by epidemics, and only a remnant arrived in the POW camps. Stalin abetted this continuation of the war of annihilation to the extent that he declared members of the Red Army who surrendered to be cowards and regarded them as outcasts who had forfeited all respect and the right to return: 'Units and troop formations who are caught in an enemy pocket should fight to the end without any thought for themselves.' Whoever chose to surrender to the enemy was with all means 'to be destroyed by land and air. But the families of the captured soldiers are to be deprived of all state support and aid', decreed the generalissimo.[419] In this way, it was hoped that the Red Army soldiers would fight fanatically and to the point of self-sacrifice. As prisoners of war, therefore, they could not expect particular consideration from anyone.

From 1943, the Soviet prisoners of war were preferably deployed in the economic enterprises of the SS around Mauthausen and its sub-camps. In order to survive, tens of thousands 'volunteered' and declared their readiness to fight alongside the German Wehrmacht in the 'Russian Liberation Army' of General Vlasov. Most of the captured Red Army soldiers remained in the camps, however, and led a miserable existence as slave labourers who were 'loaned out'. Around 80 to 90 per cent of the prisoners of war toiled for Greater Germany. Like the concentration camps inmates who were detailed to labour deployment, they were not permitted to seek shelter in the event of an air raid but had to remain at their positions. They were not even counted among the dead of the air war.

Child Soldiers

The war continued to dominate events. Some kind of 'Fortress Europe' controlled by the German Wehrmacht still existed. Thanks to the policies of conquest during the first years of the war, the resources of the occupied countries could also be exploited for the benefit of the German Reich. The war industry continued to run at full speed; the output of armaments industries reached maximum figures in mid-1944. Despite the increasingly fierce air war, a steady increase in the output of firms producing weapons was recorded. The problem of the Nazi state was not raw materials and facilities but workers. The human factor became decisive for the war. In spite of all efforts to increase labour deployment, to integrate as many female workers as possible on a compulsory basis, hire pensioners and track down those reluctant to work, the shortages became ever more acute. Foreign labourers and prisoners of war were added to the domestic workers. Their share rose in the Alpine and Danubian Gaue from ten per cent in 1942 to 36 per cent in 1944, that is, from 86,000 to 260,000.[420] Their working time comprised 72 hours a week. However, because the war had long since reached Germany and the territories occupied by her, it could only be a question of time before neither the industrial foundations nor the people would suffice to enable the Wehrmacht to continue a world war. Systematic destruction from the air was the order of the day.

The objective of destroying Germany's industrial and supply basis was joined by the intention – raised, above all by the Royal Air Force, to the status of a strategic principle – of shaking the rule of the National Socialists and the morale of the people by systematically destroying the urban centres. The raids, frequently launched by the British during the night, did not, admittedly, open up a new dimension to the war, because the German Luftwaffe had also set itself the objective of destroying residential areas. That began with the attack on Wieluń in Poland on 1 September 1939, continued with the destruction of Warsaw, the centre of Rotterdam and the bombardment of urban centres in England. As early as 1941, however, the German Luftwaffe had already lost air supremacy over the Continent, and the strategic air fleets of the British and Americans began to dominate the skies by day and night. Gradually, the Allies bombed their way towards the larger cities and industries. The circumstance that the attacks against the 'Old Reich' began earlier than those against the Alpine and Danubian Gaue had led to an industrial transfer to Austrian territory, which increased industrial potential but also multiplied the number of targets. Now it was the turn of Innsbruck, Klagenfurt, Steyr and, from March 1944, the vicinity of Vienna. Hardly any large town, noteworthy industrial plant, rail or road bridge slipped the attention of the planners of the strategic air war: Wels, Pottendorf, Türnitz, Guntramsdorf, Villach, Salzburg, Amstetten, Melk, Donawitz but also Reitern near Gföhl. No one could claim to be safe from the payloads of the bomber planes and the on-board armaments of the escort fighters. And that was ultimately one of the objectives of the air war. The purpose was not just to destroy but also to intimidate. No one should feel safe any longer in the territories dominated by National Socialist Germany.

From February 1943, the schoolchildren in post-secondary education, the 16 ½ to 17 ½ year-olds, were called up as Luftwaffe helpers. The 'total war' proclaimed by Propaganda Minister Goebbels on 18 February 1943 made it possible to draft them in the Alpine- and Danubian Gaue, too. 30,000 young people were supposed to protect something that it was ultimately not possible to protect, in spite of the tunnels built in Graz and Linz and the six nascent flak towers for Vienna as well as the fighter defence. In those regions 'vulnerable to air attack', large batteries were set up. Thus, the anti-aircraft artillery in the Vienna area was gradually increased to more than 1,400 high-calibre guns. Anti-aircraft soldiers, adolescent auxiliaries and (mostly Soviet) 'volunteers' operated them. Women were called on to serve in searchlight batteries and multiplied in this way the hundreds of thousands of women working for the Wehrmacht.

As the American bomber formations moved up to heights of over 6,000 metres, the fire from the older anti-aircraft guns could no longer threaten them. Nonetheless, the American bomber formations initially suffered heavy casualties and had to accept the loss of 54 bombers, for example, during the raid on the ball bearing works in Steyr on 2 April 1944. After the aircraft industry, the mineral oil industry was top of the Allies' list of priorities from May 1944 onwards. The German fighter defence became increasingly fragmented. Thanks to further transfers of production sites, there were still enough aircraft; but there was a shortage of pilots. Nonetheless, the leadership of the Nazi state showed no inclination to end the war. And for a long time it had no need to worry that acts of resistance might seriously threaten its exercise of power.

Austria was in their Camp

Initially, very few in Austria were willing to engage in active resistance. Just as they had belonged to different political camps before 1938 and possessed the most varied motives for opposing National Socialism and its powerholders, the opponents of the regime bore little resemblance to one another in their resistance. This was an expression not only of party-political fragmentation but also a religious differentiation extending to pacifism, which was strengthened by very diverse Austro-patriotic aspects.[421] Those who felt a bond with Dollfuß, Schuschnigg and the Corporative State could be found here, likewise legitimists and Communists. Insofar as they had not been immediately arrested, gone underground or wanted to wait and see how Nationalist Socialist rule would develop, they increasingly defied attempts to obtain their acceptance or at least tolerance. Until that happened, however, more than a few of them had been thoroughly corrupted. They had participated, for instance, in all possible forms of Aryanisation and had in this way become accomplices of the system. In view of their opposition to the Corporative State and the oppressive unemployment before March 1938, the workers had been easily won over at the moment when the National Socialists' employment policies began to bear fruit. Others regarded the years- and decades-long aim of union with Germany as having been achieved, and they perhaps did not believe in the durability of the regime. The following dictum attributed to Stalin is applicable here: The Hitlers come and go. The German people remain.

From the outset, something else had become clear: the opponents of the regime did not seek to coordinate with the resistance groups that had existed for some time in the 'Old Reich' in order to become part of some kind of Greater German resistance but instead developed into a specifically Austrian resistance.[422] There was no union in this area. Most of them paid for their resistance with their lives. Insofar as they converged in groups, they ran the risk of being infiltrated by Secret State Police informants. This resulted in legal trials for high treason. The groups disintegrated, like the Social Democrat resistance, or were decimated, like the Communists. Individual operations dissolved organised resistance. But repeated attempts were made, such as that of secondary school teacher Johann Otto Haas, who was accused following his discovery of being 'head of the Revolutionary Socialists for the Greater German Reich'.[423] He was hanged in Vienna on 30 August 1944. For Communists who wanted to oppose the Nazi regime, the Hitler-Stalin Pact of August 1939 had been an event that appeared to deprive their struggle of all purpose. This abruptly changed with the start of the campaign against the Soviet Union. The result was that in 1941, 1,507 Austrian Communists were arrested by the Gestapo in Vienna alone on the suspicion of the most varied acts of resistance. Others continued their activities underground. Between 1938 and 1943, around 6,300 people were arrested who were accused of engaging in agitation against the regime as Communists. The Secret State Police succeeded in uncovering most Communist cells.

Between 1938 and 1940, most confessional and monarchist resistance groups and their leaders, such as the Augustinian canon Karl Roman Scholz, Jacob Kastelic, Jakob Lederer or Karl Burian, were also arrested and executed. All in all, 724 Austrian priests were arrested; some of them were sent to concentration camps, 15 were executed, and about the same number died as a result of their imprisonment.[424] The parson of Vienna-Gersthof, Heinrich Maier, who – together with Franz Josef Messner and others – passed on information about armaments industries to the Americans, was the last person to be beheaded in Vienna's regional court on 22 March 1945. The nun Maria Restituta Kafka, who had circulated a poem in the hospital of her order in Mödling, was arrested for 'aiding the enemy'. The poem ran: 'Awake soldiers and be prepared / Recall your first oath / For the country in which you lived and were born / You all swore for Austria / ... We only take up arms / To fight for a free Fatherland / Against the brown Reich of bondage / For a happy Austria.'[425] Sister Restituta was beheaded in 1943 in Vienna's regional court.

But the readiness to fight against the National Socialist regime and at least weaken it by means of civil disobedience and acts of sabotage continued to exist. Three 'Austrian Freedom Movements' and around two dozen very different groups developed, at least for a period of time, activities directed against the regime. Ultimately, 9,500 Austrians were sentenced to death and executed for their activities, which were demonstrably directed against National Socialist rule and its methods. Around 32,000 were sent to prisons and concentration camps for identical reasons.[426]

In view of the war, which showed no sign of coming to an end, the readiness to oppose the regime and reveal the 'other Germany' shifted ever more to the military. This was not because there were especially many opponents in the German Wehrmacht but because only force and the removal of Hitler could bring about a radical change. In this way, the same Wehrmacht that had contributed like no other to the expansion of German rule in Europe became the most important instrument of resistance.[427] Many became victims and sufferers of the regime; many longed for an end to the war and Nazi rule, and there were also those who encouraged a disentanglement leading to a complete rejection of the regime. But there were few who resolved to act. It was not a question of wanting to murder Hitler – although a man like Erwin Lahousen from Vienna, a colonel in the General Staff, was ready to do just this[428] – but of definitively ending the rule of the National Socialists. Until 1944, few aimed at Austria breaking away from Germany, that is, at a kind of reversal of the Anschluss. Furthermore, in the self-conception of the most important protagonists, there was no special link to Austria before 20 July 1944.[429] Only after the war did it become known that a veritable Austrian network had existed within the Foreign Affairs / Counterintelligence Office under Admiral Canaris, in which Erwin Lahousen and the long-time intelligence officer Kurt Fechner, as well as a dozen Austrians played a role. From 1939, they established contact with the Allies and strove to show 'another Germany' but also the still extant Austria.[430] Ethical questions and the experiences gathered during the war played a notable role here.

At that moment when it became clear that only an act of force would be able to bring about the overthrow of the regime and that only the military was capable of neutralising the influence of the NSDAP and its military formations, it was a question of finding soldiers as senior as possible who were prepared to undertake an assassination and an overnight seizure of power. Aside from the relatively large group of military oppositionists in Berlin, similar groups existed in Paris, in Brussels and within Army Group Centre as of 1943, and the organisation gradually spread to most military districts – including Vienna. The plan of the conspirators was both simple and ingenious. In cases of 'urgent danger, e.g. for the protection of threatened borders or for combating revolutionary movements in the territories newly acquired by the Reich', the deputy general commands were to form fully operational units that would be ready for action within six hours under the code name 'Valkyrie'.[431] With their help, the conspirators wanted to seize power in the state. The author of the 'Valkyrie' plans, which Hitler had expressly approved, was Lieutenant Colonel Robert Bernardis of the General Staff, who came from Vienna. He acted in Berlin in close collaboration with Count Claus Schenk von Stauffenberg. His liaison in Vienna was Captain Carl Szokoll.

Code Name 'Valkyrie'

On 20 July 1944, the time had come. Hidden in his briefcase, Stauffenberg carried a bomb, which was supposed to kill Hitler. He activated the time fuse on the bomb, left the briefing room in the East Prussian 'Wolf's Lair' and was no longer present to witness that, though the explosion of the charge killed four people and seriously wounded others, Hitler had survived. Notification of the assassination attempt was received in Vienna at around 6 p.m. – five hours after the bomb had exploded. The chief of staff of the military district, Colonel Heinrich Kodré, who was not among the conspirators, immediately did everything to ensure the implementation of the measures foreseen in the event of 'Valkyrie'. Carl Szokoll described the situation: 'Clueless soldiers hastened everywhere to their guns, prepared units and made a grab for power in the state, without even knowing it.'[432] At the same time, a fabricated teletype message was sent from Berlin, in which the arrest of the Party leadership, the heads of the SS and the Security Police was ordered. All concentration camps were to be occupied and their commandants likewise arrested. Should the Waffen SS resist, their commanders were to be immediately replaced with army officers.

Everything passed off smoothly in Vienna during the first hour. The garrison was alarmed; the most important buildings were occupied and secured. From 8 p.m., the representatives of the political and police authorities in the military district command arrived at Stubenring one by one. Many of them were exceedingly suspicious. But the 'Valkyrie' measures continued to function, at least until a telephone call from Führer Headquarters brought the message that the assassination attempt had failed. Now the regime started to take revenge.

Lieutenant Colonel Bernardis and the vast majority of those who had agreed to follow their conscience, murder the tyrant and overthrow the reign of violence, were executed. Hardly any of the insiders survived. One of the few was Carl Szokoll, who had remained so inconspicuous that he was even promoted soon after. He was able to participate, therefore, in another phase of military resistance, which ultimately ended with the liberation of Austria.

The proceedings of the summary courts martial and People's Court that followed the attempt on Hitler's life were used for a kind of general reckoning with potential opponents of National Socialism. Arrests were carried out on a large scale and they did not fail to miss their mark as a means of state terror. For months afterwards, resistance capabilities were as good as neutralised. Ultimately, however, only a bloody example could be set, just as Hitler demanded. Proclamations of loyalty were organised.

Their success was evaluated by Joseph Goebbels as an 'unconscious plebiscite' in favour of Hitler. He was of the opinion that there was approval for a 'more strident totalisation' of the war.[433] A large manifestation of joy also took place on Schwarzenbergplatz in Vienna on 21 July 1944, and one might have gained the impression that most participants attended voluntarily. As on the day of the proclamation of the Anschluss in 1938, however, one also had to ask how many had stayed home.

Beyond the demonstrations, the chief of the German police and native of Austria, Ernst Kaltenbrunner, recorded the mood he observed in Vienna. It was, he wrote, 'poor and the attitude of almost all sectors of the population requires immediate intervention'. Furthermore, 'despondency' and 'helplessness' dominated.[434] 'The defeatist basic mood in Vienna is, therefore, very susceptible to all news from the south-east, any atrocity propaganda, certain "Austrian tendencies" and, of course, all Communist propaganda', wrote Kaltenbrunner. He believed that a substitution of certain people would make a difference. Very few wanted to accept that the collapse of National Socialist rule was already looming.

At a relatively late point in time, in winter 1944/45, representatives of various resistance groups met and overcame the shock of the failed attempt on Hitler's life. They gathered under the abbreviation O5, a synonym for Austria, and began to think about the future. But no political 'heavyweights' were among them; instead, they comprised – as Fritz Molden then put it – above all 'fools' and 'honest men'.

It seemed to be the case that the capacity for suffering was far greater than the courage to be different. Only a few, whose names have become known, made a difference, such as the garrison physician in Slutsk, south of Minsk, Erwin Leder, who saved the lives of hundreds, if not thousands, of Jews and prisoners of war (and survived),[435] or Warrant Officer (Class II) Anton Schmid, who did the same in Vilnius in 1942 (and was executed). Towards the end of the war, the cases became more frequent where attempts were made to reduce suffering and avoid destruction, just as Josef Gadolla did in preventing the destruction of Gotha. If the figures are correct, there were only 65 instances of resistance activity by native Austrians in the ranks of the Wehrmacht that clearly aimed at something one could call active resistance.[436]

13 Rubble

13 Upon liberating Mauthausen concentration camp, American troops (5th Regiment of the 11th Armoured Division) discovered only the last of the more than 69,000 dead from Mauthausen and its 48 subcamps. As the American troops withdrew again, some members of the gamp garrison armed themselves and wanted to prevent a final massacre from taking place at the moment of liberation. Mauthausen concentration camp was and remains a thorn in Austria's side. (Photo: Rauchensteiner, *1945. Entscheidung für Österreich*)

I n autumn 1944, the construction of the so-called Reich Protective Position (Reichs-schutzstellung) – the 'South-East Wall' – began along the Hungarian and Slovakian border. This was at a point in time when the troops of the Red Army were still positioned in eastern Hungary and central Poland. In Western Europe, American, British, Canadian and French troops were fighting their way forward through France, Belgium and the Netherlands. In Italy, the Germans had evacuated Rome on 6 June. The so-called Casablanca formula of unconditional surrender allowed for only one possible end to the war: if the Nazi state laid down its arms. There was still nothing to suggest, however, that the National Socialist leadership might give up the war for lost. Millions of soldiers were supposed to enable it to exercise power for a while longer. The Nazi leadership was fighting for its survival and left no doubt that it would continue to mercilessly suppress internal unrest or any absence of a will to resist. And it was in a position to do so.

Towards the end of the war, the inclination to desert increased among members of the Wehrmacht, and the Austrians did not lag behind. However, there could be no talk of mass flight.[437] The reason given by a former member of the Protection League for why he did not desert to the Americans, however, sounded very odd: 'I'm German, after all, and I just can't. ... Look, Renner, Renner was in favour. ... In the end, I'll have to shoot at my own people.'[438] In any case, most of them followed their commanders, their comrades or their oath until the unconditional surrender of the Wehrmacht. Why this was the case can be traced back to seven reasons: comradeship; the most varied forms of optimism; fear of the enemy's revenge; hatred of the enemy, who had obliterated the life of relatives and in this way turned the war into a personal affair; concern for their own homeland and its potential post-war fate; a specific soldierly ethos; and, last of all, National Socialist indoctrination.[439] Long after the war, around 40 per cent of former soldiers responded to the question 'Did you enjoy being a soldier?' with yes; 48.5 per cent with no. Most of them claimed to have fought to survive; 12.8 per cent fought for the (German) fatherland, 10.8 per cent out of a sense of duty and only 1.6 per cent for Austria.[440] To this spectrum of mental states we could add that non-compliance and desertion were regarded as offences punishable by death. Desertion was, therefore, located somewhere between cowardice and courage.[441] Somewhere within this conglomerate of sensitivities and threats, though not of prime importance, was also the concept of 'duty', which would be cause for heated debates in 1986/87. The men felt obligated; they had sworn an oath – a serious matter for many of them; while this did not mean blind obedience, they could not understand those who did not discharge this duty or changed sides and deserted. This had nothing to do with a doomsday mood, Nibelung loyalty or the Battle of Mons Lactarius in the Gothic War. And it revealed a dichotomy: between front and hinterland and likewise between the members of a community of fate and those who did not belong. Self-delusion was also a significant factor, as well as a conscious blindness towards those who became victims of this scrupulous performance of duties.

After the overthrow of the government of Admiral Horthy in Hungary and the installation of a new regime, similar to the National Socialists – the Arrow Cross Party – a frivolous bargain had been made: Germany committed itself to supplying Hungary with goods vital to the war effort, above all trucks, and received in return the promise of hundreds of thousands of Hungarian Jews as workers. Some of them would be deployed in constructing the Reich Protective Position.

Along the Reich frontier, a tank ditch was excavated and infantry positions were prepared. Aside from Jews, thousands of Hitler Youth members, employees of civilian firms and members of the final military contingent – the National Militia (Volkssturm) – dug the South-East Wall, though without coercion or any threat to their lives. By winter, most of the positions had been built – it did not become known at what human cost until much later.

Incitement to Murder

Once the ditches had been dug, the resistance nests created and the case locks concreted, the troops of the 2nd Ukrainian Front of the Red Army besieged Budapest. At the same time, the bomber formations of the American Fifteenth Air Force continued their work of destruction. The core territories of the German Reich and the Alpine and Danubian Reich Gaue with them, which were now given the designation 'Fortress', were to be subjected to a 'softening-up' barrage. After the industrial, oil and transportation targets, everything was bombarded that might serve to prevent swift reconstruction and in order to maintain the pressure. The priority objectives intermingled. Every target was attacked that could be regarded as even remotely worthwhile. No one could explain the fact that the Americans also bombarded prisoner-of-war camps and that every POW camp on Austrian soil was ultimately subjected to at least one air raid and that dead and wounded of the air war were recorded there, too. In November 1944, the Red Cross symbols were finally removed from the roofs. But the American air reconnaissance had already reconnoitred the sites.[442]

The circumstance that the devastation from the air not only exposed the targets as defenceless and was denounced as 'gangsterism' could be used by the Nazi leadership to once more arouse hatred and incite the population in a positively criminal manner to take revenge. The anti-aircraft defence and the deployment of the last fighter formations led to American bombers being shot down or damaged so badly that the crews attempted to rescue themselves with parachutes. Once they had landed on the ground, they ought to have the status of prisoners of war. But a shocked and fanatical population, who were directly called upon to kill aircrews, attempted to do just that. This first happened after devastating raids on large cities in the 'Old Reich', then in Hungary and finally in Austria. The Gauleiter of Upper Danube, August Eigruber, formulated the intention concisely and unequivocally: 'The Gendarmerie is not to intervene against lynch law carried out by the people (especially members of the NSDAP) against baled-out enemy pilots.'[443] The Gauleiter of Styria, Siegfried Uiberreither, of Tyrol-Vorarlberg, Franz Hofer, Hugo Jury in Lower Danube and Friedrich Rainer in Carinthia followed suit.[444] Finally, in May 1944, Joseph Goebbels called on the people in the entire Reich to take revenge. He arranged for all newspapers to circulate the message that the international laws of war no longer applied in cases of aerial terror; 'people's justice' was called for. It was not a direct incitement to murder but the escalation was predetermined. After an attack on Wels, the first maltreatment of American bomber crews who had rescued themselves with their parachutes had occurred on 24 February 1944.[445] On the day after Goebbels' article had appeared, the first actual murder of a member of an American bomber crew was committed in Wiener Neustadt.[446] People began to attack (sometimes wounded) Americans with iron bars, wooden slats and stones. In rural regions, scythes and pitchforks were also used. Most bombers crashed outside the cities. With increasing frequency, the crews of downed bombers were then led back to the cities, though not to show them the smoking ruins but instead to expose them to the fury of the people. On 25 July 1944, 16 American bombers were shot down over Linz. 80 crew members were able to save themselves with parachutes. 13 Americans are likely to have been murdered. And so it went on. There were repeated attempts, mostly by members of the Wehrmacht, to bring the pilots to safety, but they were of no avail. Men, women, National Militia, police, Wehrmacht soldiers and members of the Waffen SS partook in equal measure of the hunt for the only enemies they could get their hands on in the 'home theatre of war' (Heimatkriegsgebiet). And they demonstrated in a terrifying manner that it was not at all difficult for people to become murderers.[447]

In February, March and April 1945, a final escalation of violence occurred. On 12 March, the anniversary of the German invasion of Austria, 747 four-engine bombers of the American Fifteenth Air Force carried out the heaviest air raid on Vienna and not only hit their primary target, the oil refinery in Floridsdorf, but also and especially cultural buildings in the city centre. Among other things, the opera house was gutted. On 2 April, Graz suffered its heaviest air raid. And American pilots were once more beaten and shot to death. Long after the war, stock was also taken of this chapter of the war: after 556 downed aircraft on the territory of present-day Austria, there were 131 acts of violence against American bomber crews, which resulted in the deaths of at least 70 people.[448] The incitement to murder had doubtlessly succeeded.[449]

In March 1945, Vienna braced itself for the final battle. Whoever could flee did so. Women and children were called on to leave the city. Most of those who now sought shelter in the western and southern regions of the country had not realised that they were only part of a larger refugee movement.

From autumn 1944, columns of refugees were on the move with increasing frequency; they embodied another of the infinite number of fortunes of war. The German ethnic groups in Romania and Hungary, ultimately old Austrians, fled from the territories of south-eastern Europe that they had inhabited for centuries. They feared the Soviets as much as the vengeance of the non-Germans, and it was irrelevant here whether they had personally done something wrong or not: they would have to atone for the Nazi racial, settlement and resettlement policies and for the war. As many as five million German-speakers went on the move in Eastern and south-eastern Europe. On 5 October 1944, the Syrmia Germans were given the evacuation order and on 8 October those in Bačka. Around 70 per cent of the so-called Danube Swabians moved to the north and the west. In early 1945, the exodus of the Silesians began. Insofar as the refugees were able to decide on a particular territory in which they hoped to find shelter, they opted for the Alpine and Danubian Reich Gaue. Often, however, these were only transit territories, and the trek continued. More than half a million people came. Over 300,000 stayed.[450]

Among those who tried to save themselves were columns of Hungarian Jews who had survived the construction of the Reich Protective Position. Now they were no longer needed and herded to the west. The evacuation marches, which were intended to carry off tens of thousands from concentration camps in Eastern Europe and the inmates of the POW camps, labour camps and prisons, led in the same direction. The camp guards wanted to leave behind as few witnesses as possible of their unspeakable deeds. Starvation marches began. For many, above all Jews and concentration camp prisoners, they were death marches. In January and February 1945, as many as 9,000 prisoners from Auschwitz and several thousand more from Sachsenhausen, Dora-Mittelbau and Groß-Rosen concentration camps arrived in Mauthausen.[451] Neither on the move nor in the temporary reception areas was there a willingness to accept them unconditionally as suffering fellow humans and members of society. But Austria also began by way of precaution to remove traces and erase memories, as in Hartheim. In December 1944, the killing of prisoners and the sick was brought to an end. The castle was then returned to its original owner. As before, there was no place for compassion. In the vicinity of Mauthausen in February 1945, not many had hesitated to help recapture those who had not got far during the attempted outbreak of more than 400 doomed

Soviet prisoners of war.[452] By the same token, however, there were others who hid people for years and were shocked by the appearance of the terror previously carried out
somewhere far away. It contributed to strengthening a rejection of the regime and to
the feeling of consternation. It was often only subsequent generations, however, who
took up the thread again and gave expression to their horror in the form of memorials.

In February and March 1945, as many as 30,000 exhausted and apathetic Hungarian
Jews are likely to have made their way westwards. The main routes went via Graz, Eisen-
erz and Hieflau to the Danube. A third of the prisoners died in transit or were killed.[453]
The remainder reached Mauthausen. Fanatical National Socialists and officeholders,
who could work out for themselves that they would soon be brought to account, lost all
inhibitions. They ran amok and availed themselves of all available means for spreading
terror, taking revenge and dispossessing future generations of their livelihood. With his
so-called Nero Decree of 19 March, Hitler had removed any inhibitions that may still
have remained: 'All military transport, intelligence, industrial and supply installations
as well as material assets within Reich territory that the enemy could make use of to
somehow continue the fight now or in the foreseeable future are to be destroyed.' Whoever wanted to defy this order or even provided a pretext to circumvent it was shot or
hanged. Murder was the order of the day. In the penal institution in Stein an der Donau,
the prison director, Franz Kodré, released approximately 1,800 people who were serving
time mainly for minor political offences. The Kreisleiter of Krems mobilised SA, SS,
National Militia and Wehrmacht soldiers in order to recapture the people. This resulted
in a massacre. Kodré and two others were shot without any questions asked. This, however, was just one of many cases. The regime, which had used violence against its own
people from the very outset, left behind a final, bloody trail.

In February 1945, it had been claimed: 'Vienna is defended in Budapest'. After 51
days, the Battle of Budapest was over and the city had been taken by troops of the
Red Army. The Wehrmacht's Operation Spring Awakening was a fiasco. Then the Red
Army's 'Vienna Offensive' began. The Wehrmacht formations continued their struggle
in western Hungary, though it had now become hopeless, and moved ever closer to
the Reich frontier and thus Austria. The remnants of the four German armies of Army
Group South, still counting 700,000 soldiers, withdrew to the Reich Protective Position. It did not provide any defence. On 29 March 1945, the vanguard of the Red Army
crossed the 'great line', as they called it. The six-week war in Austria began, and with
it the liberation from National Socialism and its rulers. At the same time, a new era in
the history of Austria commenced, no less of an experiment than the period that had
started in 1918. And at the same time very different.

14 The Waltz of Freedom

14 Street party in front of the parliament building in Vienna on 29 April 1945. Two days after the formation of the Provisional State Government and the declaration of Austrian independence, members of the State Government moved into the badly damaged parliament building. A Soviet military band played on Ringstraße. The whole thing had the character of a popular festival. Soviets and Austrians danced. (Photo: Rauchensteiner, *1945. Entscheidung für Österreich*)

The period of the Allied occupation of Austria lends a strange weight to the history of the country after the Second World War. It is as though this Second Republic were constructed in a top-heavy way. The first ten years weigh more heavily than the decades that followed. Strictly speaking, this occupation period begins during those late afternoon hours of 29 March 1945 when the first Red Army soldiers first set foot on Austrian soil near Klostermarienberg in Burgenland.[454] The end of the Second World War was now almost close enough to touch. Initially, it was only the Rechnitz area in Burgenland that was consumed by fighting. However, just a few hours later, the fighting spread. Five armies of the 3rd Ukrainian Front drove forward what remained of the German Army Group South, which had by then been renamed the 'Eastern March' army group. In a move that was probably calculated to increase the will to resist among the population, the major formation was placed under the command of a native Austrian, General Lothar Rendulic.

The Battle for Vienna

The Soviet troops had a clear goal in mind: Vienna. They may have preferred to participate in the battle for Berlin, but they had to make do with the glory of taking the 'second capital of the Reich'. The battle for Wiener Neustadt began on 1 April. At the same time, the Russians made a deep incursion into the Raabtal area. They swerved northwards towards the Danube and began to encircle Vienna, the city that, in the opinion of the British secretary of state for war, James Grigg, would be far more important for the fate of Austria than the fate of Berlin for Germany. On 2 April, the Stavka, the supreme Soviet command, issued a call to the troops pushing forward towards Austria that they should announce the sincere objectives of the Soviets through handbills and hastily prepared posters: the Red Army was not fighting against the population of Austria, but against the German occupiers. Austrians should go about their work and do all they could to assist the Red Army. The proclaimed goal of the Red Army was to destroy the German-fascist troops and liberate Austria 'from dependence on Germany'. The Red Army stood 'firmly in support of the Moscow Declaration' and wanted merely to restore Austria. To a certain extent for internal use, the troop commanders were instructed to order their soldiers to treat the population with respect, 'to behave in the proper manner and to avoid mistaking the Austrians for the German occupiers'.[455]

This all sounded very positive, and it was intended to mitigate the fear of foreign soldiers among the people living in the regions that had gradually been liberated by the Soviets. It was assumed that everyone was familiar with the wording of the Moscow Declaration. Despite all attempts, however, fear of the Russians among those whose homelands threatened to turn into battlefields remained unabated. Whoever could do so fled – not only mayors, local group leaders and functionaries of the NSDAP, the rural emergency police (Landwacht) and teachers, but also young women and girls. The people who remained in the villages close to the front buried their valuables and prepared to set up home in their cellars. The shops were sold out. There was also no further need for ration cards. 'No post, no newspapers, no radio.' Those who had no petrol winnowed any candles they had in store. If not enough candles were available, 'funereal candles and small graveside candles were appropriated', as one teacher noted.[456] Soon afterwards, the shelling started. Towns and villages were quickly transformed into heaps of rubble.

While troops from the German Sixth Panzer Army were still preparing for the battle for Vienna, the hour of resistance struck once again. Now, the aim was no longer to remove Hitler and create a better Germany; the purpose instead was to offer resistance in support of Austria. Austrians no longer counted themselves among 'those' Germans. The man who had already played the main role in Vienna on 20 July 1944, Carl Szokoll, who had now been promoted to the rank of major, succeeded in making contact with the command of the Soviet Ninth Guards Army in Hochwolkersdorf. A confidant of Szokoll, Ferdinand Käs, informed the Soviets of the intention to start an uprising in Vienna. It is difficult to ascertain whether or not he was believed. Even so, Szokoll's emissary was sent back to Vienna and reported what the Soviets wanted. The plan for the uprising was revealed to the Security Service of the Reichsführer-SS by one of the individuals involved, Karl Biedermann. However, the demands made by the Russians exceeded the capacity of the resistance group anyway. Three officers, including the betraying officer, were hanged. Szokoll himself reached the Soviet lines. The battle could not be prevented. However, one thing was achieved: the 3rd Ukrainian Front reported to the General Staff in Moscow that there had been an attempted uprising in Vienna, in which not only 1,200 'Austrian soldiers' had wanted to participate, but also 20,000 Viennese residents. 'The planned uprising was prevented only by the betrayal of a very small number of people.'[457]

The battle for Vienna began on 6 April. The Russians fought their way forward from the south and west of the city. Finally, they crossed the Danube at Korneuburg and together with the Soviet formations advancing in the Marchfeld began to encircle the city from the east as well. The divisions of the II SS Panzer Corps surrendered one section after another, crossed the Danube Canal and finally succeeded in withdrawing from the city via the Floridsdorf Bridge, before retreating northwards. What remained was a metropolis that had not only been severely damaged by bombing, but also by street fighting. The looting began. St. Stephen's Cathedral was in flames. The battle for Vienna lasted eight days, until 13 April. Then the red flag of the Soviets was hoisted over the ruins of the government quarter. However, it was not the only flag to dominate the view of the city. Here and there, red-white-red flags could also already be seen. The Soviets allowed them to be flown – indeed, they fully approved of this. According to their own account, the attack on Vienna had cost them 18,000 lives. Since their offensive in the direction of Austria had begun, they had counted 35,000 dead. The German Wehrmacht was said to have lost 19,000 soldiers before Vienna was taken. In May, the Soviet government awarded a medal to those who took part in the battle 'For the capture of Vienna', as would later also be the case after Berlin fell. The Red Army soldiers were therefore not presented with a Liberation Medal, as they had been after the battle for Budapest or Bucharest. Consistently or otherwise, Vienna was regarded as a city of the Greater German Reich, and had therefore not been liberated, but taken.[458] No one noticed.

While the Vienna offensive was still underway, not only were further attempts made to offer resistance to 'those' Germans, but also to set the course for the political rebirth of Austria. At best, one could only guess as to the basis on which this would be achieved. While the existence of the Moscow Declaration was known, there was no precise information as to what the Allies had decided upon during 1944 and 1945. Was the Moscow Declaration more than just a declaration of intent? How would it be implemented? What contribution should and could Austria itself make towards its liberation in order to fulfil the demand that had been made in rather threatening undertones at the end of the Declaration? It was impossible to predict whether the basic assumption of the Declaration could be realised, namely that an Austrian state could be rebuilt on the same scale as it had been during the interwar years. The major warring powers, who had met to discuss their post-war plans for Austria, were able to agree only that the country should somehow be divided and subjected to Allied control for an unspecified period of time. However, there was no doubt as to their intention of giving Austria a historic chance.

Renner, Who Else?

The Soviets, British and Americans, and not least also the French, had planned for Austria's future without the country's involvement. Since January 1944, there had been discussions within the framework of the European Advisory Commission, which was now based in London, as to how Austria should be divided into zones following its full occupation, and what form Allied control should take. At first, there was talk of three, and then of four occupation zones of different sizes. Vienna presented an additional problem. One could almost gain the impression that here, a decision was deliberately being put on hold. At any rate, there was no agreement as to how to move forward. It could therefore be assumed that those who reached Austria first would put their plans into action. And those were the Soviets.

The Soviets had very precise ideas as to which areas their zone of occupation should include, namely the portion of the country that bordered Hungary and the new Czechoslovakia, as well as large areas of Vienna. The Soviet ideas as to how the administrative framework should look in order to get Austria back on its feet were far less specific. However, they were helped by the practice they had pursued thus far in East-Central Europe: they wanted to transfer responsibility for the administration of the liberated areas to local representatives as quickly as possible. Several communists returning from exile in Moscow and Yugoslavia were to ensure that developments remained on the planned course, and they were to be incorporated into a provisional government as the most important component of a 'people's front'. If no one could be found in Austria who could head such a government, the Soviets planned to install General Fritz Franek – a prisoner of war and a highly decorated officer of Austrian origin – as head of a military administration. However, in the end, he was not needed. In Gloggnitz near Semmering, under circumstances that could not be clearly explained, Soviet troops met with the state chancellor of the First Republic, Karl Renner, during the course of their advance on Vienna – in other words, the man who had already played an eminent part in establishing the Republic in 1918.[459] He quickly made it clear that he was keen to assume a similar function to the historical role he had played in 1918. He was at least willing to participate in the experiment of the state system that he quickly labelled the 'Second Republic'.

There was much about this new beginning that was strange and by no means straightforward. Austria, which had emerged from being a supranational empire and which for years had upheld the notion of union with Germany, now wanted to define itself as a nation state. As the Allies had done with the Moscow Declaration, so the events of 1938 were to be dismissed as a historical error and an act of aggression. Renner himself was an exponent and an example of much that could now be described as having been an error and based on fundamental misconceptions. And his adaptability appeared to be exemplary. In 1918, he had by all means been willing to form a final imperial government. He had opposed a revolution and a Bolshevik experiment, and he was regarded as a 'right-winger' among the 'leftists', which had led to him being branded a 'betrayer of socialism' and a 'lackey of the bourgeoisie' in the Soviet Union. Renner had been the leader of the Austrian delegation during the peace treaty negotiations in Saint-Germain, although as a parliamentarian during the 1920s, he had repeatedly given way to Otto Bauer and Karl Seitz. Finally, in March 1933, his withdrawal from the presidium of the National Council (Nationalrat) had led to its incapacity to act. In 1938 he had very clearly expressed his support for union with Germany. And now?

At first, Renner had no idea of the political events underground and of the various resistance campaigns. He assumed that there would be a swerve to the left in Austria, and he wrote to Stalin on this matter. He described the terrible situation in Austria to Stalin and concluded with the simple statement: 'The fact that the future of the country belongs to socialism stands beyond question and requires no further emphasis.'[460] He wrote to Stalin twice more and finally congratulated him in sycophantic tones on his victory over the German Wehrmacht.

Renner was the man of the hour. And indeed, he was given a chance. Before he could set to work realising the experiment of founding a new state for the second time in his life, he put his thoughts down on paper regarding the next steps needed. They focussed on the restoration of democracy, basic freedoms, elections, security, teaching, finances, the domestic economy, and also those who were to play no part in rebuilding the country:

> All fascists (members of the Home Guard [sic]), the clergy, national fascists who were more than just fellow travellers, are to be excluded from all democratic rights for a trial period of ten years; they are thus neither eligible to vote, nor can they be elected or assume public office... The universities shall be closed during the first days... the student associations that have existed to date are to be disbanded... physical exercise (sport etc.) may include elements of 'pre-military education'.[461]

With regard to other considerations, too, Renner expressed a highly idiosyncratic and personal standpoint, such as with his demand that Social Democrat workers should be returned the property that they had lost as quickly as possible, although Jewish assets should be transferred to a restitution fund in order to prevent the country from being flooded on a mass scale by those who had been expelled and who were returning to reclaim their personal property.[462] In his notes, Renner was finding ways to deal with the past, but his thoughts carried no weight for the future. He already revised them days later. The reality was now different. Renner acknowledged this fact, and since he was a political professional, he was keen to show that he was not acting on behalf of the Soviets, but on his own ideas. The Soviets agreed to this approach.

Renner therefore began to form a provisional government, which was to be compiled of former Social Democrats and revolutionary socialists who had come together to form the Socialist Party of Austria (SPÖ), as well as of former Christian Socials and other moderate right-wingers, who re-formed to create the Austrian People's Party (ÖVP), and communists. He felt that he was fully entitled to describe this government as a state government of a Second Republic. In so doing, Renner conformed to the ideas of the Soviets, which were based on the concept of forming a people's front government. Thus, all political forces, aside from the National Socialists, were represented. The country was being governed by a well-known individual, but not by a communist. Two key departments, the State Secretariat for Internal Affairs and for Schools and National Education, were to be given to the communists Franz Honner and Ernst Fischer, however. Even so, it was an auspicious start, since each of the state secretariats to be created was filled with three appointees, so that each could monitor the other. Nine ministers and sixteen permanent secretaries were initially appointed, including the first woman to join an Austrian government, Helene Postranecky (KPÖ – the Communist Party of Austria). Several positions remained unoccupied, waiting to be filled with representatives of the parts of Austria that would join later. A political advisory council was to ensure that the provisional State Chancellor did not become too high-handed – which in the case of Renner was a real danger. However, he had no power in the classic sense.

In fact, the area of responsibility of the provisional state government initially hardly extended beyond Vienna and a part of Upper Austria. However, even in this reduced portion of Austria, Renner was only granted limited power. In parallel to the negotiations with him, the Soviets had sought a mayor for Vienna and found one in the form of the former Imperial General Staff officer Theodor Körner. Renner took note of this. He also had no influence on the appointment of mayors outside Vienna. All this was taken care of by the Soviets, who primarily took communists into consideration, although only those who came from the Soviet Union or Yugoslavia. The 'Westerners' were excluded from the running.[463] In tandem with the formation of a provisional government, those forces from the Austrian resistance were excluded who might disagree with Renner and the Soviets in the future. The command of the 3rd Ukrainian Front declared that the O5 resistance organisation had been disbanded.[464]

However, it was not the provisional state government that then passed the founding document of the Second Republic, the declaration of independence, but the three political parties authorised by the Soviets. As a result, the parties were in place before the state existed. And it was they who announced the dissociation from Germany, in a declaration that was probably primarily drafted by Renner. In the preamble, the path that Austria had taken since 1938 was described. It was a highly idiosyncratic representation of events, which by no means corresponded to the historical facts, and which culminated in the claim that Hitler and the National Socialists had led 'the people of Austria, who had been rendered powerless and with no will of their own, into a senseless and futile war of conquest, which no Austrian had ever desired... to warring against peoples against whom no true Austrian had ever harboured feelings of enmity or hatred...'. Without further ado, Renner had made the victim theory put forward by the Moscow Declaration entirely his own, and he would have happily excluded the paragraph that focussed on the responsibility of Austria for what had happened. The communist members of the provisional government insisted, however, that this passage should also appear in the Austrian declaration of independence. So it was that the ambivalent nature of a document that had been consciously drafted in very general terms by the British entered Austrian post-war history. It is probable that no one thought to question the individual paragraphs in the declaration, since one thing was clear: Austria must break away from Germany and state its reasons for doing so, in order to make its break with the past entirely clear. Therefore, the long preamble, which could be considered the covering note of the declaration, was followed by the following clauses:

Article I: The democratic Republic of Austria has been restored and is to be established in the spirit of the constitution of 1920.

Article II: The union forced on to the Austrian people in 1938 is null and void.

Article III: With regard to the implementation of this declaration, a provisional state government shall be installed with the participation of all anti-fascist party orientations, and it shall be entrusted with full legislative and executive powers and subject to the laws of the occupying powers.

Article IV: From the day of the announcement of this Declaration of Independence, all military, official or personal vows pledged by Austrians to the German Reich and its leadership are null and non-binding.

Article V: From this day on, all Austrians are again in a civic relationship of duty and loyalty to the Republic of Austria.

In the mandatory consideration of the postscript of the aforementioned Moscow Conference, in which it is stated that: 'However, it is called to Austria's attention that it bears responsibility for the participation in the war on the part of Hitler Germany that it cannot evade, and that in the final regulation, its own contribution to its liberation shall ineluctably be taken into account', the state government shall immediately take such measures as are required to enable each individual to make their possible contribution to their liberation, but feels obligated, however, to determine that in light of the exhaustion of our people and the plundering of our country, this contribution can, to its regret, be only modest.

Vienna, 27 April 1945

It was a clear refutation of the Greater German Reich and its leadership. A new Austria wanted to obligate its people once again to support the country that had declared itself independent, and whose borders had not yet been clarified. Just like the state constitution of 1918, this was more a declaration of intent than a determination of facts. The release of all Austrians from their oaths even presented a real hidden risk, since if someone who was a member of the Wehrmacht refused to continue to fight in the war, referring to the declaration of independence as grounds for doing so, they risked being executed. Right at the end, an almost touching, helpless excuse was provided as to why Austria was only able to make a minor contribution to its own liberation.

However, the two first articles were important and unequivocal: Austria broke away from Germany and in so doing took an unmistakeable step. In a reversal of what had been said and asked at the end of 1938, it may have been worth wondering whether there had been a triple renunciation of the affiliation of Austria with the German Reich.[465] Naturally, the war-like occupation of the country could not be compared with the 'floral campaign' when the Germans entered the country in 1938. However, the joy over the end of the war and the end of the tyranny, which most people probably regarded as enforced rule, was deeply felt. From mid-March to mid-May 1945 – as in 1938 – people lined the streets, expressed their joy and cheered on the Allied troops as their liberators. Finally, there was also something akin to a negation of the Anschluss in the form of the creation of the provisional state government. It was probably inevitable that it had to contend with the appearance of being at best pseudo-legal, since Renner was unable to point to elections or any even rudimentary democratic procedure. He took action. Pro-Austrian forces formed a new elite and left no doubt that they, too, were aware of the necessity to act. At best, one can only guess whether the Schuschnigg formula of 1937 – one-third of the population supported the National Socialists, one-third was against them, and the remainder would adjust depending on how the land lay – could also be applied in revised form to 1945. It is not entirely implausible. With reference to the correct assertion made with regard to 1938 that it was a revolution, what happened in 1945 was a counter-revolution. In any case, one could hope to reconstruct a state system that was conceived of as a contrasting alternative to the First Republic, which was dominated by conflicts and violence. At first, it remained to be seen how consistently this would be put into practice. And the question was, whether it would succeed.

Much occurred in the space of days and hours that was unfamiliar. Not everyone could 'break back', and not without some effort. Some concepts had been discussed – albeit relatively superficially. Here, there was a tendency to adhere to Karl Renner's ideas, as had been the case in 1918. In the same way as it had been then, now, everything was provisional, there were no ministries, but state secretariats, official bodies and chancelleries. It was also interesting that the term 'Second Republic' was clearly not called into question. It was only later, once order had been brought to proceedings and to the terminology used, that people noticed that Renner's enumeration of the Austrian state forms had been adopted. Was that correct? If – as had already been recommended in 1945 – the disappearance of Austria in 1938 was an occupation and not an annexation, then continuity would have to be shown. In 1946, the first 'Austrian official directory' was published. In a consistent manner, and in line with the occupation theory, the provisional state government was termed 'Renner IV'. The uninterrupted enumeration underlined the continued existence of the state. Yet if this was accepted, and the transition laws were also taken into consideration, one could only conclude that, in fact, the First Republic still existed. Perhaps it still does today, only we don't know it.[466] The sense of a new beginning and the constitutional sequence of enumeration quite clearly fail to harmonise. Even today, the name given to the government, 'Renner IV', remains unchanged, as does the fact that the final Austrian government before the Anschluss in 1938 is listed as the 'Schuschnigg IV' cabinet. The Seyß-Inquart government, which lasted for two days, is ignored.

In keeping with the motto 'better late than never', the Soviets informed their Western allies that Karl Renner intended to form an Austrian government. The Western powers responded with a clear rejection of the idea. In particular, they were alarmed by the fact that a communist had been nominated to lead the State Secretariat for Internal Affairs. The British and Americans voiced their objections in the strongest possible terms. As a result, the Austrian state government that had been desired and installed by the Soviets was also not recognised by them. This made for a rocky start for the new Austria. To make things even worse, at some point, the original declaration of independence was lost.

Renner and the members of his government were not put off by the huge problems they faced. After they were constituted, the members of the government paraded from Vienna City Hall to the ruins of the parliament building, together with the mayor of Vienna and accompanied by march music. There, on the ramp of the former Imperial Assembly (Reichsrat) building, there was an almost grotesque meeting. Among other invitees, Cardinal Theodor Innitzer awaited the new provisional State Chancellor Renner. The two most prominent supports of the Anschluss in the spring of 1938 came together, both of them no doubt long reformed after the years of Nazi rule and war.

While all these events were taking place, the war in Austria continued. And it was not only characterised by fighting and destruction, but equally by a final upsurge of the Nazi regime. Once again, accounts were settled with no mercy shown. Where there were indications of dissolution within the Wehrmacht, and where young soldiers in particular attempted to hide, court martials were quickly convened and death sentences pronounced, which were immediately carried out after hasty trials. Perhaps more than any political change or the arrival of the first Allied soldiers, what happened here caused Austria to break away in a radical fashion. As one secondary school teacher from the Weinviertel region wrote in her diary: 'This blood must be avenged among those who

[have] brought it upon themselves… This was the work of mindless monsters. Willing instruments who believed everything and thought everything was right that was drummed into them. People who could not form their own judgement. People without their own sense of justice. God preserve us from such leadership'.[467]

The Western Allied troops had still not reached Austria at the time the government was formed and Austrian independence was proclaimed. The vanguard of the First French Army and that of the Seventh and Third United States Armies only reached the borders of Vorarlberg, Tyrol, Salzburg and Upper Austria between 28 April and 3 May.

While in the east of Austria, something approaching normality began to return, in the west, the Americans and French continued to push forward. There were no major battles to be fought here. Yet out of concern that the German Wehrmacht could again establish itself in the Alps and realise what ultimately emerged as a propaganda coup, namely the creation of an 'Alpine fortress', they advanced quickly. Salzburg and Innsbruck were given up to the Americans without a fight. Bregenz was shelled and bombarded by the French. In many places, it became evident that there were Austrians who were by all means willing to comply with the demands made in the Moscow Declaration, and who cooperated in the liberation of Austria as though it were a matter of course. Linz, too, was surrendered to the Americans without a fight. Near Linz, in Mauthausen, a particular act of liberation took place on 5 May: the survivors of the concentration camp could finally feel safe. They reported not only on the long death marches and massacres, as well as the final execution in the Mauthausen gas chamber on 28 April,[468] but also told of the unspeakable suffering that they and those who shared their fate had endured.

As the final Western Allied military force, formations from the British Eighth Army pressed forward from Italy, arriving in Carinthia on 7 May. The following day, they occupied Klagenfurt, doing so in competition with Yugoslavian formations, which had been waiting with the advance on Carinthia to revive demands that had been made during the period following the First World War. The matter in question was the state affiliation of the areas of southern Carinthia that were partly inhabited by Slovenes. The two post-war periods, after the First and Second World Wars, appeared, as it were, to shake hands.

Even the unconditional capitulation of the German Wehrmacht on 7 and 8 May 1945 did not yet lead to a full cessation of fighting in Austria. Here, it was the region around southern Carinthia in particular that saw repeated incidences of gunfire, since the remainder of the German Army Group 'E', headed by the Austrian general Alexander Löhr, planned to penetrate northwards. Only a few of them succeeded in doing so. Again, the clearest impression of the scale and size of the military activity can be obtained by taking a look at the numbers involved. In the Austrian area, the remnants of the four German army groups capitulated, with a total of one million soldiers altogether. They were joined by the remaining areas of the Hungarian, Croatian and other states and ethnic groups allied to the German Reich. Gradually, around 1.5 million soldiers laid down their arms in Austria. One can assume that the number of men marching into Austria among the Allied armies was similar in scale, whereby the Red Army also included Romanian and Bulgarian divisions, without forgetting the regular and partisan formations from Yugoslavia. Less than seven million Austrians were joined by more than three million non-Austrians, who between the end of March and mid-May 1945 laid claim to something akin to 'Lebensraum', or living space, at least on a temporary basis.

Around 4,000 Austrian civilians lost their lives during the battles that were fought from the end of March until mid-May. They joined the more than 30,000 civilians killed during the aerial war.[469] It would still be a long time before even a halfway precise estimate could be made of the number of soldiers in the German Wehrmacht who had been killed or were classified as permanently missing. The final figure calculated for the number of Austrians killed was 247,000.[470] Around 600,000 Austrians were taken as prisoners of war. 370,000 widows and orphans of soldiers that had been killed were dependent on aid. The death tally, which included all victims of the war and of National Socialist rule in Austria, could not be more terrible. The total number of people killed amounted to more than 400,000.

A Look to the Future

Following the unconditional surrender of the German Wehrmacht, the Allies could begin to shape the country that – according to the Moscow Declaration – had been the first victim of typical Hitlerite aggression in line with their ideas, and to liberate it from National Socialism. It was the last of the liberated countries of Europe. The word 'liberation' was not one with which many Austrians were comfortable, however. They remained noncommittal and preferred to speak of the end of the Second World War, which had been something that they had desired, but which they had hoped would come about in a largely painless manner. At any rate, an adjustment to the new situation was required, as well as the ability to collectively push it to the back of one's mind, if necessary. However, there was a hunger for information, and a realisation that the Soviets, Americans, British and French had sealed off the occupied zones so tightly that news was very difficult to come by. The Soviets were the first to publish a newspaper, which was available to those living in the zones occupied by the Soviet troops, and which also contained interregional news. Then, from 23 April, the first newspaper created by Austrians, for Austrians, *Neues Österreich*, was founded. So it was that a process began that has still not been concluded to this day: the discussion surrounding the Nazi period, with the role of those in power, the involvement and the part played by

Austrians during National Socialist rule, the systematic destruction of millions of lives, the war and the war crimes. The burning questions relating to guilt became dominant themes, as did those concerning personal responsibility. Just as the war had possessed a sort normality, so the search for normality in the post-war period began. And the Austrians knew that they were being monitored as never before. What was more: the total war had now turned into total control.

The country was torn apart. One could not even speak of unity with regard to the areas of command of the four occupying powers. There were the areas in the east, and particularly Vienna, that had been won after heavy fighting, the areas with a lower level of damage and fewer victims, and others that had emerged from the fighting conducted by the Allied ground troops almost unscathed, or which had not been affected by it at all. The aerial war had also left widely differing traces of destruction in its wake. The cities most affected were Wiener Neustadt, Villach and Klagenfurt, which reported that up to 88 per cent of their buildings and apartments had been destroyed or damaged. In terms of absolute figures, Vienna, Wiener Neustadt and Graz suffered the most. The war and the end of the war had triggered the migration of ethnic groups. Here, too, not all parts of the country were equally affected, by any means. However, it increasingly became clear that it made a big difference whether a zone was occupied by the Soviets, the French, the Americans or the British.

Initially, Austria resembled a transit building that was controlled by Allied armies. And in the manner in which they arrived, the Allies made an effort to turn their notions of rebuilding a democratic state system into reality. They did so in competition with each other, during the course of which a power political and ideological confrontation began to emerge. And it was a Soviet commentator who succinctly summarised the situation: Austria is a country 'where almost in laboratory conditions, the process of the battle between two systems can be observed, the Soviet and the capitalist'.[471] The 'testing-station for the apocalypse' described by Karl Kraus had become a laboratory for two societal systems.

If one excluded the 'special case' of Vienna, in Lower Austria, too, something like a hint of a future life could now be experienced. Johann Koplenig, who had flown in from exile in Moscow, and who was to take up office as state secretary for internal affairs in Renner's provisional government, had by chance met Leopold Figl, a concentration camp prisoner of many years, in the Lower Austrian regional diet (Landtag) on Herrengasse in Vienna, and had nominated him to the city commander of Vienna for the post of head of an administration for Lower Austria. Both General Alexei Blagodatov and Figl accepted. Yet what was the situation in Lower Austria? There were different Soviet areas of command to the south and north of the Danube; initially, communication was impossible. Parts of the federal state from the Lower Danube Reich Gau that had been reallocated to Lower Austria were in ruins. Hundreds of thousands of soldiers, not all of them from the Red Army, crossed the state, which initially also included the northern region of Burgenland, which had been dissolved in 1938. The southern Moravian, southern Bohemian and Slovakian territories had been informally returned to Czechoslovakia. Soon afterwards, the flight of the German-speaking inhabitants began. Those who did not flee were driven out. On 11 May, Lower Austria was officially handed over by the Soviets to the Austrian civilian administration. Violence was an everyday occurrence. The threat of starvation loomed. Ultimately, it was only the Soviets who could help.

Around two-thirds of Styria was also occupied by the Red Army. The images resembled those from Lower Austria. As was the case there, in Graz, everything possible was done in order to ensure the survival of the population. Even while National Socialist rule was collapsing, people had come together, headed by the provisional state governor, Reinhard Machold, who wanted to try to make a new start. However, the Soviets then dissolved the provisional state committee, only to reconvene it with the participation of the communists.

In Carinthia, which was slated for inclusion in the British zone of occupation, Yugoslavian formations had entered at the same time as the British Eighth Army, and they demanded to be given an active role in the occupation. In so doing, they presented demands that had already been known from the Austro-Slovene conflict in Carinthia from 1918 to 1920. The area of southern Carinthia that was partially inhabited by Slovenes was to be separated off and made a part of Yugoslavia. A long-term conflict over the issue began to brew. With this in mind, the hastily formed provisional Carinthian executive committee under Hans Piesch therefore sought British support from the first day on. The aim here was not only to liberate the state from Nazi dictatorship, but also to rebuff the Southern Slavs and to maintain Carinthia as a whole entity. It was no easy legacy. The British also ran into difficulties. They saw themselves as being challenged by the Yugoslavian formations, and ultimately directly threatened war. Thanks to an intervention by the Soviets, the Yugoslavs withdrew. The service provided by the British in return consisted of delivering the Cossacks living in Carinthia and East Tyrol to the Soviets.[472] If they had fought on the German side, this frequently amounted to nothing less than a death sentence. In turn, Yugoslavia's request for the handover of the Croatian, Serbian and Slovene collaborators who had come to Carinthia was granted. It was a merciless trade in human lives that in many parts of the new Yugoslavia went hand in hand with a regime of terror and mass murder.[473]

In Vorarlberg, which although it had suffered during the fighting at the end of April and the beginning of May had emerged comparatively unscathed, a relatively rapid arrangement was agreed with the French. Ulrich Ilg became president of the state committee. His primary goal was to create an independent Vorarlberg, separate from Tyrol. For the French, this was a matter of course.

Map 3: The
Allied Zones of
Occupation from
4 July 1945 to
27 July 1955 and
the Allied Zones
of Occupation in
Vienna from 4 July
1945 to 27 July
1955

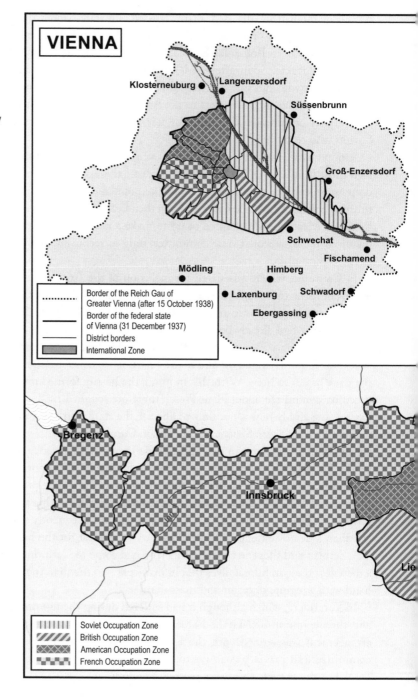

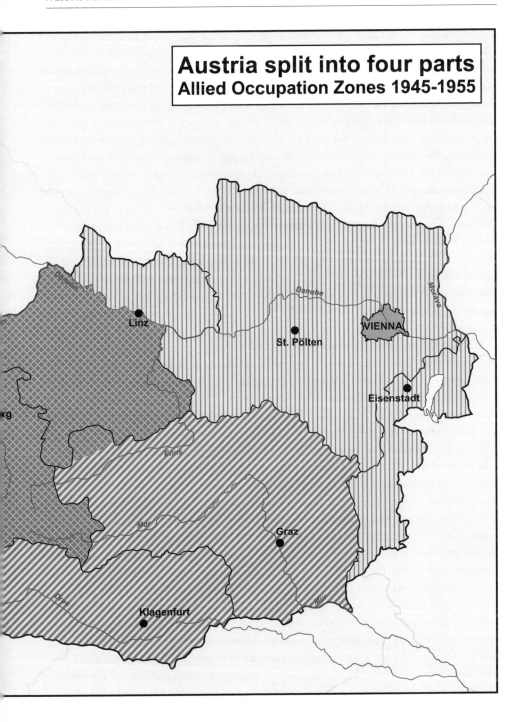

Austria split into four parts
Allied Occupation Zones 1945-1955

The process of establishing regional administrations did not run as smoothly in Tyrol, Salzburg and Upper Austria. All three federal states initially fell within the area of advance of the major American formations. However, those commanders who were least prepared for their duties as occupiers generally accepted the individuals and groups who presented themselves as willing to create new political structures, and who also had the necessary legitimisation to do so, on which the Americans in particular placed great value. They themselves faced the problem, however, that on repeated occasions, the wrong troops were in the wrong place, and as a result, it took some time before proceedings could be conducted in a halfway normal fashion. Finally, the Americans accepted the new personnel structure and in Innsbruck confirmed an executive committee headed by Karl Gruber. In Salzburg, Adolf Schemel was approved as the head of a provisional state government, with Adolf Eigl assuming the equivalent post in Upper Austria. Interestingly, the Soviets, who had not taken the approach of following the instructions given in an occupation manual, ultimately demonstrated greater skill than the Western powers in selecting the individuals tasked with forging a new Austria. As a result, while the east of the country had far greater problems resulting from the war, it almost automatically became a focal point for the reconstruction of the state.

Since at the end of the war no valid treaty had been signed regarding the division of Austria into occupation zones, it was not until the beginning of July 1945 that the requisite agreements were made, which determined both the division of Austria into occupation zones and the modalities of Allied control. Finally, the 'Austrian experiment' was established on a relatively secure foundation with the Control Agreement of 4 July and the agreement regarding the borders of the occupation zones of 9 July.

The core subject of the agreement was the planned intention to divide the country into areas of influence and to exert control jointly. For this purpose, an Allied Commission was to be created. The chairmanship was to alternate on a monthly basis. And when it came to the zones of occupation, it was determined that the Soviets should retain occupation of and control Burgenland, Lower Austria and Upper Austria to the north of the Danube (the Mühlviertel region), the Americans Upper Austria south of the Danube and Salzburg, the French Tyrol and Vorarlberg and the British Styria and Carinthia, including East Tyrol. Any minor deviations from the state borders were usually created by transport connections. The division of Vienna was a source of debate and friction up to the last, since it was evident that the Austrian capital lay deep in the Soviet zone of occupation. However, unlike Berlin, which had a similar geographical location in terms of the zones of occupation, Vienna was to be divided not into four, but five sectors. The 1st District, which contained almost all the Austrian ministries and important administrative institutions, as well as the university, was not to be permanently controlled by one of the occupying powers but would instead become an 'international zone'. There, too, a monthly change of the monitoring occupying power was intended to achieve a type of equality. A further issue was the boundaries within which the city should be divided, which airfields were to be made available to which occupying power, and which railway lines and roads, which ran right through the Soviet zone, should be authorised for use by the Western occupying powers.

However, the Allies still lacked more precise knowledge of the conditions and problems that they, like Austria, were facing. Even so, it would be unreasonable to view the Allies primarily as an obstacle to more rapid, more radical development. In light of the huge problems of 1945, which were not only characterised by questions of a new political beginning but primarily by the fundamental state of emergency in a country that had been degenerated by National Socialism and ravaged by the war, they had taken on the role of protective powers, which prevented Austria from fully imploding – a not unlikely prospect – and heading towards a state of disintegration that could have led to an entirely different course of events.

In Vienna, which had mutated from Reich Gau back to the federal capital city, the thousands of dead awaited burial after the battle, over 80,000 apartments were either partially or entirely destroyed, 35,000 people were homeless, and gas, water and electric power, if at all, were only available for an hour at a time. There were almost no means of transport, but there was starvation, the first signs of epidemics and few employment opportunities, aside from clearing rubble.[474] There was no fuel and only 40 lorries in total to supply around 1.5 million people with items that were essential for survival. Rape occurred on a mass scale. Then the Soviets began to dismantle assets, and entire factory complexes were transported to Russia. The total value of these facilities, which were seized as reparations for war damage and to rebuild the Soviet Union, was estimated at between 200 and 500 million dollars.[475] However, it was not only the Soviets who dismantled factories. The French behaved in a similar fashion. The economy had collapsed. The country had been looted bare. The attempt to stabilise the currency failed when huge quantities of Reichsmarks were brought into Austria from Czechoslovakia and Hungary, for which there was no coverage, but which were still valid as a form of payment at to their nominal value.

In the same way as the Soviets in Vienna, in the reconstructed Burgenland and in Lower Austria, the American military administration in Salzburg and Upper Austria, the French in Vorarlberg and Tyrol and the British in Carinthia and Styria had to create conditions in which people were no longer threatened with starvation. Prominent Nazis were hunted down who had gone into hiding. The mass of Wehrmacht soldiers had been taken as prisoners of war. Hundreds of thousands were distributed in camps throughout the world; around 100,000 of them had been released in Austria. In every federal state, any sense of normality was still nowhere near in sight. And beyond Vienna, the actions of the Soviets and the Red Army were followed with suspicion. Did

Karl Renner's state government really embody the new beginning that fell somewhere between yearning and compulsion?

The Parts and the Whole

While the Western Allies began to establish themselves in their zones of occupation, the provisional state government, with the aid of the Soviets, worked consistently to shape the basis of the new state. A prohibition act of 8 May drew a concluding line under the NSDAP chapter, ordered the registration of all National Socialists and former illegals, and enabled the establishment of people's courts. Those who had belonged to the NSDAP or one of its defence organisations between 1 July 1933 and 27 April 1945 were subject to punishment. Transition laws were passed in order to provide a legal basis for themselves and for the new state system. Thus, a bridge was also created between the First Republic and the post-war era, while at the same time excluding the corporative state and the Nazi period. With the Constitution Transition Act and the 'Temporary Constitution', a law designed to secure the constitutionality of the provisional state government, the way to the creation of a legislative framework was paved. The two laws agreed on 13 May were post-dated to 1 May and came into immediate effect. Five weeks later, a further special law was passed, the War Crimes Act. The rapid succession of legislative measures was reminiscent of the beginning of the First Republic, and this was only to be expected, since Karl Renner of all people had unrivalled experience when it came to founding republics. With the provisional constitution, the state government secured its considerable scope of power: it held the competencies of the National Council, the Federal Council, the regional diets and the consultative referenda. In addition, a three-member cabinet council exercised the function of the federal president. The government controlled itself. Only the term 'power' did not really fit, although a nascent state system only had a chance if it possessed at least a modicum of power. This applied internally and externally. The Communists initially attempted to assume a type of oppositional role within the provisional state government, although after receiving an 'admonition' from the Soviet army general and People's Commissar Vsevolod Merkulov, they refrained from calling into question the unanimous vote in favour of the decisions.[476] This once again underlined the fact that at least during the first few months of Allied occupation, the Soviets held sway over whether the Austrian experiment would succeed or fail.

The Legislation Transition Act of 13 May rendered a portion of the National Socialist legislation invalid.[477] And finally, the opportunity was created with the Civil Service Transition Act of eliminating the National Socialist official bureaucracy. On 10 May, public administrators were installed for 6,000 German-run companies and operations,[478] and that was just the beginning. Despite a somewhat leftist tendency and an occasionally shrill verbal radicalism, the provisional state government showed strong signs of restoration, even reaction. It was as though someone had issued the command to 'Go back to the future!'. A state territory and a state people were required, as was a government that had at least sufficient power to establish a democratic state system within the possibilities granted to it by the occupying powers. For Renner, as had been the case after the First World War, it was a matter of course to have his own military forces available to hand, since no uncontrolled growth of paramilitary formations was to be permitted. With this in mind, he also established an Army Office during his state chancellorship, whose task consisted not only of demobilising the German Wehrmacht in terms of material assets and personnel, but which also began to conduct military activities – albeit on a modest scale – with repatriate sections and railway station and building surveillance services.[479]

After months of negotiations and a certain amount of wrangling, American, British and French troops entered Vienna on 1 September. Only now was Austria completely occupied in the agreed form. And following the arrival of the Western supreme commanders, at least external appearances of the Allied presence conformed to what had been stipulated in the Control and Zone Agreement for Austria. On 11 September 1945, at 2 p.m. Moscow time (12 midday Central European Time), the Allied Council for Austria met at the Russian headquarters in the 'Imperial' hotel for its first meeting.[480] And if anyone had ever doubted it, the fact was now plainly evident that the Allied Council, which consisted of the supreme commanders of the four occupying powers, was now the highest authority in Austria. The legislative and executive frameworks were to be controlled with the aid of the Viennese Inter-Allied Command and 15 'divisions' (departments) of the Allied Commission. This was reported to the provisional state government. The Cabinet Council pledged an oath to 'loyally obey' all commands issued by the supreme Allied authority and expressed the 'deepest thanks of the Austrian people'.[481] In the federal states, military commanders were required to implement the will of the Allied Council. The room for manoeuvre for Austria was noticeably restricted. However, there were rays of light. Following an American proposal, Austria was accepted into the emergency programme of the United Nations, the UNRRA (United Nations Relief and Rehabilitation Administration), and the British, who were particularly sceptical of Renner, agreed to the holding of federal state conferences by means of which Renner intended to expand his government and prepare elections. Again, the similarity with the first post-war period was striking.

In other areas, too, one was reminded of the beginnings of the First Republic. Austria was granted aid that was not given to Germany. And Austria could start rebuilding itself as a state and drive forward the consolidation of the divided country, without this being prevented in the long term by one of the occupying powers – as was the case in Germany.

With his push for the convening of federal state conferences, Renner also wanted to take the wind out of the sails among those state politicians in Tyrol and in particular Salzburg who had very openly discussed the formation of a western counter-government. It was not the Allies, therefore, who were working to divide Austria, but Austrians themselves who conceived of such initiatives. The federal state conferences were designed to pave the way for elections at the earliest possible time, however. After all, everything in Austria was still provisional.

The provisional state government also had to tackle territorial issues. In Salzburg, there were those who wanted to annex the Berchtesgadener Land region and the Rupertiwinkel area that adjoined the Salzburg Flachgau. The Kleines Walsertal region, which had been assigned to the Swabia Gau in 1938, and which for seven years had belonged to the Upper Bavarian municipality of Jungholz, had re-joined Austria once again (and was difficult to access). In Burgenland, meanwhile, there was a yearning for the annexation of Sopron (Ödenburg), and it was not only in Tyrol that many were of the opinion that the hour had come to demand the return of South Tyrol from Italy. Yet the wishes of the others also had to be considered. Yugoslavia demanded the separation of the southern regions of Carinthia with its partially Slovene population, while Czechoslovakia wanted the northern border of Austria moved in its favour. In a report written for Renner, all demands, those of Austrians and of other nations, were rejected. 'The raising of such demands in public shakes the moral foundations of our state entity and its politics.' Austria must stand up in support of the notion that the state boundaries of 1919 in Central Europe should remain fundamentally unchanged: 'If we ourselves assert a claim to parts of Bavaria, Hungary and so on, as it were, out of the blue, what right do we have to deny the claims of Yugoslavia to Carinthia, of Czechoslovakia to north-eastern Lower Austria with its valuable mineral oil resources, or to the Upper Austrian Mühlviertel?' However, South Tyrol was a separate problem. Here, a clear line had been specified. As Renner had hoped, the federal state conference that began on 24 September produced a type of compromise. Politicians from the western zones of occupation could take up the positions that had been kept free for them in the provisional state government. The head of the provisional state administration of Tyrol, Karl Gruber, was given responsibility for the Ministry of Foreign Affairs. However, it was of particular importance that agreement be reached regarding an election date and the modalities for the election. This could not only be booked as a success by Renner; it also earned the respect of the occupying powers. They expressed their satisfaction in different ways.

On Saturday, 20 October, at midday, Schwarzenbergplatz in Vienna was blocked off. The Allied Commission moved into its joint quarters, the House of Industry. Until that point, the occupying powers had met in their respective headquarters. They had something special planned for their first meeting in the new building. The 'Any other business' item on the agenda was the visit by Karl Renner, the provisional state chancellor. The chairman, which for that period was the British general Richard L. McCreery, received him, and 'escorted him', as was reported in the *Neues Österreich* newspaper, to the three other military commissioners, who informed him of their agreement to the expansion of competencies of his government to the whole of Austria, and thus of their de facto recognition. Renner assured the Allies of his gratitude and promised to work in very close cooperation with them. The provisional state chancellor was then permitted to take a central position among the military commissioners for a first group photograph.

The path forward for the coming weeks and months was sketched out and discussed with the Allies, and it engendered a certain degree of nervousness. The forthcoming elections also constituted a test for them as to how far their measures, which had ultimately been primarily founded on force, had been accepted. It had already become clear since the summer that the attempts to establish something akin to a miniature USSR, miniature France, miniature America and miniature Britain in the zones of occupation had been met not only with agreement, but also with rejection to varying degrees. What was helpful and necessary was accepted, such as the removal of the mountains of rubble, as well as the restoration of roads, bridges and supply lines. However, if, for example, the provision of labourers was demanded day in, day out by the Soviets in order to sweep field tracks, while arbitrariness and maltreatment were the order of the day, the willingness to regard them as anything more than an occupying power dissolved rapidly. Since August 1945, therefore, the Soviets also attempted to make themselves more popular by punishing arbitrary acts and attempting to increase supply quantities. It was not really a success. However, after July, attempts by the parties authorised by the Allies to win over support increased. Voter meetings, which became more frequent in September and October, could be seen as a mood barometer. The 25th of November would provide evidence of the domestic political situation.

This was the designated date of the elections to the National Council and the regional diets, as well as municipal council elections in several towns and cities. However, elections for most of the municipal representative bodies would have to wait. National Socialists and representatives of the Corporative State were excluded from the elections. This had not been without controversy, whereby all three governing parties flirted with the option of increasing their potential number of votes with the aid of former National Socialists.[482] Finally, however, everyone came out in support of exclusion from the elections. The intention was to deny the Allies any possible reason for questioning the legality of the first democratic elections for nearly 14 years. What could not be influenced was the fact that willingness to participate in elections for another democratic state was limited. Politics had become something that had to be borne. What counted far more was an at least reasonably functional, familiar environment. Of the electorate,

63 per cent, or around 2.2 million, were female, with women even making up 68 per cent of the electorate in Vienna; 1.2 million were men. Despite the release of prisoners by the Allies, in November 1945, around half a million Austrians were still prisoners of war and thus barred from taking part in the voting.[483] Forecasts regarding the outcome of the elections bordered on star-gazing. Perhaps the elections in Hungary, which were held on 4 November, could be taken as a yardstick, in which the Smallholders' Party, which could be compared to the ÖVP received around 57 per cent of the vote. In fact, on 25 November, the People's Party achieved an absolute mandate majority in the National Council and filled the post of state governor in seven of the nine federal states; by contrast, the Communists fell far short of most forecasts, with just 5.42 per cent of the vote. Once again, a new period 'thereafter' began.

15 Stern Men

15 It took four months for the Americans, British, French and Soviets to set themselves up in Austria. It was not foreseeable how long the occupation would last. The Western occupying powers needed weeks and months to accept the fact that there had been a Provisional State Government in Austria since 27 April 1945. Finally, on 11 September 1945, the Allies moved into joint headquarters in the House of Industry in Vienna. At the end of a joint session, Provisional State Chancellor Karl Renner was invited to officially liaise with the Allies. Afterwards, photographs were taken; from left to right: Soviet Marshal Ivan Konev, Karl Renner and British Lieutenant General Sir Richard L. McCreery. (Photo: Rauchensteiner, *1945. Entscheidung für Österreich*)

During the course of 1945, it had by no means yet become clear what the next steps would be for Austria, and the first elections to the National Council (Nationalrat) could merely be understood as a sign that a sense of unity in people's thoughts and actions had begun to take form, from which one could only hope that it would ensure a new beginning for Austria. However, it must have been clear to anyone who was politically aware and active that it would be endlessly difficult to extinguish the positive memories of National Socialism, and to overcome the paralysing political apathy. The future was uncertain. Austria was kept alive through military force.

Hardship Reigns

Hunger left people emaciated. Thomas Bernhard, describing conditions in Salzburg, which were in any case 'paradisal', wrote that 'The entire population had, in the strictest sense… become criminals in order to survive'.[484] More needed to be paid for stationing the occupying troops than the amount left for the remaining state budget. In the Soviet zone, one Soviet soldier was stationed for every 15 Austrians.[485] Renner then wrote in a highly provocative manner in a letter to the Allied Council that the strong military presence had nothing to do with monitoring and security operations but served solely to create a military balance.[486] The annual accounts for 1945 showed an expenditure of 143 million schillings for the Soviet zone alone, whereby the greatest portion, 120 million, was used for the Federal Railways. They had achieved vanishingly low levels of income, and they had to conduct all transport operations for the Soviets free of charge.[487] However, there were many more reasons to complain. There were other matters, particularly the rape, looting, murder and removal of assets, that increasingly made the Soviets an object of hatred. Almost nowhere was there so little to eat than under 'the Russians'. In the elections, they and the Communists supported by them had reaped the rewards of this behaviour. The response was a type of 'withdrawal of affection'. The Soviets increased the pressure, sought to show solidarity with the Western Allies, and to reinforce their control of the political events and day-to-day processes. They also laid claims to an increasing number of companies and services, referring to the fact that at the Potsdam Conference of the 'Big Three' in August 1945 they had been promised the entire so-called German Assets in their zone. In contrast to the initial months of the occupation, the Soviets refrained from making friendly gestures.

The first federal chancellor of the second post-war period was Leopold Figl. His legitimacy was due not least to four years' incarceration in Dachau and Mauthausen concentration camps. He wanted to continue the policies of the provisional state government. Among the Austrian People's Party (ÖVP) and the Socialist Party of Austria (SPÖ), there was also agreement that – their poor showing in the elections notwithstanding – the Communists should be invited to join the government. An all-party government was also the most tried-and-tested solution for the Allies. A portion of the government members could point to years of persecution. Once again, the 'regressive break' became evident. Whether this would suffice as legitimisation would have to be seen. At any rate, the Allies were not impressed by the composition of the first elected federal government. Initially, however, they also had to clarify their own role. And several notable changes occurred in this regard.

Before the elections, it had been the British who had restricted what was in their eyes an excessively free development among the Austrians. After the elections, this role was assumed by the Soviets. At the meeting of the Allied Council of 30 November 1945, the Austrian government – Renner was still in office – was notified that the de-factor recognition of the state government that had been announced on 20 October was by no means to be interpreted as a restriction of the Allied power of control over all areas of public life.[488] Shortly afterwards, the Allied Council began to play out the power enshrined in the Control Agreement in full. The currency law, with which the schilling was introduced on 30 November, was accepted of necessity under pressure from the Allies. This was not because anyone had anything against the old currency, but because only a portion of the tide of money could be siphoned off and, above all, 2.6 billion Allied military schillings remained in circulation, which had a deflatory impact on the effects of the currency reform.[489] The military commissioners objected to the composition of the Figl government and fixated on the names of four government members. It was Julius Raab in particular whom the Soviets mistrusted, and who was baldly classified by them as an 'enemy of the Soviet Union'.[490] He had to be deleted from the government list. In the government declaration, the passage was forbidden in which Austria was described as a 'bridge' between East and West. Such a bridge was clearly not required. Figl improvised and refused to adhere to the pre-censored text. After all, this was Austria.

The Allied specialists waded deeper and deeper into the procedures of the Austrian administrative branches, which must have been difficult for them to comprehend. They made recommendations and produced assessments, and demanded large numbers of documents and reports, which required an enormous amount of work on the part of the Austrian authorities, and which frequently overextended their capacity. Quite obviously, the 'Big Four' were preparing for a longer period of stay, and they demonstrated their extensive powers and authority to make decisions. The British and Americans felt themselves required to internalise what had been presented to them in the publication 'Austria: Military Government Handbook'. And here it was stated unequivocally that the Peace Treaty of Saint-Germain had created Austria as a non-functioning state, which had become a fertile breeding ground for Nazi Pan-Germanism. And as long as the peace had not been won, it warned that the fruits of military victory would be lost and all sacrifices in vain.[491] In particular, it was important to hold all National Socialists to account.

Again, Karl Renner stepped in. He had been elected federal president on 20 December 1945, not by means of a popular vote but by the Federal Assembly of the National and Federal Councils. However, he certainly did not want to see his role in politics reduced to representative duties, even more so since he, too, was forced to recognise the fact that the Allies stood above the federal president. Thus, Renner pushed for an end to the occupation. And if this were to run into difficulties, it would be worth considering whether Austria might not be made a trust territory of the United Nations.[492] In the Chancellery, it was thought that another way out of the occupation dilemma might have been found. Austria, which was not permitted to become a member of the United Nations, could revive its membership of the League of Nations. In fact, it was a curiosity that the League of Nations still existed at all since the establishment of the UN in June 1945. However, an attempt was to be made. The Secretary General of the League of Nations was informed that Austria intended to revive its membership. The response from Geneva was sobering: Austria may only participate as an observer in the dissolution of the community of states, which now existed only formally, at best.[493] However, for the occupying powers, neither a UN seat nor membership of the League of Nations was sufficient to call into question their de-facto rule over Austria. In reality, they were confronted with other problems. At first, it was necessary to secure Austria's ability to survive before struggling with issues that may have been interesting in terms of international law, but which in the spring of 1946 were of only marginal importance to the occupying powers. In light of a looming humanitarian catastrophe, any criticism of the occupying powers would of necessity have to be suppressed, and Renner's role, too, was reduced to one of polite subservience.

Despite all assurances and sincere efforts, the daily rations continued to decrease. In a large part of Austria, particularly in the eastern regions of the country, they remained far below 800 to 1,000 calories. As in the winter of 1918/19, people went hungry. Unlike then, however, they not only had to rebuild a broken state, but also a country that had been decimated. There were still around 100,000 buildings in Austria that had been destroyed or damaged. Countless bridges, gas, water and power lines were broken, while 2,500 kilometres of railway track were unfit for use.[494] In Vienna, there was now just one bridge over the Danube remaining, and one over the Danube Canal. There were not enough machines or construction materials to conduct the rebuilding work. However, there was also a positive difference: the occupying powers regarded themselves as being responsible for preventing starvation. Their task was to bridge the period until food aid arrived from the UN, prevent outbreaks of epidemics and ensure public safety with the help of over 220,000 soldiers. The safety problem was exacerbated – and continued to be exacerbated – by the fact that due to the refugee movements at the end of the war, 200,000 people were stranded in Austria. They could not be simply expelled or refused food ration cards, like the '(old) Reich Germans', who were simply deported. 28,000 resettlers from South Tyrol and the Val Canale, or 'optants', decided to remain in Austria. The flight and expulsions continued. There were 151,000 arrivals from the Sudetenland, South Bohemia and South Moravia. In some cases, they had been driven out in pogrom-like campaigns and had been chased across the Austrian border. The Allies had given carte blanche to the eastern and south-eastern European states to expel Germans and old Austrians. Those who wished to remain and were able to do so had to suffer multiple discriminatory measures, were not permitted to use public transport, had to wear white armbands, lost what they had possessed and, in most cases, chose to flee a short time later.[495] The number of arrivals from Yugoslavia and Romania totalled 190,000, with 15,000 coming from Hungary. They could count themselves lucky that they had 'just' been driven out. Tens of thousands of people were handed over to the Soviets and were brought to the Soviet Union as slave labourers to help repair the war damage there. In Yugoslavia, thousands were herded together in at least 15 locations and executed.[496]

Finally, the refugees also included 170,00 Jews, who had been at least temporarily accommodated in Austria, mainly in the American and French zones. Only some of them had actually fled; most had been expelled. In the end, it was calculated that Austria held new arrivals from 34 nations, amounting to an estimated half-a-million refugees and displaced persons, who were usually housed in camps.[497] Unless they were Germans in the broadest sense of the word, their degree of willingness to find a permanent new home in Austria was minimal.

This applied to the Jews in particular. There was however also no willingness to integrate them, and the Austrian population was deeply relieved when the Americans took responsibility for accommodating them and arranging their onward transport. The expulsion of the Germans was presented by the Soviets and by the east-central and south-eastern European countries as an act of atonement, and as a denazification measure. In Austria, they were considered to be a disruptive factor in the search for a new, separate form of nationalism. They also exacerbated the supply problem. The result was an intensification of the anti-German sentiment that had also already been latent in Austria during the war. At the same time, in Germany, an anti-Austrian mood was cultivated, with the accusation that Austria, from one day to the next, had taken leave of its common history with Germany and emphasised its role as victim. One of the most important German historians, Gerhard Ritter, put it clearly and succinctly: National Socialism was a degenerate Bavarian-Austrian form of German nationalism. And in Munich, Erich Kästner, who is usually only known as an author of children's books, wrote a bitter, vicious text for a cabaret:

> We are the Eastern Marchers, excuse me, the Austrians / My honour, Sir Baron! / We'll send those German vagrants home. / We're a victorious nation.
> Don't you believe what you read in the papers… / The blue Danube was never brown…
> The Nibelungen loyalty is cursed legacy / Let me kiss your hand and your heart, my beautiful child! / We are a mountain people with a busy hotel trade. / In our Alps, there's no such thing as sin.

The Council of Ministers in Vienna took on the task of finding a new federal anthem, and it would have liked to have used the old melody of *Gott erhalte* (God Preserve). However, since this was still resonant in people's ears as the *Deutschlandlied* (Song of Germany) used by the National Socialists, another melody would have to be found. The text was selected by means of a competition. Austrian history was highly popular. Maria Theresia replaced Friedrich II; Radetzky and Prince Eugene were honoured anew. The 'Speech about Austria' by Anton Wildgans became one of the most important reading items in the new school textbooks. However, passages referring to Austria belonging to German culture were left out. While they may have been in keeping with the times in 1929, this was no longer the case in 1945. In September 1945, on the initiative of State Secretary for Popular Enlightenment and Education Ernst Fischer, German as a subject was described in convoluted and in unrecognisable terms on school report forms as 'language of instruction'.[498] And because it was an opportunity too good to miss, 1946 was celebrated as the 950th anniversary of Austria. To start off the festivities, the American military commissioner, General Mark W. Clark, presented to Federal Chancellor Figl the Imperial Regalia that had been stored for protection in Nuremberg, without much caring about the claims of Aachen or Nuremberg to them.[499] The insignia of the Holy Roman Empire were to remain in the Vienna treasury for ever.

Re-Austrification

Ultimately, the process of re-Austrification and the settling of accounts with the National Socialist past were moving too slowly for the Allies, however, even though without doubt everything possible was being done to impose retaliatory measures and apprehend war criminals and bring them before a court. The newspapers published lists of war criminals, and Allied and Austrian courts began to bring them to trial. In

Vienna, Graz and Linz, people's courts were set up which were designed to process 137,000 cases in just a brief period of time. They issued 43 death sentences, of which 30 were carried out, and thousands of years' worth of prison sentences. The Allies also formed their own courts, whereby the British emerged as probably the strictest occupying power. They pursued criminal charges against over 30,000 people living in the British zone, of whom a considerable portion were found guilty. 53 cases ended with the pronouncement of the death penalty. The last execution took place in February 1955.[500] Nonetheless, the accusation was repeatedly made that denazification was restricted to the 'small' Nazis, the fellow travellers, while the bigger and more prominent members of the party succeeded in making their indispensability sufficiently plausible to be left alone. As the first retaliatory measure, 537,000 members of the NSDAP were denied the right to vote. However, what to do with someone who was not a member of 'the party' or who was discovered, proverbially speaking, with a smoking gun? What happened to the pen-pushing activists? They frequently remained unpunished. And what about the 'Ariseurs' who had purchased Jewish property but who were not in possession of a party book? Did this already make them opponents of National Socialism, as many of them claimed to be? Yet it was difficult to prosecute them, since they were very keen to prove their innocence and humanitarian attitude and had no qualms in asking those whom they had persecuted or robbed to produce a 'Kassiber', or secret note, in which their good conduct and, if possible, their part in saving human lives were attested to. Many succeeded in obtaining such notes.

The members of the resistance began to feel thoroughly frustrated. They had the impression that people who had been implicated in the wide-ranging forms of persecution were able to remain in the service of the state without any further ado, while they themselves not only fought for recognition, but frequently struggled to maintain a livelihood. The government made rebuilding and suppression a priority, but also pursued several measures to prevent emigrants from returning, since they would then be in a position to contest the positions of certain neo-politicians, interfere with the political reconstruction and certainly to make claims. This had to be stopped. Thus, not only demands for reparation for those who had suffered racial persecution were put on hold, but the return of representatives of the First Republic was also prevented, as was the case, for example, with Julius Deutsch and Friedrich Adler. On this matter, the party chairman of the SPÖ, Deputy Chancellor Adolf Schärf, and Minister of the Interior Oskar Helmer were in full agreement.

As of May 1945, a request was issued to all former National Socialists to register themselves voluntarily. Then, registration was conducted 'ex officio'. In order not to lose time and to avoid providing the Allies with a reason to delay or even terminate their aid and intensify their monitoring measures, a separate ministerial committee was deployed, the purpose of which was to denazify the ministries. However, it was equally remarkable that already on 28 November 1945, the Austrian bishops approached the Allied Commission with a request for clemency for those former National Socialists who were incarcerated and had been proven to have done good deeds during the Nazi period.[501]

The purpose of the intensification of monitoring measures was not to reprieve, but to punish. The British and Americans put thousands of individuals into holding camps. Wolfsberg and Glasenbach became synonyms for this measure. They appeared not to mind that the word 'denazification' was translated as 'Entnazifizierung' in German, thereby fatally linking it to the Nazi jargon 'Entjudung', or 'de-Jewification'. In so doing, they threw the baby out with the bathwater. Those who were temporarily arrested included the first provisional governor of Styria, Reinhard Machold, and the security director of Styria, Alois Rosenwirth, who were accused of working to build up an Austrian army on Renner's behalf. The Figl government was warned, newspapers were criticised, and internal borders and transport routes were meticulously monitored. The Soviets wanted Figl to issue a declaration regarding the denazification of commercial life. They demanded the immediate sacking of all former National Socialists, and they were unimpressed by the argument that if this measure were applied to all train engine drivers who had formerly been party members, not even the most essential food transportation could be provided.[502] Since most teachers had been in 'the party', their dismissal would have led to a collapse of the school system. A partial remedy was sought through the employment of teachers who had long since retired. Naturally, measures that were possible in the public service sector differed from those of the private sector, where employment bans could be imposed, but no dismissals were possible. Indeed, in the commercial sector, as in agriculture, very few traces of the denazification process could be found.

While Austria hoped that the occupation of the country would end in the foreseeable future, the Allies were thinking no such thing. They wanted to keep the country under occupation until the political situation in Europe became clearer. And contrary to all assurances and positive signals, they were by no means convinced that Austria's ability to survive had been secured, and that it could pursue its own path. Here – as was clearly expressed in the American occupation handbook – the First Republic was a truly alarming example. Austria should be made viable and also provide stability to neighbouring states. Furthermore, the occupying powers were also convinced of their respective social systems, and they wanted to implement them at least in their own zone. When it came to 'clearing up', the Americans, Soviets and Austrian communists were of the same mind, and formed a strange coalition. Denazification was followed by re-education. In this, the American occupying organs played a leading role – and successfully so. The British and French developed far less enthusiasm. For the Soviets, it came down to another matter entirely. At that time, they clearly reckoned with a longer-lasting occupation and currently wanted to exploit the benefits. The Figl government was accused of aiming to 'prevent the democratisation of the country', and of intentionally attempting 'to create a catastrophic situation in the country and to instrumentalise this against the Allied occupation and primarily against the Red Army.'[503]

Naturally, these were formulations that had nothing to do with reality and were only intended to justify the continuation of the occupation. However, the Soviets were not immune to the necessity of changing the framework conditions of the occupation and cooperating with the other occupying powers – and without the knowledge of the Austrian government –in reviewing the occupation status. The fact that something had to be done, and that the Control Agreement that had been concluded to date was not a suitable instrument for further progress, was an open secret, and it was also viewed in this way within the Allied Commission. Again, it was the British who were the first to work towards creating a solid basis for negotiation. A short time later, the French and Soviets also developed drafts for a second control agreement, which they also exchanged with each other. On 24 December, all three drafts were sent to the head of the European section of the Soviet Ministry of Foreign Affairs, Andrei A. Smirnov, for his comments. On this matter, Mikhail E. Koptelov, the acting political advisor to the Soviet Military Commissioner for Austria, Marshal Konev, attempted to correct a whole series of distortions contained in the reports sent to Moscow and not least in the writings of the Austrian comrades.[504]

However, since the aim was not only to shape Austrian politics in a more positive way than in the immediate past, but the Allies ultimately also had to write their own instructions, the utmost care was required. On 28 June 1946, the Allied Council was presented with a new accord, the Second Control Agreement, for approval. And it meant a quantum leap. The Allied Council remained in its current structure. However, conceptually, it was upgraded, and the military commissioners were now given the title 'high commissioners', the same term used in British colonial language. Allied control was somewhat restricted. However, the real substantive change was in Article 6. The Allies wanted to relax control over Austrian legislation to a large extent. Only constitutional laws were to be dependent on the prior approval of the Allied Council. The period of validity of the Agreement was limited to six months. It was therefore only intended to apply until the end of 1946. Instead, the Agreement remained in force until 27 July 1955, the day on which the final instrument of ratification of the State Treaty was lodged, and the Allied Commission for Austria decided to disband itself.

Hand in hand with the development of a new control agreement, the Soviets prepared to seize all businesses and property that belonged to German physical and legal entities, and to which the term 'German Assets' was applied. They were to be exploited for the benefit of the Soviet Union. The corresponding order from the new Soviet military – or high – commissioner, General Vladimir V. Kurasov, was pre-dated to 27 June and was assigned the number 17.

In Austria, this was regarded as a severe blow, while the relaxation of the hold on the country by the occupying regime was all but ignored. Attempts were made to circumvent the seizure through rapid nationalisation of a portion of the raw materials industry. In itself, this would by all means have fulfilled Soviet demands for the acceleration of the path to a 'socialist' society through consistent nationalisation measures.[505] However, since the Austrian steps were directed against Soviet interests, the response was an unequivocal 'nyet'. And even when, in a concerted effort, the three Western Allies transferred the 'German Assets' located in their zones to the Austrians in trust, the Soviets did not hesitate to pursue their own path. 'Order No. 17' remained in force within the Soviet occupation zone. The political division of Austria had been prevented; the economic division, however, appeared to be unavoidable. The management of the economic assets in the Soviet zone was transferred to the administrative body for Soviet property in eastern Austria (Upravlenie Sovietskim Imushchestvom v Avstrii, or USIA). Around 280 industrial operations with over 5,000 employees were affected, as well as the Danube shipping company, the 'Donau-Dampfschifffahrtsgesellschaft', or DDSG, the Ybbs-Persenbeug Danube power station, motorway construction sites on the A1 motorway, the majority share of the mineral oil industry and 157,000 hectares of land. On 21 July, a supplementary provision added concessions, patents and trademarks, accounts and objects of value to the list.[506] In Burgenland, the Soviets expropriated a majority of the Esterházy estates, amounting to around 50,000 hectares of land. In Hungary, where this also occurred, the assets of the noble Esterházy family were seized under the pretext that they were an 'enemy of the Hungarian people', while in Austria, the reasons given were 'collaboration and Nazi connections'. In this case, too, it was not simply a matter of redistribution or the offer of a gift to small farmers, but of Soviet interests and 'silent reparations'. In the wake of these measures, the Americans felt that there was just a 50:50 chance of saving Austria for the West.

These developments amounted to the fact that the Soviets were procuring a replacement for the reparations in the case of Austria that had not been granted them at the Potsdam Conference. With their constantly repeated assurances that they did not wish to call the unity of Austria into question, the Russians continued to pursue in full the course on which they had embarked in April 1945. Measures similar to those imposed in the Soviet zone of occupation in Germany were not taken. In the interim, the division of the country into zones had become a technical problem more than anything else. The Soviets had offered no resistance to the political unification of the Austrian zones. Quite the opposite: before the elections, they had promoted such unification. For this reason, no efforts were made to realise a consistently communist-style economic and socio-political model in the Soviet zone of occupation. Indeed, it was Austria itself that through the nationalisation of large operations took steps that were not dissimilar to the eastern planned economy. This could certainly be regarded as a model in the neighbouring states of East-Central Europe. Thus, the aim was to screen off those states in order to establish the Soviet model there. And in relation to Austria, the greatest possible benefits were to be obtained from the occupation of the eastern part of the country. The term 'Iron Curtain' did the rounds. The phrase, which had been borrowed from the theatre and which had also been used by Joseph Goebbels, appeared to perfectly fit the Austrian situation. And when on 5 March 1946, the former British prime minister Winston Churchill made the phrase common property with a speech at the university in Fulton, Missouri, and described Vienna as lying behind that curtain, no one contradicted him.

Instead of pursuing a course of confrontation that would anyway have been futile, the Austrians did the only right thing: they complied with the Russians as far as possible and attempted to avoid exposing themselves to criticism. Here, denazification played a highly prominent role. However, denazification was also among the top priorities of the Western powers. So it was that everything possible was done to make the reckoning with the Nazi past as obvious as possible. After all – and this was also the opinion of the political advisor to the American High Commissioner, John Erhardt – Austria was opening itself up too much to Soviet accusations with its failure to pursue rigorous denazification.[507] The first list of war criminals of December 1945 had been followed by others. In the interim, six people's courts had been established in order to deal with the severest cases. Each individual group of incriminated individuals had to pay a penalty, which could range from a penal tax to employment bans, to measures of atonement such as forced labour and increased pressure from the people's courts. Of the total number of people employed, 7.5 per cent were dismissed or banned from their profession. They included 2,982 judges and state lawyers who were regarded as particularly incriminated. Hundreds had to be permitted to continue working, however, in order to prevent a collapse of the legal system.[508] In July 1946, Federal Chancellor Figl reported to the Allied Council 'that the Austrian administration is now free of the National Socialist spirit'. Of 299,420 public servants, 70,818 had been removed from office.[509] Yet there was still a long way to go until full denazification was achieved, and when it came to reparations, work had only just begun. Thus, the work on a denazification act was accelerated and the Austrian draft was presented to the Allied Council in July 1946. The act was intended to come into force only after it had been approved by the Allies. In fact, after nearly five months of consultations, the occupying powers demanded considerably more stringent provisions. These were granted. The National Council passed the act on 6 February 1947. It was criticised by all sides. For some, it was too mild, while for others, it was too strict. In the American zone of occupation in Vienna and Upper Austria, 25 per cent of the population had been in favour of a general amnesty; in Salzburg, the figure was 33 per cent.[510]

On the same day on which the Allied Council agreed the Prohibition Act, the deputy Soviet high commissioner, General Alexei Zheltov, attracted attention with the announcement that he assumed that the occupation of Austria would end in the autumn of 1947. Zheltov was not authorised to make such a statement, and he was even supposed to be recalled as a result.[511] However, it could not be unsaid – and Zheltov remained in office. Perhaps he had already become slightly 'Austrified'. The background to his claim was the circumstance that negotiations regarding an Austrian State Treaty were imminent. If the experiences with the Peace Treaty of Saint-Germain were transferred to the new treaty, one could indeed assume that the negotiations would be concluded within three to four months. How far this was from the truth!

The Key Territory

In January 1947, preliminary talks began regarding an Austrian state treaty. The preparations had already been made. On 2 February 1946, Foreign Minister Karl Gruber had already handed an official draft version of a 'treaty on the restoration of the legal status of Austria' to the political advisor to the British in Austria, William Henry B. Mack, the man who in 1938 had written such a touching obituary for Austria. As Karl Renner had attempted to do during his time in office with the Austrian declaration of independence, an abbreviated version of the Moscow Declaration was used, and no mention was made of co-responsibility. Instead, a thorough list was made of everything that was required to bring the first victim of Hitler's typical policy of attack back into the fold of the community of states as a member with full rights, and to provide compensation to Austria for the iniquity it had suffered. Finally, a recommendation was made to demand a settlement from Germany of over 34 billion schillings.[512] On this basis, no progress could be made.

Once again, Federal President Renner joined the fray and brought his own experience and Saint-Germain to bear. In the view of the head of state, preparations would have to be made, as had been the case at that time. However, the situation now was entirely different, and the only similarity to the preparatory phase for the Paris Peace Conference of 1919 was that in Vienna, those involved were happy to content themselves with a whole series of illusions. Gruber, the foreign minister, had also collected recommendations that were to be negotiated with the Allies. He promptly received a catalogue of wishes and measures from the ministries and federal states that still contained demands for reparations from Germany, as well as the desire for borders to be corrected in the Gmünd area and free access to the Adriatic.[513] Only the demand for the annexation of South Tyrol was omitted, and this had already become obsolete in the interim. The French and the Soviets had expressed their support for the annexation of South Tyrol to Austria, as had the British until February 1946. It was not until 4 March 1946 that the British foreign secretary, Ernest Bevin, put an end to the debate with the assertion that while the

Austrians may have had better arguments than the Italians, a loss of South Tyrol could result in Italy becoming communist. In so doing, Bevin espoused the argumentation of the United States. Under pressure primarily from the British and Americans, on 5 September 1946, Gruber had then agreed an accord with the Italian prime minister, Alcide De Gasperi, that provided autonomous regulation for South Tyrol instead of annexation to Austria. Austria was granted what was in effect the role of a protective power. And Italy was keen to portray itself in a generous light. It declared that it was willing to allow thousands of South Tyroleans, who had left the region as optants, to return home. This question was therefore no longer a subject of negotiation with the Allies.

The Federal Chancellor, Foreign Minister, federal state representatives and expert advisors came to London to discuss the regulation of all open issues, which was to be a precondition for the Allied withdrawal from Austria. As in 1919, the treaty to be developed was referred to as a 'state treaty'. However, instead of being invited to participate in regular negotiations, the Austrians were subjected to a hearing. With reference to the 'complicity clause' in the Moscow Declaration, the Soviets asked whether Austria really had made the type of contribution towards its liberation that could then be taken into account when it came to the final settlement. At issue here were not the victims, but the 'perpetrators'. How many Austrians had served in the German Wehrmacht? How high was the level of support among companies based in Austria for the German war effort? What partisan activities had taken place, and what acts of sabotage had been conducted; in short, what was the active contribution that Austria had made towards the overthrow of the National Socialist regime and the German Wehrmacht? The Soviets were very well informed, and they had also arranged for precise figures to be delivered by the Communist Party of Austria (KPÖ). The quintessence of the questions was indeed also that Austria should be aware of the fact that it also had its share of responsibility to bear. Moreover, nothing had been done in the country to clear away the remnants of National Socialism. The Soviet government newspaper *Izvestia* described Austria in bald terms as the 'Augean stables of fascism'.[514]

However, it was not only the Soviet delegation that was a source of discomfort to the Austrians. In a largely unexpected development, the Austrians realised that representatives of a whole series of states had been invited in order to clearly express their views on Austria and in some cases to voice their demands. There was shock when a Yugoslavian delegation demanded the cession of the southern area of Carinthia and smaller areas in Styria. Here, it was probably only the scale of the Yugoslavian demands that was surprising, rather than the nature of the demands itself. This had already been clear after May 1945. Now, what they wanted had been clearly laid out: 2,470 square kilometres with around 180,000 people in Carinthia, as well as 130 square kilometres with 10,000 people in Styria.[515] Then came demands for reparations totalling 150 million dollars and the desire for a separate statute for the Croats living in Burgenland.

While the British could have forced the Yugoslavian troops out of Carinthia in May 1945, they were evidently not clear themselves about the future of the southern part of the country. For this reason, a type of demarcation line was also drawn along the Gail and Drava rivers, along which the British monitored people passing through. However, there was no doubt that the question of which country southern Carinthia belonged to deserved particular attention, as did the fate of those who remained and of the Carinthian Slovenes who had been returned.

As a result of these London consultations in January and February 1947,[516] the Allies, led by the British, produced the rough structure of a treaty on Austria ('State Treaty for the Re-establishment of an Independent and Democratic Austria'). They did not waste time on subtle differentiations between a peace and a state treaty. Additionally, the Allies were still in disagreement over half of the clauses.

On 10 March 1947, consultations began in Moscow between the foreign ministers. Austria's foreign minister, Gruber, had also arrived in the Soviet capital, although as a type of observer rather than as a participant. Gruber would have welcomed it if the foreign ministers of the Western powers had shown greater accommodation of the Soviet chairman, Minister of Foreign Affairs Vyacheslav Molotov. Ultimately, however, he had to be content with what he was given, which was not difficult in the case of the territorial demands made by the Yugoslavs, which were supported by the Soviets but rejected by the Western powers. The Western Allies were also reluctant to purchase the treaty on Austria for the price of the total transfer of German Assets to the Soviet Union. On the one hand, this would have damaged Western corporate interests, while on the other, in the view of the Anglo-Americans, it could all too easily become a powerful vehicle of political control. The main opponent of such an idea was the new American secretary of state, George C. Marshall. However, the British foreign secretary, Ernest Bevin, and the French foreign minister, George Bidault, were not interested in achieving unity at any price. They regarded a breakdown in negotiations as a 'successful failure'.[517] Austria became a part of the policy of containment.

Even while the Moscow Conference of Foreign Ministers was still being held, mass demonstrations had occurred in several towns in Lower Austria, during which banners were carried bearing slogans such as 'Down with the Figl starvation government!', 'We demand new elections!', and 'We are hungry!'.[518] Farm inspections were called for in order to root out food being withheld by the farmers. Further demonstrations followed. Naturally, this was the 'accompanying music' to the first round of state treaty negotiations. Yet it came about for a specific reason. The food situation in Austria was compared with the (West) German one, and it was concluded that in the interim, Austria was generally faring worse. At the same time, the Austrians and Germans were suffering from the consequences of the war, from a lack of workers, in equal measure, and it was foreseeable that the harvest would only provide about half of what was needed.[519]

However, it was not just food that was lacking. During the winter, a coal and raw materials crisis meant that many companies had to cease production. The only blast furnace that had been kindled in 1946, had to be extinguished again. Since Austria had nothing to offer, the bartering ran into the sand. Coal was nowhere to be found, either from the Ruhr region or from Czechoslovakia or Poland. The Communists directed various accusations against the government and suspected that it was using the tactic of making Austria as poor as possible in order to enable it to come away with a 'cheaper' deal when it came to regulating the material aspects of the state treaty.[520] Whether or not such accusations were to be believed, it was clear that Austria was heading for catastrophe. The SPÖ came under strong pressure from its own left wing, which was in favour of a policy swing in the direction of the Soviet Union.[521] Deputy Chancellor Schärf then began to reassure the Americans, indicating that the majority of Socialists were unwilling to go along with the policies of its left wing under Central Secretary Erwin Scharf and the parliamentary delegate Hilde Krones.[522]

The next stage of the domestic policy distortions became clear at a Communist-led demonstration in front of the Federal Chancellery on 5 May. At this demonstration, the same slogans could be seen that had already been displayed in March. Demonstrators entered the interior of the Federal Chancellery by climbing scaffolding. The spectre of the 25th of July 1934 haunted the scene. Leopold Figl called on the police commissioner of Vienna, Arthur Klauser, to provide support. He was unable to help and instead informed the Inter-Allied Command of Vienna. The latter was unwilling to be drawn into the dispute, however. The 'four in the jeep' prudently remained at a distance. The situation calmed down. Yet it continued to fester, and while fissures became visible within the ÖVP and the SPÖ alike, the Communists resolved to drive forward the rift and to exploit it to the full. Ernst Fischer, the former state secretary for popular enlightenment and education, and an intellectual poster boy for the KPÖ, began to conduct talks with politicians from both the major parties, in particular with Federal Chancellor Figl, about stronger participation by the communists in the government. Ultimately, the possibility of Figl resigning was mooted. However, the attempt to force the coalition between the ÖVP and SPÖ apart failed. The chancellor was supported not least by the SPÖ, whose party chairman and deputy chancellor, Adolf Schärf, issued a clear statement in support of the collaboration.

So it was that in less than three months, not only were Austria's hopes for an end to Allied occupation dashed, but a deep domestic policy crisis was created. There could be no talk of stable conditions. Now, however, the occupying powers were also needed, and countless strategic decisions had to be made. Since in the interim, the USA had taken over from the British as the chief spokesperson of Western policy, the obvious step was to transfer responsibility for an assessment of the situation to the highest military committee of the USA, the Joint Chiefs of Staff (JCS). The chiefs of staff did

as requested and formulated the goals to be pursued by the USA in Austria in unequivocal terms.[523] They described the country as being of maximum political and military
interest. The USA, it was claimed, could not permit itself to allow this key territory to
fall under sole Soviet influence. If this were to occur, there would not only be consolidation of Soviet rule in the Danube basin and in the Balkans, but also a weakening
of the [American] position in Italy, Germany and even Czechoslovakia[!]. The US
government was therefore to continue to support any Austrian government who presented the prospect of an independent, neutral orientation in the country. One option
for achieving this, which was proposed by the political advisor to the American High
Commissioner, John Erhardt, was to cease demanding payment from Austria for the
cost of occupation. He pointed out that here, not only the Soviets should be kept in
mind but also the British and French. However, it was absolutely necessary that Austria
should be given a positive signal after the failure of the state treaty negotiations.[524] On
28 May, the State Department gave the green light and authorised the American high
commissioner, General Geoffrey Keyes, to refrain from demanding funds for the occupation from the Austrian government, and to arrange for the payment of services to
be provided by Austria for the stationing of US troops. In addition, all payments made
between 1945 and 30 June 1947 were to be refunded, amounting to a total of around
308 million schillings.

At the same time, on 7 May 1947, the American Congress approved a foreign aid
programme of 350 million dollars, of which 85 million were to go to Austria. During
the initial planning stages of this congressional aid, the intention had been to allocate
aid funds to China, Italy, Greece, Poland, Hungary and Austria. After a gradual adjustment of the plans and consideration of the political changes in these countries, some
received more, while others – such as Hungary and Poland – were given nothing.

However, the Americans and British stipulated specific conditions for further aid
measures and demanded a currency reform. A stable currency was also to be the condition for Austria's participation in the next major aid programme, the Marshall Plan.[525]

On 5 June 1947, American Secretary of State George C. Marshall outlined his ideas
for the economic recovery of the countries impacted by the war. The basic idea behind his proposal was that the USA and other donor countries wanted to establish
a European reconstruction programme, from which all European countries, with the
exception of semi-dictatorial Spain, and including the neutral countries of Switzerland
and Sweden, were to profit. The 'Marshall Plan' was also designed to benefit the Soviet
Union and the states under its sphere of influence. However, Moscow – not entirely
surprisingly – rejected the control mechanism that was an obligatory part of the package and forced the states of East-Central Europe to do the same. Sixteen recipient
countries remained. Austria was among them – and was to profit disproportionately –
although always with the precondition that it was willing to accept the offer of assis-

tance. The resolution on the Marshall Plan was passed by the Council of Ministers on 28 June 1947; even the only Communist minister in the government, Energy Minister Karl Altmann, was in favour.[526]

It was only in relation to the currency policy measures demanded by the USA that Altmann was of the opinion that the course taken by the government could no longer be supported, and he resigned from his government post on 20 November 1947.[527] If Altmann and the KPÖ had hoped that the resignation of the Communist minister would trigger a government crisis and lead to new elections, they were mistaken.

From now on, the government was reduced to the Grand Coalition itself. This could either be regarded as the regrettable end to the first major post-war compromise, or as a positive step, since from now on, any necessary agreements could be reached more efficiently. Furthermore, there had been a suspicion – and one that was by all means justified – that the Communist minister was revealing internal government affairs to the Soviets. Now, the government ministers were amongst themselves. However, Altmann's resignation entailed the risk that the Soviets might feel that their interests were not being sufficiently taken into account in Austria, and that they might work towards breaking the Allied agreements. 1948 was to be a landmark year.

Rumours of Partition

The New Year's speeches had been given, as had the (few) receptions. Although there was no real unrest in the air, a sense of irritability and tension could be felt. In some areas, the political environment changed dramatically. In Hungary, the Communists had taken over power. In September 1947, the Communist parties of the Soviet bloc joined those of Italy and France to form the Communist Information Bureau (Cominform). The Austrian Communists sought to find a common response to the American policy of containment and above all to the Marshall Plan. This had been a good deal, to be sure, and it would also make an impact in the Soviet zone of occupation, too. There was no indication that the Allied occupation might come to an end any time soon. A real sense of consternation was also created by the fact that in 1948, the punitive measures against 530,535 former National Socialists were to come into full effect, thus threatening to force Austria to abandon its comfortable role as victim.

The sense of confidence, which had anyway only been present to a limited degree, now disappeared entirely. Pessimism became widespread. Yet there could have been real reason to celebrate. The Soviet Union had begun to transport Austrian prisoners of war back home who had been captured as members of the German Wehrmacht. 53,000 of the 134,000 men[528] originally taken prisoner were returned. Even if the same amount again were still waiting to come home, most of them had been held out the prospect of doing so. With the start of the Marshall Plan, rebuilding work could finally begin in a much more efficient way than had been the case up until then. The functional mechanisms of the project officially known as the 'European Recovery Program' (ERP) were extremely simple. Donor countries, particularly the USA, delivered goods that were sold in the recipient countries. The profits were used to issue loans under particularly favourable conditions. With the repayment of this EPR loan (counterpart funds), the coffers began to fill again. American monitoring bodies were designed to prevent misuse and misappropriation. A certain level of 'wastage' was included in the calculations.

The Soviets had not prohibited Austria from participating in the ERP as they had done with their satellites. They were not enthusiastic, and did not refrain from issuing warnings, but in practice, they did nothing. However, the government was aware that Austria would also have to remain cautious when accepting American aid, since the Russians had it in their power to break off the state treaty negotiations even before they had properly begun. On the other hand, the Americans were the only ones who were able to provide effective help, even if they ensured that they would have significant influence over the domestic economies of the recipient countries through their aid programmes. For this reason, the instructions given to the Austrian delegation at the Marshall Plan conference in Paris in July 1947 included the following: '... in critical situations, abstain. Take a cautious approach, be aware that the whole undertaking in any case entails a great risk for us but seize opportunities that are offered'.[529] These instructions were conscientiously followed. The Soviets also did not respond with their own economic programme, but with increased propaganda.

Ultimately, they, too, would have to be content with the fact that Austria was making a rapid economic recovery with American aid. After all, the Soviet Union was planning to demand a heavy payment when the occupation of Austria came to an end. Since, in April 1947, the Soviets had not only declared themselves willing to continue to negotiate the state treaty but had also agreed to a recommendation presented by the acting French high commissioner, General Paul Cherrière, to the effect that financial compensation should be provided for German Assets, a concrete proposal was now laid on the table. A specific figure was also named: 200 million dollars. Austria offered 100 million. In the tried and tested manner, the delegates agreed to meet in the middle. A solution took form, and with it, the end of the occupation.

At the beginning of 1948, the American high commissioner, General Keyes, ran down the agenda at the Allied Council meetings in the usual way. Then, in February, the British high commissioner, Lieutenant General Sir Alexander Galloway, took over the chair. Everything seemed to follow the routine, although rumours were rife and the perceptions of the Allies could not have been more different. Since the start of the year, there had been talk of the possibility that Austria might be threatened with partition. Attempts were made to consider the advantages and disadvantages of such a development, and questions were only asked on the margins as to why Austria was suddenly at risk of disintegration. Interestingly, it was the Soviets in particular who expressed their concern. The influential secretary of the Central Committee of the Communist Party of the Soviet Union, Andrei A. Zhdanov, then summoned the head of the Austrian Communists, chairman Johann Koplenig, and Central Secretary Friedl Fürnberg, to Moscow and demanded that they act to counter the partition rumours. The fight of the KPÖ should be directed towards ensuring independence and sovereignty for Austria and 'unleashing the domestic national democratic forces'. Anything else would lead to a 'dead end' and 'a lack of prospects for the future'. In addition, the efforts of the Soviet Union were aimed at a withdrawal of its troops from Austria at the earliest possible time. Zhdanov further emphasised that the Soviet Union was quite clear that the Austrian state treaty should be signed as quickly as possible and include the best possible conditions for the Soviet Union.[530] The Austrian Communists were forced to accept this approach, even if they did not agree with the direction prescribed by Zhdanov. They did as they were told, although naturally, a partition of Austria would almost automatically have led to Communist rule in the eastern part of the country.

In this, the Austrian Communists were thinking along similar lines to several western Austrian politicians at federal state level, particularly the governor of Salzburg, Franz Rehrl, who could certainly envisage a partition taking place. Rehrl, who was not particularly popular in the federal state that he governed, perhaps thought that Salzburg could be offered as a suitable capital of western Austria, thereby gaining personal prestige along the way. He made his own contribution to the partition rumours. His thoughts, like those of the Communist leadership, could only be understood in light of the situation in other European countries, which continued to develop in a dramatic way.

In February 1948, there was a coup d'état in Czechoslovakia. The first signs had already emerged during the autumn, when the Slovakian Communists had taken over the 'Board of Commissioners' in Bratislava. Thousands of opponents of the new regime attempted to flee to Austria. Then, months later, President Edvard Beneš agreed to the formation of a Communist-led government, after massive demonstrations and the threat of invasion by Soviet troops. As a result, after Hungary, which had been dominated by the Communists since September 1947, a second neighbouring country of Austria had now been firmly anchored within the Soviet sphere of influence. In April 1948, the rumours of partition reached new heights. Following the merger of the three western zones of occupation in Germany to form the 'trizone' and a currency reform that was also designed as a prerequisite in Germany for Marshall Plan aid, the Soviets responded by sealing off their zone of occupation in the east of Germany and blocking transport access to Berlin. There were rumours flying that a blockade of Vienna was also imminent, and the Western Allies prepared for such a development. The French planned the evacuation of the most important Austrian figures; the British created an airfield near Schönbrunn and filled the depots in their zone in Vienna with stores of grain; the Americans built an additional airstrip near the Danube Canal and prepared for a dissection of the city. Yet nobody could find a plausible reason as to why Austria should take a step backwards and forfeit its head start in becoming an independent state, which it had enjoyed since 1945. The prospect remained a rumour, therefore – and did not go beyond the prepared countermeasures.

In fact, there was significant progress in one area of the state treaty negotiations. The principle of the financial compensation for German Assets and the compensation sum of 150 million dollars was met with agreement, and other specific issues could also be resolved. However, very much to the relief of the Americans, British and French, the Soviets were unwilling to renounce their support for the territorial demands of Yugoslavia, even though in the interim, a rupture had occurred in the relationship between Stalin and the Yugoslav head of state, Marshall Tito. Subsequently, once again, no agreement was reached regarding the treaty on Austria at the annual Conference of Foreign Ministers.

In June 1948, the Soviet high commissioner, General Kurasov, invited his American colleague, General Keyes to a private meeting, and put the case for a reduction in tensions.[532] Once again, in the Allied Council, the talk was of denazification, the cost of occupation, the simplification of postal and telegraph traffic, the expulsion of war criminals, censorship measures and anti-Soviet propaganda, in other words, to a certain degree of everyday matters.[533] More still: the Soviets made concessions, presented a proposal on their own initiative with the aim of offering an amnesty for 487,000 National Socialists accused of lesser crimes, and expressed their willingness for Austria to take its first steps towards rearmament in the foreseeable future.

At least in retrospect, one would be forgiven for thinking that the so-called 'Cold War' was being conducted elsewhere, and that Austria was the famous eye of the hurricane – which to a certain extent was indeed the case. Austria was a victim and at the same time a beneficiary of the Cold War and of the 'brutal form of stability' that emerged from it.[534] Since in 1948, Austria had succeeded in participating in the Marshall Plan and using American aid in order to quickly rebuild itself, a type of decoupling occurred in central Europe, since Austria gained an increasingly significant economic head start over those countries that had been prevented by the Soviet Union from benefiting from the Marshall Plan. However, there was also an east-west divide within Austria, since in eastern Austria, in the Soviet zone of occupation, the Marshall Plan aid only reached those companies that had not been seized by the Soviets under the premise of being 'German Assets'. These economic enclaves received no American investment aid, and they skidded towards a crisis.

Finally, the statistical data was there for all to see: of all the recipient countries of ERP aid, Austria received the most per capita after Norway, free of charge. The German western zones received a tenth of the figure granted to Austria. The differences within Austria were no less evident: Upper Austria and Salzburg received 44 per cent of the ERP loans, while Vienna, Lower Austria and Burgenland were assigned 16.5 per cent.[535] As a result, it was largely due to the Marshall Plan that the western regions began to be referred to as the 'Golden West' – and it was not California that was meant here.

The 'Fourth Party'

It was the Soviets who had been the first on the Allied Council to propose an amnesty of the 'lesser offenders'. This may have appeared strange, but it also had its own logic. Since 1945, groups had repeatedly been formed who were dissatisfied with the course the government was taking. Yet they had no opportunity of being permitted to form political parties.[536] Thanks to the gradual agreement among all four occupying powers that new parties should be allowed, a dam appeared to break.

The ÖVP and SPÖ passed a law according to which political groups were to be permitted to participate in elections upon the presentation of one hundred signatures of eligible voters. As an exception, this law contained a constitutional clause, in order to make it clear to distant observers that there was an interest in obtaining a unanimous resolution from the Allied Council. Shortly afterwards, the first registrations for the foundation of political parties were submitted. The occupying powers were in disagreement. The Americans were against granting permission to new parties, while the British were convinced by the argument presented by the Austrian Socialists that the party landscape was imbalanced. While there were two left-wing parties, there was just one 'right-wing' party. The argument was easy to see through, since the price of a further party on the right-wing spectrum would inevitably be paid by the ÖVP. Yet matters were in fact not that simple, since the return of the majority of the prisoners of war and the readmission of 487,000 amnestied National Socialists meant that the situation was difficult to predict. However, the Socialists could give themselves credit for promoting the reintegration of the former National Socialists. For the French, granting permission for additional parties was not a major topic of discussions. However, the sense of confusion was exacerbated by the fact that the Soviets emerged as vehement proponents of a new (right-wing) party. The new Soviet high commissioner, Major General Vadim P. Sviridov, advocated not only an amnesty for National Socialists, but also the admission of small parties. At the same time, the Soviets retained their practice of repeatedly referring to lower-level denazification and the alleged revival of National Socialism in Austria. This was a type of dual strategy that ultimately resulted in the weakening of the parties of the Grand Coalition. It was questionable whether this approach would pay off.

The main focus of interest in this game of poker was a group in Salzburg led by Herbert Kraus and Viktor Reimann. Kraus, who according to his own conviction was an impeccable monarchist,[537] presented the 'Federation of Independents' (Verband der Unabhängigen, or VdU), on 4 February 1949. It wanted to inherit the liberal and (moderate) German nationalist mantle, and it had one aim above all else: to de-criminalise the large group of those regarded as 'less incriminated' National Socialists. The association found prominent supporters, including the archbishop of Salzburg, Andreas Rohracher, the same church dignitary who had spoken up against euthanasia and the expulsion of the Carinthian Slovenes. This made him almost untouchable. Yet at the same time, the Archbishop of Salzburg had given many former National Socialists a sense of having been unjustifiably persecuted and of being victims of the new state.

Just when everything seemed to be reorganised along new lines, the president of the Federal Economic Chamber, Julius Raab, gave grounds for confusion. He persuaded one of the most prominent supporters of the VdU, the editor-in-chief of the *Salzburger Nachrichten*, Gustav Canaval, to write in opposition to the founding of the new party. Canaval was convinced by Raab's argumentation, according to which a fourth party would be 'linked to the weakening of the existing official state groups', and one should not forget that the Communists were lying in wait for their chance to take over power in the state. Canaval could no longer prevent the participation by the VdU in the next elections to the National Council, however.

The Allied Council reported its approval of the electoral law to Federal Chancellor Figl. Other parties, including those on the 'right wing' were to be permitted. In the interim, the Allies conducted the 100th meeting of the Allied Council. The British high commissioner, General Sir John Winterton, who held the position of chairman that June, stated that there was certainly no reason to celebrate. However, with the agreement of the other high commissioners, he concluded that good work had been done. On that day, the 10th of June, agenda items 1024 to 1031 of the ongoing count since 1945 were listed for discussion. Overall, negotiations were held at intervals of two weeks. To these were added several special meetings, which were counted, and several meetings behind closed doors, which were not, and which in the main dealt with the costs of occupation. The executive had been even busier. On 2 June 1949, it held its 139th meeting, and had dealt with 1,793 agenda items, including this meeting. It could therefore not be claimed that the Allied committees had made life easy for themselves. Yet equally, it was evident that the Allied Commission for Austria had outlived its purpose.

The occupying powers were all dissatisfied with what had been achieved for different reasons. And they felt overburdened. This was reflected in the details. It was not possible to simply monitor everything, and controlling bodies that had long become superfluous were kept alive at great effort. In October 1947, the Americans, in a desultory manner, calculated that within the space of two weeks, 858,887 letters had been opened, 27,365 telephone conversations had been tapped and 10,000 secret service reports had been analysed. The information obtained as a result had ultimately been inconsequential.[538] What was the point of it all? At the same time, all the occupying powers adhered to the fixed general attitude that they had forged several years previously: that they did not want to leave Austria to the others. This was not least a point of concern among the Americans, who only slowly abandoned their pessimistic assumption made in 1946 that the Soviets had the potential for a military takeover of Austria, Germany and Italy within six months. Therefore, a state treaty regulation was required that excluded all possible eventualities – at least for a foreseeable period of time.

In the spring of 1949, the Allied foreign ministers agreed that by 1 September of that year, a treaty on Austria would be produced and ready for signature. The politicians from the governing parties did not seem particularly happy at this prospect, since the burden of payments to be taken on in the long term in order to satisfy Soviet demands was considerable. There were also security policy concerns, although these were usually dismissed with the remark that sooner or later, an Austria cleared of occupying troops would join NATO, which had been founded in April 1949. And the material payments were not least to be provided with American aid. The main point was to achieve an end to the occupation of Austria.

With a view to the time 'afterwards', particular interest was therefore taken in the development of Austrian domestic politics. The permission to form eight new parties, and in particular the arrival on the scene of the VdU, which in October 1949 was renamed the 'Electoral Federation of Independents' (Wahlverband der Unabhängigen, or WdU), in the National Council elections, was intended as a challenge to the Grand Coalition. In fact, it then emerged that the 'fourth party' did indeed siphon off hundreds of thousands of votes and 14 seats from the two Grand Coalition parties. In theory, the ÖVP and the SPÖ could have formed a little coalition. However, hardly anyone considered abandoning the certain degree of certainty that had emerged and to potentially appear weakened to the Allies. Even before the elections, the ÖVP and SPÖ had more or less bindingly agreed to stay together until the end of the occupation.

The General Strike

Contrary to the mutual assurances given by the foreign ministers of the occupying powers, on 1 September 1949, no state treaty ready for signature had been produced. On the Allied Council, there was also nothing to indicate a readiness for agreement. And indeed, months passed until finally, at the beginning of 1950, it had to be acknowledged that attempts to call a treaty into existence had again failed. It was only of small comfort that the Western powers wanted to appoint diplomats in place of the military high commissioners. The Soviets had no objection to the idea but continued to employ military representatives. Even so, this marked the end of an era.

There were various different reasons for the abrupt failure of the state treaty negotiations. Primarily, however, shifts in the global power structure had an impact on Austria. Germany had – or so it appeared – been broken up for good. In the west of the country, the Federal Republic of Germany (FRG) was officially founded on 24 May 1949, while in the east, the German Democratic Republic (GDR) had existed since 7 October of that year. Soviet attempts to achieve a unified Germany had failed. Stalin's break with Tito meant that the Soviets were reluctant to withdraw their troops from Hungary, which they would in fact have been required to do when the treaty on Austria came into force. The Soviets dithered, discussed ancillary matters, began 'counting beans' and finally simply presented more excuses, particularly the increase in neo-Nazi statements and publications in Austria, in order not to conclude the agreement. The situation was exacerbated by changes of a very different nature. In the Soviet Union, war hysteria abounded. On 12 January 1950, the Presidium of the Supreme Soviet decreed that the death penalty, which had been abolished in 1947, should be reintroduced. Anti-Soviet espionage, terror and treason were to be punishable by firing squad. As a consequence, in Austria, too, at least 90 men and women were convicted by a military court in Baden near Vienna, taken to Moscow and executed.[539] The fear of spies was rampant. And the sense of nervousness increased. In June 1950, North Korean military forces attacked the south. The Korean War, which the Harvard student Henry Kissinger, like so many others, thought was a distraction offensive on the part of the Communists, had begun. In their view, the real war would take place in Europe. Suddenly, there was widespread fear of a world war, which would involve the Soviet Union, the USA and above all, China, which had become a Communist country in 1949. In Vietnam, France had become embroiled in a bloody guerrilla war, in which half a million French troops participated. Britain increasingly withdrew into its own national borders and underwent severe domestic political crises. Europe was divided; the world was divided. And Austria? Austria was a part of this division, and as in 1948, the question again arose as to why it should not be directly affected by war and tensions.

Austria made concessions. The Soviets were promised fulfilment of their material demands to a very large extent, and though there were mutterings of discontent when they presented Austria with a bill for food deliveries from May to September 1945 to the tune of four million dollars, a willingness to pay was nonetheless signalised. The Austrians wanted the Soviets out. While the USA pursued a different path, they too were offered concessions. In addition, the Western orientation appeared to be unproblematic. Who didn't love American rhythms, read American literature or try to win a scholarship to travel to the US? Who didn't regard the American occupying troops as a type of security and something akin to paying guests? What was far less self-evident was the fulfilment of a demand made by the USA that went hand in hand with preparations for a potential withdrawal of troops from Austria. The USA did not want to leave behind a defenceless country, in other words, a country that was not able to make at least some convincing effort to defend itself. There were those who opposed rearmament, to use the term applied to the Federal Republic of Germany. However, they were fewer in number on the extreme left, who had their own ideas of how to create military security. The opponents were above all those who brought the matter of the cost involved to the table, and who regarded military expenses as wasted money. However, it was clear to all opponents of rearmament that concessions would have to be made.

American authorities began to steer the Grand Coalition towards making plans for an emergency. If it were to come to a European war, the plan was to take as many male Austrians who had served in the war out of the country as possible in order to create a military component of an Austrian government-in-exile. An Austrian army of 200,000 men was to be formed, first in Italy, or – as was later proposed – possibly in North Africa, who would participate in the recapture of Austria, if necessary. In September 1950, Minister of the Interior Oskar Helmer even stated that the 300,000 refugees in Austria should not be ignored, since they represented a considerable potential that could, if necessary, be used for military purposes.[540]

Since the leaders of the coalition agreed to the proposal (more than a handful of people would not have known it), in October 1951, in cooperation with the commander of the US troops in Austria, General Stafford Leroy Irwin, a stocktake was made of the co-called 'contingent'. In each federal state of the western zones of occupation, camouflaged army record centres were established in order to record four birth cohorts. As yet, it was not clear whether this would also be possible in the Soviet zone. However, work began on the development of the emergency plans.

In light of the preconditions described above, the war in Korea, a war hysteria that now also infected Austria and increasing socio-political tensions, it did not take much to see imminent danger ahead. Those who believed in the recurrent nature of historical events presented the future in the bleakest possible terms. As was the case after the First World War, between 1924 and 1929, the Second World War was followed by a rapid economic upswing. In Western Europe, industrial production increased by twelve per cent. In 1949, it sank to five per cent.[541] The spectre of unemployment lurked everywhere. In West Germany, there were fears of a food shortage. Would events take the same turn as they had at the end of the 1920s?

One impact of the Korean War was that in Austria, too, the price of raw materials and agricultural products increased. At the same time, the USA announced a gradual phase-out of the ERP. Deliveries of American goods were significantly reduced. Since price support for foodstuffs had also been provided with the aid of counterpart means, which was now to be brought to an end, attempts were made in Vienna to cushion the impact by means of a wage and price agreement. Such social partnership agreements had already been concluded three times in the past. However, this time, the negotiations failed. The Trade Union Federation announced strikes for 26 September 1950.[542] All fractions, the Socialists, Christian trade unionists, Communists and the Federal of Independents, wanted to participate. The walkouts already began on the evening before the fourth wage and price agreement was passed by the Council of Ministers. Work was brought to a halt at the iron manufacturing plants in Styria and Upper Austria. On the following day, Vienna and the industrial plants in Lower Austria were affected by the strike. The USIA factories also participated. On the morning of 26 September, workers from the outer districts descended on the inner city of Vienna. An estimated 30,000 or so demonstrators took part. The police were instructed only to intervene when demonstrators attempted to get close to the government quarter. In fact, the strikers did begin to find their way to Ballhausplatz via Herrengasse. Once again, there were vague similarities to the 25th of July, 1934. Since the meeting of the Council of Ministers had been brought forward, the only occupant of the Chancellery was Federal Chancellor Figl. The level of police protection appeared to be insufficient. Figl arranged for the American military police to be contacted by telephone. As in 1947, they were at pains to avoid involvement at all costs. Figl refused to receive a delegation of the strikers. Now, the only likely outcome appeared to be a storming of the Chancellery and a further escalation of violence. However, no one really wanted to take this step. De-escalation was called for. However, the subsequent assessment by the British high commissioner, Lord Harold Caccia, to the effect that the Austrian government had been 'caught napping',[543] was far from the truth.

In fact, the prospect of overcoming the worst was still a long way off. The radicals, and in particular the Communists, presented a catalogue of highly exaggerated demands. At the request of the Soviets, as reported by the central secretary of the KPÖ, Fürnberg, to the Politburo on the evening of 26 September, the strike was to be interrupted. The reason given was that 'in this dangerous international situation', it was 'irresponsible to create further difficulties for the Soviet comrades'.[544] The break in activity gave the government and the non-Communist trade unions a breathing space. And following the realisation that the Communist trade unionists and the KPÖ were putting themselves at the head of a social movement and wished to use it for their own purposes, the other trade unions gradually distanced themselves. If a renewed wave of strikes and violent demonstrations were to occur, they did not wish to get involved in a joint campaign with the Communists. Within the government executive, the code word 'concert' was issued, which was to trigger the occupation and defence of the critical areas.[545] Appeals were made by the government, demanding that workers disobey the call to strike. Since during the strike on 26 September, members of the USIA factory security service had been sighted, who were variously armed, several non-Communist trade unions mobilised their 'technical emergency supports', who were willing to conduct themselves in just as violent a way as the Communists.[546] It was no coincidence that two years previously, one of the political advisors to the American high commissioner, Martin F. Herz, had referred to the 'Protection League' characteristics of the trade union armed groups, and to leaders such as Franz Olah who displayed thoroughly militant tendencies.[547] At any rate, a situation could by no means be allowed to develop in which a labour dispute incited by the Communists mutated into a putsch, or even a revolution, even if certain individuals might have had an Austrian 'October Revolution' in mind.[548] Following a final appeal by the federal government, Minister of the Interior Helmer ordered that the entire executive should be on permanent duty from 3 October, 12 midday. Then, the morning of 4 October dawned. The 'concert' began.

In Vienna, Communist strike squads went into action. Their most drastic means of attack was the filling-in of tramline tracks or the pouring of concrete into points. Whenever violence flared, the 'technical emergency supports' responded with counter-violence. In Wiener Neustadt and the surrounding area, violence also reigned. The USIA workers, who were reinforced by others from the industrial sites close by, shut down factories, occupied official buildings and finally stormed the post and telegraph office. The Soviet city commander of Wiener Neustadt prevented the deployment of police forces in Vienna. At other industrial sites in the Soviet zone of occupation, there were also walkouts and acts of violence. However, the strike collapsed on the same day. Afterwards, the question arose as to whether this really was simply a strike, or whether it was a violent uprising or even a putsch attempt. The putsch metaphor was the most widely supported explanation.[549]

The Soviets had been in a difficult situation. If they supported the Communists, they risked encouraging support of all non-Communists among the Western occupying powers. And the Soviets wanted calm. Indeed, they wanted it at almost any price. For this reason, they prevented the police from being brought in, and in some places also put a stop to countermeasures. In this way, they at least saved face. Internally, however, the detailed report by the head of the propaganda department of the Soviet section of the Allied Commission for Austria, Lieutenant Colonel Kuranov, regarding the second phase of the strike, looked much like a justification memorandum, which culminated in the following sentence: the leadership of the KPÖ had decided, after the strike had been terminated, to 'learn all the necessary lessons from the strike campaigns of September/October 1950.' The blame for the failure – as could only be expected – lay with the non-Communist workers, the government parties and the police.[550]

The Soviet high commissioner, General Sviridov, in whom decisive influence over the Communist takeover of power in Hungary in 1947 had been vested, had almost demonstratively stayed away from Austria during these critical weeks. In November, the Allied Council already presented the usual picture. There was talk of Austrian laws, denazification, technical matters and agreements. At the beginning of 1951, the Soviets claimed to have caught Federal President Renner out in an infringement of the Second Control Agreement. At the recommendation of the Minister of Justice, and on understandable humanitarian grounds, the Federal President had pardoned six former National Socialists who had been sentenced to many years in prison. General Sviridov regarded this as a transgression. The Western high commissioners voted against him. However, the most important person involved, Federal President Renner, had died on 31 December 1950.

Just a few days before his death, he had recorded a radio address that could by all means be regarded as his legacy. The intended audience were the Austrians and the Allies:

… Every Austrian thinks: leave us alone, we are capable of regulating our own affairs, we will deal with all the problems of Nazism, the war damage, our domestic democratic order, our absolute will to independence, our rejection of any union with another country, be it to the west or the east, to the north or the south. We wish to be left alone, so, leave us alone![551]

New Approach

The parties of the Grand Coalition would have liked to have had a new federal president elected in the Federal Assembly, as had been the case in 1945, and they already had a candidate waiting in the wings, whom they wanted to elect, namely Leopold Figl.[552] He let it be known that he was willing to stand in an election as a joint candidate. If, however, direct elections were to be called, Figl did not wish to stand. Already on 12 January, the National Council was presented with a joint application from the ÖVP and SPÖ for an election to be held in the Federal Assembly, which was approved by the plenum. The Allied Council could not agree, and as a result, the law was to come into force. Thankfully, there was a press that was independent of any political party. It was the press that gave warning of the breach of constitution, presenting the procedure as deeply undemocratic, and recommending with all its force that the federal president should be chosen through direct elections. The government and parliament succumbed to the pressure from the media. Finally, for the first time in the history of the Republic since 1918, the federal president was indeed appointed by direct elections, resulting in victory for the former mayor of Vienna, Theodor Körner.

The ÖVP, which had presented the governor of Upper Austria, Heinrich Gleißner, as a candidate, had evidently been too sure of victory. The blame for the defeat was placed on the shoulders of the Federal Chancellor. The criticism of Leopold Figl grew. And he was given a deputy: Julius Raab. The ÖVP nominated Reinhard Kamitz, a new minister of finance who was to steer Austria on to a course similar to the one taken by West Germany after 1947, with visible success. The primary goal of the new Minister of Finance was the fight against stagnation. And naturally, he was keen to restrict inflation, which had reached 27.8 per cent in 1951 and 17 per cent in 1952. In order to be able to take countermeasures with a sustainable impact, and to bring about a complete turnaround in developments, the framework conditions also had to change, however.

For now, there was little that could be expected of the Allies. Their topics of discussion had petered out. There were no new initiatives for the state treaty, and the Allied Commission had no real remit to offer solutions. One increasingly had the impression that the Allies met more and more frequently for mandatory exercises, and not for consultations of any substance. The writing style in the daily and weekly newspapers was discussed for the hundredth time, as were the police and Gendarmerie, the costs of occupation, alleged transgression here and there, and finally, the question of the secret rearmament of Austria emerged as a perennial issue. Such chit-chat could be dismissed as a triviality.

However, it was not just the Soviets that were regarded as the blockers. The relationship with the Americans was also not free of tension. Their demand for rearmament had been supplemented by objections to the premature amnesty of war criminals. And, finally, the Americans gave clear voice to their dissatisfaction with the compensation measures for Jewish victims of National Socialism. The Americans were not content with promises alone.[553] They exerted pressure, or – as in the case of rearmament – took the initiative themselves. The registration period for the 'contingent' had begun. As a next step, emergency formations were to be formed in the Gendarmerie of the three western zones of occupation. During military exercises in Stadl-Paura in Upper Austria in 1951, however, it became clear that this approach would not be successful. Thus, the possibility was considered of gaining war troops for entry into the new Gendarmerie formation later named the 'B-Formation'. Furthermore, as direct emergency plans, and without the knowledge of the Austrian authorities, the Americans and British began to set up stores of weapons, in order to be able to wage a guerrilla war to the rear of any enemy if the worst-case scenario came to pass. Finally, in the Alpine foothills, 33 British and 79 American depots were created where weapons were stashed, the content of which was sufficient to arm and equip 2,000 men.[554] The British depots were cleared between 1959 and 1965. In 1996, the announcement of the American stockpiles and their precise locations created a considerable stir. 64 depots were still intact. Since the Americans waived any rights of ownership, the war material they contained was handed over to the Austrians: carbines, pistols, ammunition, explosives, opiates and tools.

The 'contingent' and the weapons depots were the result of emergency planning. This turned Austria into an arena in a very different way than before. Once again, one could be forgiven for thinking that the country had been gripped by internal unrest. What was to happen now? The sense of a new beginning that had been felt during the 1940s had dissipated for good. The existential hardship had been overcome. In 1952, the rationing of food and material assets was brought to an end. The final ration cards were issued. What in 1945 had been considered a historic compromise was now the object of increasing criticism. The parties in the Grand Coalition mutually blocked each other. The first generation of post-war politicians, known in derogatory terms as the 'concentration camp generation', was increasingly called into doubt by a younger generation. For them, the concentration camps were insufficient grounds for legitimacy. An American political advisor, Johannes Imhof, baldly described the Grand Coalition as an 'unnatural alliance', and he speculated that it was only the presence of Soviet troops that forced the ÖVP and SPÖ to continue to work together. The word most frequently used by the ÖVP was 'reform', he said. However, this was mere camouflage for their desire for greater influence.[555] New people arrived, and members of the government departed. The problems remained. In the view of the political scientist and contemporary historian at the University of Chicago, Hans Morgenthau, the electorate regarded the major parties simply as organisations for economic security.[556] Some individuals demonstrated 'quasi-feudal' behaviour. There was apathy and corruption, he claimed, particularly at the municipal and federal state level. Democracy continued to be weak.

The harsh assessment of the path Austria had taken was not simply plucked out of thin air. The unease over the stagnation was palpable and was illustrated by many examples. The 'pillarization' had assumed new forms, had led to misuse and had in the interim already directly hampered progress. Now, countermeasures were to be taken. Minister of Finance Kamitz wanted to introduce a fundamental change of direction in the economy. He spoke out in favour of economic liberalism, wanted to reduce the tax burden on businesses, increase consumer taxes and if necessary also hazard the consequences of higher unemployment. In so doing, he exacerbated the tensions between the coalition partners. In October 1952, it was clear that the National Council elections would be brought forward. And on the evening of 22 February 1953, it became known that the SPÖ had gained more votes than the ÖVP, and that it was only as a result of the electoral arithmetic that the ÖVP secured a lead of just one seat.

Government negotiations began with no end in sight. Once again, the ÖVP wanted to appoint Leopold Figl as chancellor. Once again, a grand coalition was to be formed. The British and Americans were assured of this on several occasions. However, now, the tactical manoeuvring began, and there was one person pulling the strings: Julius Raab. Despite a very clear rejection by Federal President Körner, Figl was forced on behalf of Raab to suggest to the SPÖ that a type of tripartite coalition be formed with the VdU. Raab could envisage a loose connection, 'not a union, but collaboration' between the ÖVP and the VdU, a tacit agreement for which he was prepared to sacrifice the Ministry of Trade.[557] Here, it must have been clear to him that his would not be an easy task. With regard to the VdU, he noted in his diary that: 'They have all kinds of Nazi demands', while on Körner, he wrote that 'There's nothing we can do with the old gentleman, however.' The Socialists were not prepared to form a tripartite coalition under any circumstances. Little coalitions were proposed, as was a minority government. There continued to be no solution in sight.

One month after being entrusted with his office, Figl was forced to admit his failure. He did not do so voluntarily. Raab was vested with the role in his place. And in just a few days, he succeeded in forming a government, the fourth of the Second Republic. Raab had granted two additional ministerial posts to the actual electoral victor, the SPÖ, including one in the Ministry of Foreign Affairs, which was to be given to a man who had become Theodor Körner's most important advisor in previous months: Bruno Kreisky. Once again, a coalition pact was signed. To a greater extent than in the pact, however, the government declaration by the new Chancellor revealed his intention of pursuing new paths, and particularly of reviving the economy. State expenditure was to be drastically reduced, and foreign trade promoted for the long term. Trade delegates were to create additional opportunities. The occupying powers at least raised no objections, but instead waited cautiously to see what would happen. Raab had been a member of the Home Guard (Heimwehr), had never been in a concentration camp, had been named an 'enemy of the Soviet Union' by the Soviets and also enjoyed no particular support among any of the occupying powers after his nomination. However, he had been unexpectedly handed an opportunity, and he wanted to exploit it.

On 5 March, the Soviet dictator, Joseph Stalin, died, and the Soviet Union took a new direction, not only in terms of personnel. Raab made the first signs of a rapprochement. The Soviets already demonstrated a more open-minded attitude in April 1953, and they had many opportunities for presenting a friendly face. In addition, with their emphatically positive approach, they wanted to 'prevent a too distinctive interest on the part of Austria in the integration of Europe... or much worse, close political or economic ties with Germany.'[558] Thus, it became necessary to create a balance with the Western Allies. With around 50,000 men, the Red Army had far more troops stationed in Austria than all the other occupying powers put together. The payments that Austria was required to make for the cost of occupation were accordingly high. The figure was two-and-a-half times that assigned to universities and academic institutions. The control measures on the Soviet zone border were elaborate and repeatedly involved harassment. Newspapers, printed materials, letters, telegrams and phone calls were censored, and the Soviets – unlike the Western powers – were unwilling to deviate from this practice. 750 people were employed in the Allied censorship department alone. The Soviets employed an additional 170 censors in their zone. The USIA companies did not pay any taxes. Time and again, arrests were made, and arbitrary decisions were taken. There was indeed a great deal of room for improvement. And the overriding question was why all this was still necessary in the first place, and why the state treaty negotiations had not been concluded. However, something was stirring in the Soviet empire.

Within just a few weeks, the Soviets ended the controls on the zone borders, voted on the Allied Council for simplified procedures and finally waived the payment of the cost of occupation. Now, the British and French were the only ones still demanding such payment. In the same way as the Western powers had done, the military high commissioner was replaced by a civilian one of ambassador rank. Like the Western Allies, the Soviets agreed to the annulment of the visa requirement for those travelling to the Federal Republic of Germany. From 1 September 1953 onwards, there was no longer Allied censorship, and finally, the expansion of the Danube power station at Ybbs-Persenbeug was permitted, which until then had been confiscated by the Soviets as German Assets.

Raab replaced the now noisy anti-Sovietism with silent diplomacy. His inherent pragmatism led him to rethink the relationship with the Federal Republic of Germany after just a few months in office. The Allied Council was still responsible for the assumption of diplomatic relations. However, it would be possible to establish a German commercial representation. This appeared all the more important since Austria itself had already sent a consul general, Josef Schöner, to Bonn three years previously. However, what was not known was that until then, the assumption of diplomatic relations with the Federal Republic of Germany had not failed due to a lack of will among the Germans or the fear of objection by the Soviets, but to opposition from the Americans.[559] However, in November 1953, the head of the 'German Delegation to the Joint Parliamentary Committee', Hermann Müller-Graf, received instructions in Bonn to travel to Vienna in order to make contact with the Austrian authorities within the scope of the German-Austrian trade agreement. However, he was to avoid the appearance of an official representative at all costs, make no courtesy calls and to keep a low social profile.[560] Here, too, a start had been made, and Raab's goal had been achieved.

Finally, the Chancellor arranged for options to be sounded out for reviving the negotiations regarding the Austrian state treaty. And not entirely surprisingly, he raised the prospect of neutrality. However – and this could only be interpreted as a goodwill gesture towards Moscow – he did not want to pursue the new foreign policy line with Karl Gruber, the foreign minister who until that point had been regarded as pro-American, but instead handed responsibility for the Ministry of Foreign Affairs to the former federal chancellor, Leopold Figl. He was the guarantee that Raab could realise his own foreign policy ideas. With his exploration of the concept of neutrality, Raab was drawing closer to considerations that had been discussed repeatedly in the Soviet Union since 1943. After 1952, they had also become a fixed feature of Soviet propaganda. In order to move forward on this issue, the agreement of the Western Allies was of course required. Initially, however, Raab wanted to accommodate the wishes and reservations of the Soviets in a particular way.

16 A Glorious Spring Day

16 Austrian Foreign Minister Leopold Figl in front of Robert Fuchs' painting of the State Treaty. As the first official painting of the signing of the treaty conceived by Sergius Pauser did not meet the expectations of Austrian Federal Chancellor Julius Raab, Robert Fuchs was commissioned to produce a further painting, on which the facial features of those present at the signing were clearly visible. It was a group picture without women. (Photo: Leopold Figl Museum, Rust)

The wishes for the new year, 1954, were similar to those of the previous one: happiness, health and wellbeing. People could already take steps themselves to achieve the latter. The New Year speeches made by the politicians also contained nothing that differed widely from what had been said in previous years. For the first time, however, it was possible to read and listen to what Julius Raab had to say to mark the change of year in response to the wishes, hopes and reminiscences of what had recently passed. Some things had changed. That was the quintessence. For those who lived in one of the western zones, the difference from 1952 was probably less keenly felt than for the people in the 'Russian zone', and it took long train journeys to the east to discover that the zone border had disappeared, and for 'westerners' to also notice the changes in the occupation regime.

However, in their speeches, the Federal President and the Chancellor had attempted to convey another very different message: one of hope. This was only risky in that so many hopes had already been dashed, and caution was by all means prudent before new hopes were nurtured. Yet what should Theodor Körner and Julius Raab say at the beginning of a year, if not that perhaps there might be a further, and this time decisive, turn of events? The reasons for optimism were certainly there, since in Berlin, another Allied Conference of Foreign Ministers was due to be held. The conference was called in a city that was dominated by the Cold War like no other.

Gong for the Final Round

After three years, during which the treaty on Austria was not on the agenda, the Allies wanted to tackle the issue of Austria again. For the first time, Austrian representatives were also invited to join the negotiations. In the Federal Republic of Germany, there was a sense of annoyance. Once again, Austria was pursuing its own path and showing a clear inclination of wanting to achieve a withdrawal of the occupying powers, if necessary at Germany's cost. It wanted to remain a 'special case', and – as one West German politician frankly put it – 'to pass itself off as a child who has been attacked rather than recognising its complicity'.[561] Federal Chancellor Adenauer expressed open rejection, indeed disdain. His aim was to achieve the western integration of the Federal Republic, and not to follow the Austrian path and perhaps achieve a unification of the divided Germany and the withdrawal of the occupying powers at the price of a neutralisation of Germany. Adenauer wanted to subvert Austrian attempts to persuade the Soviets to back down by proposing that Austria join the European Coal and Steel Community (ECSC). This was designed to drive the neutralisation nonsense out of the heads of the Austrian government leaders. Here, Adenauer developed a veritable neutrality phobia, and was not even willing to meet with Raab. Germany wanted occupying forces to remain in the country, and Austria wanted them out.[562]

For the Austrians, the negotiations became a balancing act. There was much beating about the bush, talk of non-alignment, and a desire to please not only the Soviets, but also the Americans, who appeared none too keen on the prospect of Austrian neutrality.[563] Then, references were made to Swiss neutrality. A breakthrough appeared to be in sight when the Soviet minister of foreign affairs, Molotov, made the offer, which was easy to see through, of ending the occupation of Austria and finalising the treaty on Austria. Until a German peace treaty was signed, however, symbolic Allied troop contingents should remain in Austria. In retrospect, this would have meant that contingents of an indeterminate size might have remained in Austria until the 'Two Plus Four Agreement' was signed in 1990. The negotiations in Berlin stalled. Adenauer was satisfied. For him, it was important that it had not been possible to reach agreement over Germany, and that he could continue his course of a full integration of West Germany into the Western communities and, in particular, NATO.

In Austria, the disappointment ran deep and gave rise to all kinds of anti-Soviet sentiment. The mood in the Soviet zone of occupation was downright aggressive, which was ultimately no surprise. In Vorarlberg, the French soldiers had left, while 25,000 Red Army troops were still stationed in Lower Austria. The government gave instructions that the public buildings in Vienna should no longer be decked with flags on 13 April 1954. The anniversary of the capture of the city by the Soviets in 1945 had been marked for eight years with differing degrees of pomp. Now, however, according to the official broadcast, there was no further reason for doing any more than commemorating the victims of the battle for Vienna.[564] The Soviets gave a prompt response. The KPÖ was instructed to terminate its many years of appeals for support for neutrality from one day to the next.[565] And the Soviet high commissioner and ambassador, Ivan Ilyichev, who had in the interim become 'civilised', used the 218th session of the Allied Council to unleash his criticism of Austria. The Austrian government, he claimed, was tolerating and supporting fascist and militaristic organisations who were conducting intensive propaganda promoting a union with Germany. It was clear, therefore, who was to blame for the failure of the state treaty negotiations. It was no coincidence that it was in Berlin that the Soviet Minister of Foreign Affairs pointed to the risk of an Anschluss. Now, the evidence was there for all to see, and Austria would only have itself to blame for the consequences of its anti-Soviet policy.[566]

The 'ice age' continued for several months, and the Russians never tired of pointing out that Austria was pursuing a European course, was pushing to become a member of the Council of Europe, had appointed a European Affairs Committee in the National Council (Nationalrat) instead of a Foreign Policy Committee, and was quite clearly seeking union with Germany through the back door. One might have added that the Socialist Party executive also wanted to prohibit members of government from travelling to the Soviet Union, but the Russians were evidently unaware of this. However, it was clear that the Soviets, who were now regarded as nothing other than obstacles to progress, became even more unpopular and that an increasing number of people were moving to western Austria. Of all the federal states, Salzburg, for example, experienced the largest increase in population in relative terms, with a growth of 31.9 per cent between 1945 and 1954, while Vienna and eastern Austria saw a reduction in absolute terms.[567] In the west, there was prosperity, modern industries had been established, and employment opportunities created; the east, meanwhile, was lagging behind. The picture that emerged was highly similar to that of the Soviet zone of occupation in Germany, which had now become the German Democratic Republic. And yet it was wrong to draw parallels of any kind, since despite its division, Austria was a single state, and fought tooth and nail to retain its full sovereignty. Germany was not a model for Austria! (And conversely, Austria was no model for Germany.)

Gradually, a type of normality for everyday life under occupation set in. Raab continued, as he put it, to avoid 'pinching the Russian bear in the stub of its tail'. Quite the contrary: he expressed his gratitude several times for the fact that in July and August 1954, Soviet soldiers had helped deal with an emergency in the Danube Valley as a result of flooding. Developments in international politics occurred on almost a daily basis. In October 1954, the unification of Western Europe took a decisive step forward with the creation of the Western European Union, a military mutual assistance pact. The Federal Republic of Germany was on the way to becoming a member of NATO. The Soviets failed in their proposal of a European security conference and threatened to continue with the unification of the east and create their own military equivalent of NATO. But where did Austria belong? The Soviets revised the deliberations that had already been presented by the Litvinov Commission in 1943: Austria lay outside its direct field of interest but should not simply be left to the West. At some point, this should not just be said but also signed and sealed in a treaty.

In January 1955, the Soviets again made an offer to the West: if the Federal Republic of Germany refrained from joining NATO, the Soviet Union could agree to all-German elections under international control and the reunification of Germany. What would otherwise happen was set out in the passage that was of importance to Austria: after the signing of the Paris Accords, there would be no further negotiations regarding an Austrian state treaty. The Soviets would have to remain in Austria as protection against a union with militant West Germany. The announcement weighed all the heavier in that precisely during this time in the Federal Republic, the issue was being argued as to whether the law enshrining the Anschluss of 13 March 1938 was not still valid. Naturally, this was grist to the mill of the Soviets. Tensions between Germany and Austria became worse than they already had been.[568] The Austrian ambassador in Moscow, Norbert Bischoff, resigned. Once again, as so often in the past, developments seemed to have run into the sand.

The sense of futility was probably also the reason why Austria did not ascribe much significance to a speech held by Molotov on 8 February 1955, which contained an invitation to bilateral negotiations. The possibility was only explored further after the Soviets made further enquiries. Perhaps the auspicious moment had arrived, after all. And in London, it was the man, of all people, who had played a key role in drafting the Moscow Declaration of 1943, Geoffrey Harrison, who described the situation in unusually drastic terms, claiming that the Austrians had appeared to have decided to run towards disaster like the Gardarene swine, and that they had been possessed by the devil. To put it bluntly: Western interests could be damaged.

In consequence, it was necessary to be cautious and proceed tactically. The government wanted to agree to the Soviet offer of direct negotiations, while at the same time avoiding alienating the Americans, British and French. Quite clearly, the task in hand was to precisely define the non-alignment of Austria. Already before an Austrian delegation travelled in Moscow, perpetual neutrality in accordance with the Swiss model emerged as the most suitable norm under international law. Swiss neutrality was treated as a type of myth – and just at a time when Switzerland was not only considering the possibility of nuclear armament, but even potentially also forfeiting its neutrality. The chief of armaments of the Swiss infantry, Major General Max Waibel, put it in direct terms: 'From a purely military perspective… the expediency of neutrality in peacetime must be negated, since it leads to military isolation.' And politically, an adherence to neutrality was 'not very advisable'.[569] So it was that at the same time as Switzerland was calling its perpetual neutrality into question, Austria wanted to become neutral in accordance with the Swiss model.

An End to Jubilation

Federal Chancellor Raab, Deputy Chancellor Schärf, Foreign Minister Figl and Permanent Secretary Kreisky flew to Moscow on 11 April 1955. Two days later, the result, set down in the Moscow Memorandum, was clear: the State Treaty negotiations were to be concluded and Austria was to become neutral, like Switzerland. However, the latter would occur not as the result of a clause in a state treaty, but as the first act after the withdrawal of the Allies and the recovery of full sovereignty.

The West was not happy, and the British ambassador and high commissioner in Vienna, Geoffrey Wallinger, claimed that what had happened was exactly what had been feared: Austria had been cheated, and the settlement with the Soviets was comparable to the Munich Agreement of 1938.

In western Austria, there were declared opponents of neutrality. For the ÖVP delegate to the National Council Lujo Tončić-Sorinj, it was a 'sacrifice' that had to be made, and even among the Socialists, opinion was divided, although the majority were against neutrality. Non-alignment would have been acceptable, but the neutrality of the country, and not a clause in a state treaty, would prevent Austria from participating in European unification. For this reason, Schärf and Kreisky should not have accommodated the demands for neutrality made by the Soviets. They did so anyway. And naturally, something was offered in return: for the Austrian concession of refraining from joining NATO and potentially pursuing an anti-Soviet course after conclusion of the State Treaty, but instead remaining neutral like Switzerland, the Soviets agreed to the conclusion of the State Treaty and the revision of a whole series of State Treaty clauses. They were also willing to content themselves with lower material payments, to abandon limits on numbers for the Austrian army and to withdraw all their troops within a short period of time, and not only after a German peace treaty had been signed. All this was finally to be agreed in the form of a pact within the scope of an unscheduled meeting between the foreign ministers in Vienna. The ambassadors/high commissioners and staff at the Austrian Ministry of Foreign Affairs combed through the draft treaty item for item. Some clauses were deleted, while others were modified. The situation was entirely different to the one in Saint-Germain. On 14 May 1955, the foreign ministers met. They had been able to clear their diaries for a weekend appointment in Vienna. The three Western delegates, Secretary of State John Foster Dulles, Foreign Secretary Harold Macmillan and Foreign Minister Antoine Pinay, came directly from the NATO spring summit in Paris. Molotov came from Warsaw, where the Warsaw Pact treaty had been signed on 14 May.

All four foreign ministers of the occupying powers announced their approval of the text that had been negotiated. Finally, Leopold Figl raised a subject that had been broached at the Berlin Conference of Foreign Ministers 1954: the passage of the Moscow Declaration should be deleted from the preamble of the treaty on Austria in which Austria was described as bearing a share of responsibility for the war and National Socialist rule. The foreign ministers of the occupying powers agreed. On the afternoon of 14 May, the clean copies were produced. The three Western foreign ministers made their state seals available for use, so that the original of the treaty could be sealed beforehand and only the signatures would be required. Molotov was unwilling to let go of his seal. The fact that most of the young officials from the Ministry of Foreign Affairs took the liberty of also sealing the correction copy went unnoticed. Finally, a copy of the clean version of the treaty was brought to the party headquarters of the ÖVP and SPÖ, approved there, and signed by Leopold Figl, Julius Raab and Adolf Schärf. This copy was forgotten and was left with a taxi driver. However, naturally, this was not the official document that was to be taken to Moscow. For posterity, therefore, only the signing ceremony in the Marble Hall of the Upper Belvedere and the concluding statement by Leopold Figl, 'Austria is free!' remains as the crowning end to a ten-year story. It was a glorious spring morning.

With the signing of the treaty on 15 May 1955, a type of operational calendar came into effect, with one event leading to the next. First, the ratification debate began, which was to be conducted not only in Austria, but also in the other signatory countries in their parliaments, until finally, on 17 July, the last copy of the ratification certificate could be filed in the Soviet Ministry of Foreign Affairs. The process was completed far more rapidly than after Saint-Germain. On the same day, the Allied Council met in Vienna for its 249th session. The sole item on the agenda was the resolution regarding the annulment of the Second Control Agreement of 1946. At the same time, the 90-day period specified in the treaty for the withdrawal of the occupying troops from Austria began. In theory, the occupying powers could have left their troops in Austria for somewhat longer, since it was expressly stated in the treaty that the withdrawal of troops must be completed by 31 December 1955 at the latest. However, it was clear that they all wished to abide by the 90-day deadline, particularly the Soviets, who were the first to carry out their troop withdrawal. From 4 August to 19 September, 39,512 army personnel and a further 10,000 or so others were given the order to march, with 308 trains and six cargo barges. On 24 September, the high command of the 'Centre' group reported in 'strict confidence' to the Chief of the General Staff that the withdrawal had been completed, with the obligatory positive concluding statement: 'Our troops are leaving Austria with the sense of having fulfilled their duty and are returning to their beloved homeland with great political zeal.'[570]

While the troops of the occupying powers made preparations to leave Austria, the latter worked to complete its Law on Permanent Neutrality, which was to be passed as an independent federal constitutional law and as a sovereign act.

However, the signing of the Austrian State Treaty was followed not only by the ratification debates, the withdrawal of Allied troops and neutrality, but also jubilation and a certain sense of disbelief at all the changes taking place within the space of just a few months, which were catapulting Austria into her future. To an equal extent, Austria's neighbours and the world at large had to adjust to the new situation and, probably like Austria itself, only now became aware of the implications of some of the clauses.

The assessment that Austria was a sovereign state with a precisely defined territory, namely that which had been defined as belonging to Austria before 1937, appeared to be a matter of course. Even so, only now was the contractual security provided that resolved any open questions relating to all territorial demands, be it those made by Austria at any given time or those of its neighbours. The respect for human rights was set down as a self-evident obligation in just the same way as the protection of the Slovene and Croatian minorities and their freedom to develop their culture.

The clauses relating to the military and to air transport stood out in particular. As well as restrictions, however, there was also a concession that was offered not least as a result of the country's neutrality: Austria could establish an army on the basis of general compulsory military service and without a limitation on numbers. This meant that there was compatibility between the State Treaty on the one hand and the Law on Permanent Neutrality on the other, whereby Austria was obliged to follow the Swiss model, while at the same time defending its sovereignty and territorial integrity through the use of all military means at its disposal if need be.

Austria also undertook to recompense those who, primarily for racial reasons, had been stripped of their property after 1938 and who had been robbed of their artworks, if compensation had not already been paid. The section that had been the subject of the longest negotiations, and which ultimately merely came down to a type of cost factor of the State Treaty to be charged, dealt with the so-called German Assets (Deutsches Eigentum) and with demands by the Soviet Union regarding the manner in which it was to be recompensed for releasing them. Strangely enough, it then emerged that precisely this complex issue, which had been the subject of wrangling over many years, was only a temporary burden, since the payment of the settlement amount of 152 million dollars could also be made in the form of goods deliveries, and the ten million tons of crude oil to be delivered to the Soviet Union as agreed in the treaty were finally reduced to around 6.5 million tons in 1958. All this was feasible.

However, the State Treaty impacted bilateral relations with Austria's neighbours in many different ways, whereby for many, it came as unexpected that the Federal Republic of Germany felt not only that it had been left in the lurch by Austria, but also that the treaty had been signed at Germany's expense. Here, a potential union was the least significant issue, since in Germany, too, the question had become as good as redundant. It transpired that the issue of whether Austria's neutrality might also be a model for Germany in order to achieve reunification was also a mirage.[571] However, Federal Chancellor Adenauer made it clear that there was a sense in Germany that Austria wanted to fulfil all material demands made by its occupying powers, while overlooking the fact that the term 'German Assets' was not only a verbal construct. The British ambassador in Vienna, Geoffrey Wallinger, was of a similar view. It appeared that nobody had really read the State Treaty, he claimed, with the exception of the Germans, who discovered that the occupying powers and Austria had settled their accounts at the cost of the Germans.[572] In his opinion, the Austrians, however, were happy to be neutral like the prospering countries of Switzerland and Sweden. Here, these same Austrians were entirely unclear about what neutrality really meant. Ultimately, they wanted their borders to be guaranteed and saw this as being nothing other than justified compensation for past sufferings. In this way, they hoped to lay down in a four-poster feather bed for all eternity.

Of course, the State Treaty had been read through word for word, however. In addition, the Western ambassadors had worked to ensure that not only the material demands of the Soviets were fulfilled, but also those of Western companies whose capital was invested in 'German Assets'. On 10 May, in the 'Vienna Memoranda', they were granted compensation – to the great surprise of the Soviets. Without such concessions, the Western powers may possibly have prevented the conclusion of the treaty at the last minute. The total costs of the State Treaty thus increased, reaching 7.9 million schillings.[573] However, the German demands did indeed remain unfulfilled, all the more so since the Soviets had been assured by the Austrian delegation in Moscow that the companies to be returned by the Soviets would be nationalised. The Americans, British and French also agreed to the nationalisation of German Assets in the zones that they were due to clear.

Konrad Adenauer was enraged. Since he knew very well that the Western powers were in agreement that the former German owners should be left empty-handed, he had official protest notes delivered to the Americans, British and French. He described the actions taken in Vienna as 'Austrian dirty tricks', and on 14 May 1955, the German federal government suspended its diplomatic relations, which were anyway classified at the lowest level.[575] Hermann Müller-Graaf was ordered to return to Bonn and was faced with the difficult task of dampening the fury there. Raab expressly asked him to explain the unavoidable nature of the Austrian strategy and to seek to obtain understanding for the Austrian decision. However, in Bonn, no one could condone the fact that Austria, as in 1946/47, was arguing that the level of damage caused by the 'occupation' was far higher than the German assets due to Austria. Müller-Graaf could also not understand this point of view, and wrote to the federal minister of foreign affairs, Heinrich von Brentano, in Bonn that: 'in light of the particularly wild Austrian Nazis who once "occupied" us', the Austrian stance was 'outrageous'.[576] This could be understood as the almost objective modification of the well-known statement by Konrad Adenauer to the effect that Austrian demands directed at Germany could be answered by returning the remains of Adolf Hitler to the Alpine republic.[577] It would be weeks and even months before anything like normal relations could be reinstated. One month after his enforced departure from Vienna, Müller-Graaf urged that arrangements should be made for his return as quickly as possible. No one could really understand the reasons for the suspension of relations, he claimed, and the continuation of this unusual state of affairs would only fuel anti-German sentiment in Austria. It was time to return to normality and to take steps to counteract the definition of Germany – as published in the Austrian daily press in June 1955 – as 'the alien neighbour'.[578]

Other neighbours faced problems of a very different nature, but for all of them, the situation was new and different in that until then, it had always been taken into account that the Americans were in Salzburg, the British were in Carinthia and the Soviets were in eastern Austria. And now, for the first time since the Second World War, these neighbours faced each other directly, without a 'big brother'. In Switzerland, Austria was regarded as a military vacuum, and it was stated in no uncertain terms that the fortress at Sargans to the west of the Rhine and Liechtenstein had become a fortress on the Soviet border. Italy was able to compensate for the departure of the American/British protective shield in Austria by demanding that nuclear weapons should be stationed – a request that was also granted. The Federal Republic of Germany not only got back a further degree of sovereignty, but also became a member of the Western defence alliance. With the Warsaw Pact, however, the Soviet-dependent east was given a comparable military structure to that of NATO. In this way, the Austrian State Treaty formally ended something that belonged to the past, while at the same time opening up a path to a future that was yet to be formed.

The Challenges of the Plains

After the 'glorious spring day' recorded for posterity as the day the State Treaty was signed, a type of inventory was required. Eastern and western Austria, which since 1918 had repeatedly had problems in forming a relationship with each other, had still not really grown any closer, despite the state unity created in 1945. Characteristic of this was perhaps the telegram from Salzburg that burst on to the scene even while the State Treaty was still being celebrated, in which the federal government was asked in earnest who would compensate 'in the future the inhabitants of this federal state for the losses of income' that would occur following the withdrawal of the Americans.[579] In the zone occupied until that point by the Soviets, such a request could only be met with incomprehension. In eastern Austria, there was a huge need to catch up. There, a particular kind of redistribution was required; one which was desired in the east and feared in the west. Without doubt, every federal state and every region had its own problems and had to try to accommodate itself to the new situation, but egoism would only hinder the process of unification. The work of rebuilding the country was far from complete. War damage remained in evidence. The last prisoners of war needed to be welcomed and integrated, and naturally, the withdrawing Allies not only put on a more or less impressive show with their farewell parades, but also left behind a plethora of problems.

These were hectic times for the legislative authorities. While the Allies were packing their bags, the work was only just beginning in earnest for the Austrian National Council. Order had to be brought to the legislation. Since the strategy over the last ten years had been to only pass a small number of constitutional laws, legislation from the time of the monarchy was still in force, including the laws on management of the economy that were passed during the First World War as a result of emergency decrees. To these were added laws that were currently still being drafted, including those relating to complex issues such as the General Social Security Act. And naturally, attention was focussed on the Federal Constitutional Law relating to the perpetual neutrality of Austria, which was finally approved with a qualified majority on 26 October 1955. Only the delegates from the Federation of Independents (VdU) and a 'wild card' delegate voted against the law. For the 'Independents', there was much about the path Austria was taking that was wrong. In 1954, they had written in their manifesto that: 'Austria is a German state. Its politics must serve all of the German people and must never be directed against another German state.' This was quite simply an anachronism, and when one VdU delegate adopted even more radical tones, the Federal Republic of Germany, of all countries, issued him with an entry ban.[580] Germany officially recognised Austrian neutrality on 7 December, with a verbal note that contained the same wording as that used in the letters of recognition issued by the British and French.[581]

Austria was spared one thing, namely fresh elections, as proposed for a brief period by the ÖVP leadership. Raab was strictly against such a step, and for good reason: it would probably have been almost impossible to conduct an electoral campaign in a year that was already hectic enough. There was no doubt that the ÖVP had a chance of gaining an absolute majority, but this would have led to a humiliation of the SPÖ – despite the fact that to a degree of probability bordering on certainty the Grand Coalition would have remained intact. Raab and Schärf had assured the Americans and the British alike that this would be the case.

Although it could not have been planned in advance, the 'year of the State Treaty' was also framed by major cultural events, which again placed Austria at the centre of attention, albeit in a very different way. On 14 October, the Burgtheater, which had been severely damaged in 1945, was reopened with Grillparzer's *König Ottokars Glück und Ende* (King Ottocar: His Rise and Fall). The play had of course been chosen with care, with an Austrian writer, an Austrian theme and as a kind of climax, the 'hymn of praise to Austria', which would have been greeted with applause during the National Socialist era: '... It is a good country ... Look about you, wherever your gaze travels. Where else have you seen such sights?' Originally, the theatre was to be reopened with Goethe's *Egmont* – but that was not an Austrian play. Thus, the final line of the hymn of praise – 'Habsburg for all eternity!' – was simply omitted, and Grillparzer was performed.

Three weeks later, on 5 November, the Vienna State Opera, which had been destroyed on 12 March 1945, was reopened. Here, too, the piece to be performed was carefully selected. The opera chosen was Beethoven's *Fidelio* – not because Ludwig van Beethoven was finally to be made an Austrian citizen, but because of the third act and the chorus of the finale: 'Hail the day, hail the hour! ...'. The audience could wallow in patriotism, and the 'annus mirabilis' could be brought to a fitting end.

Even without premature National Council elections, the final months of 1956 could accurately be described as a time of intense activity. Not only did a balance need to be created between east and west in terms of intra-state structures. It was equally important that Austria's international standing was further developed. For years, membership of the United Nations had been an objective, and one that to date had still not been achieved. In September 1947, Austria was granted observer status. Henceforth, as of 14 December 1955, Austria was accepted as the seventieth state in the global organisation. This was one more item to be added to the list of accomplishments in 1955. However, all other matters were a cause of deep concern.

The end of the Allied occupation led to unexpected turbulences. Insecurity ran rife, not in the military sense, but as a consequence of the fact that without any recognisable reason, the historic compromise made by the two major political camps was called into question. As a result, sales of revolvers and pistols increased dramatically.[582] Were the Allies the only ones who could maintain calm in Austria? Were the future prospects for peace in the country so poor? Dozens of professional groups threatened to strike. There was an outbreak of real strike hysteria. Ultimately, the contentious issues were merely of a banal nature. The State Treaty, neutrality, and accession to the UN had all been accomplished. The question as to whether Austria should become a full member of the Council of Europe, contrary to Raab's wishes, was already a marginal topic. By contrast, increases in the price of tram tickets in Vienna and the cost of milk were sufficient cause for unrest.

However, there were also noticeable shifts in the spectrum of parties. The VdU, which had enjoyed unexpected success in 1949, and which also succeeded in maintaining and even further reinforcing its position in 1952/53, was in crisis. It almost appeared as though its 'purpose of business' had been removed with the withdrawal of the Allies. An equal factor in their defeat was the fact that Minister of Finance Kamitz had adopted an economic policy orientation that made it difficult for the VdU to continue its activities as an opposition party. Austria had not only made up ground but had also fully immersed itself in a new world of consumption. Items that had long been lacking were again available and affordable. The governing parties could be credited for achieving a form of quantum leap with regard to economic policy. And finally, they had successfully continued in their attempts to win the loyalty of former National Socialists and split the 'nationals'. This time, in light of the possibility that the VdU might dissolve entirely,

it was Raab who advocated the continued existence of a right-wing party. The VdU
then remained intact, and from that time on continued under the name 'Freedom Party
of Austria' (Freiheitliche Partei Österreichs, or FPÖ).

Elections were held on 13 May 1956. The outcome did not come as a great surprise.
The ÖVP just missed out on an absolute majority, with 84 seats, while the Socialists
remained at the same level, with 73. Of the 14 VdU seats, only six could be retained by
the FPÖ. The Communists, who at one time were among the founding fathers of the
Second Republic, and who were feared for a time as the spectre and long arm of the
Soviets, were marginalised and secured just three seats on the new National Council.
Since the balance of power was redistributed as a result, there was no longer any doubt
that the Grand Coalition would continue, and that everyday political activities could
resume as normal, the task was now to undertake a thorough realignment. Here, it was
noticeable that responsibility for the foreign policy agendas was divided between four
posts. First, there was the Federal Chancellor, who regarded himself as being at least
a generator of foreign policy ideas. Then there was Foreign Minister Figl. However,
in contrast to the situation since 1953, he now had two permanent secretaries at his
side, Bruno Kreisky and Franz Gschnitzer. In light of this unusual constellation, it
was not surprising that Raab included a passage in his government declaration that
made people sit up and take notice. The Chancellor noted that a shadow had fallen on
bilateral relations with Italy, since Italy had failed to fulfil a whole series of conditions
set out in the Gruber-De Gasperi Agreement of 1946. The Italians delivered a prompt
response. Minister of the Interior Franco Tambroni announced in Rome that this was a
purely domestic matter for Italy and none of Austria's business. Vienna took a different
view, and the Italians were just as aware of this fact as signatories to the State Treaty.
However, as yet, there was no sense of alarm. The matter had nonetheless at least been
addressed.

However, the Americans, British and French were disconcerted by another comment,
although one that was made by the Soviets. On the anniversary of the memorandum
that was the product of the bilateral negotiations in Moscow in April 1955, an article
in the Soviet government newspaper *Izvestia* included a reminder of one of the phrases
that it contained: Austria would make efforts to have its yet to be declared neutrality
guaranteed by the occupying powers. The matter was not pursued further by Moscow,
but the fact that a problem could arise here had long been clear to the Western powers.
Since the spring of 1955, it had been the subject of internal consultations. The Americans and British were categorically against a guarantee, and they hoped that the Austrians could talk the Soviets out of such a requirement if need be. It now emerged that
the Russians had not forgotten the matter. In Austria, opinion was divided. It was by
no means the case that such a prospect was unanimously rejected. There was one person
in particular who stood to benefit from the guarantee: Julius Raab. The same applied,

however, to the permanent secretary in the Ministry of Foreign Affairs, Bruno Kreisky. In order to at least avoid being ambushed by a one-sided guarantee assurance by the Soviets, the ambassadors of the three Western states drafted a statement that contained a 'harmless' guarantee, which was to come into effect if the Soviets decided not to remain silent.[583] According to this statement, the Security Council of the United Nations would be responsible for dealing with any threat that might arise. This would hardly have had any effect, but at least the matter could be ticked off as having been dealt with. However, it was not Moscow that again raised the issue of the guarantee, but Austria. The rejection could not have been clearer. And the British Ambassador was unequivocal in voicing his annoyance: 'Britain is being asked to guarantee a country that was a military vacuum'. A guarantee was out of the question. Austria was behaving 'like a child' and was probably planning to offer only symbolic resistance. The Chancellor, Foreign Minister Figl and Bruno Kreisky were forced to accept this response.[584] And Austria learned to live with a form of neutrality that differed from that of Switzerland, after all.

The fact that Austria was not in a position to defend itself in the long term against an attack was a fact that could not be ignored. While a start had been made in 1956 with the establishment of a federal Austrian army, the first cohort of recruits, who were to be conscripted on the basis of the military service law that had come into force on 7 September 1955, would not join up until October 1956. The first minister of defence in the Second Republic, Ferdinand Graf, attempted to circumvent the evident military inadequacy of his army by seeking – and making – contact with Italian Minister of Defence Paolo Emilio Taviani. Taviani, who was regarded as an 'Austrophile', and who in 1953 had already stated that it had been a catastrophe for the south of Italy that Austrian rule had ended after the War of the Polish Succession in 1738,[585] agreed to provide Ferdinand Graf with military support. If neutrality could not be guaranteed by the Americans, British and French, and no firm agreement could be offered to help Austria defend its territorial integrity, then Italy would play its part, and – although this remained a matter of speculation – would obligate Austria to perhaps not abide by the Gruber-De Gasperi Agreement. Even so, the notion of rekindling the Rome-Vienna-Budapest axis of the Mussolini years was an attractive one. However, the 'brakes were applied' to both Graf and Taviani by their respective heads of government, and probably also by the Americans.[586] A few months later, it appeared that the discussions had been aborted too hastily. Suddenly, something akin to a threat of imminent danger arose.

17 Between the Blocks

17 Collection for Hungarian refugees, November/December 1956. State authorities, charitable institutions and quickly-formed private organisations helped out in order to cope with the stampede of refugees. Towards the end of the year, Austria counted approximately 145,000 refugees, of which 70,000 had to be catered for. From a total of around 200,000 refugees who came to Austria, however, only 20,000 remained in the country. (Photo: Rauchensteiner, Spätherbst 1956)

On 23 October 1956, demonstrations in Budapest expanded to become a popular uprising. It was not only in Austria that too little attention had been paid to the fact that something was in the offing. Unrest in Poland might have been a warning sign. Perhaps Austria had simply been too self-absorbed to follow developments among its closest neighbours. Neither the Austrian envoy to Budapest, Walther Peinsipp, nor representatives of the media could have imagined that the occasional protests might develop into something larger. And then it happened. Only afterwards was it possible to obtain some clues about it. In late September 1956, the former Hungarian prime minister, Ferenc Nagy, had applied to the Austrian embassy in Washington for a visa for several trips to Austria. During his visit planned for October/November, the former head of the Hungarian government, who had been forced to emigrate in 1947, wanted to meet some friends. Did Nagy know that something was brewing? But there were also other indications that this was the case. There were still 158,000 refugees in Austria, whom the war and the post-war period had washed into the country, including tens of thousands of Hungarians. They sought to increase contact with their compatriots.

When a crowd of malcontents gathered on 23 October at the memorial to the Hungarian poet Sándor Petöfi and formed a protest march, the predominantly young people chanted slogans aimed at a fundamental change. They wanted different people in power, more freedom, a higher standard of living and fewer Russians. As was typical for Hungary, it started with a song. Then fiery speeches were held, the Stalin monument in Budapest was stormed and soon shots were fired. Hours later, there was a nationwide uprising. The commotion spread like wildfire.

A Myth Emerges

On the day after the revolt had flared up, the situation in Vienna was sounded out. The heads of the federal government – the Federal Chancellor and the Foreign Minister – were abroad or, like the Deputy Chancellor and the Permanent Secretary in the Foreign Ministry, about to depart. Thus, Minister of the Interior Oskar Helmer and Minister of Defence Ferdinand Graf took action. They ordered a tightened monitoring of the border. The next day, Raab cancelled the alerts. But then it happened a second time: the formations of the Soviet 'special corps' stationed in Hungary were called in to help suppress the unrest. Martial law was imposed. Neither the Hungarian government nor the insurgents, not to mention the Soviets, had the situation under control. This resulted in Austria ordering extensive measures to secure the border only 24 hours after the alerts had been revoked.

The purpose of these measures was clear: to give the Austrian people a sense of security and to establish a complete frontier protection, in order to be equipped not least for a mass exodus from Hungary. In view of events in Hungary and the unclear situation at the border, an exclusion zone was set up along the Burgenland frontier on the anniversary of the Austrian declaration of neutrality and the deployment of the Federal Army was decreed. Another two days later, on Sunday, 28 October, a special ministerial council resolved to expand the measures enacted. Furthermore, a note was sent to the government of the Soviet Union, expressing shock at the events in Hungary. It stated: 'The Austrian federal government [it was originally supposed to read: The Austrian people] has been following with painful concern the bloody and costly events that have been taking place in neighbouring Hungary for the last five days. It entreats the government of the USSR to play its part in breaking off military hostilities and ending the bloodshed.' There followed a discussion of the order to shoot received by the Federal Army and which was also valid vis-à-vis Soviet soldiers. It was in any case necessary to be resolute in order not to create the impression of neutrality with a wink of the eye. And it was high time to make this clear!

The Soviet counterstrategy consisted of shaking Austria's moral stance with the help of the Austrian media. Aid deliveries of foodstuffs and medicine, it was claimed, had been used to smuggle weapons and ammunition into Hungary. Thousands of militant Horthy supporters and émigrés had made their way to Hungary via Austria in order to stir up the 'counterrevolution'. Illegal American training centres existed in Salzburg, Linz and Graz, in which people were prepared for deployment in Hungary. It was ultimately claimed that American troops were anyhow already in Austria and directly at the Hungarian border. Such suspicions were designed to distract attention from events in Hungary and to intimidate Austria. On the last day of October, the leadership of the Kremlin resolved on military intervention in Hungary and the suppression of the uprising.

Meanwhile, the world was spellbound by the Middle East, where, on 29 October, Israel had started a war with Egypt and the British and French had intervened two days later at the Suez Canal. Events in Hungary seemed to become less important by the hour. In view of the commencing advance of Soviet troops, Hungarian Prime Minister Imre Nagy undertook an act of desperation: on 4 November, he declared the withdrawal of his country from the Warsaw Pact and the neutrality of Hungary on the model of Austria. This succeeded neither in stopping the Soviets nor in preventing the Hungarians from regarding the uprising as having failed. Whoever was able to flee, did so. Systematic disinformation claimed that Soviet formations would not be content to suppress the popular uprising in Hungary but would also invade Austria. 18 years later, the Czechoslovak General Jan Šejna, who had fled to the West, stated that the Soviet minister of defence, Marshal Zhukov, had demanded of First Secretary Khrushchev the reoccupation of Austria – which was rejected.[587] As Zhukov had been a declared opponent of the conclusion of the State Treaty in 1955 and the associated withdrawal of Soviet occupation troops, the rumour need not be pure invention. Apparently, Czechoslovakia and East Germany also demanded the reoccupation of Austria.[588] As we know, however, this did not happen.

From mid-November, Austria concerned itself less with a war of words and more with refugee questions and aid deliveries to Hungary. First hundreds and then thousands crossed the border. In early November, there were already 86,000 people. Others pressed after them. The total number rose to more than 143,000. Eventually, around 200,000 were counted. Not all of them had definitively turned their backs on Hungary, because those who initially fled to Austria did so out of fear of the insurgents. It was clear that they returned following the re-consolidation of the Communist regime. Whoever was armed when crossing the border, was interned. The barracks of the Federal Army, which were designed to accommodate its own soldiers, served as refugee camps. Discontent emerged, especially because most European countries and the USA were not prepared to accept larger contingents of refugees. They merely selected individuals. Once the USA had declared its readiness to increase their immigration quota for Hungary after a visit to Austria by American Vice President Richard Nixon, the situation relaxed somewhat. But it remained the case that Austria definitively offered more Hungarian refugees a home in 1956 and 1957 than any other country in the world.[589] As a result, a myth was born.

On 23 November, a flagrant border violation was committed by Soviet soldiers. They were pursuing Hungarian refugees near Rechnitz and advanced well into Austria. A Soviet soldier was shot in the process. Thereafter, the Eastern bloc media accused Austria of a breach of neutrality. Without prejudice to the above and somewhat surprisingly, the new Hungarian leader, János Kádár, sent official thanks to the Austrian government on 23 November 'for the highly caritative actions by means of distributing aid packages from the Austrian Red Cross, with which it went to the rescue of wounded Hungarians and children in need in the darkest of days…'. At the border, the Iron Curtain was closed again.

The End of the Fifties

It would at least be worth considering whether the period of the Allied occupation of Austrian did not reach its historical end with the State Treaty and the withdrawal of the Allies but rather in 1956, just as historical periods as a rule come to an end only with the era that follows. Austria took its first major steps on the international stage and began in the process to make up for something that had not been possible until the conclusion of the State Treaty. In its end-of-the-year review for 1956, the British embassy in Vienna stated: 'Austria starts to regard itself as the hub of Europe, as a mediator between East and West.'[590] Julius Raab travelled to Bonn, making the first state visit there during the post-war period, and strove to re-establish Austro-German relations following the turbulence of spring 1955. He succeeded by and large, and both sides were aware that it was the first visit by an Austrian head of government in Germany since the meeting of Hitler and Schuschnigg in Berchtesgaden. It was agreed that Adenauer would travel to Vienna the following year.

Foreign Minister Figl travelled to Strasbourg and held the first speech by an Austrian foreign minister to the Council of Europe, which had accepted Austria as its fifteenth member state on 16 April 1956. He was able to do this without further ado because the Council of Europe no longer developed any military ambitions. The Minister in this way made a clear pledge for Austria to the European idea. Schärf and Kreisky took part in the session of the Socialist International. Austria's acceptance into the United Nations had also enabled an enormous expansion of its room for manoeuvre in foreign policy. At the same time, however, thought patterns and approaches from the period of occupation seemed to alter only gradually. And Austria no doubt first had to secure its place in the international community.

In 1955, Austria had made an approach to the Soviets. Its conduct during the Hungarian Revolution then amounted to it distancing itself from the Soviet Union; but an attempt was soon made to correct this. The West nonetheless perceived Austria as the easternmost outpost of the Western democracies. In the eyes of the British, the accession to the Council of Europe was in fact an unmistakeable step towards the West. There were also signs that allowed for a different interpretation, however, and in April 1957 there was another opportunity to praise relations between the Soviet Union and Austria, when Deputy Soviet Premier Anastas Mikoyan visited Vienna. He found amiable words, which was all the easier for him because Austria decided not to pursue its efforts to join the European Coal and Steel Community (ECSC).[591] Ultimately, it was the case that Austria took shape both for the West and for the communist East and was the subject of attributions by both. Perhaps the image of the hub conjured up by the British was closest to the truth. Contrary to initial fears, Austria had not laid itself in a neutral 'four-poster bed', after all. Its role during the aftermath of the popular uprising in Hungary had led to a reversal of opinion. London was pleasantly surprised.[592]

Besides, the occupying powers, like most neighbouring states, were satisfied that Austrian had become calculable. The basic pattern of domestic policy had not changed. After the death of Theodor Körner, Adolf Schärf had somewhat reluctantly stood for election as federal president and then been elected. His election was interpreted as the office of a federal president from the Socialist Party being a counterbalance to the ÖVP federal chancellorship. Western observers credited the new deputy chancellor, Bruno Pittermann, with seeking an understanding with the Catholic Church and prohibiting the occasionally pugnacious attitudes of his party when it came to culture, just as the Austrian Socialists in general developed more in the direction of the Social Democrats of the Nordic states. Austria voted in the UN for a Western disarmament proposal, closed the Vienna office of the World Peace Council, much to the satisfaction of the Western powers and the chagrin of the Soviets, but shortly thereafter readmitted the society with the new designation 'International Institute for Peace'.

On the face of it, Austria's popularity did not appear to change. The State Treaty and the period that followed were a turning point for the Great Powers, too, as they had to concern themselves far less with Austria than had previously been the case. A new British ambassador in Vienna, Sir James Bowker, wrote to the Foreign Office in London that Austria only still possessed some significance because it was situated at the Iron Curtain and protruded into the Soviet bloc like a spearhead. Otherwise, he continued, it was unobtrusive, pleasant and predominantly of interest for tourists, lovers of music and friends of Central European baroque.[593]

A process of normalisation indeed began in 1956, which took its course independently of the occasional praise or rebuke from Washington, London, Paris or Moscow. Relations with West Germany were getting better. The tone had become friendlier. The return visit to Vienna of Federal Chancellor Adenauer was marked by Austria relenting in the question of German assets. It was agreed that negotiations would take place regarding compensation for owners of smaller properties. Hungary had attempted to compensate for the shock of 1956 by again becoming completely unapproachable. Relations with Czechoslovakia could only be described as chilly. The announcement that a 'Sudeten German Day' would be held in Vienna in 1959 caused further resentment. Yugoslavia had confiscated Austrian assets in 1957 and was not satisfied with the fulfilment of the provisions of the State Treaty in accordance with Article 7. Raab cancelled a visit to Belgrade planned for 1957. And Italy was enraged that Austria insisted on the fulfilment of the Gruber – De Gasperi Agreement and reacted with increasing harshness to Italy delaying tactics. Thus, there was still much to do. Foreign policy remained a major and important topic. But there were also other issues.

Under the smooth surface and beyond tourist attractions, the Viennese State Opera House and the baroque art treasures, things began to boil. Value conservatism had provided for sedation and prevented Austria from experiencing unpleasant surprises during the act of self-discovery ongoing since 1945. But it was noticeable not only in the area of youth culture that something was in the offing. And there was some doubt as to whether the state's attempted countermeasures would be successful. Perhaps the most discussed expression of the state leadership striving to celebrate peace as the citizen's first obligation and to discipline above all the youth was the passing of a Youth Protection Act by the National Council in 1957 with the aim of nipping adolescent 'immorality' in the bud. The intention was not only to preserve the youth from the dangers of the street but also to prohibit the 'indiscriminate frequenting of restaurants and events [and] the consumption of alcohol and nicotine'.[594] Concerts by American rock singer Elvis Presley were regarded as downright dangerous, because they sent the audience into a state of ecstasy. Order and subordination were, once again, regarded as a matter of course.

A gulf separated the war generation and the first post-war generation. The latter did not agree with the self-satisfaction of those who demonstrated so clearly that they had 'made it'. Was it really sufficient for the past to remain dormant? Any detailed discussion of, not to mention a thorough preoccupation with, the period of National Socialism was dismissed as inopportune. It was bad enough that it had been terrible and that the war had claimed so many victims. This view went so far that in one history of Austria from 1970 the audacious formulation appeared: 'The Second World War is part of world history, though not of Austrian heritage itself.'[595] No attempt had been made to retrieve the emigrants of 1938. They might make demands, the fulfilment of which could well have disturbed the cosiness. A third of those who fell into the category 'expelled intelligentsia' had returned and stocked up Austria's academic and cultural potential.[596] In other words: two-thirds had not returned. Their absence left a large gap. But what it came to doing more, everyone blamed someone else. In the long term, nothing could be suppressed, and one only had to look at the provisions of the State Treaty to know that much still had to be done.

But who looked at the State Treaty? It remained a more or less unread document. And very different things assumed priority for a growing generation that was hungry for life. The writer Hans Veigl counted what had become important: silent comfort, pressure cooker, washing machine, cars, nylon stockings and chipboard, illustrated magazines and *Schlager* music. People celebrated – mostly at the radio – the victories of skiing aces Anderl Molterer and Toni Sailer, went on holiday to the Upper Adriatic or Dalmatia, danced rock and roll – consumerism and the joy of living were dominant. And only as some sort of reminder did Veigl mention the 'will to unite' on which this republic had been built, consensus, the Grand Coalition and 'reconstruction work as a success story'.[597] There were no concerns about jobs; the General Social Security Act (ASVG) aimed to ensure that everyone living in Austria had access to medical insurance. Provision for old age was assured. There was little room for fears about the future.

The 'unease in the party state'

On 4 January 1957, only a few months before the end of his term in office, Theodor Körner died. He had been the first federal president to be elected in direct elections since the foundation of the Republic. His death triggered a long period of change, though this was not foreseeable at first. Following some pre-election squabbling, including a discussion of whether direct elections should not be abolished again, after all, Deputy Chancellor Adolf Schärf of the SPÖ positioned himself as a candidate. The ÖVP and the FPÖ agreed on the physician Dr Wolfgang Denk after Raab had rejected the idea, as he saw it, of retiring from public life by standing as a candidate himself. Schärf was elected and the chairman of the SPÖ parliamentary group in the National Council, Bruno Pittermann, succeeded him as deputy chancellor. This was a bitter defeat for Raab. Several months later, he suffered a stroke. He slowly recovered. At precisely this time, something began to take form which Raab and the president of the Austrian Trade Union Federation, Johann Böhm, had been contemplating for some time: they wanted to institutionalise the balance of interests. The strikes and social unrest of the previous year, 1955, and early 1956 had led to a resuscitation of something that had prevented major conflicts across the years (with the exception of autumn 1950), namely the wage and price agreements. This now became a body of rules with the creation of the Parity Commission for Wage and Price Issues. It was to comprise representatives of the federal government and advocacy groups and supposed to arbitrate when major wage conflicts loomed. In this way, not only was something strengthened that was designed to ensure a balance of interests. In addition, it was perhaps the clearest expression of that which had long since begun to develop into the Austrian form of a consensus democracy. One could regard this as conflict avoidance or as an instrument for relieving the government. In any case, it actually seemed to work. Raab also had another objective in mind. He wanted to continue shaping things and was confident, even after his sickness, of being able to make use of opportunities for talks in both the East and the West, and indeed far better than others could. Here he aimed at a sort of extension of negotiations on the State Treaty. For him, the 'aftermath' was evidently far from over.

Suddenly, however, an incident that no one had expected caused some discomfort. American military intervention in Lebanon made it necessary to swiftly transport troops to that crisis region. The necessary aircraft and soldiers were available in Bavaria. A request for flyover permission with disclosure of the actual troop strength was to be avoided. Thus, the Americans requested overflight clearance from Vienna only for a humanitarian operation, and they commenced the air transport on 16 July 1958. Around 100 transport aircraft, escorted by fighter planes, flew over Austria to Lebanon. Austria felt deceived and withdrew its permission for humanitarian flyovers. Then, on

18 July, a blockade of its airspace was announced. Austria sent a crew of its few (old and poorly-equipped) 'Vampire' jet trainers to Innsbruck and informed them that they were not to fly too closely to American aircraft. The USA pretended to be indignant but also knew very well how it would respond if Soviet aircraft were to fly back and forth over Austria. In any case, Austrian gratitude and looking away did nothing to help, especially as Austria had every reason not to be perceived as being in thrall to the Americans. The Soviet Union promptly addressed a note to the USA, in which it emphatically condemned the violation of the State Treaty and Austrian neutrality.[598] And precisely on the day on which the note was handed over in Washington, a delegation of the Austrian government with an almost identical composition to 1955 flew to Moscow. This time, however, Bruno Pittermann was on board instead of Adolf Schärf. It was the first visit by a high-ranking delegation from the West since the suppression of the Hungarian Uprising. Along the streets in the centre of Moscow hung banners stating: 'Long live the Austro-Soviet friendship.' The Austrians were greeted like representatives of a global power.[599] Finally, the Soviets were generous and reduced the deliveries of mineral oil in accordance with the State Treaty from ten million tons to 6.5 million.

Once the Austrians had returned home again, the USA responded to Moscow's note of 18 July with the observation that the flyovers had been cleared with Austria and had taken place in full agreement with Austrian wishes.[600] This was at best a white lie. Austria did not lift the blockade of its airspace for transports of wounded and sick, as well as for guests of state, until 20 August. This was the first step towards a normalisation, though not in relations to the USA.

In Moscow, Raab and his entourage had avoided addressing with the Soviets a change in the military provisions of the State Treaty or expressing their desire for an acquisition of missiles for the Federal Army. The Western powers were also disappointed that the topic was not brought up. Raab had instead stated that he was well aware that Austria had first and foremost the Soviets to thank for the conclusion of the State Treaty. The British Ambassador in Vienna commented to the effect that the Austrians had done nothing in Moscow but play the 'amiable drinking companions'.[601] Washington, however, was very irritated and it was inevitable that the USA would give utterance to their indignation.

It was noticeable how often Austria was selected by the Soviets as the recipient of messages for the West. And both Soviet Premier Nikolai A. Bulganin and First Secretary Khrushchev had made repeated use of the country's neutrality. Topics included a non-aggression pact between the two military blocs, in order to end the Cold War, a ban on additional nuclear weapons' tests, as well as the German question, in which Austria was to offer its services.[602] The responses from Vienna had remained non-committal but for the USA this evidently meant: nip it in the bud. Austria should not dare to presume that it could drive a wedge between the Western alliance partners. Thus, Vienna was forced on to the defensive and confronted with a list of its failings. Austria had been tardy in fulfilling the provisions of the State Treaty but also those of an important related agreement, the Vienna Memorandum of 10 May 1955. Those American and British mineral oil corporations were to be indemnified that had been deprived of the assets they had possessed before 1938 as a result of the transfer to state-owned industry of the conveyor plants and refineries released by the Soviets. The nature and extent of the compensation, however, were still open after two years of negotiations. It concerned an indemnification programme of around 400 million schillings.[603] Article 26 of the State Treaty had codified the reimbursement of people who had been expropriated and persecuted by the National Socialists. In this case, too, Austria had been tardy, and it was of no avail to point to domestic problems. Raab had proposed the payment of a blanket compensation amount of five million dollars, and he claimed to have already agreed on this with the president of the World Jewish Congress, Nahum Goldmann. But nothing had been paid. When Foreign Minister Figl visited Washington in late September 1958, he felt the full force of the American administration's displeasure. It was clear that it was under pressure from Jewish organisations and mineral oil corporations. But the Austrian reactions to the flyovers in July and Raab's words during his departure from Moscow had atmospherically changed several things for the worse. In brief, the Americans felt that the Austrians had been prepared to fulfil all Soviet demands but that the demands and desires of the Western powers had been repeatedly dismissed. A short time later, the Americans showed that they were serious: they blocked the disbursal of Marshall Plan funds, ignored Austrian credit applications submitted to the American Export-Import Bank, failed to deliver the already approved armaments required by the Federal Army and demonstrated in this way their options for applying pressure.[604] They turned off the money supply to Austria.

Raab blamed his coalition partner for the problems. The Grand Coalition suddenly manifested itself as a not particularly good form of government, as the partners blocked each other in important questions. It was also unmistakeable that several predominantly younger politicians wanted to force the replacement of the 'old guard'. From time to time, Raab was accused of an authoritarian style of leadership. He had made no secret that he wanted to pursue the catching-up process of the former Soviet occupation zone at the expense of the western and southern federal states. The tightening of credits, of which he was accused, had brought with it an additional aggravation and led to the postponement of projects that had already been planned. Figl was criticised for riding on the coattails of the Chancellor but not having got anywhere in the assets negotiations with Yugoslavia or in the fulfilment of Article 7 of the State Treaty. It was argued that the complete avoidance of the South Tyrol problem was almost unforgiveable. Other issues were state-owned industry, the issuing of people's shares, more or less federalism and other details of government work. There was no progress.[605] The 'unease in the party state' was articulated,[606] and the question was posed as to whether it was sensible to continue the Grand Coalition, as Bruno Kreisky wanted, or whether other combinations were not also conceivable. 25 years after the civil war of 1934, the path taken by the First Republic could of course be recapitulated at length. The fact that the European setting had fundamentally changed, as had Austria itself, even if not everything had been transformed, suggested that any parallels were dubious. However, it stoked up debate. Once again, the easiest path seemed to be that of ending the legislative period and agreeing on new elections for May 1959. There was a repetition of what was already known from the elections of 1953: the SPÖ overtook the ÖVP in terms of votes, though not in the number of parliamentary seats. As the formation of a new coalition government refused to succeed, Adolf Schärf intervened, as Theodor Körner had done before him. He again tasked Raab with the formation of a government and appealed to the SPÖ to retract some of their demands. Raab remained federal chancellor. The real victor of the government negotiations, however, was Bruno Kreisky, who replaced Figl as foreign minister. The question, however, was: What would the new government be able to do which the old one could not?

Structural problems could not be solved by continuing the old course. In the east of the country, there was stagnation and out-migration, despite all efforts. The farmers became increasingly few. Industries that had already proliferated in the west during the occupation period, perpetuated this trend. The federal states drifted apart more than during the occupation period and evinced increasing self-importance. They had existed longer than the state as a whole. The state governors insisted on their local power and capabilities and well and truly crowed. This was above all a problem of the ÖVP, which was made to discharge its duties by the state governors from its own party. Salzburg, Tyrol and Styria distinguished themselves by the criticism they voiced and fully exploited the apparent weakness of federal politics and the federal party organisation. The states gave fresh impetus but also contributed on the other hand to a hardening of the situation. Indeed, both the federal government and the states were repeatedly found guilty of something and gave rise to complaints and accusations. And let us not forget the political parties!

Power and political influence could be expressed in figures. The two biggest parties had around 700,000 members each. A comparative organisational density could be encountered at most in dictatorships and semi-dictatorships. Even the NSDAP had possessed fewer members than either of the two major parties. The huge number of party members was a legacy of the occupation period, when membership in a democratic party had been regarded as a purification process. As in previous times, party membership was cited when it was a question of apartments, appointments, pay raises, positions or benefactions of whatever kind. Use was then unashamedly made of this, not least in the area of enterprises that were state-owned or close to the state. The party membership book did not determine everything but it did determine a lot of things. Those with a lot of practice could point to two or three party membership books, while those who were capable of adapting confused benefits with character. There was nothing new about it. And the attempt of political parties to have a ready offer for as many areas of life as possible already existed. This had been common to the First Republic and the Corporative State. What had changed was only a certain pressure in those days that aimed at preventing someone from defecting from a party again. As a member of a particular social class or a professional group, one not only belonged, as before, to a party but also lived in a certain district or a region, socialised with like-minded people, took part in demonstrations and spent leisure time with one's peers. Artists and art were likewise never free from opportunism. Economic deprivation demanded the ability to adapt, first to the Republic, then to the Corporative State and finally to National Socialism. In the Second Republic, the extreme forms of pillarization disappeared only gradually but the opportunism remained. The parties knew this and they counted on it.

The Decade of the Malcontents

With the 1960s, a decade of the malcontents dawned. Raab was one of the first to learn this. In 1960, he forewent of necessity the party leadership of the ÖVP, though he did select his successor, Alphons Gorbach from Styria. Less than a year later, he would succeed him as federal chancellor. Gorbach regarded himself as Raab's trustee and he did not carry out a 'palace coup'. But a time bomb was ticking, because a group of ÖVP politicians under the leadership of Salzburg governor, Josef Klaus, called 'the reformers' no longer wanted to accept what had become a ponderous grind of politics. The SPÖ also tried out new, fresh people. The ranks of men in the federal government did not change. But it was a certain pressure from below and the youth, who were shaped least of all by the occupation period, that had an accelerating effect. Europe, which Julius Raab still eyed with a certain scepticism, became the objective. And this was more than just chasing a dream.

The European Economic Community (EEC) of six nations had existed since 1 January 1958. A year later, seven states that had for various reasons been unable to partake in the founding of the EEC resolved to establish a small European Free Trade Association (EFTA). Decisive for the formation of this coalition was first and foremost a Franco-British conflict that prevented Britain's involvement in the EEC. A consultation in Moscow also showed, however, that the Soviet Union regarded an accession to the EEC by Austria as a violation of its obligations in accordance with the State Treaty and therefore refused to allow it. Federal President Schärf had also been informed of this during a trip to Moscow in October 1959.[607] For Austria, therefore, membership in

EFTA was the only possibility to avoid a looming isolation in terms of economic policy. Ultimately, Austria had to be content with this. And Raab did not have the slightest intention of opposing the Soviets. Others in his party and, above all, among the Socialists would have been willing to attempt an accession to the EEC, though this would have been an irresponsible act of violence. The EFTA treaty was signed on 4 January 1960.

Small steps were also being taken regarding South Tyrol. All political parties in Austria had taken up the cause of South Tyrol. 'No one wants to be accused of half-heartedness', adjudged the German ambassador in Vienna, Müller-Graaf. The Communists became positively raucous and wanted in this way to at least arouse attention.[608] Until 1959, there had merely been a testing of the waters. Italy did not want negotiations but only exploratory talks. The action taken most recently by Leopold Figl had been anything but prosperous, however, and he had failed in his attempt to bring the matter in front of the Council of Europe. As a result, the Minister had been severely criticised in Tyrol. His successor, Kreisky, initially wanted secret talks but ultimately decided otherwise. He sought to internationalise the matter and chose the UN General Assembly to this end. His tactical calculation of securing himself the support of small and medium-sized states proved successful. The General Assembly resolved to invite Italy and Austria to engage in bilateral negotiations. Italy could now no longer argue that the South Tyrol affair was an internal problem. The matter was delicate because Yugoslavia began simultaneously to champion the rights of Slovenes in Carinthia, and it could not be ruled out that Yugoslavia also wanted to internationalise the matter. It was a question first and foremost of school affairs. An internationalisation could be avoided. Not by a long shot, however, could it be assumed that efforts to achieve a fulfilment of obligations in the State Treaty that also satisfied not only Yugoslavia but also and above all the Carinthian Slovenes would be successful. Negotiations became stuck when it came to the strength and regional distribution of the Slovene ethnic group: Austria wanted to make its measures dependent on the ascertainment of a minority, while the representatives of the Slovenes rejected any kind of census.

In late 1959, the period of a cooling of relations with the USA had come to an end. A proprietary agreement ended the dispute over the Vienna Memorandum. The demands of Western oil firms were satisfied. With the creation of a compensation fund endowed with six million dollars, Jewish demands could be regarded as fulfilled. The USA at least promised to drop its support of Jewish claims. It turned out shortly afterwards that the endowment of the compensation found had been far from sufficient and that it had by no means satisfied all material losses that Austria had pledged itself to settling.[609] Only the next step had been taken. But the USA had suddenly rediscovered its sympathy for Austria. The US National Security Council noted: 'Austria ... is a symbol of resistance to the Soviets. Austria is strategically important. ... A weakening of Austria's stability and pro-Western ties would constitute a serious setback for the United States.'[610] This assessment was thus based on very clear calculations, for the USA must have had the feeling that the Soviet Union was thoroughly embracing Austria.

From late June to 8 July 1960, Soviet Premier Khrushchev spent ten days in Austria, travelled through six federal states and was acclaimed by the people. The West German ambassador, like other foreign spectators, had admittedly observed a rather lukewarm reception in Vienna[611] but the mood improved, and Khrushchev claimed afterwards that a certain aloofness had been attributable to the influence of the Catholic Church and the ideological opposition of the Socialists.[612] At Leopold Figl's farmstead, the Soviet Premier and the former foreign minister betted against a pig that the harvest of Austrian maize would be higher than the Soviet yield. Khrushchev disagreed – and lost (a fact that was then discretely concealed).[613] He demonstrated generosity and once more reduced Austrian deliveries from the State Treaty by 500,000 tons of crude oil. Khrushchev's badmouthing of the USA, West Germany and Italy at various press conferences caused indignation. In Mauthausen, he referred to Adenauer as the 'reincarnation of Hitler'.[614] This was regarded as a violation of the right to hospitality and was also repudiated – albeit somewhat late – by Raab, who had accompanied the Soviet state guest during the entire visit. The Federal Republic of Germany felt compelled to issue an official protest. Even more annoying for the Austrian host, however, was the fact that the Soviet Premier had spoken of the Soviet Union being prepared to defend Austrian neutrality. This formulation must have had a positively alarming effect on both Austria and the Western powers. It was no wonder, therefore, that Washington wanted to counter this by at least attempting to stop the cooling-off process that could no longer be overlooked. For the Americans, as well as the British, however, Austria was no longer a special case but rather a state of lesser importance.[615]

Suddenly, however, Austria was assigned precisely the role that it had always wanted to play: it assumed a bridging function. It was a 'neutral zone of peace',[616] which made for a wonderful meeting place. As early as 1953, Austria had attempted to arrange a summit meeting. In 1954, Leopold Figl offered Vienna in the event of the Conference on Security and Co-operation in Europe desired by the Soviet Union taking place. Then the State Treaty had been signed. Shortly thereafter, Vienna had fallen behind Geneva and could not host the meeting of the heads of state of France, Britain, the Soviet Union and the USA planned for July 1955 due to an American protest.[617] Now, however, it looked like everything would work out. Americans and Soviets agreed to hold a meeting between American President Kennedy and Soviet First Secretary and Premier Khrushchev in Vienna. The proposal to hold the meeting in Vienna had not been made by Austria but it did use the opportunity to make clear its hub or bridging function. In any case, the Americans and the Soviets had drawn level with one another and made it clear that they did not intend to vacate the field for the other. The images of the summit meeting in Vienna were shown across the globe. It was well known that the meeting on 4 June 1961 would deal with Germany. The fact that Khrushchev's announcement to conclude a peace treaty with East Germany and rescind the Berlin Agreement with the former allies triggered shortly thereafter a mass exodus from the GDR, the response of the East German leadership to which was the construction of the Berlin Wall and a hermetic lockdown of the East, was already visible on 13 August. Khrushchev's assessment of Kennedy as a political lightweight and his attempt a year later to station missiles in Cuba was a further consequence of the Vienna summit. The world teetered on the brink of a nuclear war. And yet everything had looked so peaceful – back then in Vienna.

The militaries in the East and the West were alarmed. And Austria joined in. But the agony of the Grand Coalition manifested itself nowhere more clearly than in the matter of the country's ability to defend itself. For Austria's military conceptions, the Warsaw Pact was the measure of all things. The construction of the Berlin Wall and the accompanying war mentality appeared to underline the latent assumption of a threat from the east. The defence minister in Gorbach's cabinet, Karl Schleinzer, was not content to implement a first army reform and adapt the organisational framework of the army to at least some extent to reality. He also seized the initiative to bring about a ministerial resolution with commissions for national defence. The Minister and his permanent secretary, Otto Rösch, however, held divergent views. Rösch did not want the defensive scenario brought to the fore but rather to be able to initially deal with a situation of crisis and neutrality. At the same time, he demanded in any event that the Federal Army begin with defence 'at any rate at the border'. This boiled down to the squaring of the circle, though this was all that could be achieved within the coalition. The Federal Army was supposed to adjust its plans to defending the regions close to the border. It was unclear what conclusions should be drawn from this: that it was merely a question of symbolic defence; that an actual war scenario was not envisaged; or that investment should be made primarily in the political option? As usual in these times, operational assumptions were based on the deployment of nuclear weapons. This was realistic to the extent that NATO and, above all, Italy were focussing entirely on nuclear components at the time[618] and the Warsaw Pact was planning as a matter of course the use of nuclear weapons against Austrian targets in the context of an advance in the direction of Italy and Germany. A training exercise of the Hungarian People's Army then revealed that the destruction of Vienna by means of two 500-kiloton nuclear bombs was being considered.[619] People were thinking the unthinkable. A nuclear inferno would have wiped out Austria.

Vienna naturally occupied a special place in all deliberations on how a potential attack from the east should be dealt with. As the Austrian capital was located little more than 40 kilometres from the Hungarian and Czechoslovak borders, and the most important state institutions were to be found there, the issue of the capital city had to be addressed. The swift evacuation of Vienna was considered, though it was feared at the same time that a mass exodus from the city would seriously hamper any attempts at defence, even beyond the city itself. A relocation of the Austrian capital was then pondered in all seriousness. According to one study: 'On the basis of its geographical location, Bregenz as the federal capital would correspond to a markedly Western orientation on the part of the Republic of Austria; Vienna – if it were really the freely-elected [capital city] and not one adopted, unexamined, from the Monarchy – to a similarly Eastern orientation.'[620] Bern and Ankara were cited as examples of how a capital city should be located.

The suggestion was not followed up on. This did not mean, however, that the problem had therefore become smaller. And the plans of the Soviet General Staff and Hungarian staffs, which became known only much later, merely confirmed the scenarios on which the operational plans of the Federal Army were likewise based.

The Agony

While senior officers laboured over emergency plans, it was business as usual in Austria – or so it seemed. But following a brief acceleration of political events between summer 1959 and spring 1961, a new paralysis took hold. Proportional representation and package deals dominated. And a jealous watch was kept that no one gained an advantage that had not been agreed on. The creation of package deals degenerated into something that was termed 'Packelei' in old Austrian – a distasteful compromise: the exchange of share transfers in the mineral oil area in return for flexible tariff rates for egg imports[621] and similar things. This was not least at the expense of the state budget. The new finance minister in Gorbach's cabinet, Josef Klaus, who had switched from Salzburg to Vienna, put it to the test. He sought to put the national finances in order by means of budget cuts, redeployments and a radical policy of cutbacks. This met with a lot of approval among the people, as did his demand for an 'objectification' of politics. But within the government he was confronted in some cases with bitter resistance, and not only on the part of the SPÖ, where the president of the Austrian Trade Union Federation and second president of the National Council, Franz Olah, resigned in protest from his parliamentary function, but even more so from his own party. Minister of Education Drimmel wanted to resign. Gorbach was able to prevent this but he had to stand up to intraparty opposition with increasing frequency. He unexpectedly saw himself confronted by an 'adjacent government', for Raab – who was still president of the Federal Economic Chamber – and Olah agreed over the heads of government and parties on the development of the Parity Commission, which was supposed to discuss intervention measures in the future, predetermine them and submit them to the gov-

ernment. The Grand Coalition thus received a further pillar independent of elections
to the National Council, as though the togetherness was to be perpetuated in this way.
Raab's objective was to secure his political legacy. He did not want to leave anything to
chance and even during the period of his departure created instruments that aimed to
accomplish a type of automatism.

In 1961, the USA delivered the remaining agendas of the Marshall Plan to Austria.
Raab invested the available funds, which were being spent only slowly, in a trust of the
European Recovery Program and ensured that the mechanism of lending and repayment could be retained.[622] All attempts to convey an impression of continuity and business as usual, however, could not prevent fortuities and unforeseen events. A few days
after the end of the summit meeting between Kennedy and Khrushchev, it was not one
of the established points of contention that led to a scandal in the Council of Ministers
but rather a thoroughly remote topic. The son of the last Austrian emperor, Otto von
Habsburg, had submitted the declaration of renunciation and loyalty demanded since
1919 from members of his family. In this way, he hoped to remove all obstacles that
had hitherto prevented his entry into Austria from Bavaria. The text of the declaration
of renunciation corresponded to that which had already been submitted by numerous
members of the House of Habsburg-Lorraine. Otto von Habsburg had also received
multiple signals, including from Interior Minister Helmer and Foreign Minister Kreisky,
that gave reason to expect a smooth handling of the matter.[623] However, the Council
of Ministers was unable to agree on the validity of the declaration. The SPÖ ministers voted against it, and the permanent secretary in the Federal Ministry of Trade and
Reconstruction, Eduard Weikhart, did not shy away from publicly declaring: 'If Otto
Habsburg should dare to enter our country and bring misfortune upon us, he will receive
the kind of welcome that an undesired intruder must expect.'[624] Otto von Habsburg
did not receive the settlement he had hoped for. In response, he lodged a complaint of
unconstitutionality against the Republic. Now it was the turn of the supreme courts
and it was a question of waiting. In spring 1962, it again became clear that there was no
progress. Thus, elections were to take place once more. The date was deferred as much
as possible, in order that at least a three-year legislative period could be achieved; thus,
elections would not take place until 18 November 1962. The result was essentially more
of the same. Thereafter, four months of continuous government negotiations began.

It would again have been possible for ÖVP and SPÖ to build a little coalition.
This possibility, however, was only brought into play as a tactical element. The ÖVP,
strengthened by a gain in seats, wanted, however, to attempt to govern once again with
the SPÖ. As a result, a bid was made above all for the Foreign Ministry, less with a view
to strengthening the ÖVP and more in order to weaken the SPÖ. Eventually, Kreisky
retained this post, and he was deprived only of his competence for foreign trade. Not
the Foreign Ministry but rather the Trade Ministry would conduct prospective negotia-

tions with the EEC regarding a treaty of association. Austria wanted an exclusively economic agreement. The Soviets reacted promptly: any association with the EEC, even in conjunction with Sweden and Switzerland, was characterised as incompatible with the State Treaty and Austrian neutrality. And it was clear: the Soviets were serious! They raised the ante: Moscow, it was claimed, would no longer feel 'bound by the obligations of the State Treaty in the event of a violation of the State Treaty by Austria'.[625]

Austria was in a bind. The years of the 'Economic Miracle' had ended with a recession in 1962. Investments stagnated. Rising inflation gave cause for concern. The effects of the economic coalition in the framework of EFTA threatened to fizzle out. And as Britain wanted to leave EFTA, the moment had also come for Austria to re-orientate itself. As so often, however, attention was paid not to the parameters of a sustainable policy but to personnel decisions. For example, Franz Olah, who had fought for and with Kreisky for the Foreign Ministry, became minister of the interior. It was not the distribution of posts, however, that proved decisive for the continuation of the partnership but rather the coalition pact. This expressed like nothing else the mistrust that dominated the new/old partners and made it clear that this was not the start of a trust-based cooperation but instead that they sought to codify the most ridiculous trivialities. It was no longer the grand policy objectives that were at issue but rather the terms for a continuation of the partnership, which very few actually believed in. The members of the Grand Coalition were nonetheless content with this. Others, especially the group of 'reformers' in the ÖVP, were not. And they could not be satisfied either with the creation of a coalition-free zone. Josef Klaus withdrew from politics and wanted only to work as a lawyer in Salzburg.

Once again, the government of the two major parties was literally caught off guard by an already-known side issue. The Constitutional Court had declared itself not competent when it came to Otto von Habsburg's complaint regarding the entry ban. The Administrative Court felt competent and decided on 24 May 1963 that the Habsburg Law of 1919 had already fulfilled its requirements and that Otto von Habsburg should therefore be permitted to enter the country. The SPÖ turned the matter into a trial of strength with the ÖVP, voted twice in the National Council together with the FPÖ against a supreme court levering out the parliament. The turbulent session went down in the history of the National Council as the 'June battle' (Junischlacht).[626] Minister of the Interior Olah made a complete farce of the affair when he threatened to deploy executive forces in the event that the Habsburg should attempt to enter the country. Aside from the fact that a republic was actually acting out an undignified comedy here, one person was affected more than any other, namely the Federal Chancellor. He had been positively sidelined. In September 1963, Gorbach was voted out of office as party chairman. Klaus replaced him. The first step had been taken in the replacement of the Federal Chancellor. The second step was only a question of time.

On 8 January 1964, Julius Raab died. He had campaigned only a year earlier as the
ÖVP's candidate for the federal presidency and had been swept aside in a hopeless election campaign against the incumbent federal president, Adolf Schärf. In Raab, Alphons
Gorbach once again lost his backing. On 25 February 1964, the Federal Chancellor
resigned, only a few days after he had demonstratively met with Bruno Pittermann at
Vienna's Central Cemetery for a symbolic handshake in remembrance of the victims of
the uprising of February 1934.

Josef Klaus' hour had now come. He became federal chancellor and formed his first
cabinet. The coalition treaty remained for the most part in force but for Klaus it was
clear from the first day on that it would only be a temporary treaty. He was aided in accelerating events less by the strength of his own party and more by the self-destruction
of the SPÖ. Four incidents contributed to the sustained weakening of the SPÖ. The
first was the Olah 'affair'. The Interior Minister, who had begun to direction his department with an astonishing thoughtlessness and authoritarianism, had the ambition
of replacing Bruno Pittermann as party chairman and deputy chancellor. His downfall,
however, was the fact that he had enabled the FPÖ to conduct a lavish election campaign in 1962 with trade union funds. The aim had been clear: Olah wanted to secretly
obtain a partner for a little coalition. On top of that, Olah had also used trade union
funds to found a new newspaper, the *Neue Kronen Zeitung*. During the appraisal of
the affair, Olah did not shy away from openly arguing out the conflict with his party
colleague, Minister of Justice Christian Broda. Olah's exclusion from the party, his
replacement as interior minister, legal proceedings, conviction and prison were the consequences. The damage done to the SPÖ by this open dispute was immense, for Olah
had been very popular since his intervention in October 1950 in the strike movement
led by the Communists.

A further 'accident at work' also cost the SPÖ votes. Transport Minister Otto Probst
regarded it as the responsibility of his department to mandate the christening of a
new ship on Lake Constance in the name of *Dr Karl Renner*. The state government of
Vorarlberg, however, had unanimously resolved to name the ship *Vorarlberg*. The christening of the ship in Fußach on Lake Constance on 21 November 1964 turned into
a debacle. 30,000 demonstrators could not be held back by the executive. The guests
of honour, who had travelled from Vienna, felt hounded. The commander of the state
Gendarmerie, who no longer looked the part, called for assistance from the Federal
Army. It would have been the first time that the Federal Army had provided domestic
assistance. It was refused by Inspector General of Troops Erwin Fussenegger. The day
ended peacefully. But Otto Probst had become persona non grata. Finally, the SPÖ
also reacted wrongly in another matter. The journalists of independent newspapers, especially the editor-in-chief of the *Kurier*, Hugo Portisch, were so indignant about radio
and television being demoted to party radio broadcasting that they decided to resort

to an instrument never before used in Austria and initiate a petition for a referendum. It was to be the first petition for a referendum in the history of the Republic, for Kurt Schuschnigg's referendum had been cancelled on 11 March 1938.

The SPÖ regarded a successful petition for a referendum as a threat of a loss of potential influence in the formation of opinion, and it therefore argued against the plebiscite, which, however, with more than 800,000 signatures, unmistakeably pointed the way. The ÖVP was not particularly happy about the actions of the journalists but accepted them nonetheless. After Habsburg, Olah, *Vorarlberg* and radio, it could be assumed that the SPÖ was significantly weakened. Otherwise, however, nothing had changed, aside from the fact that vent was given ever more drastically to the unease about the Grand Coalition's way of working and its unwillingness to reform.

Within ten years since the conclusion of the State Treaty, Austria had become rigid and, in this way, almost undemocratic, as power and influence were completely divided between the two major parties. The ÖVP and the SPÖ watched, eagle-eyed, that the other did not gain an advantage or, if so, that it was compensated for. In the process, those who cultivated this system and were simultaneously trapped in it lost sight that they were about to miss out on the breaking of a new dawn. The ambassador of West Germany, Josef Löns, wrote to the Foreign Office in Bonn: 'The cabinet of Klaus/Pittermann constitutes the most barren government of the Second Republic. Almost all important tasks … get bogged down in the quarrel between the coalition partners.' And it seemed to go on for ever and ever. For this reason, no one thought much of it when Josef Klaus demanded new elections in response to the Socialists' refusal to agree to his savings plans. They were scheduled for 6 March 1966.

The British ambassador to Austria, Sir John Arthur Pilcher, found the election campaign boring even in early 1966.[627] At the end of the day, it was almost pointless, he claimed, for the end of cooperation had not been caused by a fundamental conflict or a serious rift. There had admittedly been disagreements over the budget for 1966. But Klaus and Pittermann had ultimately grown tired of working together. No progress was any longer made.

The ÖVP and the SPÖ exhausted themselves in defending traditional interests. The only unexpected turning point in the dispute had been provided by the Communists, as Sir John wrote to the British Foreign Office, when their party chairman, Franz Muhri, announced that the KPÖ intended to campaign in only three Vienna working-class districts, in which they expected to obtain a seat. Furthermore, no money should be spent on a hopeless election campaign. Instead, the comrades should vote for the SPÖ. The ÖVP promptly warned against the threat of a popular front – which did not exist. The SPÖ, in turn, did not defend itself against the Communists' ingratiation and evoked the spectre of the Habsburgs. They claimed that the ÖVP would allow Otto von Habsburg to enter the country and that this would bring about conditions akin to a civil war. This was as profound as it got, claimed His Excellence, the British Ambassador. As it had to be assumed, however, that both parties would once again form a coalition, they did not engage in any fundamental debates or conduct an aggressive election campaign. Nonetheless, it was the first time since the war that the parties did not announce in advance their intention to join forces once more. But, the ambassador continued, it would turn out as always. Sir John, like many others, would prove to be mistaken!

18 The New Style
of Dispassion

18 Josef Klaus on the balcony of Palais Todesco on Vienna's Kärntnerstraße opposite the State
Opera House on 6 March 1966. The election victory of the ÖVP, which enabled Klaus to form
a non-coalition government, ended a twenty-year period in which Austria had been governed by
a Grand Coalition. Klaus was given four years to realise his reform programme. (Photo: Portisch,
Österreich II, vol. 3)

I t was certainly not an earthquake but nevertheless a lurch that was felt by Austria on 6 March 1966. At first, many people could scarcely believe that the ÖVP had obtained an absolute majority in the elections to the National Council. Before the election, only the general secretary of the party, Hermann Withalm, had voiced this possibility. But it was a general secretary's duty to be optimistic. On election night, one saw people celebrating and others mourning and withdrawn into themselves. The polling institutes had predicted a completely different result and had to acknowledge that their demoscopic methods had not been sufficiently sound. It was then discovered, admittedly, that above all Franz Olah had cost the SPÖ a better outcome. The post-election analysis demonstrated furthermore that the SPÖ had not rejected the Communists' attempts at ingratiation but instead seen them as an opportunity to optimise their votes. The fact should not be overlooked, however, that the broad-based party had experienced a modernisation drive, which could be traced back above all to Josef Klaus. By comparison, the SPÖ simply looked 'old'. It should not be forgotten that the newspapers had stirred up public opinion against the Grand Coalition to such an extent that a retention of this form of government would have been a type of suicide in terms of communication policy. It was not yet clear, however, how far-reaching the change would be and whether a breach with everything that had been held dear and a 20-year tradition of Austrian politics would take place.

The chairman of the SPÖ, Bruno Pittermann, who had to take part of the blame for the defeat of his party, observed a 50:50 mood in his party regarding the continuation of the coalition. The older and the younger party members, he claimed, were in favour of going into opposition and fighting, while the middle generation wanted to continue working together with the ÖVP.[628] This picture might not be entirely accurate but it was clear that there were some in favour and some against. Even the still incumbent federal chancellor, Klaus, could not yet entirely gauge the consequences of the ÖVP's victory. But it was ultimately a matter of only a few days and weeks until the broad-based party demonstrated its absolute majority and made demands for the formation of a coalition government that could not be fulfilled by the SPÖ. In other words, it might have been possible to fulfil them but there was simply no desire to do so. Within the ÖVP, it was argued that anything other than a complete assumption of governmental responsibility would constitute a betrayal of the voters.

At the same time, concerns were voiced. For the Socialists, going into opposition meant a departure from several power centres. This also meant, quite banally, that they could no longer serve their own clientele and lost the information edge that a party in government automatically had. This went hand in hand with concerns about whether it would be possible in a short time to return to the corridors of power. Would an ÖVP government abandon welfare state objectives? Would full employment be maintained? Would control mechanisms work? Would there be a return to violence in what was in itself a peaceful Austria?

Government negotiations began on 14 March. They ended a little over a month later – and had failed. Socialist politicians had repeatedly leaked information about the progress of negotiations and approached the British Labour government. But the sister party in Britain was also unable to give useful advice. At a party congress of the Socialists on 15 April, the demand was made that the ÖVP must ensure that the coalition would be retained for at least 18 months; police and Federal Army were not to be combined in one department; and there could be no budget cuts. The ÖVP had no intention of agreeing to these demands. They would rather go it alone. In the SPÖ, only one person advocated an acceptance of the demands of the broad-based party: Bruno Kreisky.

Governing Alone

The new/old Chancellor was naturally aware of the upcoming problems and already attempted to provide reassurance in his government declaration. For the ÖVP, too, there were unanswerable questions: Would the Socialists accept the change? Would there be strikes and perhaps violent clashes? Would it be possible to retain the social partnership? Klaus knew that not least foreign countries were anxious to see how he pictured Austria's future path. He had big plans: an end to proportional representation, objectivity in filling posts, a reform in radio broadcasting, the conclusion of an association agreement with the EEC, the solution of the South Tyrol question, economic policy and structural reforms, the reorganisation of state-owned industry and many other things. He had clearly formulated his idealistic approach in 1965 in the context of a speech, of which he later confessed that it had been one of the few 'self-made' speeches of his political career: 'People – measure and focal point of politics.'[629] It addressed dignity and law, liberal regulations, a pluralistic society, processes of concentration and integration and the struggle against depersonalisation and levelling. This may well have had some validity as a philosophical approach. By invitation of the Chancellor, domestic and foreign academics had discussed current political issues, the consequences of a budding technological revolution and social transformations in the context of a thinktank called 'Operation 20' (Aktion 20) and laid them down in position papers. This was a base on which could be built. But Klaus knew by now only too well that the difficulties on the ground were by all means suited to removing the intellectual elites. Perhaps, however, the Chancellor was too optimistic when it came to his own approval. He was treading on very thin ice, for he had to reckon not only with an opposition that mourned its status as a party of government but also with intraparty resistance. He would soon feel its effects. Klaus allowed most of the ministers from the era of the Grand Coalition to remain in their posts and replaced only the lost SPÖ ministers. He opted not to establish his own team committed to him. It was in fact precisely some of the older and very experienced colleagues, especially Federal Minister for Trade, Business and Industry Fritz Bock, who demonstrated open antipathy. Bock was a representative of a liberal economic wing and strongly argued for a 'solo approach' to Brussels, which Klaus regarded as not very promising for foreign policy reasons. It would not be the only conflict.

It was perhaps even more surprising that Klaus resorted in his government programme to that which he had suggested to the SPÖ in the event of a coalition. Should the new/old Chancellor have thought that this would be understood as a sign of continuity and, not least, signal to the SPÖ that there was no intention to steamroll them, however, he was mistaken. The Chancellor did not need to worry that he would not be accepted abroad, for one thing because the whole world was busy with its own problems. For another, what had taken place in Austria was not a revolution and only made the country more comparable to the Western democracies, though without being understood by the Soviet bloc as a rejection of the foreign policy path taken so far.

On the evening of 18 April, Klaus presented his cabinet to Federal President Jonas. This was admittedly just a formality but it revealed a further facet of Josef Klaus' personality: he did not just show respect but actually *had* respect for the head of state. The Federal President belonged to a hierarchy that started with dear God and, a little like 'at the time of the Emperor', continued downwards via the federal president. It was only later that criticism crept in when Franz Jonas, who – despite his high office – had remained a member of the SPÖ, was accused of pursuing socialist aims or even of bias in statements released by the Presidential Chancellery. Klaus, however, retained his respectful approach to the head of state throughout. Perhaps he had expected more support from Jonas. Ultimately, however, this would not have had a lasting effect on his work.

So many things were supposed to be dealt with swiftly; some of them almost simultaneously. Klaus demanded perhaps too much of some government members and – something that was noticed just as quickly – he made it clear that he wanted to control everything, gain an insight into everything and, if necessary, decide things as he saw fit. His way of working was also a source of irritation. Problems were caused repeatedly by ministerial meetings lasting the entire day and by the demand that materials be dealt with as swiftly as possible that were no doubt so complicated that they could not be dispatched without involving parliament or even social partners. The Chancellor also caused irritation by constantly consulting his notebooks and reading out his thoughts – or often just aphorisms – and quotations, with which neither the Minister of Social Affairs Grete Rehor, the first female minister in Austria, nor her male ministerial colleagues had any idea what they should do.

The government got down to business and began to work through its projects. Even during preliminary cabinet talks and likewise at the sessions of the Council of Ministers, differences of opinion and sometimes just tactical issues came to the fore and there were heated interventions, quarrels and anything but the desired harmony that the Chancellor expected but which he was himself unable to establish. The governors of the federal states run by the ÖVP, the so-called party grandees, and above all the heads of the ÖVP associations, made it anything but easy for the Chancellor to govern. He did not belong to any of the associations himself and he had to laboriously build his own network from scratch. Of course, the lack of harmony could not remain concealed. Nonetheless: Klaus impressed people and led the German ambassador, Josef Löns, to report almost enthusiastically that the government had already achieved a huge amount in the first three months alone. More than 40 draft laws had been submitted to the National Council, including a law on growth, university and study laws and a reform of wage and income tax. A new university emerged in Linz. Price increases to accelerate road construction and higher rail fares were unavoidable. The government displayed an incredible tempo. The oppositional Socialists, however, had not yet accepted their new role. The trade unions would keep quiet, because around one million people had received wage and salary raises as a result of the government's tax and income policy measures.[630] The list of projects could have become even longer and been enriched, at least by one episode: Klaus also dealt with the tiresome problem of the entry into the country of the son of the Emperor, Otto von Habsburg, by having him issued with a passport that no longer stated: 'Valid for all countries of the world with the exception of entry into and passage through Austria.' The Habsburg soon made use of the passport.

The media naturally accompanied the first non-coalition government of the Second Republic with curiosity and eagle-eyed – depending on editorial policy. The Austrian Broadcasting Corporation, positively unleashed by the Radio Broadcasting Law of July 1966, began to play an increasingly important role and leapt at the opportunity to report by and large freely. Criticism could soon be heard. Klaus himself was uncommunicative. He had a 'paralysing shyness when faced with the interviewer, the microphone and the television camera'. And it was judged that in television he frequently made a 'defensive and mildly offended' impression.[631]

The Others and Us

While there were increasing friction losses in domestic politics, foreign relations appeared to largely run smoothly. As with the previous governments, the main interest was in relations with the signatories of the State Treaty. In the case of the Soviet Union, Klaus made every effort to reassure the government in Moscow when it came to Austrian efforts to approach the EEC. Soviet Premier Khrushchev had already accused Gorbach of attempting to destroy 'what his [Khrushchev's] friend, the "little capitalist" [Julius Raab] had built'. Gorbach had, of course, disagreed. For the Soviets, however, the topic remained on the table and returned at irregular intervals. 'That would be a type of Anschluss and, as such, a direct violation of the State Treaty', as Khrushchev had informed Gorbach. 'If you assume a difference stance, then you have abandoned the politics of neutrality.'[632] West German 'imperialism' and the threat of a strengthened neo-Nazism in Austria accompanied bilateral relations into the 1980s. The Soviets were evidently not impressed by the fact that it was Josef Klaus who declared the day of the enactment of the Declaration of Neutrality, 26 October, a public holiday and in this way signalised: the day was important and should be a central component within the collective memory of Austria.

Klaus let the Soviets know that he would not pursue an agreement with Brussels at the expense of a violation of Austria's obligations in accordance with the State Treaty and neutrality. His protestations culminated in the formulation printed prominently by the *Spiegel* in 1967: 'Poor, if need be, but neutral.'[633] An increase in the number of diplomatic visits, which was already high, was designed to further emphasise the bond to the Soviet Union, which had been regarded since Raab almost as a 'special' relationship. It was once more visits lasting a week, as had been the case in 1960 and 1961, that stressed this uniqueness and created the impression that the Soviet state leadership was just as happy to spend time in Austria as in the Crimea. The Soviet premier, Nikolai Podgorny, visited Austria for a week in November 1966; reciprocal visits at ministerial level followed, until Josef Klaus travelled to the Soviet Union for a week in mid-March 1967. In the economic sector, agreement was swiftly reached on one point: Austria received Soviet natural gas and delivered, in turn, industrial plants. The Soviets were not willing to make any concession in the question of Austria's accession to the EEC. Austria was told to defer any hopes in this respect. The Soviet Union continued to interpret Article 4 of the State Treaty in such a way that an accession to the EEC would result in close economic ties to West Germany, and this would not conform with the treaty. It was claimed that Germany would soon dominate Austria in economic terms and 'penetrate' the Danube region as far as the borders of the Soviet Union. This would destroy the entire, painstakingly established balance of power in Central Europe.[634]

In another area, too, the Chancellor found interested observers but no accommodation from the Soviets. He emphasised Austria's unbroken will to defend its neutrality with all available means but also demanded that the State Treaty be adapted or at least interpreted in a way that would allow the Federal Army to obtain surface-to-air missiles for defensive purposes. The Soviets' willingness to make concessions ended here. This was also to have been expected. Nonetheless, the two sides remained favourably disposed to one another.

Relations with the USA were similarly smooth. Austria had every reason to be grateful to the Americans for their reconstruction aid, and Foreign Minister Tončić-Sorinj did this not only in words but also by presenting a huge crystal chandelier for the Metropolitan Opera, an act that was well covered by the media. A discussion of military matters became superfluous, for the USA had never made any bones about their particular desire to equip the Federal Army with more modern weaponry. This needed, at most, to be emphasised. For Tončić, in any case, it was not an issue. It was more the concern of Defence Minister Georg Prader. In order, however, to demonstrate the equilibrium in the respective relations, Klaus visited the USA at Easter 1968 at the head of a government delegation, for a similar length of time as he had visited the Soviet Union a year earlier. While talks with the Soviets were substantial, however, and addressed neutrality and the EEC, the discussions in the USA and a meeting with President Lyndon B. Johnson remained strikingly empty. Klaus claimed that he was there 'to thank' the Americans and had no wishes, let alone demands.[635] Of course, there was still much that could be done in terms of the atmosphere. For example, the Chancellor's announcement to the effect that a Sigmund Freud Institute was being established in the former home of Sigmund Freud on Vienna's Berggasse was met with exceedingly friendly comments.[636] One thing was not addressed, which would take centre stage only a few years later. In 1965, Austria had consented to a transit camp being set up in Schönau Palace for Jews leaving the Soviet Union. Those eager to emigrate received Austrian transit visas, were brought to Austria by train and forwarded to Israel by the Jewish Agency, which had rented the transit camp in Schönau. Not all the new arrivals wanted this, because it was for them above all a question of being able to leave the Soviet Union, and many of them wanted to be brought to the USA. Austria had no reason to interfere in the debate on the onward transport of the Jews, for which reason Klaus guarded against addressing the subject. The silent diplomacy functioned in any case, and not only in the case of Israel but also that of the United States and the Soviet Union.

Should we want to compare, however, how the leading powers in East and West behaved towards Austria, the impression remained that the Soviets evinced considerable affability beyond official protocol, even where substantial matters were concerned and the two sides were not at one, whereas the Americans veered ever more towards a purely business-like tone. It should also be pointed out, however, that it evidently caused Austrian politicians no difficulty to obtain appointments with the leaders of both major powers and to meet with them for an exchange of ideas.

It was a similar situation in Britain. The still incumbent deputy chancellor, Bruno Pittermann, had been in London immediately before the SPÖ had gone into opposition. The ÖVP sent their general secretary, Hermann Withalm, to London in July 1966, though not in order to synchronise with the Conservatives but instead to find out which rights applied to the opposition in the House of Commons. He got what he wanted.[637] Indeed, during Josef Klaus' term of office, British-Austrian relations headed for a high point, which would remain unique in the history of bilateral relations: Federal President Jonas visited England in May 1966 at the invitation of Queen Elizabeth II and extended a return invitation, which the Queen paid in 1969. Beyond the niceties of diplomatic visits and commonplace bilateral contacts, there was no doubt one topic that engaged both the British and the Austrians. Both EFTA members sought a way to approach the EEC. And both must have been aware that they encountered resistance from French President Charles de Gaulle for different reasons. The British capitalised on French opposition, however, by making it clear that they, just like France, did not take any pleasure in a strengthening of the 'German' bloc in the EEC. This meant Austria, which was assigned on face value to the 'German bloc'. But as long as it could hide behind the French, London did not have to show its cards.

At the end of 1966, Klaus made a short trip to England. There was not much to be said. It was certainly not mentioned that British politicians and diplomats had played a decisive role in the drawing up of the most important documents on the organisation of post-war Austria. But perhaps by that time no one knew this any more. The fact that British diplomats in Vienna increasingly and at short intervals sent reports to London on the development of domestic affairs in Austria and were, in any case, very well informed could be concluded from the fact that the Foreign Office was outstandingly prepared on all issues. Nonetheless: the transformation from then to now could be best deduced from how extremely comprehensive the reports of the British ambassadors had been in the 1930s and above all during the period of occupation, and how thin the 'annual reviews' had now become. They now did not even comprise a tenth of what they had in the past. And this not only said something about the decreasing intensity of relations but also about how much importance Austria had lost for the British, above all since the end of the occupation period. The Austrians occasionally bought something or were at least interested in British products, for example military and civilian aircraft. Even in this area, however, there was very little to report in the late 1960s. And should Austria have hoped for support from Britain in the South Tyrol question, it was to be disappointed. It was England that had promised Italy the Brenner border in the Treaty of London from 1915, so that the 'Germanic hordes' – as they were termed by the

British throughout[638] – could not invade from the north again. And, of course, nothing would change in this respect.

Like with Britain, there was also no cause for concern regarding Austro-French relations. In cultural affairs and everyday bilateral business, everything was in order, and France signalised corresponding niceties. Austria could not expect the French to champion its efforts to approach the EEC. This may have had something to do with President de Gaulle knowing about the Soviets' strict rejection of the idea. Klaus had evidently supposed that the Soviet 'no' to an approach to the EEC would not be a definitive one. Eventually, the next French president, Georges Pompidou, was asked to intercede in Moscow. He was also unsuccessful. It is possible that he, like the successor of his successor, François Mitterand, was not all that inspired by the fear of a strengthening of the 'German bloc'. London 'hid' behind Paris; Paris 'hid' behind Moscow. The three shared the fear of an increasingly strong Germany, and little Austria felt the effects.

The government's activities in foreign policy were not limited, however, to signatories of the State Treaty. At least as important to the Chancellor, if not more so, was an intensification of contacts to Yugoslavia, Hungary and other states in the so-called Eastern bloc. The latter was a particular concern of his; more than that: it was a historical mission.[639] During a speech to the Council of Europe in 1965, he began with the observation: 'Civis Europeus sum' – I am a citizen of Europe. And when he employed the popular image of a 'House of Europe', he noted that one ought not to forget that this house also had an east wing.[640] And precisely this was sharply criticised by the 'Westerners' from both opposition parties, especially the SPÖ, but also from parts of his own party. He was accused of being 'susceptible to the East', engaging in 'attempts to ingratiate himself with Moscow's satellites', 'amateurism' and 'missionary zeal'.[641] Admittedly, zeal was not enough, for there were some fundamental issues in which the respective positions could scarcely be brought in line with each other. One of these deserves to be emphasised: Austria endeavoured to foster and develop its image of a bridgebuilder between East and West, also in the eyes of the West.[642]

An improvement of relations perhaps succeeded best in the case of Hungary. One hundred years after the Austro-Hungarian Compromise of 1867, which had led to the emergence of Austria-Hungary, Budapest could build on the former commonality on the occasion of a visit by the Federal Chancellor lasting several days. And this was far more than just an intensification of economic relations. Dealings with Yugoslavia were positively warm, whereby it would have been easy for both Tito and Klaus to ignore the question of the Slovenes in Carinthia. Tito was not interested in it.[643]

With regard to a normalisation of relations with Czechoslovakia, it was proprietary matters that constituted a nuisance factor, even if progress was made in negotiations on a property agreement. Austria was furthermore discomforted by a whole series of incidents at the Czech border, for Czech border guards repeatedly opened fire on people attempting to flee, above all in summer 1967. The shots were fired on to Austrian soil and led to formal protests. Only in the second half of the year did tensions ease. Nonetheless, relations with Czechoslovakia remained difficult, and it was not surprising that Austria followed with interest and a certain turbulence how the reform Communists under Alexander Dubček in Prague set about altering domestic conditions in the country, as well as its foreign relations. This was a cause for both hope and fear. The latter ultimately influenced the military planning of the Austrian Federal Army.

The Ministry of Defence was keen to establish new plans for military emergencies as soon as the non-coalition government was formed. The discontinuation of the Grand Coalition and governance only by the ÖVP had removed any consideration of the coalition partner to the extent that not only plans for crisis and neutrality scenarios but also for defence scenarios were now drawn up. In this way, nine comprehensive studies (named 'colour scenarios' after their markings) and corresponding directives emerged, which included all conceivable aspects, right down to questions of transport. Many things could be committed to paper, including a combined attack by Warsaw Pact states using nuclear weapons. The fact that, if the occasion arose, it would have been a classic case of 'asymmetrical warfare' was clear to everyone involved in the drawing up of such papers. Only the term had not yet been invented. Ultimately, everything boiled down to emergency planning. Theoretical vulnerability was an experience, however, that was not new but rather shared with half the world. In the Austrian case, politics with neighbouring states was supposed to make up for military efforts. If that succeeded, the foreign policy world of Josef Klaus would be in order. Indeed, for a period of two years, no crisis symptoms manifested themselves in this political field. This could not be claimed of domestic politics to the same degree.

'Power and Impotence in Austria'

Bruno Pittermann, president of the Socialist International and, as the British ambassador in Vienna, Sir Anthony Rumbold, noted, one of the last advocates of Austro-Marxism, gave birth in 1969 to a new catchphrase: 'Austro-Provincialism'.[644] He only wanted to apply it to the ÖVP but it annotated an entire nation. Decades later, Alexander Van der Bellen assigned the epitaph 'conservative provincialisation' to the years of the ÖVP government.[645]

Pittermann himself had meanwhile been put out to political pasture, and the SPÖ had obtained a new central figure in the form of Bruno Kreisky, who constituted a complete contrast to Klaus by virtue of his personality. Klaus came from a rural milieu, was strongly shaped by Catholicism, showed no affinity for the National Socialists, had been called up to the German Wehrmacht and had survived. After the war, he began a career as a lawyer, then answered the call of politics, became state governor of Salzburg in 1949, then switched to politics at federal level but always regarded his political career as only temporary. He remained bourgeois by nature and correct to the point of pettiness.[646] He made no secret of belonging to the Catholic student association 'Norica' and maintained contact with numerous Christian Socials as well as monarchist circles abroad.[647] Klaus had a sense of mission and, like Bruno Kreisky, stood for public office 'with a reformist aspiration to which the entire political work had to be subordinated', as the general director of radio and television (now the ORF), Gerd Bacher, who had been appointed by Klaus, formulated it decades later.[648] He had a pronounced awareness for the constitution and the rule of law. Politics also had to take a back seat to this. Klaus was sensitive and retreated into himself when he felt unfairly treated. And he was also indecisive, though no one would have guessed this initially.[649]

Bruno Kreisky came from a middle-, or, rather, upper-class Jewish family, was agnostic, had become involved in politics at a very early age and was a declared opponent of the Corporative State. After a short period of imprisonment, he succeeded in 1938, with some difficulty, in leaving Austria for Swedish exile. He championed a new Austria and, following his return, became deputy chief of staff to Federal President Theodor Körner. Eventually, he replaced Bruno Pittermann as party chairman of the SPÖ. Despite being a native of Vienna, he was denied a seat in the Viennese National Council. He stood on the Lower Austrian list. For Kreisky, politics was the art of the possible. He was not accustomed to subordination.

The fact that a renewal of personal was also needed in the SPÖ had been clear after the election disaster of 1966. To use a boxing term, Bruno Pittermann was down for the count. His political opponent, Franz Olah, sat in parliament as a National Council delegate for the Democratic Progressive Party (DFP), which he had founded. The SPÖ, however, had no option but to start searching for a new party chairman as soon as possible. The favourite was the last interior minister of the Grand Coalition, Hans Czettel. But he had a challenger, namely the last foreign minister of the coalition, Bruno Kreisky. Perhaps he was merely flirting with a defeat in the vote when he claimed on the way to the SPÖ party congress in St. Pölten that it was out of the question that he, a Jew, would be elected. But the opposite was the case: Kreisky obtained a convincing two-thirds majority. He was evidently not content to remain in the opposition; there had to be more. Kreisky, who was no newcomer to politics and also knew the internal dynamics of political decision-making, began to consistently adopt opposing positions. From the outset, the parliamentary interplay on the model of Western democratic rules also functioned well, and it was personified by the contrasting pair of Josef Klaus and Bruno Kreisky.

After a year of non-coalition government at the latest, Josef Klaus had to acknowledge that the difficulties had gained the upper hand and an ever-stronger wind was blowing his way from the direction of his own party. It was not for nothing that he gave his memoirs the highly associative title 'Power and Impotence in Austria' *(Macht und Ohnmacht in Österreich)*. 'It was not a brilliant year for Austria', as the British Ambassador summarised events in his report on 1967, thereby indirectly contradicting his German counterpart Löns.[650] The non-coalition government, he continued, had not achieved anything that might make it appear as the beneficiary of the new form of governance. Admittedly, he claimed, no real mistakes had been made but also no progress. The head of government was an honourable man but he lacked the necessary assertiveness, while his colleagues were mediocre and in fact unsuited to govern a modern, industrial state. The only politician of international standing was the leader of the opposition, Dr Kreisky. Klaus, however, had the problem that he was restrained whenever he wanted to reform something. Only a few months after forming the non-coalition government, he already foundered on his general secretary and the regional party leaders. The lethargic way in which the government pursued reforms had been reflected in the bitter losses in the elections of autumn 1967. And it was unclear where things would go from there. There were, the British Ambassador concluded, no prospects.

The contents of the British Ambassador's report to London were not plucked out of thin air. But he saw only the results of a political system that was not yet entirely familiar to him, as he had only taken up his post in Vienna in 1967.

However, the Chancellor did indeed have more than one problem. The desires of most cabinet ministers were regularly blocked by the Federal Chancellor. He repeatedly argued that it was necessary to economise. Incurring debts was anathema to the farmer's son Josef Klaus, who came from a humble background and was accustomed only to managing his own money. As, however, additional financial requirements – which would increase the financial debt of the federal state to 30 billion schillings – were necessary for the maintenance of full employment and the consolidation of investments, Minister of Finance Wolfgang Schmitz declared that this had to be compensated for with a shortfall in receipts and supplementary funds by means of no doubt unpopular measures. Both touched on taboos. And the government's tax and financial policies of course provided the opposition with a fantastic target. Election defeats were unavoidable. Eventually, the ÖVP's loss of votes in elections to the regional diet in Upper Austria in October 1967 was, at 3.6 per cent, sufficient to not only result in a demand for a government shake-up but also led to voices being raised to the effect that the Chancellor should vacate the field. The leaders of all three ÖVP associations, the Workers' and Employees' Association (Alfred Maleta), the Economic Association (Rudolf Sallinger), and the Farmers' Union (Josef Wallner), pushed for Klaus' replacement. He had no intention of giving in, however, and he saw the criticism less as an expression of doubt regarding his own leadership abilities and more as evidence that some members of his government team were not delivering what could justifiably be expected of them. As a result, Klaus planned a major cabinet reshuffle for 1968, which would literally leave no stone unturned. He brought General Secretary Hermann Withalm into the government as deputy chancellor, ended the unfortunate collaboration with the previous deputy chancellor and minister of trade, Fritz Bock, and instead fetched Otto Mitterer, a member of the Economic Chamber. Wolfgang Schmitz was replaced as finance minister by Stephan Koren. The pro-European federal minister for foreign affairs, Lujo Tončić-Sorinj, who had gradually lost ever more authority, had to make way for the far more assimilated Kurt Waldheim. Finally, a new permanent secretary, Karl Pisa, was to restructure information activities. Klaus would have preferred the editor-in-chief of the *Kurier* newspaper, Hugo Portisch, but he refused.[651]

Klaus wanted to unite a cabinet of 'unity and strength' under his leadership and did not grow tired of describing the successes of the first two years of his chancellorship. Who else aside from the government led by him, he asked, could have succeeded in two years in reforming the property market, reorganising the administration of state-owned industry, carrying out the promised reform of radio broadcasting, reforming wage and income tax, increasing funding for research and carrying out a reform of university studies? The answer was supposed to be self-evident. However, these reforms were in part only small steps and not far-reaching changes. In the end, more attention was gained by that which the new finance minister announced on 2 February 1968 with his 'budget policy bombshell', the Koren Plan.[652] There were mutterings of displeasure. That which Klaus and Stephan Koren did with their measures for consolidating the budget was no doubt honest and also praised in hindsight, but it did not contribute to making the government more popular. It was not a question of eliminating the predicted budget deficit but of at least reducing the looming minus by half. Koren warned of the danger of abandoning the stability of the schilling and announced tax raises and budget cuts. The ten per cent surcharge on car and alcohol tax, limited to two years, was considered especially burdensome. Shortly thereafter, Koren initiated a soft currency policy and abandoned the attachment of the schilling to the upgraded German mark. In this way, it was intended that Austrian goods would better be able to hold their own on the global markets. All these reform steps of the first weeks of the new year, 1968, were dressed up in the favourite expression of the Chancellor, namely the 'politics of dispassion' *(Politik der Sachlichkeit)*.

As was to be expected, the public, independent newspapers and above all the opposition reacted with fierce criticism. Klaus was sensitive enough to now suggest he might also resign and was prepared to hand the reins over to the next generation. Perhaps he had been overinterpreted but the indication that the Chancellor might leave politics not only stoked speculation but was also grist to the mill for his political rivals. Above all the SPÖ played its trump cards.

Like Klaus, Kreisky naturally had a series of topics he felt strongly about. And he openly focussed on the same topics that Klaus had identified. This was unproblematic when it came to domestic events and, above all, socio-political concerns. In terms of foreign policy, Kreisky had to be content to comment on the government's plans.

South Tyrol

In 1966, Klaus and Kreisky had cooperated regarding South Tyrol. The Chancellor had largely left his Foreign Minister a free hand, and in early 1965 it appeared that a solution was close at hand. The Italian and Austrian foreign ministers, Saragat and Kreisky, had, they believed, already reached extensive agreement on issues relating to South Tyrolean autonomy and the international anchoring of a South Tyrol package when cold water was poured on their plans: representatives of South Tyrol and North Tyrol rejected the result of the confidential compromise. Klaus and, above all, Minister Tončić-Sorinj took up the reins again after the change of government. Once again, secret – or, at least, non-public – discussions were to take place, though before they could start a bomb exploded at the Pfitscherjoch in the Upper Ziller Valley and killed an Italian customs officer. The talks nonetheless continued but without achieving any substantial progress. In August 1966, however, bomb attacks once more took place. The South Tyrol negotiations nonetheless went ahead and the agreement was eventually approved by the South Tyrolean People's Party, subject to a better international anchoring of the proposed solution. But the terror increased and the opponents of a compromise appeared in public. In Vienna, the offices of Alitalia were blown up. Klaus and Tončić fiercely condemned the violence. The architect of the attacks, Norbert Burger, and 14 South Tyrol activists were put on trial. As the defendants were acquitted, Burger made no secret of his intention to continue using violence and, eventually, four Italians died in June 1967 in a bomb attack on a power pylon on the Porzescharte near Obertilliach,[653] there was outrage in Italy. The government in Rome reacted by vetoing Austria's attempts at integration and halting negotiations on an association treaty with the EEC. For a short time, a visa requirement was even reintroduced at the Austrian border. The government was confronted with a shambles. Not only had the South Tyrol negotiations – at least temporarily – ended in nothing; the approach to the EEC had also failed for the time being. In a Europe that increasingly regarded itself as a blueprint for lasting peace, Austria was out of the ordinary in that certain circles evidently did not rule out the use of violence as a political tool. Klaus, however, stuck to his guns and firmly rejected violence. Tončić was fiercely attacked and later complained that the Federal Chancellor had not sufficiently supported him or come to his defence. The South Tyrol issue was naturally also a subject for the Chancellor.

In order to take countermeasures, the government resolved to request assistance from the forces of the Federal Army at the Italo-Austrian border, to the displeasure of the general inspector of troops, Erwin Fussenegger, who regarded the sufficient protection of the borders of the Republic as a task for the Gendarmerie and the customs officials. He was furthermore of the not unreasonable opinion that the army should not be deployed to assist in political issues, as it had been during the First Republic. Ultimately, it was vital that a signal was sent to Italy that Austria would do anything to fight terrorism. However, opinions diverged on the matter. Advocates of the acts of terror regarded them as an effective means to force Italy not only to fulfil the Gruber – De Gasperi Agreement but also to accommodate the further development of international law. Bruno Kreisky was likewise not disinclined to regard terror without bloodshed as a legitimate tool in the South Tyrol matter. It was possible to argue conversely, however, that this had delayed a potential earlier settlement and lastingly damaged relations between Austria and Italy. But he had to act. Until late October 1967, three battalions of the Federal Army were deployed on the Italian border. Thereafter, the securing of the border again became a matter for the Gendarmerie and the customs officials. One thing had become clear: the terror, as it repeatedly flared up between 1960 and 1967, and, likewise, the Italian counterterror, the demolition of the Andreas Hofer monument in Innsbruck and attacks in the Ebensee region led to an intensification of attempts to find a solution.[654] Tončić was able to resume negotiations with Italy in late autumn 1967 and ultimately proposed a road map for a declaration to end the dispute, which was accepted by the South Tyroleans and the government in Rome. The successful conclusion of the South Tyrol negotiations could no doubt be seen as a success for Austrian foreign policy and an expression of a mindset focussed on accommodation. Ten years later, Austria even offered the South Tyrol model as an approach to solving the Middle East conflict.

Tončić had to leave the conclusion of negotiations and the parliamentary handling of the agreement to his successor, Austria's ambassador to the UN, Kurt Waldheim, who switched to Vienna as foreign minister on the occasion of the cabinet reshuffle in 1968. He returned to a country in which it was simmering.

The revolt of a predominantly young generation did not originate in Austria but rather in Vietnam, the USA and, above all, France. But the student protests that had become a sort of global phenomenon also spread to Austria. Initially, Austrians followed events in France, where the government of Charles de Gaulle was almost toppled, and in Germany with a mixture of horror and fascination. There, the activism of 'fashionable demos' led to violent acts, during which the Austrian lyricist Erich Fried could be seen marching with motorcycle helmet and clenched fist alongside Gaston Salvatore and Rudi Dutschke, surrounded by communist banners.[655] The picture in Austria also gradually transformed. Above all in Vienna, the impression arose that an offshoot of the West German anarchist movement had also reached Austria. It was initially a question of student conditions. As early as 24 October 1967, 4,000 students and professors marched down Vienna's Ringstraße and demonstrated against the plight of the universities. Shortly thereafter, very different topics mixed with the demonstrations. People met at the State Opera House to disturb the opera ball and demonstrate against the Shah of Iran, Reza Pahlevi. Demonstrations then addressed the freedom of the press and questions of sexuality. The occasion for this was the three-month sales ban of the magazine *Der Spiegel*, which was also widely read in Austria. Two photos inside showing two bare-breasted girls, and not a depiction of the kind of 'perverse orgy' that took place at the University of Vienna, had led to an intervention by the public prosecutor.[656] The distribution of the magazine was prohibited with the argument that the publication was suited to having a 'harmful effect on the moral, mental and healthy development of adolescents, especially by stimulating the lustfulness and misdirection of their sexual appetite'. This was grist to the mill of a generation in revolt.

Adolescents made it clear that the era of reconstruction was coming to an end, that the 'times of plenty' were over and that 'the joys of the consumer culture' were already regarded as 'vapid'. A new left despised the establishment.[657] They questioned not only traditional Marxism but also values or concepts that were seen as traditional, such as 'homeland', 'fatherland', 'honour' and 'loyalty'. Those who were later referred to as the 'generation of '68' rebelled against narrow moral concepts and accused the older generation of having lost touch with the youth. The papal encyclical 'Humanae vitae' of July 1968 regarding birth control and the sales ban on the *Spiegel* seemed to be outdated. Although things revolved time and again around the war (in Vietnam), there was ultimately no trace of pacifism. Militancy was the order of the day. Even extremely conservative students and adolescents demonstrated in the streets chanting the name of the Communist leader of the North Vietnamese, 'Ho, Ho Chi Minh', were not referring, however, to the leader of North Vietnam's government, who had first led his country into a war against France and then against the USA, but the Western-capitalist system in general that should be fought. Austria suffered increasingly from an emigration of the young intelligentsia, who were veritably siphoned off, above all by the USA.[658] But the American dream of the 1940s and 1950s was over. And there was so much that was worthy of criticism.

In Austria, too, the exchange of generations was well underway and the members of the war generation of the Second World War were called into question. They were seen not least as Cold War warriors and certainly as members of a generation that regarded its moral concepts as absolute and overlooked its role after the Anschluss of Austria by the German Reich and its involvement in the Second World War. The question of resistance to National Socialism combined with other questions, including those relating to modern forms of resistance, the Easter march movement of the opponents of nuclear weapons and, above all, the demonstrations against American involvement in Vietnam. There was talk of consumerism terror, Theodor W. Adorno was quoted and Herbert Marcuse was read with reference to the 'Frankfurt School', and the 'manipulation of humans in late capitalism' as well as the 'the alienation of the individual' were discussed. So many things no longer corresponded to the traditional ideals; a critique of materialism was no longer sufficient when directed at aspects of life in which the post-war generation of reconstruction believed it had rendered a presentable, lasting service. It no longer applied. The consumerism frenzy, the dramatically increasing motorisation and the social constraints led to this criticism becoming ever louder and to historical questions also being addressed. Friedrich Torberg's *Hier bin ich, mein Vater* (Here I am, my father), Ernst Lothar's *Der Engel mit der Posaune* (The angel with the trombone) and others who dealt with National Socialism had admittedly shocked but not provided any answers to the question of 'why?' A generation of young writers and poets contributed to the emergence of a different world view, regardless of whether it was Thomas Bernhard, Peter Handke, Barbara Frischmuth, Ilse Aichinger, Wolfgang Bauer or Peter Turrini who positively dominated the German book market for a time: they all expressed that it was time to think in new dimensions and to let these dimensions flow into society, economics and politics. The latter in particular was intended to create the necessary conditions.

Josef Klaus may have been the ideal head of government for several of the guiding principles of political action demanded, for the insights of natural science, especially cybernetics, or for new philosophical ways of thinking. He occupied himself intensively with philosophy, the predictability of the future, nuclear research, space travel and empirical social research. He showed an interest in the founding of the Club of Rome and discussed limits of growth, even if this was not an issue that was 'fit for the masses'. It was a private affair and a way of expanding his horizons. Klaus also took time to think about things. Only a few days after his election victory in March 1966, he had withdrawn for three days, in order to come to terms with himself.[659] But he was unable to make it clear that he was intensely interested in the trends of the time and, above all, would have been prepared to unreservedly contribute to the start of a new era.

Perhaps Josef Klaus would have nonetheless achieved broad acceptance if he had not been accused of a lack of expertise in solving problems and of several other traits that had more to do with his character than with political strategy. Klaus suffered from the fact that he took action against breaches of trust and corruption regardless of the standing of the person involved and did not even spare prominent members of his own party. As early as October 1966, he had 21 managers of firms and several senior civil servants arrested who had enriched themselves during the construction of the A1 motorway, including a head of department from the Ministry of Trade. The scandal had become known because in the harsh winter of 1965/66 entire sections of road had been damaged by heavy frost. The construction work under the surface had not been solid, though a lot of money had been pocketed. The arrests continued. Public servants at federal, state and municipal level had received payoffs and been involved in price fixing and the manipulation of offers. The Federal Chancellor reported in the plenum of the National Council that investigations were underway against around 100 construction firms, according to a report of the public prosecutor in Innsbruck. There had been 63 house searches. The circle of suspects was so big that it was not possible to investigate all of them simultaneously.

One question that was not posed in the National Council but otherwise very openly was: Why had the scandal only surfaced in 1966? Why had Klaus not dealt discretely with the matter instead of tasking the public prosecutor with investigations? The German embassy reported to Bonn that the citizens would have remained silent, which was down to the mentality of the Austrians. Vienna was not a city 'in which the plebs practice a revolt – no more than the country itself'.[660] It was clear that the image of the government had suffered considerably. As road construction during the period concerned was the responsibility of the Trade and Reconstruction Ministry under Fritz Bock, the question of ministerial culpability was posed as a matter of course. The Chancellor's aversion to his deputy chancellor received a considerable boost but Klaus reacted for the time being only by withdrawing Bock's authority for road construction and by installing Vinzenz Kotzina as a separate minister for buildings and engineering.

Perhaps Klaus could have expected that his approach to corruption without consideration for the people involved would be seen as being to his credit. But the nice guy effect did not take hold. The industrial sector, on whose goodwill and financial donations not least the ÖVP was dependent, punished the action against its clientele by reducing the flow of funds. In December of the same year, the general manager of the Lower Austrian energy company NEWAG and NIOGAS and deputy state governor of Lower Austria, Viktor Müllner, was arrested. He was accused by the Court of Audit of serious corruption. This was the second corruption scandal to jolt the ÖVP and its chancellor. Klaus could not help but demand a complete investigation, even if in the process a complete network came to light that had arisen in a big ÖVP biotope. This time, too, neither his party nor the voting public wanted to reward him for it.

The biggest challenge for the Chancellor in 1968 would admittedly not be in the realm of domestic politics but in connection with the intervention of Warsaw Pact troops in Czechoslovakia. This was a turning point to the extent that it ruined the contacts to the countries in the Soviet sphere of influence carefully established by Josef Klaus.

The Czech Crisis

While the student unrest in Paris and the war in Vietnam evoked some excitement in Austria and also encouraged a few imitators who then spoke of '15 minutes in May', that is, a very brief period of time, during which those in Austria could also imagine that a radical alteration of political and social conditions might be achieved, that which happened to the northern neighbour got under the skin. The uproar was tangible. And the shock about events in the northern neighbour can perhaps be seen as an explanation for why Austria's 'generation of '68' are perceived least of all as 'revolutionaries' and remained on the path of political virtue. This had nothing to do with approval of political conditions but simply a certain concern that events in Czechoslovakia might also have an impact on Austria. What if the Soviets, like in Hungary in 1956, were to re-establish an order agreeable to them by means of a military intervention? What if, furthermore, the Soviets were looking for an excuse to invade Austria, too? Nothing ever suggested this might be the case but who wanted to be accused of not having demonstrated sufficient concern?

Despite neutrality and détente, the Austrians were gripped to the marrow by the Hungarian Revolution of 1956. Admittedly, nothing had happened, but it was not clear why nothing had happened or whether something might not happen the next time. For the military authorities, potential acts of aggression on the part of the Warsaw Pact provided the scenario for most operational plans. They were full of dark premonitions! Oddly enough, Czechoslovakia played for a long time only a minor role. Hungary was regarded as the spearhead of the Warsaw Pact, whereas it was said of the northern neighbour: 'An act of aggression by the ČSSR alone is regarded as unlikely, though possible ....'

Then several years passed. And the Czechs continued to be perceived as unfriendly but ultimately less harmful neighbours than the Hungarians. The reason for this was clear: a Soviet army was stationed in Hungary, while there were no Soviet troops in Czechoslovakia. The first signs that the Soviets did not trust the Czechs and wanted to station troops in Czechoslovakia emerged after the 'Vltava' manoeuvre in 1966. In fact, the Czechs did not give the Soviets any reason to do this. They never made any systematic attempts to question their role as part of the Eastern military alliance. They tolerated a large manoeuvre and a staff command post exercise, knowing full well that they were the opposing party. The political leadership was unwaveringly committed to communism and nonetheless began to restructure the political system. The Soviet state and party leaders, Leonid Brezhnev, mistrusted all assurances of continued loyalty to the Soviet bloc made repeatedly by the Czechoslovak party and government head, Dubček. Brezhnev himself was subjected to the growing pressure of the Soviet military leadership. Dubček promised to rescind reforms but nothing happened. In accordance with the motto 'nip it in the bud', the Soviets struck. They did not even try to gloss over anything. On 21 August 1968, Warsaw Pact troops marched into Czechoslovakia. The justification was similar to comparable actions, not least Germany's invasion of Austria: they were merely responding to a request for help, in order to come to the aid of the sister people of the Czechs and Slovaks. It was claimed that units of the National People's Army of East Germany were among the invading troop contingents, until it was clarified in 1990 – to the amazement of the Czechoslovaks and even the East Germans – that this had been deliberate disinformation and that no East German units had participated in the invasion of the ČSSR.

Austria had been prepared for an invasion of the ČSSR by Warsaw Pact troops. As early as spring and summer 1968, the fear grew that the events witnessed in Hungary in 1956 might be repeated in Czechoslovakia. This ultimately led to the general inspector of troops in the Federal Army, Erwin Fussenegger, preparing an order regarding the deployment of the army for securing the border with Czechoslovakia. The security mission to be triggered by the codename 'bedrock' (Urgestein) had the purpose of securing the 'northern border with the focus on the border crossing points', 'to occupy the border crossings and monitor the territory in between via patrols'. Should difficulties arise while securing the borders, it was intended 'to carry out a consolidation of border surveillance by adding additional units'. When the invasion actually occurred, the order was useless, because the Austrian federal government demanded a completely different security deployment to the one intended.

On 21 August, the Federal Chancellor was in his house in Wolfpassing near Tulln and was fetched to Vienna by his secretary, Thomas Klestil, shortly after four o'clock in the morning. Minister of Defence Prader did not have a telephone and had to be brought from his cabin on Lake Erlauf to Lunz am See by a Gendarmerie official, in order to use the telephone. Hectic deliberations began at six o'clock. Four members of the SPÖ executive committee requested the same morning that the National Defence Council be convened. The Federal Army had been alerted but not yet received any marching orders. A stream of refugees was expected. On the early afternoon, that is, after a considerable response time, measures were discussed during an extraordinary cabinet meeting. Minister of Defence Prader wanted to deploy the Federal Army in order 'to defend the borders of the Republic'. Foreign Minister Waldheim advised against any extreme measures and stated: 'It would be dangerous for our small country if we adopted a provocative tone in our declaration. ... From a military point of view, it is in my opinion best to not work too conspicuously or undertake any major troop movements near the border, for Moscow would regard that as too drastic.'[661] The Chancellor decided that there was no necessity to deploy the Federal Army to secure the border. Thus, only the large military formations were placed on alert and several units transferred to the Weinviertel, the Waldviertel and the Mühlviertel in order 'to strengthen the garrison areas north of the Danube'. As even Minister of Defence Prader was evidently not aware of the military dubiousness of this measure, it was carried out. The quintessence of this 'long day's journey into night' was that the military reaction was only very weak and everything was focussed on securing humanitarian aid and reassuring the Austrian people.[662]

Politicians, senior military officers and civil servants attempted to return from their holiday resorts as quickly as possible. Even the Austrian envoy in Czechoslovakia, Rudolf Kirchschläger, came from Yugoslavia, received final instructions from Minister Waldheim and travelled to Prague. There, he received a directive from Interior Minister Soronics the next day to discontinue the issuing of visas for Czechs, as the rumour was circulating that visa forms had fallen into the hands of the Soviets on a large scale and were being used to smuggle secret service agents into Austria. Kirchschläger objected, informed the Foreign Minister and was empowered to resume issuing visas.[663] It had been a storm in a teacup.

In Vienna, agreement was being reached on 22 August regarding a suitable reaction to the invasion of Czechoslovakia. It seemed most sensible to refer to the 'preceding act' from 1956, namely the note that had been sent to the Soviet Union at the time, which had appealed for an avoidance of bloodshed. This time, however, the text resolved on by the Council of Ministers did not contain any of the harsher formulations and it remained very noncommittal.[664]

Klaus informed Kreisky, who had also only just arrived from his holiday and later strongly criticised the inclusion of the opposition in the crisis management as well as the measures of the Federal Army. Five years later, on the occasion of an attack by Palestinians on Jewish emigrants in Marchegg, the tables were turned and the ÖVP criticised Kreisky because they had not been included in the decision-making process. Kreisky responded by saying that in Austria no one governed except the government and one could only talk if there was time and it could be expected that there would 'be a useful contribution'.[665]

Klaus also 'forgot' the opposition, however, when it came to ensuring the state's ability to act in the event of a lightning occupation of Vienna. During the course of the Warsaw Pact's invasion of Czechoslovakia, namely, a situation emerged in which the fear prevailed among the policymakers that Austria, or at least the east of the country, might be in danger, and the Federal Chancellor decided that several members of the federal government, above all the Deputy Chancellor, would remain outside of Vienna in order to ensure, if necessary, the state's ability to act without a complete evacuation of the federal government from Vienna. The opposition had to decide for itself. And the Federal Chancellor would in any case be in his summer residence in Mürzsteg.

The fear had arisen because a Czech secret service officer had combined his jump to the West with disinformation on a massive scale. He claimed to know for certain that the Soviets would invade Austria on the weekend of 7–9 September 1968. The information was systematically spread by Western secret services in Austria and was the reason for the most major instance of placing the Federal Army on alert. Many a person back then would not have bet a single schilling that Austria would emerge unscathed. They were smarter in hindsight. Furthermore, a final problem, as it were, had emerged. The best trained conscripts were to be disarmed on 12 September. Minister Prader addressed the problem in the Council of Ministers and applied for the disarmament date to be postponed by 14 days. The minister of education, Theodor Piffl-Perčević, and the Permanent Secretary for Information Karl Pisa advocated a deferral of four weeks. Foreign Minister Waldheim disagreed this time, too: 'I regard such a measure as unnecessary as regards foreign policy. If we do that, then only on the grounds that the Federal Army would not be operational in a crisis situation.'[666] As Bruno Kreisky also agreed to a onetime extension, however, the disarmament date was postponed to late October.

A comparison of the years 1956 and 1968 turns out clearly in favour of the former – however absurd that might sound. In 1956, Austria was still more or less unprotected; in 1968, it could claim a certain military potential. In 1956, Austria had acted in the tradition of the occupation period and dabbled in policies of neutrality; in 1968, there was an assured knowledge of possibilities and scope for action in perpetual neutrality. In 1956, the beginnings of a stream of refugees forced Austria to improvise; in 1968, preparations were made for a mass rush of refugees – but they did not come. There was a considerable number of Czechs and Slovaks, however, who had legally emigrated before 21 August 1968, because they had received passports and Austrian visas. Around 60,000 had gone on holiday somewhere to the south. When they heard about events in their homeland, most of them wanted to wait and see how the situation would develop. As Hungary refused the Czechoslovaks passage to their homeland, the vast majority of them gathered in Austria. But they did not flee, though they also did not want to register themselves as refugees and apply for asylum. Most of them found accommodation with relatives and friends, and only a small number of the 93,635 Czechoslovaks who would eventually arrive in Austria then decided to remain indefinitely. They comprised 1,547 people.[667] The quarters that had been created for refugees as a precaution remained empty.

In spite of the mild outcome of the Czech crisis for Austria, political aftershocks were nonetheless inevitable. The members of Klaus' government emphasised time and again that they had done everything correctly and in a timely fashion. They claimed to have remained calm and consistent. The deployment of the Federal Army had gone optimally; one could not have expected more. And there had been no war. In response, the SPÖ and Bruno Kreisky felt they had to accuse the Federal Army of pursuing a single concept, namely evacuating eastern Austria as quickly as possible, if need be, and withdrawing to the west in search of support from NATO. The accusation was unreasonable but, of course, Kreisky could not possibly know which measures the government and the Federal Army would have taken in the event of one of the 'colour scenarios' being triggered. No one could.

Although nothing had in fact happened and Austro-Soviet relations were not lastingly tarnished, either, a stale aftertaste nonetheless remained, to say the least. For Austria, at least theoretically, the potential threat had become greater, for the Soviets' invasion of Czechoslovakia had more than compensated for their withdrawal from Austria in 1955. Ultimately, the number of Soviet troops stationed in the ČSSR came to 75,000 soldiers with 1,220 tanks, 2,500 combat vehicles, 76 aircraft and 146 helicopters. Later, a brigade was added, which was capable of launching nuclear weapons.[668] Even if an immediate threat to Austria cannot be deduced from this, because the troops of group 'Centre' must have unsettled, first and foremost, West Germany and NATO, it was not possible to simply resume business as usual. It had to be kept in mind, not least, that the American government – unlike in 1956 – had initially declined to issue a statement to the effect that a violation of Austrian sovereignty and territorial integrity would bring the USA on to the scene. Evidently, Austria was expected to cope with the 'crisis situation' itself. Only two months after the invasion of Warsaw Pact troops, American Secretary of State Dean Rusk let it be known that the USA might feel called upon to take action if Soviet troops were to advance to Yugoslavia via Austria. However, when Rusk – on the occasion of a NATO conference in Brussels in mid-November 1968 – stressed the willingness of the USA to support Austria, if necessary, the Austrian government was forced to react. As well-intentioned as the remarks of the Secretary of State might have been, Foreign Minister Waldheim let it be known that Austria had to insist that it not receive any unilateral pledges of aid.[669]

Taking Stock of the Politics of Dispassion

The feeling of having to manage without external assistance could also be thoroughly unsettling. Bruno Kreisky, who had dealt with issues relating to national defence for years and in numerous seminars as foreign minister before 1966, drew the consequence from the Czech crisis, which he regarded as a crisis of Austrian national defence: he wanted to undertake a root-and-branch reform of the Federal Army and arranged for the former permanent secretary in the Ministry of Defence, Otto Rösch, to submit his concept for a transformation of the Federal Army into a militia army and for the reduction of the period of military service. As a result, the slogan 'six months are enough' emerged during the election campaign of 1970.

Klaus noticed, of course, that he was about to lose the support of his party and among the public, which had in any case rarely been certain. The imminent elections to the National Council occupied him, therefore, to an unusual degree. As early as 22 August 1968, he appeared to be preoccupied more with issues relating to the future budget than with events among neighbouring countries. He repeatedly made entries in his notorious notebook of anything that he thought worthy of consideration or fit for the future, especially when it came to scientific research, innovation, administrative reform, freedom and democracy. The list of positive aspects should have been impressive and it was also acknowledged by foreign representatives in Vienna: the economic output of the country rose by between 5.5 and six per cent in 1969. Industrial production alone had risen by eleven per cent. Exports increased by 15 per cent; wages rose quicker than prices; and pensions had been raised by five per cent. During the decade from 1960 to 1970, the 'Klaus years' in the broadest sense, politics had created conditions that made Austria very attractive. Growing affluence could be seen, for instance, in the increase in the number of motor cars. Their number had climbed from around 400,000 to 900,000. Motorways and roads had been built. The A1 motorway was regarded as finished in 1967. In Styria and Carinthia, the first sections of the A2 motorway were completed. Talks with the EEC at least showed signs of progressing. A whole series of younger politicians had begun to replace the first post-war generation of politicians, and it was expected that a man like Alois Mock, who was only 35 years old, might one day become federal chancellor. Foreign Minister Waldheim had not only brought the South Tyrol negotiations to a satisfactory conclusion but also very discretely conveyed the Warsaw Pact's interest in conducting a conference on security and cooperation in Europe. Waldheim furthermore positioned himself as a potential successor to UN Secretary General U Thant. Talks between the Americans and the Soviets on the reduction of strategic weapons had been arranged for April 1970. The image of the country could not have been better.

However, Klaus noted not only the successes but also those things that had not yet been done: an extension of the legislative period from four to five years, limited-term mandates for parliamentary delegates and postal voting.[670] The reform of criminal law had fallen by the wayside, the reform of university studies remained a torso and the Federal Army was a problem zone. Klaus arranged for the publication of a brochure that, under the title 'Success for Austria', was designed to demonstrate the fulfilment of points in his government policy statement.[671] Indeed, much had happened: there had been a juvenescence not least in the Chancellor's party, measures for administrative reform had been taken and there had been a modernisation drive. In 1970, there were around 500 computer systems in Austria, which was regarded as remarkable. In Seibersdorf, south of Vienna, a veritable atomic research institute emerged around the research reactor, which had gone into operation in 1960. In Vienna's Prater Park and in Graz, nuclear research was carried out by the universities.[672] In order to cover the electricity demand in the long term, two nuclear power plants were planned. The construction of one in Zwentendorf in Lower Austria was approved by the Council of Ministers on 11 November 1969. In 1967, the decision had also been made to accommodate the two UN organisations located in Vienna, the International Atomic Energy Agency (IAEA) and the Industrial Development Organisation (UNIDO), in a new complex in Vienna's Danube Park. Far more than the achievements, however, the opposition addressed the failure of the government in its attempt to break down established social structures. In 1964, the ÖVP had discovered the petition for a referendum as a political tool and made use of it. In 1969, it was the SPÖ that had initiated a petition for the reduction of working hours and the introduction of a 40-hour week. 890,000 registered voters had signed it. The ÖVP argued against a reduction and lost. A 43-hour week was resolved on. The SPÖ had achieved a sort of thematic leadership. The special taxes with which Klaus hoped to balance the budget were regarded as a plundering of the middle classes. Scandals had shaken the ÖVP. And the government repeatedly demonstrated a lack of unity. That was the problem!

During the campaign for the next National Council elections, a feeling of exhaustion spread within the Chancellor's party. They expected to lose their absolute majority, though they were confident of obtaining a relative one. Hardly anyone doubted it, not even the critical British Ambassador.[673] But the SPÖ of 1970 was no longer comparable with the SPÖ of 1966. Just as Klaus had done in his day, Bruno Kreisky created an advisory board described pithily as the best 1,400 brains; it was expected to find answers to all issues that were in any way relevant and make proposals for solutions. Perhaps the details of the results were less interesting than the circumstance that politics should begin to gain momentum again. Kreisky himself conveyed the image of a 'manager of a modern society'.[674] He certainly knew how to effectively make his positions clear and to emphasise the main points. Kreisky also did not want to make the same mistake as Pittermann. He, therefore, ruled out any cooperation with the Communists. Far more appealing, however, was the announcement that, in the event of a Socialist election victory, military service for those young men enlisted in the context of general conscription, around 40,000 a year, after all, would be reduced from nine to six months. The slogan 'six months is enough' was ultimately so popular that the ÖVP half-heartedly followed suit a few weeks before the election. But it was not credible. Male youth, first-time voters, felt more addressed by the SPÖ. This was not changed by the fact that Josef Klaus looked like the winner on points following the first television confrontation between the leading candidates of ÖVP and SPÖ.

The SPÖ obtained a relative majority at the elections to the National Council on 1 March 1970. It was not a single factor that had helped them achieve victory. There were many factors. Theoretically, ÖVP and FPÖ, the two losers, could have formed a little coalition. For Klaus, however, this was out of the question. He had already announced before the election that he did not intend to enter into a coalition government. In saying this, he had merely had a repetition of the Grand Coalition in mind. A little coalition was an experiment that he certainly had no intention of undertaking. A minority government seemed to him an absurd idea. 'He was not a political gambler.'[675]

Instead, he resolved on election night to withdraw from politics. He concluded his notes, which he had been making since 1949, a total of around 7,000 pages, with the for him characteristic concluding remark 'Deo Solis sit Gloria'.

What had been the Chancellor's party up to this point was now without a leader. And Kreisky did not give it a chance. On election night he already called the FPÖ party chairman, Friedrich Peter, and promised a reform of electoral law. He did not demand anything in return, though it was clear that Kreisky intended to form a minority government, for which he expected the support of the FPÖ. Peter understood this.

19 The Counter Narrative

19 Bruno Kreisky and members of the SPÖ minority government on their way from the Federal Chancellery for the inauguration ceremony in the Presidential Chancellery on 21 April 1970. On election night on 1 March, Kreisky had already been able to secure the support of the Freedom Party for a minority government and began to implement his first election goals – an electoral reform and the reform of the Federal Army – immediately after the swearing-in of his government. Other measures would follow. (Photo: IMAGNO / Votava)

Everything began more or less in the usual manner. Representatives of the two major parties, who still represented around 90 per cent of the voters, met for negotiations, only to realise after a few days that the respective standpoints were too far apart. The SPÖ wanted to realise its programme 1:1; the ÖVP likewise intended to force through its demands. As in 1962/63, there was a struggle for the distribution of power. Like in 1966, though this time with reversed omens, the ÖVP described the SPÖ's offer as unworthy of discussion. The negotiations failed on 20 April; Kreisky made certain once more of the temporally limited support of a minority government by the FPÖ and was eventually tasked by the Federal President with the formation of the same.

Let Kreisky and his team work

During the election campaign, Josef Klaus had been billed as a 'real Austrian', a statement that appeared to contain a very anti-Semitic tendency directed against Bruno Kreisky. And now the same Bruno Kreisky had become head of government. Austria had already had two chancellors who had been persecuted by the National Socialists: Figl and Gorbach. Now, for the first time in the history of the Republic, a Jew and agnostic became federal chancellor. However, this circumstance was noted more abroad than it was rated as a sensation in Austria. Kreisky's chancellorship would in any case be measured on the basis of events and not prejudices. Oddly enough, Kreisky was then characterised as the first Socialist head of government in the Second Republic,[676] which was nonsense because the Provisional State Government under Karl Renner was not taken into account. The ignoring of Renner was perhaps not a coincidence, however: the Anschluss opponent Kreisky had no sympathy for the Anschluss advocate Renner. Furthermore, he sought and found countless opportunities to draw attention to the path he, Kreisky, had personally taken. In his view, the roots of all Austrian evil were to be found in the interwar period, above all in the Corporative State. The low point was clearly the armed uprising of February 1934, which is generally characterised as a civil war. This was a traumatic experience that had shaped Kreisky far more than National Socialism and the Second World War. 'He abhorred the Christian Socials more than the Nazis', claimed Helene Maimann.[677] Accordingly, he vehemently set priorities when it came to the politics of addressing the past *(Vergangenheitspolitik)*. This corresponded to the opening of the archives, for which a ban of at least fifty years

still existed at the time. Resistance and persecution were topics that Kreisky only sporadically prioritised. With his own historicization of the years 1939 to 1945, he at
least did not provide any former members of the NSDAP or right-wing groups with a
target; it can be assumed that they would otherwise have delighted in taking a shot at
the Chancellor. An unexpected side-effect, however, was that it resulted in a backlog in
researching the Nazi period, people continued to be very content to take the view, like
Kreisky, that Austria had been the first victim of National Socialist aggression and, in
this way, indirectly paved the way for what then erupted as an unresolved past in the
mid-1980s under the catchword 'Waldheim'.

Kreisky's efforts to demonstrate no fear of contact with National Socialists and
members of the Wehrmacht was already clear in the case of the silent agreement with
Friedrich Peter. Kreisky may not have known it at the time, but Peter had been an officer in the Waffen SS and had made it his business not only to personally break with
the Nazi past and the war but also to lead his party – which still demonstrated a relatively strong affinity with the Nazi period – out of the right-wing corner. Peter wanted
to present it as a normal liberal party capable, above all, of forming coalitions. The next
time that Kreisky showed no fear of contact with the Nazi era was the appointment
of his first minister of agriculture, Johann Öllinger. He had also been an officer in the
Waffen SS. However, this was too much for his party and, above all, the media. Öllinger
was forced to resign two weeks later.

In April/May 1970, all European states and many outside Europe analysed the new
situation. London, for instance, assessed Kreisky's chances as relatively good. The British Ambassador in Vienna noticed that Kreisky had presented his government on the
symbolic day of 27 April 1970, the 25th anniversary of the formation of the first Austrian post-war government. This had also been the reason for the haste with which the
formation of the government had been concluded, according to Ambassador Wilkin-
son. From the first day on, it was noted that Kreisky kept the members of his government on a short leash. He spoke about anything and everything and developed in the
process an unflappability that allowed him to bypass factual questions and colleagues.
This could also be regarded as arrogance.[678]

In terms of foreign policy, no special innovations were expected, though by all means
a deepening of bilateral relations and a new quality thereof. Kreisky's close relations
with the Labour Party were a reason for this, according to London. Klaus had steered a
course towards Germany. He was well connected in decidedly conservative circles and
cultivated intensive contacts with them. This would change under Kreisky. This was
viewed with some concern in West Germany. What did it mean when Kreisky's foreign
minister, Rudolf Kirchschläger, floated the possibility of recognising East Germany and
did not rule out relations with the People's Republic of China? Clearly, a new direction
in foreign policy was looming.[679]

The new chancellor, who was not yet 'the old timer', dived head first into the business of governance. Kreisky had no doubt improved his image in domestic politics during his time as leader of the opposition. He knew that he did not have much time as the leader of a minority government. A concern of the Chancellor from the first day on and one used as a motto was the 'democratisation of all areas of life'. He wanted to change everyday life, to which end it was necessary to target, first of all, domestic policy objectives. Turbulent times were also ahead of him, as time would tell.

Two issues were paramount: the reform of electoral law promised by the SPÖ and the reduction of the military service period from nine to six months. Resistance to the former on the part of the ÖVP could be bypassed, for with the help of the FPÖ a small-scale reform of electoral law could be forced through, by means of which the number of delegates in the National Council was to be raised to 183 and the constituencies aligned with the nine federal states. Other matters were at stake in the case of the army reform. In fact, *more* was at stake, namely the oft-cited reduction of the vulnerability of state and society and, ultimately, the reorganisation of the Federal Army.

The catchphrase of six months was perfect. There was, naturally, much more to it, and the 'originator of the concept', Otto Rösch, had already committed it to paper in the early 1960s. At the time, it had not caused even the tiniest bit of outrage. 1970 would reveal what was behind it. At first glance, the matter looked very simple: the period of military service was to be reduced to six months. In addition, there would be a few weeks of review exercises and, in order that the soldiers were immediately deployable and sufficiently trained, there would be a standby force recruited from volunteers. The professional soldiers, above all the senior officers, were opposed to this. The whole thing, they claimed, was half-baked. As the majority of them supported the ÖVP, it was easy to dismiss them as party soldiers. But that was too easy. There was one thing that no one expected: Kreisky appointed a respected brigadier in the army, Johann Freihsler, to his cabinet as minister of defence and transferred responsibility for the army reform to him. After only a few weeks, a Federal Army Reform Commission was appointed, which included not only soldiers but also a series of civilian organisations, above all youth delegates. The target of six months remained unchanged. The work was intense, because there was doubtlessly much at stake. It was a question of whether Austria, on its own, would be capable of defending its neutrality with all means at its disposal, and do that convincingly and effectively. Thus, fundamental issues were at stake.

Kreisky intervened at regular intervals. He made reference to a 'hero' of his youth, the French socialist leader Jean Jaurès, who had been murdered in Paris in July 1914, and his ideas for a militia army, which – armed to the teeth – would act exclusively in a defensive capacity.[680] Senior officers promptly hastened to read Jaurès. It was intended that the reform be completed by the end of 1970 and that the reduction of the period of military service would come into effect as of 1 January 1971. The Minister-General

Freihsler threatened to be torn apart: as an officer, he was able to see the incomplete and thoroughly amateur aspects of the concept; as a minister, it was his job to implement the will of the head of government. He was neither physically nor mentally up to the task; he fell sick and was represented by the Chancellor. He brushed aside the opposition of the military leadership: generals, he claimed, were nothing more than uniformed civil servants of the two highest service classes, that is, they were bound by directives. The people dismissed in this way could not refuse their cooperation permanently. The respective standpoints drew nearer. A root-and-branch reform of the Federal Army took shape, even if it was clear that the army would have to be completely restructured and thus weakened for years to come. Kreisky was undeterred.

In order to silence the critics and emphasise the reasonableness of the path chosen, a 'moral rearmament' was initially pursued: a truism that can be regarded not least as the key to political success revealed itself to the military only with some delay: one does not expect to receive evidence of everything that is not possible but instead wants to know what *is* possible and how. Especially in view of the prevailing military impotence, the principle of nurturing hope applied on the threshold to the 1970s, even in affairs of national defence.

In fact, the discussion in the (first) Federal Army Reform Commission went far beyond the question of the period of service. For this reason, it cannot be denied that the dismissive reaction of the military professionals to the so-called Rösch Plan on a reduction of the service period had a positive impact. The concomitant circumstances, it must be said, were annoying. Kreisky suspended contact with the West German Bundeswehr and with Switzerland, which had been nurtured until then with differing intensity. In the first case, it was West Germany's membership in NATO that bothered him, and in the other it was Switzerland's aloofness in affairs of international security and what Kreisky then characterised as a policy of active neutrality. This was intended to signalise that Austria was beginning to take a path that amounted to military equidistance. A few weeks after the start of the army reform, operational plans in accordance with the colour scenarios were discontinued. On 25 June 1970, a 'top secret' directive stated: 'The Federal Army reform currently underway can have unforeseen consequences', which make it pointless to continue pursuing previous operational plans. 'Therefore, the reworking with the neutrality scenario north-south, security mission, will be scrapped.'[681] But how were things to proceed?

The oppositional front of officers soon began to crumble, for one thing because they became reconciled with the political terms of reference and then also because the commander of the National Defence Academy, Brigadier Emil Spannocchi, was able to demonstrate convincingly that he had begun to rethink things and did not think much of a continuation of the path taken so far. He was completely committed to a new concept.

Minister of Defence Freihsler declared his resignation in early February 1971 for health reasons. And Kreisky appointed the next general, Karl Lütgendorf, as minister. Kreisky would have preferred Hubert Wingelbauer, who had been persecuted for racial reasons during the Nazi era, but the ministerial office had rejected him. Lütgendorf, however, hastily and with a certain naivety, set about accelerating the army reform for resolution in parliament. Criticism from army circles was answered with the 'muzzle decree'. In response, 1,700 officers, around two thirds of all active officers, appealed directly to the Chancellor and presented their concerns about the future of the army in a veritable 'letter of rejection'. One of the key sentences read: 'The envisaged total service period of six months and less than 75 days of review exercises is insufficient to justify the deployment of Austrian citizens in the military defence of their country and to maintain the Reserve Army at the required size.'[682] It was of no avail.

It was a cause of lasting irritation, however, that the West German federal minister of defence, Helmut Schmidt, gave an interview on 5 March 1971 in which he made little effort to hide his criticism of the reduction in the period of military service in Austria and also addressed the expected costs for a standby force of 15,000 men. This came at an extremely inopportune moment for Kreisky, not only because of the already scheduled next election campaign but also because he feared Moscow's reaction.[683] It did not happen every day that a West German (Social Democrat) minister of defence interfered in internal Austrian affairs.

The FPÖ, which in army matters was far closer to the arguments of the ÖVP than those of the SPÖ, changed its spots and assisted in the passing of the military law, which was accompanied by an alternative to military service. Years later, in 1977, Kreisky then relented after all, arranged for the passing of an amendment to the military law and, with it, the upgrading of the standby force from a chimera to a quite presentable capacity of 15,000 men.

The FPÖ wanted to support Kreisky's minority government for as long as possible. It was the first time that the Freedom Party emerged from the political wilderness. Kreisky, however, was already speculating about an end to the cooperation. He had very visibly demonstrated that he knew how to get his own way, had little to fear in the way of internal party challenges and was also willing to address 'hot topics'. He was also not perturbed by the demonstrations against Minister Lütgendorf or that there was unrest among farmers. He had skilfully passed on the 'Old Maid' of the naysayers to the ÖVP. The consistency with which he followed his path was, furthermore, very impressive. When, after one-and-a-half years of minority government, he again scheduled elections to the National Council, which were designed to allow him to continue to pursue his policies, he did not risk much. A reduction in the period of military service had become reality; free transport for schoolchildren and schoolbooks free of charge were aimed at the poorer classes, though they ultimately benefitted all families with children. The

ÖVP provided a picture of disorientation and a dog-eat-dog struggle. The FPÖ were also in favour of new elections earlier rather than later, as they hoped to be able to enter a little coalition in the event of a relative majority for the SPÖ.

The re-election of Franz Jonas as federal president in April 1971 confirmed to Kreisky that he was at the peak of his popularity. With Kurt Waldheim, the ÖVP had fielded a far less attractive candidate than the incumbent Federal President. Nonetheless, the SPÖ did everything in order not to present the last foreign minister of the ÖVP non-coalition government as someone who had been successful in foreign affairs. Behind closed doors, rumours were circulated regarding Waldheim's wartime past, though without anyone showing much interest in them. On 10 October 1971, the SPÖ obtained an absolute majority in the elections to the National Council. Although there had been numerous shady tactical tricks in the run-up to the election, this result had been expected. Kreisky, who had dominated domestic politics since 1970, given his party the appearance of a left-liberal, cosmopolitan party and made it clear that he was not only willing to but also capable of breaking down established structures and moving forwards, was confronted by an ÖVP leadership that – after the only one-year interregnum of Hermann Withalm – again had a chairman in the form of Karl Schleinzer who was recognised but that ultimately did not make a unified impression and was always playing catch-up. The ÖVP and the FPÖ had to be content with their role in the opposition. The majority of the population had acquiesced with the SPÖ's election slogan 'Let Kreisky and his team work' and wanted – as Kreisky formulated it – to accompany him and the SPÖ on their 'journey'.

The formation of a government provided a few surprises and also showed Kreisky that he, like the ÖVP, would be well-advised to include representatives of the western federal states in his cabinet. There was one thing he did not succeed in, namely the integration of representatives of the ÖVP associations. His intention was very clear: Kreisky wanted to pry open the ÖVP and apply to political opponents, too, his adage of the journey to be taken jointly. What he did succeed in doing was – by means of skilful personnel politics – satisfying the wings within his party and securing the support of the trade unions by appointing the president of the Trade Union Federation, Anton Benya, as the first president of the National Council. Now he could return to pursuing policies with substance. It was no surprise that Kreisky regarded his beloved field of foreign policy as his own domain, despite the reappointment of Rudolf Kirchschläger. The functionaries of his party would have preferred to nail him down to issues of domestic and regional politics. Foreign policy was regarded as the Chancellor's 'hobby'.[684] But why should a federal chancellor not be permitted to ride his hobbyhorse, too?

Just as he had already established his own independent focal points in 1959 instead of waiting for someone else to do something and then responding, Kreisky also prescribed a topic in 1971: security. The Soviet Union had already in the mid-1950s begun to talk about a European security conference. Kreisky took this up again. There was surprise, above all in the West. Austria's approach to the governments of European states and the USA and the transmission of a memorandum on European security were characterised simply as 'naïve'. But perhaps there had been a misunderstanding. It had to at least be possible to talk about it. Thus, a first attempt was made. Foreign Minister Kirchschläger visited London in December 1971 and was supposed to meet with his counterpart there, Sir Alec Douglas-Home, on the occasion of an annual dinner of the Anglo-Austrian Society. Kirchschläger had been asked what he actually wanted to discuss in London. He responded by saying that it was important for him first of all to visit friends in the West after having done the same with many contacts in the East. He also wanted to discuss the now for some time pending issues of an association of Austria with the European Economic Community (EEC). A particularly important topic was also Kurt Waldheim's candidacy as UN secretary general. And then, of course, there was the question of security.

They were still feeling their way. Only in the case of support for Kurt Waldheim did things become more definite. And it looked good, just as had been the case during a visit of Kirchschläger in Paris. Waldheim was unanimously elected by the UN General Assembly on 22 December 1971. This could be regarded by all means as a major foreign policy triumph. But Austria's Chancellor wanted more, and a year later another expression was added to the initial assessments of his foreign policy and the word 'naïve': an evaluation of the British Foreign Office claimed that Kreisky was 'unpredictable'. According to this evaluation, he was beginning to pursue a more adventurous foreign policy. His scope for action was admittedly limited and left 'little room for extravagance', but it might catch the British unprepared. Several things had already made them prick up their ears. In late December 1971, Austria had assumed diplomatic relations with East Germany. The word 'recognition' had been skilfully avoided but it amounted to the same thing.[685] Austria had not restricted itself to speaking out in matters of European security but also championed a conference on security and cooperation, which was now on the verge of being realised. It was scheduled to take place in Helsinki. The Western states wanted to take part but they saw little or no sense in it and, therefore, could not understand Austria's enthusiasm. Austria had gone one step further in July 1970, however, by circulating a memorandum containing an invitation to a conference in Vienna on the reduction of conventional armed forces. NATO, which was bothered by the massive superiority of the Soviet Union in terms of conventional weapons, could do nothing but signalise its approval. The Soviet state and party leader, Leonid Brezhnev, followed suit in 1971. Vienna volunteered. The Conference on Security and Cooperation in Europe (CSCE) and the Mutual and Balanced Force Reductions (MBFR) on the reduction of conventional weapons were two parts of the same whole. Suddenly, however, the initiatives were no longer coming from the major powers but from the naive, unpredictable, small states – like Austria.

Gradually, those outside Austria also started to examine Kreisky more closely. He seemed to be omnipresent and left no doubt that he was of a mind to be heard in foreign policy matters. From 22 February to 2 March 1972, he decamped for a major European tour and sought to promote Austrian attempts to come to an arrangement with the EEC. He visited every state in the Economic Community, explained, talked, occasionally listened and simply wanted to move things forward. Despite the reservation with which he was met, above all in France, the Chancellor hoped to receive a first draft for an association treaty in June or July 1972.[686] In fact, an interim agreement was already reached in March.

'I am of the opinion'

In Austria, it was perhaps noted that things were happening in terms of security policy beyond the reduction in the period of military service. But it was not surprising that the focal points of the SPÖ government in other areas attracted more attention. The Chancellor had, after all, dedicated himself to social policy and above all welfare work. Reasonable economic growth and the willingness to increase Austria's national debt allowed for the funding of free transport for schoolchildren, schoolbooks free of charge, then the abolition of tuition fees, pension increases and higher family allowances. It was clear that this all cost money, a lot of money. Minister of Finance Hannes Androsch was tasked with procuring it by means of a tax reform and budgetary restructuring. The rest had to be borrowed.

But Kreisky was no doubt also willing to solve long-discussed problems and also did not shy away from addressing controversial topics. The absolute majority provided him with the opportunity to do this, and he wanted to take advantage of it. Unlike Josef Klaus, he gave the ministers – who were more or less handpicked by him – free rein to do this, without allowing the slightest doubt to arise that he was primus inter pares. There was, of course, occasional unrest but because the media, like the government, had moved slightly yet unmistakeably to the left, Kreisky could delight in largely unbroken sympathy. A contributory factor here was his own typical style of arranging a press foyer after cabinet meetings, engaging in question and answer sessions, accommodating the journalists and by all means giving them the feeling that they were influential. Occasional witticisms did the rounds, were greeted with smiles but did no damage. The Chancellor's solemn way of speaking was ironized (and impersonated) and his frequently used phrase 'I am of the opinion ...' became a sort of trademark.

The start of a new era was probably most visible in the codification of legal materials. Kreisky took the view that it should certainly be possible to introduce socialist principles, especially when it came to contentious subject matter. The way had already been paved to some extent by the minority government. Democratisation was the keyword. The universities were to be brought in line with the forms of co-determination on the part of students and mid-level academic staff practised above all at German universities. The professors resisted. They were sent a discussion draft as early as January 1971. In the university committees, one-third parity representation was to prevail in accordance with the ideas of Minister of Science Hertha Firnberg. In this context, Firnberg recalled her own time as a university professor, when she had been more or less completely dependent on her institute's head of department and tenured professor. Now, the position of university professors, regarded by some as the omnipotence of tenure, was to become much less important. Education, in the view of the Minister, was understood by the 'middle classes' as a weapon for securing their positions of power. This was to be counteracted by easing access to universities and allowing the students and the mid-level staff to have a say in organisational affairs and the range of courses on offer. Beyond the occasional tones of class struggle in the discussion, which was not exactly good publicity, the actual objective – easing access to the universities and making them more attractive to educationally alienated classes – was often drowned out. An increase in scholarships might have been enough to achieve this. But there was precious little democracy at the universities. The accusation of a politicisation of the universities concomitant with the academic reform, however, could not be dismissed, especially as the Ministry of Science was able to intervene more in personnel decisions and, above all, the appointment of professors. The new committees sometimes demanded endless meetings, which placed an additional strain above all on the teaching staff. In return, the academic teaching staff was considerably increased in numbers. This, combined with the growing influx of students, resulted in the universities bursting at the seams. This could only be countered by the expansion of the universities and, eventually, the establishment of an additional university in the south of the country, in Klagenfurt. Equally, however, the universities needed – and received – more funding. This was supposed to sedate at least some of the critics.

As was the case at the universities, Kreisky and his supporters detected at the Austrian Broadcasting Corporation (ORF) a 'middle-class hegemony',[687] which had to be broken. In contrast to the question of a new law on university organisation, in which case the compound word – *Universitätsorganisationsgesetz* – already had a deterrent effect, radio and television were, at the latest since the petition for a referendum on radio broadcasting, areas that could be certain of a widespread interest. The desire for a change to the legal foundation was already voiced in 1970 and 1971. Four years after the radio reform, with which a considerable autonomy for radio and television had been reached, it was comparably difficult to argue that the influence of the parties, above all the governing party, on the ORF should be increased again. The general director of the ORF, Gerd Bacher, eloquently and vehemently defied the wishes expressed above all by representatives of the trade unions. As a change could no longer be carried out due to the elections of October 1971, the topic was postponed. The aim of the SPÖ, however, was to alter the legal foundation in such a way that the 'private limited company' (Gesellschaft mit beschränkter Haftung) would be changed to a 'public-law institution' (Anstalt öffentlichen Rechts) with a supervisory board, to which the parties could then dispatch their representatives in accordance with their majority ratios. This sounded like legal jargon but it amounted to an attempt to secure the maximum possible influence on the 'greatest organ in the country', as Bacher termed it.

But there were also other and more natural things on which Kreisky and the SPÖ could leave their mark and demonstrate their will to change. At the time of the minority government, a minor reform of criminal law had been carried out with the aim of decriminalising homosexuality, marriage-wrecking and adultery. Those issues had, therefore, already been addressed. After the minor reform of criminal law, there was now to be a major reform. The key point was the issue of abortion. And here something disappeared that Kreisky in particular had taken for granted – if not the support, then at least the indulgence of the Catholic Church. The same church that had confirmed in 1945 its withdrawal from party-political events vehemently returned to politics in the question of a naturally deeply ethical and not only political matter. Minister of Justice Christian Broda had hoped that it would be possible to bring about an alteration to § 144 of the Criminal Code, which contained the ban on abortion, with the mutual consent of all parties in parliament.

The topic had been discussed for decades. There had been both a reduction and an intensification of the threat of punishment; abortion was at one point a misdemeanour, then a crime. By means of an 'indications-based solution', Broda sought to achieve exemption from punishment, where women could cite social, ethical or eugenic reasons, that is, a demonstrable impairment of the genetic makeup. Perhaps he had expected political opposition but this did not initially materialise. There was, however, an outcry on the part of Catholic, though, to begin with, not church circles. The 'Action for Life' (Aktion Leben) was set up. Were the proposals made by Broda in his draft of a new version of criminal law a relapse into National Socialist times? Was the destruction of 'unworthy' life being proposed? Where were the limits? Would the killing of mentally or physically disabled people also be enabled at some point? Was pregnancy termination to be regarded as the first step on the road to legalised euthanasia?[688] Birth control was clearly something different but this was suddenly reminiscent of killing centres like Hartheim or Vienna's Spiegelgrund. It did not help to point out that most Scandinavian countries and Britain had long since legalised abortion. It remained an ethical problem. The opposition of Catholic circles in particular brought an action committee of women on to the scene as a counteraction. They demanded, if not the abolition of § 144, then at least general impunity for abortions up to the third month of pregnancy. The political parties got involved. It looked very much as though a confrontation might develop between the ÖVP and SPÖ. Broda, in any case, was disappointed that his proposal for an indications-based solution was met with increasing resistance. And he brought himself in line with the advocates of a time-phase solution, according to which abortion should be exempt from punishment until the third month after conception.

The fronts ran right through the political parties. It was to be expected that the Catholic Church would eventually reject the time-phase solution. It was almost inevitable that the arguments flowed into sermons and finally culminated in the question as to whether a party that was willing to surrender unwanted life to annihilation was still electable for Catholics. As neither the Catholic Church nor the ÖVP was prepared to understand the increasingly heated debate on abortion as something that could again be interpreted as an entanglement of what was at root a Christian party with the Catholic Church, the two pursued identical aims in the discussion on abortion but kept their distance. Kreisky, who would have gladly arbitrated and most certainly did not want any conflict with the Catholic Church and, above all, with Cardinal Franz König, was more or less forced to follow his party's line. For a time, it looked like the standpoints of the advocates and the opponents were not so far apart. The ÖVP sought a compromise, knowing all too well that they could not simply close the window that had been flung open by the Socialists in the abortion question. However, even the broad-based party was surprised by the extraordinary reaction of the opponents. Ultimately, one could get the impression from the parliamentary debates that one was witnessing decisive moments in the history of parliamentarianism. The ÖVP, however, slid ever more into a dilemma, for the Catholic Church now officially rejected an indications-based solution, too.

On 29 November 1973, after two years of discussions and a three-day debate, a vote was taken in the National Council. The new criminal law and, with it, the revision of the 'abortion paragraph' was accepted by 93 votes to 88. Whoever believed, however, that the matter had now been dealt with was mistaken. The Salzburg state government submitted a complaint to the Constitutional Court. The Federal Council rejected the time-phase solution with a majority of one vote. The renewed discussion of the subject in the National Council resulted in a vote of persistence. In late January 1974, the Catholic Bishops' Conference intervened and declared that it intended to support the petition for a referendum sought by 'Action for Life'. Cardinal König had hesitated for a long time. But then he stated: 'After this referendum, at least no one will be able to say that the Catholics did not make every effort.'[689] The remark could also be understood as a small dig at the Protestant Church, for the Socialists had repeatedly cited the opinion of the Protestant theologist and university professor Wilhelm Dantine, who had clearly come out in favour of the time-phase solution.[690]

The Constitutional Court rejected the complaint of the Salzburg state government. The petition for a referendum was not carried out until 1976 and obtained around 800,000 signatures. As prescribed by law, the matter was discussed once more in the National Council. The decision remained unchanged. It could be regarded as a slap in the face for the opponents of a time-phase solution, however, that the majority of the population took the view that the Catholic Church should not interfere in questions of contraception and abortion.

In this way, the criminal law reform had become a long-burning issue in Austrian domestic politics and engaged both legislation and electorate from 1971 to 1976. But there were also other issues, too.

Carinthia

Perhaps surprisingly, Kreisky flung himself into another topic that was neither particularly urgent nor especially exciting, it seemed, namely the question of minority rights in Carinthia. Again, everything began very harmlessly. There was no doubt that a Slovene-speaking minority existed in Carinthia. Likewise, the fact that they were mentioned rather prominently in Article 7 of the Austrian State Treaty. According to this: 'Austrian state subjects of the Slovene and Croatian minority in Carinthia, Burgenland and Styria have the right to elementary education in the Slovene or Croatian language and to a proportional number of their own junior schools', the use of their mother tongue as an 'official language' in the territories of mixed language and the mounting of 'terms and inscriptions of a topographical nature' alongside the German designations. Some things had been achieved since 1955. The mounting of bilingual place-name signs, as the somewhat simplified portrayal of the problem ran, had not. A total of 205 localities were affected. The Carinthian Josef Klaus, in any case, had not been willing to touch the problem; the Viennese Bruno Kreisky regarded it as a point of the State Treaty that had not yet been implemented. (There were also others, which were evidently less important for him.)

It was the Carinthian state governor, Hans Sima, who had persuaded Kreisky to detect a problem in the issue. During celebrations for the 50th anniversary of the Carinthian plebiscite, on 10 October 1970, and shortly thereafter on the Austrian National Holiday, leaflets had turned up stating that calls for tolerance and fine words were not enough. Other methods were required. The State Governor then wrote to the Chancellor that one had to 'expect an escalation of the situation'.[691] In fact, there were not only threats but also the first daubing campaigns. Among others, in October and

December 1970, Slovene students added Slovene place names to German place names on the signs in the mixed-language territory. One student was placed on trial – though not convicted. In spring and summer 1971, the next – now expanded – daubing actions were carried out. Now, not only were place-name signs scrawled on but also partisan monuments and memorials for the Slovene families forcibly resettled in 1941/42. Bomb attacks followed, the authorship of which is still disputed today. One thing was certain: the conflict had attained a new quality. And both German Carinthians and Slovenes could denounce each other and accuse the other of bad intentions. For the one, the others were Greater Slovene partisans, while they in turn cited the other side as 'Nazi vermin'. An escalation appeared unavoidable, and the Chancellor did not simply want to await developments. In addition, there was a sort of parallel action, namely the Conference on Security and Cooperation in Europe. There, Austria and Yugoslavia were prominent representatives of the N+N group, namely the neutral and nonaligned states. Vienna and Belgrade, therefore, had not the slightest interest in a confrontation.

In Belgrade, however, other factors also flowed into the deliberations: President Tito was in failing health. What would happen if he were to die? There were murmurings among the nationalities of Yugoslavia. Above all in Croatia, a veritable organised resistance manifested itself against the central government and the regime. It proved possible to suppress the movement of the so-called Croatian Spring; the leaders were placed on trial and given severe penalties. However, what if the Slovenes, too, planned an uprising and sparks flew from Carinthia to the most northerly Yugoslavian constituent republic? Considerations repeatedly circulated that the Soviet Union might use unrest in Yugoslavia as an opportunity for military intervention. Belgrade, like Vienna, therefore did everything to nip the unrest in the bud.

Kreisky acted swiftly – perhaps too swiftly – and resolutely. The constitutional committee of the National Council was sent a draft of a law on place-name signs. The delegates were given less than three weeks to review the draft. The ÖVP and the SPÖ objected that insufficient groundwork had been carried out to enable an assessment and demanded that the minority be established. Kreisky regarded this as unnecessary. The law was adopted on 6 July 1972 with the votes of the governing party. In all municipalities in which there was a Slovene share in the population of more than 20 per cent, bilingual place-name signs were to be mounted. In autumn, their erection commenced. On 4 October 1972, in Škocjan v Podjuni (St. Kanzian am Klopeiner See) and Zvrhnje Žamanje (Obersammelsdorf), the signs were dismantled by demonstrators. They were reaffixed the following day, only to be torn down again. This could be interpreted as civil disobedience but also as a breach of the law. The government in Belgrade, which had not commented on the problem of the place-name signs so far, responded promptly and regarded the incident as a severe strain on bilateral relations. Belgrade, however, had less the situation in Carinthia in mind and more the situation in its own country.[692] But the matter had not yet reached its climax. During the nights before the national holiday of 1972, the 52nd anniversary of the Carinthian plebiscite of 1920, most place-name signs were dismantled and demonstratively deposited in front of the town halls and the state government in Klagenfurt. The State Governor was insulted on live television. Carinthia was suddenly perceived as a province in which not only the old Nazis but also neo-Nazis called the shots. The Slovene organisations responded by demanding that two entities perceived as anti-minority be banned. The possibility of internationalising the issue was also discussed. What if Belgrade – just as Kreisky had done with the South Tyrol problem – were to bring the demand for a fulfilment of State Treaty obligations before the United Nations? Kreisky insisted on the observance of the law on place-name signs but also made himself available for an information event in Klagenfurt. As a sort of prelude, unknown persons blew up an electricity pylon in Horce (Horzach) near St. Kanzian. It was intended as a reminder to Kreisky of the Porzescharte. On 28 October 1970, Kreisky was received in Klagenfurt with a chorus of whistles and insults. Kreisky talked for three hours, appealed for understanding and attempted to build a golden bridge to his critics, many of whom were from his own party. The turmoil did not subside. The Chancellor was advised to leave the assembly hall via the rear entrance. He refused: a chancellor of the Republic of Austria does not leave an event by the back door. Outside, he was sworn at. Perhaps his sympathy for Carinthia diminished on this day. Years later, when it became known that he had bought himself a house on Mallorca, he commented that he could not afford to holiday in Carinthia. It was clear that he was not only talking about money. Subsequently, Kreisky resorted to a method that he repeatedly applied when a notable problem emerged: he convened a group of experts to study the issue and suggest solutions. He hoped, by means of this minority commission, to sedate not only the Carinthian Slovene associations but also Yugoslavia. The former refused to cooperate and continued to vehemently resist a numerical assessment of how many Slovenes and multilinguals, termed 'Windish', lived where. Belgrade, however, had sent a diplomatic note to Vienna in early September 1972, in which the rights of the 'Yugoslav minority' were demanded, otherwise the taking of appropriate steps was threatened. The Foreign Ministry in Vienna remained calm.[693] The British, however, began to take a greater interest in the matter. Carinthia had belonged to their occupation zone and, as a signatory of the State Treaty, they were obliged to ensure that its provisions were observed. The British ambassador in Vienna, Sir Denis Laskey, reported to the Foreign Office that Yugoslavia was the only neighbour of Austria's with which problems existed, because the Belgrade government was accusing Austria of not having fulfilled its State Treaty obligations towards the Slovenes. 'But', continued the British Ambassador, 'it really cannot be claimed that the Slovenes are living in a state of misery and oppression.' Therefore, he claimed, the severity of Yugoslavian attacks was 'entirely unreasonable'.

Perhaps, when making light of the increasing violence in Carinthia vis-à-vis his ministry in London, Northern Ireland crossed the mind of the British diplomat. But the matter was certainly not as harmless as he suggested. The unveiling of the partisan monument in Robež (Robesch) in early September 1973 and a memorial to the combatants who fought the defensive battle on the Gurk Bridge east of Klagenfurt one month later was a veritable invitation to carry out actions. Two weeks after the unveiling of the monument in Robež, it was blown up. An example was made of the perpetrators.

But the affair was far from over, and the minority commission was not always of one mind and above all did not have any ready answers. It was a question of which districts and municipalities a law on ethnic groups, as it would soon be called, was to be applied and how large the minority had to be in order to have a right to bilingual topographical inscriptions and funding measures. The recommendations fluctuated between a population share of five per cent and one of 30 per cent.[694]

Kreisky was in favour of a generous solution. But it seemed that one thing could not be got around, namely an assessment of where and how many people professed themselves to be part of a minority. The conflict continued, the journey was not uneventful and time passed. In late October 1974, Minister of the Interior Otto Rösch drew up a sort of interim balance: until this point in time, he stated, there had been 50 complaints to the police against known perpetrators, while administrative criminal proceedings had been initiated in 250 cases. Suspicions were reinforced that some of the daubing actions and attacks on Slovene memorial sites had been carried out by Slovenes themselves with the intention of escalating the situation.[695] As the government did not desire an escalation, however, the proceedings were dropped. Austria proposed bilateral negotiations to Yugoslavia and, in this way, demonstrated good will. In early March 1975, Kreisky invited the Slovene representatives to the Chancellery, in order to discuss with them a special type of census, that is, the establishment of a minority. The Slovenes categorically rejected the proposal. They did offer, however, to work together with the federal government if the latter were prepared to forego the establishment of a minority. Two months later, in late May, Kreisky announced a 'special type of census' as an aid to orientation. In doing so, Vienna also ignored a further note of protest from Yugoslavia, in no way disputed its obligations from Article 7 of the State Treaty but likewise made it unmistakeably clear that every state had the right, if necessary, to gather statistical data, and indeed in secret and in such a way that was typical in democratic states. (This was a clear sideswipe.) The census was designed to provide a basis for a law on ethnic groups, though it was not expected until the following year. Yugoslavia protested yet again. This appeared to confirm what the British had already seen coming following the last annual report of Ambassador Laskey: were Yugoslavia to appeal to the London government with reference to the State Treaty, the British would have to take up a clear position. And it was precisely this that no one wanted. ('Kreisky is playing for time', it was claimed.) However, the British had been prepared since 1973 to be pulled into the conflict and had drawn up a substantial dossier on the genesis of the conflict between ethnic groups in Carinthia. The Foreign Office admittedly took the view that Yugoslavia pretended to be so flustered only because it was put out that Vienna called the tune in the matter of disinformation regarding the internal situation in Yugoslavia and, above all, speculation regarding the period after Tito's death.

The 'special type of census' was carried out. Slovene associations had called for a boycott but Kreisky was content. Now nothing stood in the way of the adoption of a law on ethnic groups. Nonetheless, only the next station in a seemingly never-ending story had been reached. And the bilingual place-name signs were a long time in coming.

Jews, Palestinians and Terror

The commotion over the minority conflict in Carinthia repeatedly invited comparisons with South Tyrol. Terrorism was also discussed. As yet, however, Austria had been least affected by this. This would also change, and Austria would unexpectedly be brought into contact with conflicts that had their roots elsewhere. To this extent, it was not true what the British Ambassador in Vienna reported to London in 1974: 'Austria is an oasis of calm.' He found that Austria had definitively bid farewell to the Habsburg Monarchy – even if it continued to bask in the splendour of imperial Vienna. This was a Vienna that the Briton considered 'grey and dying'. Austria had succeeded, he thought, in evading most of the difficulties that troubled so many industrial states. Austria had ridden out the oil shock, perhaps not completely without trace but in the main well enough. Several factors had been decisive for this remarkable success: in the energy sector, Austria produced around a fifth of its crude oil needs itself and more than half of its gas requirements. More than two-thirds of electricity came from domestic water power. Considerable amounts of the necessary oil and gas imports came from the Soviet Union, and even if its prices had risen sharply, Austria was still far less dependent on OPEC than other countries. Laskey gave the social partnership responsibility for this prosperity. Discipline in wage and price questions had contributed, he thought, to a major export success. The rate of growth would also be between 3.5 and four per cent in 1975. Measured against the economic issues, claimed His Majesty's Ambassador, the political issues fell away.

'The Socialist government under Dr Kreisky proceeds with its work with evident self-assurance, and its measures for stabilising the economy were more successful than was assumed a year earlier. Nonetheless, the popularity of the Chancellor and his party suffered.' The corporations cut staff. The employment of foreigners in industry and construction rapidly declined.[696] This could be regarded as a skilful measure of offsetting the recession, though it was ultimately an expression of declining prosperity. There were rumours that elections to the National Council, which were scheduled for October, would be moved forward to spring or summer 1975. The ÖVP pushed for this and saw themselves in the ascendant.

'In the area of international politics, Austria has retained its course of wanting to be a friend to everyone', was the British Ambassador's view, which he passed on to London. 'Relations with the West are outstanding. In the Arab-Israeli conflict, Austria has striven to remain neutral but the focus has shifted in favour of the Arabs and Iran.' It was clear what Sir Denis meant. But the reference to the Arab friendship could not simply be left uncommented.

Already in early May 1972, four hijackers of the militant Palestine organisation 'Black September' had brought an aeroplane underway from Vienna to Tel Aviv under their control. They wanted to enforce the release of imprisoned comrades-in-arms and prevent the transit of Russian Jews via Austria to Israel. At this point in time, the transit camp in Schönau an der Triesting set up in 1965 was already very well known. Leading Israeli politicians visited it. More than 160,000 emigrants had passed through it. In February 1971, there had been first warnings about potential aircraft hijackings, by means of which Austria was to be forced to suspend its support for Russian Jews. The unabashed actions of Jewish organisations were admittedly a thorn in Kreisky's side but he did not intervene. And Foreign Minister Kirchschläger had provided reassurance: Austria was neutral and, furthermore, not anti-Arab. But the Austrian state police had also received warnings, including of a splinter group, the 'Popular Front for the Liberation of Palestine'.[697] Nothing had happened. In September 1972, the Israeli embassy in Vienna warned the Ministry of the Interior about a possible attack on the camp. Security measures were strengthened. In early 1973, the first threats were directed at the Austrian address. Six suspects were arrested. The security precautions were tightened still further. Nonetheless, on 28 September, near Marchegg, two men from a Palestine terror organisation attacked a train coming from Czechoslovakia and took three Russian Jews and an Austrian official hostage in an attempt to obtain the release of kindred spirits sitting in Israel prisons.[698] Diplomats from Arab states intervened. The closure of the transit camp in Schönau was negotiated as a solution. It remained disputed from whom this proposal actually came. Kreisky, at least, claimed this step for himself. The Palestinians were flown out and the hostages released.

Kreisky's compliant stance was heavily criticised in Austria. In Israel, however, there was complete indignation over the Chancellor's decision. Israeli Prime Minister Golda Meir travelled to Vienna only days later and had a chilly discussion with the Federal Chancellor. Kreisky stuck with his decision. Schönau remained closed. Instead, a new transit camp was set up in Wöllersdorf, which was operated by the Red Cross and not the Jewish Agency. It did not bother anyone that a detention camp of the Corporative State had once existed in Wöllersdorf. For the transit of Soviet Jews, nothing had changed in practice. But Israeli-Austrian relations remained strained.

Over the course of a week, events surrounding Marchegg and Schönau attracted attention not only in Austria and, in hindsight, could almost be seen as a perfect diversionary tactic, because on 6 October 1973, on the Jewish Day of Atonement, Yom Kippur, Egyptian, Syrian and allied troops launched a surprise attack on Israel. Everyone had been watching Austria and not paid attention to the Suez Canal and the Golan Heights. Years later, the terrorist known as 'Carlos' summarised the issue from his point of view: 'Golda Meir flew into a rage at exactly the right moment .... Imagine: the Arabs are about to commence the October War against Israel and persuade the Prime Minister to fly to Austria and make a scene with Kreisky. A few days before the war, two Syrian Palestinians easily manage to distract the entire Israeli nation.'[699]

Regardless of this, it could be observed that the Middle East conflict had now, at the latest, reached Austria. As the large oil producers in the Near and Middle East imposed an embargo and throttled oil exports following the Yom Kippur War, Austria was affected by it just like other European states. For Kreisky, this was no reason, however, to change his Middle East policy. On the contrary: it was necessary to find solutions and Kreisky, in particular, wanted to do his bit. This was not, as might have been assumed, by demonstrating – as an Austrian Jew – a greater devotion to Israel but far more by evincing understanding, even sympathy, for the Arab states. He was well aware of the West's critical stance. The Netherlands, the USA, Britain and France expressed time and again 'disconcertment over the behaviour' of Austria. The closure of the transit camp in Schönau was judged to be a break with Austria's post-war humanitarian stance and a relapse into anti-Semitic traditions. Perhaps it was precisely this criticism that persuaded Kreisky to increasingly champion the cause of the Palestinians. To begin with, he took pains over the statistics: year after year, Eastern European Jews had come to Austria in large numbers and moved on. Since 1960, the number had been 164,000, as he wrote to German Federal Chancellor Willy Brandt. 74,000 had come from the Soviet Union alone.[700] Seen in this way, the Marchegg-Schönau incident appeared to be merely an anomaly. Why did other countries not share Austria's efforts to take in emigrants from the Soviet Union? 'We cannot carry the burden alone', claimed the Chancellor.[701] In 1974, around 20,000 emigrants arrived in Wöllersdorf. International perception again shifted to 'friendly'. Kreisky, however, remained true to his chosen course.

After the death of Franz Jonas, Rudolf Kirchschläger had been chosen as federal president. The long-time independent, whom Kreisky had known and valued since the 1950s, had been appointed foreign minister by him. He had loyally implemented the foreign policy guidelines of the Chancellor, which had allowed the Foreign Ministry to become an 'executive organ of the Federal Chancellery'.[702] He was not extremely well known and certainly not more so than his competitor, the Mayor of Innsbruck Alois Lugger, who attempted to score points with two Winter Olympic Games in Tyrol. But Bruno Kreisky made the case for Kirchschläger, even though Kirchschläger made no secret of having been an officer of the German Wehrmacht and having still been fighting in early April 1945 in the region of Wiener Neustadt. Lugger had also been a reserve officer and served with the anti-aircraft artillery. In the case of Kirchschläger, his wartime past was made the subject of discussion; in Lugger's case, it was immaterial. In any event, with the selection of Kirchschläger, a former officer of the German Wehrmacht became Austrian federal president for the first time. Renner had championed the Anschluss in 1938; Körner had been an inconspicuous but consistent opponent of the Nazi regime; Adolf Schärf was able to cunningly avoid membership in the National Socialist Association of Legal Professionals (Nationalsozialistischer Rechtswahrerbund) and remained unmolested as a lawyer during the war; Franz Jonas, who had worked at the locomotive factory in Floridsdorf, had been deferred from military service and did not have to join up. Kreisky made neither the one nor the other a subject of discussion.

Kirchschläger was succeeded by Erich Bielka and, as early as 1976, Willibald Pahr. Neither was a Socialist, though they did embody something like non-partisanship and accepted that Kreisky continued to establish the main focal points in foreign policy. Reference was made to détente, and Europe had indeed achieved a greater degree of security as a result of the Helsinki Final Act of 1975. It could only be hoped but not yet known that the impact of the détente process and the associated openness, as well as the demand for an observance of human rights in the countries dependent on the Soviet Union, would set a real process in motion. Austria, in any event, was a beneficiary, for in a sense in the shadow of the politics of détente an association agreement with the EEC was achieved in 1972. Even if this could only be an interim objective, Austria had to be satisfied. The Soviet Union, in any case, had not raised any objectives to this form of rapprochement, even if it had rejected an actual membership of Austria on grounds that it was not compliant with the State Treaty.

Polarka

Connecting with Europe was a process aimed primarily at securing economic development. At the same time, however, it could also be seen as something that concerned Austria's external security. Kreisky did not grow tired of emphasising that the best security policy was a good foreign policy but he was naturally unable to close his eyes to the fact that the stability and, ultimately, also the economic resilience of a country continued to be measured internationally in terms of divisions, tanks and aircraft. To this extent, nothing had changed since Mussolini's remark to Schuschnigg in 1936. Austria was admittedly catching up but its national defence continued to look like a shambles.

After the 'revolt' of officers, most of them had fallen in line and also learned to accept a certain amount of gloating at home and abroad about the almost defenceless Austria. 'In view of the absence of credible national defence, which is also limited for geographical and financial reasons, everything is focussed on politics', noted British Ambassador Laskey. Austria was proud of its role in the UN, he continued, above all of Secretary General Waldheim, as well as its participation in the UN missions in Cyprus and the Near East. Even Switzerland was unable to keep up. But, if it came down to it, Austria's only hope was NATO. And assistance from NATO would have to come after three or four days at the latest, for, it was concluded, Warsaw Pact troops would be done with Austria by then.

In 1972, this pessimistic assumption was countered, entirely in the spirit of Kreisky, by General Emil Spannocchi, who had been appointed as an army commander only after the Second World War, with his own concept. Without yet being able to resort to the terminology of Herfried Münkler, he addressed the subject of 'asymmetrical' war,[703] though all cases of asymmetry fitted the Austrian case. Austria's national defence embodied a stark disparity among the forces to be deployed, its equipment was substandard in many weapons sectors and exhibited striking shortcomings in the area of civil defence. While Vienna was still taking pains to interpret the State Treaty provisions regarding bans on 'special weapons', technology of the next-but-one generation was already stored in the arsenals of the others.

Spannocchi did not see any possibility, in the event of a defensive scenario, to withdraw combat troops in an orderly fashion or to undertake major movements in view of the massive superiority of mechanised forces and the assumed absolute air supremacy of every opponent. Thus, he no longer intended to focus any attention on stalling tactics but wanted instead to use above all the Austrian standing army (Landwehr) in predetermined regions and with the support of numerous 'fixed installations' to force the aggressor to advance slowly and, where possible, inflict damage on him and, ultimately, compel him to attack strongly-defended key zones. It was not, therefore, a question of partisan warfare but very much the deployment of regular forces. Beyond the operations themselves, the aim of all political and military efforts, that is, the overall strategy, would be to prolong a conflict to such a degree that the attacked state could be granted some form of assistance. This, at least, was the theory. But it required soldiers, forces that could be predominantly deployed as infantry and in a small-scale war, and indeed three times as many soldiers as there had so far been space for in the military organisation. Seven times as many would be better. To begin with, however, the concept appeared to be successful. The reserve army of those trained between 1956 and 1970 was more or less written off. A new reserve army first had to be established. The concern circulated that the (almost complete) military vacuum in Austria carried a high risk.[704] It also suddenly appeared that Austria had only just escaped with a bloody nose a few years earlier.

The chief secretary of the Communist Party within the Czechoslovak Ministry of National Defence, Jan Šejna, who had fled Czechoslovakia in February 1968, caused a great sensation when he claimed in February 1974 that the Soviets had already drawn up a concrete operational scenario – 'Polarka' – in order to force Yugoslavia into the socialist community of states. The most alarming aspect of this account for Austria was the fact that Šejna claimed that the operation was supposed to be carried out on Austrian territory.

Thanks to media attention accorded to the Czechoslovak party soldier, his story advanced to become the 'scenario' par excellence. While the related planning of the Federal Army had been categorised as 'top secret', all fears seemed now to be confirmed. The media had their sensation. 'Polarka' was seen as the confirmation of everything that had always been assumed.[705] The occasion for an operation by Warsaw Pact troops via Austria was to be turmoil in Yugoslavia following the death of Tito or conflicts between nationalities, which could be used as an excuse for intervention. According to the 'Polarka' plans, Czech and Hungarian troops were to occupy eastern and parts of southern Austria. Soviet troops from the Transcarpathian front would then follow and occupy southern Austria as far as the Villach region. The Graz-Thalerhof airfield was envisaged as hub and command headquarters. 'Polarka' had already been tested during exercises in the mid-1960s, explained Šejna. Czechoslovak officers had explored the routes of their units during the journey to football matches in Vienna, and the 'Vlatava' (Moldau) manoeuvre of 1965 had ultimately been based on 'Polarka'.

This in itself was nothing new, as it had been considered for a long time and constituted the theoretical background to at least four operational scenarios of the Federal Army. The interpretation of that which Šejna had not only recounted and attempted to prove but positively staged was not limited, however, to the contents of the 'scenario'. Almost more interesting was the point in time at which 'Polarka' was processed by the media and the way this was done. To begin with, the Warsaw Pact could be pilloried. This was fine with NATO, for it appeared to confirm what could be derived from a multitude of other observations. Strictly speaking, 'Polarka' was not directed against the Western alliance but the nonaligned Yugoslavia and the eternally neutral Austria. The latter was shown how vulnerable it was at the exact moment when it demonstrated a special degree of military weakness and, on top of that, left itself plenty of time for its reform measures. This was more than a thorn in the side of the Western alliance. It was not advisable, however, to voice real criticism. Concerns had of course been expressed on multiple occasions. What about letting someone have their say, however, who really ought to know, namely the Czechoslovakian General Šejna, who had defected to the

West? What if he were given the opportunity to not only serve the Western secret service but also give an interview to the magazine with the biggest circulation in Austria? During the Hungarian Revolution in 1956, there had been Western disinformation; the same had applied in 1968, after the Czechoslovakian secret service agent Ladislav Bittmann had absconded; and 'Polarka' thoroughly matched the pattern.

'Polarka' was a bluff. Behind it was anxiety. In spite of its neutrality, Austria would understand itself as part of a pan-European security structure. Ministers and generals, above all the Federal Chancellor, however, pledged themselves to this. 'Polarka' had left its mark on them.

The UN in Vienna

Kreisky's security policy measures had a further objective. Austria should become the third official seat of the United Nations, that is, in actual fact, it already was. But the two UN organisations that had relocated to Vienna, the International Atomic Energy Agency (IAEA) and the Industrial Development Organisation (UNIDO), should receive better accommodation and, potentially, bring additional institutions to Vienna. The construction of a UNO-City in Vienna's Danube Park had already been planned under the government of Klaus. It was realised from 1972 onwards. In addition, Vienna was to receive a conference centre in order to be able to host larger conferences and important meetings. A majority of the negotiations of Americans and Soviets regarding the reduction of strategic weapons had already taken place in Vienna, before the SALT I Treaty could be signed in Moscow in 1972. The continuation of talks regarding another agreement was scheduled to take place in Geneva. However, their finalisation was to take place in Vienna.

Austria's Chancellor also had something else to offer. It had nothing to do with a construction measure or the hosting of an important conference. During a visit to London in April 1973, Rudolf Kirchschläger had made a concrete suggestion for a solution to the Middle East conflict. And with this announcement, something known as the 'Austrian Middle East initiative' started, which then began to irritate not only the British. Kirchschläger stated that the same approach was called for as in the South Tyrol question. An operational calendar should be compiled and then worked through. (25 years on, this is now known as a 'road map'.)

Already the following month, in May, Kirchschläger became more definite. What if UN Secretary General Kurt Waldheim were requested by the Security Council to commission his Middle East plenipotentiary, Ambassador Jarring, to draw up such an operational calendar and submit a progress report every three to six months? Once the operational calendar was there, one would have to start dealing with the more harmless matters, place them beyond dispute, and each side would be willing to make small compromises. In this way, there would also be no necessity for formal negotiations, and neither side would have to abandon positions in a widely visible way any more. Gradually, confidence-building measures would also lead to an entry into constructive talks, until a just and sustainable solution were found on the basis of UN Resolution 242 from 1967.

The Foreign Office in London evidently did not rightly know how it should react. But shortly thereafter, the Israeli Ambassador set the tone: it was unacceptable. Israel wanted direct negotiations and was not willing to abandon this stance. This made everything clear: the plan was extremely 'amateurish' and in no way acceptable for Israel. The responsible British civil servant, therefore, openly continued in his file comment: 'My personal opinion is that the plan is the result of very naïve deliberations and is not suited as the starting point for further steps.'

Foreign Secretary Douglas-Home then responded to his Austrian colleague and courteously declined the offer as not interesting. In view of the stance displayed by Israel and Egypt, he, Douglas-Home, was anything but optimistic. But perhaps his Austrian colleague could inform him which steps he would like to take and what initial concessions might look like.

The British response was perhaps not so curt because it had in the meantime become clear that Secretary General Waldheim found positive aspects in the Austrian initiative, after all, and was having it examined for its feasibility. London, therefore, wanted to await developments. Should the matter come to nothing, they would 'not shed any tears' on the Thames.

Months later, in October 1973, Kreisky was confirmed in his endeavours. The Yom Kippur War demonstrated once again how dangerous the situation in the Middle East was and how all hopes continued to be pinned on war and not negotiations. The Chancellor had the feeling that no further progress could be made by means of traditional diplomacy. As a type of immediate measure, he agreed in October 1973 to the request of UN Secretary General Kurt Waldheim to send peacekeeping troops to the Middle East. The cooperation between Waldheim and Kreisky went smoothly. The UN asked Ireland, Finland, Sweden and Austria to send soldiers in order to carry out a disengagement of troops on the Egyptian and Syrian front following the armistice of 24 October. As Austria already had peacekeeping troops stationed in Cyprus, some of them were set in motion and began their deployment in Egypt on 27 October. Eight months later, in June 1974, the Austrian battalion was transferred to the Israeli-Syrian border and eventually took up positions at the highest point, Mount Hermon, which, for ultimately trivial reasons, was not vacated by the Austrians until 12 June 2013. For Kreisky, however, the Austrian UN contingent was part of his foreign policy activities.

In 1974, he began, in the framework of the Socialist International, with exploratory talks, which were concluded in 1976. He acted here in unison with German Federal

Chancellor Willy Brandt and Swedish Prime Minister Olof Palme. Acts of terror in Austria and Germany, above all the attack by a commando of the Palestine Liberation Organisation (PLO) of Yasser Arafat on the Israeli Olympic team in Munich, the oil crisis in the aftermath to the war of October 1973 and the situation in the Middle East, which remained explosive, forced not only him to think about possibilities for a solution to the conflict. Once again, the fact that the initiative did not come from the major powers but a network of Social Democratic parties and their political exponents was new. This approach was judged with corresponding disdain. Kreisky and Co. were not always bound in their contact to Arab statesmen to the arduous and convoluted route of foreign policy but instead strove primarily to establish trust. Of course, they would have liked to have incorporated real 'heavyweights' in their mission, above all British Prime Minister Harold Wilson. The latter, however, even once gave instructions to say he was not there when Kreisky attempted to reach him by telephone. Britain, after all, backed Israel, not the Arabs.

An operational calendar still did not exist. However, the UN Secretary General had granted Yasser Arafat's PLO observer status at the United Nations. And this was at least something where naivety and amateurism had achieved more than the Foreign Office in London had either desired or, at least, expected.

In 1973/74, Austria was a non-permanent member of the Security Council of the United Nations. A 'backbencher' of the global organisation had become a 'big player' since Kurt Waldheim's selection as UN secretary general. The construction in Vienna of the third official headquarters of the United States after New York and Geneva after countless quarrels thus fitted perfectly into a long-term concept, and likewise the accelerated realisation of other projects that were designed to correspond to what Kreisky regarded as an active politics of neutrality. The British and Americans continued to keep their distance. In the case of the British, it was possible to speak for a time of thoroughly disturbed relations. It even proved difficult to get diplomatic visits started. When Kreisky made a stopover in London on his way from a meeting of the UN General Assembly in New York, the Foreign Office was informed but there would not be any talks. It was claimed that the Chancellor was very tired after a seven-hour flight and would simply wait for his connecting flight. The last time that a British foreign secretary had been in Vienna for a working visit dated back 15 years. London was well aware of this. But the only option that was seriously discussed was the participation of Foreign Secretary Lord Callaghan in the State Treaty celebrations in May 1975. The head of the Foreign Office in London understandably wanted to make this dependent on whether the foreign ministers of the USA and the Soviet Union – Kissinger and Gromyko – would also attend. Kissinger declined. With that, the matter was decided. Finally, the compromise was chosen that representatives of the State Treaty signatories with ministerial rank would come but nothing more.

For Kreisky, the celebrations for the twentieth anniversary of the State Treaty of 1955 was nonetheless a welcome opportunity to portray his own role – which was undisputed. By now, he was also the last major Austrian protagonist, for Raab, Figl and Schärf were all dead. But in view of the limited interest that the foreign ministers of the former occupying powers showed in their trust territory, it was advisable to keep the ceremony simple.

Oppositional Formulas

Already in early 1975, unrest started to grow in domestic policies. The ÖVP pressed for new elections. The ÖVP federal party chairman, Karl Schleinzer, was confident of breaking the absolute majority of the Socialists. He was in favour of a grand coalition. Kreisky was against the idea. He spoke once again of a minority government like in 1970 or of going into opposition. Naturally, the possibility of a joint government with the Freedom Party was discussed. No one really believed this would happen, though.

There was no doubt that Kreisky wanted to remain chancellor. Otherwise, a year earlier, he would not have resisted so vehemently the in any case not very sustained attempts to banish him from the 'operating business' to the 'supervisory board'. Minister of Finance Hannes Androsch and Mayor of Vienna Leopold Gratz had advised Kreisky in 1974 to run for the post of federal president. In this way, they evidently sought to force him into a more representative role. And they argued in favour of this by pointing out that it would in any case prove impossible to obtain an absolute majority again at the next elections. Thus, perhaps there should be a little coalition with Androsch as chancellor and Friedrich Peter as his deputy. But Kreisky did not allow himself to be forced out. He openly declared that he intended to remain chancellor. But he had understood that Androsch wanted power. In this way, the breach already existed. But Kreisky did not dismiss his finance minister, although the two had actually no longer been 'able' to work with each other since early 1975. Kreisky had begun to make major deficits in order to be able to finance both his reforms and full employment. Androsch gave him the money. This led the budget deficit to shoot up from 1.3 to four per cent. For Denis Laskey, the British ambassador, this was evidently a sensible measure. Kreisky, however, began, unperturbed, to tinker with an expression that also struck the British. In 1975, the Chancellor stated: 'I prefer a few million schillings to a few thousand unemployed.' Soon, only the following variation on the theme was fitting: 'that a few billions in debts cause me fewer sleepless nights than a few hundred thousand unemployed would.'[706] For all the criticism of this credo, it was undeniable that the SPÖ had proven in the economic area that it could govern and did not distance itself from its tradition as a working-class party, increased welfare and was not willing to compromise one of the cornerstones of social harmony, the social partnership.[707]

It was time to take stock. Kreisky had made a well and truly impetuous start. During the years in opposition, he had been able to prepare himself and work out topics. Then it had been a question of implementing measures. The four years from 1971 to 1975 had admittedly sufficed to get the major penal reform, a family package, the university reform and also a solution for the minority problem in Carinthia off the ground. The reform of the broadcasting reform had taken place in 1974 and brought the SPÖ the desired supervisory board and a new director general, Otto Oberhammer. But many things were still unfulfilled. In foreign policy, Kreisky had established focal points above all in security policy and at least revealed possibilities. He had also succeeded in keeping Austria out of heated debates on the Vietnam War. And this had been anything but easy, for the sympathies of the youth in the Chancellor's party were far more on the side of North Vietnam than the USA. But the pro-Western stance of the government had asserted itself over any doubts. The quarrels over domestic policy had been limited. Here, Kreisky had no doubt benefitted from the initial absentmindedness of the ÖVP. Their search for a new chairman, personal differences within the associations, but also within the initially eight and then seven federal states governed by the ÖVP with the party at federal level allowed the SPÖ to appear to be relatively tightly managed. The allocation of posts, which was decided not least by the Chancellor, must have appeared to be a good deed. The image of the 'Sun King', who was responsible for anything and everything, was no coincidence. But an established federal chancellor also had every reason to prepare himself for the elections scheduled for autumn 1975.

During the warming-up phase for the election campaign, Karl Schleinzer died in a car crash on 19 July 1975. A whole series of Christian Social politicians or politicians close to Schleinzer, for instance the governor of Rheinland-Pfalz, Helmut Kohl, attended the funeral. The leader of the British Conservative Party, Margaret Thatcher, sent a condolence telegram. A few days later, the search began for a suitable successor. There appeared to be three candidates: Stephan Koren, Alois Mock and Josef Taus. Of Koren, the British Ambassador was able to report that he would not emphasise a generational break. Furthermore, the Ambassador continued, he was not very popular and made a 'sour' impression on television. Mock was popular, according to the Ambassador, but not across the ÖVP; for some, he was too 'left-wing' and, in intellectual terms, Kreisky would have an easy job of it. Taus was unknown, continued the Ambassador, but had a lot of experience in all economic matters. Whether he would be able to stand up to Kreisky on social issues, as well as those of national defence and foreign policy, however, was more than questionable. It was very probable, claimed the Ambassador, that he would be able to take some of the shine off the Chancellor as the Sun King. Taus was elected on 25 July, thereby becoming federal party chairman and candidate for chancellor. Erhard Busek became the new secretary general. In view of their comparative youth, the new leadership duo quickly gained the nickname 'pacifier brigade'. Taus and Busek had to dive right into the election campaign. They were given programmatic statements such as 'quality of life' and 'social market economy' along the way but it proved difficult to struggle against a widespread sense of satisfaction, and the German sociologist of law, Helmit Schelsky, who was teaching as a guest professor in Vienna in 1975, stated that the 'mentality of social support' had become a veritable profession of faith.[708] Austria was content with itself and the world.

The election campaign continued to give foreign observers plenty of material to report on. It was said of Taus that he actually succeeded for a short time in becoming the most popular politician in Austria. But then the Leopold Helbich affair happened, when the ÖVP National Council delegate attempted to bribe a journalist. After that, it was claimed, the ÖVP came under pressure. A poor television appearance by Taus during the confrontation with Kreisky and Peter had cost the party the 'middle-class' ground, it was suggested. Nonetheless, an absolute majority for the SPÖ was not expected. Once again, however, the opinion pollsters were mistaken. Kreisky and the SPÖ again obtained an absolute majority in votes and seats. Women and pensioners accounted for a considerable share in this success.[709]

Shortly before the elections on 5 October, there had been a special type of intervention. As Kreisky did not rule out the possibility of eventually having to form a little coalition with the FPÖ after all, their party chairman, Friedrich Peter, once more came into focus. He had been in the SS, specifically the 1st Infantry Brigade (Motorised), which was accused of murdering Jews and shooting hostages, charges that were then proven. The fact that Peter had been a member of this troop unit had been known since 1964, when the Soviets had passed on relevant files to the Czechs, who then shared them with Austria.[710] The following year, the diary of the brigade had been published. The head of the Jewish Historical Documentation Centre in Vienna, Simon Wiesenthal, made a scandal of something that had already been known for a long time. He had already passed on a memorandum to Josef Klaus in 1966, in which he had criticised the procedural practice on the part of jury courts in trials against people who were charged with Nazi crimes.[711] In this 'Guilt and Atonement Memorandum', he cited a number of 1,100 people who were being investigated, suggested that Austrians had comprised a disproportionately high proportion of perpetrators and, as a result of scandalous acquittals, failed to fulfil its moral and legal obligations. Klaus had responded that everything necessary was being done. In 1971, when there was an opportunity for Friedrich Peter to become deputy chancellor, Wiesenthal made another push and discovered that Austrian procedural practices had not changed. In 1975, as had been the case ten years earlier in West Germany, the intention was to discontinue the prosecution of Nazi crimes, and Wiesenthal did not exclude the possibility that Peter might become deputy chancellor, that is, a member of the Waffen SS whose unit had demonstrably been involved in murders. Therefore, Wiesenthal made a third push.

A few days before the elections to the National Council, he wrote to Federal President Kirchschläger and stated that it would be absolutely unacceptable if Friedrich Peter were to become deputy chancellor in a little coalition. As it turned out, this did not happen, but Kreisky resented Wiesenthal's intervention. He argued that the attacks had been directed exclusively against him and wanted his parliamentary immunity repealed in order that he could take legal action against Wiesenthal.[712] After the National Council did not repeal the immunity of the Chancellor, Kreisky began, for his part, with a very different sort of scandalisation: Wiesenthal was accused of having collaborated with the National Socialists. He wanted to sue Kreisky. Foreign observers like Ambassador Laskey did not know what to think about the matter. Laskey sought advice from newspaper editor and former resistance fighter Fritz Molden, who assured him that Kreisky did not have a shred of evidence that Wiesenthal had collaborated with the Nazis. What astonished the British even more, however, was the silence of the FPÖ. They had expected criticism. But, as Third Consular Secretary David Lyskom then summarised: the only SPÖ politician who had publicly commented on it was the third president of the National Council, Otto Probst. But he also refrained from voicing criticism, likewise Minister of Justice Broda and the new chairman of the SPÖ parliamentary group, Heinz Fischer: evidently, they did not want to criticise Kreisky in public. It was a point of contention whether the 'Kreisky-Wiesenthal affair' would have an impact on the international standing of Austria. The later German federal chancellor Helmut Schmidt soberly commented in hindsight: 'Conflict with Wiesenthal? I'm not familiar with that. When was the dispute?'[713]

Back then, in 1975, however, it was not plain sailing. The nationwide partisanship for Kreisky was striking, though it could not simply be reduced to latent anti-Semitism. That would ultimately have been preposterous. Kreisky suggested that Wiesenthal had inexplicably placed himself at the disposal of the Nazi regime. On the periphery, doubt was also cast on Wiesenthal's role in the identification of the whereabouts of Adolf Eichmann, thus questioning Wiesenthal's characterisation as the 'Eichmann hunter'. In short, low punches and question marks dominated proceedings, and one had to ask 'why?' The issue was no longer Friedrich Peter but now ultimately Kreisky's indignation, until the Chancellor agreed to cancel a parliamentary enquiry committee previously announced by him and Wiesenthal withdrew his lawsuit. Now everyone could return to important political matters.

Again, as in 1973, Austria unexpectedly ended up in the firing line of terror. On 21 December 1975, six terrorists not belonging to the PLO stormed the headquarters of the Organisation of the Petroleum Exporting Countries (OPEC) in Vienna, whose annual conference was taking place. Around 70 people, including several ministers, were taken hostage; three people were shot during gun battles, including an Austrian official. It never emerged what the terrorists under the leadership of Ilich Rámirez Sánchez, called 'Carlos', actually wanted. The only German in the terror commando stated that they wanted to highlight the misery of the Palestinians and the unspeakable wealth of the oil nations. For Kreisky, the whole thing was a setback to the extent that he felt his efforts to upgrade the Palestinians had not been honoured. He had to acknowledge, however, that not all Palestinians were the same and that Arafat was not the undisputed leader of anti-Israeli organisations. Remaining consistent, Kreisky did not want to see any violence used, just as he had done after the Marchegg attack. He could be certain of being criticised. The 'politics of looking away' was subjected to severe criticism, especially from Western states.[714] The terrorists were permitted to leave the country with the hostages and gradually released their prisoners. Kreisky was subjected to massive accusations. It was above all Israel that told him that one ought not to give in to kidnappers and terrorists, as it would only be understood as an invitation to carry out further attacks. German Federal Chancellor Helmut Schmidt also stated that the release had certainly been a mistake, even if Kreisky had achieved his objective of avoiding further bloodshed.[715]

'King Kreisky'

What had been expected by a majority of people could begin in October 1975: Kreisky formed his third government. Deliberations regarding the possibility of a new grand coalition or a government of national concentration with the inclusion of the Freedom Party were off the table. In view of the absolute majority, Kreisky did not waste any thought on this. And he was in a position to continue and finish any outstanding business. But a difference soon manifested itself: unlike in 1970 and 1971, Kreisky could not predetermine a whole host of topics. Now, it was increasingly others who passed on the topics to him. The ÖVP, led by Taus, were prescribed a debate on ideology. In early 1976, the SPÖ did the same thing. An era of re-ideologization appeared to have dawned. It was not yet possible, however, to speak of an impact on day-to-day politics, unless the circumstance counted that the new chairman of the ÖVP parliamentary group, Alois Mock, was invited to Washington by American President Jimmy Carter as representative of a small group of leading conservative politicians, 'Christians in Responsibility' (Christen in Verantwortung), before Bruno Kreisky was. The latter, however, continued to enjoy national and international approval. A new British ambassador in Vienna, Hugh Trevors Morgan, could not get enough of emphasising the general contentment in Austria. He did this with a certain degree of wit and wrote in early July 1976 in his six-monthly report to the Foreign Office in London: 'A holiday mood

reigns in Austria. Aside from that, it's impossible from Friday lunchtime to reach someone at his desk.'[716] It might be the case that the low level of working zeal appeared odd
to the representative of a country, Britain, that was economically anything but prosperous at that point in time, or perhaps it evoked envy. The Phaeacians on the Danube
had switched from self-sufficiency to self-satisfaction and were pleased that everything
was running so smoothly. Therefore, they did not allow themselves to be distracted by
politics and instead concentrated on 'munching its Wurst and sipping its wine', as the
Ambassador so graphically wrote. A million Austrians consumed alcoholic drinks to
excess. One third of male and female Austrians smoked and, calculated over the course
of a year, achieved herewith a theoretical daily consumption of around 20 cigarettes.
More than a third of the population was overweight. Consumption of meat soared.[717]

Austria was doing well. It had overcome the 'oil shock', had enjoyed a good laugh
about the Chancellor's recommendation to shave wet in order to save electricity, had
accepted one car-free day a week and was now once more in the fast lane.[718] The government had steered Austria through the recession with the aid of inflation and rising
budget deficits. From 1976, things were on the up and up. The figures seemed to speak
for themselves: the growth forecast was at four per cent, while unemployment was at
2.1 per cent. Who could complain? However, the cost of living had reached the level of
West Germany and Switzerland, without income having climbed to the same height.
And while matters such as deficit spending or Austro-Keynesianism were viewed critically by the foreign press, this was lost in the self-assessment. Self-confidence was the
order of the day. A contributory factor in this was not least the somewhat patronising
manner apparently evident in the conduct of West German guests. For a long time, the
problem was: 'Disrespect, primarily in the form of disregard.' More curious was the
circumstance that Kreisky could never completely free himself of the fear that Germany
would eventually demonstrate Anschluss tendencies again.[719] Towards West Germany,
he then also displayed a strange reserve, quite different to Raab, Figl and Klaus in their
day. This could be interpreted as a result of the assumption of closer relations with East
Germany. This did no harm to the popularity of the Chancellor, either.

Kreisky stood unchallenged at the forefront of politics in Austria and was omnipresent in other ways, too. The opposition, led by Josef Taus, was more or less helpless. 'As
long as King Kreisky is there and there are no external crises', the opposition parties
did not stand a chance, according to the British Ambassador. Kreisky continued to bet
on the politics of neutrality and not on military national defence. And UNO-City was
more important to him than armaments. He spoke of military equilibrium, although
Austria made practically no contribution in terms of the military and military stability,
in the opinion of the British. Only when compared with what came 'later' would it
become clear that the share of the budget for the Federal Army not only grew steadily
but – at 1.3 per cent of the gross domestic product – was the highest in the Second

Republic. The insiders knew that this was also very low in European comparison, while the foreign observers knew that it was still the case that not much could be achieved with this. The Federal Army was conceded a certain delay effect in the event of an attack from abroad but the weapons were obsolete and ammunition supplies extremely low. What was acknowledged, however, was the spirit that filled the army and made itself felt above all among the young.[720]

Kreisky had spoken out very clearly against the acquisition of interceptors, though the unofficial reason was that no modern aircraft were required if they were in any case not permitted to be equipped with missiles due to the provisions of the State Treaty. The British agreed with a Swiss assessment: militarily, Austria (still) constitutes a vacuum.

But there were also other things that occurred to those who kept Austria under observation. For one thing, there was the question of the establishment and start-up of the Zwentendorf nuclear power station. It had been planned in 1969 and construction had commenced in April 1972 but a small anti-nuclear movement continued to grow. The technology harboured too many risks, it was claimed. Gradually, arguments for and against increased, even if they did not yet have the vehemence already known from other states. But why should it be any different in Austria than in those countries in which nuclear energy divided opinions. Hugh Trevors Morgan stated that it could not have escaped the attention of even an Austrian chancellor that groups and constellations of all kinds converged in the anti-nuclear movement, not least peace campaigners, environmental activists and a new left.

However, it was not only the future to which attention was devoted. The same happened with the past. Kreisky had also not succeeded in correcting the view abroad and, above all, in Germany that Austria had not only unsubscribed from the joint past but had well and truly conned its way through. As confirmation of this, German Federal Chancellor Willy Brandt repeatedly related that the Austrians had succeeded in making an Austrian of Beethoven and a German of Hitler. Brandt's successor, Helmut Schmidt, formulated it even more drastically:

> Kreisky 'has contributed to Austria cheating its way through. Even in the consciousness of Austrian society. It has cheated its way through. It's cheated its way through not only in relation to the Nazis but also with regard to Austro-Fascism. This never existed, when I visit Vienna today, in the mind of the Austrians living there. Nor the enthusiasm for Adolf Hitler. It's nowhere to be found.'[721]

One-sidedness in passing judgement and a certain forgetfulness can also be detected in explaining why the view from abroad and the self-perception differed.

Kreisky would not have let himself be put off by such an outside perspective. He had to cope with other, far more banal, things: personnel issues repeatedly troubled him. He did not have a logical successor. It also could not be assumed, therefore, that he would truly make a reality out of his suggestion to resign from office before the 1979 elections. The succession to the Ministry of Foreign Affairs was also problematic. What Kreisky was looking for, namely, was nothing more than a post-holder. Interestingly enough, the British assumed that Kreisky therefore waited for a while before replacing Erich Bielka in 1976, because he wanted to offer the post to Kurt Waldheim in the event that he was not re-elected as UN secretary general. The Western members of the Security Council vehemently advocated Waldheim's re-election, though they were concerned that the Soviet Union might not cooperate with the reappointment. Ultimately, however, Waldheim's election to another four-year term in office was undisputed and, in Willibald Pahr, Kreisky found another man who was more convenient for the post of foreign minister than the UN secretary general. Kreisky continued to focus on Waldheim, however, with whom he was completely at one, not least in his appraisal of the Palestine problem. As UN secretary general, Waldheim had made his own contribution to rescuing the Palestinians from the sidelines and raising global public awareness of them. Kreisky had also learned the lesson from his three visits in the framework of the Socialist International that something had to happen and fast, with the involvement of Palestine leader Yasser Arafat. He was convinced that the Palestinians were ready for a peace settlement on the basis of the creation of a Palestinian state. This would stretch from the West Bank to the Gaza Strip, whereby these two territories would be connected via a corridor. The extremists outside the PLO, however, were a completely unpredictable group and anything but ready for peace. Kreisky knew this. The Palestinians were so aggressive, as the British Ambassador quoted the Austrian Chancellor, because they were shown on a daily basis how the Arab states were wallowing in luxury and bathing in oil, while they 'got the dirt'.

Kreisky's efforts at making peace in the Middle East continued to be denigrated; his endeavours to strengthen Austria's bond with the EEC were remarked on with the recommendation that those in Vienna should read *Pravda* in order to learn what the Soviets thought of these endeavours; the belief that the CSCE process had expanded Austria's room for manoeuvre in international relations was met with considerable scepticism. According to London, this amounted to presumptuousness. Not only that: those in power on the Thames were simply appalled. And in this point, they were in unison with the ÖVP.

From 'crown prince' to 'entailed estate farmer'

For years, coalition and government parties had felt themselves obligated to pursue a common foreign policy. Now, this had changed. Both Western countries and the ÖVP criticised the fact that Austria had swung into the Arab camp instead of maintaining equidistance in the Middle East conflict. Finally, it was claimed that Kreisky was neglecting relations with traditional friends in the West: the USA, Britain and France. The ÖVP's accusations were directed first and foremost at Kreisky's third foreign minister, Willibald Pahr, but it was clear that the Chancellor himself was responsible for the course steered in foreign policy. Kreisky unmistakeably demanded the right to self-determination for the Palestinians and traced terror attacks in Israel back to the Arabs being denied this right. He also saw no reason to close the office of the PLO in Vienna.[722] The Israeli Ambassador left Vienna. Kreisky appeared unimpressed. When the Austrian Foreign Minister was then quoted as having made a remark towards the USA to the effect that America should abandon the realisation of a project for the construction of neutron bombs, the Minister felt he had been misquoted but the damage was already done. Above all the chairman of the ÖVP parliamentary group in the National Council, Alois Mock, accused the SPÖ and Kreisky of having left the path of a common foreign policy. Kreisky, it was claimed, was not sufficiently nurturing good relations with the signatories of the State Treaty, and likewise policy with neighbouring states and contact to the countries of the European Community. For the sake of completeness, the ÖVP also called for the strengthening of 'development work'. Austria had also decided in favour of the objective of the OECD for increasing development aid by 0.7 per cent of the gross domestic product. Austria indeed found itself in last-but-one position and ultimately expended only 0.17 per cent.[723] There was no need for numeracy skills here.

Other things were also unsuited to being classified as successes. The head of government, who was often termed the 'media chancellor', could still be certain of the complete attention of journalists. At the same time, he had to acknowledge that the flourishing media could also turn against him and were positively greedy for investigating and processing information. And, ultimately, there were no taboos. It was no longer the case, as it had been, that scandals and corruption only seemed to affect others. The party of the Chancellor was also no longer taboo. Klaus had been forced to recognise this. During his third term in office, history caught up with the Chancellor, and he had to grapple with discord in his government team, scandals and setbacks, which no doubt troubled him. In addition, there were health-related problems.

It all started with the petition for a referendum on a time-phase solution achieving a respectable result of more than 800,000 signatures. The mandatory parliamentary handling of this case in the National Council did not change the decision that had been made or the major penal reform. However, the level of rejection had turned out to be stronger than expected. The special type of census for the establishment of a minority, which had been called due to the conflict over place-name signs in Carinthia, was only useful to a degree, though it did lead to the appointment of ethnic group advisory boards and to a gradual coming round of the Carinthian Slovenes, as well as a normalisation of relations with Yugoslavia. The actual point of contention, however, the mounting of place-name signs, could not be regarded as having been dealt with. Only in half of the originally envisaged localities could signs be mounted.

By 1977, the weaknesses of the army reform were blatantly obvious: the standby force still fell short of the envisaged 15,000 men. Obligatory review exercises had to be subsequently enacted in law. The ÖVP felt confirmed in the objections they had already voiced against the military law in 1970. However, the big opposition party picked up another topic as a matter of priority, namely state indebtedness. In 1970, Kreisky had accused the ÖVP of running up exorbitant debts. Meanwhile, the public debt increased continuously. It continued to apply, however, that the Chancellor preferred high debts to rising unemployment rates. He brushed aside concerns that there would at some point be both high debts and high unemployment. But he knew that the clock was ticking on the 'journey' to be taken jointly. And the problems multiplied.

The new building of the Vienna General Hospital (Allgemeines Krankenhaus der Stadt Wien, or AKH) not only devoured far more funds than originally estimated but had become an absolute symbol of the times. An investigation was announced. The media pounced on the case. It recalled the incidents of corruption in the First Republic, though now it concerned the Socialists. Time and again, the staffing of several state organisations give rise to criticism. Once more, it was a petition for a referendum that went against the SPÖ and eventually resulted in a resignation: the mayor of Vienna, Felix Slavik, had to go and made way for one of those men from Kreisky's entourage repeatedly termed 'crown princes', Minister of Education Leopold Gratz. In 1976, the largest Viennese bridge across the Danube, the Reich Bridge, collapsed due to undetected structural failures. The municipal building director had to step down. The political classes in Socialist-dominated Vienna had become smug and lazy. Kreisky knew this. The ÖVP also recognised that the Austrian capital, described by the British Ambassador as 'grey and dying' by all means offered possibilities to position oneself in a new and better way. Erhard Busek, hitherto secretary general of the ÖVP, became deputy mayor in Vienna. And he really mixed things up in the city. Thus, the opposition appeared to be making ground, while Kreisky's own party was heading for a crisis.

Relations between Kreisky and his finance minister, Hannes Androsch, who was also occasionally touted as his successor, deteriorated inexorably. Professionally, the dispute revolved around questions of budget and currency policy, as well as the introduction of a special car tax. In 1977, Kreisky wanted to abandon the renewed pegging of the schilling to the German mark. Androsch was opposed and clung steadfast to a hard currency policy. He advocated a reduction of social security benefits. For Kreisky, this was out of the question.[724] The atmospheric disturbances were far graver, however, than disputes over professional issues. They concerned Androsch's tax consultant office, 'Consultatio', which he operated until his ministership, as well as frequent commissions awarded to companies and people close to Androsch, who had now also become deputy chancellor. The accusation of corruption, or at least inappropriate privileging, was in the air. And the more the Deputy Chancellor attempted to brush it aside and argue by pointing to different lifestyles, the more evident the Chancellor's annoyance became.

Admittedly, he did not yet want to overly give utterance to his disapproval. But occasional comments from him could be heard, 'which were to all intents and purposes more dangerous for Androsch than the attacks of the ÖVP'.[725] In the Viennese café and pastry shop *Demel*, an SPÖ network had formed, which was then accused of all kinds of things, including criminal schemes, even if the latter concerned above all the owner of *Demel*, Udo Proksch. Years later, it was proven that he had murdered six people in connection with the sinking of the freighter *Lucona*. Many people in the Chancellor's party had been friends of his. It was never completely clarified who exactly was involved in the affair or what role Minister of Defence Lütgendorf had played, who died in 1981 'in unexplained circumstances'. At any rate, years 'after Kreisky', in 1988/89, 16 people were investigated in connection with the demise of the *Lucona* and the mayor of Vienna, Leopold Gratz, and Minister of the Interior Karl Blecha resigned. Everything had started in the setting of 'Club 45' in *Demel*.

The biggest problem for Kreisky, however, emerged in the context of the construction of the nuclear power station in Zwentendorf in Lower Austria. There was an explosion of costs. Far more serious, however, was that a small group of opponents of nuclear power plants who obtained their information primarily from Germany had become a respectable movement, the ÖVP described the question of the start-up of the power station as a matter for the government and Kreisky himself eventually started to wobble. Following an operation and whilst still in hospital, he announced that the question of the start-up would be made the subject of a plebiscite. He himself emphasised that he believed a non-start-up to be wrong and that several billion schillings – it would eventually be 13 billion – would be thrown out of the window. But no one could understand this.[726] The plebiscite was scheduled for 5 November 1978 – it would be the first since the vote for whether Austria should unite with the German Reich in 1938. Neither the ÖVP nor the SPÖ wanted to make a recommendation. Taus let it be known, however, that he would be voting 'no' due to security concerns, and Kreisky with 'yes'. The mood heated up. Advocates and opponents could be found in all political camps and knew how to put their opinion across. Pro-Zwentendorf posters were pasted over by the Socialist Youth. The trade unions lobbied for support.[727] All possible arguments could be heard. Most of them were already familiar from Germany. The vote narrowly went against the start-up, with 50.5 per cent of votes for 'no'.

This in itself would not have been regarded as a debacle but Kreisky had very clearly made his continuation at the head of the federal government dependent on a 'yes' to the use of nuclear power. And he now had to swallow a defeat that he took personally, even if he had stated in the run-up to the vote that he would 'not shoot' himself in the event of a 'no' vote. But he acted swiftly. Three days after the vote, the SPÖ initiated a 'non-proliferation law' in the National Council. The law was accepted unanimously. No one and no party wanted to oppose the result of the plebiscite. Kreisky, however, who had forced the Zwentendorf project and wanted to make his political fate dependent on the result of the vote, had no intention of resigning and, in this way, emerged from a personal defeat as the victor, because he had presented his 'no' in advance as his personal opinion and had accepted the democratic decision. Evidently, this is what counted. The clever tactician decided to act and wanted to make another go of it. But he was concerned that he might lose the voters' favour. The outcome of the plebiscite, as well as poor results in the elections to the regional diets, were a wake-up call for him.

The SPÖ began to speak of bringing forward the elections to the National Council by half a year, to 6 May 1979. The ÖVP was in agreement. This time, they would succeed in breaking the absolute majority of the Socialists. Again, there was speculation regarding the formation of a little coalition, and reports circulated of agreements between the ÖVP chairman, Josef Taus, and the new chairman of the FPÖ, Alexander Götz. Then the major topics emerged. These, however, were neither nuclear power (it had been dealt with) nor even the impact of Austrian politics abroad; instead they were job protection, the fight against inflation and tax policies.[728] The eternal triad.

On 6 May 1979, the predictions were once more proved wrong. Kreisky helped the SPÖ to their biggest election victory in Austrian history. Taus had been defeated again. As always, people puzzled over the reasons for the election result; there were explanations or at least assumptions. Repeatedly, quotes could be heard such as: 'I don't actually like the Jews but I vote for Kreisky.' The Chancellor, who, as with the Zwentendorf vote, had made his continuation dependent on the result of the election, now had no reason not to accept the mandate to form a government. But stormy times were ahead for him. However, he was not troubled by the ÖVP, which once more had to look for a new federal party chairman in summer 1979 after the resignation of Josef Taus and found one in Alois Mock, but rather corruption in his own party. And it was confirmed that in the shadow of the 'Sun King' a sort of subculture had emerged that gave the Chancellor a very hard time. Some things had been rumoured for a long time, others suddenly erupted. New things were added. And Austria suddenly appeared to be the 'republic of scandals' per se.

By April 1980, it was evident that in the case of the new building of Vienna General Hospital, not only were the procedures chaotic and the building supervision deficient. More serious were the instances of illegal awarding of commissions, bribe payments to foreign bank accounts and the loss of the taxpayers' money to the tune of billions. Parliamentary investigations and legal proceedings followed. In summer 1980, the conflict between the Chancellor and his deputy, which had been smouldering for some time, erupted. It concerned Androsch's murky company constructions, transfers of money to anonymous accounts, irregularities and circumstances that ill befitted a finance minister. In the case of the so-called AKH scandal, the ÖVP and the SPÖ agreed that there would be a complete investigation; when it came to the accusations against the Minister of Finance, the harmony was only feigned, because to the dismay of his party, Kreisky visibly distanced himself from Hannes Androsch during a special session of the National Council, so that the latter was left with no option but to resign. Last but not least, yet another scandal joined the ever longer list, though it was the ÖVP that was affected this time. It was a question of ten million schillings, which had flowed, 'off the record', into the party cashboxes in a dubious, though, as it later turned out, quite understandable way. The books simply refused to be balanced.

Beyond the criminal facts of the case, it was noted that the Federal Chancellor had, for quite some time now, forfeited the role of the one who lays down the law, and that politics in general was now regarded as a dubious, dirty business. Billions flowed; dozens of people were involved; any amount of personal advantages were obtained and, with the help of political office, which actually obligated a person to particular integrity, assets increased. Even the FPÖ had difficulty presenting itself as a 'clean' party, for their agreement in enabling the Deputy Chancellor and Finance Minister to obtain a subsequent role as president of the largest Austrian bank following his departure from government was the result of political 'horse-trading'. It had to be asked: were these typical occurrences in politics? Had Kreisky lost the overview, so that he no longer noticed what was going on? Did he no longer hold the reins?

The Chancellor responded with a ten-point programme, in which he demanded honesty in public life and a rigorous separation of politics and business. This was like an act of liberation. But, beyond the cases in question, one of course had to ask whether a government and a chancellor to which so much power had been given could not also be guilty of an abuse of power.

Before 1966, the Grand Coalition had rightly been reproached for the fact that the governing parties not only shared influence but also drew material benefits from working together, passed posts to each other and were involved in scandals, great and small. Now, one had to ask whether the coalition parties had not also monitored each other and, in this way, protected the state and its citizens from damage.

Kreisky had grown long in the tooth. He could also look back on a long 'journey', with all its ups and downs. For several hours in 1980, he would also experience something like a personal triumph. That which had not succeeded in 1975, did so in 1980 with hardly any effort: Austria could celebrate the 25-year anniversary of the signing of the State Treaty. And (almost) everyone attended: the incumbent foreign ministers of the former occupying powers and one of the two foreign ministers from back then who were still alive, the Brit Harold Macmillan. (As in 1975, Vyacheslav Molotov's

government did not permit him to take part.) Secretary of State Edmund Muskie
came from the USA, Jean François-Poncet from France and Andrei Gromyko from
the Soviet Union. Kreisky could bask in the glow of the media and the respect of his
guests. He conveyed the impression – as the British ambassador, Donald Gordon, so
graphically reported to London – that he, or rather Austria, could solve any number of
global problems without further ado.[729] Everyone – literally – presented themselves in
Vienna. Of course, the encounters were also used to discuss bilateral and global problems. And Kreisky was an ideal conversation partner for this, even if the British, for
instance, claimed that his views sometimes had 'idiosyncratic' traits.[730]

The 'old timer'

After the celebrations, the daily routine caught up with Kreisky and with Austria. In
the early 1980s, the Chancellor still led the opinion polls unchallenged, though the
ÖVP had, in Alois Mock, a young, likeable and dynamic chairman, the fourth in the
space of ten years. And, of course, not only were the scandals exploited to run down the
government but also political decisions that had been made long before but only now
took effect. The support measures for families and adolescents, the programme for full
employment and the hard currency policy caused budget deficits of a type never before
seen in the Second Republic. The flow of money showed a strong upward trend. The
trade unions were in agreement with it – and that was the main thing.[731] State-owned
industry was experiencing a crisis. It was not the seemingly 'unsinkable ship with virtually permanent jobs' that it liked to be seen as.[732] A renewed shortage of quantities
of mineral oil deliveries on the part of the OPEC states, rising prices and dwindling
demand increasingly caused Austria problems. The unemployment rate rose year after
year. Where were the times when Kreisky had been able to accuse Josef Klaus of being
wasteful and irresponsibly driving the budget deficit to three billion schillings? Now,
the budget deficit was almost ten times as high and the so-called Austro-Keynesianism
had failed. The dismal prediction that Kreisky's labour policies would ultimately lead
to high unemployment rates and budget deficits appeared to have become reality. But
was everyone willing to accept this? The journalist Alexander Vodopivec wrote about
the 'end of the illusion society'. By contrast, Ernst Hanisch wrote retrospectively: 'in
everyday life, the people behaved as though things would always be that way'.[733]

   In other European states, the pressure to re-orientate made itself felt. Austria, however, still cultivated a denial of reality. But it no longer succeeded so well. People rose up
against the fact that, by all accounts, the period of upswing, as well as the major benefits,
was over and sought to preserve what had been achieved. If need be, one could find
comfort abroad. But even the most positive ambassadors' reports could not erase the

impression that Austria did not arouse international attention for its own sake.[734] Naturally, the gaggle of reporters had come to Vienna in June 1979 when Soviet state and party leader Leonid Brezhnev and American President Jimmy Carter met to sign the SALT II Treaty and agree on a further restriction of strategic nuclear weapons. After that, however, other things were more important. Kreisky especially did everything to cultivate his efforts – dismissed as a personal hobby – to position Austria as an honest broker.

Austria was actively engaged in both the East-West and the North-South dialogue. It was also important that it was so wonderfully visible to the states of East-Central Europe as the window display of the West. And the message that was transmitted in the process was that communism did not work. Neutrality also constituted a virtue in itself. It secured the country a status that one no longer had to paraphrase by stating that it was excluded, belonged neither to NATO nor the Warsaw Pact and was also not part of the EEC or the Council for Mutual Economic Assistance (COMECON) of those states dependent on the Soviet Union. Seen like this, the feeling of self-worth was unbroken.

A change of values, environmental awareness and the central statement of the Club of Rome regarding the 'limits to growth' were perhaps cited but they were regarded least of all as an Austrian problem. And it could not fail to happen that Austria was also brought back down to earth.

Kreisky – who still possessed the charisma that kept him from losing the support of the people, of which he had been certain for so long – had to accept that the additional welfare spending needed financing. The successor to Hannes Androsch as minister of finance, former minister of health Herbert Salcher, had the thankless task of making the dawning of a new era comprehensible in such a way that he announced measures which had been set out in Kreisky's holiday home on the island of Mallorca. The 'Mallorca Package' of 1982 had a certain similarity to the special taxes that Josef Klaus had introduced 15 years earlier and had promptly cost him a great deal of support. It would be the same for Kreisky. The attempt to change course was justified in every way, because there was a veritable explosion in the budget deficit. But the special tax introduced on bank savings, which would become the capital gains tax, the increase in the tax on 'luxury goods', which had been established in 1977, and a whole host of increased charges were perceived as a grab for their wallets. Kreisky was in any case not – or not yet – willing to go any further. Androsch openly and severely criticised the government's course.

The Kreisky of the 1980s appeared tired and jaded; he struggled with an eye disease and diabetes, became a dialysis patient and, after thirty years in politics, had become egocentric and intolerant. Above all, however, the ageing statesman still had much to say, and people listened: global economy – it was in a state of crisis, claimed the Chancellor,

but Austria was doing well; the employment rate was encouraging; Middle East – the
situation was catastrophic; the world was standing 'on the edge of an abyss'; the opportunity for negotiations had passed; the moderate Arab states had been forced to abandon their restraint after Israel's invasion of Lebanon; the USA tended in the Near East,
like everywhere, to simplify things and failed to see the real problems. Kreisky himself
repeatedly sought to mediate and at least succeeded in negotiations on an exchange of
prisoners between Israel and the PLO taking place in Vienna. He also emphasised that
he was the only Western statesman who enjoyed good relations with Libya's Gaddafi.
The Libyan had spent four days in Vienna in March 1982 and been able, in this way, to
fight off increasing isolation. The USA was annoyed.[735] The images of the revolutionary leader giving Kreisky a brotherhood kiss induced Fred Zinnemann, the famous
film director who had grown up in Vienna, to return a badge of honour for services to
the Republic of Austria. Kreisky accepted it. Arafat visited Kreisky in Mallorca. King
Hussein of Jordan recuperated with his family in a villa in Vienna. What more could
one want? Kreisky was quoted as saying that the situation in Eastern Europe was very
worrying. Should the disputes in Poland worsen, the Soviets would naturally intervene.
Then not even a renewed partition of Poland could be ruled out; the American and
British stance, which aimed at bringing Poland to its knees, was 'pure stupidity'.[736] In
the Soviet Union, Yuri Andropov was the logical successor to Leonid Brezhnev, according to Kreisky. Konstantin Chernenko was not a strong candidate, he said. Kreisky
surprised people by establishing contact with Fidel Castro in Cuba and believed he had
a real chance of deploying the group of neutrals and nonaligned as mediators in induc-
ing the Soviet Union to withdraw from Afghanistan.[737] He also claimed to have been
in informal contact with Castro in 1962, when he forwarded to Washington the Soviet
proposal for solving the Cuban Missile Crisis, namely the trade-off whereby Soviet
missiles would be withdrawn from Cuba in return for the removal of American Jupiter
missiles stationed in Turkey – and in this way actually demonstrated a way forward in
solving the crisis.[738] Kreisky did not agree with the British Falklands policy, though he
was pleased that the matter had come to a good end. The British government, in any
case, had demonstrated strong leadership, something that Kreisky found lacking in the
case of other Western leaders (meaning, above all, Ronald Reagan).[739]

A contributory factor in Kreisky's verdict on American policies was admittedly not
only the fact that the Reagan administration increasingly showed its annoyance regarding Kreisky's Middle East policy and, especially, his friendship with Libyan head of
state Gaddafi but also because it assumed threatening tones regarding Austrian exports
of advanced technology to Warsaw Pact countries.[740]

As a recipient of Marshall Plan aid, Austria had been obligated to adhere to the
embargo provisions of an office established in Paris named COCOM. In the early
1980s, natural gas pipes suddenly appeared on this list. Austria delivered these to the

Eastern bloc on a large scale. In the event that a country was not inclined to adhere to
the embargo provisions, the USA threatened not to deliver any more advanced technology to the 'culprits', either.[741] Austrian firms delivered computers for Budapest Airport,
forging machines with Austrian know-how and other things, of which it was claimed
in Paris that they were on the embargo list.[742] Kreisky claimed that it was a misunderstanding and wanted to discuss the matter during his visit of President Reagan scheduled for 3 February 1983. But, while they were at it, the government in Washington
raised the ante: the USA regarded Austrian refugee policy with increasing disapproval.
As in 1956 and 1968 in the cases of Hungary and Czechoslovakia, respectively, Austria
saw itself called upon in the case of the military government established by General
Wojciech Jaruzelski in Poland in 1981 to positively respond to the requests of Poles
for asylum. The United States was prepared to take in Polish asylum seekers but was
criticised by Austria not least for not taking in more, resulting in 19,000 Polish refugees being stranded in Austria.[743] Austria also willingly accepted refugees from other
countries and switched, in the opinion of the Americans, from a liberal policy to one of
invitation. This ought to be ended as swiftly as possible, otherwise the USA would feel
compelled to refuse to take in any more eastern refugees from Austria. In the opinion
of the Americans, the failure of communist economic policy was no reason to request
asylum.[744] This was a shot across the bows.

Diplomats and foreign visitors also noticed Kreisky's dwindling vigour. And there
was really no logical successor any more – aside from Minister of Education and Deputy Chancellor Fred Sinowatz, though he remained in Kreisky's shadow. During a television discussion with Alois Mock regarding the implementation of a petition for a
referendum on the construction of a conference centre near UNO-City, which the
ÖVP rejected, Kreisky was no longer convincing. The referendum in May 1982 could
and must be rated as a rejection of the project pursued by Kreisky. 1,361,562 people
voted in favour of a 'Conference Centre Economisation Law', that is, they rejected the
building. It would be the most successful petition for a referendum in the whole Second Republic. All that now remained for Kreisky and the SPÖ if they did not want to
acknowledge defeat was to force through the construction by using their parliamentary
majority. Again, a parallel could be drawn: in 1969, the SPÖ had chased off the ÖVP
with a petition for a referendum on the introduction of a 40-hour working week. Now,
the tables were turned. And the ÖVP concluded: on a personal whim, Kreisky was
wantonly jeopardising Austria's position in the Western world. What strange friends
he had, after all: Castro and Gaddafi instead of Reagan and Thatcher; neutral and anti-Israeli sentiments instead of understanding for Israel's policies.[745]

Kreisky made his candidacy in the 1983 elections to the National Council dependent
on the advice of his doctors. They would decide. It soon filtered through, however, that
they had not deferred to their diagnosis but to the Chancellor's wishes.[746] He wanted

to give it another go. At the 1983 elections to the National Council, the SPÖ lost their absolute majority. All kinds of reasons were cited to explain the failure: the setbacks in recent times, the illness of the Chancellor and the no longer so recent conflict with Androsch, which had afflicted the Chancellor's party. After 13 years of governmental responsibility, a shift was only natural, it was claimed. Bismarck and Churchill were cited as examples; de Gaulle was the more obvious one.[747] All of them had been shown their limitations. Gratitude is not a criterion of politics. Kreisky had surely hoped to once more obtain an absolute majority. But it was only a relative majority. Before the elections, Kreisky had already ruled out the possibility of becoming leader of a grand coalition. He stated that it would be too onerous and rejected the offer of the ÖVP.[748] Kreisky had remained silent on the subject of a little coalition, though as it turned out his vigour was no longer sufficient even for that. And he had also lost his desire to govern. A minority government was now out of the question. The FPÖ wanted more. And no one could expect a minority government to last. Instead, the SPÖ wanted to take what was considered to be the easier route, include a manageable junior partner in the government and form a cabinet under Fred Sinowatz and the FPÖ of Norbert Steger. This would have been no problem in terms of electoral arithmetic. From the Social Democratic view of later years, it was the fall from grace.

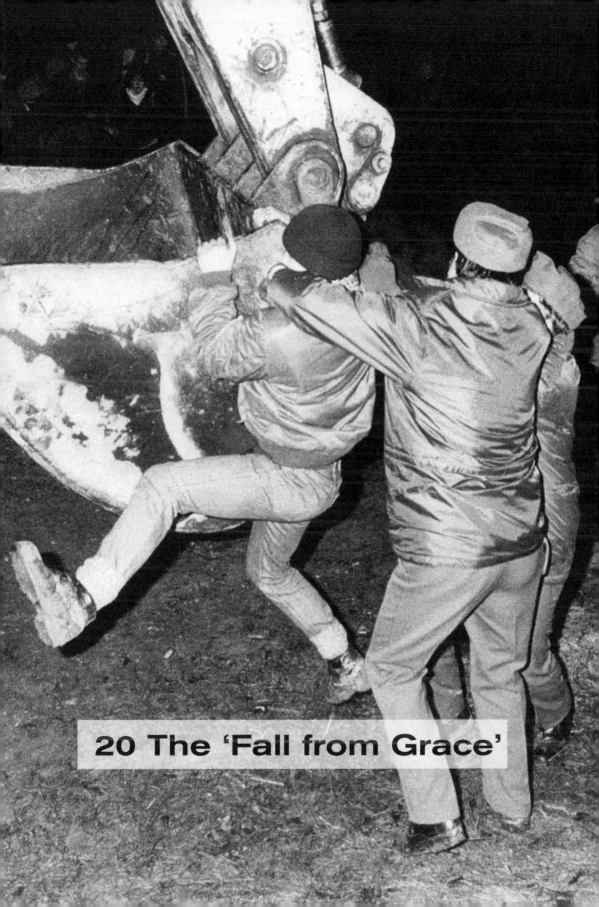

20 The 'Fall from Grace'

20 Demonstration against the construction of a Danube power plant in the Hainburg Floodplains near Stopfenreuth, 19 December 1984. After months of discussions and demonstrations for and against the construction of a Danube power plant near the Slovakian border and the occupation of the Floodplains by several hundred people, the conflict escalated. Eventually, the commencement of forestry works in the Floodplains led to run-ins between environmental activists and executive authorities. The decision of Federal Chancellor Fred Sinowatz to agree on a type of Christmas truce led to a de-escalation and eventually to a renunciation of the expansion of the power plant. (Photo: IMAGNO / Votava)

The first task was to overcome the various forms of inner resistance. The FPÖ was not 'left-wing'. Yet the Freedom Party had already been snubbed several times by the ÖVP and on the other hand had also had good experiences with the SPÖ, or more precisely, with a whole series of SPÖ politicians. One that immediately came to mind was Franz Olah, but in particular also Bruno Kreisky. And this was of greater importance that the accusation levelled against the Freedom Party that their ranks still included large numbers of the 'formers', the old Nazis. In that area, the SPÖ were by no means lagging behind, even if it had discarded its Austrian brand of German nationalism. However, there was no doubt that the dominant force in the FPÖ were the liberals surrounding Norbert Steger. The accusation levelled repeatedly against Friedrich Peter that he had been a member of the SS ran into the sand after Peter had already foregone becoming party leader in 1978, and now also declined to take up the office of third president of the National Council (Nationalrat). It therefore finally became clear to Fred Sinowatz and the SPÖ that after 13 years of bearing governmental responsibility, there was no necessity to take leave of power, and that it was possible to form a little coalition. Indeed, there was even no need for them to depart from the principles that had been applied since 1983, and the belief in progress, feasibility and social wellbeing continued to be emphasised as ideologically underpinned goals. However, it was not Fred Sinowatz who would decide what should happen in the period after Kreisky; this was done by the Chancellor himself, in whom – according to the ÖVP circles – 'the fury over his lacklustre departure' was noticeable.[749] He had been entrusted with the continuation of business, and he set about forming the Little Coalition.[750] The main decisive factor was that the People's Party continued to be kept away from important levers of power. When it came to making a decision in the party committees, the FPÖ voted unanimously for a coalition with the SPÖ; in the SPÖ, the journalist Günther Nenning voted in favour of going into opposition. No one voted for a new version of a grand coalition.

The Hainburg Floodplains

Once again, the challenges of the plains began on the day after the period of hard work had come to an end. At first, everything amounted to a continuation of the politics of the Kreisky years, with a whole series of examples acting as an exhortation, such as

Count Gyulay, who after the ousting of Radetzky as the commander of the Second Army in Italy had said in analogous terms: what the old man managed to do, I can do easily. Before the 'plains' were reached, however, the new Chancellor and Austria shone with unusual brilliance: for the first time since 1782, when Pope Pius VI came to Austria, Pope John Paul II visited Vienna. On 10 September 1983, during a mass on Heldenplatz, he modified the word directed at Austria by Pope Paul VI from 1971, 'isola felice', which under Kreisky had been translated as 'island of the blessed' and which had become a downright folkloristic phrase. John Paul II called Austria 'mirror and model', a term that was already closer to reality. John Paul read out the mass under the terrace of Vienna's Hofburg, since the Council of Ministers had agreed that the front terrace, which was still known as the 'Hitler balcony', was out of bounds.

As soon as the Pope left, political everyday life demanded its due – and soon also claimed its victims. If Fred Sinowatz might have thought that there would be plenty to go around, as had been the case during the initial Kreisky years, he was disappointed.[751] The times when relatively generous sinecures were still to be had were a thing of the past. Above all, another competitor in the form of the FPÖ had emerged, which laid claim to important positions in the public service sector, among state-owned companies and among the banks, which still lay within the sphere of influence of the ÖVP and SPÖ.[752] The four large social partnership institutions appeared to be erratic blocs, however. The desire to simply do a normal job was already thwarted after a matter of months during which staff conflicts broke out in both SPÖ and FPÖ that attracted far more attention than the work of government. Steger, the FPÖ federal party chairman, was occupied with the 'case' of Jörg Haider, who never failed to capitalise on an opportunity to cast doubt over Steger. Everyone was called to the 'witness box', including Kreisky, who had called Haider a 'young Nazi', had been sued by him, and who had lost the press court case. Even so, the 'young Nazi' moniker stuck.[753] Sinowatz had other problems. He laboured with ministerial colleagues who had been selected by Kreisky, but who increasingly exasperated the new Chancellor. Kreisky's man in the Ministry of Finance was Herbert Salcher. There were repeated indications of discord between him and the Chancellor. Sinowatz wanted to appoint Franz Vranitzky in his place, but he was considered to be part of the 'Androsch camp'. Suddenly, a chasm of personal animosities opened up, with indictments and written statements for the public prosecutor's office.

For the time being, the conflict within the FPÖ could be contained. Sinowatz allowed an intra-party rupture to develop, however, and in September 1984 reshuffled his government, with five new ministerial appointments, including the Ministry of Finance, to which he brought Franz Vranitzky, and the Ministry of Foreign Affairs, which was to be headed by Leopold Gratz, who until then had been mayor of Vienna. Kreisky did not agree to the changes and withdrew. And from then on, it was just a small step before setting aside the honorary chairmanship of his party and describing the path taken by the SPÖ since 1983 as the 'greatest disappointment of my life'.[754]

Naturally, the coalition partners had forged ambitious plans. However, the manner in which this was expressed in the government programme was fatally reminiscent of the well-worn empty phrases. The goal was 'to continue to promote the nationalised industries', and to 'retain [their] level of employment', as well as to facilitate a 'climate that is beneficial to investment', and the 'competitiveness of the small and medium-sized businesses'. One specific aim was included in the government programme: 'There is agreement that the Danube power station should be built in the Hainburg area'.[755] And this in particular was to be prevented from happening and would become a fiasco for some.

The expansion of the Danube at Hainburg had already been planned in 1952. In the interim, much Danube water had flowed downstream. Josef Klaus had the project on his agenda. In 1983, however, the expansion entered into a concrete stage. Political approval followed, although during the same year, environmental organisations began to campaign against the construction. The success of the referendum over Zwentendorf had added wind to the sails of the environmental movement. The argument that a unique floodplain landscape should be preserved found support far beyond party boundaries. The ÖVP and SPÖ were divided. The trade unions and businesses were in favour, while other groups were against the plans. A power struggle emerged. After the floodplain was occupied by opponents of the power station, and after the violent attempt to set up the construction site and fell the trees on the site of the planned power station, the conflict escalated. Sinowatz called off the project just before Christmas. After the peaceful Christmas period, the power station project was dealt the final death blow. The Trade Union Federation, primarily the construction and woodworkers' unions, could no longer understand what the Chancellor was doing and were furious. How did he think he could secure full employment and invigorate the economy if he couldn't make the first billion-schilling project a success? The decision had been made by the Chancellor and the SPÖ, but not by the government. The FPÖ had 'played dead'. Parts of the ÖVP, however, had joined in support of the environmental movement. Neither the Socialists nor the People's Party were any longer those monolithic blocs that had almost unlimited influence, as people had still wanted to believe before 1966 or 1983.

It had already become clear in 1968 that social movements, and the peace movement in particular, were also exerting an influence on Austria. With Zwentendorf, and certainly with Hainburg, features were highlighted that became models for the future. Where else in the world was an atomic power station that had already been completed not put into operation? Where else was another major power generation project stopped in its tracks? The example caught on, but probably also resulted in the fact that those who believed in progress in the world regarded the Austrians as backward.

The excitement over Hainburg had hardly died down when another event, or 'case', as
many people put it, caused a stir. In January 1985, a former member of the SS, Walter
Reder, was released from prison in Italy. Reder, who had been born in Silesia and grew
up in Austria, had been an illegal National Socialist who had fled to Germany after the
July putsch in 1934 and been stripped of his citizenship. As a member of the Waffen
SS, he had taken part in one of the dirtiest aspects of the war, in mass executions and
the shooting of hostages in the Bologna area, particularly in the village of Marzabotto.
After a doubtless problematic trial, Reder was sentenced to life imprisonment. After the Austrian State Treaty was signed, he attempted to regain Austrian citizenship,
which was also granted to him thanks to the intervention of Minister of the Interior
Helmer. From then on, he became known as 'the final Austrian prisoner of war'. At the
beginning of the 1960s, the Ministry of Foreign Affairs under Bruno Kreisky finally
came to the conclusion that Reder was due the status and the treatment of a prisoner
of war as defined in the Geneva Convention relative to the Treatment of Prisoners of
War.[757] In April 1972, during a state visit to Rome, Kreisky had intervened with Italian
President Giovanni Lenoe, but had had to make do with a vague response.[758] In particular, the Italian left wing wanted to uphold the 'myth of the resistance', according to
the Austrian embassy in Rome. However, the interventions had continued. Members of
the House of Commons in Britain, newspapers in Austria and Germany, Austrian federal presidents, cardinals and countless private individuals intervened on Reder's behalf.
On 25 January 1985, he was released and collected from the Graz-Thalerhof airfield
by Minister of Defence Friedhelm Frischenschlager, one of the three FPÖ ministers.
Since Reder had been found guilty of mass murder, and no one knew anything about his
prominent supporters – or at least, pretended not to know – a storm of indignation was
unleashed. If the minister in question, who was certainly given bad advice, had resigned
immediately, it would have saved Austria a great deal of trouble. As it was, however, a
sense of opprobrium remained, and the misdemeanours began to be catalogued: with
his support for the PLO, Kreisky had presented a challenge to the Western states, and
to Israel in particular. He, the Austrian Jew, was accused of harbouring 'hatred' towards
Israel. He had not drawn a clear boundary with the German Wehrmacht, or in fact the
SS, and had even appointed a former member of the Waffen SS to his cabinet. He had
shown flexibility with regard to the release of the terrorists of Bad Schönau. This was
clearly in line with a specific pattern. And now, of all things, a minister tolerated by
Kreisky did something that was seen as playing down National Socialist crimes. The
executive committee of the World Jewish Congress promptly cancelled a conference
that had been due to take place in Vienna at the end of January.[759] The SPÖ minister of
transport, Ferdinand Lacina, was no longer willing to share the government bench with
Frischenschlager. The ÖVP submitted a motion of no confidence against the Minister
of Defence. The SPÖ subsequently had no other choice than to side with Frischen-

schlager and accept his public apology, with the explanation that he had been guilty of an 'error of judgement'.

The Reder-Frischenschlager affair had only just subsided when the SPÖ found itself in a very different kind of predicament, since its unwavering support for nationalised industry and the repeatedly referenced workers in front of the furnaces threatened to become a fiasco. In 1984/85, Vranitzky had already recommended a reconsideration of the policy regarding nationalised industries.[760] In almost all cases, the subsidies were higher than the profits. For years, large orders from the GDR had made a positive impact and in Eisenhüttenstadt, close to the Polish border, a converted steel works had been built at a cost of twelve billion schillings, maintaining the level of employment at the United Austrian Iron and Steel Works (Vereinigte Österreichische Eisen- und Stahlwerke, or VOEST). However, it was precisely the business dealings with the GDR that were showing a deficit. And what was worse, in 1985, trade with the German Democratic Republic broke down completely.[761] The annual losses of VOEST were just as high as the share capital. Everything possible was named as the reason for the disaster: an international steel crisis, high losses at a steel works erected by VOEST in the USA and, finally, losses from speculation.[762] At the end of the day, the result remained the same, and the Director General of the group did not miss the opportunity to present the situation in dramatic terms when announcing the debacle: 'We are broke! – You must understand – We are broke!'[763] And so, the nationalised industry, the pride of the last fifty or sixty years, had to be saved. With the supplier companies included in the calculation, the number of jobs at stake was 100,000. A flagship and one of the distinguishing features of Austria was threatened with ruin. 71 billion schillings, an almost unimaginably high sum, had to be found in order to save at least parts of the group.[764] For the ÖVP in opposition, this was certainly no reason for triumph. But one thing was clear: the Little Coalition was in crisis.

And there appeared to be no end in sight to the misery. The next major issue to hit the Sinowatz/Steger government was the export of weapons to warring nations. On 12 July 1985, the Austrian ambassador to Athens, Herbert Amry, died. Ten days previously, he had reported to the Ministry of Foreign Affairs that he suspected that weapons were being illegally exported via Athens. The mystery of Amry's death could not be resolved, but journalists from the *profil* and *basta* magazines were able to corroborate the suspicions. Between 1981 and 1983, 200 'Noricum' howitzers (GHN-45) had been sent from Liezen to Iraq via Jordan. Later, it became known that supplies were also sent to Iran. Since both states had been at war since 1980, this could be classified as a clear breach of a whole series of statutory regulations, and as an endangerment to neutrality, for which politicians and managers alike were responsible before the law. The scale of the exports of howitzers, which Austria was itself forbidden from possessing due to the applicable State Treaty clauses, was still not clear. However, naturally, questions were asked as to what role had been played by the Federal Chancellor and the Minister of the Interior, who was responsible for issuing approvals for exports.[765]

Suddenly, what had been regarded as a special relationship to the Arab states as a result of Kreisky's efforts, and which it had been hoped would protect Austria against terrorist attacks, appeared no longer to hold. Far from it. In 1981, there had been clear evidence of Middle-Eastern terrorism. On 1 May, the Vienna city councillor Heinz Nittel had been shot in front of his home. News of the murder led to the cancellation of the traditional SPÖ May Day demonstrations, and it was initially regarded as a step back towards a recurrence of the civil war years of the interwar period. At first, Kreisky had wanted to link the assassination with the Viennese underworld. And although on the day after Nittel's murder, handbills appeared in Damascus in which a splinter group of the Fatah praised the murder of the 'Zionist agent' Nittel, the scepticism remained. The incident simply did not fit the image that had been cultivated in Austria, of all places, of Kreisky's Middle East policy. At least, not until 29 August 1981, when members of the same terrorist cell carried out its next serious attack, killing two people and injuring 21, when two of the perpetrators were captured. Now, at the latest, it was clear that Austria was in the cross-hairs of Middle-Eastern terrorism. In December 1982, Kreisky had received a written warning from the Abu Nidal group, which until that point was almost unknown in Austria, that Austria had become an area of operations for the Zionists and had opened its doors to the notorious traitor to the Arab cause, Yasir Arafat's Fatah, and if Austria did not revert to its former neutral course, terrible things would happen.[766] A third serious attack was carried out three years later.

On 27 December 1985, in the middle of the Christmas period, members of the Abu Nidal group stormed the check-in counters of the Israeli airline El Al at Vienna-Schwechat airport, killed three people and injured more than 40 others, some of them severely.[767] The attack came at precisely the time when an exchange of prisoners was made, with one Israeli being exchanged for 150 Palestinians. Direct warnings were issued of the attack, and it had ultimately been anticipated since 1982:[768] it had been announced that if the murderer of Heinz Nittel and perpetrator of the synagogue attack, Bahiy Younis, as well as two other members of the Abu Nidal group, were not released, further attacks would follow. Emissaries of Abu Nidal attempted to negotiate, but without success. Kreisky became involved. The Austrian ambassador in Paris, Georg Lennkh, flew to Libya and met Gaddafi – as was almost the standard procedure – in a Bedouin tent. Abu Nidal was Gaddafi's creation. Kreisky let it be known that if another attack occurred, he would be 'in a very difficult predicament', and 'would find it almost impossible to support the Palestinian cause with any degree of credibility.'[769] Furthermore, he said, Federal Chancellor Sinowatz also requested that Gaddafi intervene. However, evidently, Gaddafi's influence was insufficient, or it came too late. At any rate, he regretted in retrospect that he had not succeeded in preventing the attack. Since it was of course unclear what target the terrorists would choose, general precautionary security measures were intensified. Special security steps were taken at Schwechat airport. But they were not enough.

After three of the four terrorists had been arrested, the number of Palestinians sentenced to life imprisonment in Austria rose to six. And it had to be acknowledged that – in addition to the fact that this was quite clearly linked to the Russian Jews who were continuing to emigrate via Austria, presenting a potential risk, and also the fact that OPEC was based in Vienna, with the resulting danger of at least isolated incidents occurring – a new element had now emerged: even the best contacts with the Arab state governments and the efforts made by Bruno Kreisky and, until 1980, by UN Secretary General Kurt Waldheim, to achieve international recognition for the Palestinians, were unable to prevent dissatisfied groups from using terrorism to attract attention to themselves and disrupt Austro-Israeli relations. After London and Paris, Vienna was home to the largest Arab community in Europe. Had the Austrians been too naïve in thinking that Austria was an 'island of the blessed'? Was there really a connection between neo-Nazi groups in Austria and Arab terrorists, as had been suspected since the summer of 1982?[770] Was Kreisky correct when he said that: 'The fight against terror through the absolute refusal to comply with the demands of the terrorist has led to a capitulation of the terrorists only in extremely rare cases'?[771] Was negotiation really the better approach? In Germany, Italy, France, Britain and the USA, this view might originally have predominated, but in the interim, they had chosen to take a tougher line. The attacks in Vienna were at any rate a shock administered in doses. Yet as with comparable events, the sense of shock did not last for long. Soon, the focus of interest turned again to domestic politics. This was understandable, since the SPÖ was falling behind in terms of voter support for the first time since 1970. The downward trend that – and this fact should not be overlooked – had already begun in 1983 under Kreisky continued, and if there had been National Council elections in 1985, the People's Party would very likely have won. Elsewhere, too, the ÖVP was enjoying an improvement in its fortunes, since for the federal presidential elections due to be held in the spring of 1986, the party planned to put forward a candidate who was almost certain to win: Kurt Waldheim. The former ambassador to the USA, then minister of foreign affairs, and most recently secretary general to the United Nations for the past ten years, had been briefly considered by Fred Sinowatz as a joint candidate of the SPÖ and ÖVP. However, Waldheim then stood for election solely on behalf of the ÖVP, against the health minister in the Sinowatz/Steger government, Kurt Steyrer, who while he may have been highly regarded, was almost entirely unknown internationally. The candidate for the Green Alternative party, Freda Meissner-Blau, was still considered to be a political lightweight. The ÖVP remained confident of victory. However, the electoral campaign progressed in anything but a normal manner. And it began at least a year in advance.

Kurt Waldheim and the Watchlist

The campaign began with rumours that Waldheim had not merely been a simple officer of the German Wehrmacht, but that he had enjoyed close relations to the National Socialist regime, the precise nature of which were not known. Then, memories of the past returned. As early as 1971, when Waldheim first competed as a federal presidential candidate, documents had covertly been passed on and a photo had been shown of a strikingly tall, lean officer working as an interpreter at a meeting between Italian and German officers on the airfield of Podgorica in Montenegro. At that time, Waldheim was a member of the German Twelfth Army and later of the staff of Army Group E, the chief commander of which had been General Alexander Löhr. At the beginning of 1985, Löhr was honoured with a commemorative plaque in the National Defence Academy in Vienna's Monastery Barracks as the 'creator of the Austrian air force'. Since Löhr had been held responsible for the air attack on Belgrade in 1941 and been found guilty of war crimes by a Yugoslav military tribunal and executed, the unveiling of this plaque, which had been donated by a private club, was treated as a scandal. It had to be removed. Once again, albeit indirectly, Waldheim had been a topic of conversation. An increasing number of official bodies began to take an interest in him. Documents from the Austrian State Archives were revealed to foreign media with the aim of discrediting him, until finally, from March 1986 onwards, he was the subject of articles in the press on an almost daily basis. Since Waldheim remained silent, his autobiographical records glossed over the war years and he was unable to recall certain events, questions were asked as to why he did not speak out, why he had been unable to close the gaps in his memory earlier – and whether he should withdraw his candidacy. He did not withdraw, and on 8 June 1986, he was elected federal president.

From one day to the next, the whole of Austria was again under observation. After all, it had been the Austrians who had elected him. Anyone who thought that the excitement would gradually die down after the election would be disappointed. The tense atmosphere continued, although the individuals involved changed. Fred Sinowatz was not plagued by a bad conscience when even before the federal presidential election, he held secret talks with his minister of finance, Franz Vranitzky, and offered him his post. Vranitzky finally agreed. Waldheim's victory in the election tipped the balance: Sinowatz resigned the following day. Sinowatz had informed his predecessor, Kreisky, just shortly before resigning, and told him that Franz Vranitzky would be the new head of government. Of course, he knew that the 'new man' was not Kreisky's choice. Kreisky fumed.

Vranitzky would certainly have wished for a better start. On top of that, he knew that even from his own party he could not only expect support. He was a kind of outsider, without one of the usual party careers behind him; he was a technocrat and a banker, in other words, everything that did not fit in with a traditional socialist image.[772] Additionally, like many in business and high finance, he was a supporter of the grand coalition. However, at first, the work of government appeared to continue. Vranitzky accepted the partnership with the Freedom Party, which had been a wish of the honorary chairman of the SPÖ, Bruno Kreisky, and had been entered into by Sinowatz. It was also rumoured that he would even be willing to appoint the head of the Carinthian FPÖ, Jörg Haider, as minister of trade in place of Norbert Steger.[773] However, on 13 September 1986, everything turned out differently. Haider was elected to replace Steger as the federal leader of the FPÖ. His election was accompanied by right-wing extremist incidents and a 'Sieg Heil mood'.[774] The day after, Vranitzky announced his intention of terminating the Little Coalition and calling for new elections. These were held in November 1986. The ÖVP calculated that it had a good chance of becoming the strongest party in terms of votes and seats. This would be a vindication of the cautious, long-view strategy of Alois Mock. Vranitzky put paid to such hopes. The SPÖ remained in front. While there were some who thought that with the election of Kurt Waldheim, the ÖVP had already 'consumed' its victory, others saw the failure of the party as an act of liberation with which the SPÖ emerged from the nadir of its unpopularity with the electorate. However, ultimately, the ÖVP and SPÖ lost out against the Freedom Party, which succeeded in doubling its vote.

Vranitzky's rejection of the FPÖ was so clear that a little coalition was not possible. The far more fundamental decision was therefore that of the ÖVP, which probably also blanched at the prospect of collaboration with Jörg Haider's FPÖ, listened to the demands of business and industry, and perhaps was also happy to leave the aftershocks of Kurt Waldheim's election for Franz Vranitzky to deal with. Opinion was divided as to whether a grand coalition made sense. In the business sector, the majority approved. The grand coalition appeared to indicate stability, and there was hope that the period of economic upturn might return. Those who remembered the checkmate situation of the 1960s were of the opposite view, fearing a renewed bottleneck when it came to reforms, endless quarrels and a 'pack mentality'. However, the former order appeared to be restored. In January 1987, the grand coalition was re-launched in a new version. And 'The Two' set about steering the fate of the country for the eleventh time in the history of the Second Republic. There was plenty to do. It was expected from Vranitzky at the least that he would set about his business in an uninhibited, dynamic way. However, the still designated federal chancellor left the Ministry of Foreign Affairs to the ÖVP – or more precisely, to Alois Mock.

For Bruno Kreisky, the decision to transfer the Ministry of Foreign Affairs to one of the most consistent critics of his foreign policy was the straw that broke the camel's back. He had already informed Fred Sinowatz on 9 June 1986 that he wanted to realise a goal that he had been entertaining for some time and step down from his honorary chairmanship of the SPÖ. On 15 January 1987, he made his decision public. However, he proposed Adolf Schärf, saying that the takeover of the Ministry of Foreign Affairs by Alois Mock would be a break with the politics of the Deputy Chancellor and Federal President at that time. In reality, however, this was all about him and what he had written for the party archive just half a year previously. Kreisky settled his accounts with his party, and named those who had spoiled his honorary presidency, starting with Hannes Androsch, and no less unequivocally Fred Sinowatz, Leopold Gratz and Helmut Zilk. What particularly irked him about the latter was that he had unashamedly used television and the *Kronen-Zeitung* to his own advantage. And he did not expect Vranitzky to stand his ground against Mock. He pulled no punches.[775]

While the new Federal Chancellor regretted the decision of his predecessor, he had to accept it if he wanted to bring the new Grand Coalition into being. However, no one could claim that it made his start in the role any easier. In light of Austria's growing national debt, Vranitzky's announcement, 'The state is not a self-service store'[776] appeared more than plausible. There was nothing left to distribute, which is why a former banker and minister of finance appeared to be a good choice. However, any hopes that the new Grand Coalition would be able to hurl itself with all its energy into solving the imminent problems turned out to be unfounded. At first, the 'case' of Waldheim dominated and attracted the attention of most of the world.

In March 1986, the media had turned on the former UN secretary general Waldheim. Newspapers and magazines began to attempt to outdo each other with reports and 'revelations', until, finally, the boulevard publication, the *New York Post*, printed an article on 26 March entitled 'Papers show Waldheim was SS Butcher'.[777] This was a straightforward lie. But instead of taking the newspaper to court, there was simply a denial that this was the case. Prejudices and old enmities were revived. Who had allowed Yasir Arafat to appear before the General Assembly of the United Nations? Waldheim! Who had sharply criticised the USA for bombing northern Vietnamese dams? Waldheim! Now, attention was turned to Kurt Waldheim, the man who was running as a candidate for an office that for many was probably of little importance. Due to the fact that a portion of the suspicions, which could not initially be corroborated, regarding Waldheim's part in the war were later confirmed, and Waldheim repeatedly claimed to have gaps in his memory, gave renewed impetus to investigative journalists. Finally, Waldheim's statement, 'During the war, I only did what hundreds of thousands of other Austrians did: I fulfilled by duty as a soldier', was seen as a direct provocation. The 'case' of Waldheim took on proportions well beyond the matter itself and became a settling of accounts with the war and post-war period in Austria. In the process, no further interest was taken in the contribution made by Austrians to the German resistance, but instead, the formulation of the Moscow Declaration, according to which Austria was the first victim of the National Socialist policy of expansion, was dismissed as a sham. In reality, Austrians had played a considerable part in Germany's war effort and, in particular, in the regime's acts of mass murder. The focus was therefore not on the victims, but on the perpetrators, it was claimed. The situation was highly reminiscent of the first phase of the State Treaty negotiations, when in 1947, the Soviet representative in the State Treaty commission, Fedor T. Gusev, became increasingly insistent and reproached the Austrian foreign minister, Karl Gruber, for Austria's part in the war. This notwithstanding, for the Federal President and Federal Chancellor, for ministers and for a considerable portion of civil society, the phrase 'fulfilment of duty' had applied over the decades, at least analogously. It was only after forty years had passed that such simple answers were no longer accepted. A differentiation had already been made a long time previously, but who was interested in that? It did not take long for Waldheim to become a symbol of Austria's handling of its past. For this reason, the campaign against Waldheim soon mutated into a reckoning with the Austrian post-war era.

The simple formulation by the USA was: 'They had it too long too good.' The 'case' of Waldheim was taken as a welcome opportunity to vent the pent-up frustration over Austria. This was taken up in Austria itself, and forty years after the start of the war, a generation of young people who had been born after it ended began to ask searching questions.

'I didn't elect him' was the electoral slogan of those who wanted to distance themselves from Waldheim. Yet hardly anyone could entirely disassociate themselves from the blanket judgement that branded Austria as a Nazi country and Austrians as anti-Semites. Not even the Israelite Religious Community in Vienna managed to prevent, or at least minimise, the generalisations.[779] On 27 April 1987, the date of the Austrian declaration of independence, of all days, the Waldheim affair took a dramatic new turn, when at the request of the World Jewish Congress, the American Justice Department added Waldheim to its list of suspected war criminals, or 'Watchlist'. It was a prejudgement. Austria had been informed of the move in advance. In the event that the Chancellor or the government wanted to vouch for Waldheim having done no wrong, the measure would have been left to the American government. Yet no one was willing to vouch for him. Instead, a Historical Commission was installed, consisting primarily of the presidents and members of a UNESCO sub-commission, the International Commission of Military History. The historians were tasked with checking the facts.

From the formation of the Commission to the submission of its final report, 160 days passed. On 8 February 1988, the report was passed to the federal government. Immediately, a process of interpretation and re-interpretation began. Some people understood the report as a declaration of Waldheim's guilt by the Commission, while others saw it as confirmation that he was absolutely innocent. Only subsequently did it become known that the historians had not only been exposed to enormous public pressure, that repeated attempts were made to fob it off with falsified documents and that large bribes had also been involved.[780] The report was a verdict.

It took several days for the greatest turmoil to die down and the report could be read and analysed properly. One thing very quickly became clear, namely the fact that the question of whether Kurt Waldheim could be accused of being a war criminal was flatly denied. However, there were also formulations that did level accusations at him, and which were essentially based on the principle that knowledge is complicity. Did this apply to an entire generation? The consequence of the report was a type of condemnation of the Austrian Federal President by the Western community of states. While the same was not true of the Arab world, or the Soviet Union and the states within the Soviet sphere of influence, these were not countries to which Waldheim wished to pay a state visit.

It was only when the debate surrounding Kurt Waldheim's part in the war had come to an end that something like normality returned. The isolation of the Federal President led to a shift in duties, in that it was more or less the Chancellor and Foreign Minister alone who were now tasked with representing Austria abroad. Both had to tackle handicaps. During the 1986 election campaign, Alois Mock was diagnosed with Parkinson's disease, which took an increasing physical toll on him. However, everyday political life continued relentlessly despite this. The Chancellor, meanwhile, saw not so much himself, but his party as suffering from a depression in popularity. Vranitzky was forced to acknowledge that he was losing control over his own party. He was repeatedly compared to Kreisky, and he had to endure hearing that he was less inspiring, had no visions for the future and was probably also not the right person for presenting Austria to the world. The membership of the Chancellor's party declined steadily.[781] SPÖ members transferred their loyalty to Haider's Freedom Party and the 'Greens', which presented themselves not only as a pro-environment party, but also as a left-wing alternative. Both parties attracted increasing numbers of young people, who wanted to distance themselves from what Haider called the 'old parties'.

While both Vranitzky and Mock did battle with their respective difficulties, they were suddenly and unexpectedly faced with challenges that may well have marked the greatest watershed in Austrian post-war history since the Allied occupation and the State Treaty.

21 The Implosion in the East

21 Rejoicing over a successful escape. East German citizens after the Pan-European Picnic on the Austro-Hungarian border on 19 August 1989. The announcement of a festival on the border between St. Margarethen in Burgenland and Sopronköhida in Hungary on the birthday of the last Austrian emperor and king of Hungary, Karl I (Károly IV), was used by more than 700 East German citizens to flee. In doing so, they not only triggered a larger refugee movement but also signalised the end of Communist rule in East-Central Europe. (Photo: APA picturedesk)

Was it Friedrich Engels, Thomas Mann or Hugo von Hofmannsthal[782] who first began to use the phrase 'conservative revolution' in literature and debate? At any rate, in 1950, the term was updated by Armin Mohler. Common to most, if not all definitions was that they referred to 'right-wing' trends and movements, and that their actors were classified as anti-liberal, anti-democratic and anti-egalitarian.

In 1989, the majority of the demonstrators demanding fundamental changes in the East-Central European, Communist-ruled states within the sphere of influence of the Soviet Union would have vehemently rejected being labelled as actors of a conservative revolution. In retrospect, however, it could certainly be seen that they fitted such a description. Initially, however, they were individuals playing a part in a process that after 1914 and 1939 made 1989 the third epochal year of the twentieth century.

The Hope for Eternal Peace

In Austria, like in most countries of the world, there was astonishment at the end of the 1980s at how the changes in the Soviet Union came about. The Soviet state and party leader, Mikhail S. Gorbachev, initiated a full departure from the Brezhnev doctrine that had applied since 1968, and carried along the states of the Communist bloc in the forecourt of the Soviet Union. As a result, the Soviet community of states threatened to break up on the basis of something that had been designed to maintain their system, namely the results of the Conference on Security and Cooperation in Europe and the 'Helsinki Final Act'. However, it was without doubt more than the freedom of information, which was also slowly taking effect in the 'eastern bloc', that then led to the implosion. The USA under President Ronald Reagan had done all it could to 'downgrade' the Soviet Union, and it had achieved its aim. The political system and economic space of the eastern bloc, which could now only be kept afloat with a great deal of effort, with its cumbersome control mechanisms and egalitarian social orders, were in the throes of collapse, and could only have been maintained by means of a massive use of military force. Gorbachev was not prepared to apply such force. The result was a chain reaction.[783]

In Poland, the way was paved by the Solidarność trade union movement, while in Hungary, it was the growing economic liberalism and the memories of 1956 that led to the changes, in Czechoslovakia, the reference to 1968, and in the GDR, protests against the division of Germany and the desire, which could certainly be seen as nationalistic, for a union with the Federal Republic of Germany. For all the East-Central European states, Austria was the traditional gateway to the West, and Hungarians, Czechs and Poles had their own special relationship to it. The GDR, too, had used this 'gateway'. In 1989, neutral Austria once again offered itself up, as it had done in 1956, 1968 and 1981. It was to be the last time it would so.

Hungary was the first country that not only set about reforming its political system, but also sent out a visible signal that it wanted to abandon its isolation, which had anyway already begun to crumble. Prime Minister Miklós Németh paid his first foreign visit, not to Moscow, as 'tradition' demanded it, but to Austria. He met with Federal Chancellor Vranitzky in Rust and informed him that the border security facilities were to be dismantled. At the Romanian border, their removal was already fully underway. On 2 May 1989, work began on the border with Austria. Finally, on 27 June, the Austrian and Hungarian foreign ministers, Alois Mock and Gyula Horn, posing for the media, cut through the final section of barbed wire. Six weeks later, on 19 August 1989, around 700 GDR citizens took advantage of a Pan-European Picnic organised directly on the Austro-Hungarian border to mark the birthday of the last Austrian emperor, Karl, in order to flee. No shots were fired. Five days later, a SwissAir plane brought 108 GDR citizens to Schwechat airport in Vienna. They were taken by bus to the German border at Passau. Even while they were still in the bus, they began singing 'Deutschland, Deutschland über alles' (Germany, Germany above all else).[784] On 11 September, Hungary fully opened its borders in order to allow GDR citizens to pass through.

In Austria, there was confusion as to how to respond. It was beyond question that sympathy clearly lay with those who wanted to cast off or flee the old regime. However, in order to avoid breaching its obligations as a neutral country by transporting the refugees via the state-owned Federal Railways, the GDR citizens who had already fled on 19 August were taken to the border of the Federal Republic by bus. The same procedure was applied to the mass exodus of East Germans in September. When the numbers began to be counted, it emerged that approximately 50,000 people had found their way into the Federal Republic of Germany via Austria in all manner of ways.[785] In order to avoid the possibility of having to justify himself, Federal Chancellor Vranitzky initially cancelled a planned visit to East Berlin on 25 September.[786] Two months later, the Chancellor did decide to travel to Berlin, however. His decision was probably influenced by the assessment of Austrian diplomats, who regarded it as improbable that the GDR would collapse any time soon.[787] They were not alone in thinking this. Vranitzky indicated that he did not intend to interfere. For East Germany, this visit, as well as a return visit to Vienna shortly afterwards by the East German Prime Minister Hans Modrow, was an important signal, in that they hoped to be able to prop up their regime with Austrian assistance. For the *Berliner Zeitung*, Austria was a 'friend in difficult times'.[788] Modrow could also well imagine that the GDR, or even better, the whole of Germany, could, like Austria, be perpetually neutral. Foreign Minister Mock described the idea as 'unrealistic'. He was to be proved right, and when it came to the German unification, the issue was not whether, but rather when – all gloomy predictions and the mutterings about a 'Fourth Reich' notwithstanding.

Almost at the same time as in Hungary, in Poland, too, decisive steps were being made to end Communist rule. On 24 August 1989, one of the leading opposition politicians, Tadeusz Mazowiecki, was elected as the first non-Communist head of government. Finally, from 4 September onwards, the Monday demonstrations in Leipzig and other major cities in the GDR also ushered in the transition in East Germany. People in the GDR had been stirred up by the images of the events on the Austro-Hungarian border. With chants of 'Wir sind das Volk' (We are the people) and 'Deutschland einig Vaterland' (Germany, united fatherland), the focus of the protest and the aims behind the demonstrations were expressed in a way that could not be ignored. On 9 November, the border to the FRG was opened.

Eight days later, the protest movement in Czechoslovakia also escalated. The Czech Communists wanted to retain power. For a short period, the threat of the use of force loomed. Then a non-violent form of transition was found, and the spokesman of the Civic Forum, Václav Havel, was elected as state president. Ultimately, Romania was the only country in which the transition from Communist rule to semi-democratic conditions was of a violent nature. Over 1,000 people lost their lives. The dictator of many years, Nicolae Ceaușescu, and his wife were killed on 25 December 1989.

In Austria, developments were followed right up close in some cases. In December 1989, when the borders to Czechoslovakia were freely passable for 24 hours, hundreds of buses could be seen rolling towards eastern Austria and through Vienna. There were scenes of fraternisation as well as occasional rejection. Yet the main mood was one of joy, and the prospect of seeing the bloody twentieth century come to a peaceful close was also a reason to celebrate. The Cold War did indeed appear to have come to an end, without it being possible to assess what would come afterwards, and what would happen next. However, it was at least possible to foresee that the dawning of the end of the Warsaw Pact, COMECON and a Soviet glacis of East-Central European states could result in something that would be a turning point, and not only for Austria. Borders became porous, and border checks a mere formality. People only gradually became aware of the fact that the distance between Vienna and Cracow was less than between Vienna and Innsbruck, or that Bregenz was just as far away as Przemyśl on the Polish-Ukrainian border. Until then, all that had been known was that Bregenz was closer to Paris than it was to Vienna.

Being good neighbours was something that had to be learned, and it demanded mutual consideration of each others' needs. And this was lacking, at least initially, not

least in Austria. The fact remained largely ignored that as a result of the discussion surrounding Kurt Waldheim, there was a huge increase in the level of reflection in Austria
on modern and recent history, particularly with regard to the National Socialist period,
which was by all means paralleled in the states of East-Central Europe. In Poland, work
began on analysing more closely Poland's participation in the persecution of the Jews.[789]
In Czechoslovakia, the calling into question of the legality of the Beneš decrees, with
which the collective expulsion of the German-speaking population in 1945/46 without
compensation was justified, jarred the nation's self-image and led to harsh reactions,
including towards Austria.[790] In Hungary, the involvement of the prime minister at
the time of the revolution of 1956, Imre Nagy, in the shooting of the Czar's family
in Yekaterinburg in 1918, was furiously denied.[791] However, the 'reform states' would
certainly need to be given time in order to process their earlier past, since they were still
fully engaged with their most recent history. Ultimately, this connected them to Austria
and separated them from it at the same time. All the states had gone through traumas.

   However, the priority was to handle the changes brought about by the respective revolutions. This had its positive sides but it was also expressed in highly unattractive ways.
Among many Austrians, mainly in the east, a new type of business sense was awakened.
People travelled to Hungary and Czechoslovakia to go shopping or visit the hairdresser.
In tiny locations in Lower Austria and Czechoslovakia, TV sets, washing machines and
technical appliances of all kinds were stacked up in the hope of attracting customers
'from over there'. However, this did not mean that prejudices were broken down. Quite
the opposite: the fear of criminals, who might use the opportunity for crossing the
border unchecked, increased rapidly. In Hohenau an der March, for example, residents
prevented the construction of an emergency bridge designed to set small-scale border
traffic in motion. The forthcoming regional diet (Landtag) elections led the governor
of Burgenland, Hans Sipötz, to demand the deployment of Federal Army assistance
troops in September 1990. The Council of Ministers agreed to his request. As had
already occurred in 1967, the army was brought in to provide what was ultimately an
assistance deployment motivated by domestic politics. This deployment would last for
21 years, until 2011... Finally, 450 kilometres of state border were guarded.

   In fact, nothing expressed the change more clearly. Until 1989, the 'East' had been
hermetically sealed off; in 1990, eastern Austria began to unbar its gates. And without there being a direct connection, Austria regained a piece of its sovereignty. On 12
September 1990, the so-called 'Two Plus Four Agreement' was signed in Berlin, which
ended the division of Germany and gave the unified country its full sovereignty. As a
result, the clause in the Austrian State Treaty no longer applied according to which
Austria was obliged to prevent a rearmament of Germany. On 6 November 1990, the
Austrian federal government sent the four other signatories of the State Treaty a note,
in which it was stated that a change had occurred not only in relation to Germany, but

that it was no longer in keeping with the times that Austria should continue to be subject to military and air traffic regulations that had hypothetically become outdated.[792] These regulations were set out in Articles 13 to 16 of the State Treaty. Since the former Allies acknowledged this note, and gave their approval, most of the regulations relating to 'special weapons' and the prohibition on the acquisition of 'civil aircraft which are of German or Japanese design' or such aeroplanes of which, like the 'Airbus', important parts were of German or Japanese origin, no longer applied. Austria still had no desire to possess nuclear weapons and weapons of mass destruction, or chemical weapons. However, now it was permitted to purchase guided anti-tank missiles, air defence rockets and artillery that could fire over 30 kilometres. The fact that Austria was also permitted to possess sea mines, torpedoes and submarines could be taken with a small pinch of salt.

It might also have been worth declaring other articles in the State Treaty to be obsolete, such as the provision in Article 10, point 2, which regulated the modalities of expulsion from the country and the deterioration of assets of the Habsburgs in a similar manner to the federal law of 3 April 1919. However, the SPÖ at least were not prepared to interfere with these. The regulation therefore remained valid at constitutional level. Austria, therefore, was still required to undertake 'to maintain the law of 3rd April, 1919, concerning the House of Hapsburg-Lorraine'. The titles and privileges of the nobility also remained abolished. However, Article 22, point 13 certainly was revoked. Here, it was determined that Austria should undertake not to sell or to restore to their former owners that property to which the term 'German Assets' was applied. Now, these businesses and capital were permitted to be outsourced from the nationalised industrial administration and sold. As a result, the upheaval in Europe was not just limited to the states of the Soviet bloc. And Austria was one of the major beneficiaries – without having done any more than exploiting its geographical and security policy position. Its function as a bridge was no longer relevant. In 1990, it had already been replaced by a very different one: Austria became a springboard. While economic relations between Austria and the COMECON countries had already been very good prior to 1989, now competition set in for securing new sales markets. This began with direct investments in Hungary and was to be followed by the other reform states.[793] And at first, it appeared that the growth knew no limits. It was no matter that the exports to most of the East-Central European states declined in 1990. These levels would soon recover.

However, the elimination of the bridge function also led to the loss of something else that had contributed like almost nothing else to Austria's self-understanding. It was such an attractive metaphor. American presidents and Soviet state and party leaders had made use of it and had met in Vienna. The UN organisations based in Vienna made it clear that the global organisation was also at home in the forecourt of the eastern bloc, in a country that considered itself to be a part of the West, but which had longer and more extensive relationships with the Communist states of eastern-central and south-eastern Europe than most Western states. Trade and cultural exchange flourished. Austria also offered travel opportunities that were highly valued. When, for example, Polish Catholic priests wished to travel to Rome and the Vatican in order to request an audience with Pope John Paul II, they had to fly via Vienna, since no direct flights were available. Now, however, there was suddenly no more 'East'. The question also arose as to whether anyone still needed the 'bridge' at all. Of course, the answer, 'no!', was a disappointment. In Budapest, Prague and Warsaw, no bones were made of the fact that it was not Vienna, but Berlin, Paris and London that were now the focus of orientation. The American government, at least under President George Bush sen., gave its full backing to the potential new allies in Europe. While Austria played a role as a foothold and a base for company headquarters, it no longer did so when it came to military plans.[794] Nonetheless, for a time, the Pentagon sent its best people to Austria – a country that had to redefine itself, just like East-Central Europe.

A Decidedly Patient Wait

On 17 July 1989, the federal government submitted a request for the assumption of negotiations regarding membership of the European communities. Three weeks after Alois Mock and Gyula Horn had undertaken the symbolic act of cutting through the Iron Curtain, a step was made, after thorough consideration and preparations, that had been the subject of deliberations and negotiations for almost exactly a quarter of a century, disappointments included. At this point in time, the step still appeared risky, and without a clear prospect of success. However, it had been planned in advance. Franz Vranitzky, who in October 1988 had met with Mikhail Gorbachev in Moscow, had taken soundings and came back home with a nice anecdote. Gorbachev had asked him several times: 'Do you know Margaret Thatcher?' Vranitzky had said that he did. 'Do you know her well?' The Chancellor had again replied in the affirmative. Then, Gorbachev had said: 'And you still want to join the EEC?'[795] However, what was of far greater importance was what the Soviet prime minister, Nikolai Ryzhkov, had given him to think about on the plane journey back home: the government of the Soviet Union acknowledges the Austrian desire to join the EEC, but 'assumes that Austria will meet all its requirements'. No further information was provided as to what this might mean. Now, the Austrians could choose to make of it what they would.

In Brussels, the reaction was not one of joy. The attitude of the French president of the European Commission, Jacques Delors, and 'the cool to dismissive behaviour of French diplomacy', as well as the no less unequivocal rejection by Belgian politicians, spoke volumes.[796] The former Belgian foreign minister, Mark Eyskens, also responded promptly with the notion, which was not meant to be taken seriously, that now, the European Community should negotiate with the Soviet Union regarding Austrian neutrality.[797] Austria, he claimed, wanted to be treated as a 'special case', as so often in the past.

Since the first soundings had been taken by Foreign Minister Kreisky in 1959 and Federal Chancellor Gorbach in 1963, Austria had consistently been refused permission to become full members by the Russians. In doing so, they referred alternately to neutrality and to the State Treaty, which denied Austria the right to a union with Germany – including economic union. The membership of EFTA was accepted, but the association agreement with the EEC had not elicited any further response aside from warnings. Now, however, the SPÖ/ÖVP coalition went all out. There was a desire to be involved in European unification, with a reluctance to continue accepting recognisable economic disadvantages, and precisely in light of the attitude of the West towards the Federal President, not to run the risk of being forced into isolation. Franz Vranitzky and the foreign ministers of the two first cabinets, Peter Jankowitsch and Alois Mock, did their best to exploit the opportunities that arose from the changes brought about by Mikhail Gorbachev. There was a ray of light seen in the change in the Soviet attitude, perhaps again – as had already been the case in 1955 – the 'favourable moment'. So it was that Austria formally requested that accession negotiations with the European Economic Community begin. This made it the first neutral state to take such a step. All the others followed, including Switzerland.

However, the Soviets were not impressed by the fact that in the Austrian note in which the request was made to start accession talks, there was reference to the fact that Austria assumed that in the case of an agreement with the European Economic Community, the continuing neutral status of the country should as a matter of course be taken into consideration. In August 1989, the Soviet Union protested against the Austrian intention of starting negotiations with the European Communities. Even if it was only a formal protest, it caused the willingness of the EEC to start negotiations to flag. One would have to wait and see how things developed.

In light of the attempts to join the EEC and the awakening in the east, other regions naturally faded somewhat into the background. Yet it was precisely here that entirely new, unusual experiences would follow. Austria, which liked to think of itself as 'everybody's darling', could also become a bogeyman.

In the spring of 1991, a paper did the rounds of the staffs of the Yugoslavian People's Army. It was not entirely clear whether it was the basis for military exercises or was intended as a document to be produced on some kind of particular day 'X'. It was the scenario 'Bedem-91' (protective shield-91), and what it described was particularly appalling. Hungary, Bulgaria and Albania had, it claimed, set themselves the goal, with the aid of NATO, of 'realising their territorial claims in relation to Yugoslavia'. Slovenia, Croatia and Macedonia would call NATO to their aid in order to accelerate their detachment from the Federation of Yugoslavia. Austria, it said, had decided 'to annul the State Treaty and enter into the NATO Alliance'. Austrian soldiers had also participated in NATO exercises. The supreme command of the north-western army group was in Klagenfurt. If massive air attacks on targets in Serbia and Montenegro failed to deliver the desired success, ground troops would be deployed, and so on, and so forth. The paper was passed on to Austria by Slovene authorities. Yet this targeted disinformation was not needed in order to attract Austrian attention to developments in Yugoslavia and the danger that they presented.[798] The atmosphere had been tense for a long time, and Europe remained in a process of upheaval.

Slovenia and Croatia prepared their declarations of independence for the end of June 1991. However, they also wanted to be recognised internationally as quickly as possible, and they looked for support. The USA, the Soviet Union and, what counted most, the states of the European Community, showed Ljubljana and Zagreb the cold shoulder. A single state expressed sympathy towards them: Austria. A cautious, then increasingly stormy rapprochement began, and caused consternation all round.

The Yugoslavian news agency 'Tanjug' gave voice to the fear that: 'If Slovenia were to become independent, it would sooner or later become the tenth federal state of Austria.'[799] France accused Austria of facilitating the breakup of Yugoslavia. Italy urgently advised the Slovenes not to listen to any 'ambiguous messages from Vienna'. The USA sent a special envoy to Vienna; the Soviet prime minister, Valentin S. Pavlov, invoked the unity of Yugoslavia; the Italian prime minister, Giulio Andreotti, spoke of the danger of a 'pan-German' union between Germans and Austrians, which would threaten Italy and Yugoslavia alike; German Foreign Minister Genscher telephoned the Austrian Federal Chancellor and warned of the necessity of maintaining a united Yugoslavia.[800] Even the Vatican expressed its concern.[801]

By contrast, the Ministry of Foreign Affairs in Vienna repeatedly stressed that, naturally, steps would be taken in harmony with the major powers, and with Europe in particular, and that no attempt would be made to go it alone. This assurance had a specific and also a banal background. In its letter to Brussels, in which Austria had requested the assumption of accession negotiations with the EEC, it had still not received a substantive answer. And so, the order of the day was to think and act in a 'European' way. And it was precisely this that led to the decisiveness with which Vienna chose to support Slovenia and Croatia in the long term to ebb away, making way for a period of cautious waiting. What was more, opinions were also divided in Vienna. Federal Chancellor Vranitzky made it clear that he regarded the unity of Yugoslavia as essential, while Deputy Chancellor and Foreign Minister Mock maintained his support for Ljubljana and welcomed its desire for independence.

However, everyone, the Americans, the Soviets, the Europeans in the EEC and Austria, were overrun by events. Croatia and Slovenia declared their independence on 25

June. And the Yugoslavian People's Army did exactly what had been feared: it intervened. What was to be done?

The disintegration of the eastern bloc had been a surprise. The Warsaw Pact was in the midst of being dissolved. Yugoslavia was not affected by this. It was not part of the eastern bloc, was not a member of the Warsaw Pact, and was one of the most important of the nonaligned states. At the latest following the death of State President and Marshal Josip Broz-Tito in 1980, the southern Slav state, which was so popularly compared to the Habsburg Monarchy, had become increasingly unstable. The republics strove to gain independence and wanted to reorient themselves. The economy went downhill. The disintegration of the Federation was imminent. And Austria was prepared – like never before! Only when the event actually happened, once again, what had been planned on paper did not tie in with reality. There was shooting close to the border. Yugoslavian aeroplanes repeatedly infringed Austrian air space, and finally flew over Graz. Yet the government in Vienna could not decide what to do. Hunters in Styria then announced that they would take self-defence measures. Finally, on 28 June 1991, Minister of Defence Werner Fasslabend gave the instruction for the army to be deployed. However, this was not an assistance deployment as had been the case in Burgenland, where refugees were picked up, but a security deployment, with everything that this entailed: tanks, aeroplanes and 4,000, then later, 6,000 soldiers.

While Federal Army forces moved forward to the areas bordering Yugoslavia, the diplomatic measures also began. The Austrian Ambassador in Belgrade demanded information about the military activities of the People's Army. Belgrade provided reassurance. Yet it emerged that the government no longer had any influence over the military. The leadership of the armed forces had no intention of breaking off its campaign in Slovenia. There was talk of war. Austria's media, particularly the tabloid press, were happy to take up this theme, and shortly afterwards, there were reports of a 'total war'. Emotions ran high. It was assumed that streams of refugees would cross the border, although, thank God, they did not materialise. The Federal Army, the members of which were not so sure whether or not this was war, prepared two internment camps in case war really had broken out. The international law experts, who were not sure themselves at first, provided assurance, however: this was not war, since for this to be the case, two sovereign states were required, and Slovenia was not yet such a state. Confusion continued to reign.

Austria found itself pursuing a unilateral path. The USA, the (still extant) Soviet Union and the European Community continued to back the unity of Yugoslavia. Hungary did not concentrate military forces along its southern border; while Italy had taken emergency measures and was preparing to accept refugees, it did not display any particular sense of alarm. And in Vienna, the question was asked, probably quite rightly, as to why the rest of Europe was doing nothing.

For Serbia and the Yugoslav People's Army, therefore, Austria was an easy target for attack and suspicion. And the date was inviting in every way. It was Friday, 28 June. Probably, hardly anyone in Austria had thought of honouring this day in any particular way. However, for the Serbs in Yugoslavia, the situation was entirely different. The 28th of June was 'Vidovdan', St. Vitus' Day. It was said that on this day, in 1389, after the Battle of Kosovo Field, the victorious Sultan Murad had been murdered by the Serb Miloš Obilić. On 28 June 1914, and this should in fact have been more likely to be in people's memory, the Austro-Hungarian heir to the throne, Archduke Franz Ferdinand, was shot in Sarajevo on this same St. Vitus' Day. The day had a certain aura about it. The central government in Belgrade therefore made use of the date and in a verbal note and in its media accused Austria of creating an escalation by moving troops to the border, thus engendering a dangerous situation. In addition, it was claimed that Austria had recognised Slovenia at a diplomatic level, which was utterly untrue.

On 28 June and the days that followed, information and disinformation went hand in hand. It was only on 1 July that there was a de-escalation, but the situation had by no means become clear. All that was unequivocally known was that the troops from the Yugoslav People's Army had not only failed to achieve their goal of re-occupying the borders with Austria, Hungary and Italy, but that they were now in a serious predicament. All conflicting parties finally agreed to an immediate ceasefire and the return of the troops to their barracks. In return, Slovenia and Croatia were to put the consequences of their independence on hold for three months.

This notwithstanding, the next steps were taken in the Ministry of Foreign Affairs in Vienna. All 35 member states of the Organisation for Security and Cooperation in Europe (OSCE) were requested to attend an urgent meeting at the Conflict Prevention Centre in Vienna. It was the first time that such an event had been held.

It is likely that the diplomats' banter went unnoticed amid the general agitation. Equally, almost no attention was paid to the fact that on 2 July, Minister Fasslabend dissolved the army command, one of the achievements of the army reforms of the 1970s. On 5 July and after the EC and Yugoslavia, together with the secessionist republics, had reached agreement in Brijuni regarding an orderly dissolution of the Federal Republic, the conflict could be regarded as having been resolved. One EU state after another expressed support for recognising the independent states of Slovenia and Croatia. They were joined by Austria on 17 January 1992. The Socialist Federal Republic of Yugoslavia was consigned to history.

If anyone had believed that the secession of Slovenia and Croatia would mark the end of the disintegration of Yugoslavia, they were to be proved thoroughly wrong. The process of disintegration continued. However, there was a reluctance to talk of war, or at least, not yet. However, this was indeed war. So began an object lesson that could not have been more bitter, not only for the states emerging from the Yugoslavian federation, but also for the whole of Europe. People had become so used to the idea of Europe being divided into blocs, which repeatedly forced each other with threatening gestures to uphold the power political conditions that had applied since 1945. If attention was paid to anything, then to a major war. A 'small' war was a 'sandbox game'. In the interim, on 25 February 1991, the six states that still belonged to the Warsaw Pact signed a protocol regarding the end of the military agreements that had been valid until that point. One month later, the Pact was formally dissolved. Half a million Soviet soldiers, some of whom were stationed close to Austria, withdrew. It had been repeatedly feared that the Soviets, together with other Pact members, would march into Yugoslavia and force the Balkan state to join the Eastern alliance system.

Instead, on 7 December 1991, in a hunting lodge in Belarus, the Union of Socialist Soviet Republics decided to discontinue its 'existence as a subject of international law and as a geopolitical reality'.[802] Thus ended a threat that had hung over Yugoslavia for years, as well as a compulsion for it to stay together. And what people had hoped to prevent for so long then occurred: Yugoslavia disintegrated and became consumed by a war that would create unrest in the Balkan region for almost ten years to come. The secession of Slovenia had still somehow been manageable. The war in Croatia, and certainly the war in Bosnia, soon got out of control. They culminated in genocide and forced displacements. The shocking thing about it was that people who were thought to be peaceful neighbours began attacking each other and showing no inhibitions. The situation was reminiscent of the Balkan Wars of 1912/13, when local massacres and mass murders had also taken place. The Austrian freedom movement led by Bertha von Suttner had argued at that time that such atrocities could only take place in countries that lay outside the Western cultural sphere. The great cultured nations would continue to uphold their obligation to find peaceful ways of resolving disputes. A fundamental error, both then and during the subsequent course of the twentieth century. This final decade was to be no exception.

For Austria, there was an emotional side to events from the start. Not only Slovenia, but also Croatia, Bosnia and Herzegovina had been part of the Habsburg Monarchy. Sympathy was therefore directed mainly towards the Slovenes, Croats and Bosnians. Reports about massacres of the Croatian population in urban and rural regions, the start of systematic expulsions and finally the beginning of the siege of Sarajevo by Serb insurgents and forces of the Yugoslav Army triggered outrage and were reminiscent of events that had long been consigned to the past: the war waged by the Imperial and Royal Army against Serbia during the First World War and the partisan fighting during the Second World War, which was regarded as a war without fronts. It was of course pure coincidence that the Austrian Federal President, who had been accused not least of participating in the Balkan war of 1943 to 1945, began the final months of his period of office at the same time as the first climaxes of the Croatian and Bosnian war and declined to run for a further term.

This brought a presidency to an end that had not only begun with nothing less than a hate-filled dispute, but which had also left deep scars in Austria. Since 1986, the focus had been not only on reconsidering the National Socialist period and the World War away from debates on the subject among historians, but also on starting a new discussion about victims and perpetrators. This discussion was now in full swing and had also made an impact on politics. Most noteworthy was the speech by Federal Chancellor Vranitzky on 8 July 1991 in the National Council (Nationalrat). In what was to a certain extent intended to replicate a throwaway comment made by FPÖ leader and now governor of Carinthia, Jörg Haider, about the 'orderly employment policy' of the National Socialists, Vranitzky noted that:

> We acknowledge all the facts of our history and the acts carried out by all sections of our population, the good and the evil. And in just the same way that we claim the good for ourselves, so we must apologise for the evil, to the survivors and to the descendants of the dead. This acknowledgement has been repeatedly omitted by Austrian politicians. I would like to do this today, expressly also in the name of the Austrian federal government: as a standard for the relationship that we must have to our history today, in other words, as a standard for the political culture in our country, but also as our contribution to the new political culture in Europe.[803]

This speech was intended to present a clear position by Austria and bring an end, to a certain degree, to the debate surrounding Kurt Waldheim. The aim was to make it clear that Austria accepted without reservation the basic consensus of the post-war era: the renunciation of fascist tendencies of all kinds. Three weeks later, Austria was invited to Brussels for negotiations.

The modalities were clear and new at the same time. Since Portugal and Spain had entered the European Economic Community in 1986, they had enjoyed considerable upward development. In the interim, the Community had become the European Union (EU). An arduous and above all, lengthy process of negotiation began, together with the other applicants for entry, Norway, Sweden and Finland. Chapter for chapter had to be worked through and negotiated. Ultimately, in the case of Austria, the issue was not individual items, rights and limitations, indeed no longer even the amounts that the new member had to pay into the Community pot, but the relationship with Germany and neutrality. Sweden and Finland were also neutral. Austria, however, was perpetually neutral. And, of course, the fact could not be ignored that Austria's efforts had been met with resistance from the Soviet Union since the 1960s, which suspected a type of union with Germany by the back door if Austria entered the EEC. People were well aware of this in Vienna, Moscow and Brussels.

The Soviet Union had collapsed in 1991. Nonetheless, the matter had to be considered as to how relations with the post-Soviet Commonwealth of Independent States (CIS), and particularly Russia, should develop. Was the Russian Federation legitimised to also assert its right as successor state in the matter of the State Treaty? Once again, opinions within the government were divided. On 4 February 1992, the Russian ambassador in Vienna, Valeri N. Popov, handed Foreign Minister Alois Mock the draft of a paper in which the Russian Federation provided assurance that it wished to uphold all international agreements, particularly the State Treaty. Since the situation was still volatile in Russia, and each of the individual successor states to the Soviet Union wanted to be recognised, the Austrians could take their time. However, playing dead for an unlimited length of time was also not an option. In the Ministry of Foreign Affairs, however, there were concerns that arose not so much from bilateral relations but from the fear that Brussels might get the idea that Austria was restricted in its capacity to act. So Austria further delayed on the issue of recognition, but certainly showed itself willing to act as though nothing had changed. Austria had no objection to Russia or the Russian Federation joining the United Nations Security Council and taking its place in the plenum that had previously been occupied by the Soviet Union. Caution was only displayed when it came to the State Treaty. The German question had faded into the background, however, since Austria had no intention of forming a union with Germany, and the more states that entered the Community, the less significant each individual one became. This possibly also reassured the Russians, who had already opened up a new chapter in world history with their agreement to the reunification of West and East Germany. Even so, in Vienna, there was no desire to take any risks.

Relations between Russia and Austria were certainly of a symbolic nature, and it could no doubt be argued that there had been phases of what could be termed special relations. What was new was that Russia gave the impression that it was more interested in maintaining the status quo than Austria itself. In fact, there was even a certain contradiction in this. Russia was considerably in debt to Austria, to the tune of 53 billion dollars, and could not pay Austria back. This was embarrassing. If Austria wished not to forego the payment, it would, for better or worse, be forced to recognise the Russian Federation as the successor state.[804] However, this did not apply to the State Treaty. This was a real balancing act. When Federal Chancellor Vranitzky visited Moscow for the second time after short intervals in April 1992, the topic of discussion was not, however, only Islamic fundamentalism, as brought to the table by Boris Yeltsin and classified as dangerous by Russia, but a great deal of money. This had also been the case two years previously when Deputy Chancellor Josef Riegler had visited.[805] For this reason, generosity was required on both sides, and at the same time the turning of a blind eye to certain issues. This was understood in Vienna. A visit by the Russian State President was to serve to underline the continued existence of excellent relations. On 28 July 1993, Boris Yeltsin was formally invited to pay a visit to Austria. At the same time, the head of the political section in the Ministry of Foreign Affairs, Albert Ro-han, modified the issue of recognition to the extent that on behalf of Foreign Minister Mock, he stated that the State Treaty would remain in force whatever happened. The other signatories and those who entered the treaty at a later stage were still in existence. Yet the Treaty was taking on 'an increasingly historical character through its fulfilment, obsolescence and the passage of time'. For this reason, the Russians should be informed 'in an unspectacular manner' that Austria accepted the demand for continuation. It would have no practical consequences.[806]

However, the matter could not be resolved quite so easily. The Russian Federation insisted on a treaty of friendship. And if there was to be no treaty, a 'joint declaration' would be sufficient. In January 1994, the Russians delivered the text of such a declara-tion. And the State Treat and neutrality promptly appeared as the basis for the bilateral relationship. This by no means concurred with what the Austrians wanted, and a coun-ter-draft was edited in May which referred to all possible elements of commonality, and not only to the Belvedere treaty of 1955 and neutrality. Austria continued to be in no hurry. Quite the opposite. Time was intentionally allowed to pass, with the primary aim of achieving one thing: to bring the agreement with the European Union to conclusion.

There was already a sense of joy at the start of negotiations with the Union, and at the same time, expectations increased. Above all, domestic politics would be given greater impetus. As Andreas Khol, a delegate in the National Council put it, '1992 was the year in which the Grand Coalition reaped its reward'.[807] There was widespread satisfaction. The Grand Coalition used its constitutional majority, passed a new voting law with modified electoral districts and preferential voting, set about institutional reform, suc-ceeded in announcing that the dispute with Italy over South Tyrol had been resolved, and was satisfied with the ongoing economic boom. Once again, the annual financial statements were dominated by one word. Unlike in previous years, however, this word was not 'crisis', but 'reform'. The reform of the National Council electoral regulations, reform of the Court of Audit, reform of agricultural market regulations, reform of the Austrian Federal Railways, pension reform, university reform and reform of the army – to name just the most important areas. Finally, a tax reform, science reform and a federal state reform were to be added. While some of these proposals would in the end turn out to be 'mini-reforms', the collaboration between the coalition parties worked.

There was a sense of progress. Then, issues relating to security policy constituted the greatest hurdles, and suddenly, the issue of neutrality was up for discussion. It was argued that it was no longer in keeping with the times. The Western European Union was praised as the military arm of the EU, and was to develop into an organisation that, like the United Nations, would act as an instrument of collective security. In this area, too, a sense of optimism dominated, and people looked to the future with confidence.

We are Europe

After Kurt Waldheim's decision not to run for re-election, the remainder of the fissure had also been overcome that had for a time felt like a deep chasm. Old and young, left and right were pitted against each other as they had been before on repeated occasions, but in 1986, a new form of aggressiveness had come into play. The so-called 'war generation', which in some cases saw itself exposed to undifferentiated accusations of being a generation of war criminals, was increasingly silenced by the discussions surrounding the war history of the Federal President. When the president of the National Council, Heinz Fischer, declared of the outgoing Federal President when the latter was bid farewell in the Federal Assembly 'that as an individual and as federal president, Kurt Waldheim was done an injustice when actions – indeed, even war crimes – were attributed to him which according to all the historical evidence ... he did not commit',[808] this was a gesture of goodwill with which the now former federal president and the war generation could be satisfied. Waldheim's successor, Thomas Klestil, who like Waldheim came from diplomatic circles, and who therefore also wished to enter office as an independent candidate, was a further indication of a new beginning in this political field. He was the first federal president not to be from the generation that lived through the Second World War.

However, Klestil had not been 'the' candidate from the very beginning. To a greater extent, the SPÖ and ÖVP discussed the issue for quite a long time as to whether they could agree on a joint candidate. Names such as Hugo Portisch, Herbert Krejci, Ludwig Steiner, Heinrich Neisser, Helmut Zilk and Alois Mock were mentioned. Klestil was also considered. Vranitzky, who had been encouraged to put himself forward by the president of the National Council, Anton Benya,[809] had declined to do so. The comparison with Kreisky forced its way out into the open. However, Vranitzky was neither inclined to submit his candidacy himself nor to have a joint candidate, and he decided that Minister of Transport Rudolf Streicher should run as a candidate for the SPÖ. Deputy Chancellor Erhard Busek backed Klestil. Klestil then won with a respectable majority. In light of the necessity for Austria to attract greater attention again internationally, this step was almost essential. The task in hand was to take steps towards Europe. And Austria had now become interesting for other reasons than in 1986. However, this was not because it was an object of suspicion, but because it played a geopolitical role. There were an increasing number of comments coming from the USA that honoured Austria's importance for building up contacts with East-Central Europe. Occasionally, it was also mentioned that perpetual neutrality could become a model for the so-called 'reform states'.[810] However, that might have been worthy of consideration in 1956, and perhaps still in 1968, and in the case of Poland, in 1981. However, the situation at the start of the 1990s was different: the states that had detached themselves from the Soviet bloc wanted to become members of NATO as quickly as possible, and not to enter into any security risk. In Austria, this might have been met with disappointment, but perhaps in this way, a neutral Austria also gained additional security. At any rate, it lost its exposed position, and now began to steer an unmistakeable course towards the European Union.

On 25 February 1994, the final round of negotiations over the accession to the European Union began. During the long period of grovelling, and in light of the changes that the European Community had undergone from the time in which the accession request was sent and the assumption of negotiations, Austria had repeatedly hastened to make it clear that it wished to also join a transformed Community. The Common Foreign and Security Policy (CFSP) was to be no obstacle. Several aide-mémoires were passed on to Brussels, in which reference was made to the matter. There was no further talk of the proviso of maintaining neutrality.[811] The final areas of dispute that also led to fears that the negotiations might fail at the last moment were the common market, the Alpine transit and the free movement of goods.[812] The Austrian Foreign Minister Alois Mock, who was now suffering severely from Parkinson's disease, brought the negotiations to a positive conclusion with the help of his ministerial colleagues and the members of the Austrian negotiating delegation. On 12 April 1994, the resolution of all points of dispute was formally announced.

There was one hurdle left to be cleared: the accession was to be decided in a plebiscite, since this ultimately amounted to an overall change to the federal constitution. Countless small, medium-sized and large events prepared the public for the plebiscite on Austria's accession to the EU. In the end, around two-thirds of the electorate voted in favour of the accession. Those in favour were satisfied, while the majority of opponents of accession, including Jörg Haider's FPÖ, came to accept it. Brussels was finally to become the main goal for Austrian foreign, economic and security policy. On 24 June 1994, the accession agreement was signed on Corfu. Thomas Klestil did not want to pass up the opportunity to sign the agreement himself. However, he had to demur and give precedence to Federal Chancellor Vranitzky, Foreign Minister Mock and two officials, and limit himself to a brief address. At the beginning of 1995, Austria became a member of the European Union.

From this moment on, the priorities with regard to political activity at all levels shifted in a decisive manner. In the future, what was important would be what Austria did within the framework of the European Union. The past was regarded as having been dealt with. In the case of Russia, this was demonstrated extremely clearly. At the end of 1994, Moscow definitively wanted to know what Austria's position was with regard to the proposed 'joint declaration'. Boris Yeltsin had been invited to Vienna, and the visit was due to take place in April or May 1995. Fifty years of the Second Republic were just as good a reason for coming as the 40 years of the State Treaty. The Russians also built a type of golden bridge by stressing that even if the American, British and French heads of state and government might not come to Vienna, Yeltsin would. However, he also wanted to sign something; if not a treaty of friendship, then at least a 'joint declaration'. The Ministry of Foreign Affairs in Vienna again played down the issue, and this time in a very decisive way: there were so many opportunities for maintaining the existing contacts, it stated, and no separate declaration was required for the purpose. Austria had already declared the validity and continued existence of two dozen agreements in June 1993, during an exchange of notes, and converted them into new Austro-Russian treaties. This must surely be enough to uphold existing friendly connections. The Russians got the message and Yeltsin cancelled his visit to Austria. Now, notice had been taken elsewhere, too, and even in one of the most popular Chinese newspapers, the *Guanming Ribao*, it was reported on 25 March 1995 that a shadow had fallen over Russo-Austrian relations. In Vienna, the approach taken was to stand one's ground. Even before the summer, Klestil, Vranitzky and Mock agreed to inform the Russian side 'that Austria is no longer interested in a joint political declaration with Russia'. This message was delivered to the Ambassador of the Russian Federation on 20 June. In Moscow, this was acknowledged with the word 'unfortunate'.[813] And from then on, the formulation 'quite good' was used to describe the state of relations. However, in the words of Deputy Foreign Minister Sergei B. Krylov in October 1995, if Austria were to attempt to join NATO, that would be 'the straw that breaks the camel's back'.

If anyone had told Julius Raab or Bruno Kreisky that Moscow was no longer important for Vienna, they would probably have vehemently disagreed. However, Raab had died in 1964, and Kreisky in 1990. These were different times.

An Intermezzo

With EU accession, Austria had again achieved a major goal. Depending on how you counted, this was the second or third time in the history of the Second Republic that there had been a turning point on this scale. The end of the war in 1945 had arguably been the most important and consequential watershed. This was followed by the State

Treaty of 1955 and the departure of the Allies. Now, in 1994/95, there was again cause for celebration. The feeling dominated that something had been achieved, and that despite all the perils that had arisen at times in connection with the Waldheim years, Austria had placed itself at the forefront. In no other European country was the sense of pride so strong as in Austria.[814] In this regard, Austria was even a contender for the USA, which was at the top of the list when it came to patriotism. It was only gradually that a slight sense of a hangover emerged. And as in 1955, suddenly, a feeling of emptiness became widespread. 'We are Europe' sounded all well and good but, of course, it was not enough to preserve the euphoric mood.

For many people, the change of perspective came too abruptly. A great deal had happened within a short period of time, the impact of which was not yet possible to comprehend: the end of Soviet dominance in East-Central Europe, the disintegration of Yugoslavia, and finally, accession to a political union that was dominated above all by the major Western European states whose broader goals were obscure for the large majority of people. This could certainly lead to a certain amount of confusion.

After all, all this had happened in the space of just six years. The economic benefits of accession to the Union had already been laid out in detail. Here and there, scepticism remained. And even the political banner bearers, delegates, federal state politicians and politically-minded members of the general public were not always clear about what aspects of life would now be decided by EU committees, for which the synonym 'Brussels' became established. Was this a return to those times when League of Nations commissars monitored Austria's development? Would the unison that was required even mean an abandonment of neutrality? Would Austria be obliged to participate in military campaigns? At any rate, the step had been taken, and was arguably irreversible.

The Grand Coalition had done what had been expected of it. Almost immediately, the will to collaborate had dissipated. After just over a year, on 17 December 1995, there were new elections. As had been the case with the State Treaty in 1955, the Chancellor and his party were able to exploit their success. The SPÖ gained six seats, while the ÖVP had to make do with just one additional seat. In March 1996, a new coalition pact was agreed. However, while during the first half of the 1990s, there had been a sense of euphoria in the coalition, too, from 1996 onwards, the objectives were to do no more than repair and plug holes. Certainly, the sense of satisfaction that might have been expected took root, and the adaptation to the regulations issuing from Brussels was a repeated cause for resentment. It was necessary to orient oneself to the rules from Brussels down to the tiniest detail. And so, the country had to find a way of dealing with the new conditions and learn to think in a European way. And in order to further underline the new situation, the word was soon that foreign policy was European domestic policy. From 2007, therefore, there would also no longer be a 'Federal Ministry for Foreign Affairs', but a 'Federal Ministry for European and International Affairs'.

After his EU success, Franz Vranitzky could not expect to enjoy any comparable political achievement again. No wonder, therefore, that in 1996, he already considered taking his leave as chancellor and party chairman.[815] His first two years in government had been dominated by the endless discussions around Kurt Waldheim's role in the war. Then there had been the turning point in 1989. At the SPÖ party conference in mid-June 1991, the party name had been changed to the 'Social Democratic Party of Austria'. Kreisky had already dallied with the idea, but now, the name had been adjusted to match Western European practice. In Britain, however, the Labour Party retained is original title, and did not have to fear being punished for having such an old-fashioned name.

However, in Austria, there was the renunciation of what had previously been held dear, even though this was a break with the compromise of 1945, when the Social Democrats and the Revolutionary Socialists joined together under a new party name. Now the revolutionary element appeared once and for all to be no longer relevant. And this was entirely in line with the wishes of the Federal Chancellor.

Then, Austrian attempts to obtain full membership of the European Union were successful. And even if Vranitzky did not have to bear the full burden of the negotiations, as the head of government, he was of course strongly involved during all phases. That, too, was a thing of the past, and after ten years in government, he became increasingly weary of the resistance against him that came not only from the opposition, but also from his coalition partner, and above all, from his own party. Membership numbers had continued to decline. While they still totalled around 670,000 when he took over office, now, there were just 457,000.[816] This was a far cry from the halcyon days of the Kreisky era, with over 720,000 party members. By contrast, the proven number of party members of the ÖVP amounted to 700,000.[817] A cause for alarm! The workers, who had traditionally been regarded as Social Democratic, had switched to the FPÖ led by Jörg Haider in increasing numbers, which Vranitzky could only describe as 'marginalising'.

Had the Chancellor and the government gone too far with their concessions to the EU? Had the most possible benefit really been extracted? Did the willingness to become involved in the security policy of the Community and to play a role in the Western European Union, the European Defence Community, nolens volens entail Austrian membership of NATO? Such a step was still opposed by 65 per cent of the population, but in the spirit of 'little strokes fell great oaks', the majority might disintegrate. The fact that Austria had joined the NATO Cooperation Council in 1995 was here not seen as being of significant consequence, since Russia was also a member of this round table, which was regarded as the 'antechamber' to the military alliance. At any rate, in November 1996, Foreign Minister Wolfgang Schüssel and Minister of Defence Fasslabend signed a security agreement with the Western European Union. It was clear to everyone that this would strengthen the European part of NATO, and the limitation to an obligation to participate in peacekeeping operations, which Austria had already been practising for years anyway, was a rather arbitrary interpretation. Austria was not yet a member, however. Even so, the governing parties agreed to produce an options report designed to present and evaluate all feasible security policy possibilities. Ultimately, the result would have to be a recommendation. At first, however, a decision was put off for the time being. Even so, the mood within the coalition was fractious.

The Family Silver

The Chancellor could not simply defy the rejection of the security policy demands among some members of his party. However, this was just one point about which opinions were divided. Another resulted from the economic policy measures taken by the government that were branded 'selling the family silver'. In light of the budget deficit that threatened to explode, as well as the budget discipline demanded by the EU, all possible countermeasures had to be taken. Primarily, these were measures relating to the new regulation of the banking and state-owned industrial sectors. In order to be able to tackle the problems that had plagued the state-owned industrial sector for more than ten years, steps began to be taken to sell part of the group of companies. The side effects, namely a radical reduction in the number of workers, made life difficult, particularly for the Chancellor and the SPÖ. Even in his original field of employment, the banking sector, Vranitzky was forced to take action and implement reorganisation measures. There, too, the question was asked whether the Social Democrats had not simply succumbed to the goals specified by the ÖVP.

Only gradually did people begin to accept the idea of selling state-owned assets. The annulment of the State Treaty regulations of Article 22 created an opportunity for doing so. Once again, the Grand Coalition took on the characteristics of a reform partnership and could be regarded as a thoroughly suitable form of collaboration. After all, there were still major goals that were to be achieved together. At first, therefore, consolidation was required. In 1994, the Austrian Federal Railways had already been outsourced. They were followed in 1996 by the postal and telegraph service. That same year, Vranitzky announced that the Republic would surrender its shares in Austria's largest bank, Bank Austria, as well as the Creditanstalt bank, in the coming years. In 1997, road works planning was outsourced to the motorway and major road-building finance company ASFINAG (Autobahn- und Schnellstraßen-Finanzierungs-AG).[818]

Liberalisation and privatisation were diametrically opposite to the trend towards nationalisation that had been pursued until that point. Here, it was overlooked by the critics that the nationalisation of the basic materials industry and the energy sector during the years of the Allied occupation had quite clearly been designed to deny access to these areas by the Allies, primarily the Soviets. The second major surge in nationalisation was also connected to this, since in 1955, Austria had entered into an obligation with the Soviet Union not to transfer the restituted companies labelled as German Assets to their former owners, but to nationalise them. During the 1970s, steps had been taken to further enlarge state-owned industry through concentration measures. However, instead of increasing performance and becoming more powerful internationally, the nationalised businesses skidded towards a crisis, together with a series of parastatal companies. From now on, it was decided that the state should not regulate matters that did not belong to its core areas of responsibility. The purpose of privatisation and outsourcing was dual in nature: the state would to lose a millstone around its neck and the sale of companies in which the state participated as an owner, either entirely or in part, would be used to consolidate the budget and pay off debts. For the Chancellor, this was a necessary economic policy step. However, naturally, he was shaking the very foundations of socialism.

A federal chancellor who appeared tired of his office, and who was accused of being responsible for the performance of his party in the first European parliamentary elections and above all for the major losses suffered by the SPÖ in the Viennese municipal council elections in 1996, prepared to step down. His decision was also influenced by the fact that he did not know how to deal with Jörg Haider. The latter had, in a relatively cavalier manner, played every card that he thought might benefit him. He spoke of the 'Third Republic', allowing associations to be formed such as that of the 'Third Reich'. Haider exploited the former National Socialists, before casting them aside again, was happy to give voice to Greater German ideas, and could lead his party not only with authority, but in an authoritarian manner. He claimed that foreigners were responsible for the rise in crime, repeatedly led xenophobic campaigns and attracted attention with his racist comments, in order to then contradict himself with philo-Semitic and anti-racist statements.[819] The petition for a referendum initiated by Haider in 1992 against the influx of foreigners had gathered 417,000 signatures. Although this meant that it was only moderately successful, there was no doubt that slogans and posters such as 'Vienna must not become Chicago' had been effective and attracted a great deal of support.[820] The fact that there had been a strong counter-movement, and that a series of prominent members had left the FPÖ, including the deputy party leader Heide Schmidt, was seen as a party-filtering measure. The adaptability of the FPÖ leader was a repeated source of astonishment. Only one thing stayed the same: Haider's battle against, as he called them, the 'old parties'. At times, there appeared to be no recipe for handling him, with his well-constructed, youthful, fresh image, and how long the 'marginalisation' of Haider could continue to function was questionable. For Franz Vranitzky, however, this was not in any doubt. Ultimately, it came down to the question: him or me?

On 18 January 1997, Vranitzky announced his resignation, also to the surprise of his party, and proposed to the party presidium of the SPÖ that the minister of finance to date, Viktor Klima, should be his successor. For Deputy Chancellor Schüssel, this was no reason to end the coalition.[821] However, he wanted to set the conditions and for a very specific project – the cancellation of the sale of Creditanstalt and Bank Austria – he sought the support of Haider. The project failed, forcing Schüssel to swallow his fury over the sale of the 'black' Creditanstalt and the 'red' Bank Austria, as well as the displeasure of only finding out about the Chancellor's intention to resign after the fact. This was mitigated by the fact that Klima offered him a new form of collaboration, and the replacement of most of the SPÖ members of government was announced. In this way, one might have assumed, the cards had been reshuffled.

What began so harmoniously and appeared to be so simple was accompanied by several small-scale eruptions, however. Klima wanted to continue Vranitzky's policy of marginalising the FPÖ. For the mayor of Vienna, Michael Häupl, this was – at that time – by no means a clear-cut matter. He demanded that his party reconsider its approach.[822] And the claim made by the chairman of the SPÖ parliamentary group, Peter Kostelka, that the Grand Coalition had no alternative, either numerically or politically, was also not true. There were certainly other factors at play. The left-wingers in the party had felt that the SPÖ had been too conformist for a long time, and they were by no means afraid of going into opposition. Quite clearly, they did not agree with Vranitzky's departure from revolutionary socialism. Here, references to the electoral successes of Tony Blair and his New Labour Party in Britain, or of Gerhard Schröder's Social Democrats in Germany, who had both made efforts to attract neo-liberal voters, were of no help. Why should the British and Germans be models for Austria at any price? Klima would start to feel the dissatisfaction among young members of his party in particular. But first, the coalition parties wanted to continue as before. After all, these had just been smaller eruptions, and not yet an earthquake.

Federal Chancellor Klima 'could clearly work with everyone and was omnipresent'. He had already achieved considerable popularity before becoming chancellor as minister of the public Economy and transport, and from 1996 as minister of finance, at a cost to Vranitzky. At any rate, his world appeared to be in order. The economic upturn, which had begun with the opening up of the east in 1989, continued, even if there were budget problems. Austrian banks and corporate groups expanded. A gold digger mentality emerged to a slight degree, even if the feeling of having arrived in a peaceful world was already long dissipated. The war in Yugoslavia was a huge presence, especially in Austria. The siege of Sarajevo had also led to an emotional reaction.

Just how close the war was could be seen in the daily reporting and by the fact that at weekends, buses departed close to Vienna's South Station, transporting not only people bringing urgently needed supplies to their relatives but also weekend fighters to the various theatres of war. It appeared that this was part of normal life during the war in the neighbouring country. Also, not much fuss was made of the fact that mass flows of refugees came from the war zones and were accepted by Austria. They would return to their homeland when the war was over – or so it was hoped. During the course of the war in Yugoslavia, about 13,000 people fled to Austria from Croatia.[824] After 1992, around 90,000 arrived from Bosnia and Herzegovina. Approximately 60,000 remained. 9,000 were expelled. The remainder returned voluntarily.[825] In Austria, too, it would therefore be a long time before there could be a return to normal everyday life. Not only that, but there was an emotional pressure, since repeated reference was made to the historical role played by Austria in the western Balkans.

In 1998, Austria took over the chair of the European Council for the first time. This, too, was something in which one could certainly get the feeling of making up for lost ground. As a result, there was planning down to the last detail, and everything was done in order to make the procedures during the smaller and larger-scale meetings a success. This was done even though it could not be expected that a breakthrough could be achieved with regard to the serious issues. Yet the framework was perfect, and Austria made a clear mark by supporting the acceptance of six East-Central European states. Elsewhere, solidarity was demonstrated. Franz Vranitzky was sent to Albania in March 1997 by the OSCE as a special coordinator, and when, on 21 April 1997, 'Operation Alba' began, and an international peacekeeping force was stationed in Albania in order to bring the chaos in the country under control, the Austrian Federal Army participated with a medical contingent. From the autumn of 1998, Austria built a refugee camp for Albanians fleeing from Kosovo. Finally, in 1998, 5,000 refugees also came to Austria from Albania.[826] The federal government, the federal states and above all charitable organisations helped, and there were only a small number of people who did not support the effort. However, there could be no question of this being an ideal situation, and despite all attempts, also domestically, to evince the dawn of a new era and at least normality, there was something brewing that would again hurl the country into severe turmoil.

The Grand Coalition, which in reality existed as such only in name, went into a tail-spin, since both governing parties were coming under increasing pressure and were losing support. The fact that Austria had caught up internationally was repeatedly stressed, yet the collapse of businesses and the gradual infiltration of foreign companies that pushed aside old and well-established Austrian ones attracted a great deal more attention. Small and medium-sized businesses were forced to file for bankruptcy. Dismissals, the buying up of companies and corporate mergers increased. This was distressing to watch. People looked around for guilty parties. The government found itself being pilloried.

Since 1945, the ÖVP and SPÖ had formed a coalition 15 times. Historical reminiscences of successes achieved through joint effort were restricted mainly to the periodic State Treaty celebrations in 1980 and 1995. The social partners appeared to continue to guarantee social peace, even if Franz Vranitzky now referred to them as 'social enemies' and had also got to know them as such.[827] And the image presented by Viktor Klima and Wolfgang Schüssel was devastating. Time and again, an eagerness for reform was invoked. Then differences of opinion arose, and the social partners in particular prevented reforms that were already urgently needed. At issue here, time and again, were jealously guarded interests; arguments were based on acquired rights and attempts were made to pander to their own clientele. And while this was happening, the benefits were reaped by those who castigated the moribund political system and made reference to topics that were becoming increasingly important, and which the holders of key positions of power were accused of ignoring: the environment, transport, privileges and so on. Here, there were points to be scored. What the coalition parties continued to praise as consensus democracy was regarded as shying away from conflict. Alternatives began to be considered, and the SPÖ soon began to regard the Greens as ready for government. This would mean the possibility of a form of consonance *(Gleichklang)* with Germany (no-one cared to mention the similar word that was used by the National Socialists, *Gleichschaltung,* meaning 'enforced coordination'). The German cabinet cooperation between Gerhard Schröder and Joschka Fischer was also possible in Austria with Viktor Klima and Alexander Van der Bellen. And as in Germany, people in Austria began to dream of a new political culture. The term 'reform partnership' very quickly became hackneyed, and the attempts to take pioneering decisions were lost in the ongoing sense of dissatisfaction. Perhaps it was intended as a reminder of the early Kreisky years when under the auspices of distributive justice, 'benefits' were disbursed among the people. There were tax reductions without a new savings package, pensions were increased, parental leave was granted to all, in other words, not only working women, and the debate over security policy was put to rest with a clear commitment to neutrality.[828] And this even though the chairman of the ÖVP parliamentary group, Andreas Khol, had unequivocally stated in July 1998 that Austria would be a member of NATO in 2003.[829] However, questions such as the maintenance of prosperity and full employment were classified as far more important.

Wolfgang Schüssel wanted to conduct a far more fundamental debate than the one over well-being and percentages, and he created a think tank designed to discuss future-related issues and processes. While the concept was not entirely new, it had gone out of fashion somewhat. With his 'Operation 20', Josef Klaus had started something similar. Bruno Kreisky had followed him with his best 1,400 minds and the 'Alternative for a modern Austria'. Now, however, the discussion was slow to move forward, although certainly, thorough consideration was given to it. Once again, the situation was reminiscent of episodes from the chancellorship of Josef Klaus, when three federal state governors began to think aloud as to whether the triple role that Schüssel had assumed, of deputy chancellor, foreign minister and federal party leader, might not have become too much of a burden. The public spat between ÖVP politicians may have been fun to watch – and in Kreisky's words, politics should have a certain entertainment value – but it resulted in a fair amount of damage.

The ÖVP world still appeared to be more or less intact. At the federal state level, there were increases in membership and electoral victories in Upper Austria and Lower Austria, and there was no question that Thomas Klestil would not be re-elected as federal president in 1998. The SPÖ had even declined to put forward its own candidate. However, there were also signals to the contrary, above all in Carinthia, where Jörg Haider, who in 1991 had been forced to resign due to his statements regarding the 'orderly employment policy' in the 'Third Reich', celebrated a triumph in the elections to the regional diet in 1999, reducing the ÖVP to the size of a small-scale party.

Haider so visibly embodied a different type of politician that the parties of the Grand Coalition, with their orientation towards solidity, tradition and continuity, that he must have appeared as a complete contrast. If there was anything that repeatedly caused him problems, then it was his ill-considered statements and the human deficiencies of a considerable number of his party members, who hoped to exploit the momentum he created to climb the professional ladder. Then there were disputes over the direction to be taken, with a departure announced from the fundamental German nationalist concept of the party and a relapse into just this same concept, then an emphasis on the basic Christian values of the country and party and, in response to this, the stressing of its free-thinking roots. The clean-living image also failed to hold water, since the FPÖ itself experienced scandal after scandal. Some national organisations were deeply involved in dubious business dealings, while countless party members were guilty of corruption. Sub-organisations were disbanded and re-staffed, only to be turned inside out immediately afterwards. Some followers of the FPÖ, which had increasingly become simply the Haider party, appeared to be immune to harm, even when they called the Federal President a 'thug'. As an individual, Haider continued to be regarded as a decent and upright fellow and as a hope for the future. He may even have enjoyed being downright hounded, both domestically and abroad. What did it matter when in Serbia, 'Haider = SS' was daubed on the sides of the street? Who was supposed to take that seriously, not least in that country? And the states of East-Central Europe would anyway do well to behave themselves, since they would need Austria's support in their attempts to join the EU. Haider and 'his' FPÖ, from which the liberals had already separated, brought foreign countries into Austria in that they led a systematic battle against 'excessive foreign infiltration', and in so doing brought several factors into play: concern about employment, the homeland and the Christian Western world. At the same time, such campaigns were also directed at the parties of the Grand Coalition, to whom these values allegedly meant nothing, or at least, too little.

Klima and Schüssel were clearly pro-European. They spoke out in favour of the 'eastward expansion' of the EU and were reminded of a traditional role played by Austria when during the course of the 'great' Balkan war, Austria repeatedly acted as a broker. However, their relationship became increasingly strained. Both were forced to admit, however, that if the National Council elections were brought forward, they would suffer more or less heavy losses. As a result, they could only hope that they could find a way out of the misery of having to work with each other. All attempts to disseminate a sense of optimism and a new beginning, and to focus on future-oriented issues, led to nothing. And so, elections were called. In August 1999, Schüssel publicly considered taking the ÖVP into opposition if his party did not come second in the National Council elections. In September, he reaffirmed his statement with a view to the electoral forecasts. His fears were substantiated in the weeks that followed. On 3 October, the election was held: the FPÖ overtook the ÖVP. The outcome was decided by just 415 votes.

22 Under Observation

22 On 18 February 2000, extensive demonstrations took place in the vicinity of parliament, Federal Chancellery and Heldenplatz in Vienna against the Little Coalition led by Wolfgang Schüssel. Even schoolchildren who were unable to vote at the time were permitted to skip school in order to participate in the protests. The comment of the president of Vienna's Municipal School Council, Kurt Scholz, to the effect that schoolchildren ought to be in the classroom during lesson time and not on the street was one of the reasons for his subsequent dismissal. The demonstrations against the coalition of ÖVP and FPÖ reached their climax with a mass rally on 19 February 2000. (Photo: APA picturedesk)

Already on the day 'afterwards', the commentators in foreign newspapers claimed that there had been a swing to the right in Austria, and that a neo-Nazi hydra had raised its head. A direct line was quickly drawn between the Waldheim years and the electoral success of the Freedom Party. Since their victory quite clearly stood or fell with Haider as an individual, the obvious reaction was to conjure up a type of new 'Führer myth'. In fact, it was not easy to differentiate between a right-wing opposition party, a right-wing populist party and a right-wing nationalist party that was quite happy to use racist platitudes. The simplest solution appeared to be to throw everything into one pot. Not the ossified system of government, the horse-trading, the dissipating ability to find solutions to problems or even personal animosities were to blame for the defeat of the coalition parties, it was claimed, but rather the aggressive campaigning of a party that had succeeded in spreading in the ineradicable right-wing biotope that had existed in Austria since the 1930s. This was attributed to 'ignorance with regard to foreign countries' and the 'return of the old demons'. [830] Suddenly, Austria had become 'Haider country'. Here, however, it must have been also clear to the foreign observers that there were very different reasons for the success of the FPÖ. And the accusation that Austria had never dealt with its past ran completely into the sand. The core issue could rather be described as a lack of repentance. The Federal President, the Federal Chancellor and any number of prominent political and academic personalities were at any rate at pains to counter the emotional response with objective explanations. Again, the question arose as to what should happen next.

The 'Sanctions'

On the evening of the election, there were celebrations in the ÖVP headquarters 'as though the party had won the election'. A period in opposition would enable 'all-round renewal'. The party would not 'die a slow death' in the 'halter' of the coalition, and it would no longer be the 'stirrup holder for the SPÖ' – as the deputy president of the National Council (Nationalrat), Andreas Khol, described the mood. [831]

In the National Council election, the Greens under their new federal spokesman, Alexander Van der Bellen, had, for the first time after a long period, recorded an increase in their number of votes, although – unlike in Germany – it was not possible to form a red-green government, since it would not have had a majority. The group that had splintered off from the Freedom Party, the Liberal Forum, was no longer represented in the National Council. The SPÖ stood by its word and was not willing to enter into a coalition with the Freedom Party, while the ÖVP wanted to keep its word and go into opposition if it fell behind the Freedom Party... The theoretical possibility, at least, of the formation of a minority government remained, although this would have required one of the two other, now equal-sized parties to indicate its willingness to provide support and to also accept the designated chancellor. Suddenly, the SPÖ also expressed the possibility of going into opposition, since it did not want to allow itself to be blackmailed by the ÖVP.[832] Clearly, no one was any longer either willing or able to govern the country. The option remained of holding fresh elections. But would they bring a different result?

Initially, the ball lay in the court of Federal President Klestil, who entrusted Viktor Klima with the continuation of government business and exploratory discussions regarding the formation of a government. At the same time, Klestil made no secret of the fact that he was interested in a continuation of the Grand Coalition. There was talk of a stable government for the next four years, and of a fair and sensible approach. The best the country had to offer was mentioned, and references were made to other countries. The Federal President did all he could to encourage Klima and Schüssel to begin proper exploratory discussions, and even presented them with nine items for a catalogue of reforms. The mood between the Chancellor and Deputy Chancellor alternated between constructive and icy.[833] Meanwhile, relations between Schüssel and Haider became increasingly friendly. The latter declared his willingness to accept the eastward expansion of the EU desired by Schüssel as a common goal, and he also distanced himself from the xenophobic posters that had been put up by the Viennese federal state organisatin.[834] Since the FPÖ also approached the SPÖ during the course of exploratory discussions, however, one could have been forgiven for thinking that Jörg Haider wanted to participate in government at almost any price. The question was whether the Vranitzky formula, 'No coalition with Haider's FPÖ' would continue to hold. Then, the negotiating and manoeuvring began. However, the coalition partners to date had hardly taken two steps towards each other before taking one step back again. The SPÖ trade unionists created all kinds of problems and wanted reassurance that their demands would be met under all circumstances. It was not until 9 December that Viktor Klima was formally requested to form a government. Schüssel declared himself willing in principle to enter into negotiations and renounce his statement of wishing to go into opposition. However, he named his price, which included the settlement of a budget that had already run out of control, postal voting, a harmonisation of the pension system and a clear commitment to Europe, and not least also a joint security and defence policy.

The attitude of the ÖVP was mixed. There were supporters and opponents of negotiations with the SPÖ. Among the Social Democrats, too, the gulf ran right through the federal states and organisations. The Federal President became directly threatening in his tone: if the ÖVP were to refuse, he would approve the formation of an SPÖ minority government. This – and this was the horror scenario for large numbers of ÖVP federal state governors – would lead to fresh elections one year later and probably to an even worse defeat for the People's Party. The manoeuvring continued, yet it became clearer every day that there was by all means an alternative to a grand coalition, since the FPÖ remained willing to fully and entirely accept Schüssel's demands. Additionally, Jörg Haider did not wish to enter government, but to remain governor of Carinthia. Yet neither Schüssel nor Haider were requested by Klestil to conduct negotiations regarding government cooperation. And so the painstaking search for 'areas of overlap' between the ÖVP and the SPÖ continued. At times, it seemed as though the issue of NATO accession could become the key topic; then, however, the budget situation emerged as the real point of debate. As had been the case during the Kreisky years, money had been spent in an easy manner, and the extremely high debts of state-owned industry and several parastatal companies had been taken into account. To this was added an enormous number of early retirees, since office workers and public servants had also been told that they had an extremely tough job to do, and that they had the option of taking retirement long before they reached the statutory pensionable age. Already at the start of negotiations, the SPÖ minister of finance, Rudolf Edlinger of all people, had announced the necessity of making drastic savings. At the same time, he was faced with the considerable financial demands being made by his own party. The ÖVP were furious and referred to the proposed introduction of the euro as the common currency within the EU and the necessity of adapting Austria's finances to the requirements for this. Since the trade unions were unwilling to accept an increase in the pensionable age and considered the pension reform of 1997 to be adequate, Viktor Klima also showed an inclination to resign. On the question of possible NATO accession, a compromise was finally found which again put off making a decision on the matter, and, with regard to the budget, it appeared that an agreement would be reached imminently. Once again, the SPÖ trade unionists were resolutely against the proposals. They fully opposed the planned exchange of ministries, although such a move had already been made in the past.[835] The so-called hereditary leases were to remain intact. Under no circumstances was the Ministry of the Interior, let alone the Ministry of Social Affairs, to be placed in the hands of the 'class enemy'. The year 1934 was explicitly mentioned.[836] Even after 66 years, the trauma had clearly not been healed. Or rather: this argument, too, was welcomed in order to prevent any further concessions from the Chancellor. In both coalition parties, there were ultimately those who supported the continuation of the Grand Coalition and those who opposed it. For the ÖVP, the decisive issue was that the Faction of Socialist Trade Unionists (Fraktion Sozialistischer Gewerkschafter) led by the head of the metalworkers' trade union, Rudolf Nürnberger, refused to sign the last-ditch compromise and approve pension reform and a different distribution of ministries to the one that had been expressly demanded by the ÖVP. Supporters and opponents of the coalition agreement, regarding which negotiations had already come to an end, expressed their points of view via the media. On the evening of 20 January 2000, there was no option but to accept that the negotiations had failed. There was nothing left to negotiate.

On the following day, Wolfgang Schüssel informed the Federal President about the end of discussions with the SPÖ. Thomas Klestil refused outright, however, to entrust Schüssel with the task of forming a government. However, Klestil no longer had the option of ordering another election immediately, since he, too, was aware of the poll results, which indicated a clear majority for the FPÖ. And if there was one thing that he absolutely did not want, then it was to ask Jörg Haider to form a government. He again tasked Klima with doing so. In order to make the renewed assignment appear as plausible as possible, a type of extended minority government was proposed, in which experts nominated by the ÖVP and the FPÖ were to be involved. The suggestion may have been meant well, but it had no chance of being realised. Finally, it was Karl Korinek, the president of the constitutional court, who dissuaded Klestil from further pursuing the idea that followed next of forming a civil service cabinet. The criticism of the Federal President increased. He was forced to hear repeatedly that his office was merely representative in nature, and that his effective capacity for action was extremely limited. Klestil refused to believe this. A comparison with Wilhelm Miklas was inappropriate, yet the assertion that the Federal President was suddenly no longer required as a solver of problems but had instead become a part of a significant problem had not been plucked out of thin air. Soon, it would be four months that Austria had been without a functioning government, and the question had to be asked, with a certain degree of impatience, as to what the way forward could possibly be.

Haider announced that he was not willing to form a minority government. Again, political games were played. Klima was prepared to conduct coalition talks with Haider, but the majority of his party opposed such a move. The Greens wanted to support a minority government with the involvement of experts but were unable to help Klima achieve a majority with this suggestion. The ÖVP refused to cooperate and referred to the negotiated but unsigned coalition pact. Time was running out, since if no budget could be produced, the Republic was threatened with insolvency.

Now, other countries intervened and expressed their concern. Klestil offered Franz Fischler, the former minister of agriculture and now agriculture commissioner at the EU, the opportunity of becoming chancellor.[837] Together with the former deputy chancellor and minister of finance, Hannes Androsch, he was to form a government, over the heads of Schüssel, Klima and the others. This was anything but a helpful idea, since how did Fischler and Androsch plan to gain the support of the parties? Klestil argued with the international image of Austria if the FPÖ were to become involved in government. The warning did not come from out of the blue. The prime minister of Luxembourg, Jean-Claude Juncker, had already informed Wolfgang Schüssel in October 1999 that participation in government by the FPÖ could lead to negative reactions within the EU. The governments of a whole series of states were at precisely this time fighting the rise in right-wing, nationalist, xenophobic parties and therefore feared the example that might be set by a little coalition in Austria. The number of warning voices increased. Over the years, Haider and his imitators had made use of verbal radicalisms and used all types of derogatory slurs. The fact that anti-Semitic and anti-Israeli sentiments had led to outrage and disgust had not been forgotten. And hardly had expressions of regret been made, then the next insulting and extremely disconcerting statements were made at 'Ash Wednesday speeches', meetings and festive gatherings, which were consumed by those present with clearly visible and audible signs of approval. What had been said and done could not so easily be erased from memory. Already during a meeting of the OSCE states in Istanbul in November 1999, Federal President Klestil and the French President Jacques Chirac spoke about the Austrian situation. During a meal, Chirac switched to the table where Deputy Chancellor Schüssel, who was also present, was sitting, and issued a direct warning.[838] It was probably intended as a shot across Austria's bows. The year came to an end without a solution appearing to be in sight. It was not until the end of January 2000 that events began to follow in rapid succession and threatened to disintegrate into irrationality. On 26 January 2000, an International Holocaust Conference began in Stockholm. There were 48 states present, represented by numerous heads of government.[839] Viktor Klima spoke on behalf of Austria, and warned against anti-Semitism and xenophobia, with a reference to the possible participation in the government of Austria by the FPÖ. Here, he must surely have spoken the minds of most of the delegates, who were quickly willing to make a threatening gesture. The French prime minister, Lionel Jospin, proposed that António Guterres, who was president of the EU Council and president of the Socialist International at the same time, should appeal to the anti-fascist conscience of the Austrians, but also inform them of the possible consequences if Jörg Haider's FPÖ were allowed to join the government. Other positions were formulated in far sharper tones. Subsequently, the question was asked as to whether the international excitement had been generated or even initiated by Austria. This was highly unlikely. Yet there is no doubt that nothing was done to dampen this tension. Finally, the Federal President urged the presidency of the Council to publish in advance the text of a resolution written in an abrasive tone by Federal Chancellor Gerhard Schröder, which had also been sent to French Prime Minister Lionel Jospin and Council President Guterres. Ultimately, it is of no consequence whether other members of the EU agreed with the statement spontaneously or only after some deliberation. Everyone, including the prime ministers and premiers of

Denmark, Finland, Ireland and Luxembourg, bent under the pressure of the majority and signed. The disaster took its course, and one could be forgiven for thinking that Austria was the causa prima of European politics. The rejection by the Federal President of entrusting anyone other than Viktor Klima to form the government led to a response that was hardly surprising: Schüssel and the FPÖ closed ranks. Two days before Viktor Klima rose to speak in Stockholm, Schüssel and Haider informed the Federal President that they had begun coalition talks. They intended to bring a process to conclusion that had already begun to emerge on the sidelines. Schüssel had not yet convinced everyone in the ÖVP that there was no other way than to form a little coalition, but for the first time during the four-month post-election period, the Federal Party Chairman had the (almost) resolute backing of the federal state governors from his party.

Haider declined to enter government. It was hoped that other countries would be reassured as a result. The FPÖ accepted the goals laid out by the ÖVP as central items of a government programme, particularly the stipulations regarding European policy and the eastward expansion of the EU. The latter also meant that the FPÖ saw no obstacle with regard to the issue of the expulsion of the German-speaking population from those countries that now had the status of accession candidates to the EU, and that it might possibly demand an Austrian veto. Schüssel also called for the approval of a generous reparation package for the victims of National Socialism. In so doing, he circumvented an issue that Viktor Klima had warned on the previous day was still un-resolved. The Freedom Party agreed. In the European state chancelleries, the alarm bells were ringing, however. Thomas Klestil, who had still not yet presented Schüssel and the FPÖ with a request to conduct coalition talks and to form a government, was forced to accept one telephone call after another, and listen to warnings that Austria risked drifting towards isolation. It was easy, to draw a direct line from Hitler via Waldheim to Austria in January 2000. The tenor of the reporting, even in highly-regarded newspa-pers, was 'Once a Nazi country – always a Nazi country'. The reply: 'Once unobjective – always unobjective!' would probably have been rejected as being too polemical, however.

Schüssel knew that the EU was considering enforcing measures that he described as sanctions.[840] Israel presented the prospect of recalling its ambassador from Vienna. Before the formation of the government had even been brought to a conclusion, the EU published the declaration of sanctions of 14 member states against the fifteenth. Yet there was no turning back.

On 2 February, Wolfgang Schüssel and Jörg Haider reported to Federal President Klestil and handed him a 100-page coalition agreement and a list of ministers. The latter was intended as a recommendation. Klestil probably realised that he had few options left for making changes, let alone preventing anything. Another way forward had been offered to him directly by Schüssel and Haider. A passage could be inserted in front of the government agreement in which it was stated, among other things, that:

'The federal government works on behalf of an Austria in which xenophobia, anti-Semitism and racism have no place. It will take systematic measures to counteract all forms of ideology that show contempt for other human beings, together with its dissemination .... The federal government is committed to protecting and promoting human rights', as well as to a pluralistic democracy and to a critical reappraisal of the National Socialist past. 'With regard to forced labour under the National Socialists, the federal government ... shall make efforts to find appropriate solutions.'[841] Klestil agreed. In addition, the wish of the Federal President for a change to be made to the composition of the federal government should also be taken into account. Klestil demanded that instead of Thomas Prinzhorn and Hilmar Kabas, of whom he did not approve, Karl-Heinz Grasser should be instated on the list of ministers as finance minister and Herbert Scheibner as minister of defence. Susanne Riess-Passer was to become deputy chancellor. However, naturally, it could be assumed that Jörg Haider would not lose his influence over the party that he continued to lead from Carinthia. To the end, Klestil did not consider giving Schüssel a direct mandate to form a government. He simply acknowledged what could no longer be prevented and created the impression that the preamble had been set at the front of the coalition pact at his request. No one contradicted him. On 4 February, the government accord was signed and the 16-head Schüssel I government was sworn in. There were demonstrations on Ballhausplatz, with people shouting and violence in the air: 'Widerstand, Widerstand. Schüssel, Haider an die Wand!' (Resist, resist. Schüssel, Haider against the wall!). It looked as though Austria was heading for turbulent times.

The Thursday Demonstrations

The members of the newly-formed government opted for an underground passage to take them from the Federal Chancellery to the Presidential Chancellery. They did not want to risk being heckled and possibly spat on. Thomas Klestil made his reluctance at having to swear in a government that he did not want abundantly clear. An unmistakeable, deep chasm ran between the Federal President and the Federal Chancellor. It was a reflection of the situation in a country in which the population was just as riven. The phrase 'nip the problems in the bud' ran through the media and the groups of demonstrators, as did references to Dollfuß and the Corporative State as the prelude to the seizure of power by the National Socialists. 'Everyday fascism' was invoked by those who suddenly couldn't cope with the situation. It was as though people had always been expecting this. A later winner of the Nobel Prize for Literature allegedly even considered suicide. It was said that there had been a break in the system, a renunciation of consensus democracy.[842] On 19 February, a large demonstration was held on

Heldenplatz in Vienna, with 150,000 people attending. It was clearly designed to act as a reference to the demonstration against Kurt Waldheim on 11 March 1998. After Erhard Busek had already written of the 'Third Republic' many years previously, and this was also postulated by Jörg Haider, for the SPÖ visionary Egon Matzner, the year 2000 really did mark the end of the Second Republic.[843] Events were followed by countless comments in the Austrian and foreign media. Once again, Austria had become the focus of attention, and the fight against the ÖVP-FPÖ coalition took on mass psychotic traits.

Perhaps the rift would have become even deeper if the EU sanctions had not triggered a very different and unexpected form of solidarity. The measures had been announced, with the formulation:

> The governments of the 14 member states shall neither conduct nor accept any official bilateral contacts at the political level with an Austrian government with the involvement of the FPÖ. No support shall be given to Austrian candidates who wish to attain positions in international organisations; Austrian ambassadors in the capital cities of the EU shall from now on only be received at the technical level.

However, what followed went far beyond downgrading bilateral contacts.[844] The Portuguese state president, Jorge Sampaio, cancelled a visit to Austria. The British heir to the throne, Prince Charles, who was due to open the British Weeks in Vienna, sent his apologies on 8 February; the British Weeks were cancelled. Two weeks later, countless schools in France announced that they would forego their school exchanges with Austria.[845] Academics were no longer invited to conferences – or were 'disinvited'; conferences that had nothing at all to do with politics were called off; student-exchange programmes stalled; suddenly, taking a winter holiday in Austria was considered objectionable. The poster of a Belgian youth organisation showed Hitler in the snow of the Austrian Alps.[846] San Remo, which for decades had delivered flowers to decorate the Vienna Opera Ball, declined to deliver. Belgium disinvited Austria from the opening ceremonies of 'Brussels: European Capital of Culture'. The grotesque situation reached its zenith when, on 4 July 2000, the long-planned 'European Monitoring Centre on Racism and Xenophobia' (EUMC) was opened in Vienna. The president of the European Commission, Romano Prodi, the President of the European Parliament and the Austrian Federal President came, but Foreign Minister Benita Ferrero-Waldner had not been invited. She came anyway and sat down demonstratively in the front row.[847]

The rejection that Austria was made to feel was directed primarily at the ÖVP-FPÖ coalition. The fact that, here, a sideways look was taken at the respective domestic policy problems could be seen as causative, or at least as a type of explanation, however. Yet what only gradually began to be understood between Lake Constance and

Lake Neusiedl was the fact that, suddenly, resentments that went back many years were coming out into the open. The degree of popularity of Austria was after all quite a bit less than the pessimists had already assumed anyway. At a conference of internationally highly-regarded historians, for example, the French historian and diplomat Jacques Le Rider or the Belgian philosopher and prime minister of Wallonia, Hervé Hasquin, could not have made themselves clearer. Even assertions that were intended as half-questions, such as 'Austria is thoroughly bad', or 'Austria as ideal anti-country' were deeply unsettling. Austria had become 'the ideal successor to prejudices against Germany',[848] and there was the almost unavoidable trio: Hitler – Waldheim – Haider. However, it was also noticeable that the Slovene historian Dušan Nećak, as well as historians from Hungary and Poland, were by no means singing the same tune.[849]

Since the measures taken by the EU 14 were expressly directed at the Austrian government, Federal President Klestil was demonstratively exempted. For his part, he also did not wish to comment on what was happening. And when on the day the government was sworn in the BBC asked him to comment, he refused, saying only: 'Take a look at the photos of the swearing-in of the new federal government. My facial expression is my comment.' Klestil then began a period of intensive travel. He travelled to talks in Munich, came to the swearing in of President Stjepn ('Stipe') Mesić in Zagreb, visited Commission President Romano Prodi in Brussels and the European Parliament in Strasbourg in April, and otherwise had a considerable presence abroad.

There were some things about which one could have laughed, or at least smiled, such as the inflammatory and cruel caricatures, which reduced Schüssel, who always appeared in public wearing a bow tie, to this accessory. This misfired when Schüssel began wearing a tie from one day to the next. Otherwise, the Chancellor, who had quite clearly become the 'front man', attempted to dodge criticism and suspicion. The task at hand was in fact to conduct a new kind of politics and to unclog the blockage of reforms, while at the same time demonstrating to other countries and above all the EU 14 how unjustified their measures were. However, the sticking point lay somewhere entirely different: all this could only succeed as long as Haider really did keep out of government politics.

One of the first measures was designed to not only present the preamble of the government agreement as a chastity belt or beauty spot, but to provide evidence of the fact that it was meant seriously. As early as February 2000, Maria Schaumayer, formerly a city councillor, then president of the Austrian National Bank and now something akin to the conscience of the nation, became the government commissioner for the compensation of forced labourers during the National Socialist period. She determined that while such compensation did not result from any responsibility on the part of the state, it was a moral obligation. Three months later, the government named the director of the Diplomatic Academy, Ernst Sucharipa, as the Austrian 'special envoy with regard to restitution'. Most of the negotiations were conducted in the USA, where President Bill Clinton entrusted them to the special envoy for Holocaust issues, Stuart Eizenstat. In the decision to take up these two troublesome topics, a continuation of the path on which Franz Vranitzky had set out could be seen, as well as the frequently announced willingness not to present Austria primarily as a victim, but also to refer to the perpetration of offences and the responsibility of many Austrians. However, there were also practical reasons: in the USA, class actions were brought against Austria. Currently, however, there was another factor at play. The USA did not chime in with the chorus of the EU 14, but quite evidently wanted to make its behaviour dependent on the action taken by the government. However, the speed and methods came as a surprise. Schaumayer had at his disposal six billion schillings that had been paid onto an account for forced labourer compensation from the budget and by those companies that had employed forced labourers between 1939 and 1945. 149,000 people, of whom it was not initially known how many were still alive, were to receive financial dona-tions. In the countries from which the forced labourers originated, organisations were created – if they were not already in existence – and the modalities were determined for the assertion of claims and the collection of documents began. Unmistakeable advertisements in newspapers and appeals attracted attention to the opportunity for receiving payments from the fund. Already in May 2000, a 'reconciliation conference' was called in the Hofburg Palace in Vienna. Shortly afterwards, the reconciliation fund act was passed in the National Council. In the years that followed until 2005, 132,000 applications for the compensation of former slave and forced labourers were brought to a positive conclusion, and 352 million euros (around 4.9 billion schillings) were paid out.[850]

The negotiations regarding the creation of a compensation fund were conducted at a similar speed, and finally, in 2001, with Stuart Eizenstat, an amount of 210 million dollars were decided on, with which the consequences of acts of persecution conducted by the National Socialist regime in Austria that had not yet been settled were to be dealt with. The amount was finally topped up to 400 million dollars.[851] The payments, which were from now on to be processed via the 'General Compensation Fund for the Victims of National Socialism' (Allgemeiner Entschädigungsfonds für Opfer des Na-tionalsozialismus), were to be the final chapter in a never-ending story and to honour the obligations of Austria as set out in Article 26 of the State Treaty of 1955.

Time and again, in stages, with delays and under pressure, some areas were regulated during the course of restitution and compensation. Now, finally, the hope was that there would be legal certainty in the USA. However, since not all class actions had been with-drawn, the payments of the reconciliation fund were delayed. Yet no one could accuse Austria of not showing goodwill. Together with the art restitution act that had already been passed in 1998, and which was systematically implemented, something was now definitively to be brought to conclusion that had long been awaiting completion. In multiple ways, it was an act of liberation: for Austria and for the government.

One more signal was sent, particularly in the direction of the EU, that Austria was aware that it had joined not only a community of interests but also a community of values: on 3 May 2000, the Council of Ministers drafted a resolution for the development of a new security and defence doctrine. This once again put Austria's neutrality up for discussion, and it was intended to demonstrate that a policy of 'keeping on the sidelines' and being a 'fellow passenger' was to be replaced by a policy of solidary co-involvement. Austria did not wish to close its mind to an obligation to provide assistance among the EU states.[852]

The image that the cabinet presented to Schüssel was certainly not the one that his critics had already painted in advance. Demonstrations by thousands of people, occasional outbreaks of violence, bags of paint thrown at government buildings and, finally, hostilities that now occurred only periodically appeared not to throw the government off course. The 'Thursday Demonstrations', which in 2000 and 2001 first attracted thousands, and then only hundreds of people, lasted the longest, before then only being called on the anniversaries. At first, there were demonstrations against the government and above all against the FPÖ; then, topics were included that at best were only indirectly connected to Wolfgang Schüssel's government. People demonstrated against cuts in social services and the weakening of employee representations, or for an extension of the legal time limit on abortions, and more rights for homosexuals.

Although the government did not issue any criticism of the EU, the number of voices among the general public that were critical of the EU increased. The EU 14 had been joined by the Czech Republic, Canada, Israel and then also Norway. However, since the Austrian government behaved so very differently than had perhaps been expected, and simply undermined the 'sanctions', the question of how it would be possible to return to normality became more pressing than ever before. Jean-Claude Juncker called the measures 'excessive', and the Greek Foreign Minister described them as 'a dangerous precedent'. Athens distanced itself formally.[853] Other states, primarily Belgium, France and Germany, appeared unimpressed. There was a search for an exit strategy. It was not until July that the President of the European Court of Justice for Human Rights commissioned the former Finnish state president, Martti Ahtisaari, to produce a report on Austrian commitment to the common European values. On 8 September, the report was submitted. The conclusion was unequivocal: 'We are ... of the view that the measures taken by the XIV Member States ... should be ended. The measures have already stirred up nationalist feelings in the country, as they have in some cases been wrongly understood as sanctions against Austrian citizens.'[854] At the same time, Austria was also praised because it intended to build a 'House of History'.

In October, the measures known as sanctions were lifted and a type of European normality was restored. This was also regarded as a signal in the USA, and the Federal
Chancellor was invited to Washington.[855] For some, this was a matter of course, while
for others, it was no reason to abandon their rejection. For the French minister for
European affairs in the Jospin cabinet, Pierre Moscovici, it was therefore also true that
'the evil' in the Austrian government would continue to be kept under surveillance.[856]
Israel also delayed a resumption of diplomatic relations, although Israel of all countries
must have realised that the measures to compensate victims of National Socialism were
more than just a gesture.

Positive signs from the European sphere only came gradually. No doubt, it was not
easy to acknowledge that they had acted wrongly. The fact that the Commission and
the member states showed generosity in the face of real violations of EU law and human rights was certainly not a helpful lesson, however. In Austrian domestic politics,
the basic principle applied from the start that the government should not be measured
according to its composition, but according to which reforms it introduced and how
it implemented them. The coalition had embarked on a rigorous policy of dismantling
the state debt. And then the measures came hailing down: taxes and fees were raised
and new ones were introduced, the pensionable age was increased, and early retirement
due to invalidity was abolished or made very difficult. The influence of the social partners, which in some cases had even been involved in producing the budget, was to be
pushed back. Privatisation measures continued to be regarded as a good opportunity for
making money, even if there were only one-off effects. Here, the object was above all to
test the room for manoeuvre that was still available at all after the largest privatisation
measures had been completed in the second half of the 1990s. Yet how was a turning
point to be understood, if not the pushing back of state influence? 'Less state – more
market', a restriction on public spending, and a departure from 'Austro-Keynesianism'
were the slogans used to gloss this over. Now, at least parts of the SPÖ were by no
means opposed to this path, but increasingly referred the benefits that would arise if
the central supply areas were not simply left to the 'market'. The speed set by the government from 2000 onwards was a cause of consternation, and it was akin to an own
goal when the chairman of the ÖVP parliamentary group, Andreas Khol, one of the
architects of the Little Coalition, was quoted as saying 'speed kills'.

The suspicion, which did not abate, that the ÖVP-FPÖ coalition was helping populist and even authoritarian tendencies in Austria to break out, would not go away, and
made the tax policy and economic measures in particular look like something that was
consciously and sustainably weakening the social partnership, and that an entirely new
path should be taken. Yet ultimately, the government was only continuing something
that had already been begun a long time before. State-owned and parastatal companies
were to be sold off and, in particular, the federal states and municipalities were to be

obliged to be involved in helping to consolidate the budget. It appeared that no stone had been left unturned. For the SPÖ, this appeared to confirm gloomy predictions, and for the ÖVP, it was a logical continuation of its course of privatisation, liberalisation and deregulation.

Had Austria really changed in 2000? For the opponents of the Little Coalition, countless numbers of whom remained hostile, this was certainly true, and to Austria's disadvantage. For those who had placed at least some hopes in the altered political constellation and above all the end of the Grand Coalition, this was also certainly true, and to its benefit. The FPÖ watched the rapid changes taking place with a mixture of pleasure and pain. For years, Jörg Haider had polemicized against corruption and waste with regard to national administration, the National Bank and above all the companies that belonged to the nationalised sector. Now, mismanagement in the areas that had been sold off was at best a case for the state prosecutor, but it was not a matter for political discourse. On the other hand, great business deals could be done as a result of the sell-off. Yet the success of the measures, which was regarded as a return to the 'Austrian school of national economy',[857] was evident. In 2001, the goal of presenting a balanced state budget appeared to have been achieved. Thus, Austria also fulfilled all preconditions in order to take the next step towards the creation of a standardised economic and monetary union, as had already been agreed at a meeting of the heads of state and government of the EU on 9 and 10 December 1991: the introduction of a common currency. At that time, however, one could be forgiven for doubting whether all the states of the EU would agree to pursue the path that had been taken. The loss of their own currency was seen by some states, particularly Britain, as the moment in which they would say: up to this point, and no further! However, twelve states, including Austria, switched their monetary transactions to the euro in 1999. From 1 January 2002, the new currency was valid for 'the twelve' as the sole means of payment.

Both within and outside the currency bloc, the EU was enjoying a continuous upward trend. And not least the Austrian government saw itself as confirmed in having taken the right course, and it intensified its commitment to also enable the East-Central European countries to join the EU. The role of the advocate, however, was not undisputed. And the scepticism regarding the path taken by Austria and above all regarding government policy continued within and outside Austria and was repeatedly linked to a name that had already been well known for some time: Jörg Haider.

The Troublemaker

Haider, who by now had become, according to his own definition, an 'ordinary party member' of the FPÖ, and who had also given up the leadership of the FPÖ after the formation of the Little Coalition, was not in favour of the effects of the consolidation policy. In his view, the burden of the consequences had been borne mainly by the 'ordinary man on the street'. Haider demanded a change of direction in the government, and in his party in particular, which was faced with dwindling support. The Governor of Carinthia rejected the attempts by the government to pave the way into the EU for the Czech Republic, Poland, Slovakia and Hungary. These states in any case showed no willingness to enter into the 'strategic partnership' desired by Austria, and instead pinned their hopes on Germany and France. It was a form of unrequited love. What was more, the Czech Republic took part in the sanctions of the EU 14 without being a member itself and was in dispute with Austria over the Temelin nuclear power station. It was obvious that the FPÖ would also support a petition for a referendum against the commissioning of the Czech nuclear power station and would take the credit for the participation of over 915,000 people.

Haider entirely disapproved of the fact that the government put off a tax reform that it had already agreed to, because the damage from flooding in the late summer of 2002 totalling around three billion euros had used up the funds set aside for the tax reduction. In September 2002, Haider managed to call a special party conference in Knittelfeld. There, an outburst occurred. Haider wanted to return to national politics and demanded the right to participate in meetings of the coalition committee. Leading representatives of the FPÖ, including the deputy chancellor, Riess-Passer, and the finance minister, Karl-Heinz Grasser, then left the party. They no longer wanted to be a part of 'Haider's FPÖ', as the junior partner to Wolfgang Schüssel was still regarded as being. The Chancellor drew the consequences and exploited his opportunity, informing the Federal President that his government had failed and demanding new elections. Klestil had no qualms about dismissing the government he so detested. On 24 November, elections to the National Council were held again. The FPÖ suffered a heavy defeat. By contrast, the ÖVP enjoyed its best electoral victory since 1966, but only achieved a relative majority, causing Schüssel to seriously consider changing his coalition partner. From February, he negotiated with the federal spokesman of the Greens, Alexander Van der Bellen, who may have seen this as a great opportunity for his party, but who failed in the end to win over that same party. He could find no support for the non-negotiable demands made by the Chancellor for the agreement to purchase 18 'Eurofighters', the upholding of university tuition fees and a pension reform. On 16 March 2003, Van der Bellen had to inform Schüssel: 'It was not enough.' Schüssel then briefly negotiated with the party chairman of the SPÖ, Alfred Gusenbauer, who was however also told by his party that the demands made by the Chancellor were unacceptable. And so the ÖVP renewed the coalition with a severely weakened FPÖ.

Again, the government placed its main emphasis on financial and economic policy. Liberalisation and reregulation were continued. The arguments against these appeared to be repeated just as often as the measures: 'sell-off of showcase companies', 'squandering of public property', 'family silver'.[860] However, it was difficult to argue when one took into account the VOEST disaster in the past and the huge deficits being run up by several state-owned operations. The downside, however, was that the dismantling of personnel was dramatic, and in the years that followed 2000, the number of people in work was now only just over half of the figure for 1985.[861]

The success of the restructuring of the enterprises and businesses that had long shown a deficit was noticeable. They required no further subsidies, or, like the Austrian Industry Administration Ltd (Österreichische Industrieverwaltungs-Aktiengesellschaft, or ÖIAG), they made profits that then boosted the budget as dividends. Even before this development, full privatisation was introduced. The crude oil company OMV, Telekom Austria and Austrian Airlines (AUA), were the next 'candidates'. The Postal Service was to be listed on the stock market, and so on. The fact that this meant saying goodbye to a large number of corporations, firms and businesses that really had become part of the country's identity, had to be accepted. After all, the SPÖ had also been forced to acknowledge that the *Arbeiter-Zeitung*, the Vorwärts publishing house, the Consumers' Cooperative (Konsum-Genossenschaft) and other traditionally 'red' enterprises had become financial burdens that could no longer be supported, and that they had to be liquidated, in some cases under dramatic circumstances.

The changes brought about by the sale of large, now privately-managed areas, would have been seen as a real catastrophe decades earlier. German enterprises purchased shares in Austria's economy on a grand scale, and in some commercial sectors even gained a supremacy that went far beyond that which had been classified as German Assets in 1945, for example. The British, Dutch and Italians strengthened their presence in Austria, so that in the end, over 10,000 foreign companies in Austria generated on-third of the turnover of all companies operating in the country.[862] As an equivalent, reference was made to the 'eastward expansion', in which 6,400 credit institutions and companies based in Austria had played a leading role,[863] and for their part were regarded as emissaries of a globalised, but not always welcome, world. This notwithstanding, some enterprises threatened to become non-Austrian ones within a short period of time. In the food trade sector, any thinking along national lines faced the imminent threat of having to be discarded. Most food chains that took over from the retailers were German-owned. The concentration on the newspaper market led to a takeover of the titles with the highest circulation by German enterprises. German television programmes took up more and more broadcasting slots, and pushed back the monopolist, the Austrian Broadcasting Corporation. One only had to look at the television adverts to see where the euro was rolling. And the young people left in the hands of the 'infant care institution' began to use language brimming with German idioms such as 'Schnäppchen' (bargain), 'nö' (no), 'lecker' (yummy) and 'dufte' (great).

The globalisation of the neighbouring region was a side effect of the changes that had begun to take place during the 1990s. German students flooded Austrian universities. Any attempts at limiting numbers were objected to as being non-EU conformant. When it came to appointing staff at university teaching faculties, it was equally noticeable that Germany once again had the advantage, with ten times the number of intellectuals on offer. A similar phenomenon applied to the major cultural institutions, museums and theatres. For some long-serving actors with a sense of Austrian patriotism, such as Fritz Muliar, this was a horrific scenario. He had already expressed his frustration in writing in 1993:

> There is no more Burgtheater. There is just a building of the same name, opposite the City Hall in Vienna, where a lot of foreign people perform plays. Since the takeover of the directorship by the theatre-makers from Bochum (four of them!), our national theatre has become a city theatre in line with the West German model... The imperial crown has been pushed aside by the spiked helmet, and with German thoroughness...[864]

The balance was therefore mixed, although the complaints ran at a high level. It was indisputable that 'backward' Austria, as one German magazine had described it, had become a model: 'How on earth have they managed it? Good mood, more growth, new jobs... Hard to imagine, but it's true: the eternally backward Austrians really have outdone the Germans when it comes to economic figures.'[865]

This assertion had the capacity to act like balsam on the wounds inflicted on Austria in the European political arena. The penalties had not stopped with the measures taken by the EU 14. Austria was always reminded of its outsider role when it was felt appropriate to critically refer to the 'different nature' of the small Alpine state. After all, Austria had also become an obstacle. This was unwillingly acknowledged by NATO during the second Iraq war, and particularly as a side effect of the NATO air attacks against targets in Yugoslavia in 1999, when Austria prevented NATO transport convoys from crossing the country and forbade flights over its air space.

Austria was also repeatedly harshly criticised because it still adhered to the 'Atomsperrgesetz', the act prescribing a non-nuclear Austria passed in 1978, and not least with the catastrophe at the Chernobyl nuclear power station in Ukraine in mind, was also opposed to the construction of nuclear power stations near its borders. This was a source of irritation for all those who continued to promote nuclear energy. Austria was also regarded as an obstacle when it came to asserting the free movement of goods in Europe, and it put up considerable resistance against the approval of heavy goods vehicle traffic through Tyrol. Time and again, Austria was urged to become more pliable by EU headquarters in Brussels. At the same time, a pro-EU mood was to be nurtured in the country, and those countries that were not good neighbours were also to be treated like friendly ones. This was not least the case with Germany, too, whose red-green, Schröder-Fischer, government displayed unequivocal antipathy, quite unlike the previous governments under Helmut Kohl. The 'one against all' mentality appeared not to have changed when Austria was unsuccessful in asserting its desire to offer Turkey a 'privileged partnership', but not to begin real accession negotiations. In Vienna, Turkey's size, its socio-economic backwardness, its dubious human rights situation, high costs and above all the risk of mass immigration, were used as arguments. But, naturally, for Turkey's NATO partners, almost all of whom were Europeans, these arguments did not sufficiently hold water. Furthermore, Turkey had been promised that accession talks would begin. No EU country shared Austria's opinion.[866] The criticism of Vienna was unavoidable. Austria's now poor image was not helped by the fact that elections to the European Parliament were not used by all parties as a reason for sending their best minds to Brussels, but that alongside good candidates, some rather dubious characters also obtained a seat.

At the end of 2003, Austria broke away again when it urged that no obligation to provide military assistance on the part of the neutral countries should be adopted in the EU Constitutional Treaty. This was however a view that was also shared by Sweden, Finland and Ireland. The Iraq war of 2003 contributed more than anything else to increasing awareness of the value of perpetual neutrality. Austria did not join the 'coalition of the willing' demanded by the USA and was immediately demoted to the status of a part of 'old' Europe. However, it was in good company with countries such as Germany and France. For those who supported Austria's joining NATO, this war put a definitive end to all their efforts. There was no point in fighting against it.

However, there was one back door available. In 2003, the minister of defence of the Schüssel II government, Günther Platter, publicly considered the option of abandoning general conscription in favour of a professional army.[867] This did not appear to be such a bad idea, considering the fact that looking around, more and more countries were converting their military forces into professional armies. Seven years later, in 2010, the mayor of Vienna, Michael Häupl, gave an abrupt impetus to the holding of a plebiscite on the abandonment or retention of general conscription. However, the introduction of a professional army – not least according to the observations of a large number of proponents of the idea, and particularly among the ranks of the Federal Army – would sooner or later lead to Austria joining NATO and put an end to its hybrid existence of 'I'd like to, but I can't'. Above all, as so many members of the military hoped, NATO would urge Austria to better materially equip its notoriously under-funded army. The Federal Army had become smaller and smaller. Organisational changes were made at increasingly short intervals.[868] Finally, the total period of service was reduced to six months. Repetition exercises were no longer required. However, while heavy weapons and armoured vehicles were purchased, there was a quantum leap in the air force, which for so long had been the poor relation. Austria wanted to order 24 of one of the most modern planes in the world, the 'Typhoon' Eurofighter. Soon, however, the financial problems became clear: 24 planes were too expensive, and 18 would have to suffice. And a few technical refinements would also have to be left out. In this way, the government not only responded to the constantly dwindling budget funds, however, but also to the desire expressed by the opposition to roll back the purchase entirely. As was natural with such an expensive and controversial purchase, there was quickly talk of corruption. The accusation turned out to be unfounded, however. In 2002, it could not be foreseen that problems of a very different nature abounded and that in 2017, the manufacturing company would be accused of fraud.

Measured against the first months of the ÖVP-FPÖ coalition, the government had already lost a great deal of momentum by 2003. As was normal, the attempt had been made to implement as many measures as possible, and not only popular ones, within the first few months, in order to be able to then work under less pressure. The EU sanctions had led to an increase in the extent to which processes were accelerated. This period was now a thing of the past, and it had in theory become 'normal' in Austria – to the extent that developments within the FPÖ could be described as 'normal'. After the elections, the FPÖ had shrunk considerably, but it still existed, and was still represented in government. In April 2005, Jörg Haider set about establishing a new party, however, which he called the 'Alliance for the Future of Austria' (Bündnis Zukunft Österreich, or BZÖ). Schüssel briefly considered calling new elections, but it was likely that not least the Chancellor's party would bear the consequences for the turbulence within its coalition partner. However, another reason that this was not an opportune moment to call new elections was that the celebrations to mark the fiftieth anniversary of the State Treaty of 1955 were due to be held soon, and Austria did not want to present an image of political disintegration and chaos in the domestic political arena.

The State Treaty celebrations could certainly be regarded as a barometer of the regard in which Austria was held internationally, and as a reflection of how the country positioned itself on the international stage. The main celebration in the Upper Belvedere on 15 May was attended by the Russian foreign minister, Sergei Lavrov, and the French foreign minister, Michel Barnier. Britain sent its minister of state for Europe, Douglas Alexander, and the USA send Rudy Boschwitz, a former senator and the son of an American occupation officer. However, this could probably merely be interpreted in such a way that for Russia and France, the Austrian State Treaty continued to be important, while for the USA it had become an annoying reminiscence. Here, it could be seen very clearly what value the small neutral country had for one country or another in the complex European situation. The USA was content to send an ex-senator.

After the agreement regarding compensation for forced labourers, and above all after the conclusion of the Washington Agreement on the General Settlement Fund, bilateral relations between the USA and Austria had remained without any particularly positive developments. The description given a short time later in the relations summary applied: in the eyes of the Americans, Austria was a 'self-absorbed, comfortable and due to the prevailing circumstances economically successful country', which sold itself below its value'.[869] Such an appraisal could have been applied to a series of other countries, too. And it was not the least complimentary. Austria had actively supported the acceptance of those states that were now termed as 'central European' – Hungary, the Czech Republic, Slovakia and Poland – into the EU in 2004. The same applied to Slovenia. And for Croatia, there were at least real prospects in sight. Yet what would be described ten years later as a 'welcome culture' only applied in part. These states, too, were only welcome in Austria to the extent that they opened up the Austrian version of 'turbo-capitalism' and ensured external security – and this they then indeed did. The inevitable consequence was that Austria again reduced its defence spending. Anyway, there had never been any real effort directed towards building up a defence. And in order to avoid becoming the destination for uncontrolled migration and being obliged to take in a large number of workers who were looking for the chance to earn better wages, the Austrian labour market was blocked to migrants from the east for a period of ten years.

23 The Relapse

23 Soldiers of the Austrian Federal Army during an assistance operation for the monitoring of the Austro-Hungarian border near the Loipersbach-Schattendorf railway station, August 1992. The dismantling of border fortifications in Hungary and the possibility of crossing the border unchecked resulted in September 1990 in the deployment of soldiers of the Federal Army for an intended ten weeks. The deployment ultimately lasted for 21 years and was not ended until 15 December 2011. (Photo: Federal Army)

Should anyone have been able to remember that far back, he might have been reminded in 2006 of the end of Josef Klaus' period of government. Wolfgang Schüssel took stock of his time in office. Positive aspects dominated, and the Chancellor had his achievements of the past six years printed on posters and in brochures in such a way that one must have believed Austria had completely changed. True enough, much had happened. The somewhat bumpy start was no longer very relevant. It was a question of the 'eco-social market economy' invoked years earlier, deregulation, liberalisation, budget consolidation – and whatever else was worthy of emphasising. In contrast with what had been present at the beginning – fears about the sustainability of domestic peace, suspicion over the collaboration with the Freedom Party, social conflicts and, above all, damage to Austria's international standing – things had developed far more moderately. By virtue of privatisation and the state's withdrawal from important, albeit not always profitable economic sectors, money had flowed into the coffers. A long-burning issue in domestic policy and one with relevance for foreign policy, namely the tiresome question of the mounting of bilingual place-name signs in southern Carinthia, could be regarded as almost solved. Jörg Haider's FPÖ had disintegrated. Haider himself had become inconceivable as a partner. One of the main sceptics vis-à-vis the Little Coalition, Federal President Thomas Klestil, was dead. He had died on 6 July 2004, two days before the completion of his second term in office. The Second President of the National Council, Heinz Fischer, had been elected as his successor. He had achieved a comfortable victory over his opponent, Foreign Minister Bernita Ferrero-Waldner. This seemed to re-establish the old formula that federal president and federal chancellor belonged in different parties. Despite the defeat of 'his' candidate, Schüssel could be content that the relationship with Federal President Klestil, which had never been entirely free of tension, was over. Things would run more smoothly with Heinz Fischer.

The Unloved

Foreign countries had come to terms with the Little Coalition in Austria and demonstrated increasing friendliness, for Austria had developed into a model pupil of the EU. Relations with the USA, as well as Russia, were more or less free of tension. For those who were due to vote in 2006, however, other issues were in any case more important, namely – in descending order – combating criminality, political integrity, preventing the relocation of Austrian businesses abroad, improving care for the elderly, stopping the EU's exertion of influence, which was regarded as patronising, and, finally, a whole host of material objectives, ranging from an increase of pensions to benefits for families with many children.[870]

The SPÖ intervened above all regarding the latter challenges. They felt like they were in the ascendant. Under their new party chairman, Alfred Gusenbauer, the Social Democrats had conquered the traditionally black federal states of Styria and Salzburg and now provided the governors in both provinces. For the Austrian Social Democrats, therefore, the record of the government did not, by any means, look so positive. The following issues were denounced as unfulfilled and unsociable: questions of basic social security benefits, a major tax reform, the privileges of the rich and the 'super rich', the abolition of tuition fees, etc. This could be processed in such a way that not only was a position adopted but also fears might be aroused. It amounted to a direct confrontation between the traditional parties, as the Freedom Party could be largely excluded this time following their internal quarrels and the Greens rated as bothersome rather than dangerous. Yet the outcome could be predicted even in the run-up to the elections: there would be another grand coalition. There would be a return to the basic model of the Second Republic and a little coalition would once again be no more than an episode. A grand coalition as an expression of puzzlement, however, was surely not a good prerequisite for renewed collaboration.

Wolfang Schüssel must have regarded it as the second-best solution imaginable but, on the assumption that he would continue to lead a coalition government, it was for him at least a conceivable model for cooperation. What he did not want, however, was to play second fiddle in a grand coalition. He felt sure of victory – and would be proved wrong: by 1 October 2006, everything had changed again. The SPÖ had the edge. And Schüssel resigned. However, he did not respond like Josef Klaus had done in 1970 and withdraw overnight; instead, he wanted to explore and agree on conditions for a collaboration in the negotiations with the designated chancellor, Alfred Gusenbauer. This was done in good faith, for it gave Finance Minister Wilhelm Molterer – Schüssel's successor as federal party chairman – the possibility to join a new government unburdened and unscathed, as it were. But it would prove to be much more difficult than anticipated. Gusenbauer and Schüssel did not accommodate each other, just like Klima and Schüssel in their day, but instead distanced themselves ever more from one another. Instead of a process of 'overcoming the past' (Vergangenheitsbewältigung), a not entirely suitable term, as addressed by Gusenbauer or the 'disarmament talks'[871] called for by the Salzburg governor, Gabi Burgstaller, there was an escalation. Verbally and in terms of content. Gusenbauer did not hesitate to agree to an enquiry committee on the acquisition of 'Eurofighters' already demanded during the election campaign by his campaign manager and federal whip, Norbert Darabos, and – if possible – to cancel the purchase. He willingly complied with the demand for an enquiry committee on banking. Both times, the SPÖ was supported by the FPÖ under its chairman, Heinz-Christian Strache, who had been elected in 2004, and by the Greens of Alexander Van der Bellen. The ÖVP regarded this as an affront and the coalition talks developed into a bitter confrontation. They were ultimately on the verge of failing when the Federal President began to intervene in a sustained manner. He naturally knew about the scenarios of an at least theoretically conceivable three-way coalition, though this – if at all – would have been more easily possible under ÖVP leadership. Gusenbauer responded with the possibility of forming a minority government.[872] It was again the example of Bruno Kreisky that was employed here, because Gusenbauer strove to emulate what Kreisky had achieved in 1970. The ÖVP saw this by all means as an option with an uncertain outcome, even for a broad-based party with mass appeal. Heinz Fischer took a different few. He was against it. Gusenbauer and the SPÖ complied.

It was January 2007 before at least a framework agreement began to take shape. The mistrust and personal aversion remained. And that was a poor basis for a renewed collaboration in an unloved coalition born of necessity. There were also enough questions awaiting an answer. Fears for the future were being voiced. Instead of starting with the positive features of earlier Grand Coalitions, however, those concerned acted as though it was necessary to skip the era of the ÖVP-FPÖ coalition and continue where the quarrels of 1999 had left off. The day in 2001 on which Finance Minister Grasser had announced that a zero budget deficit had been achieved was long past. In other areas, too, the discrepancy between the new/old partners was striking: on the one hand, there was the demand for a reduction in the exertion of state influence, whereas the SPÖ felt obligated to a state that was responsible for everything. Not least for immigration.

'Pummerin rather than muezzin'

The change of subject had been coming for a long time. Now it had arrived: if the fear of foreign domination had already been addressed in the late 1980s and early 1990s, it now increasingly hardened. The FPÖ focussed above all on Islamisation and awakened both concerns and fears. Rhymes on posters such as 'Pummerin rather than muezzin', referring to one of the largest bells in the history of St. Stephen's Cathedral, or 'Better homeward bound than entry admission' *(Lieber Heimreise als Einreise)* were openly used already during election canvassing in Vienna in 2005 in order to stir up emotions. The masses of immigrants, the circumstance that they came from foreign cultures and the fact that their ability and willingness to integrate were sometimes non-existent[873] were discomforting. Attempts had repeatedly been made to take countermeasures but the number of immigrants kept growing. Austria did not select its refugees but only took them in. Family reunions and the abundance of children foiled attempts to place limits on immigration. Children born in Austria were Austrians. Wars and civil wars in the Caucasus republics of the former Soviet Union resulted in an influx of refugees. Chechens, who arrived in Austria via Hungary and, mostly, Slovakia often only had to say one word – 'asylum' – in order to be taken in and receive refugee status.

An even bigger headache was caused by the influx from Turkey. The integration of immigrants from Turkey became an ongoing topic, because it simply refused to succeed. Something evolved here that was in principle already known, namely 'pillarization', but it received a completely different content to the term originally coined by the major parties. The understandable tendency of the new arrivals to concentrate in the urban centres, especially Vienna but also Graz, Linz and western Austria, initially manifested itself. The result was the formation of something like ghettos. The infrastructure changed; stores and service providers served first and foremost to satisfy the needs of the migrants. Markets soon offered more 'oriental' products than such from regional farmers. The dietary rules of devout Muslims encouraged this. School attendance became a problem. Older immigrants did not even try to acquire the language. In the school classes of individual districts and regions, the children of long-time residents were in the minority. Whoever was able to move away, did so. The integration package passed by the Schüssel government called for obligatory German courses for immigrants. The language competence of the younger ones was successfully improved, though many older ones did not even make an attempt to learn German.

At the end of the first decade of the twenty-first century, the number of people living in Austria with a so-called immigrant background came to 1.5 million, which corresponded to 18.6 per cent of the total population. 516,000 of them were Muslims.[874] (In 2017, their number was estimated at around 700,000.)[875] Half of them had Austrian citizenship. In this respect, Austria was the undisputed leader among European states. Islam had become the second biggest religious community after the Catholic Church. The ground was laid for a growing xenophobia. This was not limited, however, to the 'long-time residents' but also embraced the immigrants of earlier waves of immigration. As they were threatened by unemployment to a far greater extent than before, they supported xenophobic parties for existential reasons and turned above all to the FPÖ. It was believed that they were most likely to prevent a further influx. The other parties were admittedly able to oppose this with their arguments and retaliate by pointing to human rights and EU guidelines, but they were able to convince with these tactics only sporadically and in the case of the benevolent-natured.

The solidarity that had certainly functioned during the wars in Yugoslavia was rapidly on the wane. The multicultural society invoked after 1989 ('Multikulti') became a fiction. This was only the beginning of a debate; attempts were made to tinker with the symptoms, though without there being any easy answers on hand. The migration problem interlaced with other issues, above all the growing scepticism towards the EU. The introduction of the euro had been acclaimed in 2002. Scarcely was the question of EU expansion addressed, however, and noticeable resistance promptly bestirred itself. The barometer of public opinion showed Austria in an inglorious last place in October/ November 2005. Only 24 per cent of the population were unreservedly positive towards the EU. In an internal comparison, it was noticeable that approval in Salzburg was still at 59 per cent, while it had sunk to 14 per cent in Burgenland, a region that particularly benefitted from EU funding. Frustration spread. There was opposition to an early accession on the part of Romania and Bulgaria, not to mention Turkey. For many things, there was little understanding. Seeds of conflict aplenty arose from the spatial and, above all, emotional distance to the European institutions.

The EU wanted to adopt a constitution. In itself, this was merely the logical continuation of the work of unification.[876] In France and the Netherlands, plebiscites were held on the subject. They resulted in a vote against the constitution. Thus, plan B was devised: instead of a constitution treaty, there would be a reform treaty. Now Ireland voted against it. A day later, on 15 June 2008, the *Kronen-Zeitung* stated: 'The angry Irish gave the EU a black eye.' And what of Austria? For the EU sceptics, and all the more so for its opponents, a single article of the reform treaty agreed on in Lisbon appeared significant: Article 50, which regulated a withdrawal from the union.

The coalition dealt with the process of parliamentary treatment of the Treaty of Lisbon and arranged for the necessary approval. Almost simultaneously, however, the Federal Chancellor and his new party chairman, Werner Faymann, distanced themselves in sensational fashion from what had just been resolved. On 1 July 2008, both of them wrote a letter to the editor of the *Kronen-Zeitung*, Hans Dichand, with whom above all Faymann was on good terms, stating:

> In the discussion on the Treaty of Lisbon, great unease became apparent. Like in Ireland, in Austria, too, there is a widespread scepticism towards the EU. After an overwhelming majority of Austrians voted to join the European Union in 1994, today we encounter a mood of uncertainty and sometimes also rejection. Many people are disappointed and annoyed about the limited progress the EU has made on the path to becoming a social union.

And then stakes were veritably driven in:

> The EU is hostile to democracy and does not address the real problems. The Austrian job market must remain 'protected' by means of 'grace periods' .... 'In the context of the struggle against climate change, the transit problem must finally be solved collectively, too.' Future treaty amendments 'that affect Austrian interests' should 'be decided on by a plebiscite ....

This also applies for a possible accession of Turkey, which, in our view, would overwhelm the current structure of the EU.'[877]

Thus, the interlacement was complete, and the ÖVP, who had to read this in the newspapers, was duped. The point described by Franz Vranitzky as 'the tabloidization of politics and politicians' had been reached.[878]

24 'It's enough'

24 Refugees in the clearance zone at the Austro-Hungarian border near Spielfeld, 26 October 2015. In late autumn 2015, the flow of refugees from the Near and Middle East reached its peak. The partial closing of the border along the motorway from Budapest to Vienna resulted in a shift to the so-called Western Balkan route, until free passage was also halted here. During the course of the year, around 700,000 people passed through Austria on their way to Germany or Sweden. 88,000 of them, ten per cent of which were unaccompanied adolescents, applied for asylum in Austria. (Photo: Army Photo and Film Office (HBF) / Gunter Pusch)

Approval of politics had been on the wane for years and faith in politicians was extremely low.[879] The sympathies of leading politicians for one another was limited. Nonetheless, the coalition agreement of 9 January 2007 had been signed. The ÖVP had achieved what had been said of the SPÖ in 1963: in the negotiations, they had easily compensated for their defeat. Resentment understandably dominated the ranks of the SPÖ. Organisations of his own party held demonstrations against Gusenbauer – but the party youth had also demonstrated against Kreisky. The media did not pull any punches with unflattering words. The SPÖ party chairman put up with it. Alfred Gusenbauer wanted to become federal chancellor. And he did so, in defiance of all invectives from around 2,000 demonstrators on Ballhausplatz. Since the formation of a government in 2000, however, even this was no novelty any more.

It lasted only a few weeks until the past caught up with the governing parties. In the pre-election period, they had shown no restraint in attempting to outbid each other and made promises that would result in additional burdens of several billion euros for the budget. The matter of saving 30 billion euros by 2016 was off the table. The extension of provisions for early retirement, which had been intended for heavy workers, had in the meantime become a farce; the abolition of tuition fees, improvements in the school and social sectors, as well as the acquisition of Eurofighters were all supposed to be financed without additional burdens – this was impossible. At the same time, there was talk of achieving a zero budget deficit. It was understandable that massive cuts were discussed. Norbert Darabos, who had advanced from SPÖ election campaign manager to minister of defence, believed he knew where: the Eurofighters. Parallel to the enquiry committee that was supposed to uncover irregularities in the procurement order, in other words 'bribes', negotiations began regarding a further reduction in the quantity, the first – that is, not the most modern – production series and lesser features. The enquiry committee brought to light several inconsistencies in expense accounts, though these had not influenced the type selection and the overall costs. But no misconduct could be established that would have justified a cancellation of the purchase contract. Minister Darabos dismissed the argument that a further reduction of the envisaged 18 aircraft would call into question the entire purchase and was ultimately content to have forced through the acquisition of 15 planes that were no longer very modern and had a considerably shorter lifespan and a reduced set of systems. It was merely a question of monitoring air space and not of 'war', he said in 2017. Talk of 'flying hazardous waste' did the rounds.

Clearance Sale

Aside from the not only atmospheric disturbances in the collaboration between the governing parties, events surrounding the acquisition of Eurofighters cast a harsh light on the country's and the government's understanding of neutrality and defence readiness. The years in which the Federal Army had no longer regarded itself as a point of dispute, following Kreisky's army reform, but could rejoice in the approval of large swathes of the population were well and truly over. Cuts had resulted in a steady decrease in expenditure for the army. The abolition of the Warsaw Pact and the accession of eastern and south-eastern European states to NATO had revived the question of the necessity of an army. There was only one perceived threat, which could be generated only with some difficulty. The coming into force of the Schengen Agreement on the monitoring of the external borders of the European Union and their protection by the states located on the periphery of the EU removed the necessity for defence of the internal frontiers.

Burgenland and Lower Austria rendered the army a service by arguing that a monitoring of the eastern border was still necessary. On 21 December 2007, therefore, an 'assistance deployment of the security police on the basis of an extension of the Schengen area' came into effect. The soldiers were withdrawn from the state border and patrolled the interior of the country. However, this was not a deployment for a fully-fledged perceived threat. A new threat scenario, which focussed above all on terrorism and infrastructural dangers, would replace the old one. Furthermore, the recommendations of a Federal Army Reform Commission from 2004 had to be implemented. Conceived as 'Federal Army 2010', it was very quickly overtaken by reality. Thus, the army was thinned out further and the sale of barracks and property continued as a way of raising funds. Criticism of the army, which should really have been directed at those politically responsible, was dismissed with the argument that Austria's army continued to play an exceptional role in international missions, above all in Bosnia but also on the Golan Heights or in Mali.

The latter was indeed worth emphasising, for it could be regarded as a foreign policy activity that contributed, among other things, to Austria once more successfully applying in 2009 for a seat as a non-permanent member of the Security Council of the United Nations. Whether this was enough to qualify the 'lull in Austrian foreign policy'[880] described shortly thereafter by the American Ambassador in Vienna remained to be seen.

In the meantime, the Gusenbauer–Molterer government continued its own work of destruction. The budget preparation turned into a squaring of the circle, as both governing parties wanted to deliver on their election promises and at the same time achieve funding in the budget. The government became somewhat driven, as it had to respond to an insight of the Constitutional Court, which had repealed the provisions in place for inheritance tax and gift tax as unconstitutional. The result was the abolition of both taxes. Then it was a question of the tax and contribution ratio, as well as the financial adjustment with the federal states and municipalities. And it was demonstrated time and again that there was approval for the foregoing of revenue on the part of the federal state in light of the fact that one could not oppose a good deed, for one would otherwise have a poor hand at the inescapable next elections. Compensation measures would offset inflation – one could feel transported back to the time of the wage and price agreement. In February 2008, the Federal Chancellor wanted to grant 100 euros to every income earner and pensioner. The 'Gusi hundred' became a topic of conversation. Deputy Chancellor and Finance Minister Molterer categorically rejected it. On 24 February, Gusenbauer demanded that the tax reform be brought forward to 1 January 2009. Molterer rejected this. With increasing regularity, the Chancellor and the Deputy Chancellor communicated their intentions via the media. And the media thoroughly exploited their position as the 'Fourth Estate' in the state. In the shadow of federal politics, the consciousness of the states – if necessary – also increased once more. The state governors became increasingly self-assured and communicated their wishes to the federal government time and again. The Conference of State Governors (Landeshauptleutekonferenz), a body not envisaged in the constitution, was already regarded as a substitute for the Federal Council (Bundesrat). This no longer bore any relation to federalism, however; instead, it was a reaction to the lack of leadership on the part of the federal government. The latter could easily be blamed for the consequences of negative developments, while the federal states appeared to embody an ideal world.

The next notable occurrence was that another icon began to totter: the Austrian airline company AUA could no longer offset the rising costs, suffered mounting losses and could only have been rescued by means of a re-nationalisation. The SPÖ wanted to adhere to an Austrian solution; the ÖVP had a 'strategic partnership' or a sell-off in mind. In May 2008, the entire airline was only worth the equivalent of two jumbo jets.[881] Ultimately, the only way out was the sale of the airline to the German Lufthansa and the transfer of the bulk of the AUA's debts to the Republic.

The next sell-offs and privatisation measures concerned the Austrian Postal Service and Telekom Austria. Ultimately, transactions on the Austrian financial market did not make things easier. Bad speculations and losses to the tune of hundreds of millions in the case of the Bank for Labour and Business (Bank für Arbeit und Wirtschaft, or BAWAG), the Hypo Alpe-Adria and the Carinthian Regional Mortgage Bank (Kärntner Landeshypothekenbank) caused a stir and led to investigations. It was not the management errors that were of consequence, however, but the interlacing of politics and finance that again became apparent. In the case of BAWAG, it was above all the link with the Austrian Trade Union Federation that was rated as a scandal, triggered a flood of legal procedures and turned the Trade Union Federation into a 'giant with feet of clay'.[882] In the Carinthian case, Governor Jörg Haider spared no effort in exerting political pressure and leaving the supervisory body, the Financial Market Authority (Finanzmarktaufsicht), looking like the guilty party. The true extent of the debacle admittedly remained unclear for a long time. Shortly thereafter, the pack was reshuffled. Transport and Infrastructure Minister Werner Faymann had already come increasingly to the fore in connection with the sale of the AUA and likewise the Postal Service and the Telekom. He used market-dominating media, above all the *Kronen-Zeitung*, to present himself as someone who had an ear for the public. Like many others, he also knew too well that the discontent in the SPÖ regarding the Federal Chancellor could scarcely be contained any more. Alfred Gusenbauer had been willing time and again to accept positions of the ÖVP and had acted in a way that was anything but favourable. And what was more: the SPÖ lost the elections to the regional diet in Tyrol. The SPÖ chairman was criticised by several regional organisations and he had to acknowledge that Faymann and the president of the SPÖ Pensioners' Association, Karl Blecha, had bypassed him in resolving on a pension reform and that his popularity was steadily decreasing. He had also 'had enough', as he subsequently confessed.[883] On 16 June 2008, Werner Faymann took over leadership of the SPÖ as acting chairman. Ten days later, he and Gusenbauer directed their aforementioned letter to the editor of the *Kronen-Zeitung*, Hans Dichand, criticising the EU. The ÖVP perceived this as a violation of a common foreign policy, which was not, in itself, regarded as a point of dispute. Gusenbauer and Faymann rejected the criticism. On 7 July 2008, Deputy Chancellor Molterer ended the collaboration with two words: 'It's enough!' The Gusenbauer–Molterer government had failed after 544 days.

Betrayal of Red-White-Red?

It was not the first time that Austrian politics had been dominated by European issues. The impression could not be denied that ultimately something was being used as an excuse here to serve as a justification for displeasure and an almost tangible aversion. It was clear that the media and, above all, a few newspapers played a decisive role. The term 'newspapers' was misleading, however, to the extent that it was only a handful of journalists who had thoroughly acquired a taste for engaging in politics. They were opinion-forming and perceived as 'the good guys', whereas those who advocated other opinions were consigned to the ranks of 'the villains'. With the help of criticism of developments taken by the EU, and which were very suited to furnishing existing stereotypes with even broader brushstrokes, it was ultimately not so difficult to obtain rapid feedback. The EU was also 'bad', indeed especially so. A paltry 58 per cent of the people were still of the opinion that Austria should remain in the European Union.

Those, however, who continued to be committed to the European institutions appeared dubious, to say the least. The EU was suddenly denounced as a 'fascistic project' and a 'betrayal of Red–White–Red'.[884] Criticism of the EU was exaggerated to the point of absurdity by virtue of sometimes humoristic and sometimes serious reports being put into circulation: it was claimed that the EU intended in the future to introduce a female quota among choirboys; that the largest bell of Vienna's St. Stephen's Cathedral, the 'Pummerin', was no longer allowed to be rung on New Year's Eve night, as 'noise pollution' was supposedly too excessive, and so on. Werner Faymann took part in the anti-movement to the full.

In this way, one arrived right back at the governing Grand Coalition. It was concluded that its continued existence had initially been 'forcibly induced by the media', only to then end 'full of hatred' one year later.[885] Thus, that was done which was already a good Austrian tradition: no attempt was made to reshuffle the government; instead, the National Council was dissolved. It was also traditional that both coalition partners gave each other the blame for the failure. Something, in any case, had to change. Other, new leading figures would have to attempt to begin what had been so keenly termed a reform partnership. As the National Council had already agreed in 2007 to extend the legislative period to five years, it was eagerly awaited whether the intention and possibility of a longer and more intensive collaboration not dictated by election dates were also viable. The experiences of the preceding years indicated otherwise.

Elections took place on 28 September 2008. For the first time, 16-year-olds were entitled to vote and there was the option of a postal vote. Josef Klaus had already had the latter on his agenda. Now, almost thirty years later, it became reality. All good things need time, after all. The election results were regarded as a disaster for the governing parties. The SPÖ and the ÖVP had to accept significant losses. The Freedom Party of Austria was able to double its total seats. Haider's 'Alliance for the Future of Austria' (Bündnis Zukunft Österreich, or BZÖ) came in fourth and overtook the 'Greens'. Two days after the elections to the National Council, Federal President Heinz Fischer tasked the SPÖ chairman, Werner Faymann, with forming a government. Faymann was still regarded as a bearer of hope. He knew that the whole SPÖ stood united behind him; he had been voted in with 98.36 per cent and was expected to turn the tide. In the Federal President's letter to Faymann, he not only called on all sides to collaborate but also sent a reminder about the federal state reform and furthermore emphasised the importance of education, science and research as well as the struggle against disenchantment with politics. And it went without saying that there ought to be a new form of cooperation.

The ÖVP's enthusiasm for a continuation of the coalition was limited. The government did not have a constitutional majority and would have to repeatedly seek out a willing third party in order to regulate fundamental issues. Three enquiry committees,

which had been applied for by the SPÖ and forced through with the help of the opposition, curbed the willingness of the ÖVP to make another go of it with the SPÖ. Again,
albeit theoretically, the ÖVP negotiators suggested that there were also other coalition
options. This was perhaps not a serious proposal but it could not be paid back in kind
by the SPÖ. There was nothing left for them to do but make an attempt at forming a
new grand coalition. That which Chancellor Vranitzky had said a dozen years earlier
still applied: it was not possible to work with the FPÖ. This had applied to the Freedom
Party when they had still been under the leadership of Jörg Haider, and it was still valid
for the party led by Heinz Christian Strache, and likewise for the BZÖ.

Then came the shock. On 11 October 2008, Jörg Haider was killed in an accident.
His BZÖ was without a leader. The death of the Carinthian State Governor, who had
played such an extraordinary role in Austrian politics for so many years and could at
least be regarded as having provided some salt for the rather dreary 'soup', gave rise to
much speculation. Had it just been an accident? Had someone given a helping hand?
Conspiracy theories circulated. Haider had repeatedly made waves, had made no secret
of his occasionally extravagant lifestyle and had turned not only the FPÖ and then the
BZÖ into 'his' party but also Carinthia into 'his' federal state. Now he was dead.

While people still puzzled over his fatal journey to the south of Klagenfurt, a completely different catastrophe was looming. In the USA, one of the largest banks, Lehman Brothers, went bankrupt. An empire collapsed. In the USA, and not only there,
cheap loans had been issued lightly for properties. The solvency of many borrowers was
not fulfilled. When the interest rose, the debtors were unable to pay their instalments.
The bubble burst. Banks had uncollectible loans galore, Lehman Brothers most of all. It
proved impossible to sell the properties that were intended as collateral, and the longer
the objects that reverted to the lenders stood empty, the more value they lost. Then
there was a shortage of loans, followed by stagnation. The problems that arose in the
USA spread. Growth sunk to zero; this was a contradiction in terms – because at zero,
there is no growth.

Initially, it seemed like the collapse of a major bank had only triggered a financial
crisis, yet what followed was an economic crisis unknown since the late 1920s and early
1930s. And this of course set the alarm bells ringing worldwide.

Perhaps it was really the financial crisis that gave the SPÖ and the ÖVP another
chance. In times of uncertainty, people always tend to fall back on proven remedies. Not
only had Alfred Gusenbauer resigned. Now Wilhelm Molterer also threw in the towel,
and the minister of agriculture, Josef Pröll, assumed leadership of the ÖVP.

Counting the cash was not a pleasant business. National debt was higher than first
assumed. The SPÖ nonetheless wanted to bring the tax reform forward to 2009. In the
middle of the negotiations, the news exploded that the Postal Service would be dismissing 9,000 employees. Who was to blame? The ÖVP suspended negotiations and

addressed ten questions to the designated federal chancellor, making their willingness to continue negotiations dependent on the answers they received. The EU was also at issue, above all the Treaty of Lisbon. The still incumbent foreign minister, Ursula Plassnik, wanted to enforce that EU resolutions could be ratified by parliament without the need for a plebiscite. It was a question of fundamental principles. Again, it was above all the print media that created an atmosphere and demanded that a binding plebiscite also be carried out for Austria. Was this not precisely what Faymann had written to the *Kronen-Zeitung*? In order to prevent the coalition from failing yet again, a way out was sought and found, namely: only the National Council would vote on the reform steps stipulated in the Treaty of Lisbon. For the future, however, plebiscites were planned. Furthermore, use was made of the so-called Ireland clause, which left it up to each state obligated to participate in the Common Foreign and Security Policy to decide for itself whether it really wanted to do so. It could not get any more casual. Minister Plassnik announced that they no longer wanted to be part of a future government.[886]

Ideology came into play, for instance when the SPÖ demanded the abolition of tuition fees. Clearly, this would apply not only to Austrians but also students from the entire EU zone. The argument that this would enable those from low-income backgrounds to study at university was not persuasive. Gusenbauer had promised and then shelved it. Legally recognised refugees, however, had to pay, which in turn brought the High Commissioner for Refugees on to the scene. In fact, during government negotiations the time had actually already come to say once again: it's enough.

The government was blemished before it had even begun to work. It might have been well advised to brace itself against Brussels' obsession with regulations. To question the Common Foreign and Security Policy, however, threw a strange light on the political decision-makers. How reliable was Austria? In 2000, the ÖVP-FPÖ coalition had proposed for the first time the inclusion of a mutual assistance obligation in the EU treaty. In 2001, the Council of Ministers had adopted a new security and defence doctrine in Vienna, in which Austria was interestingly characterised as 'nonaligned'. Social Democrats and Greens had been attuned to a further softening of neutrality if a common European army should exist by 2015. Austria still appeared to be fully on track. It was then in any case not security but the financial and economic crisis that caused the call to Brussels. It did not seem possible to solve the problems alone. One could only attempt to make a contribution and struggle against the rampant pessimism. This was the most important task of the Faymann government – Pröll, therefore, constituted a moral rearmament. Josef Pröll formulated it in four words: 'Austria after the crisis.'[887] But had the crisis really already passed? The problems were too deep-seated to be simply brushed aside. Something akin to national character also played a role here.

After years of progress, faintheartedness was taking hold. Every day, one could read and hear that all kinds of things in this country were not just in need of repair but, indeed, in bad shape. Now, as there was truly a whole host of problems, many still felt inspired to cite them and attest to the government's lack of competence in finding solutions. Werner Faymann, the 'bearer of hope', was suddenly characterised as the 'administrator of stagnation'.[888] Evidently, however, problem-solving expertise had gone astray worldwide. Looking for someone to blame appeared to be the easiest path. In connection with the financial and economic crisis, the governing parties also took up an issue that had until now been reserved above all for the FPÖ: foreigners. They were allegedly stealing scarce jobs from the natives: 'This indirect consequence of the financial crisis seems more menacing than the direct consequence', it was claimed.[889]

It had been known for some time that the largest group of immigrants in Austria were German citizens. But they and other immigrants coming from the EU zone evaded to a large extent the state tax mechanisms. Thus, the aim was to focus on the ten per cent of people coming from beyond the EU. In this way, domestic politics addressed the dominant topic of the coming years, and it hardly occurred to anyone that they were on the verge of falling back into patterns of thinking and acting from the interwar period and of distinctly assigning all misfortune and all problems to one group. What had once been the Jews were now the foreigners.

The situation deteriorated further, and in 2010 the financial and economic crisis became a debt and euro crisis. This was not just invented, however. It really existed, at least in parts of Europe. It was not clear how one could get out of it. None of the remedies seemed to take hold, aside from saving. The individual member states attempted it; the union as a whole attempted it. The appeal to the EU to demonstrate its political ability to act and fulfil its global political responsibility sounded good but the acid test was taken by the national governments. It was striking, in any case, that Federal Chancellor Faymann had transformed as early as 2009 from a critic of the EU to a 'fierce advocate' of the union.

Eventually, one country had all eyes on it: Greece. It was threatened with insolvency and, after a fashion, placed in receivership. Austria could watch all this with a certain astonishment and ought to have been reminded of the period of League of Nations supervision after 1922. Naturally, however, the cases of Greece and Austria were not comparable. Greece was helped far more willingly than post-war Austria, which was afflicted by war guilt. Even in Austria, though, the alarm signals multiplied. The Maastricht criteria valid for the eurozone allowed for a maximum new indebtedness of three per cent and a debt ratio of no more than 60 per cent of economic output. Austria had a new debt of 3.3 per cent and a 72 per cent debt ratio, with an upward trend.[890] And the dissatisfaction grew. This was not only due to the image of the coalition and individual members of the government, however, but also the result of a lack of prospects, against which ongoing action was taken but in vain. Not even the preoccupation with the past went smoothly, for the valiant announcements of the late 1990s and above all in the setting of the State Treaty celebrations in 2005 to the effect that Austria – like

Germany – would build a House of History had come to nothing in spite of four such pronouncements in the various government manifestos. When it came down to it, there was a lack of money for this. And whereas a building of this kind intended not only for Lower Austria emerged in St. Pölten and was opened in 2017, the projects at federal level were repeatedly restructured and eventually resulted in the announcement that a special exhibition would be organised for 2018 in the Corps de Logis of Vienna's Hofburg. This could certainly be perceived as an example of the failure of a whole series of federal governments to realise their grand plans.

Instead, the successive withdrawal from central and southern Europe began, into which one had set forth so full of hope after the events of 1989. It was then above all a type of legacy of the dead Carinthian governor, Jörg Haider, that was troubling. The Carinthian bank Hypo Alpe-Adria was faced with insolvency. The intention was to save the bank with eight to ten billion euros and the financial centre of Austria with it. It was no wonder that there was soon criticism along the lines of: money is available for banks; for the lowest income groups, social projects and a repeatedly called for education reform, however, there is no money. Everyone directed their discontent at the government. There were certainly some successes here though. The biggest was perhaps a solution to the problem of the Carinthian place-name signs, which had caused unrest and setbacks time and again since Kreisky's early years, and indeed since 1955.[891] It was a sheer never-ending story.

For almost forty years, there had been a struggle for compromises. There had been round table discussions, consensus talks, the so-called Karner package and endless negotiations. Occasionally, the new Slovenia had also been a source of irritation, for instance when the Carinthian 'Prince's Stone' was depicted on the currency introduced in 1991, the tolar. In 2007, the Prince's Stone was transferred to the two-cent coins and thus lost its optical presence.

Ultimately, a compromise formula drawn up by historian Stefan Karner provided the basis for one of the most determined opponents of the proposed solution, the 'Carinthian Homeland Service' (Kärntner Heimatdienst), ending its resistance. It had subsequently been accused by State Governor Haider of a 'betrayal of Carinthia'.[892] Haider was now dead. On 26 April 2011, the permanent secretary in the Federal Chancellery, Josef Ostermayer, and the Carinthian governor, Gerhard Dörfler, announced that they had reached an agreement: in 164 localities with a minimum share of 17.5 per cent Slovenes, bilingual place-name signs would be mounted – insofar as this had not already been done. There would also be accompanying measures and, above all, the anchoring of the solution in the federal constitution. The fact that the 'Council of Carinthian Slovenes' (Rat der Kärntner Slowenen) was still not satisfied simply had to be accepted.

Austria's past also played a role in another area: on 4 July 2011, Otto von Habsburg died. In 1963, his intention of travelling to Austria had triggered a veritable government crisis; in 1966, he had actually begun visiting Austria. This resulted in mass protests. But then people grew accustomed to him. Following a meeting with Kreisky, during which the Chancellor and the Emperor's son shook hands, Otto visited Austria with increasing frequency. Here, in the Capuchin Crypt in Vienna, the last crown prince of Austria-Hungary wanted to, and would be buried. As expected, Otto von Habsburg's funeral was a major event. His father, Karl, though beatified by the Catholic Church in 2004, remained in Madeira. Perhaps the burial of the Emperor's son beyond the social event could be regarded as a sort of pinnacle in the course of the year, because the political arena was denied comparable 'events'. It was difficult to govern without a constitutional majority. Both the Chancellor and the government knew this; the Federal President knew it, too. In order to demonstrate a little harmony, the SPÖ and the ÖVP had agreed in 2010 to jointly recommend Heinz Fischer for re-election. He was then confirmed in officer with an approval rating of almost 80 per cent. But even the Federal President could not ensure that the day-to-day of political life remained free of conflict. The mistrust that had existed for years continued, and the recent past was a repeated source of trouble. There was one parliamentary enquiry committee after another. They addressed privatisation measures during the government's time in office, the Eurofighters, advertisements, Telekom and party donations. In order not to become open to legal challenge, the catchword 'The presumption of innocence applies' became established among the media, which were always well fed with inside information. It even became the 'non-word' of the year in 2010.

The 'discontent over the party state' that spread ever further was tangible. Both governing parties struggled against it but they naturally had to ask themselves whether the historical justification for their existence had not long since ceased to exist.[893] The SPÖ was no longer a workers' party and the ÖVP was not a Christian-social collective movement, as it had lost the farmers and, for long periods, the Christians. Evidently, the established opposition parties were also regarded as so unattractive that a solution was sought in the form of new parties breaking down existing structures. As early as 2005, 'The Christians' (Die Christen) had made an attempt to do this and failed. Then an Austrian offshoot of the German Pirate Party (Piratenpartei) had tried and likewise failed. Ultimately, a great deal of money came into play.

In September 2012, the Austro-Canadian Frank Stronach proclaimed the launch of an as yet unready party, with which he wanted to successfully compete in the forthcoming elections. He was a billionaire and had made an enormous contribution with his Magna corporation not only to Austria and, above all, Styria. As a result of politicians from other parties joining 'Team Stronach', the latter reached a respectable size. A few weeks later, the Vorarlberg entrepreneur Matthias Strolz presented a new liberal party, NEOS. There was evidently considerable potential and the willingness to search for new solutions. This could, of course, be commented on in various ways. The sociologist and opinion pollster Peter Filzmeier pointedly stated: every party participating in the elections has a real chance as long as it is different. Perhaps 'Winnetou's Apaches' would also win.[894] In any case, the next elections to the National Council promised to be exciting.

In autumn 2012, however, not only the launch of new parties proved to be a talking point but also a motion by the mayor of Vienna, Michael Häupl, dating back to 2010. During the course of the campaign for municipal and regional diet elections in Vienna, he had advocated the abolition of general conscription. In doing so, he had not addressed a Viennese topic but he had caused something of a stir. However, he was unable to achieve his objective of securing for the SPÖ the absolute majority in Vienna. For the second time since 1996, Häupl had to find a partner, which he did in the form of the Greens. But the city's special status remained, as did the circumstance that no SPÖ chancellor could get around the city. Federal Chancellor Faymann also began to warm to the idea of the Mayor of Vienna. Eventually, even Minister of Defence Darabos made the case for a nationwide consultative referendum and promptly lodged his preference for a professional army, which he had strictly rejected up to this point. After the ÖVP under their fourth party chairman in the space of five years, Foreign Minister Michael Spindelegger, had also spoken out in favour of a consultative referendum, this was scheduled for 12 January 2013.

Plebiscitary proceedings were gradually mounting up. In addition to the plebiscite on the use of nuclear power, keyword 'Zwentendorf', there had been the plebiscite on Austria's accession to the European Union in 1994. From the petition for a referendum on radio broadcasting in October 1964 to the year 2013, there had already been 35 referendums or initiatives for them. A consultative referendum was comparatively new. Now this variety of direct democracy was also to be tested. The last time that the 'people' were to have been asked was on 13 March 1938.

The mood heated up. The military demonstrated a clear preference for a professional army, although its financing was questionable; the opponents, Federal President Fischer among them, who cited the arguments of a fair draft selection, higher costs of a professional army and cherished traditions, pointed above all to the function of an army of general conscription in the context of natural disasters and rescue. The reference to civilian service also played a role in the arguments, for it was conceived as an alternative to military service and would, therefore, have required a revision. One question was consistently avoided: whether, in the event of a retention of general conscription, young women should not also be included in deliberations, and whether perhaps a general community service ought to be striven for. The referendum was limited, however, to the six-month compulsory military service for men, and almost 60 per cent of plebiscite participants ultimately voted in favour of its retention.

In early March, after a certain time lag, Minister Darabos transferred charge of the defence department to Gerald Klug. It was incumbent on him to pour oil on the troubled waters within the Federal Army, though it lasted only three months until this minister also drew attention to himself with a conceivably controversial decision. After hostilities in the Syrian-Israeli border area, the Minister decided to withdraw the Austrian troop contingent on the Golan Heights from the position held by the Austrians there since 1974 and for them to return to Austria as soon as possible. The Austrian soldiers should not be potentially exposed to the threat of fighting. Soldiers from Fiji and India precipitately took over the mountain position. In the meantime, things had quietened down in the border region.[895] Was the decision for withdrawal correct? Was it premature? No one wanted to assume responsibility for the life and wellbeing of volunteers. The blame for the insufficient protective measures was, in any case, shifted on to the UN. Admittedly, with the withdrawal of the Austrians from the Israeli border area something had once again been lost that had already become positively identity-building, namely Austria's role in the provision of troops for the United Nations' peacekeeping operations. Only the missions in Bosnia and Kosovo remained. The withdrawal fitted the mould – at least for the American diplomats – to the extent that they had already in confidential reports from 2010 remarked on the Chancellor's lack of interest in foreign policy and expressed doubts about the long-term funding of foreign missions.[896] This was not because the necessary funds were lacking but because the will was threatening to disappear.

While the soldiers were still withdrawing from the Golan, Austria made preparations for the next elections to the National Council. On 29 September, the time had come. The governing parties suffered losses once again. In the 1970s, the ÖVP and the SPÖ had still received a 93.1 per cent share of the votes. In 2013, their share had sunk as low as 50.8 per cent. The Freedom Party were close on their heels with 24 per cent; the Greens received 12.4 per cent, Stronach's list 'Frank' 5.7 per cent and NEOS five per cent. The FPÖ, as well as the smaller parties, had 'helped themselves' to the governing parties' voters. They had long since ceased to be major parties. On the contrary, they conveyed the impression of drowning people who were clinging to each other. Andreas Khol characterised the new government alliance as a 'Medium-sized Coalition' (Mittelgroße Koalition, or MIGROKO).[897] Daily newspapers and magazines predicted that this would be the last MIGROKO. There would inevitably be a change in five years.[898]

There was certainly much need for reform. At the same time, however, it was doubted that the governing parties still possessed sufficient potential for political reform in order to not only announce projects but also implement them. Impatience, and indeed annoyance, could be discerned in the election result on which the MIGROKO was based. Economic growth was not sufficient for an upturn. State debt had reached a level that had cost Austria the highest bond credit rating, the much-cited AAA; unemployment figures were on the rise; expenditure per schoolchild may have been the highest in Europe but the results of the regular PISA tests were sobering. Austria was mid range. Contributions to development aid were at an absolute low; the gap between rich and poor continued to grow, etc. The only thing that helped was a comparison with countries that came off worse, and Austria was still not accustomed to doing this. It seemed that faith in progress, on the one hand, and solidarity, on the other, did not blend well. But this ought to have been well known. At any rate, solutions were sought, and likewise the 'other politics', which had been demanded and announced for decades. One sobering analysis ran: 'A "new style" of collaboration between Werner Faymann and Michael Spindelegger was announced, they hung on until the European elections in 2014 but were disposed of after the elections were won by the People's Party.'[899] Thus, the 'new style' was again replaced by a coalition dispute.

The federal states insisted with increasing frequency on their independence and were entirely unwilling to unreservedly cooperate with the politics of the federal government. This was particularly striking in the case of the meanwhile seven states governed by the ÖVP. Above all the Lower Austrian governor, Erwin Pröll, also occasionally defied national demands. Michael Spindelegger consequently threw in the towel. The federal minister of science, education and economics, Reinhold Mitterlehner, became his successor as deputy chancellor and federal party chairman, the fifth in short order. The rapid changes at the head of parties and departments signalised dissatisfaction and a lack of continuity. One imperial prime minister of the nineteenth century, Eduard Taaffee, was repeatedly cited, as well as the quote attributed to him and passed down by Heinrich Friedjung: 'I'll somehow muddle along.'[900] The witticism was promptly applied to several federal governments in the twenty-first century. But contentment looked very different. Calls for a strong man (it could also be a woman) became ever louder. Having said that, the federal government achieved several things in 2014 that had been repeatedly demanded and announced, above all a tax reform that was worthy of the name. At the same time, holes opened up time and again and above all the now nationalised Carinthian Hypo Alpe Adria bank, the liquidation of which had been the dictate of the moment, threatened to tear open a billion-euro hole. The zero budget deficit targeted for 2016 had turned into a balanced budget in accordance with Maastricht criteria – which was not the same thing. While budgets, achievements and mistakes, federal level and provinces were still being debated, Austria was abruptly dragged into a frequently repressed global reality.

Mass Migration

It had all started with something happening far away. Then the catastrophes intermingled. War and civil war were raging in Iraq and in Syria. In the Maghreb states, with the exception of Morocco, there were wars, insurrections and terror. Conflicts for resource allocation grew in intensity. Reports resembled each other; the participants were always different and yet somehow alike. And the consequences were flight and expulsion. Everyone watched it happen but no one could believe it. What was looming there was recognised 'neither by the politicians nor by the public in Europe'.[901]

Austria was no exception, and perhaps the account of a Swiss journalist had some merit when – expressing himself in a very similar way to a British ambassador almost forty years earlier – he wrote: 'A beautiful, peaceful summer, and the Republic cosily drifts along, in crowded swimming baths, at lavish open-air events, in wine bars.'[902] The joke had not taken hold back then and it was the same story in late summer 2015. Mingling with the war refugees were hosts of people seeking to escape starvation and misery. They began to migrate northwards. Their goal was Europe. They only had to reach Italy or – even nearer – get to one of the Greek islands from Turkey, in order to be safe and – more to the point – well provided for. The Mediterranean became the main exodus route. The human traffickers of the twenty-first century, the smugglers, were enjoying peak season. The residents of Sicily and Lampedusa but also Lesbos, Leros, Chios and other islands situated close to Turkey, were accustomed to refugees, though not in such numbers. Further to the north of Europe, also and especially in Austria, the people were likewise accustomed to refugees. After Hungarians, Czechs and Slovaks, Poles and Bosnians, people from Eastern Europe and, above all, the Caucasus region had arrived. Now they came from the south, and there seemed to be no end to them. As soon as German Federal Chancellor Angela Merkel, faced with the first hundred thousand, said the understandable but politically questionable sentence 'We can manage this!' *(Wir schaffen das!)*, more and more people came via the so-called Balkan route. They trekked across Greece, Macedonia, Serbia, Croatia, Hungary and Slovenia to Austria, Germany and Sweden. Several states were omitted along the route from the south, for instance Montenegro and Albania but also Bulgaria and Romania. There could be no question of a securing of external borders of the European Union. One state after another signalised their overload or lack of jurisdiction, for most of the refugees indicated that they intended to continue on to Germany or Sweden. Initially, Austria was not the number one destination, though it did at least offer possibilities for onward travel and did not refuse admission to refugees. Hungary eventually blocked one branch of the Balkan route by erecting a fence on its southern border. There was a great outcry on the part of a whole series of states, including Austria.

Nonetheless, there was vacillation between anxiety and compassion, xenophobia and openness. Clearly, only some of the refugees were what one might call 'genuine' war refugees. Others were economic migrants who simply wanted to be provided for and hoped for a better life in the rich countries of the north. Around 1.4 million people took to their heels in 2015/16. A large proportion of them passed through Austria. Perhaps this would have gone on for quite some time, had German federal states, above all Bavaria, not also put a check on the refugees. In view of the imminent loss of control over state territory, this was no doubt justifiable. And it had a direct impact on Austria. The same Germany that had made a significant contribution to the tide of refugees flooding northwards suddenly blocked it. Those fleeing hesitantly but increasingly applied for asylum elsewhere, not least in Austria. The number would come to around 88,000[903] and allowed the total immigration in 2015 to reach the figure of 130,000 people.[904]

The helpfulness and dedication of thousands of Austrians could best be compared to 1956. It was they who prevented a humanitarian catastrophe and ultimately also accomplished a major feat of security policy. And they also played a huge role in the subsequent round, namely when it came to language acquisition, educational opportunities and employment. As people had already beforehand begun to talk of a 'lost generation' in view of growing youth unemployment, it was foreseeable that it would not get any easier. 'Opportunities in life for all' sounded good but it was utopian.

What had initially been a European problem mutated into a domestic political powder keg. The state appeared incapable of taking corrective action. The federal government, the provinces and the municipalities blamed each other. As one Protestant theologian caustically commented, it was 'organised irresponsibility'.[905] Tragedies like the death of 71 people, who suffocated in a refrigerator truck and were simply parked on the motorway near Nickelsdorf in Burgenland on 26 August 2015, led less to questions regarding the causes of the exodus and more to demands for action against the smugglers. But there were also other consequences. The Social Democrats and the People's Party had to acknowledge that, with their reference to human rights, conventions and ethical standards, they were on the verge of losing their relative majorities, which were in any case dwindling. Measures designed to control the flow of refugees, to deploy executive forces and the army, were taken only gradually; transport and the supply of refugees were outsourced to a substantial degree. Eventually, use was made of civil society by virtue of the appointment of former Raiffeisen advocate general Christian Konrad as refugee coordinator, in order to ensure reasonably organised procedures.

The main beneficiary of the belated reaction to the migration movement was clearly the FPÖ, who saw no reason to intervene as a political organisation and, therefore, largely limited itself to declamatory interventions. It felt confirmed in its warnings to the effect that 'a further influx of the predominantly illegal immigrants deserves to be halted yesterday rather than today'. The FPÖ claimed that the uncontrolled inflow, above all from the Middle East, would lead to the emergence of parallel societies, to the detriment of the system of values that had evolved in Austria over the course of centuries.[906] The relatively objective discussion was swiftly interspersed with conspiracy theories, claiming that the ruling classes at home and abroad intended to bring about 'national death' and were preparing 'the great exchange'.[907] There was little in the way of facts that could be said in response to this but such nonsense also contributed to an emotionalization of the issue.

What now followed was a chain reaction, which began in the federal states and brought about an accelerated shift in internal political conditions. It started in Burgenland, where the people were justifiably proud of a long tradition of providing aid to refugees, yet in view of the immigrants from Eastern Europe in 1990 had called on the Federal Army and achieved assistance deployment of the army lasting 21 years. It had ended in December 2011. Four years later, the time had come again. The army once again had to prepare for deployment on the Burgenland border. After regional diet elections, which brought the SPÖ and the ÖVP a marked loss in votes and seats, the Burgenland governor, Hans Niessl, formed a coalition with the FPÖ in July 2015. This violated a fundamental decision of the SPÖ from the time of Franz Vranitzky not to form any coalition with the FPÖ, but Niessl opted to disregard this. It was all the easier for him to do this because the Federal Chancellor and Party Chairman did not offer any effective resistance. Werner Faymann had increasingly internalised the stance of the German Federal Chancellor. He was not rewarded for this in domestic politics. However, what was branded as a sin against the (Social Democratic) spirit, also befell the ÖVP. At the elections to the regional diet in Upper Austria, the ÖVP suffered heavy losses and switched coalition partners. In place of the Greens, the FPÖ was also able to govern here.

Grumbling in the federal states strengthened Foreign Minister Sebastian Kurz and Interior Minister Johanna Mikl-Leitner in their resolve to bypass the Chancellor in pursuing policies. At a conference of the Western Balkan states, it was decided to effectively block the Balkan route for refugees. As expected, the reaction to this measure varied. Greece, who had not been invited to the conference, was fuming, recalled its ambassador from Austria and cancelled a visit to Athens by Mikl-Leitner. Most Balkan states, as well as Germany, signalised their approval, though some of them did so behind closed doors. In the *Spiegel*, one could read that 'the fact that Austria sets the tone on the diplomatic stage as it has done in recent days is rare …. It was as though Austria wanted to swing the sceptre once more in its former sphere of influence, like during the times of the Habsburgs, as the protective power of the Slav Balkan countries.'[908] Serbia and Montenegro, above all the latter, which had already erected border fortifications previously and from the outset only wanted to let refugees pass through, likewise reacted as one might have expected: they did not let any more refugees enter their countries and forced them to remain in Greece. Austria went one step further and set up a border fence and a clearance zone at the main crossing point to Slovenia on the southern Styrian border. Finally, the federal government set for 2016 a maximum number of 37,500 people who were to be granted asylum each year. The figure was misleading to the extent that asylum seekers were guaranteed family reunions by international law; but alone the establishment of this maximum number had the effect of the numbers of refugees dropping abruptly. For the first time, however, it was not Germans, Romanians and Hungarians – regarded as economic migrants – who topped the statistics. Instead it was 22,600 Syrians, almost 20,000 Afghans and 10,000 Iraqis. In early 2016, the influx tapered off.[909] The restrictive measures began to take effect. For smugglers, this was an obstacle but not an insurmountable one. It was only a question of cost, and it had already been determined in the 1980s that more money could be earned with the modern form of human trafficking than with narcotics.

All things new …

The refugee crisis shook Europe to its very foundations. That which had been started in 1957 and had developed via expansions into a European whole was suddenly no longer valid. It was above all states that had been members of the EU for a comparatively short length of time that signalled a breakdown in solidarity. But Britain also did not hesitate to place its own interests above those of the European Union. Trust in EU institutions deteriorated across the EU to 31 per cent. Only a third of people in the member states were still willing to unreservedly affirm European integration. The feeling that it was necessary to work together disappeared. The lack of solidarity went hand in hand with the growth of a historical force that had long been thought dead: nationalism.

The fact that Austria had long hesitated to address this historical phenomenon and to strike up nationalist tones itself was of course a product of its history. Prior to 1918, nationalism had been played down. As a multi-ethnic state, the Habsburg Monarchy's only chance of survival had been to subordinate nationalism to the union. German nationalist tendencies had existed but were not decisively enhanced until the First World War. The Anschluss idea was subsequently an expression of German nationalism, pettiness and economic deprivation. In 1945, a period of Austrification began. This was new to the extent that similar attempts during the interwar period were viewed under the pretext of so-called Austrofascism and regarded, therefore, as exceedingly contaminated. Then the era of solidarity with Europe arrived. Catalogues of core values were enacted and Austria accepted them without reservation as this allowed final doubts to be overcome regarding a renunciation of Nationalism Socialism. Increased attempts followed to demonstrate Europeanness and solidarity. But the sword of Damocles of being more right-wing than the right-wingers in France, the Netherlands, Belgium and elsewhere, continued to hang over Austria, who was given the title on face value of being one of the last strongholds of National Socialism. The country was at the centre of attention. It appeared so easy to distract from one's own developments and problems and draw a seemingly straight line from Hitler via Waldheim and Jörg Haider to – yes, to whom, actually? And now?

EU Council President, Commission and Parliament had long since been forced to acknowledge that they could not induce the member states to show solidarity on the refugee issue, let alone force them to take in refugees and migrants. Thus, something different was attempted, and here Turkey began to play a central role. It had the status of an accession candidate and therefore ought to demonstrate solidarity. In negotiations with Turkey, it was achieved on 18 March 2016 that the Turks agreed to guarantee a better protection of their Mediterranean coast and take in illegal immigrants, predominantly from Greece. There was a high price to pay in return but it would be paid. For its part, Turkey committed itself to observing human rights and statutes that should actually have applied since Turkey joined the Council of Europe and altogether from the point at which Turkey had been given the status of an EU applicant country. It was an agreement with many question marks.

After an attempted coup by soldiers on 15 and 16 July 2016, there were mass arrests in Turkey and President Recep Tayyip Erdoğan blatantly demonstrated his intention to establish an authoritarian regime. The EU responded hesitantly and only one state demonstrated open rejection and opposition: Austria. It was not only events in Turkey themselves, however, that were regarded as vexing but a mixture of long-standing anti-Turkish and anti-Islamic sentiments. Finally, it was also a question of not relinquishing this issue with majority appeal to the FPÖ. Austro-Turkish relations were characterised by open criticism, diplomatic unfriendliness and a distinct hardening.[910]

As soon as Austria commenced nationalist wanderings, it risked being marginalised as extreme right-wing and jeopardising everything that had been built up over decades and filled with the spirit of a core European country. Werner Faymann, therefore, set an example of fundamental social democratic beliefs as well as European norms and values that were for him still intuitively valid when he even obstructed his own party and, like Angela Merkel had done, let it be understood: we can manage this! He became a shining example for it not being possible to manage it, as one might have expected.

The 1st of May 2016 turned into a debacle for the Chancellor. During the almost sacred May celebrations of the Social Democrats on Vienna's Rathausplatz, of all things, he was booed and thoroughly ridiculed. A political problem became a human problem. The Federal Chancellor experienced first-hand how pitiless politics can be and how profound disappointment can be. On 9 May 2016, he unexpectedly and hastily resigned as federal chancellor and SPÖ chairman. A week passed before a proper transition took place and a new federal chancellor – Christian Kern – could be sworn in. Even more so than Franz Vranitzky had been, Kern was a so-called lateral entrant. He had been able to gather some political experience, though he had most recently been chairman of the supervisory board of the Austrian Federal Railways and not a 'party soldier'. After two chancellors who had worked their way up the SPÖ, a comparatively young manager, who had never held any political office, was supposed to bring fresh impetus to politics. He knew the statistics: only every fifth voter in Austria still trusted the problem-solving competence of politicians and parties.[911] The political 'elite' was on the verge of becoming a term of abuse.

Scarcely was the affair with the chancellor over, when the next cause for excitement arrived. At the end of his second term in office, Heinz Fischer had to leave the Presidential Chancellery. Many would have liked to grant him a third term but the federal constitution said different. Lower Austrian Governor Erwin Pröll, who had been the favourite of the ÖVP in 2015, rejected a candidacy. Instead of him, former president of the National Council Andreas Khol declared his readiness to run for office. The SPÖ candidate was Federal Minister for Labour and Social Affairs Rudolf Hundstorfer. In addition, there were the candidates regarded as outsiders. The Greens were able to persuade their former federal spokesman, Alexander Van der Bellen, to run; the Freedom Party nominated the third president of the National Council, Norbert Hofer; finally, the former president of the Supreme Court, Irmgard Griss, intended to run as an independent candidate. With the ÖVP and the SPÖ, things proceeded as they traditionally did. Yet the results of the opinion polls were poor and they remained so to the end. Both candidates of the governing parties fared badly. Hofer, Griss and Van der Bellen engaged in a head-to-head race, which ended in favour of Hofer and Van der Bellen. Something that had been dismissed during the course of the Second Republic and treated as a means of being politically put out to pasture now attracted the utmost attention: who would become federal president? It was almost inevitable that people abroad began to take an interest in the election in Austria. The situation was depicted as a shift to the right. Anti-European remarks made by Hofer were not compared with what could long since be heard in many European Union states. Hofer was also in good company when he put the case for a revolt against 'Brussels'. And there was any number of voices warning against a relapse into the Waldheim years and the beginnings of the Little Coalition of 2000. Austria would inevitably be 'under observation' again in the event of a victory for Hofer, according to the former Czech foreign minister Karel Schwarzenberg. He knew what he was talking about.

Van der Bellen eventually won in the second ballot by a margin of around 30,000 votes. A stark urban-rural divide was noted. Hofer was most successful in small, rural communities; Van der Bellen, by contrast, in the large cities and, above all, in Vienna. Those who doubted the EU's sustainability voted for Hofer; the others voted for Van der Bellen. But the decision had not yet been made. The Freedom Party objected to the result with the argument that there had been irregularities during the counting of the votes. Eventually, the Constitutional Court was called on. As in other cases, judges were required to adjudicate on politics. Their majority vote was that even the appearance of irregularities seemed to justify a repetition of the election. There would be a re-vote. As if this was not enough, the first of the scheduled dates could not be kept. Defects were found in the envelopes for the postal vote. A glue did not hold. Austria threatened to become a laughing stock. Finally, the election was re-scheduled for 4 December 2016. In the interim, there had been less impassioned and more polemical discussions as to whether Austria even needed a federal president. But it was not really clear to anyone why a mishap should occasion a constitutional question.

The re-vote ultimately took place in a very different political environment. The EU, Turkey and the USA had changed. Britain had resolved to leave the EU ('Brexit') following a referendum on 23 June 2016. The European institutions, Commission and Parliament, demonstrated their inability to implement resolutions on the refugee issue against the stance of member states. The influx of refugees continued to possess an explosive power. Attacks by Islamists in a series of European states – Belgium, France, Italy and Germany – strengthened the call for isolation, controls and an inevitable intensification of surveillance measures. To this were added the permanent financial crisis of several member countries and the inequality between the prosperous states, above all Germany, and the southern member states, which had enormous financial problems to contend with. And Austria, which had played such an important role in building bridges and arranging compromises until into the 1990s, at times accomplished nothing more than to admonish others and manifest its own disappointment and apprehensiveness, though it had scarcely any opportunity to intervene.

The victory of American presidential candidate Donald Trump over Hillary Clinton on 8 November 2016 lastingly changed the USA, too. Trump's success was understood as the victory of a populist against the establishment. And this event was also evaluated as something that affected Austria in one way or another. In view of the no longer so young billionaire Trump, a conflict of generations was identified and a revolt of youth posited, though above all of the socially underprivileged, against 'the affluent'. It would be more fitting, however, to stress as a motivation the struggle against the feeling of superiority on the part of the establishment. Norbert Hofer and Alexander Van der Bellen suddenly appeared to fit into a pattern and likewise embody the revolt against the political establishment.

But it was not only the European neighbours and the USA who changed – priorities also shifted in Austria; less spectacularly, perhaps, but nonetheless noticeably so. The wave of refugees had weakened not only the EU but also Austria. It ultimately matched Hungary, who had previously been lambasted, and built a south-eastern wall. There were no tank ditches, like at the time of the Reich Protective Position, but rather a barrier. This time it was directed against Syrians, Afghans and, as a precaution, all other peoples in Africa and Asia who had set out on the great migration. Ultimately, Foreign Minister Sebastian Kurz became the forerunner of the group in the EU that not only voiced its unease about the increasingly authoritarian Turkey in general terms but also openly articulated it. If necessary, Vienna wanted to again make itself a bastion, though not of Christianity but instead against a type of politics that unashamedly amounted to the blackmailing of Europe. The threat of the Turkish President to 'unleash' millions of people on Europe if the EU did not fulfil the agreement concluded with Turkey on the paid return of refugees was namely unsurpassable in terms of bluntness and brutality. Austria demanded the discontinuation of accession negotiations with Turkey. Of course, this was partially due to the domestic political situation. But there was also another aspect: Austria, which was often accused of a sloppy approach to fundamental rights and values and had been criticised for its contact with authoritarian regimes and dictatorships, called a spade a spade. Even in Austria itself, this was not uncontroversial and was regarded as a conscious challenge. But the time had now come to nail one's colours to the mast.

On 4 December 2016, Van der Bellen won the third round of the presidential election, thus ending an election campaign that had placed Austria under observation to a greater extent than at any time since 2000. The election result was rated, with a certain relief, as a pro-European vote. Perhaps, however, it was merely a question of perspective that created this impression. At any rate, the attentiveness of the 'observers' caved in the same day.

In January and February 2017, one might have got the impression that the Grand Coalition had pressed the reset button. What one did not know, however, was how many times this had been done. Federal Chancellor Kern and Deputy Chancellor Mitterlehner promised not to openly argue out differences of opinion, to pull together and thus increase the acceptance of cooperation as well as rescue their own parties from the low approval ratings. For the governing parties, namely, it must have been unsettling but also motivating that the FPÖ was well ahead of the SPÖ and the ÖVP in the opinion polls. There were rumours of early elections but there was no real reason to prematurely end the legislative period. Perhaps it would prove possible to catch up a bit by 2018. There was any number of projects and just as many ideas for tackling the problems. And domestic and foreign policy issues were on a par with each another. It was necessary to take advantage of the tentative upswing in order to build on the 1990s, during which Austria – even measured against Germany – had not only been stable but thoroughly exemplary. Another factor were European issues. As Austria was somewhat unexpectedly due to assume EU chairmanship as early as the second half of 2018 as a result of Britain's planned withdrawal from the EU, it was necessary to orientate political processes to that. In addition, as it was already foreseeable in 2017 that the most important rounds of negotiations on the so-called Brexit, above all on Britain's future relationship with the EU, would fall during the period of Austrian chairmanship, it was necessary to take account of this.

In spite of all deliberations to this effect and contrary to the efforts of Federal Chancellor Kern and Deputy Chancellor Mitterlehner, it was proving impossible to restore calm to the work of the coalition. There were a great many self-destructive tendencies. Eventually, Reinhold Mitterlehner threw in the towel. With reference to Wilhelm Molterer's statement 'It's enough', aimed at the SPÖ, Mitterlehner told his own party on 10 Mai 2017: 'I think it's enough', and announced his prompt withdrawal from all political offices.

It was foreseeable that this new domestic policy crisis would not be settled by the coalition continuing with new personnel, as the Federal Chancellor hoped. Foreign Minister Kurz was regarded as the logical successor to the outgoing party chairman but he did not want to follow in the latter's footsteps without further ado. He embodied the increasingly common view that the existing political system no longer had a future. The desire for change had become an obsession with change. Kurz intuitively grasped this and initially wanted to first alter the ÖVP before addressing the continuation of the government programme. He made far-reaching demands designed to secure him direct access and limit the power of the ÖVP governors as well as the associations. Kurz wanted to give rise to a new political force. Approval of the demands ultimately submitted by him was given three days later. Eventually, everyone pushed for new elections. They were scheduled for 15 October.

Up to this point, it had been regarded as necessary to more or less continue the work, for none of the governing parties wanted to be accused of not working constructively. Thus, long-discussed issues were prepared for decision, a Eurofighter enquiry committee was set up for the second time and money was spent that the Republic did not actually have. Yet the economy was revitalised and the renowned silver lining appeared on the horizon. However, personnel changes were not yet finished. On 18 May, the party leader of the Greens, Eva Glawischnig, also announced her withdrawal from politics. Her reasoning was similar to that of Reinhold Mitterlehner. She no longer felt equal to the multiple pressures, as well as the intraparty opposition and media slurs. Ingrid Felipe was chosen to succeed her as federal spokesperson. Thus, within the space of one year, three party leaders were finished. This could not be explained by pointing to a weak constitution; instead, it was indicative of a much more fundamental problem. Could someone survive in politics only if he or she was not only authoritative but also capable of taking authoritative action, in order to master the challenges of a democracy in the twenty-first century? During the crisis of spring 2017, the end of consensus democracy became apparent. The obituaries for the political 'world of yesterday' were composed swiftly. Looking ahead was combined with taking stock of what had been.

It could be assumed in advance that, in 2018, Austrian history would pass by as though in fast motion. There would be talk of a country that had been equated with the imperial commemoration of the Habsburg Monarchy for the last hundred years. The memory of the founding of the Republic in 1918 could link up with these major narrative arcs. This was supposed to provide a frame of reference. Austria was and still is exemplary for the destruction of the imagined peace settlement after the First World

War and for the self-destruction of a state. It provided one of many examples of dicta-torship and war, of passion and perpetration. However, it can naturally also serve as a convincing example of the successful reconstruction of a state, which benefitted from the fact that it was indispensable neither for the East nor for the West. During the era of the Cold War, it was time and again a meeting place and liked to see itself in the role of bridgebuilder. This bestowed self-confidence. The loss of the bridge function led to an identity crisis.

The Austrian example allows us to surmise many things about an era that is not en-tirely ours. New forms of nationalism, violence and the 'clash of civilisations' described by Samuel Huntington were also 'rehearsed' in Austria. Austria has constantly changed, sometimes drastically so. On two occasions, it was major wars that brought about this change. In recent times, very different events cause these shifts. It is a very particular type of give and take.

What can be regarded as the start of a new age certainly does not have its roots in Austria. But the country is part of it. It is the same country as before – but it is also very different. The population has grown by more than two million people in the space of one hundred years. Statistics can record in dry facts how they are distributed and structured according to background. It is almost inevitable, however, that a feeling of vulnerability has also crept in as a result of major changes. A feeling of powerlessness would only emerge, though, if Austria were to be left alone – as in 1938 – or abandon itself. Ultimately, any comparison of these two worlds is out of the question, even if long-term historical experiences shape collective memory.

The country has been criticised and this will continue to happen. It has been praised and called exemplary and this, too, will continue to happen. This is all embedded in current problems and will also remain relevant in the future. There will be answers to many kinds of questions. Whether they are the correct answers will again only become clear, of course, after a considerable time lag. In the stream of time, even a hundred years are, at most, rapids.

25 Afterword

25 Vienna's Heldenplatz is one of Austria's central memorial sites. Since 1918, countless events have taken place on this square that have shaped it in a special way. Nonetheless, time and again there are discussions regarding how one could alter the square, how its role as the central memorial site of the Republic could be emphasised even more and whether it should be renamed or at least uncluttered. The square is more than a conceptual building site. However, the monument of Archduke Charles will probably be left untouched. (Photo: Albrecht Rauchensteiner)

The rebuilding has started; indeed, it started some time ago. This is not the type of rebuilding that involves pulling down houses and changing rooms but instead the work of directing a country towards new historical points of reference. Some things are disposed of and others replace them. But many things are dragged along that have lost their importance. It is a process – and it takes a long time. And every locality, however small, every district, every federal province and the state itself, which has possessed a non-negotiable size since 1955, became during the course of time a site of events, fates, things worth emphasising and things that have been neglected. In the search for a place that can be regarded as the focal point of most important events, where politics, culture and spiritual life meet, where, however, the question is also asked about Austria's collective memory and an answer is found, one will very likely end up on Vienna's Heldenplatz.

Heldenplatz

To begin with, Heldenplatz invites us to make a banal observation: it is a site of memory, it is obligated to the past for long stretches and it allows many things. This furnishes it with a profile and with significance, just as it conveys an attribute of memorial sites: they are scenes of events and they offer themselves up, without actually having to take action. Heldenplatz has the same fate as other 'lieux de mémoire' (P. Nora) for which no value-free attribution is possible. This makes the search for memorial sites and spaces that elude the classical trio of museums, archives and libraries an adventure of the mind. Something that is initially value-free is compelled to make a statement. Things that were once thought or done are fitted in and arranged according to an endless scale from good to bad. For a long time now, the commonly used phrase from Chilon of Sparta – 'de mortuis nil nisi bene' – no longer applies here. It is very much a question of the 'good guys' and the 'bad guys'. Precisely when one avails oneself of history, considerations of usefulness play their part and the vote of our ancestors mentioned in the Foreword is not simply accepted. Heldenplatz was and is harnessed and gives those a voice who have sought to make use of the willingness of the square on the most varied occasions.

The square is surrounded by buildings that correspond to the classical definition of memorial sites. Libraries, museums and archives can be found here. It is not they, however, that have dominated events on the empty space in front. But to whom would it occur today to regard Heldenplatz as an area of combat in an actual and not a metaphoric sense: part of the city fortifications, heavily bombarded, destroyed and blown up in 1683. It was levelled and, in 1860 and 1865, equipped with monuments to two heroes of the Habsburg Empire. From the moment this happened, the name of the square was fixed. It was Heldenplatz – Heroes' Square – and it became a reflective space for political symbolism and significance. Initially, nothing about it was politically contaminated. This would happen only very much later. Having said that, a few decades after the erection of the equestrian statues the question was raised as to whether that was really the right place for them. In 1916, the funeral process of Emperor Franz Joseph crossed the square. During the Corpus Christi procession of 1917, Emperor Karl followed the 'canopy' and prayed in front of Heroes' Gate. In 2011, it was no coincidence that the funeral cortege of the last successor to the Austro-Hungarian throne, the Emperor's son Otto von Habsburg, took the same route, flanked by Prince Eugene of Savoy, who had transformed the Habsburg Monarchy from a comparatively modest Central European empire into a major south-eastern European power, and Archduke Charles of Austria who, with the inscription 'To the tenacious fighter for Germany's honour', promptly gives the Prince opposite notice of the claim to power of times gone by. In 1918, the square was simply left there, uncultivated, unwelcome. Use of the square increased only in the 1930s, when a large, open space was sought for the large-scale celebrations on the occasion of the 250th anniversary of the lifting of the Turkish siege in 1683. The square appeared ideal, for it was supposed to illustrate a return to the past and portray Austria both as a bulwark of Christianity and as a bulwark against National Socialism. One year later, hundreds of thousands gathered for a funeral rally for Engelbert Dollfuß. Curiously enough, Adolf Hitler drew on this on 15 March 1938. He evidently felt no shyness about going to the place where tribute had been paid to the Chancellor whom Hitler's followers had murdered. For the new state of Austria, the terrace of the New Hofburg was subsequently regarded, however, as exterritorial. It was not permitted to set foot on it. In any case, both the war and the Soviets had brushed this aside and superimposed the past. The Soviets planted their victory flag on the roof of the Hofburg in 1945 and subsequently lodged in the partially destroyed palace. The Republic shied away, however, from using Heldenplatz and the Hofburg for signing the State Treaty, although this would have made it clear that National Socialism had been overcome and the memory of Hitler obliterated. Instead, the official Austria fell back on Belvedere Palace. It was only later that the square began to play a role whenever it came to cultivating national memory, swearing in soldiers, making a commitment to something or, simply, demonstrating. The terrace remained taboo.

The New Castle (Neue Burg) ensured that the horizon of the square was limited on one side. Catholic Congress, commemoration of Dollfuß but also Hitler no longer play any role. The Republic limits itself to use by the hour. This was also done in 1983, when Pope John Paul II said Mass on the square and hundreds of thousands celebrated with him or just came to watch. And people could just let their eyes wander.

The Square of Earthly Strife

Everything in sight lends itself as a backdrop: the New Hofburg, the Corps de Logis with its multiple historical reference points; the entrance to the Inner Courtyard, in which the boundary poles still exhibit bite marks from the horses that were tied up there during the changing of the guard in the Emperor's day but also in 1945, when troops of the 3rd Ukrainian Front seized possession of the Hofburg; the elongated Leopold Tract of the Hofburg, where Federal President Renner moved in in 1946 and which, as the official residence of the federal president, has since become a symbol for the hierarchy of power; the Amalie Tract, in which Emperor Karl I had his city residence until his abdication; Ballhausplatz, which – along with Kaunitz Palace – embodies a repeatedly fractured history: initially office of the Imperial and then the German-Austrian Ministry of Foreign Affairs, from 1923 Federal Chancellery, briefly headquarters of the Gau administration, partially destroyed, then again Federal Chancellery and Foreign Ministry, until the latter relocated in 2005 to a building on nearby Herrengasse. The balcony of the Chancellery is not associated with all that many historical events: a proclamation by Otto Bauer on a union of German-Austria with the German Reich in 1919, the ovation received by the last federal chancellor of the First Republic, Arthur Seyss-Inquart, during the night of 11/12 March 1938 and the bashfulness of all federal chancellors of the Second Republic to emulate the last chancellor of the Corporative State. Only the skiing ace Karl Schrank was permitted on 9 February 1972 to receive the cheers of 80,000 people for their idol on the balcony; finally, on the west side of Heldenplatz, the Outer Castle Gate bears testimony to those who were killed in action in the two World Wars and the victims of Austrian resistance against National Socialism. Until recently, the section of the Heroes' Monument referred to as the Crypt was the interior of a church. Now, it is a secularised embarrassment.

Thus, a considerable proportion of political and spiritual Austria stands alongside Heldenplatz and one can let their eyes wander, provided that the view is not obscured or one does not obscure the view oneself. Evidently, however, it still requires some effort to cope with the cumulative historical burden of the square. This is, of course, nothing new. Ever since it has existed, designers and architects have grappled with it. Thought was given to 'rotating' the square. The equestrian statues were to be relocated and the square not used primarily as a lapidarium. The most common objection to the outward appearance of the square was to the effect that it was supposedly incomplete and did not have a border on the side opposite the Corps de Logis. There have been (and still are) many plans to block this end but the 'Imperial Forum North' is so far yet to be built.

There are multiple irritations when it comes to Heldenplatz: the name, the vastness of the space and that terrace, which has undergone a linguistic minimisation as 'Hitler's balcony'. On the first point, it can be said that every era has its heroes. They occasionally lose their importance. Then they are merely part of the past and are abandoned to inconspicuousness, even when memorials are erected in their honour. In this way, they correspond to the fine quote from Musil: 'The most conspicuous thing about monuments is that no one notices them.' Only building development can be recommended as a way of combating the vastness of the square. As a result, restrictions would replace the possibility of allowing the eyes to wander. Regarding the third objection, one can only quote Karl Kraus and the start of *Die Dritte Walpurgnisnacht* (The Third Walpurgis Night): 'When I think of Hitler, nothing springs to mind.' One option would perhaps be to remove the terrace. To continue deferring to the one-hour appearance of te dictator borders on the ridiculous.

Jörg Mauthe called Heldenplatz the 'most absurd and most beautiful square in the world'. Marlene Streeruwitz wanted to dig it up and make it inaccessible for all times, thus allowing the production of dozens of definitions and recommendations and the depiction of even more scenarios for turning the square into a memorial site. It was no coincidence that Peter Stachel described it as the 'main square of the Republic of Austria and modern European history'.[912] It is an ideal location for blaring out news, proclaiming objectives, being in favour of or against something or celebrating a festival of joy. And we can safely assume that the square will be used for many more important and unimportant encounters. The Republic also needs its open spaces; it has its heroes and its memorial sites. It is necessary to become aware of them and confront them.

Acknowledgements

This book is the result of an occupation with Austrian history in modern and contemporary times lasting many years and, in fact, decades. I have dedicated a whole series of books, lectures and presentations to several temporal episodes, various individual questions and figures. The opportunity to contribute to the four ground-breaking television series by Dr Hugo Portisch and, ultimately, conduct countless interviews considerably expanded my knowledge and taught me humility for the work of a great journalist. For a general survey, however, I was, of course, lacking many aspects that needed to be added and amended. It was above all necessary to take a leap into the present. It was appealing to fill gaps and attempt to develop a fresh perspective, (examining and correcting myself in the process), to continue writing what I had begun earlier and to take into account the extensive knowledge that historical research furnishes every day. It was also necessary, not least, to allow the knowledge and recollections of those people to flow in who were formerly and until the most recent past protagonists.

Important stimuli for this study came from five visits to London for the purpose of carrying out research at The National Archives, in order to view Austria through outside eyes and in this way gain an additional perspective and correct my own sensitivities. Results of earlier research trips in the USA and, unfortunately, far too few in Moscow also flowed into the book, as did research in German files in Bonn and Berlin. The external perspective was significantly expanded by work in Austrian archives. I will address this further below. Ultimately, however, this was everyday work for a historian.

The final stimulus for this book came from Böhlau Verlag, which requested a sort of sequel to my book on the First World War. I commenced the work three years ago; the time has come to conclude it. The book had to be manageable in terms of its scope, allow an easy orientation by means of numerous sketches and be rounded off with a few photos, which should by all means have a signal effect. It goes without saying that it contains the normal elements of a verifiable study and one that ultimately serves as further reading. As always, I would like to thank those people, colleagues, friends and institutions to whom I am indebted for their help, patience, material support and for reading individual parts of the book.

Georg Rütgen very laudably enabled me to use files from the Federal Archives in Berlin by photographing the relevant record groups and placing them at my disposal. He, for his part, was assisted by Dr Maximilian Graf and Dr Andrea Brait and this, in turn, benefitted me. This research in German file collections was facilitated by the Future Fund of the Republic of Austria, for which I am grateful to the board of trustees of the Fund and, especially, its chairman, Dr Kurt Scholz, and the general secretary, Professor Herwig Hösele. The not inconsiderable costs of the archival trips to London were substantially minimised by the Austrian Cultural Forum, whose guest I was during all my research stays. The visits to the USA, in order to carry out research in the National Archives, were made possible for me quite some time ago already by the Anniversary Foundation of the Austrian National Bank and, in a wider sense and for many years, the generosity and friendship of the Austrian military attaché in Washington, Brigadier Christian Clausen, and his wife Annerose, to whom I will always be particularly indebted.

To return to the archival research: the Austrian State Archives with the Archives of the Republic, the War Archives and, above all, their library, also gave me the feeling of preferential treatment, for which I am exceedingly grateful, because it saved me an inordinate amount of time. Not least in the interests of wider research, I would like to unsubtly point out that the opening hours of the archives, the ban on photography and, above all, the very halting delivery of files on the part of the central departments are a hindrance to any type of continuous research. However, Dr Gottfried Loibl in the Federal Ministry for Europe and Integration (and its forerunners) actively helped me to offset the non-transfer of files by allowing me to carry out research myself in the central office and clarify questions of detail.

The general thanks directed at archives and libraries must be supplemented with one particular institution and one of the most important memorial sites in Austria: the Austrian National Library. I was tirelessly and generously given the opportunity to use substantial numbers of books, without which historical research is impossible. It is not a team of monkeys or a group of anonymous student assistants who make books available but rather particularly estimable and always friendly members of staff, who deserve to be mentioned with thanks.

With particular feelings of gratitude, I would also like to mention those who assisted me in obtaining material beyond the state archives and libraries, first and foremost Envoy Dr Stephan Scholz, who faithfully allowed me to use the family and estate papers of former federal chancellor Dr Josef Klaus. In contrast to the papers of Josef Klaus, which have been awaiting processing for some time, the papers of Dr Bruno Kreisky in the Kreisky Archives are for the most part accessible and, like the extensive diaries of long-time minister of trade Josef Staribacher, were made available to me. For this, I am grateful not only to Dr Maria Steiner and Maria Mesner but also, once more, to Georg Rütgen, who assisted my research.

I am no less grateful for the help that I received from Dr Johannes Schönner at the Karl von Vogelsang Institute. With untiring willingness, Dr Elisabeth Klamper from the Documentation Centre of Austrian Resistance answered my questions regarding correct figures and current aspects of research on resistance. Dr Günther Haller in the archives of *Die Presse* and Helmut Hüttl in the National Defence Academy allowed me to delve into their treasure trove and demonstrated in impressive fashion how electronic search options can considerably accelerate academic work.

The acquisition of lead photographs for the individual chapters was substantially facilitated by the Picture Archives of the Austrian National Library and by the Army Photo and Film Office of the Austrian Federal Army. This also applies to the Picture Archives of the Austria Presse Agency (APA) and the Museum of Military History. Stefan Lechner drew the maps for me with his unique expertise. I wanted to pay particular attention to the cover image, for which the painting by Otto Dix could eventually be found with the commendable help of Klaus Pokorny from the Leopold Museum.

Now it is necessary, insofar as it has not been done already, to also mention those who took the trouble to read individual chapters or entire sections of the manuscript. First and foremost, and, to some extent, in chronological order, I would like to extend my thanks to former federal chancellors Dr Franz Vranitzky and Dr Wolfang Schüssel. Both of them provided me with various pieces of information, thus saving me from avoidable errors. I am no less indebted to my long-time friend and former president of the Viennese Municipal School Council Dr Kurt Scholz, who not only allowed me to share his encyclopaedic knowledge and his multifaceted ideas but also repeatedly counselled me after reading individual chapters. Former ambassador Dr Karl Peterlik, Professor Gabriele Kucsko and Professor Wilhelm Brauneder readily granted me their assistance on individual questions. A variety of colleagues, friends and students allowed me to profit from their knowledge. There is not enough space here to mention them all by name.

The penultimate and by no means blanket thanks go to the team of Böhlau Verlag, whom I am particularly close to. Dr Peter Rauch encouraged me to write the book and also read all parts of it in advance. Dr Eva Reinhold-Weisz was a never-faltering pillar of strength, as were Julia Beenken in Cologne, Stefanie Kovacic in Vienna and the production manager Michael Rauscher, who no doubt had the most work with my text and special requests. Particular thanks go not least to Christiane Braun and, above all, Elisabeth Dechant, who always gave me the feeling that this was the book they had been waiting for.

Lastly – and I cannot stress this often enough – I would like to thank my wife Marianne for her support, for reading and re-reading the book and, above all, for never complaining when I hid myself away for days and weeks on end in archives, libraries and, finally, during the writing process. Ultimately, it was she who made this book possible.

Notes

1 The quote can be found in Walter Lukan, Die slowenische Politik und Kaiser Karl, in: Karl I. (IV.). Der Erste Weltkrieg und das Ende der Donaumonarchie, edited by Andreas Gottsmann (Vienna, 2007), 181.

2 The term 'October Diploma', which is occasionally used, is confusing. See Hanns Haas, Historische Einleitung. Staatsbildung als Programm. Der österreichische Staatsrat im November 1918, in: Der österreichische Staatsrat. Protokolle des Vollzugsausschusses, des Staatsrates und des Geschäftsführenden Staatsratsdirektoriums 21. Oktober 1918 bis 14. März 1919, vol. 1, edited by Gertrud Enderle-Burcel, Hanns Haas and Peter Mähner (Vienna, 2008). October Diploma is generally used to refer to the law of 20 October 1860, with which the main features of a constitution for the Austrian Empire were decreed.

3 On military events: Manfried Rauchensteiner, Der Erste Weltkrieg und das Ende der Habsburgermonarchie 1914–1918 (Vienna/Cologne/Weimar, 2013), 1039–1042.

4 Bruno Wagner, Der Waffenstillstand von der Villa Giusti 3. November 1918, doctoral thesis, University of Vienna (1970).

5 The important work on the founding of the state, not least because of its comments on legal history: Wilhelm Brauneder, Deutsch-Österreich 1918. Die Republik entsteht (Vienna/Munich, 2000), here 31.

6 Strangely enough, the data on the number of German delegates varies. Walter Goldinger, Geschichte der Republik Österreich (Vienna, 1962), 10, cites 208 delegates, whereas Brauneder, Deutsch-Österreich 1918, 26, cites 206, and Oliver Rathkolb, Erste Republik, Austrofaschismus, Nationalsozialismus 1918–1945, in: Geschichte Österreichs, edited by Thomas Winkelbauer (Stuttgart, 2016), 487, cites 220 delegates.

7 In the Christian Social parliamentary group in the Imperial Assembly, Prelate Johann Nepomuk Hauser tabled the motion on 9 October. See: Dieter A. Binder, Fresko in Schwarz. Das christlichsoziale Lager, in: Das Werden der Ersten Republik. Der Rest ist Österreich, edited by Helmut Konrad, Wolfgang Maderthaner, 2 vols. (Vienna, 2008), here vol. I, 253. The Social Democrat delegate Otto Bauer argued in a similar fashion on 11 October. See: Ernst Hanisch, Im Zeichen von Otto Bauer, Deutschösterreichs Außenpolitik in den Jahren 1918 bis 1919, in: Das Werden der Ersten Republik, vol. I, 216.

8 Brauneder, Deutsch-Österreich 1918, esp. 19–60.

9 Walter Goldinger and Dieter A. Binder, Geschichte der Republik Österreich 1918–1938 (Vienna/Munich, 1992), 15.

10 Hanisch, Im Zeichen von Otto Bauer, 210.

11 It is probably impossible to verify the quote in this form. See Manfred Zollinger, 'L'Autriche, c'est moi'? Georges Clemenceau, das neue Österreich und das Werden eines Mythos, in: Österreich – 90 Jahre Republik. Beitragsband der Ausstellung im Parlament, edited by Stefan Karner (Innsbruck/Vienna, 2008), 621–632.

12 Gerald Stourzh, Erschütterung und Konsolidierung des Österreichbewußtseins. Vom Zusammenbruch der Monarchie bis zur Zweiten Republik, in: Was heißt Österreich? Inhalt und Umfang des Österreichbegriffs vom 10. Jahrhundert bis heute, edited by Richard Georg Plaschka (Vienna, 1995), 290. The names were proposed as the result of a competition organised by the *Innsbrucker Nachrichten* in March 1919.

13 Karl Renner, Österreichs Erneuerung. Politisch-programmatische Aufsätze von Dr. Karl Renner, Reichsratsabgeordneter (Vienna, 1916), 41.

14 Michael Hainisch, 75 Jahre aus bewegter Zeit. Lebenserinnerungen eines österreichischen Staatsmannes, edited by Friedrich Weissensteiner (Graz/Vienna/Cologne, 1978), 207.

15 Haas, Historische Einleitung, Staatsbildung, LVI.

16 Der österreichische Staatsrat, 347–348.

17 Wolfgang Maderthaner, Die eigenartige Größe der Beschränkung. Österreichs Revolution im mitteleuropäischen Spannungsfeld, in: Das Werden der Ersten Republik, I, 198. Also Manfried Rauchensteiner, Landesverteidigung und Sicherheitspolitik 1918–1934, in: Handbuch des politischen Systems Österreichs. Erste Republik 1918–1933, edited by Emmerich Tálos, Herbert Dachs, Ernst Hanisch and Anton Staudinger (Vienna, 1995), 602–617, esp. 604–605. A largely positive picture of the People's Militia is painted by Peter Broucek, Über Prätorianergarden und Legionen in und um Österreich, in: idem, Militärischer Widerstand. Studien zur österreichischen Staatsgesinnung und NS-Abwehr (Vienna/Cologne/Weimar, 2008), esp. 232–255.

18 The rhyme, handed down by Peter Broucek, supposedly originated with the poetry-writing General Staff officer of the Imperial and Royal Army Karl Schneller. See Broucek, Über Prätorianergarden, 254.

2 The Impeded Revolution

19 According to Wilhelm Brauneder, Deutsch-Österreich 1918. Brauneder argues in his book from the perspective of constitutional history and very consciously uses the painting by Max Frey on the front cover.

20 Florian Wenninger, Von 'Monarchenfressern' und 'Habsburg-Agenten'. Der 12. November als politischer Erinnerungsort der Zweiten Republik, in: zeitgeschichte, vol. 41, no. 6 (2014), 400–414.

21 The painting by Frey can be found in the Museum of Military History, Vienna. The picture by Konopa and likewise the one by Ledli are in the collections of the Vienna Museum.

22 The phrase is used by Ernst Hanisch, Der große Illusionist. Otto Bauer (1881–1938) (Vienna/Cologne/Weimar, 2011), 144.

23 Binder, Fresko in Schwarz, 244.

24 Staatsdruckerei 2639 19 (copy in the author's possession).

25 Otto Bauer, Die österreichische Revolution (Vienna, 1923), 147–148.

26 Robert Hoffmann, Die Mission Sir Thomas Cuninghames in Wien 1919. Britische Österreichpolitik zur Zeit der Pariser Friedenskonferenz, doctoral thesis, University of Salzburg (1971), 43.

27 Andreas Hillgruber, Das Anschlussproblem (1918–1945) – aus deutscher Sicht, in: Deutschland und Österreich. Ein bilaterales Geschichtsbuch, edited by Robert A. Kann (Vienna, 1980), 161–178, here 162.

28 Hanns Haas, Österreich und die Alliierten 1918–1919, in: Saint-Germain 1919 (= Veröffentlichungen der Wissenschaftlichen Kommission zur Erforschung der Geschichte der Republik Österreich, vol. 11, Vienna, 1989).

29 Klaus Schwabe, Deutsche Revolution und Wilson-Friede. Die amerikanische und deutsche Friedensstrategie zwischen Ideologie und Machtpolitik 1918/19 (Düsseldorf, 1971), 174.

30 Haas, Österreich und die Alliierten, 27.

31 Haas, Ein verfehlter Start, 375.

32 Haas, Österreich und die Alliierten, 33.

33 The National Archives (hereafter TNA), Kew, Foreign Office (hereafter FO) 608/27, dispatch, dated 19 March 1919.

34 Brauneder, Deutsch-Österreich 1918, 207.

35 Staatsgesetzblatt für den Staat Deutschösterreich, vol. 1919, issue 54, no. 174.

36 Renner claims to have spoken to the Emperor; it seems far more likely, however, that the State Chan-

cellor was not allowed to see the Emperor. See the interesting remarks by Clemens Jabloner, Person, Amt und Institutionen, in: idem, Methodenreinheit und Erkenntnisvielfalt. Aufsätze zur Rechtstheorie, Rechtsdogmatik und Rechtsgeschichte, edited by Thomas Olechowski, Klaus Zeleny (= Schriftenreihe des Hans-Kelsen-Instituts, vol. 35, Vienna, 2013), 354, note 8.

37 Brauneder, Deutsch-Österreich 1918, 141–142.

38 Stefan Zweig, Die Welt von Gestern. Erinnerungen eines Europäers, paperback edition (Frankfurt am Main, 1989), 323– 327.

39 Kaiser und König Karl I. (IV.). Politische Dokumente aus Internationalen Archiven, edited by Elisabeth Kovács, vol. 2 (Vienna/Cologne/Weimar, 2004). The handwritten text appears in facsimile on the book cover.

40 See the very illuminating article by Georg Frölichsthal, Die Mitgliedschaft zum Haus Österreich nach 1918, in: Adler no. 6/7 (2016), 342–357.

41 Law from 3 April 1919 on the Exile and the Takeover of the Assets of the House of Habsburg-Lorraine, in: Staatsgesetzblatt für den Staat Deutschösterreich, vol. 1919, issue 71, no. 209.

42 Adalbert Graf Sternberg 1868–1930. Aus den Memoiren eines konservativen Rebellen, edited by Hans Rochelt (Vienna, 1997), 7.

43 Hoffmann, Mission Cuningham, 127.

44 See Gerhard Botz, Die 'Österreichische Revolution' 1918/19. Zu Kontexten und Problematik einer alten Meistererzählung der Zeitgeschichte in Österreich, in: zeitgeschichte, vol. 44, 2014, no. 6, 359–370.

45 TNA, Kew, FO 608/27, Intelligence Report, dated 24 March 1919.

46 Hoffmann, Mission Cuningham, 14.

47 Haas, Österreich und die Alliierten, 33.

48 Hoffmann, Mission Cuningham, 111.

49 Fritz Keller, Die Arbeiter- und Soldatenräte in Österreich 1918–23. Versuch einer Analyse (Vienna, 1998), 19–21.

50 Hans Hautmann, Die Geschichte der Rätebewegung in Österreich 1918–1924 (Vienna/Zurich, 1987), 329–330.

51 Austrian State Archives, Vienna (Österreichisches Staatsarchiv, hereafter ÖStA), New Political Archive (Neues Politisches Archiv), box 788, Liasse Ungarn I/1. Staatsamt für Äußeres, I-3676/4, dated 4 May 1919.

3 Saint-Germain: The End of Illusions

52 Christian Koller, '… Der Wiener Judenstaat, von dem wir uns unter allen Umständen trennen wollen'. Die Vorarlberger Anschlussbewegung an die Schweiz, in: Das Werden der Ersten Republik, vol. I, 86–87.

53 The quote can be found in Hanisch, Der lange Schatten des Staates (Vienna, 1994), 270.

54 Goldinger and Binder, Geschichte der Republik Österreich, 54.

55 Hermann Kuprian. Der Tiroler Separatismus der Ersten Republik, in: 1918/1919. Die Bundesländer und die Republik. Protokollband des Symposiums zum 75. Jahrestag der Ausrufung der 1. Republik am 12. und 13. November im Grazer Stadtmuseum, edited by Gerhard Michael Dienes (Graz, 1994), 51.

56 Ute Weinmann, Die südslawische Frage und Jugoslawien. Grenzziehung im Süden Österreichs unter besonderer Berücksichtigung der Kärntenproblematik, in: Das Werden der Ersten Republik, vol. I, 127.

57 Goldinger and Binder, Geschichte der Republik Österreich, 55–62; Erwin Steinböck, Die Kämpfe im Raum Völkermarkt 1918/19 (= Militärhistorische Schriftenreihe, vol. 13, Vienna, 1969).

58 Charles Kingsley Webster, The Congress of Vienna 1814/1815 (Oxford, 1919). Several reprints. Webster
    also published a comprehensive collection of sources on the Congress of Vienna in 1921.

59 Fritz Fellner, Die Pariser Vororteverträge von 1919/20, in: Versailles – St. Germain – Trianon. Umbruch
    in Europa vor fünfzig Jahren, edited by Karl Bosl (Vienna/Munich, 1971), 7–23. In his observation, Fell-
    ner relies above all on André Tardieu, who provides an exact listing of the thousands of sessions.

60 Richard Saage, Die deutsche Frage. Die Erste Republik im Spannungsfeld zwischen österreichischer
    und deutscher Identität, in: Das Werden der Ersten Republik. Der Rest ist Österreich, edited by Helmut
    Konrad and Wolfgang Maderthaner, vol. 1 (Vienna, 2008), 65–82, here 78.

61 Francis L. Carsten, The First Austrian Republic: A Study based on British and Austrian Documents
    (Aldershot/Brookfield, 1986), 5.

62 Hoffmann, Mission Cuninghame, 188.

63 Walter Reichel, Tschechoslowakei – Österreich. Grenzziehung 1918/1919, in: Das Werden der Ersten
    Republik, vol. I, 163.

64 Ludwig Jedlicka, Aufteilungs- und Einmarschpläne um Österreich 1918–1934, in: idem, Vom alten zum
    neuen Österreich. Fallstudien zur österreichischen Zeitgeschichte 1900–1975 (St. Pölten, 1975), 148.

65 See the detailed analysis by Stefan Malfèr, Wien und Rom nach dem Ersten Weltkrieg. Österre-
    ichisch-italienische Beziehungen 1919–1923 (= Veröffentlichung der Kommission für neuere Geschichte
    Österreichs, vol. 66, Vienna/Cologne/Graz, 1978).

66 Fritz Fellner and Heidrun Maschl, Saint Germain im Sommer 1919. Die Briefe Franz Kleins aus der
    Zeit seiner Mitwirkung in der österreichischen Friedensdelegation, Mai–August 1919 (= Quellen zur
    Geschichte des 19. und 20. Jahrhunderts, vol. 1, Salzburg, 1977), 113.

67 Hanisch, Der große Illusionist, 164–165.

68 See Haas, Ein verfehlter Start, 374. The question of a union was not central throughout, but it did domi
    nate domestic politics at least for a period of time.

69 Gerald Stourzh, Um Einheit und Freiheit. Staatsvertrag, Neutralität und das Ende der Ost-West-Be-
    setzung Österreichs 1945–1955 (Vienna/Cologne/Graz, 1998), 244–246. See also Stephan Verosta, Für
    die Unabhängigkeit Österreichs, in: Österreich November 1918. Die Entstehung der Ersten Republik.
    Wissenschaftliche Kommission zur Erforschung der Geschichte der Republik Österreich, Veröffentli-
    chungen, vol. 9 (Vienna, 1986), 41–48, here 44–45.

70 Hanisch, Im Zeichen von Otto Bauer, 220.

71 Peter Burian, Österreich und der Völkerbund, in: Nation, Nationalismus, Postnation, edited by Harm
    Klueting (Cologne/Vienna, 1992), 111.

72 See Rolf Steininger, 1918/1919: Die Teilung Tirols. Wie das Südtirolproblem entstand, in: Das Werden
    der Ersten Republik, vol. I, 115–117.

73 Brauneder, Deutsch-Österreich 1918, 104.

74 Gerald Schlag: Die Grenzziehung Österreich-Ungarn 1922/23, in: Burgenland in seiner pannonischen
    Umwelt. Festgabe für August Ernst (Eisenstadt, 1984), 333–346; idem: Die Kämpfe um das Burgenland
    1921 (= Militärhistorische Schriftenreihe, vol. 16, Vienna, 1970). The most important documents are
    in: Außenpolitische Dokumente der Republik Österreich 1918–1938, vol. 4: Zwischen Staatsbankrott
    und Genfer Sanierung 11. Juni 1921 bis 6. November 1922, edited by Klaus Koch, Walter Rauscher and
    Arnold Suppan (Vienna/Munich, 1998).

75 More precise figures were not available. Ultimately, we must be content with overall numbers and per-
    centages. For the Habsburg Monarchy, losses in military dead were calculated at around 1.2 million, of
    which the Austrian half of the Empire accounted for 51.52 per cent and the Hungarian half of the Em-
    pire for 42 per cent. The rest can be attributed to Bosnia-Herzegovina. Three times as high as the losses
    in dead was the number of wounded, of which, in turn, around one third were permanently disabled. It

has been calculated that, on average, 23.3 from every 1,000 people fell victim to the war. See Wilhelm Winkler, Die Totenverluste der öst.-ung. Monarchie nach Nationalitäten (Vienna, 1919). Furthermore: Statistisches Handbuch für die Republik Österreich, edited by the Statistische Zentralkommission, vol. 3 (Vienna, 1923), 9. The most recent statistics, which admittedly still have to be added together, can be found in the painstakingly researched volume: Die Habsburgermonarchie und der Erste Weltkrieg, vol. XI/2: Weltkriegsstatistik Österreich-Ungarns 1914–1918, series editor Helmut Rumpler, volume editors Anatol Schmied-Kowarzik and Helmut Rumpler (Vienna, 2015).

76   Mark Mazower, Der dunkle Kontinent. Europa im 20. Jahrhundert (Berlin, 2000), 120.

77   Laurence Cole, Der Habsburger-Mythos in: Memoria Austriae I. Menschen, Mythen, Zeiten, edited by Emil Brix et al. (Vienna, 2004), 473–504; Bela Rasky, Erinnern und Vergessen der Habsburger in Österreich und Ungarn nach 1918, in: Österreich 1918 und die Folgen. Geschichte, Literatur, Theater und Film, edited by Karl Müller (Vienna, 2009), 25–58; Martin Reisacher, Die Konstruktion des 'Staats, den keiner wollte'. Der Transformationsprozess des umstrittenen Gedächtnisorts 'Erste Republik' in einen negativen rhetorischen Topos, diploma thesis, University of Vienna (2010).

78   Rolf Steininger, 12. November 1918 bis 13. März 1938: Stationen auf dem Weg zum 'Anschluss', in: Österreich im 20. Jahrhundert, vol. 1: Von der Monarchie bis zum Zweiten Weltkrieg, edited by Rolf Steininger and Michael Gehler (Vienna/Cologne/Weimar, 1997), here esp. 107–109.

79   Malfèr, Wien und Rom, 60.

80   Mazower, Der dunkle Kontinent, 31.

81   Wolfgang Doppelbauer, Zum Elend noch die Schande. Das altösterreichische Offizierskorps am Beginn der Republik (= Militärgeschichtliche Dissertationen österreichischer Universitäten, vol. 9, Vienna, 1988).

82   Ernst Hanisch, Männlichkeiten. Eine andere Geschichte des 20. Jahrhunderts (Vienna/Cologne/Weimar, 2005), 50.

83   Christoph Gütermann, Die Geschichte der österreichischen Friedensbewegung 1891–1985, in: Überlegungen zum Frieden, edited by Manfried Rauchensteiner (Vienna, 1987), 63; Walter Göhring, Verdrängt und vergessen. Friedensnobelpreisträger Alfred Hermann Fried (Vienna, 2006), 240.

84   Peter Broucek and Kurt Peball, Geschichte der österreichischen Militärhistoriographie (Cologne/Weimar/Vienna, 2000), 77.

85   Joachim Giller, Hubert Mader and Christina Seidl, Wo sind sie geblieben …? Kriegerdenkmäler und Gefallenenehrung in Österreich (= Schriften des Heeresgeschichtlichen Museums, vol. 11, Vienna, 1992).

86   Mazower, Der dunkle Kontinent, 142.

87   Brauneder, Deutsch-Österreich 1918, 85.

88   Within the space of a few years, there were around 50,000 so-called dispensation marriages.

89   A German study can at least be taken as an indicator: Sabine Kienitz, Der Krieg der Invaliden. Helden-Bilder und Männlichkeitskonstruktionen nach dem Ersten Weltkrieg, in: Militärgeschichtliche Zeitschrift, edited by the Militärgeschichtliches Forschungsamt, vol. 60, no. 2 (2001), 367–402.

90   Friedrich Hacker, Die Entwicklung der Psychoanalyse in der Zwischenkriegszeit, in: Das geistige Leben Wiens in der Zwischenkriegszeit, edited by Norbert Leser (= Quellen und Studien zur österreichischen Geistesgeschichte im 19. und 20. Jahrhundert, vol. 1, Vienna, 1981), 133–143, here 141.

4 The End of Commonality

91   Robert Kriechbaumer, Welcher Staat? Die Christlichsoziale Partei und die Republik 1918–1920, in: Der Forschende Blick. Beiträge zur Geschichte Österreichs im 20. Jahrhundert. Festschrift für Ernst Hanisch zum 70. Geburtstag, edited by Reinhard Krammer et al. (Vienna/Cologne/Weimar, 2010), 40.

92   Goldinger and Binder, Geschichte der Republik Österreich, 92.

93   Roman Sandgruber, Ökonomie und Politik. Österreichische Wirtschaftsgeschichte vom Mittelalter bis zur Gegenwart (Vienna, 1995), 346.

94   Hanisch, Der große Illusionist, 167.

95   Goldinger and Binder, Geschichte der Republik Österreich, 103.

96   Adam Wandrusza, Deutschliberale und deutschnationale Strömungen in: Das geistige Leben Wiens in der Zwischenkriegszeit, 28–33, here 30.

97   Goldinger and Binder, Geschichte der Republik Österreich, 109.

98   Sandgruber, Ökonomie und Politik, 383.

99   See the biographical novel by Georg Ransmayr, Der arme Trillionär. Aufstieg und Untergang des Inflationskönigs Sigmund Bosel (Vienna/Graz/Klagenfurt, 2016). In general: Peter Melichar, Verteilungskämpfe. Bemerkungen zur Korruption im Österreich der Zwischenkriegszeit, in: Korruption in Österreich. Historische Streiflichter, edited by Ernst Bruckmüller (Vienna, 2011).

100   Hanisch, Der lange Schatten, 282.

101   Felix Butschek, Österreichische Wirtschaftsgeschichte. Von der Antike bis zur Gegenwart (Vienna/Cologne/Weimar, 2012), 200.

102   Malfèr, Wien und Rom, 103–104.

103   On the basis of the Geneva Protocols of 4 October 1922, Austria was awarded a guaranteed loan of 650 million gold crowns from the governments of Britain, France, Italy and the Republic of Czechoslovakia, for which Austria was obliged to pledge the revenue from customs and its monopoly on tobacco. The League of Nations loan was to run for a period of 20 years. It was issued in ten different currencies at eleven financial centres, and yielded a net revenue of 611 million crowns, or 880 million schillings. The effective interest rate varied between 8.6 and 10.2 per cent. The money was used in part to cover the income deficit of 1922 and 1923, and around 50 per cent of the net revenue had to be deposited in foreign banks, at interest rates of 3-4 per cent. Thus, the interest rate did not even remotely reach the amount that Austria had to pay the creditors, in some cases the same banks. The remaining loan was used for the period 1924-1927 for production investment by the federation, and 50 million schillings were taken to reduce the federal debt at the National Bank of Austria. Austria cancelled this League of Nations loan on 1 December 1934. A 'guaranteed Austrian conversion loan, 1934–59' of 567 million schillings was issued for repayment. See: Hans Kernbauer, Eduard März and Fritz Weber, Die wirtschaftliche Entwicklung, in: Österreich 1918–1938, edited by Erika Weinzierl and Kurt Skalnik, vol. 1 (Vienna, 1983); also Grete Klingenstein, Die Anleihe von Lausanne. Österreich Archiv (Vienna, 1965).

104   Arbeiter-Zeitung, 15 October 1922, 1.

105   The quote can be found in Saage, Die deutsche Frage, 80.

106   Alphons Lhotsky, Die Verteidigung der Wiener Sammlungen durch die Erste Republik, in: idem, Die Haupt- und Residenzstadt Wien, Sammelwesen und Ikonographie. Der österreichische Mensch (= Alphons Lhotsky, Aufsätze und Vorträge, edited by Hans Wagner and Heinrich Koller, vol. IV, Vienna, 1974), 164–210.

107   Hanisch, Der große Illusionist, 217.

108   Arbeiter-Zeitung, 17 October 1922, 1.

109   Othmar Plöckinger, Geschichte eines Buches: Adolf Hitlers 'Mein Kampf', 1922–1945 (Munich, 2006), 59.

5 Marching Season

110 Helmut Konrad, Das Rote Wien. Ein Konzept für eine moderne Großstadt?, in: Das Werden der Ersten Republik, vol. I, 230.

111 Konrad, Das Rote Wien, 238.

112 Rathkolb, Erste Republik, 494.

113 On the history of the Heimwehr: Walter Wiltschegg, Die Heimwehr. Eine unwiderstehliche Volksbewegung? (= Studien und Quellen zur österreichischen Zeitgeschichte, vol. 7, Vienna, 1985).

114 Finbarr McLoughlin, Der republikanische Schutzbund und gewalttätige politische Auseinandersetzungen in Österreich 1923–1934, doctoral thesis, University of Vienna (1990).

115 Goldinger and Binder, Geschichte der Republik Österreichs, 140.

116 Doppelbauer, Zum Elend noch die Schande, 79–101.

117 Wo sind sie geblieben …? Zeichen der Erinnerung. Catalogue of the special exhibition at the Museum of Military History, 22 October 1997 to 22 February 1998 (Vienna, 1997), 14.

118 Butschek, Österreichische Wirtschaftsgeschichte, 205.

119 Beatrix Hoffmann-Holter, 'Abreisendmachung'. Jüdische Kriegsflüchtlinge in Wien 1914 bis 1923 (Vienna/Cologne/Weimar, 1995), 211–212.

120 'Dieses Österreich retten ….' Die Protokolle der Parteitage der Christlichsozialen Partei in der Ersten Republik, edited by Robert Kriechbaumer (Vienna/Cologne/Weimar, 2006), 307.

121 Kurt Bauer, Die kalkulierte Eskalation. Nationalsozialismus und Gewalt in Wien um 1930, in: Kampf um die Stadt. Exhibition catalogue Wien Museum, edited by Wolfgang Kos (Vienna, 2010), 39.

122 https://de.wikipedia.org/wiki/Linzer_Programm_(Sozialdemokratie) [last accessed on 23 June 2017].

123 The best account of the events in Schattendorf and the fire at the Palace of Justice is by Gerhard Botz, Gewalt in der Politik. Attentate, Zusammenstöße, Putschversuche, Unruhen in Österreich 1918 bis 1938 (Munich, 1983).

124 Arbeiter-Zeitung, 15 July 1927, 1–2.

125 Neue Freie Presse, 18 July 1927, 1.

126 Tagblatt, Linz, 19 July 1927, 1.

6 Civil War Scenarios

127 Botz, Gewalt in der Politik, 166. Also Christiane Rothländer, Die Anfänge der Wiener SS (Vienna/Cologne/Weimar, 2012), 85–87.

128 Tálos, Das austrofaschistische Herrschaftssystem, 14.

129 Goldinger and Binder, Geschichte der Republik Österreich, 159.

130 Neue Freie Presse, 19 August 1929, 1–2.

131 Goldinger and Binder, Geschichte der Republik Österreich, 162.

132 Raab left the Heimwehr in December 1930 when it decided to campaign as an electoral party in competition with the Christian Socials. In 1931, he founded a separate 'Lower Austrian Heimwehr', which in May 1932 merged with the Eastern March Stormtroopers.

133 https://de.wikipedia.org/wiki/Joseph_Schumpeter [last accessed on 23 June 2017].

134 Peter Eigner, Absturzgefahr und Sanierungsversuche. Zur wirtschaftlich ambivalenten Situation um 1930, in: Kampf um die Stadt, 25.

135 Hillgruber, Das Anschlussproblem, 165.

136 Franz Mathis, Wirtschaft oder Politik? Zu den wirtschaftlichen Motiven einer politischen Vereinigung

1918–1938, in: Ungleiche Partner? Österreich und Deutschland im 19. und 20. Jahrhundert, edited by Michael Gehler (Stuttgart, 1996), 412.

137   Goldinger and Binder, Geschichte der Republik Österreich,178.

138   Burian, Österreich und der Völkerbund, 116.

139   Peter Eigner and Peter Melichar, Das Ende der Boden-Credit-Anstalt 1929 und die Rolle Rudolf Siegharts, in: Bankrott. Österreichische Zeitschrift für Geschichtswissenschaften, vol. 19, no. 3 (2008), 56–114.

140   Butschek, Österreichische Wirtschaftsgeschichte, 221.

141   Goldinger and Binder, Geschichte der Republik Österreich, 182.

142   The figures can be found in Walter Kleindel, Österreich. Daten zur Geschichte und Kultur (Vienna/ Heidelberg, 1978), 338. Further figures under the keyword 'unemployment'.

143   Josef Hofmann, Der Pfrimer-Putsch. Der steirische Heimwehrprozeß des Jahres 1931 (= publications by the Österreichisches Institut für Zeitgeschichte, vol. 4, Graz, 1965); Bruce F. Pauley, Hahnenschwanz und Hakenkreuz. Steirischer Heimatschutz und österreichischer Nationalsozialismus 1918–34 (Munich, 1972).

144   The text of the appeal of the federal government is in Goldinger and Binder, Geschichte der Republik Österreich, 186. Sequence of events and comments also in the daily press, e.g. Neue Freie Presse, 14 September 1931, 1.

145   Rothländer, Die Anfänge der Wiener SS, 94-95.

146   Goldinger and Binder, Geschichte der Republik Österreich, 190-191.

147   Mazower, Der dunkle Kontinent, 45.

148   Ernst Bruckmüller, Nation Österreich. Kulturelles Bewußtsein und gesellschaftlich-politische Prozesse (Vienna/Cologne/Graz, 1996), 307.

149   The term is used by Emmerich Tálos, Das austrofaschistische Herrschaftssystem. Österreich 1933–1938 (= Politik und Zeitgeschichte, vol. 8, Vienna, 2013), 22.

150   Grete Klingenstein, Die Anleihe von Lausanne. Österreich Archiv (Vienna, 1965). About him as a person: Peter Berger, Im Schatten der Diktatur. Die Finanzdiplomatie des Vertreters des Völkerbundes in Österreich Meinoud Marinus Rost van Tonningen 1931–1936 (Vienna/Cologne/Weimar, 2000), 24–27.

151   Goldinger and Binder, Geschichte der Republik Österreich, 197.

7 The Trauma

152   https://de.wikipedia.org/wiki/Bundespr%C3%A4sident_(%C3%96sterreich)#Notverordnungsrecht [last accessed on 23 June 2017].

153   Most clearly at a farmers' meeting in Villach on 5 March 1933. See: Robert Kriechbaumer, Die Nebel der Begrifflichkeit oder vom schwierigen Umgang mit dem Ständestaat und der Vaterländischen Front. Introduction to: Österreich! Und Front Heil! Aus den Akten des Generalsekretariats der Vaterländischen Front. Innenansichten eines Regimes, edited by Robert Kriechbaumer (Vienna/Cologne/Weimar, 2005), 27.

154   Arbeiter-Zeitung, 18 March 1933, 1.

155   Ibid.

156   TNA, Kew, WO 190/210, Note on the situation in Austria, January–July 1933, 30 August 1933.

157   Speech by Deputy Chancellor Winkler during the 9th party conference of the Rural League on 14 May 1933, in: Wiener Zeitung, 16 May 1933, 5.

158 Winfried R. Garscha, Der Terror der illegalen Nationalsozialisten vor 1938: Wer waren die Opfer?

159 Kurt Bauer, 'Heil Deutschösterreich!'. Das deutschnationale Lager zu Beginn der Ersten Republik, in: Das Werden der Ersten Republik, vol. I, 278.

160 Hanisch, Der lange Schatten, 296.

161 Sandgruber, Ökonomie und Politik, 377.

162 Goldinger and Binder, Geschichte der Republik Österreich, 206.

163 TNA, Kew, WO 190/210, Note on the situation in Austria.

164 TNA, Kew, WO 190/204 (June 1933).

165 According to Gerhard Botz during a dispute with Robert Menasse: Das Dollfuß-Regime verstehen. Available at http//derstandard.at/r1246543999319/Nachlese-Kontroverse-Botz-Menasse, 1 September 2010, and ibid., 18 February 2004.

166 Goldinger and Binder, Geschichte der Republik Österreich, 208.

167 Kriechbaumer, Die Nebel der Begrifflichkeit, 22.

168 Hanisch, Der große Illusionist, 291.

169 Helmut Rumpler, Der Ständestaat ohne Stände, in: Der forschende Blick. Beiträge zur Geschichte Österreichs im 20. Jahrhundert. Festschrift für Ernst Hanisch, 229–245, here 237.

170 Quoted from Tálos, Das austrofaschistische Herrschaftssystem, 586.

171 Hanisch, Der lange Schatten, 290.

172 The range of meanings of the term by Erika Kustascher in her comprehensive postdoctoral thesis: 'Berufsstand' oder 'Stand'. Ein politischer Schlüsselbegriff im Österreich der Zwischenkriegszeit (= Veröffentlichungen der Kommission für neuere Geschichte Österreichs, vol. 113, Vienna/Cologne/Weimar, 2016), 24. Also dedicated to the semantics: Kriechbaumer, Die Nebel der Begrifflichkeit, 35–36.

173 Bruckmüller, Nation Österreich, 308.

174 Goldinger and Binder, Geschichte der Republik Österreich, 211.

175 Austrian State Archives, War Archives (hereafter KA), BMfLV/Abt. 1, IntZl. 890-1/1933: Record 'Innenlage – Bewaffnete Verbände', 12 December 1933, where 'persons of ill repute and with previous convictions' are mentioned.

176 Ibid.

177 Indictment in the Protection League trial, Regional Criminal Court, Vienna, 8 Vr/3553/34 = Documentation Centre of Austrian Resistance, Vienna, 5593 b.

178 Walter Rauscher, Die Entwicklung des vaterländischen Regimes, in: Außenpolitische Dokumente der Republik Österreich 1918–1938, vol. 9: Österreich im Banne des Faschismus, edited by Walter Rauscher (= Fontes Rerum Austiacarum, 2nd section, vol. 95, Vienna, 2014), 16.

179 See also Lajos Kerekes, Abenddämmerung einer Demokratie. Mussolini, Gömbös und die Heimwehr (Vienna/Frankfurt/Zurich, 1966), part. 166–167. On the foreign policy situation overall: Karl Stuhlpfarrer, Österreichs außenpolitische Lage 1934, in: Österreich 1927 bis 1938, 144 ff.

180 See also Walter Goldinger, Geschichte der Republik Österreich (Vienna, 1962), 192.

181 Kurt Peball, Die Kämpfe in Wien im Februar 1934 (= Militärhistorische Schriftenreihe, vol. 25, Vienna, 1974), 16.

182 Der Februar-Aufruhr 1934. Das Eingreifen des österreichischen Bundesheeres zu seiner Niederwerfung. (Only for official use), as printed manuscript (Vienna, 1935), 157.

183 On these two individuals, see the works by Eric C. Kollman, Theodor Körner, Militär und Politiker (Vienna, 1972), and Helmut Tober, Alexander Eifler. Vom Monarchisten zum Republikaner, doctoral thesis, University of Vienna (1966).

184 (A. Neuberg), Hans Kippenberger, M. N. Tuchatschewski and Ho Chi Minh, Der bewaffnete Aufstand.

Versuch einer theoretischen Darstellung. Eingeleitet von Erich Wollenberg (Frankfurt am Main, 1971), XXXIII.

185   Tober, Alexander Eifler, 510–511.

186   Peball, Die Kämpfe in Wien, 21.

187   This was the case with the 'Sandleiten' complex. See also Februar-Aufruhr, 53.

188   On the Viennese communal buildings, see the unprinted doctoral thesis by Renate Schweitzer, Der staatlich geförderte, der kommunale und der gemeinnützige Wohnungs- und Siedlungsbau in Österreich bis 1945, College of Technology (Vienna, 1972).

189   Barry McLoughlin, Die Partei, in: Kommunismus in Österreich 1918–1938, edited by idem, Hannes Leidinger and Verena Moritz (Innsbruck/Vienna/Bolzano, 2009), 311.

190   Tálos, Das austrofaschistische Herrschaftssystem, 51.

191   TNA, Kew, FO 341/18350/3894, pp. 205–206.

192   KA, BMfLV/Abt. l, Zl. 5341-1/1934.

193   Ibid.

194   KA, BMfLV/Abt. l, Zl. 4606-1/1934.

195   TNA, Kew, FO 341/18350/3904, pp. 161 ff.

196   TNA, Kew, FO 341/18350/3894, p. 236.

8 Corporative State without Corporations

197   Mazower, Der dunkle Kontinent, 54.

198   Rothländer, Die Anfänge der Wiener SS, 419.

199   Ludwig Reichhold, Kampf um Österreich. Die Vaterländische Front und ihr Widerstand gegen den Nationalsozialismus 1933–1938 (Vienna, 1984). See also Kriechbaumer, Die Nebel der Begrifflichkeit, 45–49.

200   'Dieses Österreich retten', 467.

201   Hanisch, Der lange Schatten, 293.

202   The ratification of the Concordat required constitutionality, that is, a two-thirds majority in the National Council, which still formally existed and was only prevented from convening. The Vatican repeatedly urged the ratification of the treaty signed on 5 March 1933 but was put off until 1 May 1934. See: Erika Weinzierl, Das österreichische Konkordat von 1933 von der Unterzeichnung bis zur Ratifikation, in: 60 Jahre österreichisches Konkordat, edited by Hans Paarhamer, Franz Pototschnig and Alfred Rinnerthaler (Munich, 1994), 119–134.

203   Mazower, Der dunkle Kontinent, 57.

204   Rathkolb, Erste Republik, 504. A detailed explanation and critical analysis of the discussion, which has been very strongly shaped by the differing terms, is provided by Erika Kustascher, 'Berufsstand' oder 'Stand', 19–24.

205   Anton Philapitsch, Wöllersdorf. Trauma oder Mythos, in: Geschosse – Skandale – Stacheldraht. Arbeiterschaft und Rüstungsindustrie, edited by Leopold Mulley (Vienna, 1999); Gerhard Jagschitz, Die Anhaltelager in Österreich, in: Vom Justizpalast zum Heldenplatz. Studien und Dokumentationen 1927 bis 1938, editd by Ludwig Jedlicka and Rudolf Neck (Vienna, 1975), 128–151. In October 1934, the numbers peaked with 4,794 detainees and prisoners (4,256 National Socialists, 538 Social Democrats and Communists).

206   Hans Schafranek, Söldner für den Anschluss. Die österreichische Legion 1933–1938 (Vienna, 2011), 29.

207   Schafranek. Söldner für den Anschluss, 30.

208 Dušan Nećak, Die österreichisch-jugoslawischen Beziehungen im 20. Jahrhundert, in: Außenansichten. Europäische (Be)Wertungen zur Geschichte Österreichs im 20. Jahrhundert, edited by Oliver Rathkolb (Innsbruck/Vienna/Munich, 2003), 185.

209 Wolfgang Neugebauer, Das Standgerichtsverfahren gegen Josef Gerl, in: Sozialistenprozesse. Politische Justiz in Österreich 1870–1936, edited by Karl R. Stadler (Vienna, 1986), 369–370.

210 On the prehistory and course of the attack on Engelbert Dollfuß: Kurt Bauer, Hitlers zweiter Putsch. Dollfuß, die Nazis und der 25. Juli 1934 (St. Pölten/Salzburg, 2014). The book is more solidly based on the sources than the older work by Gerhard Jagschitz, Der Putsch. Die Nationalsozialisten 1934 in Österreich (Graz/Vienna/Cologne, 1976). Important aspects, for instance Hitler's role or that of the Austrian SA leader Hermann Reschny, are still based on clues and inferences.

211 Bauer, Hitlers zweiter Putsch, 172–177.

212 Ibid., 19.

213 In 1938, Siebensterngasse in Vienna's 7th District was renamed 'Straße der Julikämpfer' (Street of the July Fighters), and in the gallows courtyard of Vienna's regional court, where the rebels were executed, a memorial was erected. It was destroyed in 1945. Its ruins were used as filling material for the construction of the underground railway. Some pieces were preserved in the Museum of Military History.

214 Goldinger and Binder, Geschichte der Republik Österreich, 238.

215 Rothländer, Die Anfänge der Wiener SS, 454.

216 Kurt Bauer, Sozialgeschichtliche Aspekte des nationalsozialistischen Juliputsches 1934, doctoral thesis in humanities and cultural sciences, University of Vienna (2001); Der Putsch von Lamprechtshausen. Zeugen des Juli 1934 berichten, edited by Andreas Maislinger (Salzburg, 1992), 35–39.

217 After the Anschluss, Otto Steinhäusl became police commissioner in Vienna and president of the International Criminal Police Commission (Interpol).

218 Jagschitz, Der Putsch, 174.

219 *Die Fackel*, nos. 917–922, 102–103.

220 Bauer, Hitlers zweiter Putsch, 222.

221 Die Großglockner Hochalpenstraße, edited by Johannes Hörl and Dietmar Schöndorfer (Vienna/Cologne/Weimar, 2015); Clemens M. Hutter, Großglockner Hochalpenstraße (Salzburg, 2007).

222 Gabriele Volsansky, Pakt auf Zeit. Das Deutsch-Österreichische Juli-Abkommen 1936 (Vienna/Cologne/Weimar, 2001), 13.

223 Volsansky, Pakt auf Zeit, 13.

224 Goldinger and Binder, Geschichte der Republik Österreich, 243.

225 Haas, Anschluß, 8.

226 Texts, including those of the démarches from the states of the Little Entente, can be found at http://www.zaoerv.de/06_1936/6_1936_1_b_578_2_582_1.pdf [last accessed on 23 June 2017].

227 Malachi Haim Hacohen, Kosmopoliten in einer etnonationalen Zeit? Juden und Österreicher in der Ersten Republik, in: Das Werden der Ersten Republik, I, 289.

228 Tálos, Das austrofaschistische Herrschaftssystem, 74–75.

229 Schulchronik Rabensburg, vol. 1 (1902–1940), 149.

230 Heinz Stritzl, Der Zeitzeuge im Gespräch mit Thomas Cik (Graz, 2016), 21.

231 Schulchronik Rabensburg, vol. 1, 147.

232 Sandgruber, Ökonomie und Politik, 400.

233 Mazower, Der dunkle Kontinent, 142–143.

234 http://sciencev1.orf.at/science/news/68025 [last accessed on 23 June 2017].

235 Lothar Höbelt, Die Heimwehren und die österreichische Politik 1927–1936 (Graz, 2017), 367.

236 Klaus Koch, Zwischen Mussolini und Hitler. August 1934 – Juli 1936, in: Außenpolitische Dokumente

der Republik Österreich 1918–1938, vol. 10: Zwischen Mussolini und Hitler, edited by Klaus Koch and Elisabeth Vyslonzil (= Fontes Rerum Austriacarum, 2nd section, vol. 96, Vienna, 2014), 22.

237 Hillgruber, Das Anschlussproblem, 169.

238 Volsansky, Pakt auf Zeit, 23.

239 Radomir Luža, Österreich und die großdeutsche Idee in der NS-Zeit (Vienna/Cologne/Graz, 1977), 37.

240 Volsansky, Pakt auf Zeit, 37 and 41.

241 Ibid., 42.

242 Außenpolitische Dokumente 10/1528 (discussion between Schuschnigg and Mussolini, undated – May 1935), 142.

243 Helge Lerider, Die Wehrpolitik der ersten österreichischen Republik im Spiegel der operativen Vorbereitungen gegen die Nachfolgestaaten der Monarchie, military studies term paper, National Defence Academy (Vienna, 1975).

244 Quoted from Ingrid Mosser, Der Legitimismus und die Frage der Habsburgerrestauration in der innenpolitischen Zielsetzung des autoritären Österreich (1933–1938), doctoral thesis, University of Vienna (1979), 42.

245 Koch, Zwischen Mussolini und Hitler, 21, and Außenpolitische Dokumente 10/1577, discussion between Schuschnigg and Hodža, dated 17 January 1936.

246 Helmut Wohnout, Das Traditionsreferat der Vaterländischen Front. Ein Beitrag über das Verhältnis der legitimistischen Bewegung zum autoritären Österreich, in: Österreich in Geschichte und Literatur, vol. 36, no. 2 (1992), 65–82, here 73.

247 Goldinger and Binder, Geschichte der Republik Österreich, 272.

248 The so-called 'Hoßbach Memorandum', in: Hans-Adolf Jacobsen, 1939–1945. Der Zweite Weltkrieg in Chronik und Dokumenten (Darmstadt, 1961), 97–104.

249 TNA, Kew, FO 371/22310, R 1193/G, 2 February 1938, Secret.

250 Hochverratsprozess gegen Dr. Guido Schmidt vor dem Wiener Volksgericht (Vienna, 1947), 676.

251 TNA, Kew, FO 371/22310, Schuschnigg to Sir George Franckenstein, 27 January 1938.

252 TNA, Kew, FO 954/1A/49, 4 February 1938.

253 Ein General im Zwielicht. Die Erinnerungen Edmund Glaises von Horstenau, edited by Peter Broucek, vol. 2 (Vienna/Cologne/Graz, 1982), 222.

254 On the presence of senior officers, see Ein General im Zwielicht, vol. 2, 222. Identical names cited by Kurt Schuschnigg, Im Kampf gegen Hitler. Die Überwindung der Anschlussidee (Vienna/Munich/Zurich, 1969), 216–251, here esp. 233. It was, therefore, not the commanders of all three branches of the Wehrmacht, as is occasionally claimed.

255 TNA, Kew, FO 371/21750, William Henry Bradshaw Mack to Lord Halifax, 8 April 1938.

256 TNA, Kew, FO 371/22310, Enclosure despatch No 56 E, 22 February 1938.

257 In Salzburg, for example. See Robert Kriechbaumer, Zwischen Österreich und Großdeutschland. Eine politische Geschichte der Salzburger Festspiele 1933–1944 (Vienna/Cologne/Weimar, 2013).

258 TNA, Kew, FO 371/21750, Mack to Halifax, 8 April 1938, 7.

259 Wiener Zeitung, 25 February 1938, 2–8.

260 Goldinger and Binder, Geschichte der Republik Österreich, 281.

261 Gerhard Botz, Die Eingliederung Österreichs in das Deutsche Reich. Planung und Verwirklichung des politisch-administrativen Anschlusses (1938–1940), 2nd expanded edition (Linz, 1976), 25.

262 Karner, '… Des Reiches Südmark'. Kärnten und Steiermark im Dritten Reich 1938–1945, in: NS-Herrschaft in Österreich 1938–1945, edited by Emmerich Tálos, Ernst Hanisch and Wolfgang Neugebauer (Vienna, 1988), 457–486, here 467.

263 Haas, Anschluß, 13.

264 *Wiener Zeitung*, 10 March 1938.

265 TNA, Kew, FO 371/21750, Mack to Halifax, 8 April 1938, 13.

266 TNA, Kew, FO 371/21750, Telegram from Sir Nevile Henderson to the Foreign Office (Sir William Strang), 7 April 1938.

267 Erwin A. Schmidl, Der 'Anschluss' Österreichs. Der deutsche Einmarsch im März 1938 (Bonn, 1994), 111.

268 Peter Broucek, Militärischer Widerstand. Studien zur österreichischen Staatsgesinnung und NS-Abwehr (Vienna/Cologne/Weimar, 2008), 143.

269 Hochverratsprozess gegen Dr. Guido Schmidt, 684. The information on the strength of the Federal Army is based on a statement made by Alfred Jansa, who had been relieved as chief of the General Staff shortly before.

270 Jonny Moser, Österreichs Juden unter der NS-Herrschaft, in: NS-Herrschaft in Österreich, 185–198, here 187.

271 Ibid.

272 Thomas Riegler, Im Fadenkreuz: Österreich und der Nahostterrorismus 1973 bis 1985 (= Zeitgeschichte im Kontext, vol. 3, Göttingen, 2011), 20–21. The figures originally compiled by Richard Bender and In-gried Gabriel (Terror in rot/weiß/rot, Zurich, 1989, 20–21) do not differentiate between terror, putsch attempts and civil war, and need to be adjusted upwards, as there is a considerable number of unknown cases, above all in relation to the armed uprising of February 1934 and the attempted putsch of July 1934.

273 TNA, Kew, PRO 30/69/705, Letter from Selby to Eden, 8 December 1934 (correct: 1933).

274 TNA, Kew, FO 371/21750, Mack to Halifax, 8 April 1938, 4.

275 Winston S. Churchill, His Complete Speeches, edited by Robert Rhodes James, vol. VI, 1935–1942 (New York/London, 1974), 5923–5926.

276 TNA, Kew, FO 371/21750, Mack to Halifax, 8 April 1938, 19–20.

277 Stefan Müller, Die versäumte Freundschaft. Österreich-Mexiko 1901–1956. Von der Aufnahme der Beziehungen bis zu Mexikos Beitritt zum Staatsvertrag (= Lateinamerikanistik, vol. 3, Vienna, 2006). For an account of the Mexican protest, its prehistory and consequences, see 132–204. The text of the protest note is on page 332.

278 Schmidl, Der 'Anschluß' Österreichs, 244–245.

279 Rudolf Agstner, Handbuch des Österreichischen Auswärtigen Dienstes, vol. 1: 1918–1938. Zentrale, Gesandtschaften und Konsulate (Vienna, 2015), 57; Erwin Matsch, Österreich und der Völkerbund, in: Conturen, vol. I (Vienna, 1994), 79–85.

280 Rahkolb, Erste Republik, 516.

281 Rudolf Neck, Wilhelm Miklas und der 'Anschluss' 1938, in: Arbeiterbewegung, Faschismus, National-bewusstsein (= Festschrift zum 20-jährigen Bestehen des Dokumentationsarchivs des Widerstandes), edited by Helmut Konrad and Wolfgang Neugebauer (Vienna, 1983), 99–113.

282 Thomas R. Grischany, Der Ostmark treue Alpensöhne. Die Integration der Österreicher in die großdeutsche Wehrmacht, 1938–45 (= Zeitgeschichte im Kontext, vol. 9, Göttingen, 2015), 59.

283 The text of the entire speech can be heard in the Österreichische Mediathek 99-38007_003_b03_k02. mp3 [last accessed on 23 June 2017].

284 Joseph Roth, Der neunte Feiertag der Revolution, in: *Frankfurter Zeitung*, 14 November 1926.

285 Grischany, Der Ostmark treue Alpensöhne, 54–55.

286 School essay, including photos, in the author's ownership.

287 TNA, Kew, FO 371/21750, Telegram from Sir Nevil Henderson (Berlin) to the Foreign Office, 3 April 1938.

288 Andreas Natter, 'Verlieren wir uns nicht in Sentimentalitäten', in: Edith Hessenberger (ed.), Grenzüberschreitungen. Von Schmugglern, Schleppern, Flüchtlingen (Schruns, 2008), 127–134. Until 1944, people who attempted to flee to Switzerland for reasons of race were considered 'not political refugees'.

289 Johannes Eidlitz (1920–2000), himself a member of one such 'scrubbing crew', mentioned this in 1988 at a conference in the National Defence Academy in Vienna with the succinct formulation: 'If it's not you, it'll be someone else. When we saw that, we didn't think anything of it.'

290 Grischany, Der Ostmark treue Alpensöhne, 23, note 7.

291 Luža, Österreich und die großdeutsche Idee, 247, note 42.

292 Valentin Sima, Die Deportation slowenischer Familien aus Kärnten I. Rahmenbedingungen, Präludium und Vorbereitung, in: Die Deportation slowenische Familien aus Kärnten 1942. Eine Dokumentation (Vienna, 2003), 64.

293 TNA, Kew, FO 371/21750, Telegram from Sir Nevil Henderson (Berlin) to the Foreign Office, 4 April 1938.

294 Maximilian Liebmann, Kirche und Anschluss, in: Kirche in Österreich 1938–1988, edited by idem, Hans Paarhammer and Alfred Rinnerthaler (Graz/Vienna/Cologne, 1990), 212–229.

295 Liebmann, Kirche und Anschluss, 228–229.

296 Ibid., 211.

297 Klaus-Dieter Mulley, Modernität oder Traditionalität? Überlegungen zum sozialstrukturellen Wandel in Österreich 1938 bis 1945, in: NS-Herrschaft in Österreich, 25–48, here 42.

298 Engelbert Dollfuß had been buried in 1934 in Hietzing Cemetery, was transferred in September 1934 to the Memorial Church and returned to Hietzing Cemetery in 1939. From the 1950s, the grave was regarded as an 'honorary grave', which ensured its upkeep. Following the completion of the report of a commission for the examination of graves of honour and honorary graves in Vienna (2003), it was rededicated – like many other gravesites – as a 'historic burial site' in 2012.

299 Lucile Dreidemy, Der Dollfuß-Mythos. Eine Biographie des Posthumen (Vienna/Cologne/Weimar, 2014), 192.

300 TNA, Kew, FO 371/21646, House of Commons session on 21 June 1938; comments by Hjalmar Schacht and memorandum about payment terms for Austrian loans. After the war, the Republic of Austria had to resume settling pre-war debts. The Rome Agreement on Austria's external debt, signed in 1952, fixed the interest rate for the conversion loan, 1934–1959, at 4.5 per cent. The loan arrears for the years 1945–1953 were covered by generalised payments; the repayment of remaining loan issues was ultimately extended to 1980.

301 Norbert Schausberger, Rüstung in Österreich 1938–1945. Eine Studie über die Wechselwirkung von Wirtschaft, Politik und Kriegführung (= Publikationen des österreichischen Instituts für Zeitgeschichte, vol. 8, Vienna, 1970), 254–255.

302 Sandgruber, Ökonomie und Politik, 423–424.

303 Karner, '… Des Reiches Südmark', 461.

304 Dietmar Petzina, Autarkiepolitik im Dritten Reich. Der nationalsozialistische Vierjahresplan (= Schriftenreihe der Vierteljahrshefte für Zeitgeschichte, vol. 16, Stuttgart, 1968).

305 Hans Kernbauer, Fritz Weber, Österreichs Wirtschaft 1938–1945, in: NS-Herrschaft in Österreich, 49–67, here 55.

306 Michael Mooslechner and Robert Stadler, Landwirtschaft und Agrarpolitik, in: NS-Herrschaft in Österreich, 69–94 and 82–83.

307 Karner, '... Des Reiches Südmark', 461.

308 Mooslechner and Stadler, Landwirtschaft, 85–86.

309 Until 1945, between 1.2 and 1.3 million Austrian men served in the Wehrmacht. This information can be found time and again, for example in Grischany, Der Ostmark treue Alpensöhne, 61, note 146, but is lacking in clarity. The best approximate values have no doubt been calculated on the basis of the meticulous work of the Wehrmacht Information Office (WASt), which carried out its work throughout the war and resumed it after the war's end. According to this, the total number of those called up included the approximately 67,000 members of the Waffen SS. It cannot be determined whether the members of the National Militia (Volkssturm) were recorded. The figure, according to which 83.2 per cent of Austrians served with the army, 13.3 per cent with the Luftwaffe and 3.5 per cent with the navy, only serves as an indication. See Grischany, Der Ostmark treue Alpensöhne, 61. The most precise survey of total numbers, regional distribution and losses can be found in Rüdiger Overmans, Deutsche militärische Verluste im Zweiten Weltkrieg (Munich, 1999), esp. 215–228.

310 Grischany, Der Ostmark treue Alpensöhne, 62–63.

311 See also Richard Germann, Neue Wege in der Militärgeschichte. Regionale Zusammensetzung 'ostmärkischer' Einheiten am Beispiel dreier Kompanien, in: Politische Gewalt und Machtausübung im 20. Jahrhundert. Zeitgeschichte, Zeitgeschehen und Kontroversen. Festschrift für Gerhard Botz (Vienna/Cologne/Weimar, 2011), 175–191.

312 Hanisch, Männlichkeiten, 71–76.

313 Ibid., 74–75.

314 Das Kleine Volksblatt, 14–20 April 1938, and Kronen-Zeitung, 24 April 1938.

315 Gerhard Jagschitz, Von der 'Bewegung' zum Apparat. Zur Phänomenologie der NDSAP 1938 bis 1945, in: NS-Herrschaft in Österreich, 487–516, here 503.

316 Elisabeth Maißer and Christine Roiter, 'NS Frauenschaft' und 'Deutsches Frauenwerk' in Oberdonau: Strukturen, Aktivistinnen und Tätigkeiten am Beispiel des Kreises Wels, in: Frauen im Reichsgau Oberdonau. Geschlechterspezifische Bruchlinien im Nationalsozialismus, edited by Gabriele Hauch (Linz, 2006), 43. The figure of half a million organised women cited here is bewildering because the National Socialist Women's League had only 2.2 million members in the entire Greater German Reich in 1939. The number only becomes more plausible if we include the League of German Girls (BDM) and other organisations close to the NSDAP.

317 Bertrand Michael Buchmann, Österreicher in der Deutschen Wehrmacht. Soldatenalltag im Zweiten Weltkrieg (Vienna/Cologne/Weimar, 2009), 22.

318 Mazower, Der dunkle Kontinent, 61.

319 Quoted from Herbert Dachs, Schule und Jugenderziehung in der 'Ostmark', in: NS-Herrschaft in Österreich, 217–242, here 217.

320 Reichsgesetzblatt (RGBL) I 1939, 777.

321 Maren Seliger, NS-Herrschaft in Wien und Niederösterreich, in: NS-Herrschaft in Österreich, 397–416, here 405.

322 Das Kleine Volksblatt, 9–11 October 1938, front pages.

323 Luža, Österreich in der NS-Zeit, 114.

324 Johannes Martinek, 'Auf zum Schwure ...'. Das Rosenkranzfest vom 7. Oktober 1938 (Vienna, 1998), 9.

325 Luža, Österreich und die großdeutsche Idee, 123–124.

326 Ibid., 179 and 187.

327 Moser, Juden, 187.

328 Gerhard Botz, Nationalsozialismus in Wien. Machtübernahme, Herrschaftssicherung, Radikalisierung 1938/39 (Vienna, 2008), 206.

329 Österreichs Hochschulen und Universitäten und das NS-Regime, in: NS-Herrschaft in Österreich, 269–282, here 271.

330 Johannes Koll, Arthur Seyß-Inquart und die deutsche Besatzungspolitik in den Niederlanden 1940–1945 (Vienna/Cologne/Weimar, 2015), 59–60.

331 Moser, Juden, 190.

332 *Frankfurter Allgemeine Zeitung*, Feuilleton, 27 January 2011: Arno Lustiger, Der Kommerzialrat [Berthold Storfer] charterte die rettende Flotte. On the Évian Conference see also Doron Rabinovici, Eichmann's Jews. The Jewish Administration of Holocaust Vienna 1938–1945 (Cambridge, 2011). Furthermore: https://de.wikipedia.org/wiki/Konferenz_von_%C3%89vian#Verlauf_und_Ergebnis_der_ Konferenz [last accessed on 23 June 2017). I am very grateful to Dr Kurt Scholz for information on the Évian Conference and the roles of Heinrich Neumann von Hethars, Berthold Storfer and Josef Löwenherz, as well as Hans Habe.

333 Hans Witek, 'Arisierungen' in Wien. Aspekte nationalsozialistischer Enteignungspolitik 1938–1940, in: NS-Herrschaft in Österreich, 199–216, here 200.

334 Seliger, Wien und Niederösterreich, 403.

335 On the term and its various interpretations and fields of application: Berthold Unfried, Anwendungsorientierter Antisemitismus, in: Politische Gewalt und Machtausübung im 20. Jahrhundert. Zeitgeschichte, Zeitgeschehen und Kontroversen, in: Politische Gewalt und Machtausübung, 215–234.

336 Moser, Juden, 193.

337 https://de.wikipedia.org/wiki/Blockleiter#Bezeichnung_.E2.80.9EBlockwart.E2.80.9C [last accessed on 23 June 2017].

338 Maißer and Roiter, 'NS Frauenschaft', 29–75.

339 Rabensburg school chronicle for 1940/41.

340 Luža, Österreich in der NS-Zeit, 135.

341 Karner, '… Des Reiches Südmark', 474.

342 Quoted from Ernst Hanisch, Westösterreich, in: NS-Herrschaft in Österreich, 437– 456, here 442.

343 Jagschitz, Von der 'Bewegung' zum Apparat, 505.

344 Christina Altenstraßer, Zwischen Ideologie und ökonomischer Notwendigkeit. Der 'Reichsarbeitsdienst für die weibliche Jugend', in: Frauen in Oberdonau, 107–129, here 107.

345 On Max Weiler, see the foreword from Ilse Krumpöck in the catalogue of the special exhibition in the Museum of Military History, 1 December 2004 – 6 February 2005: Krisenjahre. Max Weiler und der Krieg (Vienna, 2004), 11–40; furthermore: Nicht größer als eine Ameise. Oskar Laske und der Erste Weltkrieg. Katalog zur Sonderausstellung im Heeresgeschichtlichen Museum 11. April bis 28. Juni 2002 (Vienna, 2002), 3–4.

346 Kurt Mühlberger, Vertriebene Intelligenz 1938. Der Verlust geistiger und menschlicher Potenz an der Universität Wien von 1938 bis 1945 (Vienna, 1993).

347 Ulrich Weinzierl, Österreichische Schriftsteller im Exil, in: NS-Herrschaft in Österreich, 571–576, here 572.

348 Johann Christoph Allmayer-Beck, Die Österreicher im Zweiten Weltkrieg, in: Unser Heer. 300 Jahre österreichisches Soldatentum in Krieg und Frieden (Vienna/Munich/Zurich, 1963), 342–375, here 346.

349 Overmans, Deutsche militärische Verluste, 225.

350 Adam Tooze, The Wages of Destruction: The Making and Breaking of the Nazi Economy (London, 2006), 513–514.

351 Johann Gross, Spiegelgrund. Leben in NS-Erziehungsanstalten (Vienna, 2013).

352 Neugebauer, Der österreichische Widerstand, cites 25,000 to 30,000. The total number of people killed in the 'euthanasia' killing centres in the Greater German Reich is estimated at 70,000.

353 The whole text can be found, among other places, in Neugebauer, Der österreichische Widerstand, 128. On Bishop Memelauer, see also the diploma thesis from Dieter Seybold, Michael Memelauer – ein unpolitischer Seelsorgebischof? Eine vergleichende Untersuchung der Enunziationen eines österreichischen Diözesanbischofs (1933–1934), diploma thesis, University of Vienna (1998). Hartheim began to destroy files in autumn 1944. For the most varied reasons, the main perpetrators could not be put on trial.

354 Roman Sandgruber, Die NS-Konzentrationslager Mauthausen und seine Nebenlager, in: Oberösterreichische Nachrichten, 10 May 2008, 6.

355 https://de.wikipedia.org/wiki/KZ_Mauthausen_Errichtung_des_Lagers [last accessed on 23 June 2017].

356 Wolfgang Neugebauer, Das NS-Terrorsystem, in: NS-Herrschaft in Österreich, 163–183, here 171. The number of Austrians who lost their lives in Mauthausen amounted to 1,650 people.

357 Enzyklopädie des Nationalsozialismus, edited by Wolfgang Benz (Stuttgart, 1997), 730. Neugebauer, Der österreichische Widerstand, 236, cites 9,000 to 10,000 victims, a figure that is far higher than that given by Benz and one that would mean that most Austrian Roma and Sinti were killed. Erika Thurner, Nationalsozialismus und Zigeuner in Österreich (Vienna/Salzburg, 1983), assumes, in turn, that half the Austrian Roma and Sinti were killed or died. Ultimately, all of these figures are estimates.

358 Wolfgang Etschmann, Rüstungswirtschaft und KZ-System in Österreich 1938 bis 1945, in: Walküre und der Totenwald, 102–118, here 111.

359 Hans Maršálek, Die Geschichte des Konzentrationslagers Mauthausen. Dokumentation (Vienna, 2006), 85.

360 Ibid., 122.

361 Ibid., 151.

362 A definitive assessment of how many prisoners and POWs were taken to Mauthausen from 1938 to 1945, how many were transferred, died during death marches or were killed, is no longer possible. The entries in the camp physician's books of the dead are not complete; entire categories are missing. Ultimately, all figures can only serve as indications. See Maršálek, Mauthausen, esp. 140–154.

363 Hubert Speckner, Kriegsgefangenenlager in der 'Ostmark' 1939–1945. Zur Geschichte der Mannschaftsstammlager und Offizierslager in den Wehkreisen XVII und XVIII, doctoral thesis in humanities, University of Vienna (1999), 38.

364 Hubert Feichtlbauer, Fonds für Versöhnung, Frieden und Zusammenarbeit. Späte Anerkennung, Geschichte, Schicksale (Vienna, 2005), 54.

365 Robert Stadler and Michael Mooslechner, St. Johann i. Pg. 1938–1945. Der nationalsozialistische 'Markt Pongau'. Der '20. Juli 1944' in Goldegg. Widerstand und Verfolgung (Salzburg, 1986), 98–115.

366 Sebastian Haffner, Anmerkungen zu Hitler (Munich, 1978), 55.

367 Grischany, Der Ostmark treue Alpensöhne, 232–243, lists numerous examples for this fact.

11 The War of Attrition

368 On the entire course see: Uwe Maydell, Der Aufmarsch zum Balkanfeldzug 1941 mit besonderer Berücksichtigung des österreichischen Raums, military studies term paper, 6th General Staff Course (Innsbruck, 1972).

369   On the German occupation of Slovenia and the subsequent bloody history of the country see Tamara
      Griesser-Pečar, Das zerrissene Volk. Slowenien 1941–1946. Okkupation, Kollaboration, Bürgerkrieg,
      Revolution (Vienna/Cologne/Graz, 2003).

370   Hitler passed the plaque on to the Berlin Armoury, where it was destroyed during the bombing of
      Berlin. It thus suffered a similar fate to the train carriage of Compiègne, in which Germany had signed
      the armistice with the Allies on 11 November 1918 and which had been used on 22 June 1940 to accept
      France's surrender. As the original carriage was destroyed in Berlin, France had a replica displayed in
      Compiègne after the Second World War. No comparable reproduction of the Princip plaque was made.

371   Richard Germann, Österreichische Soldaten in Ost- und Südosteuropa 1941–1945. Deutsche Krieger –
      nationalsozialistische Verbrecher – österreichische Opfer? PhD thesis, University of Vienna (2006),
      146–151.

372   Walter Manoschek, 'Serbien ist judenfrei'. Militärische Besatzungspolitik und Judenvernichtung in Ser-
      bien 1941/42 (Munich, 1995). Also Walter Manoschek and Hans Safrian, Österreicher in der Wehr-
      macht, in: NS-Herrschaft in Österreich, 331–360. In the case of the latter, it is noticeable that the
      authors do not deal comprehensively with the topic but instead focus on Yugoslavia. See also Buchmann,
      Die Österreicher in der Wehrmacht, chapter 23, 'Partisaneneinsatz und Repressalien', 190–196.

373   Quoted from Josef Rausch, Der Partisanenkampf in Kärnten im Zweiten Weltkrieg (= Militärhistor-
      ische Schriftenreihe, vol. 39/40, Vienna, 1979), 6.

374   Das Kleine Volksblatt, 23 June 1941.

375   Johann Christoph Allmayer-Beck, 'Herr Oberleitnant, det lohnt doch nicht!'. Kriegserinnerungen an
      die Jahre 1938 bis 1945, edited by Erwin A. Schmidl (Vienna/Cologne/Weimar, 2013), 168.

376   Christina Altenstraßer, 'Wir haben das sehr gut gemacht das Ganze.' Erinnerungen einer ehemaligen
      Nationalsozialistin, in: Frauen in Oberdonau, 77–88, here 81.

377   Allmayer-Beck, Die Österreicher im Zweiten Weltkrieg, 335.

378   Examples are cited in Buchmann, Österreicher in der Deutschen Wehrmacht, chapter 'Kriegsverbre-
      chen', 178–189.

379   Grischany, Der Ostmark treue Alpensöhne, 228.

380   Overmans, Deutsche militärische Verluste, 216–228.

381   Maria Fritsche, Österreichische Deserteure und Selbstverstümmler in der Deutschen Wehrmacht (Vi-
      enna/Cologne/Weimar, 2004), 25. Fritsche calculates a total number of around 1,100 deserters from the
      Eastern March who were also executed for the offences they were charged with. Here, a clear numerical
      increase in the second half of the war and, above all, during its final months were recorded.

382   Siegfried Beer, Stefan Karner, Der Krieg aus der Luft. Kärnten und Steiermark 1941–1945 (Graz,
      1992), 24.

383   See Markus Reisner, Bomben auf Wiener Neustadt. Die Zerstörung eines der wichtigsten Rüstungsz-
      entren des Deutschen Reiches – Der Luftkrieg über der 'Allzeit Getreuen' von 1943 bis 1945 (Wiener
      Neustadt, [2013]).

384   Manfried Rauchensteiner, Der Luftkrieg gegen Österreich im Kontext des Zweiten Weltkriegs, in:
      Zeitenwende 1943, 50–66, here 53.

385   Thomas Albrich, Luftkrieg über der Alpenfestung 1943–1945. Der Gau Tirol-Vorarlberg und die Op-
      erationszone Alpenvorland (Innsbruck, 2014), 39.

386   Rauchensteiner, Der Luftkrieg, 62.

387   Germann, Österreichische Soldaten, 55.

388   Bruckmüller, Nation Österreich, 349.

389   Sima, Die Deportation, 68.

390   Rausch, Partisanenkampf, 13.

391 Buchmann, Österreicher in der Deutschen Wehrmacht, 195.

392 Siegwald Ganglmair, Österreicher in den alliierten Armeen, 1939 bis 1945, in: Walküre und der Toten-wald. Das Kriegsjahr 1944, exhibition catalogue of the Museum of Military History (Vienna, 1994), 42–70, here esp. 44–52. A very different figure is given by Peter Eppel, Österreicher im Exil 1938–1945, in: NS-Herrschaft in Österreich, 553–570, here 554.

393 Buchmann, Österreicher in der Deutschen Wehrmacht, 110.

394 Ganglmair, Österreicher, 64–66.

395 The following thesis deals with this at length: Willibald Ingo Holzer, Die österreichischen Bataillone im Verband der NOV I POJ. Die Kampfgruppe Avantgarde Steiermark. Die Partisanengruppe Leo-ben-Donawitz, PhD thesis, University of Vienna (1971).

396 Christoph Hatschek, Alfred Palisek, Landesverräter oder Patrioten (Graz/Vienna/Cologne, 2001). The book with the names of the signatories can be seen in the permanent exhibition of the Museum of Military History on the Second World War and the Nazi era.

397 Ganglmayer, Österreicher, 56–61. A higher figure, namely 6,703 people, is cited by Florian Traussnig, Militärischer Widerstand von außen. Österreicher in US-Armee und Kriegsgeheimdienst im Zweiten Weltkrieg (Vienna/Cologne/Weimar, 2016), 18, note 21. The information that this figure refers to those 'born in Austria' gives an indication of the vagueness, because people were also included who had per-haps already for some time possessed US citizenship.

398 Traussnig, Militärischer Widerstand von außen, 20.

399 Moser, Österreichs Juden, 194.

400 The other victims of racial and political persecution should be added to this figure.

401 See Irene Suchy, Strasshof an der Nordbahn. Die NS-Geschichte eines Ortes und ihre Aufarbeitung (Vienna, 2012).

402 Helene Maimann, Vergangenheit, die nie vergeht. NS-Herrschaft in Österreich 1938–1945, in: Das Neue Österreich. Begleitband zur Sonderausstellung im Oberen Belvedere, edited by Günter Dürigl and Herbert Frodl (Vienna, 2005), 79–87, here 85–86. The statements of Simon Wiesenthal are con-tained in his so-called Guilt and Atonement Memorandum for Josef Klaus, which will be dealt with in more detail later.

403 Oliver Rathkolb, Die paradoxe Republik. Österreich 1945 bis 2015 (Vienna, 2015), 377–383.

404 Brigitte Bailer, Bertrand Perz, Aleksander Lasik, Winfried Garscha, Claudia Kuretsidis-Haider, Johannes Laimighofer, Siefried Sanwald and Hans Schafranek, Endbericht Österreicher und Österreicherinnen als TäterInnen im Lagerkomplex des KZ Auschwitz. Forschungsprojekt für einen Teilbereich der Neu-gestaltung der österreichischen Gedenkstätte im Staatlichen Museum Auschwitz-Birkenau (Projekt P 12-1089 des Zukunftsfonds der Republik Österreich, 2013), 168–171 and 174–179, cited and placed in the context of other studies in: Peter Schwarz, Der Anteil der Österreicher am Holocaust. Endbericht zum Projekt P16-2561 des Zukunftsfonds der Republik Österreich, January 2017. Enquiries about the background of guards in Auschwitz were carried out by the Polish historian Aleksander Lasik.

405 Freund, Perz, Industrialisierung durch Zwangsarbeit, in: NS-Herrschaft in Österreich, 95–114, here 110.

406 For this figure, I am very grateful to Dr Elisabeth Klamper from the Documentation Centre of Austrian Resistance.

407 Karola Fings, Sklaven für die 'Heimatfront', in: Das Deutsche Reich und der Zweite Weltkrieg, ed-ited by the Militärgeschichtliches Forschungsamt, vol. 9/1: Die deutsche Kriegsgesellschaft 1939–1945 (Munich, 2004), 269–270.

408 Maršálek, Mauthausen, a facsimile of the order can be found on page 322.

409 All headlines from *Das Kleine Volksblatt*, 31 January, 2 February, 4 February, 19 February, 2 June, 14 August, 26 October, 31 October and 3 November 1943.

410 Wolfgang Mueller, Die sowjetische Besatzung in Österreich 1945–1955 und ihre politische Mission (Vienna/Cologne/Weimar, 2005), 19.

411 Churchill, Complete Speeches, vol. VI, 6593.

412 Mueller, Die sowjetische Besatzung, 23.

413 Charles de Gaulle's French government-in-exile acceded to the Declaration on Austria in December 1943.

414 Manfried Rauchensteiner, Der Sonderfall. Die Besatzungszeit in Österreich 1945 bis 1955 (Graz/Vienna/Cologne, 1979), 57.

415 See, especially for the focus on Austria: Nadine Hauer, Gefangene Psychiatrie. Soldaten und Kriegstrauma (Vienna, 1997).

416 See Burkhart Mueller-Hildebrand, Das Heer 1933–1945, vol. III: Der Zweifrontenkrieg (Frankfurt am Main, 1969), esp. 260–266. The figures ascertained for the losses of the army and the Waffen SS are vague in some respects and must in any case be supplemented by the figures for the Luftwaffe and the navy. The total number is ultimately only an approximate value.

417 For the exact figures see Speckner, Kriegsgefangenenlager in der 'Ostmark', 45–46.

418 Speckner, Kriegsgefangenenlager in der 'Ostmark', 212.

419 Ibid., 281–282.

420 Freund and Perz, Industrialisierung, 104.

421 For a full discussion see Wolfgang Neugebauer, Der österreichische Widerstand 1938–1945 (Vienna, 2008), 46.

422 Ernst Hanisch, Gibt es einen spezifisch österreichischen Widerstand?, in: Widerstand. Ein Problem zwischen Theorie und Geschichte, edited by Peter Steinbach (Cologne, 1987), 163–176, here 173.

423 Neugebauer, Der österreichische Widerstand, 56–57.

424 For the figures see Erika Weinzierl, Kirchlicher Widerstand gegen den Nationalsozialismus, in: Themen der Zeitgeschichte und der Gegenwart. Arbeiterbewegung – NS-Herrschaft – Rechtsextremismus. Ein Resümé aus Anlass des 60. Geburtstags von Wolfgang Neugebauer (Vienna, 2004), 78.

425 For the text see Neugebauer, Der österreichische Widerstand, 124.

426 The figures for Austrian victims of resistance and persecution have repeatedly been and remain the subject of debate. The statistics generally demonstrate a steady increase, which can be traced back to additional sources and more differentiated analytical methods. The Polish foreign minister, long-time ambassador to Austria and later president of the International Auschwitz Council, Władisław Bartoszeswski, cited during a speech to the Austrian parliament on 4 May 2000 around 86,800 Austrians as victims of the Nazi regime, including 51,500 Jews. This figure was inexplicable and obsolete even then. Recent research by the Documentation Centre of Austrian Resistance, above all the collection of names of Jewish victims, yielded more than 63,000 people. If we add those whose names could not be determined, as well as the up to 9,000 Roma and Sinti, 25,000 people who were victims of medical experiments, as well as 9,500 political persecutees, a total number of around 110,000 people emerges. See Brigitte Bailer and Gerhard Ungar, Die namentliche Erfassung der österreichischen Holocaustopfer und Namentliche Erfassung der österreichischen Opfer politischer Verfolgung, in: Opferschicksale. Jahrbuch 2013 des Dokumentationsarchivs des Österreichischen Widerstandes (Vienna, 2013), 63–124.

427 Steinbach, Der militärische Widerstand und seine Beziehungen zu den zivilen Gruppierungen des

Widerstandes, in: Aufstand des Gewissens. Militärischer Widerstand gegen Hitler und das NS-Regime 1933–1945, edited by the Militärgeschichtliches Forschungsamt (Herford/Bonn, 1987), 238.

428 See Peter Broucek, Ein Verschwörer gegen Hitler und für Österreich. Der Generalstabsoffizier Erwin Lahousen, in: idem., Militärischer Widerstand, 310–344.

429 Radomir Luža, Der Widerstand in Österreich 1938–1945 (Vienna, 1983). This account, however, provides very little information on the military resistance. Worth consulting are also the volumes *Widerstand und Verfolgung in … 1933–1945*, issued since 1975 by the Documentation Centre of Austrian Resistance.

430 Broucek, Ein Verschwörer gegen Hitler und für Österreich. Der Generalstabsoffizier Erwin Lahousen, in: Österreich in Geschichte und Literatur, vol. 49, no. 2 (2005), 76–97.

431 The file with the designation 'Chef der Heeresrüstung und Befehlshaber des Ersatzheeres, AHA Ia VIII Nr.4500/41 gKdos, Berlin 16. Oktober 1941', a copy of which is in the study collection of the Museum of Military History / Military History Institute, Vienna, MWI 1945/14 P.

432 Lecture manuscript of Carl Szokoll for a speech to the Berlin State Centre for Political Education on 16 June 1980.

433 Gerd R. Ueberschär, Stauffenberg. Der 20. Juli 1944 (Frankfurt am Main, 2004), 173.

434 Ludwig Jedlicka, Ein unbekannter Bericht Kaltenbrunners über die Lage in Österreich im September 1944, in: Österreich in Geschichte und Literatur (Vienna, 1960), no. 2, 82–87, here 84.

435 Germann, Österreichische Soldaten, 186–198.

436 Grischany, Der Ostmark treue Alpensöhne, 275–276.

13 Rubble

437 Aside from desertion, there were the much more numerous cases of withdrawal, which aimed at evading service in the Wehrmacht by the most varied means. Some of the Carinthian Slovenes who joined the partisans also belonged in this category. In any case, the figures cited by Maria Fritsche and the data of Grischany contrast starkly with the numbers given by Thomas Geldmacher, according to whom there were 4,000 documented cases of desertion and 30,000 to 40,000 withdrawals. Of those deserters who were caught again, between 1,200 and 1,400 were executed, according to Geldmacher. See Thomas Geldmacher, 'Auf Nimmerwiedersehen'. Fahnenflucht, unerlaubte Entfernung und das Problem, die Tatbestände auseinander zu halten, in: Opfer der NS-Militärjustiz. Urteilspraxis, Strafvollzug, Entschädigungspolitik in Österreich (Vienna, 2003), 133–194. Fritsche, Österreichische Deserteure, 24–25, calculated 1,100 death sentences carried out for desertion, as well as 456 executions for undermining military morale.

438 Fritsche, Österreichische Deserteure, 33.

439 Grischany, Der Ostmark treue Alpensöhne, where this list appears in approximately the same word order.

440 Germann, Österreichische Soldaten, 264–281.

441 Hanisch, Männlichkeiten, 90.

442 Speckner, Kriegsgefangenenlager, 218–219. Here is also a reproduction of a map of the camps with American inmates.

443 Georg Hoffmann, Fliegerlynchjustiz. Gewalt gegen abgeschossene alliierte Flugzeugbesatzungen 1943–1945 (= Krieg in der Geschichte, vol. 88, Paderborn, 2015), 173.

444 Ibid., 316.

445 Ibid., 182–183.

446 This, therefore, took place months before the first known instances of lynch law in the 'Old Reich',

namely in Rüsselsheim (26 August 1944) and Essen (December 1944). See Ralf Blank, Luftkrieg und Heimatfront, in: Das Deutsche Reich und der Zweite Weltkrieg, vol. 9/1: Die deutsche Kriegsgesellschaft 1939 bis 1945 (Munich, 2004).

447 This question and many answers can be found in Harald Welzer, Täter. Wie aus ganz normalen Menschen Massenmörder werden (Frankfurt am Main, 2005).

448 Hoffmann, Fliegerlynchjustiz, 233–234.

449 See also Altenstraßer, '… wir haben das sehr gut gemacht…', 86.

450 Manfried Rauchensteiner, Flucht und Vertreibung, in: exhibition catalogue of the Museum of Military History: Der Krieg in Österreich '45 (Vienna, 1995), 91–92.

451 Maršálek, Mauthausen, 151.

452 On what was commonly called the 'Mühlviertel hare hunt' see Matthias Kaltenbrunner, Flucht aus dem Todesblock. Der Massenausbruch sowjetischer Offiziere aus dem Block 20 des KZ Mauthausen und die 'Mühlviertler Hasenjagd'. Hintergründe, Folgen, Aufarbeitung. (= Der Nationalsozialismus und seine Folgen, vol. 5, Innsbruck, 2012).

453 An Austrian historical commission appointed in 1998 ascertained that, of 55,000 Jews who were involved in the construction of the Reich Protective Position and forced to partake in the subsequent evacuation marches, 28,600 lost their lives on Austrian territory.

14 The Waltz of Freedom

454 On the military events: Manfried Rauchensteiner, Der Krieg in Österreich 1945 (= Schriften des Heeresgeschichtlichen Museums, vol. 5, Vienna, 1984; reprint 2015).

455 Rauchensteiner, Der Krieg in Österreich, 491.

456 Diary of Marie Kobsik, Rabensburg (copy in the author's possession).

457 Die Rote Armee in Österreich. Sowjetische Besatzung 1945–1955, vol. 2: Dokumente, edited by Stefan Karner, Barbara Stelzl-Marx and Alexander Tschubarjan (Graz/Vienna/Munich, 2005), 69.

458 This interesting statement is made by Wolfgang Wagner, Die Besatzungszeit aus sowjetischer Sicht. Die Errichtung der sowjetischen Besatzungsmacht in Österreich von 1945 bis 1946 im Spiegel ihrer Lageberichte, diploma thesis, University of Vienna, 1998, 30.

459 Renner is said to have already announced his intention on 2 April of playing an active part in creating a new Austria. At any rate, he reported to the Soviet command. On the following day, the soundings began. According to a Soviet source, Stalin ordered that Renner should be sought out. This version has now been called into doubt. See also Mueller, Die sowjetische Besatzungspolitik, 75–77.

460 The Russian translation and German reverse translation in: Die Rote Armee in Österreich, 102–105, here 105.

461 Archives of the Austrian Institute of Contemporary History, Vienna, Inv.Nr. 535/NL-2/Renner.

462 Oliver Rathkolb, Die Zweite Republik (seit 1945), in: Geschichte Österreichs, edited by Thomas Winkelbauer, 356.

463 Franz Marek. Beruf und Berufung Kommunist. Lebenserinnerungen und Schlüsseltexte, edited by Maximilian Graf and Sarah Knoll (Vienna, 2017), 48.

464 Wilfried Aichinger, Sowjetische Österreichpolitik 1943–1945, doctoral thesis, University of Vienna, 1977, 169. The command in question is in Appendix II/10.

465 The thoughts of Ernst Hanisch on the 'triple Anschluss' will be considered further below. See also Hanisch, März 1938: eine Salzburger Perspektive, in: Der März 1938 in Salzburg. Symposion Feindbilder (= Salzburger Diskussionen, vol. 10, Salzburg, 1988), 20–28.

466 For explanations of this highly confusing matter, I am grateful to Professor Wilhelm Brauneder. See also Wilhelm Brauneder, Österreich 1918 bis 1938. 'Erste' oder wie viel 'Republiken'?, in: Studien, vol. IV (Frankfurt am Main, 2011), 299–300.

467 Diary of Marie Kobsik, Rabensburg.

468 Mitteilungen des Dokumentationsarchivs des Österreichischen Widerstands, vol. 229, December 2016, 6–7.

469 The data is extremely imprecise, since concentration camp prisoners, refugees and resettlers were not included. The figures therefore fluctuate between 24,000 and 35,000. See also Johann Ulrich, Der Luftkrieg über Österreich 1939–1945 (= Militärhistorische Schriftenreihe, vols. 5/6, Vienna, 1967), 40. Individual items of evidence can be found in the history of the federal states published by the Dr Wilfried Haslauer Library, Salzburg, and in the studies produced in the individual states on the aerial war.

470 The figures in Rauchensteiner, Der Krieg in Österreich, 391–394.

471 Mueller, Die sowjetische Besatzung, 27.

472 Nikolai Tolstoy, Die Verratenen von Jalta. Englands Schuld vor der Geschichte (Munich, 1977).

473 Grießer-Pečar, Das zerrissene Volk, 425–470.

474 See also Theodor Körner, Zwei Monate Aufbauarbeit in Wien. Sozialistische Hefte, 2nd series (Vienna, 1945).

475 Mueller, Die sowjetische Besatzungsmacht, 114.

476 Sowjetische Politik in Österreich, document no. 19: Stenograph of the report on the domestic political situation in Austria (General Svevolod Merkulov), after 18 August 1945, 183–205, here 191.

477 The wording of this law and of the others named below can be found in the Staatsgesetzblätter (StGBl) 1945.

478 StGBl, no. 9/1945.

479 On this subject, see Rauchensteiner, Nachkriegsösterreich, 416, and Hans Michael Roithner, Österreichische Wehrpolitik zwischen 1945 und 1955, teacher training term paper, University of Vienna, 1974.

480 Ibid., session of 4 September 1945.

481 Protokolle des Kabinettsrats, vol. 3 (Vienna, 2003), 3 ff.

482 Letter from Johann Koplenig and Friedl Fürnberg to Stalin, 14 October 1945, in: Sowjetische Politik in Österreich, 211–219.

483 It will never be possible to calculate precisely the actual number of prisoners of war. Ultimately, here, too, all figures given are approximate values.

15 Stern Men

484 Quoted in Ulrike Engelsberger and Robert Kriechbaumer, Als der Westen golden wurde (= Schriften des Forschungsinstitutes für politische-historische Studien der Dr.-Wilfried-Haslauer-Bibliothek, vol. 25, Vienna/Cologne/Weimar, 2005), 12.

485 Austrian State Archives, Archives of the Republic (hereafter AdR), Pol. 1946, Österreich 15, Zl. 111.977.

486 Manfried Rauchensteiner, Stalinplatz 4. Sitz des Alliierten Rates 1945–1955, in: 100 Jahre Haus der Industrie 1911–2011 (Vienna, 2011), 294.

487 Protokolle des Ministerrats der Zweiten Republik, Kabinett Leopold Figl I, 20. Dezember 1945 bis 8. November 1949, edited by Gertrude Enderle-Burcel, vol. I/1 (Vienna, 2004), 305.

488 Austrian National Library, Microfilms, Allied Commission Austria (hereafter ALCO), P(45)22, Serial No. 1, 28 November 1945, and ALCO, M(45)10, unofficial US transcript.

489 Sandgruber, Ökonomie und Politik, 464.

490 Die Rote Armee in Österreich, Bericht Merkulov, 301.

491 James Jay Carafano, 'Waltzing into the Cold War'. US Army Intelligence Operations in Postwar Austria, 1944–1948, in: The Vranitzky Era in Austria, edited by Günter Bischof, Anton Pelinka and Ferdinand Karlhofer (= Contemporary Austrian Studies, vol. 7, New Brunswick/London, 1999), 165–189, here 166.

492 AdR, PräsKzl Zl. 476/PrK/46.

493 Burian, Österreich und der Völkerbund, 121.

494 Ulrich, Der Luftkrieg, 57–64.

495 The figures in Thomas Albrich, Exodus durch Österreich (Innsbruck, 1987); Mazower, Der dunkle Kontinent, 315.

496 Nečak, Die österreichisch-jugoslawischen Beziehungen, 196.

497 See the article by Gabriele Stieber, Die Lösung des Flüchtlingsproblems 1945–1960, in: Österreich in den Fünfzigern, edited by Thomas Albrich, Klaus Eisterer, Michael Gehler and Rolf Steininger (= Innsbrucker Forschungen zur Zeitgeschichte, vol. 11, Innsbruck/Vienna, 1995). Also Thomas Albrich, Asylland wider Willen. Die Problematik der 'Displaced Persons' in Österreich 1945–1948, in: Die bevormundete Nation. Österreich und die Alliierten 1945–1949, edited by Günter Bischof and Josef Leidenfrost (= Innsbrucker Forschungen zur Zeitgeschichte, vol. 4, Innsbruck, 1988), 217–244. Specifically regarding the Sudeten Germans: Cornelia Znoy, Die Vertreibung der Sudetendeutschen nach Österreich 1945/46. Unter besonderer Berücksichtigung der Bundesländer Wien und Niederösterreich, diploma thesis, University of Vienna (1995).

498 Rathkolb, Die paradoxe Republik, 37. The author hereby corrects the view that it was Minister of Information Felix Hurdes who introduced the phrase.

499 Regarding the dispute over the Imperial Regalia, see Matthias Pape, Ungleiche Brüder. Österreich und Deutschland 1945–1965 (Cologne/Weimar/Vienna, 2000), 173–180.

500 Siegfried Beer, Die Besatzungsmacht Großbritannien, in: Österreich unter alliierter Besatzung 1945–1955, edited by Alfred Ableitinger, Siegfried Beer and Eduard G. Staudinger (= Studien zu Politik und Verwaltung, vol. 63, Vienna/Cologne/Graz, 1998), 65.

501 Salzburger Nachrichten, 14 December 1945.

502 Ministerratsprotokolle Figl, I/1, 320.

503 Die Rote Armee in Österreich, vol. 2, 683.

504 Die Rote Armee in Österreich, 329–331, doc. no. 71.

505 Mueller, Die sowjetische Besatzung, 41.

506 A list of the companies affected is appended to the thesis by Waltraud Brunner, Das Deutsche Eigentum und das Ringen um den österreichischen Staatsvertrag, doctoral thesis, University of Vienna (1976).

507 Report by John Erhardt on the situation in Austria, in: Foreign Relations of the United States (hereafter FRUS), 1946/V (Washington, DC, 1975), 376–383.

508 Neugebauer, Das NS-Terrorsystem, 177.

509 Klaus-Dietmar Henke and Hans Woller (eds.), Politische Säuberungen in Europa. Die Abrechnung mit Faschismus und Kollaboration nach dem Zweiten Weltkrieg (Munich, 1991), 292.

510 Kriechbaumer, Politische Kultur, 45.

511 Mueller, Die sowjetische Besatzungsmacht, 57.

512 Butschek, Österreichische Wirtschaftsgeschichte, 251.

513 AdR, PräsKzl Zl. 239/47, 6. I. 1947.

514 Mueller, Die sowjetische Besatzungspolitik, 161.

515 On the Yugoslavian territorial demands, see Gerald Stourzh, Um Einheit und Freiheit, 63–67. The Yugoslavian publication designed to substantiate the claim is entitled: The Question of 200,000 Yu-

goslavs in Austria. The Slovene Carinthia and the Burgenland Croats (Belgrade, 1947). The following year, an even more comprehensive publication was presented: Documents on the Carinthian Question (Belgrade, 1948). The Austrian counterstatement was written by Max Hoffinger. Hoffinger was also a member of the Austrian delegation in London.

516 The printed conference protocols of the London and the later Moscow round of negotiations, with the most important annexes, are in the AdR, Pol 1946, P-St.

517 Wilfried Loth, Stalins ungeliebtes Kind. Warum Moskau die DDR nicht wollte (Berlin, 1994), 83–88.

518 Lower Austrian Regional Archives (NÖ LA), 339-Pr. 1/47.

519 Sandgruber, Ökonomie und Politik, 449.

520 Letter by Johann Koplenig and Friedl Fürrnberg to Stalin, 31 March 1947, in: Sowjetische Politik in Österreich, 363–371, esp. 363–365.

521 Regarding this issue, see the doctoral thesis by Friedrich Weber, Die linken Sozialisten in Österreich 1945–1948, University of Salzburg (1977).

522 FRUS, 1947/II, 1172, Erhardt to Marshall, 7 May 1947.

523 FRUS, 1947/II, 1176, Erhardt to Marshall, 16 May 1947.

524 FRUS, 1947/II, 1180, Marshall to US legation in Vienna, 28 May 1947.

525 See Wilfried Mähr, Von der UNRRA zum Marshallplan. Die amerikanische Wirtschafts- und Finanzhilfe an Österreich 1945, doctoral thesis, University of Vienna (1985), 199–231.

526 Mähr, UNRRA, 247.

527 Ibid.

528 The figure can be found in Stefan Karner, Zu den Rehabilitierungen von Kriegsgefangenen und Zivilisten in der Sowjetunion unter Chruschtschow und in den 1990er-Jahren. Dargestellt am Beispiel von deutschen und österreichischen Kriegsgefangenen, in: Sowjetische Schauprozesse in Mittel- und Osteuropa, edited by Csaba Szabó (= Publikationen der ungarischen Geschichtsforschung in Wien, vol. XIII, Vienna, 2015), 40–49, here 32.

529 Florian Weiß, 'Gesamtverhalten: Nicht sich in den Vordergrund stellen'. Die österreichische Bundesregierung und die westeuropäische Integration 1947–1957, in: Österreich und die europäische Integration seit 1945. Aspekte einer wechselvollen Entwicklung, edited by Michael Gehler and Rolf Steininger (Vienna/Cologne/Weimar, 2014), 25–26.

530 Protocol of the discussion between A. Zhdanov, Johann Koplenig and Friedl Fürnberg regarding the prospects and tactics of the KPÖ, 13 February 1948, in: Sowjetische Politik in Österreich, doc. 48, 453–465.

531 Erwin A. Schmidl, 'Rosinenbomber' über Wien? Alliierte Pläne zur Luftversorgung Wiens im Falle einer sowjetischen Blockade 1948–1953, in: Österreich im frühen Kalten Krieg, edited by Erwin A. Schmidl (Vienna/Cologne/Weimar, 2000), 171–192.

532 National Archives and Records Administration, College Park, Maryland (hereafter NARA), 740.00119 Control (Austria) 6-1948, Telegram from Keyes to Secretary of State Marshall, 19 June 1948.

533 ALCO, 73rd to 78th meetings, 30 April to 16 July 1948, protocols and unofficial US transcript.

534 Mazower, Der dunkle Kontinent, 352.

535 Sandgruber, Ökonomie und Politik, 452.

536 Peter Autengruber, Kleinparteien in Österreich 1945 bis 1966 (Innsbruck/Vienna, 1997).

537 See: Aufstieg und Fall des VdU. Briefe und Protokolle aus privaten Nachlässen 1948–1955, edited by Lothar Höbelt (Vienna/Cologne/Weimar, 2015), esp. 19–20 and 33.

538 Carafano, 'Waltzing into the Cold War', 173.

539 Wolfgang Mueller, Gab es eine 'verpasste Chance'? Die sowjetische Haltung zum Staatsvertrag 1946 – 1952, in: Der Österreichische Staatsvertrag (The Austrian State Treaty), edited by Arnold Suppan, Gerald

Stourzh and Wolfgang Mueller (= Archiv für österreichische Geschichte, vol. 110, Vienna, 2005), 89–120, here 110–113. Also Brigitte Bailer-Galanda, Winfried Garschah, Der österreichische Staatsvertrag und die Entnazifizierung, in: Der Österreichische Staatsvertrag, 629–654. On the escalation of Soviet punitive measures: Barbara Stelzl-Marx, Zum Tode verurteilt. Die sowjetische Strafjustiz in Österreich im frühen Kalten Krieg, in: Sowjetische Schauprozesse in Mittel- und Osteuropa, edited by Csaba Szabó (Publikationen der ungarischen Geschichtsforschung in Wien, vol. XIII, Vienna, 2015), 273–292.

540 NARA, 763.00/9-1350, Kidd to Williamson, 18 August 1950.

541 Mazower, Der dunkle Kontinent, 417.

542 The controversy surrounding the evaluation of the strike movement has continued since 1950. Even if the valid assessment is represented below that this was not a Communist coup attempt, it should equally be stressed as a matter of course that the in some cases very violent actions and counteractions were dangerous developments which at that time were certainly subjectively perceived differently from today, after an interval of more than 67 years. An outstanding example of subjective perception is the autobiography of Franz Olah, Die Erinnerungen (Vienna/Munich/Berlin, 1995), esp. 134–143.

543 Günter Bischof, Austria looks to the West. Kommunistische Putschgefahr, geheime Wiederbewaffnung und Westorientierung am Anfang der fünfziger Jahre, in: Österreich in den Fünfzigern, edited by Thomas Albrich, Klaus Eisterer, Michael Gehler and Rolf Steininger (= Innsbrucker Forschungen zur Zeitgeschichte, vol. 11, Innsbruck/Vienna, 1995), 194.

544 Ernst Fischer, Das Ende einer Illusion. Erinnerungen 1945–1955 (Vienna/Munich/Zurich, 1973), 311.

545 The documents relating to the deployment of the executive and the situation reports for the period from 26 September to 7 October, together with the final and testimonial reports, are in the AdR in the files of the Directorate General for Public Safety under the number 214.187-5/50.

546 Ibid. For details, see also the corresponding section in Karl Gruber, Zwischen Befreiung und Freiheit. Der Sonderfall Österreich (Vienna, 1953), chapter: 'Massenstreik'. For Lower Austria, esp. the chronicle of the federal state Gendarmerie detachment for Lower Austria, entries from 26 September to 6 October 1950. Also Wilhelm Svoboda, Die Partei, die Republik und der Mann mit den vielen Gesichtern. Oskar Helmer und Österreich II. Eine Korrektur (= Böhlaus zeitgeschichtliche Bibliothek, vol. 26, Vienna, 1993), 108– 123, and Reinhard Meier-Walser, Die gescheiterte Machtergreifung der österreichischen Kommunisten im Herbst 1950 (= Christliche Demokratie, vol. 2, 1990).

547 Understanding Austria. The Political Reports and Analyses of Martin F. Herz, Political Officer of the US Legation in Vienna 1945–1948, edited by Reinhold Wagnleitner (Salzburg, 1984), 454: Special Report No 7, 30 July 1948, and 589: Compendium of Austrian Politics, 2 December 1948.

548 The extent to which the political rhetoric exploited the putsch and revolution metaphor was noticeable in light of the parliamentary aftermath of the October strike. The highly readable reminiscences of the parliamentary stenographer at the time, Dietrich Hackl, can be regarded as a testimony that is beyond suspicion: Im Zentrum der Politik. Als Parlamentsstenograph im Hohen Haus (Vienna/Cologne/Graz, 1984), 65–74.

549 For the terms used, the individual phases of events and above all also for a portrayal of Franz Olah as an individual, see Michael Ludwig, Klaus Dieter Mulley and Robert Streibel, Der Oktoberstreik 1950. Ein Wendepunkt der Zweiten Republik (Vienna, 1991).

550 Sowjetische Politik in Österreich, doc. no. 71, 685–711.

551 Manfred Jochum: 80 Jahre Republik Österreich (Vienna, 1998), 61.

552 On the selection of candidates, NARA, 763.00/2-151, Desp. 757, Dowling to Department of State, 1 February 1951.

553 See two memoranda from Ambassador Llewellyn Thompson dated 4 September 1952, NARA, 763.00/9-452.

554 Sorry guys, no gold. Die amerikanischen Waffendepots in Österreich. Catalogue accompanying the special exhibition in the Museum of Military History (Vienna, 1998).

555 Manfried Rauchensteiner, Die Zwei. Die Große Koalition in Österreich 1945–1966 (Vienna, 1987), 169–170.

556 Rauchensteiner, Die Zwei, 172.

557 Helmut Wohnout and Johannes Schönner, Das politische Tagebuch von Julius Raab 1953/1954. New insights into the first years of his chancellorship in: Demokratie und Geschichte. Jahrbuch des Karl-von-Vogelsang-Instituts zur Erforschung der christlichen Demokratie in Österreich, vols. 7/8 (2003/2004), 13–71, here 55.

558 Dispatch from Legation Secretary Gerhard Gmoser to the Federal Ministry for External Affairs, 15 June 1953, quoted in Weiß, 'Gesamtverhalten: Nicht sich in den Vordergrund stellen', 45.

559 Pape, Ungleiche Brüder, 134–139 and 211–225.

560 Political Archives of the Federal Foreign Office, Berlin (hereafter PA AA Berlin), Nachlass Hermann Müller-Graaf, vol. 2, AA 2010-02/55, 12 November 1953.

16 A Glorious Spring Day

561 Quoted from Rathkolb, Die paradoxe Republik, 23.

562 German-Austrian relations during the phase of the conclusion of the State Treaty are discussed by Michael Gehler, for example in his work: Modellfall für Deutschland? Die Österreichlösung mit Staatsvertrag und Neutralität 1945–1955 (Innsbruck, 2015).

563 Oliver Rathkolb, Washington ruft Wien. US-Großmachtpolitik und Österreich 1953–1963 (Vienna/Cologne/Weimar, 1997), 61–65.

564 Monthly situation report by the federal police department in Vienna for April 1954, 3. Here, it is also reported that the wreath-laying ceremony took place despite the absence of the Soviet representatives, which was a form of protest against the now known government measure.

565 Marek, Beruf und Berufung, 51.

566 ALCO, 218th session, 14 May 1954, Minute 1872 and unofficial US transcript.

567 See also Liebe auf den Zweiten Blick, edited by Robert Kriechbaumer (= Geschichte der österreichischen Bundesländer seit 1945, Vienna, 1998).

568 Pape, Ungleiche Brüder, 264–272.

569 Roland Beck and Peter Braun, Die schweizerische Landesverteidigung im Spannungsfeld von nuklearen Gefechtsfeldwaffen und bewaffneter Neutralität 1955–1961, in: Die Schweiz und der Kalte Krieg, edited by the Association suisse d'histoire et de sciences militaires (Bern, 2003), here 51–54.

570 Die Rote Armee in Österreich, 863.

571 See Gehler, Modellfall für Deutschland?, 667–912.

572 TNA, Kew, FO 371/124080/RR 1011/1, Annual report 1955, 18 January 1956.

573 Butschek, Österreichische Wirtschaftsgeschichte, 310. Also Rudolf Jeřábek, Vermögensfragen im deutsch-österreichischen Verhältnis 1955–1957, in: Der Österreichische Staatsvertrag 1955 (The Austrian State Treaty), 563 ff.

574 Pape, Ungleiche Brüder, 319 and 332–333.

575 See Rolf Pfeiffer, Eine schwierige und konfliktreiche Nachbarschaft – Österreich und das Deutschland Adenauers 1953–1963 (Münster/Hamburg/London, 2003), esp. 35–60.

576 PA AA Berlin, Nachlass Müller-Graaf, vol. 2, letter dated 31 May 1955.

577 Hans-Peter Schwarz, Adenauer, vol. 2: Der Staatsmann 1952–1967 (Stuttgart, 1991), 309.

578   PA AA Berlin, TB 12, vol. 127, FS 20 June 1955.

579   Heinrich Drimmel, Österreichs Geistesleben zwischen Ost und West, in: Österreich. Die Zweite Republik, edited by Erika Weinzierl and Kurt Skalnik, vol. 2 (Graz/Vienna/Cologne, 1972), 555–596, here 565–566. Very similar is the situation report of the security department in Salzburg for July 1955 in: Neues aus dem Westen. Aus den streng vertraulichen Berichten der Sicherheitsdirektion und der Bundespolizeidirektion Salzburg an das Innenministerium 1945 bis 1955, edited by Robert Kriechbaumer (Vienna/Cologne/Weimar, 2016), 457.

580   Rauchensteiner, Die Zwei, 298.

581   PA AA Berlin, Bestand B 310, vol. 47, 1.1.-31.12.1955, 304.211-00/94.19/1995/55.

582   Rauchensteiner, Die Zwei, 297.

583   Michael Gehler, 'to guarantee a country which was a military vacuum'. Die Westmächte und Österreichs territoriale Integrität 1955–1957, in: Zwischen den Blöcken. Nato, Warschauer Pakt und Österreich, edited by Manfried Rauchensteiner (Vienna/Cologne/Weimar, 2010), 89–133.

584   TNA, Kew, FO 371/124097 RR 1071/89, Wallinger to Foreign Office, 27 April 1956.

585   Adam Wandruszka, Die Epoche der Sukzessionskriege, in: Österreich und Italien. Ein bilaterales Geschichtsbuch (Vienna/Munich, 1973), 46.

586   See Bruno Thoß, Österreich in der Entstehungs- und Konsolidierungsphase des westlichen Bündnissystems (1947–1967), in: Zwischen den Blöcken, 19–87, here esp. 80–81. See also Rathkolb, Die paradoxe Republik, 287.

17. Between the Blocs

587   *Profil*, no. 6 (1974), 32. The suggestion was made in the context of later Soviet plans for the 'Polarka' scenario. Šejna repeated his portrayal in his 1982 book We Will Bury You (London, 1982), 119. On the crisis situation on 5 November 1956 see Rauchensteiner, Spätherbst 1956. Die Neutralität auf dem Prüfstand (Vienna, 1981), 68–75.

588   See David Dallin, Sowjetische Außenpolitik nach Stalins Tod (Cologne/Berlin, 1961), 310.

589   For the figures see Ibolya Murber, Ungarnflüchtlinge in Österreich 1956, in: Ibolya Murber and Zoltán Fónagy, Die ungarische Revolution und Österreich 1956 (Vienna, 2006), esp. 358–361.

590   TNA, Kew, FO 371/130273, Annual Review for 1956.

591   Even if the connection assumed by Michael Gehler between the Hungarian Revolution and the end of efforts to join the ECSC cannot be proven, the temporal correlation is striking. See Michael Gehler, Vom Friedensvertrag von Saint-Germain bis zum EU-Vertrag von Lissabon, in: Österreich und die europäische Integration, 543.

592   TNA, Kew, FO 371/136578, Annual Review for 1957, 1–2.

593   TNA, Kew, FO 371/144862, Annual Report: 1958, 1.

594   Karin Schmidlechner, Youth Culture in the 1950s, in: Austria in the 1950s, edited by Günter Bischof, Anton Pelinka and Rolf Steininger (= Contemporary Austrian Studies, vol. 3, New Brunswick, 1995), 116–137.

595   Ernst Joseph Görlich and Felix Romanik, Geschichte Österreichs (Innsbruck/Vienna/Munich, 1970).

596   Mühlberger, Vertriebene Intelligenz, 7–8.

597   Testbild, Twen und Nierentisch. Unser Lebensgefühl in den 50er Jahren, edited by Ernst Grissemann and Hans Veigl (Vienna/Cologne/Weimar, 2002), 16–23.

598   For the text of the note see Rauchensteiner, Die Zwei, 385.

599 Wolfgang Mueller, A Special Relationship with Neutrals. Krushchev's Coexistence, Austria and Switzerland, 1955–1960, in: zeitgeschichte, vol. 41, no. 5 (2014), 286.

600 TNA, Kew, FO 371/136617. The note was delivered on 30 July 1958.

601 TNA, Kew, FO 371/144862, Annual Review for 1958, pt. 4.

602 Wolfgang Mueller, A Good Example of Peaceful Coexistence: The Soviet Union, Austria, and Neutrality, 1955–1991 (= Österreichische Akademie der Wissenschaften, Zentraleuropa-Studien, vol. 15, Vienna, 2011), 103–104.

603 Butschek, Österreichische Wirtschaftsgeschichte, 310.

604 Rauchensteiner, Die Zwei, 380–388.

605 Ibid., 392–393.

606 In: *Die Zukunft*, 1959, nos. 4 and 5.

607 PA AA Berlin, Bestand B 130, Band 3271A, 203-83.20/ 94.29, 477/59, various reports on Schärf's visit and the perception of several NATO states, 28 October 1959.

608 PA AA Berlin, B 3, Bd. 3271A, 203-81.10/94.19/87/60, 'Österreich am Anfang des Jahres 1960. Gesamtbericht', 16–18.

609 Rauchensteiner, Die Zwei, 424–425.

610 NARA, National Security Council NSC 6020 'US Policy towards Austria', 6 December 1960.

611 PA AA Berlin, B 130, Band 3271A, 203-83.20, 94.29, 398/60, Telegram from 1 July 1960.

612 Silke Stern, 'Eine Höflichkeitsvisite mehr protokollarischer Natur'. Der Staatsbesuch Nikita Chruščevs in Österreich 1960, in: Der Wiener Gipfel 1961. Kennedy – Chruschtschow, edited by Stefan Karner, Barbara Stelzl-Marx, Natalja Tomilina, Alexander Tschubarjan et al. (Innsbruck/Vienna/Bolzano, 2011), 735–756, here 740. Additional aspects of the visit can be found in Mueller, A Good Example, 117–120.

613 Stern, 'Eine Höflichkeitsvisite', 743–744.

614 Mueller, A Good Example, 118.

615 Rathkolb, Washington ruft Wien, 93–94.

616 Bruckmüller, Nation Österreich, 125.

617 See the introduction in: Der Wiener Gipfel 1961, 24–25.

618 See Dieter Krüger, Brennender Enzian. Die Operationsplanung der NATO für Österreich und Norditalien 1951 bis 1960 (= Einzelschriften zur Militärgeschichte, vol. 46, Freiburg im Breisgau/Berlin/Vienna, 2010).

619 The plans of the Warsaw Pact, which have in any case only partially become known, were first addressed by Hungarian General Robert Széles during a conference in Vienna in 1992: R. Széles, Die strategischen Überlegungen des Warschauer Paktes für Mitteleuropa in den 70er Jahren und die Rolle der Neutralen, in: Tausend Nadelstiche. Das österreichische Bundesheer in der Reformzeit 1970–1978, edited by Manfried Rauchensteiner, Wolfgang Etschmann and Josef Rausch (= Forschungen zur Militärgeschichte, vol. 3, Graz/Vienna/Cologne, 1994), 25–46. The accompanying maps with target regions for nuclear weapons marked on them were shown in a special exhibition by the Museum of Military History on the Iron Curtain / A vasfüggöny in 2001. See also Wolfgang Mueller, Der Warschauer Pakt und Österreich 1955–1991, in: Zwischen den Blöcken, 165–166.

620 Museum of Military History / Military History Institute, Vienna (hereafter HGM/MHI), Nachlass Horst Pleiner, Ordner 29, Operation 'Prišok'. See also Manfried Rauchensteiner, Operative Annahmen und Manöver des Bundesheers 1955–1979, in: Zwischen den Blöcken, 292.

621 Alexander Vodopivec, Die Balkanisierung Österreichs. Folgen einer großen Koalition (Vienna/Munich, 1966), 208.

622 Günter Bischof, Anton Pelinka and Michael Gehler, Austrian Foreign Policy in Historical Context, in: Contemporary Austrian Studies, vol. 14 (New Brunswick, 2006), 113–169.

623 PA AA Berlin, B 83, Nr. 183, 203/81/00/94.18, Draft by Study Group South-East for the Foreign Office, Bonn, 21 May 1963.

624 *Arbeiter-Zeitung*, 12 November 1960, quoted from Wenninger, Von 'Monarchenfressern', 406.

625 Stephan Hamel, 'Eine solche Sache würde der Neutralitätspolitik ein Ende machen'. Die österreichischen Integrationsbestrebungen 1961–1972, in: Österreich und die europäische Integration, 72.

626 Maria Wirth, Christian Broda. Eine politische Biographie (= zeitgeschichte im Kontext, vol. 5, Göttingen, 2011), 254.

627 TNA, Kew, FO 371/185600, Letter from J. A. Pilcher to D. S. E. Dodson, Chief Central Department Foreign Office, 26 February 1966.

18 The New Style of Dispassion

628 TNA, Kew, FO 371/185605, Memorandum of a meeting between Pittermann and Prime Minister Harold Wilson on 4 April 1966.

629 Josef Klaus, Macht und Ohnmacht in Österreich. Konfrontationen und Versuche (Vienna/Munich/Zurich, 1971), 53–61.

630 PA AA Berlin, Bestand B 26, Bd. 313, 1.1.–31.12.1966, Report from 23 August 1966.

631 Reinhard Meier-Walser, Die Außenpolitik der monocoloren Regierung Klaus in Österreich 1966–1970 (= tuduv Studien, vol. 27, Munich, 1988), 122.

632 Hamel, 'Eine solche Sache', 63. The remarks were, remarkably enough, repeated in *Izvestia* on 16 June and in *Pravda* on 26 June 1966 in advance of the visit of Soviet Premier Nikolai Podgorny to Austria.

633 *Der Spiegel*, vol. 21, no. 18 (1967), 129–132.

634 Hamel, 'Eine solche Sache', 81.

635 Klaus, Macht und Ohnmacht, 332–337.

636 Nachlass Josef Klaus, Letter from Irvin Stone, Beverly Hills, to Paul Koretz, Los Angeles, 6 May 1968. The realisation of the project, however, was delayed until 1971. I am especially grateful to Ambassador Dr Stephan Scholz for the opportunity to use the family and estate papers of Josef Klaus.

637 TNA, Kew, FCO 371/185605, CA 1051/5, 25 July 1966.

638 TNA, Kew, FO 371/185600, Central Department A 1015/11, The first six months of one-party conservative rule in Austria, 7.

639 See Maximilian Graf, Österreichs 'Ostpolitik' im Kalten Krieg. Eine doppeldeutsche Sicht, in: Österreich im Kalten Krieg, edited by Maximilian Graf and Agnes Meislinger (= zeitgeschichte im Kontext, vol. 11, Göttingen 2016), 145–173.

640 Quoted from Helmut Wohnout in: *Die Furche*, 12 August 2010.

641 Meier-Walser, Außenpolitik, 346.

642 TNA, Kew, FCO 9/11, Austria: Annual review for 1967, signed A. Rumbold.

643 According to Lujo Tončić in: Die Ära Josef Klaus, edited by Robert Kriechbaumer, vol. 1, 17.

644 TNA, Kew, FCO 33/843, Austria: Annual Review for 1969.

645 Robert Kriechbaumer, '... ständiger Verdruss und viele Verletzungen'. Die Regierung Klima/Schüssel und die Bildung der ÖVP-FPÖ-Regierung. Österreich 1997–2000 (Schriften der Dr.-Wilfried-Haslauer-Bibliothek, vol. 47, Vienna/Cologne/Weimar, 2014), 232.

646 As expressed by Heinrich Neisser, in: Die Ära Josef Klaus, vol. 2: Aus der Sicht von Zeitgenossen, 182.

647 Josef Klaus' contact with the Centro Europeo de Documentación e Información (CEDI) was repeatedly the subject of speculation. See Stefan A. Müller, Die Beziehungen Österreichs zu Spanien 1945–1978, in: Stefan A. Müller, David Schriffl and Adamantios T. Skordos, Heimliche Freunde. Die Beziehungen

Österreichs zu den Diktaturen Südeuropas nach 1945: Spanien, Portugal, Griechenland (Vienna/Cologne/Weimar, 2016), 45 and 74–75.

648 Gerd Bacher, in: Die Ära Josef Klaus, vol. 2, 162.

649 This is the conclusion drawn by Willi Sauberer from his analysis of incidents in the ÖVP leadership at federal level and, above all, on the basis of so-called post sessions from 1967 to 1970. See Die Ära Josef Klaus, vol. 1, 101–228.

650 TNA, Kew, FCO 9/11, Austria: Annual review for 1967.

651 Meier-Walser, Außenpolitik, 123.

652 The text of the Koren Plan can be found in: Die Ära Josef Klaus, vol. 1: Dokumente, 358–369.

653 See, on the basis of Austrian sources, Hubert Speckner, Von der 'Feuernacht' zur 'Porzescharte'. Das 'Südtirolproblem' der 1960er Jahre in den österreichischen sicherheitsdienstlichen Akten (Vienna, 2016). Three people charged with this attack in Austria were not convicted, because their guilt could not be proven. – By the same author: Der Sicherungseinsatz des Österreichischen Bundesheeres an der Grenze zu Südtirol 1967 (= Schriften zur Geschichte des Österreichischen Bundesheeres, vol. 19, Vienna, 2012). Also discussed in: Rolf Steininger, Die Südtirolfrage, part 1.

654 Horst Christoph, Terror um Tirol. Feuernächte und Folterknechte, in: *profil*, 14 May 2011.

655 Mazower, Der dunkle Kontinent, 455 (photo).

656 *Der Spiegel*, 19/1968, 6 May 1968, 123. See Paulus Ebner and Karl Vocelka, Die zahme Revolution. '68 und was davon blieb (Vienna, 1998), 94–95.

657 Hanisch, Männlichkeiten, 114.

658 TNA, Kew, FCO 371/185600, Central Department A 1015/11, The first six months of one-party conservative rule in Austria, 9–10.

659 Diaries of Josef Klaus, vol. LVII (17.11.1965 – 15.4.1966), 66, entry for 7 March 1966.

660 PA AA Berlin, Bestand B 26, Bd. 313, 1.1.–31.12.1966, Report from 23 November 1966.

661 AdR Ministerratsprotokolle Regierung Klaus II, Protokoll Nr. 91a, Transcript of the extraordinary proceedings of the Council of Ministers on 21 August 1968. See also Horst Pleiner and Hubert Speckner, Zur Verstärkung der nördlichen Garnisonen .... Der 'Einsatz' des österreichischen Bundesheeres während der Tschechenkrise im Jahr 1968 (= Schriften zur Geschichte des Österreichischen Bundesheeres, vol. 15, Vienna, 2008), esp. 127–144.

662 Diaries of Josef Klaus, vol. LXV (26.5. – 22.9.1968), 68–71. The entries are in part difficult to decipher, though the changes made for the first radio broadcast are still visible. The main intention was to appease.

663 The events surrounding the temporary discontinuation of the issuing of visas has been described on many occasions in such a way that Foreign Minister Waldheim had ordered the cessation and Envoy Dr Kirchschläger had acted in opposition to him. Kirchschläger expressly contradicted this depiction, though without successfully achieving a correction. See Klaus Eisterer's article, which is based on the files: Die österreichische Gesandtschaft in Prag und die Krise in der Tschechoslowakei 1968, in: Contemporary Austrian Studies, vol. 9, edited by Günter Bischof, Anton Pelinka and Ruth Wodak (New Brunswick/London, 2001), 13–17. See, furthermore, the interview with Karl Peterlik, 5000 Visa pro Tag ausgestellt, in: *Academia*, May 2008.

664 Reiner Eger, Krisen an Österreichs Grenzen. Das Verhalten Österreichs während des Ungarnaufstandes 1956 und der tschechoslowakischen Krise 1968. Ein Vergleich (Vienna/Munich, 1981), 89. The text of the Federal Chancellor's declaration, which was not a note addressed to the Soviet Union, can be found on page 195.

665 Manuscript by Gabriele Anderl, Evelyn Klein and Hannes Leidinger, Österreichs Rolle bei der jüdischen Emigration aus der Sowjetunion. Projekt 08-422 des Zukunftsfonds der Republik Österreich (Vienna, 2011), 104. Copy in the author's possession.

666 AdR Ministerratsprotokolle Regierung Klaus II, Prot. Nr. 92, Transcript of proceedings of the Council of Ministers on 10 September 1968.

667 Ibid. Somewhat different figures in Rathkolb, Die paradoxe Republik, 289.

668 The figures plus those of the Czechoslovak army can be found in Martin Malek, Österreich und der Auflösungsprozess des Warschauer Paktes (1989–1991), in: Zwischen den Blöcken, 557–614, here 559; furthermore: http://www.radio.cz/de/rubrik/geschichte/voruebergehend-bedeutete-21-jahre-die-sowjettruppen-in-der-cssr [last accessed on 23 June 2017].

669 TNA, Kew, FCO 33/428, Sir A. Rumbold to the Foreign and Commonwealth Office, 18 November 1968.

670 Diaries of Josef Klaus, vol. LXXI, (1969–1970), 7–9.

671 Die Ära Josef Klaus, vol. 2, 370–386.

672 Christian Forstner, Kernspaltung, Kalter Krieg und Österreichs Neutralität, in: Österreich im Kalten Krieg, 73–96.

673 TNA, Kew, FCO 33/843, Austria: Annual review for 1970.

674 Mazower, Der dunkle Kontinent, 445.

675 Leo Wallner, in: Die Ära Klaus, vol. 2, 29.

19 The Counter-Narrative

676 Elisabeth Röhrlich, Kreiskys Außenpolitik. Zwischen österreichischer Identität und internationalem Programm (= zeitgeschichte im Kontext, vol. 2, Göttingen, 2009), 270.

677 Helene Maimann, Über Kreisky. Gespräche aus Distanz und Nähe (Vienna, 2011), 18.

678 TNA, Kew, FCO 33/1274, Austria: Annual review for 1970.

679 PA AA Berlin, Bestand 309, 82.SL/94.19, Aktuelle Probleme der österreichischen Außenpolitik, 24 November 1970.

680 Jean Jaurès, Die neue Armee (Jena, 1913).

681 HGM/MHI, Nachlass Pleiner, Ordner 5, BMLV 129-strgeh/Fü/70.

682 Peter Corrieri, Der Brief der 1700. Demokratischer Offizierswiderstand gegen politischen Populismus 1970/71 (= Schriften zur Geschichte des Österreichischen Bundesheeres, vol. 21, Vienna, 1913). A facsimile of the letter is on 284–287.

683 PA AA Berlin, Bestand 130, Bd. 9818A, 82.00/94.19/460/71, FS 5.3.1971.

684 Franz Vranitzky, Foreword, in: Maimann, Über Kreisky, 8.

685 Maximilian Graf, Österreich und die DDR 1949–1989/90. Beziehungen – Kontakte – Wahrnehmungen, doctoral thesis, University of Vienna (2012).

686 TNA, Kew, FCO 33/1679, J. Hartland-Swann to the European Integration Department, 10 March 1972.

687 Robert Kriechbaumer, Österreichs Innenpolitik 1970–1975 (= Österreichisches Jahrbuch für Politik Sonderband, vol. 1, Munich/Vienna, 1981), 335.

688 Kriechbaumer, Österreichs Innenpolitik, 221. The initiators of resistance were above all Walter Csoklich and Anton Pelinka.

689 Quoted from Kriechbaumer, Österreichs Innenpolitik, 243.

690 Ibid., 232–234.

691 Alfred Elste and Wilhelm Wadl, Titos langer Schatten. Bomben- und Geheimdienstterror im Kärnten der 1970er Jahre (Klagenfurt am Wörthersee, 2015), 228.

692 Ibid., 156–157.

693 On the contents of the notes and, above all, the text of the Austrian answer see: Kriechbaumer, Österreichs Innenpolitik, 192.

694 Kriechbaumer, Österreichs Innenpolitik, 201–202.

695 Elste and Wadl, Titos langer Schatten, 241.

696 Butschek, Österreichische Wirtschaftsgeschichte, 359.

697 PA AA Berlin, Bestand 130 Bd. 9818A, 82.00/94.19/460/71, FS 3.2.1971.

698 On the press coverage of the incident: Johanna Feifel, Schönau und das Österreichbild in der hebräisch-, deutsch- und englischsprachigen Presse, doctoral thesis, University of Vienna (2002).

699 'Carlos', actually Ilich Rámirez Sánchez, to British author David A. Yallop, quoted in: Anderl, Klein and Leidinger, Österreichs Rolle bei der jüdischen Emigration aus der Sowjetunion.

700 Anderl, Klein and Leidinger, Österreichs Rolle, 67.

701 AdR, BMfA II-pol, Israel 1974, Zl. 88.03.10/72-6/74.

702 The witticism can be found in: Die Ära Kreisky. Österreich 1970–1983 in der historischen Analyse, im Urteil der politischen Kontrahenten und in Karikaturen von Ironimus, edited by Robert Kriechbaumer (= Schriftenreihe des Forschungsinstitutes für Politisch-Historische Studien der Dr.-Wilfried-Haslauer-Bibliothek, vol. 22, Vienna/Cologne/Weimar, 2004), 261.

703 Herfried Münkler, Der Wandel des Krieges. Von der Symmetrie zur Asymmetrie (Weilerswist, 2006).

704 One example of many politicians, military professionals and commentators who argued in this vein is the Weißbuch zur Lage der Landesverteidigung in Österreich, edited by Felix Ermacora (Vienna, 1973).

705 Profil (Vienna), nos. 4, 5, 6 and 7 (14, 21 and 28 February and 7 March 1974): Moskaus Aufmarschpläne gegen Österreich. The editor of profil, Werner Stanzl, strove for a long time to arrange an interview with J. Šejna after the latter had given a first interview to the magazine Paris Match. In December 1973, the American authorities in whose custody Šejna found himself in Washington allowed Stanzl to conduct an interview. – Šejna provided a briefer account in his 1982 book: We Will Bury You (London, 1982), here 120–121.

706 http://www.krone.at/nachrichten/bruno-kreisky-in-zitaten-beruehmte-bonmots-story-242002 [last accessed on 23 June 2017].

707 Barbara Liegl and Anton Pelinka, Chronos und Ödipus. Der Kreisky-Androsch-Konflikt (Vienna, 2004), 90.

708 Helmut Schelsky, Von Kreisky zu Taus, Politische Eindrücke aus Österreich, quoted in Gerald Stifter, Die ÖVP in der Ära Kreisky 1970–1983 (Innsbruck/Vienna, 2006), 239 and 339, note 855.

709 Kriechbaumer, Österreichs Innenpolitik, 429–430.

710 Ladislav Bitman, Geheimwaffe 'D' (Bern, 1973), 66–79.

711 Sabine Loitfellner, Simon Wiesenthals 'Schuld und Sühne Memorandum' an die Bundesregierung 1966. Ein zeitgenössisches Abbild zum politischen Umgang mit NS-Verbrechen, in: Kriegsverbrechen, NS-Verbrechen und die europäische Strafjustiz von Nürnberg bis Den Haag, edited by Heimo Halbrainer and Claudia Kuretsidis-Haider (Graz, 2007), 281–288. The memorandum can be found in the Documentation Centre of Austrian Resistance, Sign. 27.386.

712 Association for the History of the Labour Movement, Vienna (hereafter VGA), Tagebücher Josef Staribacher, 1 August – 26 October 1975, Closed meeting of the SPÖ, 22 October 1975.

713 Maimann, Über Kreisky, 75.

714 Riegler, Im Fadenkreuz, 453.

715 Maimann, Über Kreisky, 78–79.

716 Manfried Rauchensteiner, König Kreisky und die Briten, in: Die Presse, Spectrum, 31 May 2008, 3–4.

717 TNA, Kew, FCO 33/4301, C. D. Lush, 23 December 1971.

718 Roman Sandgruber, Die Industrie in Österreich 1911 bis 2011. Eine Erfolgsgeschichte auf Umwegen, in:100 Jahre Haus der Industrie 1911–2011 (Vienna, 2011), 172–275.

719 PA AA Berlin, B-130, 203-81.10/94.19/87/60, Österreich am Anfang des Jahres 1960. Gesamtbericht, 20–22.

720 TNA, Kew, FCO 33/5393, Annual Report 1971, 4.

721 Maimann, Über Kreisky, 75. Dr Helene Maimann kindly made an unredacted transcript of the interview with Helmut Schmidt available to the author.

722 Stifter, Die ÖVP, 145 ff.

723 Ibid., 150.

724 Wirth, Christian Broda, 493.

725 Heinz Fischer, Reflexionen (Vienna, 1998), 270.

726 Stifter, Die ÖVP, 192; also Heinz Fischer, Die Kreisky-Jahre 1967–1983 (Himberg, 1993), 157.

727 VGA, Tagebücher Josef Staribacher, 14 October – 22 December 1978, here 17 October. At this point in time, Minister of Trade Josef Staribacher did not believe it would be endorsed.

728 Stifter, Die ÖVP, 212.

729 TNA, Kew, FCO 33/4601, Annual report on Austria 1980, 3.

730 Ibid., 5.

731 Butschek, Österreichische Wirtschaftsgeschichte, 354–355.

732 Stifter, Die ÖVP, 247, and Ernst Hanisch, Der lange Schatten, 474.

733 Hanisch, Der lange Schatten, 475.

734 Surely one of the most positive and, in places, enthusiastic reports was written by the British ambassador in Austria, Donald McDonald Gordon, on the occasion of his departure from Austria on 12 August 1981: TNA, Kew, FCO 33/4602.

735 TNA, Kew, FCO 33/5376, Reports from the embassy in Vienna to the Central Department, above all the report of Ambassador Michael O'D B. Alexander on Gaddafi's visit, 17 March 1982.

736 TNA, Kew, FCO 33/5375, Alan Free-Gore to A. E. Montgomery, 6 August 1982.

737 TNA, Kew, FCO 33/4321, Telegram from 29 April 1980. For the State Department in Washington and the Foreign Office in London, this was more proof of Kreisky's naivety.

738 Rathkolb, Washington ruft Wien, 55. Likewise Rathkolb, Die paradoxe Republik, 293.

739 TNA, Kew, FCO 33/5391, Michael O'D B. Alexander, Record of Conversation between Edward Heath and Kreisky (15 June 1982), 18 June 1982.

740 TNA, Kew, FCO 33/5369, Austria: Annual review for 1982, 4.

741 Andreas Resch, Der österreichische Osthandel im Spannungsfeld der Blöcke, in: Zwischen den Blöcken, 497–556, esp. 536–540.

742 VGA, Tagebücher Josef Staribacher, 4 March – 21 December 1982, several entries. When the supplying companies submitted End-user certificates, they automatically received an export licence from the Ministry of Trade.

743 TNA, Kew, FCO 33/5399, Embassy Vienna to A. E. Montgomery, 3 June 1982, 10.

744 TNA, Kew, FCO 33/5399, D. G. Blunt to T. Gallagher, 10 September 1982.

745 TNA, Kew, FCO 33/5376, passim.

746 TNA, Kew, FCO 33/5369, Austria: Annual review for 1982, 3.

747 Pelinka, Chronos und Ödipus, 9–10.

748 Stifter, Die ÖVP, 287.

749 Stifter, Die ÖVP, 298.

750 See Anton Pelinka, Die Kleine Koalition. SPÖ–FPÖ 1983–1986 (= Studien zu Politik und Verwaltung, edited by Christian Brünner, Wolfgang Mantl and Manfried Welan, vol. 48, Vienna/Cologne/Graz, 1993), 21.

751 Thus, for example, a resolution was passed that the thirteenth and fourteenth monthly salaries were to be tax-free. The FPÖ took the credit for this initiative.

752 Hubert Sickinger, Politische Korruption und der Wandel der Rahmenbedingungen für politisches Skandale in der Zweiten Republik, in: Korruption in Österreich. Historische Streiflichter, edited by Ernst Bruckmüller (Vienna, 2011), 123.

753 Maimann, Über Kreisky, 43, conversation with Oliver Rathkolb.

754 http://www.news.at/articles/1103/11/286793/ein-vereinfacher-historiker-rathkolb-interview-100-jahrenkreisky (news 27 January 2011).

755 Pelinka, Kleine Koalition, 42.

756 Ibid., 43.

757 https://de.wikipedia.org/wiki/Walter_Reder [last accessed on 23 June 2017].

758 PA/AA Berlin, Bestand 130, Bd. 3892A, 117–251, Teletype message from the embassy in Vienna to the German Foreign Office, 12 April 1972.

759 Pelinka, Kleine Koalition, 47.

760 Butschek, Österreichische Wirtschaftsgeschichte, 379.

761 Graf, Österreich und die DDR, 843.

762 Pelinka, Kleine Koalition, 50–51.

763 Sandgruber, Die Industrie in Österreich, 218.

764 Peter Rosner, Alexander Van der Bellen and Georg Winckler, Economic and Social Policy of the Vranitzky Era, in: The Vranitzky Era in Austria, 137–164, here 145.

765 https://de.wikipedia.org/wiki/Noricum-Skandal [last accessed on 23 June 2017]. Further: Die Presse, 2 April 2010: 20 Jahre 'Noricum': Waffen, Spione, Tote und Millionen.

766 TNA, Kew, FCO 33/5391, M. O'D B. Alexander to Central Department, 5 November 1982.

767 Thomas Riegler, Im Fadenkreuz. Österreich und der Nahostterrorismus 1973 bis 1985 (= Zeitgeschichte im Kontext, vol. 3, Göttingen, 2011), 230–277.

768 TNA, Kew, FCO 33/5391 M. O'D B. Alexander, Record of Conversation with Mr. Lanc, 5 November 1982.

769 Riegler, Im Fadenkreuz, 290.

770 TNA, Kew, FCO 33/5391 Alan L. Free-Gore to Tracy Gallagher (Foreign and Commonwealth Office), 2 August 1982.

771 Riegler, Im Fadenkreuz, 404.

772 Kurt Richard Luther, Austria's Social Democracy During The 'Vranitzky Era', in: The Vranitzky Era in Austria, 5–30, here 5.

773 Pelinka, Kleine Koalition, 58.

774 Ibid., 59, with reference to Norbert Steger, Friedrich Peter and Walter Grabher-Mayer.

775 Kreisky's letter to Sinowatz and the 'letter of refusal' for the party archive are in the third volume of Kreisky's memoirs: Der Mensch im Mittelpunkt, edited by Oliver Rathkolb, Johannes Kunz and Margit Schmidt (Vienna, 1996), 317–323.

776 Irene Etzersdorfer, From the Sphinx with – to the Spinx without a Puzzle. A Subjective Leader-

ship-Perceptions Comparison between Bruno Kreisky and Franz Vranitzky, in: The Vraitzky Era, 56–77, here 66.

777   Michael Gehler: '... eine grotesk überzogene Dämonisierung eines Mannes ...'? Die Waldheim-Affäre 1986–1992, in: idem and Hubert Sickinger, Politische Affären und Skandale in Österreich. Von Mayerling bis Waldheim (Thaur/Vienna/Munich, 1995), 614–665. Facsimile on 663.

778   AdR, BMaA 28-Res/93, 26 January 1993, Resumé of American-Austrian relations, 4.

779   Helga Embacher, Neubeginn ohne Illusionen. Juden in Österreich nach 1945 (Vienna, 1995), 259.

780   Manfried Rauchensteiner, Die Historikerkommission, in: Österreichisches Jahrbuch für Politik, 1988 (Vienna/Munich, 1989), 335–377, here 350–351.

21 The Implosion in the East

781   Kurt Richard Luther, Austria's Social Democracy During the 'Vranitzky Era'. The Politics of Assymmetrical Change, in: The Vranitzky Era in Austria, 5–30. The party membership statistics from 1945–1996 are on page 8.

782   Hugo von Hofmannsthal, Das Schrifttum als geistiger Raum der Nation (Munich, 1927), 31.

783   In summary: Österreich und die Ostöffnung 1989 (= historisch-politische Bildung, vol. 8, Vienna, 2015).

784   Dietrich Graf Brühl, Flucht in die Freiheit. Die Flüchtlingsbewegung aus Ungarn im Jahre 1989. Ein Bericht, in: Aufbruch in eine neue Zeit. 1989 im Rückblick, edited by Manfried Rauchensteiner (Vienna, 2000), 9.

785   Brühl, Flucht in die Freiheit, 27.

786   Graf, Österreich und die DDR, 810.

787   Andrea Brait, 'Österreich hat weder gegen die deutsche Wiedervereinigung agitiert, noch haben wir sie besonders begrüßt'. Österreichische Reaktionen auf die Bemühungen um die deutsche Einheit, in: Deutschland Archiv, 23 September 2014, 82–102.

788   Ibid.

789   Norman M. Naimark, Historical Memory and the Debate about the Vertreibung Museum, in: Austria's International Position after the End of the Cold War, edited by Günter Bischof and Ferdinand Karlhofer (= Contemporary Austrian Studies, vol. 22, New Orleans, 2013), 228–241. On the case of Jedwabne, provided as an example here, see https://de.wikipedia.org/wiki/Massaker_von_Jedwabne [last accessed on 23 June 2017].

790   Peter Wassertheurer, Die Beneš-Dekrete im Kontext des öffentlichen und politischen Diskurses in Österreich 1989–2003. Traditionen – Geschichtsbilder – Stereotype, doctoral thesis, University of Graz (2006).

791   Elisabeth Heresch, Nikolaus II. Feigheit, Lüge und Verrat (Munich, 1992), 376–378.

792   The wording of the message and the responses of the Soviet, American and French governments can be found in Stourzh, Um Einheit und Freiheit, Appendix 8, 776–779. The British government merely stated verbally that it had no objection.

793   Andreas Resch, Austrian Foreign Trade and Austrian Companies' Economic Engagement in Central and Eastern Europe (CEE) since 1989, in: Austria's International Position after the End of the Cold War, 198–223, 203.

794   Günter Bischof, Of Dwarfs and Giants: From Cold War Mediator to Bad Boy of Europe. Austria and the U.S. in the Transatlantic Arena (1990–2013), in: Austria's International Position after the End of the Cold War, 14–15.

795 Franz Vranitzky, Politische Erinnerungen (Vienna, 2004), 316.

796 Gehler, Vom Friedensvertrag von Saint-Germain, 557.

797 Martin Eichtinger, Helmut Wohnout, Alois Mock. Ein Politiker schreibt Geschichte (Graz, 2008), 245.

798 Manfried Rauchensteiner, Entschlossenes Zuwarten. Österreich und die Unabhängigkeit Sloweniens 1991 (Klagenfurt, 2011).

799 The original opinion can be found in 'Politika', 8 February 1991, 5.

800 Information kindly given by former federal chancellor Dr Franz Vranitzky to the author.

801 Rauchensteiner, Entschlossenes Zuwarten, 12–13 and 61.

802 Andreas Kappeler, Todesstoß für eine Weltmacht im Jagdhaus, in: Die Presse, Gastkommentar, 7 December 2016, 32–33.

803 Jochum, 80 Jahre Republik, 165.

804 The issue of recognition is addressed, for instance, in the memoirs of the former ambassador to the Soviet Union and later Russia, Friedrich Bauer: Russische Umbrüche. Von Gorbatschow über Jelzin zu Putin (Vienna, 2008), 110–136.

805 AdR, BMaA 106-Res 91, 302-GS/93 and 517-266/93.

806 AdR, BMaA 517.266/8-II.3/93, Information for the Federal Minister, 3 November 1993.

807 Österreichisches Jahrbuch für Politik, 1992 (Vienna, 1993), 8.

808 https://www.parlament.gv.at/ZUSD/PDF/19920708_Gemeinsame_Sitzung_XVIII_GP., 8 July 1992 [last accessed on 23 June 2017]

809 Vranitzky, Politische Erinnerungen, 226.

810 AdR, BMaA Pol 517.224/6-II.9/91, 5 March 1991, Resumé protocol of Envoy Prohaska.

811 Gehler, Österreich und die europäische Integration, 560.

812 Michael Gehler, Vom EU-Beitritt zur Osterweiterung, in: Die umstrittene Wende, 461–550.

813 AdR, BMaA Zl. 517.266/1 - /94 and Moscow embassy, Zl. 3.1/4/95, 25 October 1995.

814 Rathkolb, Die paradoxe Republik, 27.

815 Robert Kriechbaumer, '… ständiger Verdruss und viele Verletzungen. Die Regierung Klima/Schüssel und die Bildung der ÖVP-FPÖ Regierung. Österreich 1997–2000 (= Schriften der Dr.-Wilfried-Haslauer-Bibliothek, vol. 47, Vienna/Cologne/Weimar, 2014), 141.

816 Luther, Austria's Social Democracy, 8.

817 Der Standard, 31 October 2008.

818 Christian Dirninger, Mehr Markt und weniger Staat. Die ordnungspolitische Wende in der Wirtschafts- und Finanzpolitik in einer längerfristigen Perspektive, in: Die umstrittene Wende. Österreich 2000–2006, edited by Robert Kriechbaumer and Franz Schausberger (Vienna/Cologne/Weimar, 2013), 235 and 225.

819 Sonja Puntscher Riekmann, The Politics of Ausgrenzung, the Nazi-Past and the European Dimension of the New Radical Right in Austria, in: The Vranitzky Era, 78–105, here 86–87.

820 In Chicago, there was resentment lasting several years as a result of the comparison. See AdR, BMaA 517.224/29-II.9/96, Report by the embassy in Washington, 19 December 1996.

821 Federal Chancellor Dr Wolfgang Schüssel expressly contradicts depictions in which he is alleged to have spoken with Jörg Haider about a 'quick transfer'. Their conversation concerned only the bank problem described here. (Information kindly provided by Dr Schüssel to the author on 26 April 2017.)

822 Kriechbaumer, '… ständiger Verdruss', 146.

823 Ibid., 162.

824 On how events unfolded: Branka Magaš, Noel Malcolm and Ivo Žanić (eds.), The War in Croatia and Bosnia-Herzegovina, 1991–1995 (London, 2001).

825 Bruckmüller, Nation Österreich, 140.

826 http://medienservicestelle.at/migration_bewegt/2011/06/21/kriege-in-ex-jugoslawien-fuhrten-
      zu-drei-grosenfluchtlingswellen [lasted accessed on 23 June 2017].
827 Vranitzky, Politische Erinnerungen, 219.
828 Kriechbaumer, '… ständiger Verdruss', 164–165.
829 Bischof, Of Dwarfs and Giants, 27.
830 Kriechbaumer, '… ständiger Verdruss', 299.

22 Under Observation

831 Andreas Khol, Veritas filia temporis. Die Wahrheit ist eine Tochter der Zeit, in: Österreichisches Jahr-
      buch für Politik, 2009 (Vienna, 2010) 379–398, here 381.
832 Kriechbaumer, '… ständiger Verdruss', 304.
833 For a detailed account of the exploratory talks and the negotiations see: Heinz Fischer, Wende-Zeiten.
      Ein österreichischer Zwischenbefund (Vienna, 2004), 40–104.
834 Kriechbaumer, '… ständiger Verdruss', 315.
835 A detailed account of the negotiations and the issue of the exchange of portfolios is provided in Wolf-
      gang Schüssel, Offengelegt. Aufgezeichnet von Alexander Purger (Salzburg, 2009), 90. In the Vranitzky
      IV cabinet (29 November 1994 – 18 December 1995), Federal Ministers Erhard Busek and Rudolf
      Scholten swapped the portfolios Education and Science, respectively.
836 Kriechbaumer, '… ständiger Verdruss', 353.
837 Ibid., 384.
838 Schüssel, Offengelegt, 103–104.
839 Heinz Fischer, Wende-Zeiten, 96, rightly disagrees that the Stockholm Conference was a conference of
      the Socialist International.
840 On the change of terminology see: Rosa Winkler-Hermaden, Als Österreich der Buhmann der EU war,
      in: Der Standard, 21 January 2010.
841 The entire text of the preamble of the government declaration can be found in: Die Presse, 4 February
      2000, 4.
842 Wolfgang C. Müller and Marcelo Jenny, Demokratischer Rollentausch oder Systembruch, in: Die um-
      strittene Wende, 53–80.
843 Robert Kriechbaumer, Von Faschisten, Austrofaschisten und Alltagsfaschisten, in: Die umstrittene
      Wende, 183–210, 189.
844 For the genesis and scale of the 'measures' see Michael Gehler, Präventivschlag als Fehlschlag. Motive,
      Intentionen und Konsequenzen der EU-14 Sanktionsmaßnahmen gegen Österreich im Jahr 2000, in:
      Eine europäische Erregung. Die 'Sanktionen' der Vierzehn gegen Österreich im Jahr 2000. Analysen
      und Kommentare, edited by Erhard Busek and Martin Schauer (Vienna/Graz/Cologne, 2003), 19–74.
845 Österreichisches Jahrbuch für Politik, 2000 (Vienna/Munich, 2001), Jahreschronik (7, 8 and 21 Febru-
      ary 2000).
846 Schüssel, Offengelegt, 108.
847 Ursula Plassnik, On the Road to a Modern Identity: Austrian Foreign Policy from the Cold War to the
      European Union, in: Austria's international Position, 55–107, here 86.
848 According to the lecturer teaching in the Netherlands, Karin Jušek, in her article: Eine trügerische
      Idylle? Das Bild Österreichs in den Niederlanden, in: Außenansichten. Europäische (Be)Wertungen
      zur Geschichte Österreichs im 20. Jahrhundert, edited by Oliver Rathkolb (Innsbruck/Vienna/Munich,
      2003), 223.

849 Außenansichten, passim.

850 Hubert Feichtlbauer, Fonds für Versöhnung, Frieden und Zusammenarbeit. Späte Anerkennung, Geschichte, Schicksale (Vienna, 2005).

851 Gehler, Vom EU-Beitritt, 507.

852 Paul Luif, Die Diskussion über die Neutralität, in: Die umstrittene Wende, 551–584, here 563.

853 Gehler, Präventivschlag als Fehlschlag, 25.

854 The text of the report can be found at http://images.derstandard.at/upload/images/bericht.pdf [last accessed on 23 June 2017].

855 Bischof, Of Dwarfs and Giants, 36.

856 Schüssel, Offengelegt, 147.

857 Dirninger, Mehr Markt, 239.

858 Gehler, Vom EU-Beitritt, 515.

859 Schüssel, Offengelegt, 170.

860 The quotes primarily from Alfred Gusenbauer in Dirninger, Mehr Markt, 255.

861 Peter Rosner, Alexander Van der Bellen and Georg Winckler, Economic and Social Policy of the Vranitzky Era, in: The Vranitzky Era, 136–164, 145.

862 Study by the CRIF credit agency, excerpts published in: Die Presse, 20 December 2016.

863 The data of the statistics on Austria can be accessed annually. http://www.stat.at/web_de/statistiken/wirtschaft/unternehmen_arbeitsstaetten/auslandsunternehmenseinheiten/in dex.html [last accessed on 23 June 2017].

864 Fritz Muliar, Das Burgtheater gibt es nicht mehr …, in: Österreichisches Jahrbuch für Politik, 1993 (Vienna, 1994), 139–143.

865 Stern, 24 June 2005, quoted in Dirninger, Mehr Markt, 266.

866 Albert Rohan, Österreich und die Türkei. Ein gestörtes Verhältnis, in: Österreichisches Jahrbuch für Politik, 2016 (Vienna/Cologne/Weimar, 2017), 137–138.

867 Gunther Hauser, Äußere und Innere Sicherheit, in: Die umstrittene Wende, 622.

868 Schmidl, Austrian Security Policy, 114–120.

869 Final report by former ambassador Dr Christian Prosl, undated [2003] draft.

23 The Relapse

870 Kriechbaumer, 'Es reicht!' Die Regierung Gusenbauer – Molterer. Österreich 2007/2008 (= Schriftenreihe des Forschungsinstitutes für Historisch-Politische Studien der Dr.-Wilfried-Haslaur-Biblitohek, vol. 55, Graz/Vienna/Cologne, 2016), 24.

871 Kriechbaumer, 'Es reicht!', 331.

872 Ibid., 344–345.

873 Alexander Janda and Mathias Vogl, Islam in Österreich (Vienna, 2010), 8.

874 Kriechbaumer, 'Es reicht!', 44.

875 This is the figure determined by the Integration Fund in: Die Presse, 14 April 2017, 9.

876 Michael Gehler, Österreich als Mitglied der Europäischen Union 1995–2005, in: Tschechien und Österreich nach dem Ende des Kalten Krieges. Auf getrennten Wegen in ein neues Europa, edited by Gernot Heiss et al. (Ústí nad Labem, 2009), 53.

877 Letter to the editor of the Neue Kronen Zeitung from Alfred Gusenbauer and Werner Faymann; the complete text can also be found in: APA, derStandard, 1 July 2008.

878 Vranitzky, Foreword, in: Über Kreisky, 9.

879 Rathkolb, Die paradoxe Republik, 27.

880 This was the interpretation of the dispatches of the American embassy in Vienna published during the WikiLeaks revelations. See: http://kurier.at/nachrichten/2055732.php, 6 December 2010.

881 Kriechbaumer, 'Es reicht!', 531.

882 This phrase can be found in Kriechbaumer, 'Es reicht!', 471.

883 Ibid., 754.

884 Othmar Karas, Österreich und Europa. Ein Aufbruch zu neuer Dynamik?, in: Österreichisches Jahrbuch für Politik, 2008, edited by Andreas Khol et al. (Vienna/Cologne/Weimar, 2009), 251–265.

885 Österreichisches Jahrbuch für Politik, 2008, Introduction, XI.

886 Martin Falb, 'Die Herausforderungen an die Politik sind groß'. Die Regierungsverhandlungen 2008 zwischen Werner Faymann und Josef Pröll, in: Österreichisches Jahrbuch für Politik, 2008, 137–152.

887 Josef Pröll, Österreich nach der Krise, in: Österreichisches Jahrbuch für Politik, 2009 (Vienna/Cologne/Weimar, 2010), 9.

888 Oliver Pink, Die Ära Faymann. Wer war Werner Faymann? Und was bleibt von seiner Kanzlerschaft?, in: Österreichisches Jahrbuch für Politik, 2016, 231–235, here 232.

889 Alexander Jand, Die internationale Finanzkrise, in: Österreichisches Jahrbuch für Politik, 2009, 84.

890 Österreichisches Jahrbuch für Politik, 2011 (Vienna, 2012), Foreword.

891 The stages of the conflict are briefly summarised in: Stefan Karner, Die Lösung der Kärntner Ortstafelfrage, in: Österreichisches Jahrbuch für Politik, 2011 (Vienna, 2012), 213–240.

892 Andreas Khol, Persönliche politische Randnoten zur Lösung der Ortstafelfrage, in: Österreichisches Jahrbuch für Politik, 2001 (Vienna, 2012), 249.

893 This is the phrase of Rudolf Burger in the Wiener Zeitung, 8 December 2016.

894 Peter Filzmaier, Winnetous Apachen würden gewinnen? Neue Parteien in Österreich – Morphologie und Perspektiven, in: Österreichisches Jahrbuch für Politik, 2012 (Vienna, 2013), 409–429, here 409.

895 See the very critical article by Stefan Thaller, Abzug vom Golan. Was wirklich geschah, in: Truppendienst, 4/2014. The article can also be read at: http://www.bundesheer.at/truppendienst/ausgaben/artikel.php?id=1732 [last accessed on 23 June 2017]. More nuanced and positive regarding the withdrawal: Paul Schneider, AUSCON und AUSBATT/UNDOF. Das rasche Ende einer langen Ära, in: Truppendienst, 5/214, 462–469. The situation no doubt developed into a state of complete confusion.

896 Excerpts of the dispatches and personal evaluations from Ambassador William C. Eacho published by WikiLeaks are reproduced in: Kurier, 5 December 2010. The reaction of several members of the government was published the following day, on 6 December.

897 Andreas Khol, MIGROKO vor dem Ende? Auf dem Weg in eine neue Republik, in: Österreichisches Jahrbuch für Politik, 2013 (Vienna/Cologne/Weimar, 2014), 3–14.

898 Peter Pelinka, Zur Koalition zwischen ÖVP und SPÖ: Hat 'Neu regieren' eine Chance?, in: Österreichisches Jahrbuch für Politik, 2013 (Vienna/Cologne/Weimar, 2014), 181–184.

899 Österreichisches Jahrbuch für Politik, 2014 (Vienna/Cologne/Weimar, 2015), Foreword, XI–XII.

900 Heinrich Friedjung, Das Zeitalter des Imperialismus 1884–1914, vol. 2 (Berlin, 1922), 169.

901 Lothar Rühl, Die strategische Lage zum Jahreswechsel, in: Österreichische Militärische Zeitschrift (ÖMZ), 1/2016, 13. More in-depth and with numerous bibliographic references: Heinz Brill, Globale Migrationsströme der Gegenwart. Die neue geopolitische Dimension der Sicherheitspolitik, in: ÖMZ, 5/2016, 604–613.

902 Charles E. Ritterband, Österreich. Stillstand im Dreivierteltakt (Vienna/Cologne/Weimar, 2016), 70.

903 Sebastian Kurz, Von der Lösung zum Problem, in: Österreichisches Jahrbuch für Politik, 2016, 254.

904 Mathias Vogl, Aktuelle Herausforderungen für die österreichische Asyl- und Fremdenpolitik, in: Österreichisches Jahrbuch für Politik 2015 (Vienna/Cologne/Weimar, 2016), 399–323, here 313.

905 Ulrich H. J. Körtner, Gesinnungs- und Verantwortungsethik im Widerstreit. Anmerkungen zur Debatte um Einwanderungs-, Asyl- und Integrationspolitik, in: Österreichisches Jahrbuch für Politik, 2015 (Vienna/Cologne/Weimar, 2016), 279–289, here 288.

906 Johann Gudenus, Die österreichische Flüchtlings-, Einwanderungs- und Integrationspolitik aus freiheitlicher Sicht. Ziele, Zielerreichung sowie künftige Herausforderungen, in: Österreichisches Jahrbuch für Politik, 2015 (Vienna/Cologne/Weimar, 2016), 347–356, here 348.

907 Peter Gridling, Extreme in Österreich. Identitäre und extreme Linke, in: Österreichisches Jahrbuch für Politik, 2016 (Vienna/Cologne/Weimar, 2017), 329.

908 *Der Spiegel*, 10/216, 19.

909 Iris Bonavida and Julia Neuhauser, Braucht Österreich eigentlich Einwanderung? Ja, aber ..., in: *Die Presse*, 16 December 2016, 8–9.

910 Albert Rohan, Österreich und die Türkei. Ein gestörtes Verhältnis, in: Österreichisches Jahrbuch für Politik, 2016 (Vienna/Cologne/Weimar, 2017), 134.

911 Fritz Plasser and Franz Sommer, Bundespräsidentenwahlen 2016: Politische Einstellungen und Motive der Wähler, regionale Trends und Wählerströme, in: Österreichisches Jahrbuch für Politik, 2016 (Vienna/Cologne/Weimar, 2017), 5.

25 Afterword

912 All quotations are taken from Peter Stachel, Mythos Heldenplatz (Vienna, 2002), 7.

Bibliography

This bibliography lists only works cited in the endnotes, predominantly monographs with their bibliographic information and edited collections according to main title. Individual chapters in edited collections as well as journal articles are included here only when mentioned once but are otherwise generally omitted, in which case they can be found only in the endnotes. The same applies to newspaper and magazine articles.

Agstner, Rudolf, Handbuch des Österreichischen Auswärtigen Dienstes, vol. 1: 1918–1938. Zentrale, Gesandtschaften und Konsulate (Vienna, 2015)

Albrich, Thomas, Exodus durch Österreich. Die jüdischen Flüchtlinge 1945–1948 (Innsbruck, 1987)

Idem, Asylland wider Willen. Die Problematik der 'Displaced Persons' in Österreich 1945–1948, in: Die bevormundete Nation. Österreich und die Alliierten 1945–1949, edited by Günter Bischof and Josef Leidenfrost (= Innsbrucker Forschungen zur Zeitgeschichte, vol. 4, Innsbruck, 1988)

Idem, Luftkrieg über der Alpenfestung 1943–1945. Der Gau Tirol-Vorarlberg und die Operationszone Alpenvorland (Innsbruck, 2014)

Allmayer-Beck, Johann Christoph, Die Österreicher im Zweiten Weltkrieg, in: Unser Heer. 300 Jahre österreichisches Soldatentum in Krieg und Frieden (Vienna/Munich/Zurich, 1963)

Idem, 'Herr Oberleitnant, det lohnt doch nicht!' Kriegserinnerungen an die Jahre 1938 bis 1945, edited by Erwin A. Schmidl (Vienna/Cologne/Weimar, 2013)

Aufstieg und Fall des VdU. Briefe und Protokolle aus privaten Nachlässen 1948–1955, edited by Lothar Höbelt (Vienna/Cologne/Weimar, 2015)

Außenansichten. Europäische (Be)Wertungen zur Geschichte Österreichs im 20. Jahrhundert, edited by Oliver Rathkolb (Innsbruck/Vienna/Munich, 2003)

Außenpolitische Dokumente der Republik Österreich, vol. 4: Zwischen Staatsbankrott und Genfer Sanierung. 11. Juni 1921 bis 6. November 1922, edited by Klaus Koch, Walter Rauscher and Arnold Suppan (Vienna/Munich, 1998)

Austrian Foreign Policy in Historical Context, edited by Günter Bischof, Anton Pelinka and Michael Gehler (= Contemporary Austrian Studies, vol. 14, New Brunswick, 2006)

Austria's International Position after the End of the Cold War, edited by Günter Bischof and Ferdinand Karlhofer (= Contemporary Austrian Studies, vol. 22, New Orleans, 2013)

Autengruber, Peter, Kleinparteien in Österreich 1945 bis 1966 (Innsbruck/Vienna, 1997)

Bailer, Brigitte, and Gerhard *Ungar*, Die namentliche Erfassung der österreichischen Holocaustopfer und Namentliche Erfassung der österreichischen Opfer politischer Verfolgung, in: Opferschicksale. Jahrbuch 2013 des Dokumentationsarchivs des Österreichischen Widerstandes (Vienna, 2013)

Bauer, Friedrich, Russische Umbrüche. Von Gorbatschow über Jelzin zu Putin (Vienna, 2008)

Bauer, Kurt, Sozialgeschichtliche Aspekte des nationalsozialistischen Juliputsches 1934, doctoral thesis in humanities and cultural sciences, University of Vienna (2001)

Idem, Hitlers zweiter Putsch. Dollfuß, die Nazis und der 25. Juli 1934 (St. Pölten/Salzburg, 2014)

Bauer, Otto, Die österreichische Revolution (Vienna, 1923)

Beck, Roland, and Peter *Braun*, Die schweizerische Landesverteidigung im Spannungsfeld von nuklearen Gefechtsfeldwaffen und bewaffneter Neutralität 1955–1961, in: Die Schweiz und der Kalte Krieg, edited by the Association suisse d'histoire et de sciences militaires (Bern, 2003)

Beer, Siegfried, and Stefan *Karner*, Der Krieg aus der Luft. Kärnten und Steiermark 1941–1945 (Graz, 1992)

Berger, Peter, Im Schatten der Diktatur. Die Finanzdiplomatie des Vertreters des Völkerbundes in Österreich Meinoud Marinus Rost van Tonningen 1931–1936 (Vienna/Cologne/Weimar, 2000)

Botz, Gerhard, Die Eingliederung Österreichs in das Deutsche Reich. Planung und Verwirklichung des politisch-administrativen Anschlusses (1938–1940), 2nd expanded edition (Linz, 1976)

Idem, Gewalt in der Politik. Attentate, Zusammenstöße, Putschversuche, Unruhen in Österreich 1918 bis 1938 (Munich, 1983)

Idem, Nationalsozialismus in Wien. Machtübernahme, Herrschaftssicherung, Radikalisierung 1938/39 (Vienna, 2008)

Idem, Die 'Österreichische Revolution' 1918/19. Zu Kontexten und Problematik einer alten Meistererzählung der Zeitgeschichte in Österreich, in: Zeitgeschichte, vol. 44, no. 6 (2014)

Brauneder, Wilhelm, Deutsch-Österreich 1918. Die Republik entsteht (Vienna/Munich, 2000)

Idem, Österreich 1918 bis 1938. 'Erste' oder wie viel 'Republiken'?, in: Studien, vol. IV (Frankfurt am Main, 2011)

Broucek, Peter, Ein Verschwörer gegen Hitler und für Österreich. Der Generalstabsoffizier Erwin Lahousen, in: Österreich in Geschichte und Literatur, vol. 49, no. 2 (2005)

Broucek, Peter, Militärischer Widerstand. Studien zur österreichischen Staatsgesinnung und NS-Abwehr (Vienna/Cologne/Weimar, 2008)

Bruckmüller, Ernst, Nation Österreich. Kulturelles Bewußtsein und gesellschaftlich-politische Prozesse (Vienna/Cologne/Graz, 1996)

Brühl, Dietrich Graf, Flucht in die Freiheit. Die Flüchtlingsbewegung aus Ungarn im Jahre 1989. Ein Bericht, in: Aufbruch in eine neue Zeit. 1989 im Rückblick, edited by Manfried Rauchensteiner (Vienna, 2000)

Brunner, Waltraud, Das Deutsche Eigentum und das Ringen um den österreichischen Staatsvertrag, doctoral thesis, University of Vienna (1976)

Buchmann, Bertrand Michael, Österreicher in der Deutschen Wehrmacht. Soldatenalltag im Zweiten Weltkrieg (Vienna/Cologne/Weimar, 2009)

Burian, Peter, Österreich und der Völkerbund, in: Nation, Nationalismus, Postnation, edited by Harm Klueting (Cologne/Vienna, 1992)

Butschek, Felix, Österreichische Wirtschaftsgeschichte. Von der Antike bis zur Gegenwart (Vienna/Cologne/Weimar, 2012)

Carafano, James Jay, 'Waltzing into the Cold War'. US Army Intelligence Operations in Postwar Austria, 1944–1948, in: The Vranitzky Era in Austria (= Contemporary Austrian Studies, vol. 7, edited by Günter Bischof, Anton Pelinka and Ferdinand Karlhofer, New Brunswick/London, 1999)

Carsten, Francis L., The First Austrian Republic. A Study based on British and Austrian Documents (Aldershot/Brookfield, 1986)

Churchill, Winston S., His Complete Speeches 1897–1963, edited by Robert Rhodes James, vol. VI, 1935–1942 (New York/London, 1974)

Cole, Laurence, Der Habsburger-Mythos, in: Memoria Austriae I. Menschen, Mythen, Zeiten, edited by Emil Brix (Vienna, 2004)

Corrieri, Peter, Der Brief der 1700. Demokratischer Offizierswiderstand gegen politischen Populismus 1970/71 (= Schriften zur Geschichte des Österreichischen Bundesheeres, vol. 21, Vienna, 2013)

Dallin, David, Sowjetische Außenpolitik nach Stalins Tod (Cologne/Berlin, 1961)

Das Bundesheer der Zweiten Republik. Eine Dokumentation, edited by Manfried Rauchensteiner (= Schriften des Heeresgeschichtlichen Museums, vol. 9, Vienna, 1980)

Das Deutsche Reich und der Zweite Weltkrieg, edited by the Militärgeschichtliches Forschungsamt, vol. 9/1: Die deutsche Kriegsgesellschaft 1939–1945 (Munich, 2004)

Das geistige Leben Wiens in der Zwischenkriegszeit, edited by Norbert Leser (= Quellen und Studien zur österreichischen Geistesgeschichte im 19. und 20. Jahrhundert, vol. 1, Vienna, 1981)

Das Werden der Ersten Republik. Der Rest ist Österreich, edited by Helmut Konrad and Wolfgang Maderthaner, 2 vols. (Vienna, 2008)

Der Februar-Aufruhr 1934. Das Eingreifen des österreichischen Bundesheeres zu seiner Niederwerfung. (Nur für den Dienstgebrauch), as printed manuscript (Vienna, 1935)

Der österreichische Staatsrat. Protokolle des Vollzugsausschusses, des Staatsrates und des Geschäftsführenden Staatsratsdirektoriums, 21. Oktober 1918 bis 14. März 1919, edited by Gertrud Enderle-Burcel, Hanns Haas and Peter Mähner, vol. 1 (Vienna, 2008)

Der Österreichische Staatsvertrag (The Austrian State Treaty), edited by Arnold Suppan, Gerald Stourzh and Wolfgang Mueller (= Archiv für österreichische Geschichte, vol. 110, Vienna, 2005)

Der Putsch von Lamprechtshausen. Zeugen des Juli 1934 berichten, edited by Andreas Maislinger (Salzburg, 1992)

Der Wiener Gipfel 1961. Kennedy – Chruschtschow, edited by Stefan Karner, Barbara Stelzl-Marx, Natalja Tomilina, Alexander Tschubarjan et al. (Innsbruck/Vienna/Bolzano, 2011)

Die Ära Josef Klaus, edited by Robert Kriechbaumer, vol. 1: Dokumente; vol. 2: Aus der Sicht der Zeitgenossen (Vienna/Cologne/Weimar, 1998)

Die Ära Kreisky. Österreich 1970–1983 in der historischen Analyse, im Urteil der politischen Kontrahenten und in Karikaturen von Ironimus, edited by Robert Kriechbaumer (= Schriften-

reihe des Forschungsinstitutes für Politisch-Historische Studien der Dr.-Wilfried-Haslauer-
    Bibliothek, vol. 22, Vienna/Cologne/Weimar, 2004)

Die Großglockner Hochalpenstraße, edited by Johannes Hörl and Dietmar Schöndorfer (Vienna/
    Cologne/Weimar, 2015)

Die Habsburgermonarchie und der Erste Weltkrieg (= Die Habsburgermonarchie 1848–1918,
    edited by the Österreichische Akademie der Wissenschaften, vol. XI/2: Weltkriegsstatistik
    Österreich-Ungarns 1914–1918, edited by Helmut Rumpler, with the assistance of Anatol
    Schmied-Kowarzik and Helmut Rumpler (Vienna, 2015)

Die Kreisky-Jahre 1967–1983, edited by Heinz Fischer (Himberg, 1993)

Die Nebel der Begrifflichkeit oder vom schwierigen Umgang mit dem Ständestaat und der Va-
    terländischen Front, in: Österreich! Und Front Heil! Aus den Akten des Generalsekretariats
    der Vaterländischen Front. Innenansichten eines Regimes, edited by Robert Kriechbaumer
    (Vienna/Cologne/Weimar, 2005)

Die Rote Armee in Österreich. Sowjetische Besatzung 1945–1955. Dokumente, edited by Ste-
    fan Karner, Barbara Stelzl-Marx and Alexander Tschubarjan, 2 vols. (Graz/Vienna/Munich,
    2005)

'Dieses Österreich retten'. Protokolle der Christlichsozialen Parteitage der Ersten Republik, edi-
    ted by Robert Kriechbaumer (Vienna/Cologne/Weimar, 2006)

Doppelbauer, Wolfgang, Zum Elend noch die Schande. Das altösterreichische Offizierskorps am
    Beginn der Republik (= Militärgeschichtliche Dissertationen österreichischer Universitäten,
    vol. 9, Vienna, 1988)

Dreidemy, Lucile, Der Dollfuß-Mythos. Eine Biographie des Posthumen (Vienna/Cologne/
    Weimar, 2014)

Drimmel, Heinrich, Österreichs Geistesleben zwischen Ost und West, in: Österreich. Die Zweite
    Republik, edited by Erika Weinzierl and Kurt Skalnik, vol. 2 (Graz/Vienna/Cologne, 1972)

Duchhardt, Heinz, Der Wiener Kongress. Die Neugestaltung Europas 1814/15 (Munich, 2013)

Ebner, Paulus, and Karl *Vocelka*, Die zahme Revolution. '68 und was davon blieb (Vienna, 1998)

Eger, Reiner, Krisen an Österreichs Grenzen. Das Verhalten Österreichs während des Ungarn-
    aufstandes 1956 und der tschechoslowakischen Krise 1968. Ein Vergleich (Vienna/Munich,
    1981)

Eichtinger, Martin, and Helmut *Wohnout*, Alois Mock. Ein Politiker schreibt Geschichte (Graz,
    2008)

Eigner, Peter, and Peter *Melichar*, Das Ende der Boden-Credit-Anstalt 1929 und die Rolle Ru-
    dolf Siegharts, in: Bankrott (= Österreichische Zeitschrift für Geschichtswissenschaften, vol.
    19, no. 3, 2008)

Ein General im Zwielicht. Die Erinnerungen Edmund Glaises von Horstenau, edited by Peter
    Broucek, vol. 2 (Vienna/Cologne/Graz, 1982)

Elste, Alfred, and Wilhelm *Wadl*, Titos langer Schatten. Bomben- und Geheimdienstterror im
    Kärnten der 1970er Jahre (Klagenfurt am Wörthersee, 2015)

Embacher, Helga, Neubeginn ohne Illusionen. Juden in Österreich nach 1945 (Vienna, 1995)

Enzyklopädie des Nationalsozialismus, edited by Wolfgang Benz (Stuttgart, 1997)

Etschmann, Wolfgang. Rüstungswirtschaft und KZ-System in Österreich 1938 bis 1945, in:

Walküre und der Totenwald. Das Kriegsjahr 1944. Katalog zur Sonderausstellung des Heeresgeschichtlichen Museums (Vienna, 1994)

Feichtlbauer, Hubert, Fonds für Versöhnung, Frieden und Zusammenarbeit: Späte Anerkennung,
Geschichte, Schicksale (Vienna, 2005)

Feifel, Johanna, Schönau und das Österreichbild in der hebräisch-, deutsch- und englischsprachigen Presse, doctoral thesis, University of Vienna (2002)

Fellner, Fritz, Die Pariser Vororteverträge von 1919/20, in: Versailles – St. Germain – Trianon.
Umbruch in Europa vor fünfzig Jahren, edited by Karl Bosl (Vienna/Munich, 1971)

Fellner, Fritz, and Heidrun *Maschl*, Saint Germain im Sommer 1919. Die Briefe Franz Kleins
aus der Zeit seiner Mitwirkung in der österreichischen Friedensdelegation, Mai–August 1919
(= Quellen zur Geschichte des 19. und 20. Jahrhunderts, vol. 1, Salzburg, 1977)

Fischer, Ernst, Das Ende einer Illusion. Erinnerungen 1945–1955 (Vienna/Munich/Zurich,
1973)

Fischer, Heinz, Wende-Zeiten. Ein österreichischer Zwischenbefund (Vienna, 2004)

Foreign Relations of the United States (= FRUS), 1945/III, 1946/V, 1947/II, 1948/III, 1950/
IV, 1955/V, 1955-1957/Central and SE Europe, 1961 – 1963/XVI (Washington, DC, 1968–
1994)

Frauen im Reichsgau Oberdonau. Geschlechterspezifische Bruchlinien im Nationalsozialismus,
edited by Gabriella Hauch (Linz, 2006)

Fritsche, Maria, Österreichische Deserteure und Selbstverstümmler in der Deutschen Wehrmacht (Vienna/Cologne/Weimar, 2004)

Frölichsthal, Georg, Die Mitgliedschaft zum Haus Österreich nach 1918, in: Adler, vols. 6/7
(2016)

Furlani, Silvio, and Adam *Wandruszka*, Österreich und Italien. Ein bilaterales Geschichtsbuch
(Vienna/Munich, 1973)

Ganglmair, Siegwald, Österreicher in den alliierten Armeen 1939 bis 1945, in: Walküre und der
Totenwald. Das Kriegsjahr 1944. Ausstellungskatalog Heeresgeschichtliches Museum (Vienna, 1994)

Geldmacher, Thomas, 'Auf Nimmerwiedersehen'. Fahnenflucht, unerlaubte Entfernung und das
Problem, die Tatbestände auseinander zu halten, in: Opfer der NS-Militärjustiz. Urteilspraxis, Strafvollzug, Entschädigungspolitik in Österreich, edited by Walter Manoschek (Vienna,
2003)

Gehler, Michael, '… eine grotesk überzogene Dämonisierung eines Mannes …'? Die Waldheim-
Affäre 1986–1992, in: Michael Gehler and Hubert Sickinger, Politische Affären und Skandale in Österreich. Von Mayerling bis Waldheim (Thaur/Vienna/Munich, 1995)

Idem, Präventivschlag als Fehlschlag: Motive, Intentionen und Konsequenzen der EU-14 Sank-
tionsmaßnahmen gegen Österreich im Jahr 2000, in: Eine europäische Erregung. Die 'Sank-
tionen' der Vierzehn gegen Österreich im Jahr 2000. Analysen und Kommentare, edited by
Erhard Busek and Martin Schauer (Vienna/Graz/Cologne, 2003)

Idem, Österreich als Mitglied der Europäischen Union 1995–2005, in: Tschechien und Österreich nach dem Ende des Kalten Krieges. Auf getrennten Wegen in ein neues Europa, edited
by Gernot Heiss et al. (Ústí nad Labem, 2009)

Idem, 'to guarantee a country which was a military vacuum'. Die Westmächte und Österreichs territoriale Integrität 1955–1957, in: Zwischen den Blöcken. NATO, Warschauer Pakt und Österreich, edited by Manfried Rauchensteiner (Vienna/Cologne/Weimar, 2010)

Idem, Modellfall für Deutschland? Die Österreichlösung mit Staatsvertrag und Neutralität 1945–1955 (Innsbruck/Vienna/Bolzano, 2015)

Germann, Richard, Österreichische Soldaten in Ost- und Südosteuropa 1941–1945. Deutsche Krieger – nationalsozialistische Verbrecher – österreichische Opfer?, doctoral thesis, University of Vienna (2006)

Idem, Neue Wege in der Militärgeschichte. Regionale Zusammensetzung 'ostmärkischer' Einheiten am Beispiel dreier Kompanien, in: Politische Gewalt und Machtausübung im 20. Jahrhundert, Zeitgeschichte, Zeitgeschehen und Kontroversen. Festschrift für Gerhard Botz, edited by Heinrich Berger et al. (Vienna/Cologne/Weimar, 2011)

Geschichte Österreichs, edited by Thomas Winkelbauer (Stuttgart, 2016)

Giller, Joachim, Hubert *Mader* and Christina *Seidl*, Wo sind sie geblieben …? Kriegerdenkmäler und Gefallenenehrung in Österreich (= Schriften des Heeresgeschichtlichen Museums, vol. 11, Vienna, 1992)

Göhring, Walter, Verdrängt und vergessen. Friedensnobelpreisträger Alfred Hermann Fried (Vienna, 2006)

Goldinger, Walter, Geschichte der Republik Österreich (Vienna, 1962)

Goldinger, Walter, and Dieter A. *Binder*, Geschichte der Republik Österreich 1918–1938 (Vienna/Munich, 1992)

Grischany, Thomas R., Der Ostmark treue Alpensöhne. Die Integration der Österreicher in die großdeutsche Wehrmacht, 1938–45 (= zeitgeschichte im Kontext, vol. 9, Göttingen, 2015)

Gross, Johann, Spiegelgrund. Leben in NS-Erziehungsanstalten (Vienna, 2013)

Gruber, Karl, Zwischen Befreiung und Freiheit. Der Sonderfall Österreich (Vienna, 1953)

Grubmayr, Herbert, 'In zwei Wochen gehst du nach Moskau', in: Demokratie und Geschichte, edited by Helmut Wohnout (Vienna/Cologne/Weimar, 1999)

Gütermann, Christoph, Die Geschichte der österreichischen Friedensbewegung 1891–1985, in: Überlegungen zum Frieden, edited by Manfried Rauchensteiner (Vienna, 1987)

Haas, Hanns, Österreich und die Alliierten 1918–1919, in: Saint-Germain 1919 (= Veröffentlichungen der Wissenschaftlichen Kommission zur Erforschung der Geschichte der Republik Österreich, vol. 11, Vienna, 1989)

Hackl, Dietrich, Im Zentrum der Politik. Als Parlamentsstenograph im Hohen Haus (Vienna/Cologne/Graz, 1984)

Haffner, Sebastian, Anmerkungen zu Hitler (Munich, 1978)

Hainisch, Michael, 75 Jahre aus bewegter Zeit. Lebenserinnerungen eines österreichischen Staatsmannes, with the assistance of Friedrich Weissensteiner (Graz/Vienna/Cologne, 1978)

Hanisch, Ernst, Gibt es einen spezifisch österreichischen Widerstand? In: Widerstand. Ein Problem zwischen Theorie und Geschichte, edited by Peter Steinbach (Cologne, 1987)

Idem, März 1938: eine Salzburger Perspektive, in: Der März 1938 in Salzburg. Symposion Feindbilder (= Salzburger Diskussionen, vol. 10, Salzburg, 1988)

Idem, Der lange Schatten des Staates. Österreichische Gesellschaftsgeschichte im 20. Jahrhundert (Vienna, 1994)

Idem, Männlichkeiten. Eine andere Geschichte des 20. Jahrhunderts (Vienna/Cologne/Weimar, 2005)

Idem, Der große Illusionist. Otto Bauer (1881–1938) (Vienna/Cologne/Weimar, 2011)

Hatschek, Christoph, and Alfred *Palisek*, Landesverräter oder Patrioten? Das österreichische Bataillon 1943 bis 1945 (Graz/Vienna/Cologne, 2001)

Hautmann, Hans, Die Geschichte der Rätebewegung in Österreich 1918–1924 (Vienna/Zurich, 1987)

Heresch, Elisabeth, Nikolaus II. Feigheit, Lüge und Verrat (Munich, 1992)

Herz, Martin F, Understanding Austria. The Political Reports and Analyses of Martin F. Herz 1945–1948, edited by Reinhold Wagnleitner (= Quellen zur Geschichte des 19. und 20. Jahrhunderts, vol. 4, Salzburg, 1984)

Höbelt, Lothar, Die Heimwehren und die österreichische Politik 1927–1936 (Graz, 2017)

Hoffmann, Georg, Fliegerlynchjustiz. Gewalt gegen abgeschossene alliierte Flugzeugbesatzungen 1943–1945 (= Krieg in der Geschichte, vol. 88, Paderborn, 2015)

Hoffmann, Robert, Die Mission Sir Thomas Cuninghames in Wien 1919. Britische Österreichpolitik zur Zeit der Pariser Friedenskonferenz, doctoral thesis, University of Salzburg (1971)

Hoffmann-Holter, Beatrix, 'Abreisendmachung'. Jüdische Kriegsflüchtlinge in Wien 1914 bis 1923 (Vienna/Cologne/Weimar, 1995)

Hofmann, Josef, Der Pfrimer-Putsch. Der steirische Heimwehrprozeß des Jahres 1931 (= Publikationen des Österreichischen Instituts für Zeitgeschichte, vol. 4, Graz, 1965)

Holzer, Willibald Ingo, Die österreichischen Bataillone im Verband der NOV I POI. Die Kampfgruppe Avantgarde Steiermark. Die Partisanengruppe Leoben-Donawitz, doctoral thesis, University of Vienna (1971)

Hutter, Clemens M., Großglockner Hochalpenstraße (Salzburg, 2007)

Houlihan, Patrick J., Was There an Austrian Stab-in-the-Back Myth? Interwar Military Interpretations of Defeat, in: From empire to republic: Post-World War I Austria, edited by Günter Bischof, Fritz Plasser and Peter Berger (= Contemporary Austrian Studies, vol. 19, New Orleans/Innsbruck, 2010)

Jabloner, Clemens, Methodenreinheit und Erkenntnisvielfalt. Aufsätze zur Rechtstheorie, Rechtsdogmatik und Rechtsgeschichte, edited by Thomas Olechowski and Klaus Zeleny (= Schriftenreihe des Hans-Kelsen-Instituts, vol. 35, Vienna, 2013)

Jacobsen, Hans-Adolf, 1939–1945. Der Zweite Weltkrieg in Chronik und Dokumenten (Darmstadt, 1961)

Jagschitz, Gerhard, Der Putsch. Die Nationalsozialisten 1934 in Österreich (Graz/Vienna/Cologne, 1976)

Janda, Alexander, and Mathias *Vogl*, Islam in Österreich (Vienna, 2010)

Jedlicka, Ludwig, Ein Heer im Schatten der Parteien. Die militärpolitische Lage Österreichs 1918–1938 (Graz/Cologne, 1955)

Idem, Ein unbekannter Bericht Kaltenbrunners über die Lage in Österreich im September 1944, in: Österreich in Geschichte und Literatur, vol. 2 (Vienna, 1960)

Idem, Aufteilungs- und Einmarschpläne um Österreich 1918–1934, in: Ludwig Jedlicka, Vom alten zum neuen Österreich. Fallstudien zur österreichischen Zeitgeschichte 1900–1975 (St. Pölten, 1975)

Jochum, Manfred, 80 Jahre Republik Österreich (Vienna, 1998)

Kaltenbrunner, Matthias, Flucht aus dem Todesblock. Der Massenausbruch sowjetischer Offiziere aus dem Block 20 des KZ Mauthausen und die 'Mühlviertler Hasenjagd'. Hintergründe, Folgen, Aufarbeitung (= Der Nationalsozialismus und seine Folgen, vol. 5, Innsbruck, 2012)

Kampf um die Stadt. Ausstellungskatalog Wien Museum, edited by Wolfgang Kos (Vienna, 2010)

Karner, Stefan, Die Steiermark im 'Dritten Reich' 1938–1945 unter besonderer Berücksichtigung ihrer wirtschaftlichen und sozialen Entwicklung (Graz, 1983)

Idem, Die Bemühungen zur Lösung des Kärntner Minderheitenproblems 2005, in: Die Ortstafelfrage aus Expertensicht, edited by Peter Karpf (= Kärnten Dokumentation, special vol. 1, Klagenfurt, 2006)

Idem, Zu den Rehabilitierungen von Kriegsgefangenen und Zivilisten in der Sowjetunion unter Chruschtschow und in den 1990er-Jahren. Dargestellt am Beispiel von deutschen und österreichischen Kriegsgefangenen, in: Sowjetische Schauprozesse in Mittel- und Osteuropa, edited by Csaba Szabó (= Publikationen der ungarischen Geschichtsforschung in Wien, vol. XIII, Vienna, 2015)

Keller, Fritz, Die Arbeiter- und Soldatenräte in Österreich 1918–23. Versuch einer Analyse (Vienna, 1998)

Kerekes, Lajos, Abenddämmerung einer Demokratie. Mussolini, Gömbös und die Heimwehr (Vienna/Frankfurt/Zurich, 1966)

Kernbauer, Hans, Eduard *März* and Fritz *Weber*, Die wirtschaftliche Entwicklung, in: Österreich 1918–1938, edited by Erika Weinzierl and Kurt Skalnik, vol. 1 (Vienna, 1983)

Kienitz, Sabine, Der Krieg der Invaliden. Helden-Bilder und Männlichkeitskonstruktionen nach dem Ersten Weltkrieg, in: Militärgeschichtliche Zeitschrift, vol. 60, no. 2 (2001)

Klaus, Josef, Macht und Ohnmacht in Österreich. Konfrontationen und Versuche (Vienna/Munich/Zurich, 1971)

Kleindel, Walter, Österreich. Daten zur Geschichte und Kultur (Vienna/Heidelberg, 1978)

Klingenstein, Grete, Die Anleihe von Lausanne (Österreich Archiv, Vienna, 1965)

Koch, Klaus, Zwischen Mussolini und Hitler. August 1934–Juli 1936, in: Außenpolitische Dokumente der Republik Österreich 1918–1938, vol. 10: Zwischen Mussolini und Hitler, edited by Klaus Koch and Elisabeth Vyslonzil (= Fontes Rerum Austriacarum, 2nd section, vol. 96, Vienna, 2014)

Kollman, Eric C., Theodor Körner, Militär und Politiker (Vienna, 1972)

Körner, Theodor, Zwei Monate Aufbauarbeit in Wien. Sozialistische Hefte, vol. 2 (Vienna, 1945)

Korruption in Österreich. Historische Streiflichter, edited by Ernst Bruckmüller (Vienna, 2011)

Kreisky, Bruno, Zwischen den Zeiten. Erinnerungen aus 5 Jahrzehnten (Berlin, 1986)

Idem, Im Strom der Politik. Erfahrungen eines Europäers (Berlin, 1988)

Idem, Der Mensch im Mittelpunkt. Der Memoiren dritter Teil (Berlin, 1996)

Kriechbaumer, Robert, Österreichs Innenpolitik 1970–1975 (= Österreichisches Jahrbuch für Politik, special issue, vol. 1, Munich/Vienna, 1981)

Idem, Liebe auf den Zweiten Blick (= Geschichte der österreichischen Bundesländer seit 1945, edited by Herbert Dachs, Ernst Hanisch and Robert Kriechbaumer, Vienna, 1998)

Idem, Welcher Staat? Die Christlichsoziale Partei und die Republik 1918–1920, in: Der Forschende Blick. Beiträge zur Geschichte Österreichs im 20. Jahrhundert. Festschrift für Ernst Hanisch zum 70. Geburtstag, edited by Reinhard Krammer et al. (Vienna/Cologne/Weimar, 2010)

Idem, Zwischen Österreich und Großdeutschland. Eine politische Geschichte der Salzburger Festspiele 1933–1944 (Vienna/Cologne/Weimar, 2013)

Idem, '… ständiger Verdruss und viele Verletzungen'. Die Regierung Klima/Schüssel und die Bildung der ÖVP-FPÖ Regierung. Österreich 1997–2000 (= Schriftenreihe des Forschungsinstitutes der Dr.- Wilfried-Haslauer-Bibliothek, vol. 47, Vienna/Cologne/Weimar, 2014)

Idem, 'Es reicht!' Die Regierung Gusenbauer – Molterer. Österreich 2007/2008 (= Schriftenreihe des Forschungsinstitutes für Historisch-Politische Studien der Dr.-Wilfried-Haslaur-Bibliotohek, vol. 55, Graz/Vienna/Cologne, 2016)

Krisenjahre. Max Weiler und der Krieg. Katalog zur Sonderausstellung im Heeresgeschichtlichen Museum 1.12.2004–6.2.2005 (Vienna, 2004)

Krüger, Dieter, Brennender Enzian. Die Operationsplanung der NATO für Österreich und Norditalien 1951 bis 1960 (= Einzelschriften zur Militärgeschichte, vol. 46, Freiburg im Breisgau/Berlin/Vienna, 2010)

Kuntner, Wilhelm, Die strategische Situation, in: Handbuch der geistigen Landesverteidigung (Vienna, 1974)

Kuprian, Hermann, Der Tiroler Separatismus der Ersten Republik, in: 1918/1919. Die Bundesländer und die Republik. Protokollband des Symposiums zum 75. Jahrestag der Ausrufung der 1. Republik am 12. und 13. November im Grazer Stadtmuseum, edited by Gerhard Michael Dienes (Graz, 1994)

Kustascher, Erika, 'Berufsstand' oder 'Stand'. Ein politischer Schlüsselbegriff im Österreich der Zwischenkriegszeit (= Veröffentlichung der Kommission für neuere Geschichte Österreichs, vol. 113, Vienna/Cologne/Weimar, 2016)

Lhotsky, Alphons, Die Verteidigung der Wiener Sammlungen durch die Erste Republik, in: Die Haupt- und Residenzstadt Wien, Sammelwesen und Ikonographie. Der österreichische Mensch (= Alphons Lhotsky, Aufsätze und Vorträge, edited by Hans Wagner and Heinrich Koller, vol. IV, Vienna, 1974)

Liebmann, Maximilian, Kirche und Anschluss, in: Kirche in Österreich 1938–1988, edited by Maximilian Liebmann, Hans Paarhammer and Alfred Rinnerthaler (Graz/Vienna/Cologne, 1990)

Liegl, Barbara, and Anton *Pelinka*, Chronos und Ödipus. Der Kreisky-Androsch-Konflikt (Vienna, 2004)

Loitfellner, Sabine, Simon Wiesenthals 'Schuld und Sühne Memorandum' an die Bundesregierung 1966. Ein zeitgenössisches Abbild zum politischen Umgang mit NSVerbrechen, in: Kriegsverbrechen, NS-Verbrechen und die europäische Strafjustiz von Nürnberg bis Den Haag, edited by Heimo Halbrainer and Claudia Kuretsidis-Haider (Graz, 2007)

Ludwig, Michael, Klaus Dieter *Mulley* and Robert *Streibel*, Der Oktoberstreik 1950. Ein Wendepunkt der Zweiten Republik (Vienna, 1991)

Lukan, Walter, Die slowenische Politik und Kaiser Karl, in: Karl I. (IV.). Der Erste Weltkrieg und
das Ende der Donaumonarchie, edited by Andreas Gottsmann (Vienna, 2007)

Luža, Radomir, Österreich und die großdeutsche Idee in der NS-Zeit (Vienna/Cologne/Graz,
1977)

Ideme, Der Widerstand in Österreich 1938–1945 (Vienna, 1983)

Malfèr, Stefan, Wien und Rom nach dem Ersten Weltkrieg. Österreichisch-italienische Beziehungen 1919–1923 (= Veröffentlichung der Kommission für neuere Geschichte Österreichs,
vol. 66, Vienna/Cologne/Graz, 1978)

Maršálek, Hans, Die Geschichte des Konzentrationslagers Mauthausen. Dokumentation (Vienna, 1980)

Matsch, Erwin, Österreich und der Völkerbund, in: Conturen, vol. I (Vienna,1994)

McLoughlin, Finnbar (Barry), Der Republikanische Schutzbund und gewalttätige politische Auseinandersetzungen in Österreich 1923–1934, doctoral thesis, University of Vienna, (1990)

Idem, Die Partei, in: Kommunismus in Österreich 1918–1938, edited by Barry McLoughlin,
Hannes Leidinger and Verena Moritz (Innsbruck/Vienna/Bolzano, 2009)

Mähr, Wilfried, Von der UNRRA zum Marshallplan. Die amerikanische Wirtschafts- und Finanzhilfe an Österreich 1945, doctoral thesis, University of Vienna (1985)

Maimann, Helene, Vergangenheit, die nie vergeht. NS-Herrschaft in Österreich 1938–1945, in:
Das Neue Österreich. Begleitband zur Sonderausstellung im Oberen Belvedere, edited by
Günter Dürigl and Herbert Frodl (Vienna, 2005)

Idem, Über Kreisky. Gespräche aus Distanz und Nähe (Vienna, 2010)

Manoschek, Walter, 'Serbien ist judenfrei'. Militärische Besatzungspolitik und Judenvernichtung
in Serbien 1941/42 (Munich, 1995)

Marek, Franz, Beruf und Berufung Kommunist. Lebenserinnerungen und Schlüsseltexte, edited
by Maximilian Graf and Sarah Knoll (Vienna, 2017)

Martinek, Johannes, 'Auf zum Schwure …'. Das Rosenkranzfest vom 7. Oktober 1938 (Vienna,
1998)

Mathis, Franz, Wirtschaft oder Politik? Zu den wirtschaftlichen Motiven einer politischen Vereinigung 1918–1938, in: Ungleiche Partner? Österreich und Deutschland im 19. und 20.
Jahrhundert, edited by Michael Gehler (Stuttgart, 1996)

Mazower, Mark, Der dunkle Kontinent. Europa im 20. Jahrhundert (Berlin, 2000)

Meier-Walser, Reinhard, Die Außenpolitik der monocoloren Regierung Klaus in Österreich
1966–1970 (= tuduv Studien, vol. 27, Munich, 1988)

Idem, Die gescheiterte Machtergreifung der österreichischen Kommunisten im Herbst 1950 (=
Christliche Demokratie, vol. 2, 1990)

Mosser, Ingrid, Der Legitimismus und die Frage der Habsburgerrestauration in der innenpolitischen Zielsetzung des autoritären Österreich (1933–1938), doctoral thesis, University of
Vienna (1979)

Mueller, Wolfgang, Die sowjetische Besatzung in Österreich 1945–1955 und ihre politische Mission (Vienna/Cologne/Weimar, 2005)

Idem, A Good Example of Peaceful Coexistence. The Soviet Union, Austria, and Neutrality, 1955–1991 (= Österreichische Akademie der Wissenschaften, Zentraleuropa-Studien, vol. 15, Vienna, 2011)

Idem, A Special Relationship with Neutrals. Krushchev's Coexistence, Austria and Switzerland, 1955–1960, in: zeitgeschichte, vol. 41, no. 5 (2014)

Mueller-Hildebrand, Burkhart, Das Heer 1933–1945, vol. III: Der Zweifrontenkrieg (Frankfurt am Main, 1969)

Mühlberger, Kurt, Vertriebene Intelligenz 1938. Der Verlust geistiger und menschlicher Potenz an der Universität Wien von 1938 bis 1945 (Vienna, 1993)

Müller, Stefan, Die versäumte Freundschaft. Österreich-Mexiko 1901–1956. Von der Aufnahme der Beziehungen bis zu Mexikos Beitritt zum Staatsvertrag (= Lateinamerikanistik, vol. 3, Vienna, 2006)

Müller, Stefan A., David *Schriffl* and Adamantios T. *Skordos*, Heimliche Freunde. Die Beziehungen Österreichs zu den Diktaturen Südeuropas nach 1945: Spanien, Portugal, Griechenland (Vienna/Cologne/Weimar, 2016)

Münkler, Herfried, Der Wandel des Krieges. Von der Symmetrie zur Asymmetrie (Weilerswist, 2006)

Murber, Ibolya, and Zoltán *Fónagy*, Die ungarische Revolution und Österreich 1956 (Vienna, 2006)

Natter, Andreas, 'Verlieren wir uns nicht in Sentimentalitäten', in: Grenzüberschreitungen. Von Schmugglern, Schleppern, Flüchtlingen, edited by Edith Hessenberger (Schruns, 2008)

Neck, Rudolf, Wilhelm Miklas und der 'Anschluss' 1938, in: Arbeiterbewegung, Faschismus, Nationalbewusstsein (= Festschrift zum 20-jährigen Bestehen des Dokumentationsarchivs des Widerstandes, edited by Helmut Konrad and Wolfgang Neugebauer, Vienna, 1983)

(*Neuberg*, A.), Hans Kippenberger, M. N. Tuchatschewski und Ho Chi Minh, Der bewaffnete Aufstand. Versuch einer theoretischen Darstellung. With an introduction by Erich Wollenberg (Frankfurt am Main, 1971)

Neues aus dem Westen. Aus den streng vertraulichen Berichten der Sicherheitsdirektion und der Bundespolizeidirektion Salzburg an das Innenministerium 1945 bis 1955, edited by Robert Kriechbaumer (Vienna/Cologne/Weimar, 2016)

Neugebauer, Wolfgang, Das Standgerichtsverfahren gegen Josef Gerl, in: Sozialistenprozesse. Politische Justiz in Österreich 1870–1936, edited by Karl R. Stadler (Vienna, 1986)

Idem, Der österreichische Widerstand 1938–1945 (Vienna, 2008)

Nicht größer als eine Ameise. Oskar Laske und der Erste Weltkrieg. Katalog zur Sonderausstellung im Heeresgeschichtlichen Museum 11. April bis 28. Juni 2002 (Vienna, 2002)

Olah, Franz, Die Erinnerungen (Vienna/Munich/Berlin, 1995)

Österreich 1918–1938, edited by Erika Weinzierl and Kurt Skalnik, 2 vols. (Vienna, 1983)

Österreich – 90 Jahre Republik. Beitragsband der Ausstellung im Parlament, edited by Stefan Karner (Innsbruck/Vienna, 2008)

Österreich Lexikon, edited by Richard and Maria Bamberger, Ernst Bruckmüller and Karl Gutkas, 2 vols. (Vienna, 1995)

Österreich im Kalten Krieg, edited by Maximilian Graf and Agnes Meislinger (= Zeitgeschichte
    im Kontext, vol. 11, Göttingen, 2016)

Österreich und die europäische Integration seit 1945. Aspekte einer wechselvollen Entwicklung,
    edited by Michael Gehler and Rolf Steininger (Vienna/Cologne/Weimar, 2014)

Österreich und die Ostöffnung 1989 (= historisch-politische Bildung, vol. 8, Vienna, 2015)

Overmans, Jürgen, Deutsche militärische Verluste im Zweiten Weltkrieg (Munich, 1999)

Pape, Mathias, Ungleiche Brüder. Österreich und Deutschland 1945–1965 (Cologne/Weimar/
    Vienna, 2000)

Pauley, Bruce F., Hahnenschwanz und Hakenkreuz. Steirischer Heimatschutz und österreichi-
    scher Nationalsozialismus 1918–1934 (Munich, 1972)

Peball, Kurt, Die Kämpfe in Wien im Februar 1934 (= Militärhistorische Schriftenreihe, vol. 25,
    Vienna, 1974)

Pelinka, Anton, Die Kleine Koalition. SPÖ–FPÖ 1983–1986 (= Studien zu Politik und Verwal-
    tung, edited by Christian Brünner, Wolfgang Mantl and Manfried Welan, vol. 48, Vienna/
    Cologne/Graz, 1993)

Petzina, Dietmar, Autarkiepolitik im Dritten Reich. Der nationalsozialistische Vierjahresplan (=
    Schriftenreihe der Vierteljahrshefte für Zeitgeschichte, vol. 16, Stuttgart 1968)

Pfeiffer, Rolf, Eine schwierige und konfliktreiche Nachbarschaft. Österreich und das Deutsch-
    land Adenauers 1953–1963 (Münster/Hamburg/London, 2003)

Philapitsch, Anton, Wöllersdorf. Trauma oder Mythos, in: Geschosse – Skandale – Stacheldraht.
    Arbeiterschaft und Rüstungsindustrie, edited by Leopold Mulley (Vienna, 1999)

Pleiner, Horst, and Hubert *Speckner*, Zur Verstärkung der nördlichen Garnisonen .... Der 'Ein-
    satz' des österreichischen Bundesheeres während der Tschechenkrise im Jahr 1968 (= Schrif-
    ten zur Geschichte des Österreichischen Bundesheeres, vol. 15, Vienna, 2008)

Plöckinger, Othmar, Geschichte eines Buches: Adolf Hitlers 'Mein Kampf', 1922–1945 (Munich,
    2006)

Politische Säuberungen in Europa. Die Abrechnung mit Faschismus und Kollaboration nach
    dem Zweiten Weltkrieg, edited by Klaus-Dietmar Henke and Hans Woller (Munich, 1991)

Portisch, Hugo, Österreich II. Die Wiedergeburt unseres Staates (Vienna, 1985)

Idem, Österreich II. Der lange Weg zur Freiheit (Vienna, 1986)

Idem, Österreich I. Die verkannte Republik (Vienna, 1989)

Idem, Österreich II. Jahre des Aufbruchs. Jahre des Umbruchs (Vienna, 1996)

Rasky, Bela, Erinnern und Vergessen der Habsburger in Österreich und Ungarn nach 1918, in:
    Österreich 1918 und die Folgen. Geschichte, Literatur, Theater und Film, edited by Karl
    Müller (Vienna, 2009)

Rathkolb, Oliver, Washington ruft Wien. US-Großmachtpolitik und Österreich 1953–1963 (Vi-
    enna/Cologne/Weimar, 1997)

Idem, Die paradoxe Republik. Österreich 1945 bis 2015, expanded new edition (Vienna, 2015)

Idem, Erste Republik, Austrofaschismus und Nationalsozialismus (1938–1945); Die Zweite
    Republik (seit 1945), in: Geschichte Österreichs, edited by Thomas Winkelbauer (Stuttgart,
    2016)

Rauchensteiner, Manfried, Die Kämpfe in Wien im Februar 1934, in: Wiener Geschichtsblätter, vol. 29 (1974)

Idem, Der Sonderfall. Die Besatzungszeit in Österreich 1945 bis 1955 (Graz/Vienna/Cologne, 1979)

Idem, Spätherbst 1956. Die Neutralität auf dem Prüfstand (Vienna, 1981)

Idem, Der Krieg in Österreich 1945 (= Schriften des Heeresgeschichtlichen Museums, vol. 5, Vienna, 1984; reprint 2015)

Idem, Die Zwei. Die Große Koalition in Österreich 1945–1966 (Vienna, 1987)

Idem, Die Historikerkommission, in: Österreichisches Jahrbuch für Politik 1988 (Vienna/Munich, 1989)

Idem, Der Luftkrieg gegen Österreich im Kontext des Zweiten Weltkriegs, in: Zeitenwende 1943. Katalog zur Sonderausstellung des Heeresgeschichtlichen Museums (Vienna, 1993)

Idem, Flucht und Vertreibung, in: Der Krieg in Österreich '45. Ausstellungskatalog des Heeresgeschichtlichen Museums (Vienna, 1995)

Idem, Landesverteidigung und Sicherheitspolitik 1918–1934, in: Handbuch des politischen Systems Österreichs. Erste Republik 1918–1933, edited by Emmerich Tálos, Herbert Dachs, Ernst Hanisch and Anton Staudinger (Vienna, 1995)

Idem, Stalinplatz 4. Österreich unter alliierter Besatzung (Vienna, 2005)

Idem, Entschlossenes Zuwarten. Österreich und die Unabhängigkeit Sloweniens 1991 (Klagenfurt, 2011).

Idem, Der Erste Weltkrieg und das Ende der Habsburgermonarchie 1914–1918 (Vienna/Cologne/Weimar, 2013)

Rausch, Josef, Der Partisanenkampf in Kärnten im Zweiten Weltkrieg (= Militärhistorische Schriftenreihe, vols. 39/40, Vienna, 1979)

Reichhold, Ludwig, Kampf um Österreich. Die Vaterländische Front und ihr Widerstand gegen den Nationalsozialismus 1933–1938 (Vienna, 1984)

Renner, Karl, Österreichs Erneuerung. Politisch-programmatische Aufsätze von Dr. Karl Renner, Reichsratsabgeordneter (Vienna, 1916)

Idem, An der Wende zweier Zeiten. Lebenserinnerungen (Vienna, 1946)

Reisacher, Martin, Die Konstruktion des 'Staats, den keiner wollte'. Der Transformationsprozess des umstrittenen Gedächtnisorts 'Erste Republik' in einen negativen rhetorischen Topos, diploma thesis, University of Vienna (2010)

Reisner, Markus, Bomben auf Wiener Neustadt. Die Zerstörung eines der wichtigsten Rüstungszentren des Deutschen Reiches. Der Luftkrieg über der 'Allzeit Getreuen' von 1943 bis 1945 (Wiener Neustadt, undated [2013])

Riegler, Thomas, Im Fadenkreuz. Österreich und der Nahostterrorismus 1973 bis 1985 (= Zeitgeschichte im Kontext, vol. 3, Göttingen, 2011)

Röhrlich, Elisabeth, Kreiskys Außenpolitik. Zwischen österreichischer Identität und internationalem Programm (= Zeitgeschichte im Kontext, vol. 2, Göttingen, 2009)

Rothländer, Christiane, Die Anfänge der Wiener SS (Vienna/Cologne/Weimar, 2012)

Rumpler, Helmut, Der Ständestaat ohne Stände, in: Der forschende Blick. Beiträge zur Geschichte Österreichs im 20. Jahrhunderts, Festschrift für Ernst Hanisch zum 70. Geburtstag, edited by Reinhard Krammer, Christoph Kühberger and Franz Schausberger (Vienna/Cologne/Weimar, 2010)

Sandgruber, Roman, Ökonomie und Politik. Österreichische Wirtschaftsgeschichte vom Mittelalter bis zur Gegenwart (Vienna, 1995)

Idem, Die Industrie in Österreich 1911 bis 2011. Eine Erfolgsgeschichte auf Umwegen, in: 100 Jahre Haus der Industrie 1911–2011, edited by Veit Sorger (Vienna, 2011)

Schafranek, Hans, Söldner für den Anschluss. Die österreichische Legion 1933–1938 (Vienna, 2011)

Schausberger, Norbert, Rüstung in Österreich 1938–1945. Eine Studie über die Wechselwirkung von Wirtschaft, Politik und Kriegführung (= Publikationen des österreichischen Instituts für Zeitgeschichte, vol. 8, Vienna, 1970)

Schlag, Gerald, Die Kämpfe um das Burgenland 1921 (= Militärhistorische Schriftenreihe, vol. 16, Vienna, 1970)

Idem, Die Grenzziehung Österreich-Ungarn 1922/23, in: Burgenland in seiner pannonischen Umwelt. Festgabe für August Ernst (Eisenstadt, 1984)

Schmidl, Erwin A., Der 'Anschluss' Österreichs. Der deutsche Einmarsch im März 1938 (Bonn, 1994)

Idem, Für Südtirol in den Kongo? Der Beginn der österreichischen Beteiligung an den friedenserhaltenden Operationen der Vereinten Nationen, in: Österreich in den Fünfzigern, edited by Thomas Albrich, Klaus Eisterer, Michael Gehler and Rolf Steininger (Innsbruck/Vienna, 1995)

Idem, 'Rosinenbomber' über Wien? Alliierte Pläne zur Luftversorgung Wiens im Falle einer sowjetischen Blockade 1948–1953, in: Österreich im frühen Kalten Krieg, edited by Erwin A. Schmidl (Vienna/Cologne/Weimar, 2000)

Schmidlechner, Karin, Youth Culture in the 1950s, in: Austria in the 1950s, edited by Günter Bischof, Anton Pelinka and Rolf Steininger (= Contemporary Austrian Studies, vol. 3, New Brunswick, 1995)

Schuschnigg, Kurt, Im Kampf gegen Hitler. Die Überwindung der Anschlussidee (Vienna/Munich/Zurich, 1969)

Schüssel, Wolfgang, Offengelegt. Aufgezeichnet von Alexander Purger (Salzburg, 2009)

Schwabe, Klaus, Deutsche Revolution und Wilson-Friede: Die amerikanische und deutsche Friedensstrategie zwischen Ideologie und Machtpolitik 1918/19 (Düsseldorf, 1971)

Schwarz, Hans-Peter, Adenauer, vol. 2: Der Staatsmann 1952–1967 (Stuttgart, 1991)

Schweitzer, Renate, Der staatlich geförderte, der kommunale und der gemeinnützige Wohnungs- und Siedlungsbau in Österreich bis 1945, doctoral thesis, Technical University of Vienna (1972)

Šejna, Jan, We Will Bury You (London, 1982)

Seybold, Dieter, Michael Memelauer – ein unpolitischer Seelsorgebischof? Eine vergleichende Untersuchung der Enunziationen eines österreichischen Diözesanbischofs (1933–1934), diploma thesis, University of Vienna (1998)

Sickinger, Hubert, Politische Korruption und der Wandel der Rahmenbedingungen für politisches Skandale in der Zweiten Republik, in: Korruption in Österreich. Historische Streiflichter, edited by Ernst Bruckmüller (Vienna, 2011)

Sima, Valentin, Die Deportation slowenischer Familien aus Kärnten I. Rahmenbedingungen, Präludium und Vorbereitung, in: Die Deportation slowenische Familien aus Kärnten 1942. Eine Dokumentation (Vienna, 2003)

Sorry guys, no gold. Die amerikanischen Waffendepots in Österreich. Katalog zur Sonderausstellung im Heeresgeschichtlichen Museum (Vienna, 1998)

Speckner, Hubert, Kriegsgefangenenlager in der 'Ostmark' 1939–1945. Zur Geschichte der Mannschaftsstammlager und Offizierslager in den Wehkreisen XVII und XVIII, doctoral thesis in humanities, University of Vienna (1999)

Idem, Der Sicherungseinsatz des Österreichischen Bundesheeres an der Grenze zu Südtirol 1967 (= Schriften zur Geschichte des Österreichischen Bundesheeres, vol. 19, Vienna, 2012)

Idem, Von der 'Feuernacht" zur 'Porzescharte'. Das 'Südtirolproblem' der 1960er Jahre in den österreichischen sicherheitsdienstlichen Akten (Vienna, 2016)

Stadler, Robert, and Michael *Mooslechner*, St. Johann i. Pg. 1938–1945. Der nationalsozialistische 'Markt Pongau'. Der '20. Juli 1944' in Goldegg. Widerstand und Verfolgung (Salzburg, 1986)

Statistisches Handbuch für die Republik Österreich, edited by the Statistische Zentralkommission, vol. 3 (Vienna, 1923)

Steinböck, Erwin, Die Kämpfe im Raum Völkermarkt 1918/19 (= Militärhistorische Schriftenreihe, vol. 13, Vienna, 1969)

Steininger, Rolf, 12. November 1918 bis 13. März 1938. Stationen auf dem Weg zum 'Anschluss', in: Österreich im 20. Jahrhundert, vol. 1: Von der Monarchie bis zum Zweiten Weltkrieg, edited by Rolf Steininger and Michael Gehler (Vienna/Cologne/Weimar, 1997)

Stelzl-Marx, Barbara, Zum Tode verurteilt. Die sowjetische Strafjustiz in Österreich im frühen Kalten Krieg, in: Sowjetische Schauprozesse in Mittel- und Osteuropa, edited by Csaba Szabó (Publikationen der ungarischen Geschichtsforschung in Wien, vol. XIII, Vienna, 2015)

Sternberg, Adalbert Graf, 1868–1930. Aus den Memoiren eines konservativen Rebellen, edited by Hans Rochelt (Vienna, 1997)

Stieber, Gabriele, Die Lösung des Flüchtlingsproblems 1945–1960, in: Österreich in den Fünfzigern, edited by Thomas Albrich, Klaus Eisterer, Michael Gehler and Rolf Steininger (= Innsbrucker Forschungen zur Zeitgeschichte, vol. 11, Innsbruck/Vienna, 1995)

Stifter, Gerald, Die ÖVP in der Ära Kreisky 1970–1983 (Innsbruck/Vienna, 2006)

Stourzh, Gerald, Erschütterung und Konsolidierung des Österreichbewußtseins. Vom Zusammenbruch der Monarchie bis zur Zweiten Republik, in: Was heißt Österreich? Inhalt und Umfang des Österreichbegriffs vom 10. Jahrhundert bis heute, edited by Richard Georg Plaschka (Vienna, 1995)

Idem, Um Einheit und Freiheit. Staatsvertrag, Neutralität und das Ende der Ost-West-Besetzung Österreichs 1945–1955, 4th revised and expanded edition (= Studien zu Politik und Verwaltung, vol. 62, Vienna/Graz/Cologne, 1998)

Suchy, Irene, Strasshof an der Nordbahn. Die NS-Geschichte eines Ortes und ihre Aufarbeitung (Vienna, 2012)

Svoboda, Wilhelm, Die Partei, die Republik und der Mann mit den vielen Gesichtern. Oskar

Helmer und Österreich II. Eine Korrektur (= Böhlaus zeitgeschichtliche Bibliothek, vol. 26, Vienna, 1993)

Széles, Robert, Die strategischen Überlegungen des Warschauer Paktes für Mitteleuropa in den 70er Jahren und die Rolle der Neutralen, in: Tausend Nadelstiche. Das österreichische Bundesheer in der Reformzeit 1970–1978, edited by Manfried Rauchensteiner, Wolfgang Etschmann and Josef Rausch (= Forschungen zur Militärgeschichte, vol. 3, Graz/Vienna/Cologne, 1994)

Tálos, Emmerich, Das austrofaschistische Herrschaftssystem. Österreich 1933–1938 (= Politik und Zeitgeschichte, vol. 8, Vienna, 2013)

The Vranitzky Era in Austria, edited by Günter Bischof, Anton Pelinka and Ferdinand Karlhofer (Contemporary Austrian Studies, vol. 7, New Brunswick/New Jersey, 1999)

The War in Croatia and Bosnia-Herzegovina, 1991–1995, edited by Branka Magaš, Noel Malcolm and Ivo Žanić (London, 2001)

Tober, Helmut, Alexander Eifler. Vom Monarchisten zum Republikaner, doctoral thesis, University of Vienna (1966)

Tolstoy, Nikolai, Die Verratenen von Jalta. Englands Schuld vor der Geschichte (Munich, 1977)

Tooze, Adam, The Wages of Destruction: The Making and Breaking of the Nazi Economy (London, 2006)

Traussnig, Florian, Militärischer Widerstand von außen. Österreicher in US-Armee und Kriegsgeheimdienst im Zweiten Weltkrieg (Vienna/Cologne/Weimar, 2016)

Tuider, Othmar, Die Wehrkreise XVII und XVIII 1938–1945 (= Militärhistorische Schriftenreihe, vol. 30, Vienna, 1983)

Idem, Die Luftwaffe in Österreich 1938–1945 (= Militärhistorische Schriftenreihe, vol. 54, Vienna, 1985)

Ueberschär, Gerd R., Stauffenberg. Der 20. Juli 1944 (Frankfurt am Main, 2004)

Ulrich, Johann, Der Luftkrieg über Österreich 1939–1945 (= Militärhistorische Schriftenreihe, vols. 5/6, Vienna, 1967)

Verosta, Stephan, Für die Unabhängigkeit Österreichs, in: Österreich November 1918. Die Entstehung der Ersten Republik (= Wissenschaftliche Kommission zur Erforschung der Geschichte der Republik Österreich, Veröffentlichungen, vol. 9, Vienna, 1986)

Vodopivec, Alexander, Die Balkanisierung Österreichs. Folgen einer großen Koalition (Vienna/Munich, 1966)

Volsansky, Gabriele, Pakt auf Zeit. Das Deutsch-Österreichische Juli-Abkommen 1936 (Vienna/Cologne/Weimar, 2001)

Vom Justizpalast zum Heldenplatz. Studien und Dokumentationen 1927 bis 1938, edited by Ludwig Jedlicka and Rudolf Neck (Vienna, 1975)

Vranitzky, Franz, Politische Erinnerungen (Vienna, 2004)

Wagner, Bruno, Der Waffenstillstand von der Villa Giusti 3. November 1918, doctoral thesis, University of Vienna (1970)

Wagner, Wolfgang, Die Besatzungszeit aus sowjetischer Sicht. Die Errichtung der sowjetischen Besatzungsmacht in Österreich von 1945 bis 1946 im Spiegel ihrer Lageberichte, diploma thesis, University of Vienna (1998)

Wassertheurer, Peter, Die Beneš-Dekrete im Kontext des öffentlichen und politischen Diskurses in Österreich 1989–2003. Traditionen – Geschichtsbilder – Stereotype, doctoral thesis, University of Graz (2006)

Weber, Friedrich, Die linken Sozialisten in Österreich 1945–1948, doctoral thesis, University of Salzburg (1977)

Webster, Charles Kingsley, The Congress of Vienna 1814/1815 (Oxford, 1919)

Weißbuch zur Lage der Landesverteidigung in Österreich, edited by Felix Ermacora (Vienna, 1973)

Weinzierl, Erika, Das österreichische Konkordat von 1933 von der Unterzeichnung bis zur Ratifikation, in: 60 Jahre österreichisches Konkordat, edited by Hans Paarhamer, Franz Pototschnig and Alfred Rinnerthaler (Munich, 1994)

Idem, Kirchlicher Widerstand gegen den Nationalsozialismus, in: Themen der Zeitgeschichte und der Gegenwart. Arbeiterbewegung – NS-Herrschaft – Rechtsextremismus. Ein Resümé aus Anlass des 60. Geburtstags von Wolfgang Neugebauer (Vienna, 2004)

Wiltschegg, Walter, Die Heimwehr. Eine unwiderstehliche Volksbewegung? (= Studien und Quellen zur österreichischen Zeitgeschichte, vol. 7, Vienna, 1985)

Winkler, Wilhelm, Die Totenverluste der öst.-ung. Monarchie nach Nationalitäten (Vienna, 1919)

Wirth, Maria, Christian Broda. Eine politische Biographie (= Zeitgeschichte im Kontext, vol. 5, Göttingen, 2011)

Wo sind sie geblieben …? Zeichen der Erinnerung. Katalog zur Sonderausstellung des Heeresgeschichtlichen Museums 22. Oktober 1997 bis 22. Februar 1998 (Vienna, 1997)

Wohnout, Helmut, Das Traditionsreferat der Vaterländischen Front. Ein Beitrag über das Verhältnis der legitimistischen Bewegung zum autoritären Österreich, in: Österreich in Geschichte und Literatur, vol. 36, no. 2 (1992)

Wohnout, Helmut, and Johannes *Schönner*, Das politische Tagebuch von Julius Raab 1953/1954. Neue Erkenntnisse zu den ersten Jahren seiner Kanzlerschaft, in: Demokratie und Geschichte. Jahrbuch des Karl-von-Vogelsang-Instituts zur Erforschung der christlichen Demokratie in Österreich, vols. 7/8 (2003/2004)

Znoy, Cornelia, Die Vertreibung der Sudetendeutschen nach Österreich 1945/46. Unter besonderer Berücksichtigung der Bundesländer Wien und Niederösterreich, diploma thesis, University of Vienna (1995)

Zweig, Stefan, Die Welt von Gestern. Erinnerungen eines Europäers, paperback edition (Frankfurt am Main, 1989)

Zwischen den Blöcken. NATO, Warschauer Pakt und Österreich, edited by Manfried Rauchensteiner (= Schriftenreihe der Dr.-Wilfried-Haslauer-Bibliothek, vol. 36, Vienna/Cologne/Weimar, 2010)

Index

Unless otherwise stated, the people listed are Austrians. The functions given are based on the role they play in the book.

MANFRIED RAUCHENSTEINER'S FASCINATING
STANDARD WORK IN ENGLISH

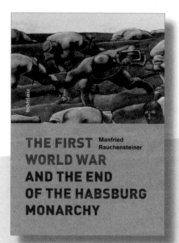

THE FIRST WORLD WAR AND THE END OF THE HABSBURG MONARCHY

Manfried Rauchensteiner

The First World War

and the End of the Habsburg
Monarchy, 1914–1918

translated by Anna Güttel and Alex J. Kay

2014. 1.181 pages with 13 illustrations, b/w,
hardcover
€ 55,– D | 57,– A
ISBN 978-3-205-79588-9

The well-respected historian Manfried Rauchensteiner analyses the outbreak
of World War I, Emperor Franz Joseph's role in the conflict, and how the
various nationalities of the Habsburg Monarchy reacted to the disintegration
of this 640-yearold empire in 1918. After Archduke Franz Ferdinand"s assassination in Sarajevo in 1914, war was inevitable. Emperor Franz Joseph intended
it, and everyone in Vienna expected it. How the war began and how Austria-
Hungary managed to avoid capitulation only weeks later with the help of German troops reads like a thriller. Manfried Rauchensteiner"s book is based on
decades of research and is a fascinating read to the very end, even though the
final outcome, the collapse of the Austro-Hungarian Dual Monarchy, is already
known. Originally published in German in 2013 by Böhlau, this standard work
is now available in English.

Vandenhoeck & Ruprecht Verlage
www.vandenhoeck-ruprecht-verlage.com

STALINIST RULE IN ESTONIA, LATVIA AND LITHUANIA

Olaf Mertelsmann (ed.)

The Baltic States under Stalinist Rule

2016. 257 pages,
paperback
€ 35,– D | 36,– A
ISBN 978-3-412-20620-8

Das Baltikum in Geschichte und Gegenwart – volume 4

In the history of Estonia, Latvia and Lithuania the period of Stalinist rule marked the time of loss of independence, Sovietization and enormous political, social and cultural change. Large segments of the population fell victim to repression or forced deportation. Some Balts fought in a partisan war against the Soviets, others fled in 1944. Until today, those events are present in Baltic societies. The volume assembles thirteen historians from eight countries discussing in their contributions different aspects of Stalinist rule in the annexed Baltic states. The authors make extensive use of recently opened archives.

Vandenhoeck & Ruprecht Verlage
www.vandenhoeck-ruprecht-verlage.com

SOUND RECORDINGS OF INFORMANTS IN GERMAN PRISONER-OF-WAR-CAMPS DURING WORLD WAR I

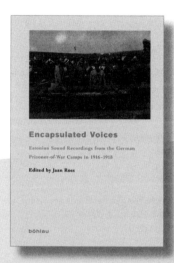

Jaan Ross (ed.)

Encapsulated Voices

Estonian Sound Recordings from the
German Prisoner-of-War Camps in
1916-1918

2012. 257 pages + audio cd,
paperback
€ 35,– D | 36,– A
ISBN 978-3-412-20911-7

**Das Baltikum in Geschichte und
Gegenwart – volume 5**

This book focuses on the sound recordings of ethnic Estonian informants,
prepared between 1916 and 1918 in five German prisoner-of-war camps. Before
1918, Estonia was part of the Russian empire, and during World War I ethnic
Estonian conscripts fought in the Russian army. The duration of available
audio material is about one hour and it is presented on the CD accompanying
the book. The original audio material is preserved in two archives: wax rolls
at the Ethnologisches Museum in Berlin-Dahlem (Phonogramm-Archiv) and
shellac discs at the Humboldt-Universität zu Berlin (Lautarchiv). This volume
consists of nine chapters written by authors working in diverse fields such as
archival or folklore studies, history, linguistics, and musicology.

Vandenhoeck & Ruprecht Verlage
www.vandenhoeck-ruprecht-verlage.com

AN ILLUMINATION OF THE CRITICAL PROBLEMS
THREATENING THE HABSBURG MONARCHY

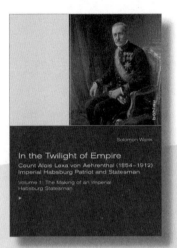

Solomon Wank

In the Twilight of Empire

Count Alois Lexa von Aehrenthal (1854-1912). Imperial Habsburg Patriot and Statesman

2009. 292 pages with illustrations, b/w, paperback
€ 45,– D | 47,– A
ISBN 978-3-205-78352-7

Veröffentlichungen der Kommission für Neuere Geschichte Österreichs – volume 102,1

Count Aehrenthal, Austro-Hungarian foreign minister (1906-1912), is well-known to diplomatic historian for the annexation of Bosnia-Herzegovina in 1908. Solomon Wank"s biography, the first since 1917, shows that Aehrenthal"s life and work transcend diplomatic history and illuminate critical problems threatening the viability of the Habsburg Monarchy. Wank focuses on the inseparable connection between foreign and internal affairs in Aehrenthal"s thinking, his involvement in domestic politics, his attempt to transform the office of the foreign minister into that of an imperial chancellor, his grand scheme of constitutional reform to solve the South Slav problem within the empire, and his personality. The work is based on unpublished documents in Austrian and Czech archives, as well as recently published correspondence with Habsburg diplomats and aristocratic relatives and friends, and with his parents. Volume I covers the history of the Aehrenthal family, Aehrenthal"s early years and education, his personality and political outlook, his diplomatic career and his involvement in domestic politics from 1878 to the eve of appointment as foreign minister.

Vandenhoeck & Ruprecht Verlage
www.vandenhoeck-ruprecht-verlage.com